The Chicago Manual of Style

Fourteenth Edition

The University of Chicago Press Chicago and London

The University of Chicago Press, Chicago 60637
The University of Chicago Press, Ltd., London
© 1969, 1982, 1993 by The University of Chicago
All rights reserved
First edition published 1906. Twelfth edition 1969
Thirteenth edition 1982. Fourteenth edition 1993
Printed in the United States of America

02   10 9 8

ISBN (cloth): 0-226-10389-7

Library of Congress Cataloging-in-Publication Data

University of Chicago Press.
    The Chicago manual of style — 14th ed.
    p.   cm.
  Includes bibliographical references and index.
    1. Printing, Practical—United States—Style manuals.
2. Authorship—Handbooks, manuals, etc.   3. Publishers and
publishing—United States—Handbooks, manuals, etc.   I. Title.
Z253.U69   1993
808′.027′0973—dc20   92-37475
                                                CIP

♾ The paper used in this publication meets the minimum
requirements of the American National Standard for
Information Sciences—Permanence of Paper for Printed
Library Materials, ANSI Z39.48-1992.

Contents

Preface

A century ago, in the proofroom of the then very young University of Chicago Press, a solitary proofreader began jotting down on a single sheet of paper a few basic style rules. Within a few years this modest list of rules had grown into a multipage collection titled *Style Book,* and within a few more years—by 1906—a still larger collection was published, this time bearing the title *Manual of Style.* From such early beginnings the collected guidelines of the University of Chicago Press have continued to grow in quantity and breadth of coverage, and although the purpose was, and remains, to establish rules, the renunciation, in the preface to the 1906 edition, of an authoritarian position in favor of common sense and flexibility has always been a fundamental and abiding principle. At the heart of that principle is a respect for the author's individuality, purpose, and style, tempered though it is with a deeply felt responsibility to prune from the work whatever stylistic infelicities, inconsistencies, and ambiguities might have gained stealthy entrance.

By the 1960s, significant changes in usage and style, as well as in manufacturing technology, had become so commanding that a radically new approach seemed an imperative. The reply to that imperative was the twelfth edition of *A Manual of Style,* which reflected those many changes and advances, and which was itself, little more than a decade later, superseded by an even more advanced embodiment, the thirteenth edition, whose title was, finally, *The Chicago Manual of Style.* These two groundbreaking editions were prepared under, and very largely by, Bruce Young and Catharine Seybold, and the exceptional edifice they painstakingly constructed is still to be encountered in almost every aspect of this fourteenth, and centennial, edition, incorporating though it does the even newer usages and technological advances that enrich or encumber, as various minds may regard them, the final decades of the twentieth century.

For this fourteenth edition, the number and variety of examples have been increased throughout, and there is augmented discussion of the role of computers in nearly every aspect of publishing, beginning with the preparation of manuscripts, from straightforward expository text to complicated mathematical material, and continuing through editing (both on "hard copy" and on-line), designing, typesetting, indexing, and printing. Recognizing, too, that over the years the *Chicago Manual* has come to be regarded, and used, as a publishing reference work of much broader scope than one devoted solely to editorial procedures, we have extended the discussion of the parts of a book to include its exterior—covers (both hard and soft), jackets, and the text and artwork proper to them. Included in this discussion are explanations of the purpose of EAN bar codes and ISBNs and how to obtain and display them on these "outward walls."

The most thoroughly revised portion of the manual is that dealing with documentation. Formerly distributed through three chapters, the material has been rewritten, modified, expanded, and reorganized into two chapters. The aim was to make progress through the myriad topics less stressful, individual cases easier to find, and the whole more unified. To this effect, a complete treatment of the humanities style of documentation is presented in a single chapter. Notes and bibliographies are separately discussed, and then individual entries for the multitude of sources are illustrated in simultaneous display of documentary notes and bibliographic entries for the same item. The chapter also offers a brief comparison of the humanities style and the author-date system. The author-date system is then presented in full in the following chapter. Text citations and reference-list entries are first discussed separately, and individual examples of both are then illustrated in pairs. In both chapters, special types of reference materials, including medieval references, public documents, sound and video recordings, performance reviews, and computer programs, are given more attention and are augmented with more examples, and guidelines for the citation of electronic documents have been added.

Another major change involves the chapter on copyrights and permissions, which has been thoroughly revised by William Strong to reflect the most recent law and the most sensible current procedures. The discussion now offers a fuller interpretation of "fair use."

For this edition, the chapter on quotations has been revised to offer an expanded discussion of speech, especially in regard to narrative conversation. In addition to an extensive treatment of the use of quotation marks in setting off dialogue, the discussion now covers, and exemplifies, such alternatives as the Franco-Joycean dash and the revived use of nothing-at-all. Thought, interior monologue, and stream of consciousness are also now treated in this chapter.

A few of the many other changes to be found in the new edition are the following: The tabular spelling guide for compound words and words with prefixes and suffixes has been extensively revised and expanded to reflect contemporary usage, and its arrangement has been made more systematic. The chapter on names and terms now provides an expanded and updated version of terms for nationalities, tribes, races, and other groups. A new section on Hebrew has been added to the foreign language chapter, and the chapter itself has been reorganized to place language discussions in alphabetical order within each group. And, of course, the bibliography and glossary have been extensively revised and updated.

Throughout all of this, strenuous effort has been made to keep the vast quantity of material accessible and its method of presentation useful.

It now appears, not unexpectedly, an impossible task to give proper acknowledgment to all of the magnificent assistance received in the preparation of this fourteenth edition, to trace precisely the many intelligent reviews, the innumerable and invaluable suggestions, additions, deletions, and modifications provided by associates at the Press, by colleagues at other publishing houses, and by independent users and devotees of the *Manual*. But special acknowledgment must be made to William Strong, who thoroughly revised the chapter on copyrights and permissions, to Dennis Pardee, who contributed the new section on Hebrew, and to Nancy Mulvany for her expert advice on indexing. Particular acknowledgment must also be given to many members of the Press staff, past and present, especially to Alice Bennett, for her splendid checking, copyediting, and intelligent suggestions; to Claudia Rex for her skillful digitizing of the manuscript and for her valuable recommendations; and to Estelle Stearn for added help with copyrights. For valued assistance in matters in general, grateful acknowledgment must also be given to Susan Abrams, Joseph Alderfer, Dennis Anderson, Bruce Barton, Geraldine Brady, Joseph Claude, Gabriel Dotto, Jean Eckenfels, Beth Garrison, Sylvia Hecimovich, Penelope Kaiserlian, Jo Ann Kiser, William Knapp, Kathryn Kraynik, Kathryn Krug, Jennie Lightner, Juliana McCarthy, John McCudden, Margaret Mahan, Manuel Moyado, Anita Samen, John Spottiswood, Lila Weinberg, and, finally, others too numerous to mention.

John Grossman
Managing Editor

Part 1

Bookmaking

1   *The Parts of a Book*

PAGES, LEAVES, VERSOS, AND RECTOS

1.1   The trimmed sheets of paper that make up a book are often referred to as *leaves*. A *page* is one side of a leaf. The front of the leaf, the side that lies to the right in an open book, is called the *recto* page (or simply *recto*). The back of the leaf, the side that lies to the left when the leaf is turned, is called the *verso*. Rectos are odd-numbered pages; versos are even-numbered.

OUTLINE OF DIVISIONS

1.2   The interior of a book usually comprises three major divisions: the *front matter*, or *preliminaries* (often called *prelims*); the *text;* and the *back matter, end matter,* or *reference matter.* The three main divisions in turn comprise several parts. A customary and efficient sequence for all the parts is presented below; some parts have alternative placements. Few books contain all of these parts, and some books have parts not listed. All the listed parts and some unlisted ones will be discussed in the text that follows.

1.3   The column at the right in the list indicates the usual page numbers assigned to the various parts. Note that lowercase roman numerals are assigned to pages in the front matter and arabic numerals to all the rest (but see 1.101). Starting pages that cannot be determined because of the variable lengths of certain parts are simply indicated as *recto,* the right-hand page being the traditional choice, or as *verso,* a sometimes useful alternative if space must be strictly conserved. Note also that

4

every page is counted in the page sequence, even those that have no *folio* (page number) *expressed* (printed) on them, such as the title and half-title pages, copyright page, and blank pages.

FRONT MATTER (PRELIMINARIES)

Book half title i
Series title, list of contributors, frontispiece,
    or blank ii
Title page iii
Copyright notice, publisher's agencies, printing
    history, country where printed, ISBN, CIP iv
Dedication (or epigraph) v
Blank vi
(Table of) Contents .... v or vii
(List of) Illustrations .... recto or verso
(List of) Tables .... recto or verso
Foreword .... recto or verso
Preface.. recto or verso
Acknowledgments (if not part of preface) .... recto or verso
Introduction (if not part of text) .... recto or verso
(List of) Abbreviations or chronology............. recto or verso

TEXT

First text page (introduction or chapter 1) 1
    or
Second book half title or first part title 1
Blank 2
First text page................................... 3

BACK MATTER

Appendix(es) .... recto or verso
Notes .... recto or verso
Glossary .... recto or verso
Bibliography .... recto or verso
(List of) Contributors .... recto or verso
Index(es).. recto or verso

FRONT MATTER

Half-Title Page

1.4 The *half title* (on p. i, the first recto) normally consists only of the main title. The subtitle is omitted, and the author's name does not appear. The half-title page sometimes carries a series title or an epigraph (see 1.6, 1.38).

Verso of Half-Title Page

1.5   The verso of the half-title page (p. ii) is often blank, but the designer may make the title page a two-page spread across pages ii and iii.

1.6   If the book is part of a series, the title of the series, the volume number in the series, the name of the general editor of the series, and sometimes the titles of the books already published may appear on page ii:

> Women in Culture and Society
> A Series Edited by Catharine R. Stimpson

A series title may appear alternatively on the title page, copyright page, or half-title page.

1.7   In a multiauthor book with too many authors (contributors) to be accommodated on the title page (but not more than, say, fifteen), the contributors are occasionally listed, usually in alphabetical order, on page ii. Far more commonly, the list of contributors, along with addresses or brief biographical notes, is placed in the back matter preceding the index (see 1.56).

1.8   If the book is the published proceedings of a symposium, the title of the symposium, the name of the city where it was held, and the date may appear on page ii. The committee that planned the symposium and edited the volume may be identified here, sometimes with the sponsor of the symposium.

1.9   Some publishers list an author's previous publications on page ii; the University of Chicago Press generally lists these on the copyright page or the jacket, along with a brief statement of the author's background (called the *author blurb*).

1.10   Page ii sometimes carries an illustration, called a *frontispiece*. Whether the illustration is actually printed on page ii or is tipped in so that it faces the title page depends on the quality of reproduction required. The offset printing process, now used on nearly all books (see 11.5, 19.49), permits either a line drawing or a halftone (photograph) to appear on regular text paper along with the other prelims; if a sharper halftone image is necessary or desired, however, or if the halftone is to print in color, offset printing of the frontispiece should be done on coated paper, which is then tipped in (glued to the next page at the inner margin).

Title Page

1.11   The title page (p. iii) presents the full title of the book, the name of the author, editor, or translator, and the name and location of the publishing house. The designer often specifies a type size or style for the subtitle different from that of the main title, in which case no colon or other mark of punctuation is needed to separate the two parts of the title.

1.12 If the book is a new edition of a work previously published, the number of the edition (e.g., "Third Edition") may also appear on the title page, usually following the title (see also 1.20–22).

1.13 The author's name, or authors' names, may be printed below or above the title (placement and type style are determined by the book designer). Given names should not be shortened to initials unless, like V. S. Pritchett and others, this is how the author prefers to be known. European authors, many of whom are accustomed to using only one initial with their surnames, can usually be persuaded by their American publishers to permit spelling out their given names on the title page. The University of Chicago Press does not print academic degrees or affiliations after an author's name on the title page, with the exception of "M.D.," which may be retained in the field of medicine.

1.14 The usual form for giving the name of a volume editor or translator on the title page is

> Edited by John Doe (*not* John Doe, Editor)
> Translated by Eric Wachthausen

1.15 The publisher's full name *(imprint)* should be given on the title page, usually followed by the name of the city (or cities) where the principal offices are located. The publisher's device or emblem (colophon) may appear on the title page as an embellishment. Some publishers give the year of publication on the title page.

Copyright Page

COPYRIGHT NOTICE

1.16 The Copyright Act of 1989, which brought U.S. practice into agreement with the Berne Convention, does not require that published works carry a copyright notice in order to secure copyright protection. Nevertheless most publishers continue to carry the notice, and the practice is strongly advised as a means of discouraging infringement under the smoke screen of ignorance (see 4.23–26). Some publishers, in fact, now carry the additional notice, "Protected under the Berne Convention." The usual notice consists of three parts: the symbol ©, the year the book is published, and the name of the copyright owner (see fig. 1.1). (The law permits the word *Copyright* or the abbreviation *Copr.* to be used instead of the c in a circle, but since the symbol suits the requirements of the Universal Copyright Convention, to which the United States, most European countries, and many Asian nations belong, it is greatly preferred. There is no point in using both symbol and

The University of Chicago Press, Chicago 60637
The University of Chicago Press, Ltd., London
© 1992 by The University of Chicago
All rights reserved. Published 1992
Printed in the United States of America

01 00 99 98 97 96 95 94 93 92   5 4 3 2 1

Fig. 1.1. Copyright notice, publishing history, and impression line

word, as some publishers do.) Most publishers add to the notice the phrase "All rights reserved" to ensure protection for the book under the Buenos Aires Convention, to which the United States and most Latin American countries belong.

1.17   A typical copyright notice might then read

© 1992 by Jonathan Agonistes. All rights reserved

Every effort should be made to ensure that the date given is actually the year of publication (this is sometimes troublesome when a book is scheduled for publication near the end or beginning of a year). A date that is no more than a year off is not disastrous, however, and the publisher need take no action except to see that the proper date is recorded when the copyright is registered. A date that is more than a year *later* than the actual publication date should be corrected. On this, and for other information concerning the copyright notice, see 4.23–31. It is also important that the name of the copyright owner be given correctly; consequently the person preparing the copyright page for the typesetter should always consult the publishing contract before completing the copy for the notice.

1.18   Subsequent *editions* (as distinct from *new impressions,* that is, reprintings) of a book are each copyrighted, and their dates should appear in the copyright notice (see fig. 1.2). If the new edition is so extensive a revision as virtually to constitute a new publication, all previous copyright dates may be omitted, as was done in the thoroughly new twelfth edition of this manual, published in 1969 (hence, the earliest copyright date appearing in both the thirteenth edition and this fourteenth edition of the manual is 1969).

1.19   The date of copyright renewal or a change in the name of the copyright owner (copyright may be assigned to the author or someone else after the initial copyright has been registered and printed in the first impression) may be reflected in the copyright notice if the book is reprinted. Copyright renewal is indicated in the following manner:

© 1943 by Miriam Obermerker. © renewed 1971 by Miriam Obermerker

The University of Chicago Press, Chicago 60637
The University of Chicago Press, Ltd., London
© 1937, 1955, 1967, 1973, 1987 by The University of Chicago
All rights reserved. First edition 1937
Fifth edition 1987
Printed in the United States of America

96 95 94 93 92 91 90 89   10 9 8 7 6 5

Library of Congress Cataloging-in-Publication Data

Turabian, Kate L.
  A manual for writers of term papers, theses, and dissertations.
  (Chicago guides to writing, editing, and publishing)
  Bibliography: p.
  Includes index.
  1. Dissertations, academic.   2. Report writing
I. Honigsblum, Bonnie Birtwistle.   II. Title.
III. Series.
LB2369.T8   1987   808'.02   86-19128
ISBN 0-226-81624-9
ISBN 0-226-81625-7 (pbk.)

Fig. 1.2. Copyright page of a fifth edition, fifth printing. Note ISBNs for both cloth and paperback editions.

To indicate a change in copyright ownership, the name of the new copyright owner is substituted for that of the previous owner. The copyright date remains the same unless the copyright has been renewed. (For more on the copyright laws see 4.1–31.) If the book is not reprinted, any renewal or reassignment of copyright is legally valid even though it does not appear on the copyright page.

PUBLISHING HISTORY

1.20 The publishing history of a book usually follows the copyright notice, although it may appear elsewhere on the copyright page, or it may be omitted, except for the line indicating the country where the book was printed (see 1.24). The publishing history of a book begins with the date (year) of original publication. Reprintings, or new impressions, of the original edition may subsequently be made, in which case the number and date of the current impression are usually indicated. Corrections are sometimes made in new impressions, but no significant revisions. Should such revisions be made, the result may be a new edition, and the number and date of the new edition become part of the publishing history. Each new edition may be granted a new copyright, and the copyright dates of all editions are accumulated in the copyright notice, but usually only the original and latest editions are reflected in the publishing history (see fig. 1.2).

1.21   What constitutes a new edition? Surely extensive changes or additions may be said to do so, but what if the text remains substantially unchanged and only a new foreword or preface is added? What if only a few significant modifications have been made to the text? The University of Chicago Press prefers to define a new edition as one in which a *significant or substantial change* has been made in one or more of the essential elements of the work: the text itself, the introduction, notes, appendixes, or, if they are integral to the text, illustrations. Additions to or deletions from a bibliography would not in themselves make a new edition, unless the changes were so extensive as to result in an essentially new bibliography. The mere addition of a new foreword or preface, whether in hardcover or paperback reissue, the correction of a dozen or so lines, changes in nonintegral illustrative content, or all of these combined will not constitute a new edition. Such minor changes may be announced on the title page by some such expression as "With a new preface" or "With a new foreword and new illustrations," but the edition remains the same. Something subjective and unquantifiable persists in this definition, but that is because the decision is ultimately judgmental, not mathematical. *Edition* in yet another sense is used by publishers to designate reissues in paperback, in special ("deluxe") hardcover versions, or in paperback or hardcover through licensing agreements with other publishers—all, however, without change to the essential text, albeit with perhaps a new foreword or preface, or with changes in nonessential illustrative material. These reissues are often identified in the publishing history in some such way as "Paperback edition 1987," "University of Chicago Press edition 1991," "First Petrine edition 1988," and so forth. In such cases acknowledgment may be given to the original publication. But these reissues are not new editions in the sense defined above and are therefore not counted in the numeration of any series of truly new editions.

1.22   How, then, should the new edition be characterized on the title page? Publishers designate new editions in a variety of ways including *new edition; revised edition; revised and expanded edition; second edition, revised and expanded; third edition;* and so on. The University of Chicago Press recommends that all such designations be simplified and regularized as a concise statement of the number of the edition: *second edition, third edition, fourth edition,* and so on. Should the publisher wish to emphasize the extensiveness of revision or expansion, that may be described in promotional copy rather than being part of the official identification. So long as alternative designations are used, however, documentation of sources should reproduce the publisher's terminology, except that such expressions as "second edition, revised and expanded" may be simplified to "second edition" (avoiding the possible misinterpretation that what is offered is a third edition).

1.23 The sequence of items in the publishing history is as follows: date (year) of the first publication or first edition; number and date of current edition; number and date of impression if other than the first (but see 1.25). These items may each be on a separate line, or they may be run together. There should be no period at the end of a line, but if the items are run together, they are separated within a line by a period (see figs. 1.1, 1.2).

1.24 Although the country in which a book is printed need no longer be identified in the work, most publishers continue the practice of displaying it, usually on the copyright page and frequently as part of the publishing history (see figs. 1.1, etc.). It may also be displayed on the jacket.

Printed in the United States of America
Printed in Great Britain

1.25 The impression is often identified by a line such as the following:

Third impression 1992

This method, however, requires that the line be reset for each new impression. The present widespread use of offset printing, in which printing plates are made photochemically from photographic negatives of camera-ready page proof, has made it possible to change the impression number and date many times without such resetting. In this system a line of numerals runs below the publishing history (see fig. 1.1). The first group of numerals, reading from right to left, represents the last two digits of succeeding years starting with the date of original publication. The second set of numerals, following a space of an em or more, and again reading from right to left, represents the numbers of possible new impressions. The lowest number in each group indicates the present impression and date. In figure 1.1, therefore, the impression is identified as the first, and the year of printing as 1992. New impressions are printed from new plates made from the stored negatives. The printer simply paints out the obsolete numerals in the impression line on the copyright page negative, and what remains shows the correct impression number and date. The impression line in figure 1.2 is appropriate for a fifth impression printed in 1989.

1.26 If the book is a translation, the original title, publisher, and copyright information should be recorded on the copyright page, usually apart from the domestic publishing history (see fig. 1.3).

PUBLISHER'S ADDRESS

1.27 The publisher's address—and sometimes the addresses of overseas agents—may also be given on the copyright page. The University of

Originally published as *Entre l'église et l'état*,
© 1987 Editions Gallimard

The University of Chicago Press, Chicago 60637
The University of Chicago Press, Ltd., London
© 1991 by The University of Chicago
All rights reserved. Published 1991
Printed in the United States of America

00 99 98 97 96 95 94 93 92 91   5 4 3 2 1

Library of Congress Cataloging-in-Publication Data

Guenée, Bernard.
   [Entre l'église et l'état. English]
   Between church and state: the lives of four French
prelates in the late Middle Ages / Bernard Guenée;
translated by Arthur Goldhammer.
     p.   cm.
   Translation of: Entre l'église et l'état
   Includes bibliographical references.
   Includes index.
   ISBN 0-226-31032-9
   1. Bernardus Guidonis, Bishop of Lodve, 1261 or
62–1331.   2. Le Muisit, Gilles, 1272–1353?   3. Ailly,
Pierre d', 1350–1420?   4. Basin, Thomas, 1412–1491.
5. Catholic Church—France—Bishops—Biography.
6. Church and state—France—History.   7. France—
Church history—Middle Ages, 987–1515.   I. Title.
BX4682.G8413   1991
282'.092'244—dc20   90-35045
[B]   CIP

Fig. 1.3. Copyright page of a translation

Chicago Press usually puts these above the copyright notice. An address may be abbreviated, consisting, for example, only of city and perhaps zip code, or it may be the complete mailing address.

CIP DATA

1.28   Since 1971 most publishers have printed the Library of Congress Cataloging-in-Publication (CIP) data on the copyright pages of their books. If the copyright page is too crowded, the information may appear elsewhere in the book, so long as a note is added to the copyright page telling where it may be found (see fig. 1.6). The Library of Congress does not provide CIP data for serial publications (see 1.32).

1.29   The cataloging data printed in a book correspond substantially to the catalog card in the Library of Congress. The *CIP Publishers Manual*, issued by the Library, provides information and instruction for participants in the program and summarizes the program's function as follows:

> The purpose of the Cataloging-in-Publication (CIP) program is to prepare prepublication cataloging records for those books most likely to be widely acquired by the nation's libraries. These records (CIP data) are printed in the book and greatly facilitate cataloging activities for libraries. They are also distributed prior to the books' publication in machine readable form via the MARC (*M*achine *R*eadable *C*ataloging) tapes, alerting libraries and other bibliographic services around the world to forthcoming titles.[1]

Examples of CIP data may be found in figures 1.2–8.

1.30   To obtain the CIP data for a book, the publisher—as soon as the final title has been decided upon, the contents page completed, and the ISBN (see 1.31) assigned—may fill out a form provided by the Library of Congress and send it to the Library of Congress, Cataloging in Publication Division, Washington, D.C. 20540, together with either a complete set of proofs or enough material from the manuscript to enable the Library to classify the book properly (title page, table of contents, preface, sample chapter, summary of text) and the ISBN. The Library requires ten working days after receiving the material to complete the cataloging and send the data to the publisher. To discharge its purpose the printed CIP data should appear substantially as received from the Library. After the data have been received, changes in title, ISBN, or listing of authors' names, inclusion or exclusion of an index or a bibliography, or other such changes in fact should be communicated to the Library along with a request for revised CIP copy. Such changes as deleting the price or the author's birth year or adding ISBNs for other volumes below the CIP data may, however, be made without notifying the Library. If the author's date of birth is deleted, the Library of Congress requests that the word *date* be used in its place.

ISBN

1.31   An International Standard Book Number (ISBN) is assigned to each book by its publisher under a system set up by the R. R. Bowker Company and the International Standards Organization (ISO). The ISBN uniquely identifies the book, thus facilitating order fulfillment and computer tracking of inventory. For example, in ISBN 0-226-07522-2, the first digit, 0, tells us that the book was published in an English-speaking country; the second group of digits, 226, identifies the publisher (in this instance the University of Chicago Press); the third group identifies the book; and the last digit is the *check digit,* which mathematically

---

1. The manual may be obtained from the Library of Congress, Cataloging in Publication Division, Washington, D.C. 20540.

discloses any error in the preceding group. The ISBN is included in the CIP data received from the Library of Congress (see figs. 1.2–7). If the CIP data are printed elsewhere in the book, or not included at all, the ISBN should nevertheless be included on the copyright page. The ISBN should also be printed on the book jacket and on the back cover of a paperback book. If a book is issued in both clothbound and paperback editions, a separate ISBN is assigned to each (see fig. 1.2). When a work comprises two or more volumes, separate ISBNs are assigned to individual volumes that are likely to be sold separately (see fig. 1.4). If the complete work is to be sold as a set only, the same ISBN applies to all volumes. Additional information about the assignment and use of ISBNs may be obtained from the ISBN United States Agency, R. R. Bowker/Martindale-Hubbell.[2]

ISSN

1.32 Serial publications, which include journals, magazines, yearbooks, and certain monograph series, are each assigned an International Standard Serial Number (ISSN). The ISSN remains the same for each issue of the publication and is printed either on the page containing the copyright notice for the issue or with the instructions for ordering the publication. If the publications are books, each is also assigned an International Standard Book Number, and both the ISSN (for the series) and the ISBN (for the book) are printed in the book. Journals and other nonbook serial publications are not assigned an ISBN. Each issue of such a series carries only an ISSN.

PRIOR PUBLICATION, PERMISSIONS, AND ACKNOWLEDGMENTS

1.33 If portions of a book have been previously published, even in slightly different versions, an acknowledgment, including copyright information if required, should be added to the copyright page (fig. 1.5) or provided in a source note in the text (see 2.171–73, 15.50).

1.34 It is sometimes desirable to acknowledge on page iv permission to publish extensive quotations from copyrighted works (fig. 1.6), but do not duplicate acknowledgments given elsewhere, such as in the preface or acknowledgments section of the prelims (1.48) or in notes (15.50). Special grants and assistance may be acknowledged on the copyright page (fig. 1.7), and photo credits may also appear there instead of in the legends to the illustrations (fig. 1.8).

2. ISBN U.S. Agency, R. R. Bowker/Martindale-Hubbell, 121 Chanlon Road, New Providence, N.J. 07974.

Library of Congress Cataloging-in-Publication Data

Theoretical issues in sign language research / edited by Susan D.
  Fischer and Patricia Siple.
    Includes bibliographical references.
    Includes index.
    Contents: v. 1. Linguistics. —v. 2. Psychology.
    1. Sign language. I. Fischer, Susan D.
II. Siple, Patricia.
HV2474.T44 1990   419   90-10997
ISBN 0-226-25149-7 (v. 1 : alk. paper)
ISBN 0-226-25150-0 (pbk. : v. 1 : alk. paper)
ISBN 0-226-25151-9 (v. 2 : alk. paper)
ISBN 0-226-25152-7 (pbk. : v. 2 : alk. paper)

Fig. 1.4. Cataloging-in-Publication data for a two-volume work having separate ISBNs for each volume. Note the added reference to alkaline paper (see 1.35).

The University of Chicago Press, Chicago 60637
The University of Chicago Press, Ltd., London

© 1977 by The University of Chicago
All rights reserved. Published 1977
Printed in the United States of America

82 81 80 79 78 77   5 4 3 2 1

Library of Congress Cataloging-in-Publication Data

Krieger, Leonard.
  Ranke: the meaning of history.

  Bibliography: p.
  Includes index.
  1. Ranke, Leopold von, 1795–1886. 2. History
—Philosophy. 3. Historicism. 4. Historians—
Germany—Biography.
D15.R3K74   907'.2'024   76-25633
ISBN 0-226-45349-9

Parts of chapters 7 and 8 of the present work appeared
in a slightly different version in *History and Theory,*
Beiheft 14 (1975): 1–15. © 1975 by Wesleyan University.

Fig. 1.5. Copyright page acknowledging partial earlier publication

The University of Chicago Press, Chicago 60637
The University of Chicago Press, Ltd., London
© 1976 by The University of Chicago
All rights reserved. Published 1976
Printed in the United States of America
83 82 81 80 79 78 77 76   5 4 3 2 1

ISBN: 0–226–09867–2 (cloth)

The publishers have generously given permission to use extended quotations from the following copyrighted works. From *Farewell, My Lovely,* by Raymond Chandler. Copyright 1940 by Raymond Chandler and renewed 1968 by the Executrix of the Author, Mrs. Helen Greene. Reprinted by permission of Alfred A. Knopf, Inc. From *Red Harvest,* by Dashiell Hammett. Copyright 1929 by Alfred A. Knopf, Inc. and renewed 1957 by Dashiell Hammett. Reprinted by permission of the publisher. From *I, The Jury* by Mickey Spillane. Copyright 1947 by E. P. Dutton & Co.; renewal © 1975 by Frank Morrison Spillane. Reprinted by permission of the publishers, E. P. Dutton & Co., Inc.

**Library of Congress Cataloging-in-Publication Data will be found
at the end of this book.**

Fig. 1.6. Copyright page acknowledging permission to quote extensively and notifying libraries where to find the CIP information.

The Society for the History of Discoveries and The Newberry Library wish to acknowledge the help of Mr. Paul Mellon in the publication of this book.

The University of Chicago Press, Chicago 60637
The University of Chicago Press, Ltd., London

© 1975 by The University of Chicago
All rights reserved. Published 1975
Printed in the United States of America

Library of Congress Cataloging-in-Publication Data

Cavendish, Thomas, 1560–1592.
   The last voyage of Thomas Cavendish, 1591–1592.

   (Studies in the history of discoveries)
   Includes index.
   1. Cavendish, Thomas, 1560–1592.   2. America—
Discovery and exploration—English.   I. Quinn, David
Beers, ed.   II. Newberry Library, Chicago.
III. Title.   IV. Series.
G246.C38A34   1975   910'.41[B]   74–11619
ISBN 0–226–09819–2

Fig. 1.7. Copyright page with special acknowledgment

The University of Chicago Press, Chicago 60637
The University of Chicago Press, Ltd., London

© 1976 by The University of Chicago
All rights reserved. Published 1976
Printed in the United States of America

83 82 81 80 79 78 77 76   5 4 3 2 1

Photo credits: p. ii—Henriette Castex Epstein
(courtesy *Albany Times-Union*); pp. 8, 36,
104, 186—Nate Fine Photo

Library of Congress Cataloging-in-Publication Data

Pratt, Henry J.   1934–
The gray lobby.

Bibliography: p.
Includes index.
1. Aged—United States—Political activity.
2. Aged—Legal status, laws, etc.—United States.
1. Title.
HQ1064.U5P68   301.43′5′0973   75–43232
ISBN 0-226-67917-9

Fig. 1.8. Copyright page with photo credits

PAPER DURABILITY STATEMENT

1.35 One more item that may be included on the copyright page is a statement relating to the durability of the paper on which the book is printed. Much of the paper used in books has some degree of acidity, which shortens its life. Acid-free paper has a longer life expectancy, and paper that is somewhat alkaline is more durable still. Other factors, such as tear resistance and durability under folding, also affect longevity. Durability standards for paper have been established by the American National Standards Institute (ANSI), which has issued statements to be included in books meeting these standards.[3] These statements are usually displayed on the copyright page. For uncoated paper that is alkaline and that meets the standards for folding and tearing, the following notice is authorized (note that it is preceded by a circled infinity symbol):

∞ The paper used in this publication meets the minimum requirements of the American National Standard for Information Sciences—Permanence of Paper for Printed Library Materials, ANSI Z39.48-1984.

3. Further information on paper durability standards and notices may be secured from the American National Standards Institute, 11 W. 42d St., New York, N.Y. 10036.

17

Similar standards have not yet been set for coated paper, but if the paper itself, the *base stock,* is acid free (most coatings are alkaline), the following notice may be carried:

This book is printed on acid-free paper.

Dedication

1.36   Whether a book includes a dedication, to whom a dedication is made, and the phrasing of the dedication are matters for the author to determine. It may be suggested, however, that the word *Dedicated* is superfluous; a simple *To* is sufficient. It is not necessary to identify (or even to give the full name of) the person to whom the work is dedicated, nor is it necessary to give the life dates of a person who has died; but both are permissible.

1.37   It is not customary for editors of contributed volumes to include a dedication unless it is jointly offered by all contributors.

Epigraph

1.38   An author may wish to include an *epigraph*—a pertinent quotation—at the beginning of the book. If there is no dedication, the epigraph may be placed on page v. When there is also a dedication, the epigraph may follow on a new recto page (p. vii) or, to save space, may be put on page vi or on a blank verso page facing the first page of the text. Less customary but possible in certain books is the placement of an epigraph on the title page or half-title page. Epigraphs are also occasionally used at chapter openings and even, although rarely, at the beginnings of subsections within chapters.

1.39   The source of a quotation used in this way is given on a line following the quotation and is usually set flush right, with no parentheses or brackets, but sometimes preceded by a dash. Only the author's name (only the last name of a well-known author) and, usually, the title of the work need appear. No page or line numbers and no bibliographical details are necessary or desirable. Since an epigraph is not part of the text, it should never bear a reference number to a note giving its source. Should the author believe that an explanation of an epigraph is essential, the explanation may appear in the preface or other introductory matter. (For examples of epigraphs see 10.33.)

Table of Contents

1.40   The table of contents (usually titled simply Contents) begins on page v or, if page v carries a dedication or an epigraph, on page vii. (Some publishers place the table of contents at the end of the preliminary matter, so that it immediately precedes the text.) The University of Chicago Press prefers to have the table of contents precede, and therefore include, all preliminary material discussed in the following paragraphs.

1.41   The table of contents should include the title and *beginning* page number of each section of the book: front matter, text divisions, and back matter, including the index. If the book is divided into parts as well as chapters, the part titles should appear in the contents, but their page numbers are not essential if the page numbers of the chapters following them are sufficient indication of where the parts begin (see fig. 1.9). If the parts have separate introductions, these should also be shown in the table of contents. Page numbers in the manuscript of the table of contents are indicated by *000,* and the actual numbers are inserted after pages have been made up. Subheads within chapters may be included in the table of contents, particularly in technical books and in books with long chapters divided into sections defined by meaningful subheads. When subheads are included, they are indented differently than are the chapter titles and are often set in another type style (see figs. 1.10, 1.11). In a long table of contents the subheads may be run in, each followed by its page number.

1.42   In a volume consisting of chapters by different authors, the name of each author should be given in the table of contents with the title of the chapter:

> The Supreme Court as Republican Schoolmaster
> *Ralph Lerner* 127
> *or*
> Self-Incrimination and the New Privacy, *Robert B. McKay* 193

List of Illustrations

1.43   The list of illustrations (usually titled Illustrations but entered in the table of contents as List of Illustrations) should match the table of contents in type size and general style. In books containing various kinds of illustrations, the list may be divided into sections headed, for example, Plates, Figures, Maps (see fig. 1.12). Page numbers are given for all illustrations printed with the text and counted in the pagination, even when folios are not expressed on the page (see 1.99). When pages of illustrations are not counted in the pagination—either because they are tipped in between signatures or because they are added after the book is made up into pages—their location is indicated by *Facing page 000* or *Following page 000* in the list of illustrations. *Facing page* is used for illustrations on a single leaf, each side of which faces a page of text. *Following page* is used for four or more pages (two or more leaves) where inner illustrations do not "face" a page of text (see

Contents

Fig. 1.9. Table of contents showing parts, chapters, preface, and back matter

Contents

Fig. 1.10. Partial table of contents for a historical work divided into books,
parts, chapters, and subsections

Contents

Fig. 1.11. Partial table of contents for a scientific work, showing chapter titles, A- and B-level subheads, and back matter

Illustrations

Figures

Maps

Fig. 1.12. List of illustrations including figures, maps, and page numbers

11.45). *Following page 000* may be set above a group of illustration
titles so that the same page number need not be repeated for each (see
fig. 1.13). A frontispiece, because of its prominent position at the front
of the book, is customarily not assigned a page number: its location is
simply given as *frontispiece*.

1.44   Titles given in the list of illustrations need not correspond exactly to the
captions or legends printed with the illustrations themselves. If the captions are long, shortened forms should be given in the list of illustrations. (See also 11.44–45, 11.46.)

Illustrations

Following Page 46

1. Josaphat's first outing
2. Portrait of Marco Polo
3. Gold-digging ant from Sebastian Münster's *Cosmographei,* 1531
4. An Indian "Odota" from Sebastian Münster's *Cosmographei,* 1531

.   .   .   .

Following Page 520

84. *Doctrina christam* printed at Quilon
85. First book printed at Macao by Europeans, 1585
86. First book printed in China on a European press, 1588
87. Title page of *Doctrina Christiana* printed at Manila, 1593, in Tagalog and Spanish
88. Final page of above
89. Title page of *Doctrina Christiana* printed at Manila, 1593, in Spanish and Chinese

---

Fig. 1.13. List of illustrations showing placement of unpaginated plates

1.45 In a book with either very few or very many illustrations, all of which are tied closely to the text, it is not essential to list them in the front matter. Multiauthor books, proceedings of symposia, and the like commonly do not carry lists of illustrations.

List of Tables

1.46 A list of tables (titled Tables but entered in the table of contents as List of Tables) follows the table of contents or, if there is one, the list of illustrations. Listing tables in the front matter is helpful mainly in technical books with many tables and frequent textual references to them. The titles may be shortened if necessary.

Foreword

1.47 A foreword is usually a statement by someone other than the author or editor, sometimes an eminent person whose name may be carried on the title page: With a Foreword by ——. The author's own statement about the work is called a preface. Both are set in the same size and style of type as the text. A foreword normally runs only two to four pages, and its author's name appears at the end, often in caps and small caps and indented one em from the right. The title or affiliation of the author of a foreword may appear under the name, in smaller type on the left side of the page. If a foreword runs to a substantial length, with or without a title of its own, its author's name may be given at the beginning instead of at the end. (For place and date with a foreword, see 1.49.)

Preface and Acknowledgments

1.48   Material normally included in an author's preface includes reasons for undertaking the work, method of research (if this has some bearing on the reader's understanding of the text), acknowledgments, and sometimes permissions granted for the use of previously published material (see 4.68–69). If the acknowledgments are long, they may be put in a separate section following the preface; if a preface consists only of acknowledgments, its title should be changed to Acknowledgments. Acknowledgments are sometimes put at the back of a book, preceding the index. In multivolume works, acknowledgments that apply to all volumes need appear only in the first. Should they vary from volume to volume, separate acknowledgments will be required in each. If special acknowledgments are required for one of the volumes, they may be included in the general acknowledgments, or separate acknowledgments may be added to that volume.

1.49   A preface should be signed by its author (name at the end, as described above for the author of a foreword) only when there might be some doubt about who wrote it. The reader logically assumes that an unsigned preface was written by the author whose name appears on the title page. The University of Chicago Press discourages the inclusion of place (city) and date at the end of a preface or a foreword. When these facts are given, however, they are set flush left, with a line space between them and the text.

1.50   When a new preface is written for a new edition, for a paperback edition of a book already published in hardcover, or for a reprinting of a book long out of print, the new preface precedes the original preface. The original preface is then usually retitled Preface to the First Edition, and the new preface may be titled Preface to the Second Edition, Preface to the Paperback Edition, or, for example, Preface 1993. In a book containing both an editor's preface and an author's preface, the editor's preface, which may be titled as such, comes first and should bear the editor's name at its conclusion.

Introduction

1.51   Material very relevant to the text, material that should be read before the rest of the book—an account of the historical background of the subject of the book, for example—should not be relegated to a preface but should be printed as an introduction at the beginning of the text proper. Text matter should not be mixed with acknowledgments, methodology or history of a research project, or other information concerning the writing of the book.

1.52   A relatively short introduction that is relevant to but not part of the text itself should be paginated with the preliminaries, that is, with roman numerals. A long introduction or one that actually begins the subject matter of the text or that the author uses to set the scene—to give, for example, the historical background of the subject—should be part of the text, paginated with arabic numerals.

Other Front Matter

1.53   Edited texts and other kinds of scholarly works often require additional material in the preliminary pages—a list of abbreviations, for example, or biographical information about the author of an edited text, or any explanation of editorial procedures or peculiarities of apparatus that the reader needs to understand before encountering the text proper.

LIST OF ABBREVIATIONS

1.54   In some heavily documented books, especially where there are many references to a few easily abbreviated sources, it may be a convenience to the reader to list abbreviations for these sources before the text rather than in the back matter. If no more than one page long, such a list may be placed on the verso facing the first page of text. A long list of abbreviations used in notes and bibliography, and sometimes in the text, is generally best placed in the back matter, preceding the notes (see 15.25).

EDITORIAL METHOD

1.55   An explanation of an editor's method or a discussion of variant texts, often necessary in scholarly editions, may constitute a large part of the preliminary pages. Such material is essential for the user of edited texts and is therefore often placed at the end of the prelims, just before the text proper. Short, uncomplicated remarks about editorial method, however—such as noting that spelling and capitalization have been modernized—should be incorporated in the editor's preface, not put in a separate section.

LIST OF CONTRIBUTORS

1.56   In a multiauthor book, such as a festschrift or the proceedings of a symposium, it is often desirable to list the contributors separately, with only the editor or editors appearing on the title page (see 1.7). The list may be headed "Contributors," "Participants," or whatever suits the particular work. An alphabetical arrangement is the usual practice (do not invert the names: Andrew D. White, not White, Andrew D.); in some cases a geographical or other arrangement may be more suitable. Academic rank and affiliation may be given for each contributor, and sometimes short biographies are appropriate. (Such a list is often placed at the back of the book rather than in the front matter.) (For examples see figs. 1.14 and 1.15.)

1.57   A book with several authors does not necessarily carry a list of contributors. Often it is enough simply to give the authors' names in the table of contents and at the heads of their contributions, with perhaps an unnumbered note at the beginning of each chapter identifying the author (see 1.42, 1.63, 15.51).

CHRONOLOGY

1.58   A chronological list of events important in a person's life or over a certain period may be useful in a volume such as a collection of letters or other documents where the sequence of events is not clear in the text itself. For easy reference, a chronology should appear immediately before the text. It is also possible to place it after the text, in the back matter, or wherever it will be most helpful (for two examples see figs. 1.16 and 1.17).

TEXT

1.59   In general, the preliminary pages serve as a guide to the contents and nature of the book, and the back matter provides reference material. The text proper should contain everything necessary for a reader to understand the author's argument. The organization of the text material can help or hinder comprehension. The following paragraphs deal with divisions commonly found in most books, not with substantive organization. Details of handling special elements in the text—quotations, illustrations, tables, mathematics, and notes—are discussed in part 2 of this manual.

1.60   In a book containing extensive preliminaries, a second half title, identical to the one on page i, may be added at the beginning of the text proper. The second half title is ordinarily counted as page 1, the beginning of the pages bearing arabic-numeral folios, although in this case

Contributors

DERK BODDE, professor of Chinese at the University of Pennsylvania, has written *China's First Unifier, Peking Diary,* and many other books, including *Law in Imperial China* (with Clarence Morris). He has translated from the Chinese the standard two-volume work, *A History of Chinese Philosophy,* by Fung Yu-lan. He is a member of the American Philosophical Society and the American Academy of Arts and Sciences.

JEROME ALAN COHEN, professor of law at Harvard University, is the author of articles on Chinese law and *The Criminal Process in the People's Republic of China, 1949–1963: An Introduction.*

HERRLEE G. CREEL, the Martin A. Ryerson Distinguished Service Professor of Chinese History at the University of Chicago, is the author of *The Birth of China; Studies in Early Chinese Culture; Confucius, the Man and the Myth;* and *Chinese Thought from Confucius to Mao Tse-tung.*

ROBERT DERNBERGER, assistant professor of economics and chairman of the Committee on Far Eastern Studies at the University of Chicago, is former editor of *Economic Development and Cultural Change* and has contributed articles on China's contemporary economy to *Three Essays on the International Economics of Communist China, Contemporary China,* and *Economic Nationalism in the New States.*

ALEXANDER ECKSTEIN, professor of economics and director of the Center for Chinese Studies at the University of Michigan, has written, among others, *The National Income of Communist China* and *Communist China's Economic Growth and Foreign Trade.*

Fig. 1.14. Partial list of contributors to a multiauthor work. Names here are set in caps and small caps but might be set in caps and lowercase roman or italic.

the folio is unexpressed. The verso of the second half title is counted as page 2, although it is usually blank and bears no folio. In this case the first chapter begins on page 3. If at a later stage, after the text pages have been numbered, a second half title is added to fill out even signatures (see 19.66), that half title may be regarded as a continuation of the roman-numbered pages so that the number of the first page of text may remain 1.

Contributors

Arthur W. H. Adkins
Professor of Greek, Philosophy, and New Testament,
the University of Chicago

Hans Dieter Betz
Professor of New Testament,
the University of Chicago

Sheryl L. Burkhalter
Graduate student in History of Religions,
the University of Chicago

Wendy Doniger
Mircea Eliade Professor of History of Religions and Indian
Studies, the University of Chicago

Norman J. Girardot
Associate Professor of Religion Studies,
Lehigh University

Douglas A. Knight
Associate Professor of Old Testament,
Vanderbilt University

Robin W. Lovin
Associate Professor of Ethics and Society,
the University of Chicago

Frank E. Reynolds
Professor of History of Religions and Buddhist
Studies, the University of Chicago

Douglas Sturm
Professor of Religion and Political Science,
Bucknell University

Lawrence E. Sullivan
Associate Professor of History of Religions,
the University of Chicago

Kay Barbara Warren
Associate Professor of Anthropology,
Princeton University

Lee H. Yearley
Associate Professor of Religious Studies,
Stanford University

Fig. 1.15. Simplified list of contributors showing names, academic ranks, and affiliations.

MADISON CHRONOLOGY
1787

27 May– 17 September	JM attends Federal Convention at Philadelphia. Takes notes on the debates.
29 May	Virginia Plan presented.
6 June	JM makes first major speech, containing analysis of factions and theory of extended republic.
8 June	Defends "negative" (veto) on state laws.
19 June	Delivers critique of New Jersey Plan.
27 June–16 July	In debate on representation, JM advocates proportional representation for both branches of legislature.
16 July	Compromise on representation adopted.
26 July	Convention submits resolutions to Committee of Detail as basis for preparing draft constitution.
6 August	Report of Committee of Detail delivered.
7 August	JM advocates freehold suffrage.
7 August– 10 September	Convention debates, then amends, report of 6 August
31 August	JM appointed to Committee on Postponed Matters.
8 September	Appointed to Committee of Style.
17 September	Signs engrossed Constitution. Convention adjourns.
ca. 21 September	Leaves Philadelphia for New York.
24 September	Arrives in New York to attend Congress.
26 September	Awarded Doctor of Laws degree in absentia by College of New Jersey.

Fig. 1.16. First page of a chronology at the end of the front matter in a volume of letters

Chronological Guide to the Track Chart of Cavendish's Last Voyage

1591

Five ships leave Plymouth, August 26: *Galleon Leicester* ("admiral," namely, flagship), *Roebuck* ("vice-admiral"), *Desire, Daintie, Black Pinnace*

They pass down the Spanish and Portuguese coast

They sight the Canaries, September 14

They probably pass into the ocean by the western Cape Verdes

They are becalmed on or near the equator

They make landfall, November 29, at Salvador, about 36 miles north of Cabo Frio

They arrive at Placencia (Ilha Grande), December 5

They sail December 11

They arrive at Ilha de São Sebastião, December 14

Desire and *Black Pinnace* attack and occupy Santos, December 15

Cavendish in *Galleon Leicester* arrives and occupies Santos, December 16 (or later)

1592

They set sail from Santos and burn São Vicente, January 24

Fleet separated in storm, February 7–8

Daintie loses contact and sails under her master to England; track conjectural

Roebuck and *Desire* arrive at Port Desire, March 6

Black Pinnace reaches Port Desire, March 16

Galleon Leicester arrives, March 18

They leave Port Desire, March 20, and encounter gales

They "fell with" the Strait of Magellan, April 8

They pass through the First Strait, April 14

They pass through the Second Strait, April 16

They double Cape Froward, April 18

They put in to a small cove on the south side of Port Tobias, April 21

They set out on return eastward, May 15

They clear the Strait, May 18

Ships are separated off Port Desire, May 20

Desire and *Black Pinnace* enter Port Desire

In May, Cavendish in *Galleon Leicester* is driven far out to sea and makes for Brazil

Roebuck also driven by storm on course presumably similar to *Galleon Leicester*'s and reaches Brazil somewhat later

Davis quells possible mutiny on *Desire* and *Black Pinnace*, June 2

From May onward (no dates available), Cavendish reaches Baia de São Vincente, near Santos; attempts to raid São Vicente; remains in Canal de Bertioga and is joined by *Roebuck*

The two ships go north to Ilha de Espírito Santo and attempt to attack the town of Espírito Santo

Roebuck returns to England alone, her track being conjectural

Galleon Leicester goes south to Ilha de São Sebastião

Galleon Leicester works up coast from lat. 29° to 20°S on first stage homeward

Desire and *Black Pinnace* leave Port Desire, August 6, to go to Penguin Island to salt food

The two vessels sail southward, August 7

Driven out to sea, they sight unknown islands (Falklands?), August 14

Fig. 1.17. Chronology accompanying a map of a sixteenth-century voyage. The large page of this book suggested a two-column format.

Chapters

1.61   Most prose works are divided into chapters, often, though not necessarily, of approximately the same length. Chapter titles should be similar in tone, if not in length. Each title should give a reasonable clue to
what is in the chapter; whimsical titles in a serious book, for example,
can be misleading. Many potential readers scan the table of contents to
determine whether a book is worth their time (and money). Relatively
short titles are preferable to long, ungainly ones, both for appearance
on the page and for use in running heads (see 1.92–98).

1.62   In the printed book, each chapter normally starts on a new page, verso
or recto, and its opening page carries a drop folio and no running head.
The first chapter ordinarily begins on a recto. The *chapter display* usually consists of the chapter number (the word *chapter* is often omitted)
and chapter title and sometimes an epigraph as well (see 1.39, 10.33
for treatment of epigraph sources). In titles of two or more lines, punctuation should be omitted at the end of a line unless it is essential for
clarity. Footnote reference numbers or symbols should not appear anywhere in the chapter display. A note that refers to the chapter as a whole
should be unnumbered and should precede the numbered notes,
whether it appears on the first page of the chapter or in the endnotes
(see 15.50–52).

1.63   In books consisting of chapters contributed by different authors, chapter
numbers are sometimes omitted. The author's name is always given in
the display. An affiliation or other identification is usually not considered part of the display but is put in an unnumbered footnote on the
first page of the chapter (see 2.171–73, 15.51) or in a list of contributors
(1.56). An unnumbered footnote is also used to disclose the source of
a chapter or other contribution that is being reprinted from an earlier
publication. When both the author's affiliation and the source of the
contribution are given in the note, it is customary, but not essential, that
the affiliation come first.

1.64   When offprints, or reprints, of individual chapters are planned, as in a
conference volume, each chapter should begin on a recto page so that
the pages of the chapter may simply be gathered and bound without
having to be reimposed or rearranged.

Parts

1.65   When text material may be logically divided into sections larger than
chapters, the chapters may be grouped in parts. Each part is normally
numbered and given a part title, as in this manual. The part number and

title appear on a recto page preceding the first chapter of the part. The back, or verso, of this page is usually left blank. Chapters within parts are numbered consecutively through the book (*not* beginning over with 1 in each part).

1.66 Part titles and their versos are counted in the pagination, even though their folios are unexpressed.

1.67 Each part may have an introduction, usually short, and titled, for example, Introduction to Part 2. The part introduction may begin on a new recto following the part title or, to conserve space, on the verso of the part title. Occasionally it will even begin, with a suitable drop, on the part-title page itself.

1.68 A text introduction to a book that is divided into parts precedes part 1 and needs no part-title page to introduce it. Also, no part title *need* precede the back matter of a book divided into parts, but part titles may be used for each section of the back matter: for example, Appendixes, Notes, Bibliography, Index.

Other Divisions

POETRY

1.69 In a book of previously unpublished poetry, each poem usually begins on a new page. Any part titles provided by the poet need not carry page numbers but should appear on separate pages (rectos) preceding the poems grouped under them. Normally the first poem in the collection and the first following each part title begin on a recto. In a collection of previously published poems, the poems may follow one another on the same page.

LETTERS AND DIARIES

1.70 Correspondence and journals are usually presented in chronological order, seldom conducive to division into chapters or parts. Dates, used as guidelines rather than titles, are often inserted above relevant diary entries. The names of the sender and the recipient of a letter may serve the same function in published correspondence. In a collection of letters written by (or to) a single person, however, the name of that person is not used each time. For example, in *The Papers of James Madison,* "To Edmund Randolph" and "From Edmund Randolph" are sufficient. The date of a letter may be included in the guideline if it does not appear in the letter itself. Such guidelines in diaries and correspondence do not begin a new page in the book unless page makeup demands it.

Subheads

1.71 In prose works where the chapters are long and the material complicated, the author (or the editor) may insert *subheads,* or *subheadings,* in the text as guides to the reader. Subheads should be short and meaningful; and, like chapter titles, they should be similar in tone.

1.72 Many scholarly works require only one level of subhead throughout the text. Some, particularly scientific or technical works, require sub-subheads and even further subdivisions. Where more than one level is used, the subheads are referred to as the *A-level* subhead (the principal subhead), the *B-level* (the secondary subhead), the *C-level,* and so on (or *A-head, B-head, C-head,* etc.). Only in the most complicated works does the need for more than three levels arise.

1.73 When a section of text is subdivided, there should ordinarily be at least two subsections. One subhead in a chapter or one B-level subhead under an A-level subhead may be viewed as illogical and asymmetrical.

1.74 Subheads, except the lowest level, are each set on a line separate from the text, the levels differentiated by type style and placement (specified by the book designer; see 18.28–29). The lowest level is often run in at the beginning of a paragraph, set in italics and followed by a period. It is then referred to as a *run-in sidehead.*

1.75 In some works the number of subhead levels required may vary from chapter to chapter; that is, one or two chapters may need three levels, the rest only one or two. Some material may require run-in subheads, for example, while the rest of the book is clear, and better off, without them.

1.76 Unless sections in a chapter are cited in cross-references elsewhere in the text, numbers are usually unnecessary with subheads. In general, subheads are more useful to a reader than numbers alone.

1.77 In scientific and technical works, however, the numbering of sections, subsections, and sometimes sub-subsections provides easy reference and may be a true convenience to the reader. There are various ways to number sections. The most common is the *double-numeration* system, perhaps more properly called the *multiple-numeration* system. In this system sections are numbered within chapters, subsections within sections, and sub-subsections within subsections. The number of each division is preceded by the numbers of all higher divisions, and all divisional numbers are separated by periods. Thus the numbers 4.8 and 4.12, for example, signify the eighth section and the twelfth section of chapter 4. The series 4.12.3 signifies the third subsection in the twelfth section of chapter 4, and so on.[4] The multiple-numeration system may

4. Multiple numeration should not be confused with decimal fractions. In multiple numeration, periods separate ordinal numeral designations of sectional levels. In such a

also be used for illustrations, tables, and mathematical equations (see, respectively, 11.27, 12.18, and 13.24–25). Another system, used in some monographs, is to ignore the chapter numbers (which should here be roman numerals to prevent confusion) and to number A-level subheads consecutively through the book, B-level subheads consecutively under each A-level, and C-level subsections under the B-level: 25.10.7 thus might occur in chapter V. This manual employs still another system—chapter number followed by *paragraph* number—to facilitate cross-referencing.

1.78 No note reference number should appear within or at the end of a subhead. Such a reference number should be placed at an appropriate location in the text.

1.79 The first sentence of text following a subhead should not contain a pronoun referring back to a word in the subhead; the word itself should be repeated where necessary. For example:

> SECONDARY SPONGIOSA
> The secondary spongiosa is a vaulted structure . . .
>> *not*
> SECONDARY SPONGIOSA
> This is a vaulted structure . . .

1.80 Instead of subheads, extra space or a type ornament between paragraphs may be used to mark text divisions or to signal changes in subject or emphasis. Usually one blank line is enough for this purpose. If such a space falls between pages, however, it will be lost in makeup; an ornament will preserve the division.

Epilogues, Afterwords, and Conclusions

1.81 *Epilogues* and *afterwords* are relatively brief concluding sections with which an author may occasionally end the text. They bear no chapter numbers. *Conclusions* tend to be more extensive and may assume the significance and proportions of final chapters, with or without chapter numbers. In such concluding sections the author may make some final statement about the subject presented, the research conducted, the decisions or conclusions to which the author has been led, the implications of the study, or questions inviting further investigation. Epilogues, afterwords, and conclusions may begin either recto or verso, and typographically they are usually treated like chapters, forewords, or prefaces.

---

system, 4.9 may be followed by 4.10, which in the decimal-fraction system would represent four and ten-hundredths or four and one-tenth, that is, a number less than 4.9. In multiple numeration, 4.9 might also be followed by 4.10.1, which does not exist in the decimal-fraction system.

BACK MATTER

Appendix

1.82 Although an appendix is not an essential part of every book, the possibilities and uses of the device are many. Some kinds of material properly relegated to an appendix are explanations and elaborations that are not essential parts of the text but are helpful to a reader seeking further clarification; texts of documents, laws, and so forth, illustrating the text; and long lists, survey questionnaires, or sometimes even charts or tables. The appendix should not be a repository for raw data that the author was unable to work into the text.

1.83 When there are two or more appendixes in a book, they should be numbered like chapters (Appendix 1, Appendix 2, etc.) or designated by letters (Appendix A, Appendix B, etc.), and each should be given a title as well. The first appendix usually, but not necessarily, begins on a recto page; subsequent appendixes may begin verso or recto.

1.84 An appendix may be placed at the end of a chapter if what it contains is essential to understanding the chapter. Here it may start on a new page, recto or verso, or may run on at the end of the chapter following a suitable space, perhaps three or four lines. (The interruptive effect of this placement should be carefully weighed, however: most appendixes belong at the end of a book.) In multiauthor books and in books from which offprints of individual chapters will be required, any appendix *must* follow the chapter to which it pertains.

1.85 The text of appendixes may be set either in the same size type as the text proper or in smaller type.

Notes

1.86 The note section follows any appendix material and precedes a bibliography or reference list. The notes are arranged by chapters, with chapter numbers and perhaps chapter titles serving as subheads, usually A-level; the chapter groupings follow one another, with a line or two of space between groups, to the end of the note section. The running heads in the note section should help identify the text pages to which the notes apply. (For a discussion of endnotes versus footnotes see 15.44–45; of unnumbered notes and notes keyed to line numbers, 15.50–52; of running heads in a section of endnotes, 1.97 and 15.37–40.)

Glossary

1.87 A glossary is a useful tool in a book containing many foreign words or in a technical work, such as this manual, intended for the general reader who may be puzzled by terms not in the common vocabulary. Words to be defined in a glossary should be arranged in alphabetical order, each on a separate line and followed by its definition. A glossary precedes a bibliography.

Bibliography or Reference List

1.88   The form of a bibliography or list of references varies with the nature of the book, the inclination of the author, and often the guidance of the publisher. It may be a single listing of sources, arranged alphabetically by author. It may be broken into sections, by subject or by kinds of materials (primary and secondary sources, etc.). It may be a selected bibliography (preferable, as a rule, in a published book as opposed to a doctoral dissertation). It may be an annotated bibliography, with the annotations sometimes indented under each entry and set in smaller type. Or it may be a discursive "bibliographical essay" in which the author discusses the most useful sources.

1.89   Bibliographies and reference lists are normally set in smaller type than the text and in flush-and-hang style (except the bibliographical essay). (For examples see chapters 15 and 16.)

Index

1.90   The index, or the first of several indexes, usually begins on a recto page; subsequent indexes begin verso or recto. If there are both name and subject indexes, the name index precedes the subject index. (For acceptable kinds and forms of indexes see chapter 17.) Indexes are normally set two columns to a page and in smaller type than the text (see 17.136).

Colophon

1.91   An embellishment sometimes added on the last page of a specially designed and produced book is the colophon, in this sense not simply the publisher's emblem (1.110) but an inscription including the facts of production (fig. 1.18). This practice is no longer common in book publishing.

RUNNING HEADS

1.92   Running heads, the headings at the tops of pages in a book, are signposts telling readers where they are. For this purpose running heads are

THE CHRISTIAN TRADITION

Designed by Joseph Alderfer
Composed by Typoservice Corporation
in Linotype Garamond with display lines
in Foundry American Garamond
Printed by Halliday Lithograph Corporation
on Warren's Olde Style
Bound by Halliday Lithograph Corporation
in Joanna Arrestox Vellum and
stamped in purple and gold

Fig. 1.18. Colophon printed at the end of each volume of a five-volume work

useful in most scholarly works, textbooks, and the like. They may be omitted where they serve no practical purpose—in a novel or a book of poems, for example. Running heads are sometimes placed at the bottoms of pages, where they may be referred to, with circumstantial humor, as running feet. (For preparation of running-head copy see 2.159–61.)

Front Matter

1.93   Running heads should never be used on display pages (half title, title, copyright, dedication, epigraph) or on the first page of the table of contents, preface, and so forth. An element in the prelims that runs more than one page must carry running heads if the design calls for running heads in the text. Each element in the front matter normally carries the same running head on verso and recto pages.

Verso	Recto
Contents	Contents
Preface	Preface

Text

1.94   Chapter openings and other display pages in the text do not require, and should not have, running heads. The choice of running heads for other text pages is governed chiefly by the structure and nature of the book. Some acceptable arrangements are the following:

VERSO	RECTO
Part title	Chapter title
Chapter title	Subhead
Chapter title	Chapter title
Chapter title	Chapter subtitle
Chapter number	Chapter title
Subhead	Subhead
Author (multiauthor books)	Chapter title

Putting the book title on the verso page is no longer common practice. Reasons against it are that the title may be changed while the book is in production and that most readers know what book they are reading and prefer running heads telling them where they are in it.

1.95 When subheads in the text are used as running heads on the recto pages and when more than one subhead falls on a single page, the *last* one on the page is used as the running head. When subheads are used as running heads on verso pages, however, the *first* of several subheads to appear on the page is used as the running head. (The principle is the same as that used for dictionary running heads.)

Back Matter

1.96 Some acceptable arrangements for running heads in the back matter are the following:

VERSO	RECTO
Appendix A	Title of appendix
Appendix	Appendix (if not titled)
Glossary	Glossary
Bibliography	Bibliography
Bibliography	Section title
Index	Index
Subject Index	Subject Index

1.97 The running heads for a section of notes in the back of the book are especially important and a definite convenience to readers. They should give either the inclusive text-page numbers or the chapter number where the relevant note references are found. Thus, two facing running heads might read:

VERSO	RECTO
Notes to Pages 2–10	Notes to Pages 11–25

or

VERSO	RECTO
Notes to Chapter One	Notes to Chapter Two

(For a fuller explanation and more examples see 15.37–40.)

Omission of Running Heads

1.98 Certain pages do not take running heads. In addition to display pages in the front matter (see 1.93), these include part titles, chapter openings, and any page containing only an illustration or a table. A running head should be used, however, on a page containing both an illustration (or a table) and lines of text.

PAGE NUMBERS

1.99 All modern books are paginated consecutively, and all leaves in a book (except endpapers) are counted in the pagination, whether folios are expressed or not, except photo galleries and full-page illustrations tipped in between signatures or inserted after pages have been made up (see 1.43). Various locations on the page are acceptable for the folio. The most common, and perhaps the most easily found, is at the top of the page, flush outside (left on verso pages, right on recto pages). The folio may also be printed at the bottom of the page, and in that location it is called a *drop folio*. Drop folios may appear flush outside, in the center, or indented from the outside.

Front Matter

1.100 The preliminary pages of a book usually, especially in United States publications, are paginated with lowercase roman numerals (see 1.3). The practice is due partly to tradition and partly to expedience: some of these pages (the table of contents and the lists of illustrations and tables) cannot be finally made up until the text is in page proofs, and others (the preface, acknowledgments, and dedication) are often heavily revised or even added by the author at the last moment, after the rest of the book is in pages. Thus, separate numbering for the prelims makes good sense.

1.101 In some books, however, arabic numbering begins with the first page (half title) and continues straight through the book. This system, more common in Great Britain than here, should be held in mind as a sometimes useful alternative. When prelims are unusually long, use of arabic numerals eliminates the awkwardness of roman folios running up through xlviii, xlix, and so on. But since this system affects the pagination of the entire book, the author must understand that there is no possibility of adding a dedication page or an additional page of acknowledgments or, indeed, anything else once paging has begun.

1.102 Whether roman or arabic folios are used, no folio is expressed on display pages (half title, title, copyright, dedication, epigraph), and a drop folio (or none) is used on the opening page of each succeeding section of the prelims.

Text and Back Matter

1.103   Following the prelims, arabic numerals are used throughout the book. When roman folios are used in the prelims, the text begins with arabic folio 1. If the text begins with a second half title (the same as that on page i) or with a part title, the half title or part title counts as folio 1, its verso as folio 2, and the first folio to be expressed is the drop folio 3 on the first page of text (but see 1.60). If there is no part- or half-title page, the first page of the text proper becomes page 1. Subsequent part titles (1.65) are counted in the pagination, but the folios are not expressed.

1.104   The opening page of each chapter and of each section in the back matter carries a drop folio or no folio at all (unexpressed). Folios are not usually expressed on pages containing only illustrations or tables, except in books containing long sequences of figures or tables.

More Than One Volume

1.105   When a work runs to more than one volume, the publisher must decide how to paginate volume 2: Begin with folio 1 on the first page of text, or carry on from where the numbering left off in volume 1? The chief consideration is probably the index. When an index to two volumes is to appear at the end of volume 2, it is often useful to paginate consecutively through both volumes so that the index need not include volume numbers as well as page numbers. More than two volumes, however, regardless of index placement, are best paginated separately, both because page numbers in four digits are unwieldy (though necessary in large reference works) and because, for the reader's convenience, any reference to a specific page in a work of more than two volumes should include the volume number as well as the page number.

1.106   Note that whether the pagination is consecutive or by volume, the preliminary pages in each volume begin with page i. In rare cases where back matter, such as an index or tabular material, must be added to volume 1 later in the production process, lowercase roman folios may be used; these should continue the sequence from the prelims in that volume—if, for example, there are twelve preliminary pages, even though page xii is blank, the back matter would start with page xiii. Again, this is not common practice but is a useful alternative.

ERRATA

1.107   *Errata,* lists of errors and their corrections, may take the form of loose, inserted sheets or bound-in pages. An *errata sheet* is definitely not a usual part of a book. It should never be supplied to correct simple typographical errors (which may be rectified in a later printing) or to insert additions to, or revisions of, the printed text (which should wait for the next edition of the book). It is a device to be used only in extreme cases where errors severe enough to cause misunderstanding are detected too late to correct in the normal way but before the finished book is distributed. Then the errors may be listed with their locations and their corrections on a sheet that is tipped in, either before or after the book is bound, or laid in loose, usually inside the front cover of the book. (Tipping and inserting must be done by hand, thus adding considerably to the cost of the book.) The following form may be adapted to suit the particulars:

ERRATA

Page	For	Read
37, line 5	Peter W. Smith	John Q. Jones
182, line 15	is subject to	is not subject to
195, line 8	figure 3	figure 15
23, 214	Transpose legends of plates 2 and 51.	

1.108   The inclusion of an errata page may be justified when all or part of a book is photographically reproduced from an earlier publication in which there are a few easily correctable errors. There should be a head-note explaining the matter (see fig. 1.19). Such a page must be prepared in time to be set in type and printed and bound with the book. It may be placed either at the end of the prelims or at the end of the book and should be listed in the table of contents.

EXTERIOR STRUCTURE

Cover

1.109   A book is protected, identified, and often promoted by its cover. The cover may be hard or "soft," that is, pliable. Hard covers are usually constructed of laminated cardboard over which is stretched an integument of cloth, treated paper, vinyl, or some other plastic. Books bound in hard covers are said to be *case bound.* Pliable covers are usually made of rather thick but flexible paper whose printed and decorated outside is coated with varnish or with a synthetic resin or plastic laminate.

1.110   A book cover has three parts, front, back, and spine. In hardcover books the spine is most often printed with the name of the author and

Errata

Chapters 1 through 6 and chapters 8 and 9 have been photographically reproduced from the original journal articles. The following are corrections for typographical errors in those articles.

Chap. 1
P. 43, n. 16: "*wirtschaftsmenschen*" should be capitalized.
P. 72, line 12: "1226" should read "1225."

Chap. 2
P. 91, n. 2: "Appendix IV" should read "Appendix III."
P. 91, n. 4: "Appendix IV" should read "Appendix III."
P. 96, line 19: "*stamai uoli*" should read "*stamaiuoli.*"
P. 107, n. 3: "Appendix IV" should read "Appendix III."
P. 114, Appendix II: "Vencenzo" should read "Vincenzo."

Chap. 3
P. 130, line 19: "*sopracorpo*" should read "*sopraccorpo.*"
P. 134, line 31: "*sovracorpo*" should read "*sovraccorpo.*"
P. 155, n. 1: "Accerito" should read "Accerrito"; the date of Folco's death should be 1431.
P. 158, line 24: "*sopracorpo*" should read "*sopraccorpo.*"

Chap. 4
P. 198, col. 1, line 21: "enforcible" should read "enforceable."

Chap. 5
P. 201, line 1 : "*bancum*" should read "*bancus.*"
P. 202, line 1: change "sought" to "found."
P. 203, line 20: "became" should read "become."
P. 208, n. 31: "*Verlagsystem*" should read "*Verlagssystem.*"
P. 213, n. 51: "*Tujdschrift*" should read "*Tijdschrift.*"
P. 216, n. 64: "Maine" should read "Maino."
P. 221, n. 107: "*Sicilio*" should read "*Sicilie*"; "*1908*" should read "*1808.*"
P. 227, n. 125: "Publication" should read "Publicatiën."
P. 237, line 15: "wors" should read "worse."

Chap. 6
P. 240, line 22: "Masarozzo" should read "Masaiozzo"; insert "Martellini" after "d'Agnolo."
P. 240, n. 3: "wich" should read "wish."

Fig. 1.19. Page of errata printed and bound with photographically reproduced material

publisher and the title of the book (see 2.158). Sometimes only the last name of the author is given; the University of Chicago Press, however, recommends including the full names of authors if there is room enough. If there is a subtitle, that is usually omitted to conserve space. For the same reason, the publisher's name is often shortened or replaced by initials or by the publisher's emblem or device, known as a *colophon* (for another type of colophon see 1.91). The front cover is often devoid of printing, especially when there is a jacket, but it may also bear stamped or printed material, such as author and title or the publisher's colophon or some other decoration. The back cover, although it too might bear some printing or stamping, is more commonly blank.

1.111   Paperback covers usually carry printing on all three parts. The author's name, the publisher's name or colophon, or both, and the title are ordinarily printed on the spine, and some or all of these may be repeated on the front cover. A subtitle, if there is one, is also carried on the front cover. Promotional copy, such as a discussion of the book or quotations from reviews, and perhaps a brief biographical statement about the author or a list of some of the author's other works may be printed on the back cover. Artwork may appear on any or all of the cover parts.

Jacket, or Dust Wrapper

1.112   Hardcover books are often further protected, and promoted, by a coated paper jacket, or dust wrapper. In addition to the three parts to be found on the book cover itself, the jacket also has *flaps* that fold around and tuck inside the front and back covers. These front and back flaps may also carry printed promotional matter. The spine and the front and back panels of the jacket carry material similar to that on the cover of the paperback book: title, author, publisher, colophon, reviews and other promotional copy, and artwork.

Copy and Artwork for the Cover and Jacket

1.113   The promotional copy that appears on the cover or jacket of the book is usually prepared by the publisher's marketing staff, and in many publishing houses the copy is read by the editors to ensure grammatical correctness and stylistic consistency and to verify that the copy accurately reflects the substance of the book. Such matters as size and style of type, cover and jacket design, and illustration are the responsibility of the design staff. Although the designer may choose the size, style, and placement of type for the author's name and the title, the editor should see that the spelling and content of these are correct.

1.114   If a credit line for artwork included on the cover or jacket is required or desirable, it is usually printed on the back cover of a paperback book or the back flap of the jacket. Credit for artwork imprinted on the cover of a case-bound book may be carried on the copyright page or in the acknowledgment section of the book. Credit for art on paper covers may also be carried inside the book. Credit for jacket art, however, is not ordinarily carried in the book itself, because the jacket may be lost or destroyed.

1.115 Two additional elements appear more and more frequently on the back cover or the back panel of the jacket. The first of these is the International Standard Book Number (ISBN), which serves as a convenient and useful identifier of both publisher and title (for further discussion of this identifier see 1.31). On the cover or jacket, the ISBN is usually given in numerals that are both machine readable and optically readable. The second and more recent device is the Bookland EAN bar code, which is similar to the Universal Product Code printed on merchandise packages and used by retailers to identify item and price and record each item sold. The Bookland EAN bar code presents a thirteen-digit number in laser-readable form (see fig. 1.20). The first three digits of the number identify the item either as a book (978) or as a periodical (977). Following this prefix are the first nine digits of the ISBN, with hyphens omitted. The last digit of the ISBN, the check digit, is replaced by a new check digit mathematically related to the composite number represented by the bar code.

Fig. 1.20. A Bookland EAN bar code and a five-digit side-bar, or add-on, code. Above the bar codes, in numerals that are "optically readable" as well as "machine readable," is the ISBN. The bar codes are also presented in optically readable numerals. In this example the price is identified as $20 in U.S. dollars.

1.116 The basic Bookland EAN code is now augmented by a five-digit bar code used primarily, but optionally, as a currency and price indicator (fig. 1.20). The first digit identifies the currency in which the price is specified (e.g., the digit 5 stands for U.S. dollars); the following four digits represent the price. The digits 0695, following a currency digit of 5, indicate a price of $6.95, and 59998 would indicate a price of $99.98 in U.S. dollars. A price exceeding this limit is indicated by the four-digit series 9999, in which case the actual price must be entered manually. Some publishers use the five-digit side-bar code for other purposes. If the publisher does not wish to use this auxiliary bar code, the digits 90000 are entered (fig. 1.21).

1.117 In printing the bar codes, the precision with which the thickness of the bars is reproduced is critical, as are the dimensions of the code itself.

ISBN 0-226-73670-9

Fig. 1.21. A Bookland EAN bar code with a five-digit side-bar code of 90000, indicating that this auxiliary bar code is not being used by the publisher

For this reason it is usually best for the publisher to obtain negative film or positive prints from specializing suppliers. Standard locations for the codes are the bottom of the back cover of a paperback book or the bottom of the back panel of the jacket of a hardcover book. An alternative location on hardcover books without jackets is the back cover, where it may be either printed or applied in the form of a stick-on label. Wherever it appears, the code must be printed against a white or very light-colored background, and the surface must be smooth enough to accept the printing effectively. (Additional information about the Bookland EAN bar code system may be obtained from the Book Industry Study Group.)[5]

5. Book Industry Study Group, Inc., 160 Fifth Avenue, New York, N.Y. 10010.

2 *Manuscript Preparation and Copyediting*

INTRODUCTION

2.1   The discussion in this chapter revolves around two main concerns. Portions of the chapter are addressed to authors (conceived broadly to include translators, compilers, volume editors—all who create material for publication). These portions recount what publishers expect in the physical preparation of manuscripts. Other portions of the chapter are addressed to publishers' copyeditors, who complete the preparation of manuscripts for the typesetter; these parts explain not only what editors do to manuscripts but how they do it. These two operations, author's and editor's, are interrelated because the copyeditor must often perform functions that the author has neglected, and because the author's responsibilities for preparing the manuscript are not fully met until he or she has responded to the editing and answered all queries on the manuscript. The word *editor* in these pages means *copyeditor,* or manuscript editor; other kinds of editors are generally subsumed under the umbrella term *publisher* (but see 2.179–82 for discussion of the *volume editor*).

2.2   Today, with electronic word processors and computerized typesetting and page makeup, machines play a significant third role in this author-editor relationship. Because there is, and will continue to be in the near future, wide variation in the requirements of electronic devices developed by different manufacturers, both author and editor must know which process is to be used and how it will affect the preparation of the final typescript or disk (or both). Whatever its final form is to be, however, the manuscript initially submitted to the publisher should be a complete and readable typescript or paper printout prepared according to rules outlined in the following paragraphs.

THE AUTHOR'S MANUSCRIPT

Components

2.3   The parts of a book outlined in chapter 1 (1.2–3) are, in general, what publishers expect to find in manuscripts submitted for publication. The

In the preparation of this chapter, some material has been adapted from *A Manual for Writers of Term Papers, Theses, and Dissertations*, by Kate L. Turabian, revised and expanded for the fifth edition by Bonnie Birtwistle Honigsblum, © 1987 by The University of Chicago.

publisher will furnish the half-title page, the copyright page, and the copy for running heads. The author is responsible for providing the following:

Title page
Table of contents
Any other preliminaries (dedication, epigraph, preface)
All text matter
Tables, if any, on separate pages
Notes, or footnotes, in a separate section
All end matter (appendixes, bibliography, etc.), except the index[1]
All illustrations
Caption or legend copy for illustrations, on separate pages
All permissions, in writing, that may be required to reproduce any illustrations or to reproduce or quote from any previously published material (see chapter 4)

Number of Copies Required

NEW MANUSCRIPTS: TYPED OR COMPUTER GENERATED

2.4 Most publishers, including the University of Chicago Press, require two copies of the manuscript. The first copy ordinarily consists of the original typescript or, in the case of computer-generated material stored on a magnetic disk, a paper printout, often referred to as *hard copy*. The second copy may consist of a carbon copy or, more commonly today, a photocopy of the typescript or an additional computer printout. However it is made, the second copy, like the first, must be clearly readable. (A third copy of the manuscript should, of course, be retained by the author.) The first copy is used by the manuscript editor for editing and markup, and then by the typesetter for the production of the book. The second copy goes to the publisher's production department for design and estimate. Editorial and preliminary production processes may thus proceed simultaneously. (In the case of computer-generated manuscripts, a copy of the disk is also commonly sent to the publisher for testing and, with increasing frequency, for eventual use in typesetting.) Only one set of illustrations—halftones or prepared artwork—is necessary, although a set of photocopies is helpful (see chapter 11 for preparation of illustrations). The publisher normally requires only one copy of the index manuscript, since its length has been estimated in advance, but the author should keep a copy.

---

1. The index is also the author's responsibility, unless other arrangements are made with the publisher. The index manuscript cannot of course be completed until the author has all the page proofs.

2.5 Previously published material in the form of printed pages is sometimes submitted as part or all of a manuscript, as for anthologies or collected works. Two copies of such a manuscript are also required. The first copy is prepared either by photocopying or by pasting or taping printed pages on standard-size paper; a photocopy may be made for the second copy of the manuscript. (For instructions on preparing a manuscript of this sort see 2.166–76.)

Numbering Pages

2.6 The author need number preliminary pages only if some element, such as a preface, occupies more than one manuscript page. The sequence of pages within this element may then be indicated by ordinary arabic numerals, for example, "Preface 2." Before the manuscript goes to the typesetter, the editor will number the preliminaries as they are to appear in the printed book (see 2.153), indicating verso pages that are to remain blank.

2.7 To avoid great difficulty restoring scattered or disordered pages to their proper order, and to facilitate estimating the length of the manuscript, the author should number all pages containing text, notes, and back matter consecutively from the first page to the last. The University of Chicago Press will also accept manuscript pages numbered by chapter if the chapter number is included with every page number: for example, 3-25 or III 25 (chapter 3, page 25). Pages added after the first typing of the manuscript may be numbered, for example, 55a, 55b, and so on, following page 55; alternatively, old page 55 may be renumbered 55a and the new pages numbered 55b, 55c, and so on. To afford the editor, or anyone else going through the pages, assurance that nothing is missing, following-page numbers may be written at the bottom right corner of all additional or renumbered pages and the page that precedes them. Thus, at the bottom right of page 54 may be written "page 55a follows" or "→ 55a" and so forth to "page 56 follows" or "→ 56." After the manuscript has been edited and the author has made all final corrections, the editor will usually renumber the pages with a numbering machine just before sending the manuscript to the typesetter (see 2.152–56).

2.8 Tables and illustrations are estimated separately and therefore are not numbered consecutively with the manuscript pages. The estimate for these is based on the number and complexity of each.

2.9 Index copy, prepared after the rest of the book has been made up in pages, is numbered separately. Even though an index is in alphabetical order (the sequence of pages presumably obvious), its manuscript pages must be numbered.

Preparing the Manuscript

2.10 The following discussion of manuscript preparation, unless otherwise specified, applies equally to manuscripts prepared by typewriter and those prepared by computer. The verb *type* may also be taken, in this discussion, to include computer keyboarding.

PAPER

2.11 It is essential that the first copy, and desirable that the second copy as well, be on good-quality paper of standard size—in the United States, 8½ by 11 inches. Neither copy should be double-sided.

TYPEWRITER

2.12 Whenever possible, the same typewriter or at least the same type size (pica, being larger, is better than elite) should be used for an entire manuscript. The type should be clean and the ribbon fresh. When using a typewriter with changeable typefaces, use the same typeface throughout.

2.13 A correct letter should never be typed over an incorrect one; erase the error and insert the correction, or strike out the incorrect letter and type (or write) the correct one above it.

2.14 A typewriter equipped with the diacritical marks and symbols occurring frequently in a manuscript is most desirable. In the absence of needed symbols, a capital *L* with a hyphen through it may be used to represent a British pound sign, a double quotation mark may be typed above a letter to indicate a diaeresis or an umlaut, and a comma under a letter may indicate a cedilla. A single quotation mark, however, which is apt to be perpendicular rather than curved or inclined, should not be used to indicate an accent, because it does not differentiate between grave and acute. These and other diacritical marks or symbols not available on the typewriter must be inserted by hand by the author or typist—in ink and accurately placed. A handwritten Greek letter or any possibly ambiguous symbol should be identified by its name, written and circled in the margin next to the line where it occurs (*alpha, sigma, times* or *mult* for an *x* used as a multiplication sign, etc.; for typing mathematics see chapter 13). Typists should know that if a typewriter lacks the numeral 1, the proper substitute is not a capital "eye" (I) but a lowercase "ell" (l), and if there is any likelihood of confusion, the numeral should be identified in the margin: "one," for instance. The typist should also remember the difference between the zero (0) and the letter "oh" (o, O).

COMPUTER

2.15   A great many, perhaps a preponderance, of manuscripts are now prepared by computerized word processing. This process not only offers the considerable advantage of greatly facilitating revision, but also provides a much broader range of characters and functions than those offered by even the most sophisticated electronic typewriters. With some computer systems, function keys, combinations of keys, or special codes can be used to enter diacritical marks, non-Latin characters, and math symbols. There are also systems that allow the "remapping" of standard keyboards (alternative keyboard functions) to make it easier to enter text that requires special characters. Such systems may display the alternative keyboard layout on the screen. Not all systems have the capability of displaying all the special characters that have been entered, but in that case it may be possible to gain some reassurance before printout by displaying and verifying the codes for such special characters. Not every printer, moreover, is capable of reproducing all of the characters displayed on the screen, and it may therefore be important to find a printer that is sufficiently versatile. Special characters may sometimes be represented by combinations of standard characters. It is also possible to find software that can create individual special characters and, indeed, complete fonts. Some software packages are capable of setting up tables; such programs can, for instance, produce multiple tabs, make columnar adjustments, perform spreadsheet management functions, and provide vertical as well as horizontal rules.

SPACING

2.16   All copy intended for publication must be *double-spaced or triple-spaced—never single-spaced or space-and-a-half.* Single-spaced material is not only impossible to edit clearly but difficult to follow in typesetting. The rule about double-spacing applies not only to the text but also to block quotations and case histories within the text, to notes, to appendix material, to bibliographies and indexes—in other words, to *all* parts of the manuscript.[2] Double-spaced means a full blank line (not a half-line) *between all typed lines,* not just between notes or between items in a bibliography.

2.17   Generous margins—at least an inch—should be left on both sides and at the top and bottom of every page. Chapter openings should begin at least three inches from the top of the page.

---

2. A possible exception is tabular material made up of groups of words, where each group may be single-spaced with a double space between groups.

CHAPTER TITLES AND SUBHEADS

2.18 Chapter titles and subheads in the text will be printed in a style specified by the book designer, who may decide to put them in full capitals or in capitals and lowercase, in italic or roman or boldface type. The typist, not knowing what style will be selected, should type them with initial capitals only—that is, capitalize the first letter of the first word and of all other words except prepositions, articles, and coordinating conjunctions (see 7.127–28). Chapter titles and subheads should not be underlined or italicized.

2.19 Subheads of different levels (see 1.71–72) may be differentiated in manuscript by their placement on the page. The first-level subhead, for example, may be centered; the second-level subhead may be typed *flush left,* that is, it may begin at the left margin; a third-level subhead may then be indented a few spaces or it may be *run in* at the beginning of a paragraph. A subhead that begins a paragraph should, of course, end with a period. No period follows a subhead typed on a line by itself. The various levels of subheads may also be indicated by writing circled letter or numeral designations (A, B, C or 1, 2, 3, etc.) in the margin of the typescript or, in the case of electronically generated manuscripts, by including generic codes in the computer files (see 2.56).

EXTRACTS

2.20 *Extracts* (block quotations, case histories, poetry, and the like) should be double-spaced and set off from the text by indention on the left and extra space above and below. Prose extracts should reflect the paragraphing of the original (see 10.20 for fuller discussion). Quoted poetry may be either centered on the page or aligned a short distance from the left margin, the indention of individual lines and the spacing between stanzas reflecting the pattern of the original (see 10.22–24). The omission of a line or more of poetry is indicated by a single line of spaced periods approximately the length of the line above it. (For omissions in prose extracts see 10.48–63; for source citations following block quotations and poetry see 2.139, 10.81–83.)

NOTES

2.21 Whether they are to appear at the back of the book or at the foot of the page, notes should be typed separately, as a group, *with all lines double-spaced.* With the sole exception of unnumbered source or author-affiliation footnotes (see 2.145, 15.50–51), notes should never be typed at the foot of the page or interlineated with the text.[3] The

3. In dissertations and other academic papers *not intended for publication,* footnotes are commonly typed single-spaced at the foot of the page for the convenience of the

number and title of a chapter should appear at the head of its notes. Each note should begin on a new line, with a paragraph indention, and each should end with a period.

2.22 Notes to the text are numbered consecutively through each chapter (beginning with 1 for the first note in a chapter). Note numbers in the text are typed above the line, with no parentheses, periods, or slash marks. The numbers introducing the notes themselves should be typed on the line and followed by a period, as they are in this manual. (See 2.44 and examples of notes in chapter 15.)

TABLES

2.23 Tables should be typed on pages separate from the text. The word *Table* and the table number, an arabic numeral, are typed on a line above the table. The table title is typed on the line below the number, with only initial capital letters—that is, the first word and all other words except coordinating conjunctions, prepositions, and articles should be capitalized (see 7.127–28). Table titles should never be typed in full capitals, and no period should follow a title. Explanatory matter applicable to the entire table, such as "in millions," may be enclosed in parentheses below the title, but longer explanations should be put in a note. The table number, title, and subtitle (if any) may be centered or typed flush left. (For examples of correctly typed tables see chapter 12.)

2.24 Brief tabular material—not more than, say, four lines and two columns—if it does not include vertical lines or braces, should be typed with the text. Lists consisting of one or two columns that may be broken (continued on the next page) should also be typed with the text.

2.25 Columns in a table must be precisely aligned; column headings and stub entries must leave no doubt about what belongs with what. Horizontal rules may be used above and below the column headings, within the body of a table to show totals, and at the foot of a table, but vertical rules should not be used unless required for clarity (see 12.14). All typing is double-spaced (but see note 2 above).

2.26 Footnotes to a statistical table are typed (double-spaced) below the table. Source notes and other general notes are not indexed in the table but are introduced below by the terms *Source* and *Notes*. Specific notes are indexed in the table and introduced below by symbols or letters. (See 12.46–52.)

---

readers. Such a practice is not acceptable in manuscripts submitted for publication. (For typing dissertations, see Kate L. Turabian, *A Manual for Writers of Term Papers, Theses, and Dissertations,* 5th ed.)

GLOSSARIES

2.27 Words to be defined in a glossary should be arranged in alphabetical order and typed flush left. They are often followed by a period (sometimes a dash or colon). Definitions begin with capital letters and usually end with periods (see the glossary in this manual). Whatever style is adopted, punctuation and capitalization must be consistent throughout. Runover lines should be indented three or four spaces.

LISTS OF ABBREVIATIONS

2.28 Abbreviations and their definitions are typed in two columns, the abbreviations, in alphabetical order, on the left and the definitions on the right. Leave two to four spaces between the longest abbreviation and its definition and align the rest of the definitions accordingly. (For examples see figs. 15.1, 15.2.) An acceptable alternative style is to run abbreviation and definition together, separating them by a colon.

BIBLIOGRAPHIES AND REFERENCE LISTS

2.29 Each item in a bibliographical list should begin flush left (with no paragraph indention). In entries requiring more than one line, runover lines should be indented three or four spaces. All bibliographical material must be *double-spaced*.

2.30 Authors' names in an alphabetical list are typed last name first. If a work has more than one author, however, only the name of the first-mentioned author is inverted. If several works by the same author or authors are listed, a long dash (three typed hyphens) is used in place of the authorial name or names for each item following the first. If a period follows the author's name in the first item, a period follows the dash as well. (For capitalization, punctuation, and other matters of bibliographical style see chapters 15 and 16.)

INDEXES

2.31 The index manuscript should be double-spaced, one column to a page, on standard-sized paper. The author should retain a copy of the index manuscript and all the index cards (if these have been used) until the index has been printed. (For a discussion of the preparation of indexes and of the use of computers in indexing see chapter 17.)

Computer Printouts

2.32 All manuscripts in the form of computer printouts must be clear and easy to read, and on good paper. Letter quality or near letter quality printouts are preferred—that is, letters very much like those in the present text. If dot-matrix printouts are used, the dots must abut or overlap, and all letters, diacritics, and punctuation must be completely legible. (For a discussion of coding and electronic manuscripts see 2.56.) In addition, the text in computer printouts should not be justified (aligned right margins with, consequently, irregular word spacing), but should be printed with ragged-right margins. If various fonts are available, a large font that is not too tightly spaced should be selected, since this makes editing much easier.

Photocopies

2.33   Most publishers will accept photocopies made from clean typescript that meets all the other requirements of manuscript preparation (ample margins, double-spacing, etc.). The image must be crisp, not blurred, and the paper of good quality and suitable for marking with the editor's pencil. Photocopies of printed matter—for anthologies or other works containing excerpts from previously published material—are also acceptable, provided the image is clear and the type lines are straight (see 2.169), and provided the material is not to be edited. Photocopies of artwork are rarely acceptable as camera-ready copy.

Author's Changes and Corrections

MANUSCRIPTS FOR TYPESETTING

2.34   On a manuscript to be typeset, corrections may be made by hand provided they are brief and clearly written. All corrections must be easily readable by editor, typesetter, and proofreader.

2.35   An added or altered word or phrase may be written—with a sharp black pencil or pen and in a legible hand—directly above the line or in the margin adjacent to the intended location. Corrections must be written in clear upper- and lowercase letters, never in all capitals. Words, sentences, or whole paragraphs may be deleted by drawing a firm line through them. Pages containing such corrections need not be retyped.

2.36   Corrections longer than a word or short phrase must be typed and inserted where they belong. The best way to insert such material in a typewritten manuscript is to cut the page where the insertion is to be made and paste or tape[4] the pieces of text in the desired order on fresh sheets of paper. All pages of a typescript must be the same size, but the

---

4. Use transparent tape with a dull finish that can be written on with a pencil; staples, pins, or paper clips should never be used to fasten manuscript material intended for typesetting.

amount of material on them may vary from page to page. It is not necessary to renumber an entire manuscript because of a few added pages, but any new page must be numbered to show where it belongs— if two extra pages are added between pages 24 and 25, for example, they may be numbered 24a and 24b; alternatively, 24 may be changed to 24a and the two additional pages numbered 24b and 24c (see also 2.7, 2.152).

2.37 Corrections made in any of the following ways are *unacceptable* to publishers and typesetters:

> Writing or typing on the backs of pages
> Writing vertically in the margins
> Typing inserts on slips attached to pages
> Pasting an addition to the bottom of a page and folding it up
> Directing the typesetter to insert a passage from another page
> Writing illegibly or with a dull pencil
> Writing in capital letters
> Drawing lines across the text to show placement of a change written in the margin

COMPUTER PRINTOUTS

2.38 When a computer-generated manuscript is to be set from the magnetic disks or tape, short corrections and changes on the computer printout must be eminently noticeable so that they will not be missed when all changes are entered on the disks or tapes. In this respect printouts resemble proofs more than manuscripts, since the operator entering the changes does not read the material word for word, as in typesetting, but looks only for changes. Changes should be marked boldly in red or some other bright color, and it is often helpful to mark them in the margins as is done on proofs (for discussion of marking changes in proof see 3.15–36). Longer changes should be entered in the file, and a new printout made. Changes should not be superimposed on the original printout by cutting and pasting, because the original text, even though portions of it may be crossed out, must remain visible until changes have been incorporated in the file.

Correlating Parts of a Manuscript

2.39 References in one part of a manuscript to other parts of the manuscript provide a fertile ground for error, as any copyeditor well knows. The careful author will check the *final* manuscript for any discrepancies that may have crept in during the various stages of preparation. The manuscript editor should also check all such references and query the author regarding any discrepancies found in them.

TABLE OF CONTENTS AND CHAPTER TITLES

2.40   The table of contents lists the titles of all sections of the book (see 1.40–42) and must therefore be checked against the text to see that the wording is identical in both places and that nothing has been omitted from the table of contents. If a later decision is made to alter a chapter title or to add or delete an appendix, the change must also be made in the table of contents.

2.41   Placing manuscript page numbers in the table of contents is helpful to publishers and readers. If the author supplies them, however, the editor must remember to circle them before the manuscript goes to the type-setter so that they will not be set (see 2.66). The printed-page numbers will of course be quite different and cannot be added to the table of contents until the pages have been made up. Page numbers to be sup-plied are normally indicated by zeros (000) in manuscript and galley proofs. Leaders (rows of evenly spaced dots) should not be used in tables of contents.

CROSS-REFERENCES

2.42   Any reference in the text to a specific part of the work—a chapter, a section, an appendix, even a sentence of text—should be verified. A chapter number, or its title, may have been changed or an appendix dropped after the author made reference to it. References to tables, figures, or plates must be checked carefully against the actual table or illustration. Cross-references from one note to another are especially hazardous because notes are frequently renumbered in the course of preparing a manuscript.

2.43   Cross-references to specific pages in a book should be avoided when-ever possible. They cannot be filled in until pages have been made up, and in many kinds of composition an entire line must be reset to accom-modate each one—a costly process. It is preferable to refer, if reference must be made, to a chapter or a section. Authors who find themselves including a great many cross-references to other pages might do well to consider whether they have organized the material as efficiently as pos-sible and whether readers would not rather use the index to find related material than be interrupted by frequent admonitions to turn to another page. Where a page reference seems absolutely necessary, it may be indicated by zeros or dashes (e.g., "see p. 000"), not by manuscript page number. Zeros in the text alert the proofreader to the fact that a number is to be inserted in final page proof, and they also reserve space in the printed line for that number. Some typesetters use black squares (en quads) for this purpose, and the editor may wish to request these, since they are much easier to spot when adding the page references. If someone other than the author is to insert the page numbers in the page proofs, the author should give the appropriate manuscript page number, and circle it, in the margin of the manuscript next to the line including the reference.

NOTES AND THEIR REFERENCES

2.44   In a work containing numbered notes to the text—either at the foot of the page or at the back of the book—there must be a number in the text referring to each note and a note corresponding to each number. Obvious as this seems, all notes should be checked against the text to make sure that every note has a corresponding number in the text and that each note is the one intended for that spot in the text. Note numbers are often inadvertently omitted when a manuscript is retyped, and the sequence of notes may be affected by any rearranging of material. Except in certain specialized works and in tabular matter, no note should have more than one text reference to it; when it is desirable to refer to exactly the same material given in an earlier note, the later note may simply give a cross-reference:

> 75. See note 3 above.

No two notes should bear the same number, such as 15 and 15a. If a note must be added, two notes may be run together to accommodate the addition; otherwise all subsequent notes in the chapter must be renumbered.

NOTES AND BIBLIOGRAPHIES

2.45   In a work containing both notes and bibliography, sources cited in the notes should be checked against the bibliography. If the same source appears in both places, the note citation may be shortened (see 15.57, 15.248–61). Author's name and title of the work must be spelled and punctuated the same way in both places. If the publication facts are given in both notes and bibliography, the facts must be checked for agreement.

TEXT CITATIONS AND REFERENCE LISTS

2.46   In a work using the author-date system of citing references (see chapter 16), each citation must be checked against the reference list, where it should appear in full. The author's name and the date of publication must agree.

TABLES AND TEXT

2.47   Tables typed or pasted on separate sheets must be identified, in the margin, by the manuscript page number of the text that each is to accompany. The manuscript text page also must have the table number noted in the margin next to the passage where the author wishes the table to appear in the printed book. A table usually follows as closely as practicable the first reference to it. Text references must be by table number, not by a phrase such as *the following table* or *the table above.* Nor should a colon be used to introduce a table. In page makeup a table may not fall exactly where the author wants it, but it will be placed as close to the spot as possible.

2.48   A final check of tables in a manuscript should ascertain that they are numbered consecutively either through the entire book or through each chapter (see also the double-numeration system, 1.77, 2.185); that each bears the manuscript page number of the relevant text; and that the placement of each is noted in the margin of the text. If there is a list of tables in the front matter, it should also be checked against the tables themselves (see 1.46).

ILLUSTRATIONS, LEGENDS, AND TEXT

2.49   Text figures (illustrations that print with the text) and maps are handled in much the same way as tables. Author or editor must insert marginal notations, widely referred to as *call outs* (e.g., "fig. 1," "fig. 2"), indicating where each belongs. Since figure captions and legends are typed separately, each figure must bear a penciled notation giving the figure number and the manuscript page where it belongs. Such notations should never be written within the boundaries of the drawing, but should go in the upper or lower margin. If the figure is a glossy print, it is best to type the notation, or write it in pencil, on a self-sticking label that is then applied to the back of the print. If the back of the print will take pencil marks the notation may be written there, but it must be done very lightly with a soft pencil so that the pressure will not mar the print surface. Writing with ink, felt-tip marker, or grease pencil on either a label or the back of the print is not recommended, since these media may smear or transfer to other prints (see also 11.10 and 11.16).

2.50   Plates (illustrations—usually halftones—that print separately from the text) are gathered in sections, or *galleries,* within the text. If plates are numbered, they are numbered separately from the text figures, but if they are not referred to in the text, they need not be numbered at all, except for identification during editing and manufacture. For that purpose a number should be attached to, or very lightly written on, the back of each print (see 2.49); the same number, circled, should be written next to the corresponding caption or legend. Also, if there is room for doubt, the top of the illustration should be indicated.

2.51   A final check of illustrations should ascertain that each has a caption or legend and that each bears a number corresponding to that of its caption or legend. If there is a list of illustrations in the front matter, it should be checked against the captions or legends (see 1.43–45). (For a more detailed description of handling illustrations see chapter 11.)

ABBREVIATIONS

2.52   If a list of abbreviations is included in a book (see 1.54), any abbreviation used in notes, bibliography, or elsewhere should be checked against the list. Any abbreviation, such as that for the title of a work, should be consistent throughout a book. Aside from a list of abbreviations, other indications of intent to abbreviate—such as "hereafter cited as"—should also be checked by the author and the editor: are all subsequent references indeed abbreviated, or shortened, as the author stipulates?

THE EDITORIAL FUNCTION

2.53   By the time the editor begins work on a manuscript, a decision on how to produce it will probably have been made by the publisher, and the amount of copyediting deemed necessary will have been a factor in that decision. Production from electronic media such as magnetic disks should be restricted to works that require relatively light editing. If more editorial work than anticipated proves necessary on a manuscript intended for computer typesetting, it may be less costly and less time consuming to have the material typeset by conventional methods (see chapter 19, especially 19.3, 19.9–24).

Types of Manuscripts

ELECTRONIC MANUSCRIPTS

2.54   Editing an electronic manuscript—a work produced on a computer and stored magnetically on a disk—is done either manually on a paper printout (known as *hard copy*) or electronically on a video display terminal. When the editing is done on a printout, all changes approved by the author are then entered on disk by the author, the publisher, or the typesetter. The corrected disks are then used by the typesetter to drive the typesetting equipment.

2.55   If the editing is done electronically, or *on-line*—that is, on a computer video display terminal—a new printout is produced containing all editorial changes. Queries to the author may also be added to the printout electronically, and it is sometimes possible to highlight the changes so that the author can find them more easily. The edited printout is then sent to the author for approval. Authors may wish to compare the new printout with their copy of the original in order to better understand the editing. When the author returns the approved printout, the editor makes the final check and enters final revisions on the disk.

2.56 To command typesetting equipment to produce properly formatted material, electronic manuscripts must be outfitted with typesetting codes. Generic codes, which identify the various elements of the manuscript (for example, chapter numbers, chapter titles, subheads, block quotations, notes, bibliographic entries, italics, and special characters), are usually added by the author or the publisher. The following are a few of the generic codes recommended by the University of Chicago Press:

CODE	END CODE	
\<CN\>	\</\>	chapter number
\<CT\>	\</\>	chapter title
\<A\>	\</\>	first-level subhead (A-head)
\<B\>	\</\>	second-level subhead (B-head)
\<BQ\>	\</\>	block quotation, or extract
\<PO\>	\</\>	poetry extract
\<SC\>	\</\>	small capitals
\<mac\>	none	macron on following letter
@-	none	en dash
\<!help!\>	\<!help!\>	signal to the typesetter to consult, or set from, the hardcopy at this point

The generic codes added by author or publisher are converted by the typesetter to specific typesetting or formatting codes following the specifications chosen by the designer. Typesetters now work with a wide range of commercial software programs, and it is wise to consult with your typesetter, when using an unfamiliar program, to determine what kind of coding is needed.[5]

MANUSCRIPTS TO BE TYPESET

2.57 For manuscripts full of complicated material or in need of considerable editorial attention, and for all manuscripts not on magnetic media, the editing is done on the copy that is to go to the keyboard operator (the typesetter, or compositor).

Copyediting

2.58 Copyediting—also, mainly in newspaper offices, called *copyreading*— is the editor's most important and most time-consuming task. It requires

5. For a detailed account of electronic manuscripts see *Chicago Guide to Preparing Electronic Manuscripts*.

close attention to every detail in a manuscript, a thorough knowledge of what to look for and of the style to be followed,[6] and the ability to make quick, logical, and defensible decisions. For the most part, the following discussion of copyediting applies to electronic manuscripts as well as to typewritten manuscripts. The specialized discussion of marking a manuscript (2.65–94), however, applies to electronic manuscripts only when the editing is done on a paper printout. It does not apply when electronic manuscripts are edited on-line, for then the editorial changes are actually achieved on the disk rather than being merely indicated on paper (see 2.55).

2.59 Copyediting is distinct from manuscript markup, which consists of adding type specifications, chapter-title and subhead styling, indication of spacing, and so forth. Markup of book manuscripts usually cannot be done at the editing stage because the designer will not yet have prepared the design. (For a discussion of markup procedures see 2.133–48.)

PRELIMINARY INFORMATION

2.60 Most editors prefer to read quickly through a manuscript before they begin editing it. The kind and amount of editing to be done depend on the nature of the material, the audience for whom it is intended, and the author's skill in preparing the manuscript—all factors that can be determined by a first reading, or sampling. Also essential to the editor are correspondence between author and publisher and any readers' reports on the manuscript, as well as the author's contract with the publisher. These should be examined for anything pertinent to the editing. The editor should of course know whether the manuscript is part of a series with a particular style of its own. If the manuscript is a later volume of a work whose earlier volumes were published a number of years before, the editor should, insofar as possible, follow the style of the earlier volumes.

ESTIMATING TIME

2.61 In many publishing houses editors are required to estimate the amount of time they will need to complete the editing on each manuscript. No editor should attempt such an estimate before having worked for a while on a manuscript. Until at least twenty-five pages of an average manuscript have been edited and the notes and other apparatus closely examined, the editor cannot, with any accuracy, prophesy how many hours the whole will take.

---

6. For rules regarding style see the chapters in part 2 of this manual.

MECHANICAL EDITING

2.62 The editorial function is in effect two processes. The first, because it is concerned with the mechanics of written communication, may be called *mechanical* editing. This process involves a close reading of the manuscript with an eye to such matters as consistency of capitalization, spelling, and hyphenation; agreement of verbs and subjects, and other matters of syntax; punctuation; beginning and ending quotation marks and parentheses; number of ellipsis points; numbers given as numerals or spelled out; and many similar details of style.

STYLE

2.63 The word *style* means two things to an editor. The first meaning is that implied in the title *The Chicago Manual of Style*. Publishers refer to style in this sense as *house style* or *press style*—rules regarding the mechanics of written communication detailed in part 2 of this manual. Authors more often think of style in its other sense, as a way of writing, of literary expression. Editors are of course also aware of this meaning of style when they undertake the second, nonmechanical, process of editing.

SUBSTANTIVE EDITING

2.64 This second editorial process may be called *substantive* editing—rewriting, reorganizing, or suggesting other ways to present material. The editor will know by instinct and learn from experience how much of this kind of editing to do on a particular manuscript. An experienced editor will recognize, and not tamper with, unusual figures of speech and idiomatic usage and will know when to make an editorial change or simply to suggest it, when to delete a repetition or simply to point it out to the author, and many other matters. Since every manuscript is unique in the amount and kind of substantive editing desirable, no rules can be devised for the editor to follow. Except for certain magazine publishers, no publishing house has a house literary style.

EDITORIAL MARKING

2.65 The following paragraphs concern the "mechanics" of mechanical editing—how to make the actual marks on the typescript or computer printout. They are addressed primarily to the inexperienced editor unsure of how to indicate a change and alarmed at the prospect of putting pencil to someone else's paper.

2.66   Editorial and typographic signs, queries to the author, notes to the type-setter, and similar communications are usually circled to inform the typesetter that they are not to be set. There are, however, several other reasons for circling material: for example, a circle is also used to enclose material that is to be transferred (2.69); to show that a dot or comma is to be a period (2.71, 2.74); and to indicate that an abbreviation is to be spelled out (2.84).

2.67   *Insertions and deletions.* To add a missing letter, word, or phrase, insert a caret (∧) where the addition belongs and write the correction above the line.

picnic*k*ing   rapproch*e*ment

Access *to the facility* was denied her on the pretext *that* the environment might be hazardous.

To correct a misspelling or to change a word or phrase, cross out (draw a line through) precisely what is not wanted and insert the change directly above the line.

~~As she~~ *Corbet* had already ~~noted,~~ *quoted* Senator Baker ~~said:~~ *'s remark,* "The Ervin Committee did not invent the leak, but we ~~ollivated~~ *elevated* it to its highest *art* ~~form~~."

To delete a word, phrase, or sentence, draw a horizontal line through the unwanted words and through any surrounding punctuation to be deleted as well. To delete several lines or a paragraph or more, the material to be deleted may be circled and marked with a delete sign (𝄞 or ȼ).

This was ~~in effect,~~ the ~~undisputed~~ end of the matter.

Morgenthaller and Henrici had devised a procedure that they believed flawless. ~~So satisfied were they with themselves that they invited Wellington to look at their outline. He did and was unable to restrain a snicker. Henrici turned white and demanded an explanation. Morgenthaller demanded an apology. After managing to affect a serious and sympathetic tone,~~ Wellington ~~did apologize and~~ managed to convince them that their procedure might end in disaster. He then offered to help the two scientists revise their plan and even to help them carry it out. In the end, after much discussion, ~~some of it heated,~~ all three did achieve the desired result.

When the deleted material is followed by a mark of punctuation that is to be retained, a close-up mark should be added above the deleted material:

Don't say that again ~~ever~~!

To delete a single letter in the middle of a word, draw a vertical line through it and make a close-up mark above the deleted letter:

> In my judgement, you are quite misstaken.

To delete a mark of punctuation, or a letter at the beginning or end of a word, make a delete mark through it; be sure to put the vertical part of the mark through the bit to be deleted and the hook part above the line, where it can be seen:

> Either one of her brother-in-laws or her brother was always in the kitchen to annoy her.

Do not write a correction in the margin unless you cannot write it legibly between the lines (as in single-spaced typescript).

2.68   *Transposition.* To change the order of, or transpose, letters, words, or phrases, draw a line over and under the affected elements, thus:

> from   struggle

> She only gave two examples.

> Earth, air, water, and fire

In the last example above, *water* and *fire* are to trade positions; the comma and the conjunction are to remain in place.

2.69   To move a word or phrase to a different line of the typescript, circle it and draw a line to the spot where you want it to be. Do not draw the line through or across any words or punctuation. And do not forget to adjust any punctuation or capitalization involved in the change.

> At first no one wanted to try it. However, after the demonstration by the professional actors, everyone was eager to do it too.

2.70   *Closing up or separating words.* To close up, or "pull together," two words or other elements you want the typesetter to set with no space between them, use close-up marks:

> worth while   any one   "What else ?"

To separate, or make a space between, two words or other elements typed without the required space, draw a vertical line between them:

> for awhile   "No," she replied.

A space mark may be added to the vertical line (although most typesetters will understand the line alone):

> moondog

(See also 2.77 on inserting or deleting a hyphen.)

2.71   *Punctuation changes.* Whenever possible, additions or changes in punctuation should be made in the line at the place of occurrence, not below it and not in the margin. For example, to add a comma, insert the mark where you want it and, to make sure the typesetter will see it, put a mark like a caret over it. This symbol, when used over a comma (it is also used to mark subscript letters and numbers), may be referred to familiarly as a "roof," a "house," even a "doghouse." If there is insufficient room to insert the mark of punctuation in place, it may be drawn in the space above the line, with a caret to indicate its exact location.

> Flopsy, Mopsy and Cottontail

To add a period, make a dot and circle it:

> He preferred opus no 45.

> All is well

2.72   To add quotation marks, an apostrophe, or a missing note reference, use an inverted caret (**V**) (the symbol used also for a superscript letter or numeral):

> The Declaration asserted that Americans were entitled to "a separate and equal station among the nations of the earth.

> states rights   Young's recent work.

2.73   Other marks of punctuation (colon, semicolon, question mark, exclamation point) should be inserted without any additional marking. (For the dash see 2.75.)

2.74   To change one punctuation mark to another, either cross out the wrong one and write the correct one beside or above it or alter the existing one as follows:

> A comma to a semicolon, add a dot above the comma: , to ;
> A semicolon to a comma, make a caret through the dot: ; to
> A comma to a period, circle the comma: , to
> A period to a comma, add a tail to the period and put a caret over the new mark: . to
> A period to a question mark or exclamation point, draw the necessary mark above the period: . to ? or !
> A comma to a colon, enlarge the comma into a dot and draw a matching dot above it: , to :
> A period into a colon, draw a second period above the first: . to :
> A semicolon into a colon, enlarge the comma into a dot and enlarge the dot above to match it: ; to :
> A double quotation mark to a single one, draw an inverted caret under one of the marks and through the other mark (the remaining mark may also be enlarged), or delete the double quotation mark

and draw a single one above an inverted caret: " to $\lor\!\!\!\!/$ or $\lor\!\!\!\!\!/$; or " to $\backslash \lor$

A single quotation mark to a double, add a second mark and draw inverted carets under both: ' to $\lor$

Parentheses to square brackets, or vice versa, make a firm mark through the existing characters, or cross out the existing characters and insert the correct ones: ( ) to [ ] , [ ] to ( ) ; or ( ) to [/)], [ ] to (/ /)

2.75 *Dashes and hyphens.* After mastering the distinctive uses of dashes of varying lengths (5.105–19), especially how the en dash differs from the hyphen in form and function (5.115), remember to identify the dash when necessary. The em dash, being a common mark of punctuation, need not be marked after its first occurrence in the text, but many editors mark it every time anyway. A pair of typed hyphens is usually taken to represent an em dash. The typesetter will understand any of the following:

-- M̲ I̲/M em

Longer dashes in the text should always be marked. In a bibliography, where 3-em dashes are used in place of the name of an author repeated in successive entries, only the first dash need be identified (see 15.66).

2̲/M 2M 2-em 3̲/M 3M 3-em

For electronic manuscripts it is recommended that hyphens and the various dashes be distinguished in the following manner:

- The hyphen is simply represented by a hyphen, without coding, and with no space before or after.

\<n> The en dash, with no space before or after, is coded to distinguish it from a hyphen.

-- The em dash is represented by two hyphens with no space before or after.

\<2m> The 2-em and 3-em dashes are coded as shown.

\<3m>

Editors should watch spacing around dashes. Hyphens and en dashes, and em dashes within sentences, should be set with no extra space on either side, that is, no more space than naturally occurs between letters. If they have been typed incorrectly, with spaces, put close-up marks with the first occurrence of the dash and write a note in the margin to the typesetter:

. . . subjects ‿ -- ‿ math, French . . . (*Typesetter: No space with em dashes*)

(For spacing around 2- and 3-em dashes see 5.118–19.)

2.76   Where a hyphen in the typescript is to be set as an en dash, it should be marked:

pre-Civil War;   1978-80

If an en dash is to be used between inclusive numbers throughout a section of a book, such as the index or the notes, you need only mark the first two or three and write an instruction to the typesetter on the first page of the section:

Typesetter: en dashes between numbers throughout

2.77   To insert a hyphen, use two short parallel lines.

two-thirds   ground-breaking   open air

To delete a hyphen and make two words, use a vertical line and a space mark:

fellow student

To delete a hyphen and make one word, put a vertical line through the hyphen and add a close-up mark:

four fold

2.78   When a hyphen appears at the end of a manuscript line, dividing a word that might be so hyphenated, the editor should indicate whether to keep the hyphen (underline it) or to close the word (line through the hyphen and close-up marks; see fig. 2.1). One need not, however, and indeed should not, either underline or delete end-of-line hyphens where it is obvious whether the word should be hyphenated or closed.

2.79   *Operational signs.* To change a capital letter to lowercase, draw a slant line through it:

H

To lowercase a whole line of capitals, or all letters except the first, draw a slant line through the first letter you want to lowercase and extend it horizontally across the top of the letters until the next capital or the end of the line:

STORIES FROM THE UNDERWORLD

To make doubly sure of the correct result, many editors also mark the capitals (see 2.80):

STORIES FROM THE UNDERWORLD

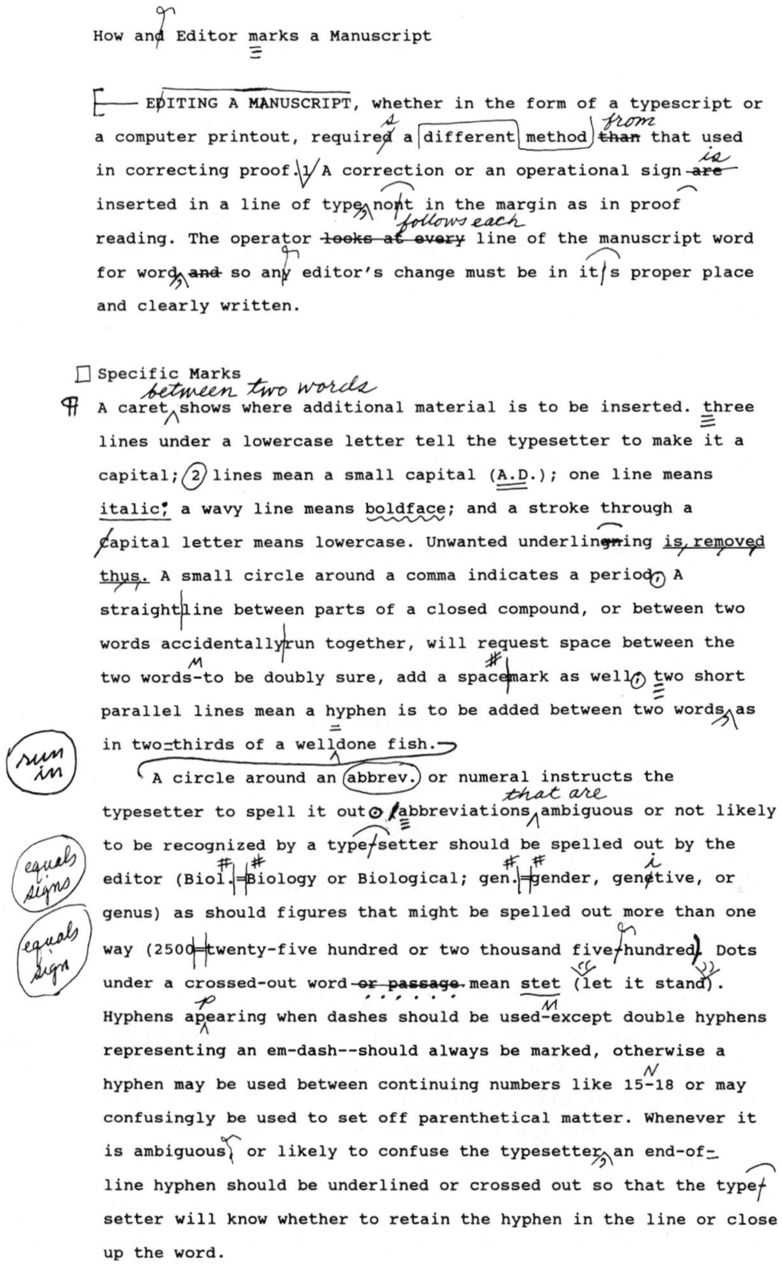

EDITING A MANUSCRIPT, whether in the form of a typescript or a computer printout, requires a different method than that used in correcting proof. A correction or an operational sign are inserted in a line of type, not in the margin as in proof reading. The operator looks at every line of the manuscript word for word and so any editor's change must be in it/s proper place and clearly written.

Specific Marks

A caret shows where additional material is to be inserted. three lines under a lowercase letter tell the typesetter to make it a capital; 2 lines mean a small capital (A.D.); one line means italic; a wavy line means boldface; and a stroke through a capital letter means lowercase. Unwanted underlinening is removed thus. A small circle around a comma indicates a period. A straight line between parts of a closed compound, or between two words accidentally run together, will request space between the two words-to be doubly sure, add a space mark as well. two short parallel lines mean a hyphen is to be added between two words as in two thirds of a welldone fish.

A circle around an abbrev. or numeral instructs the typesetter to spell it out. abbreviations ambiguous or not likely to be recognized by a type setter should be spelled out by the editor (Biol.—Biology or Biological; gen.—gender, genetive, or genus) as should figures that might be spelled out more than one way (2500—twenty-five hundred or two thousand five hundred. Dots under a crossed-out word or passage mean stet (let it stand). Hyphens apearing when dashes should be used—except double hyphens representing an em-dash--should always be marked, otherwise a hyphen may be used between continuing numbers like 15-18 or may confusingly be used to set off parenthetical matter. Whenever it is ambiguous or likely to confuse the typesetter, an end-of-line hyphen should be underlined or crossed out so that the type setter will know whether to retain the hyphen in the line or close up the word.

Fig. 2.1. An example of edited manuscript

2.80 To indicate *full capitals* (i.e., regular capital letters), draw *three* lines under the letters:

the middle ages   Gatt

the Middle Ages   GATT

To indicate *small capitals,*[7] draw *two* lines under the letters. For words to be set in small capitals with an initial full capital (caps and small caps), draw three lines under the initial letter and two under the rest of the word:

46 B.C.   Lady Bracknell

46 B.C.   LADY BRACKNELL

2.81 To indicate *italics,* draw *one* line:

Tolkien's The Hobbit

2.82 To indicate *boldface* type, draw a *wavy* line:

Section 3

Do not mark for boldface unless your type specifications (book design or journal format) call for it.

2.83 To delete underlining in the typescript, make several short vertical lines through it:

As Publius said

To read is not always to understand

If any part of the underlined material is to remain designated italic, however, place stet dots beneath it and do not draw a vertical "strike" through that segment of the line:

To read is not always to understand.

To change words typed in an italic typeface, underline or circle the words and write "rom" or "roman" in the margin. For longer underlined passages that are to be set in roman type (not italicized), circle the text involved and write a note to the typesetter in the margin:

set roman

2.84 To tell the typesetter to spell out an abbreviation or a number, draw a circle around it:

vol.   N.Y.   2   13

7. Small caps have specific uses (see index) and are not available in some kinds of typesetting.

When you circle an abbreviation or a number, be sure that there is only one way to spell it out; do not ask the typesetter to choose between alternative spellings. For example, "10-fold" might be "tenfold" or "ten-fold"; "100" might be "one hundred" or "a hundred"; "7,500" might be "seven thousand five hundred" or "seventy-five hundred." If there is any ambiguity, cross out the abbreviation and write the spelled-out version above it. If the same abbreviation occurs frequently, you may spell it out the first time it appears and circle it thereafter; but if several pages have elapsed since its last occurrence, spell it out again. Similarly, if the abbreviation is uncommon or in a foreign language, spell it out.

2.85 To indicate a paragraph indention where the manuscript does not show one, use a paragraph mark (¶) right before the first word (see fig. 2.1, second paragraph). Use the paragraph mark also to break a long paragraph into two or more shorter ones. Be sure to put it right before the sentence you select to start a new paragraph:

        . . . tempo and volume.¶One of the musically important aspects . . .

To "run in" a paragraph with the one preceding it ("no paragraph"), draw a line from the last word of one paragraph to the first word of the next (see fig. 2.1).

2.86 To show that you want a paragraph to start flush left (with no indention), make a mark like a square bracket where the paragraph should start and draw a line from it to the first word (see fig. 2.1, first paragraph). If you want to indicate that something should be set flush right, use the same mark in reverse:

        (MND 3.2.396). ⸻⫞

A vertical line, instead of a square bracket, also works if carefully done:

        ⊢Editing . . .   (396) ⸻⊣

2.87 To center a heading or other unit on the page, use marks that look like reversed square brackets on both sides and, to be doubly sure, write "ctr" and circle it:

        ⸥Tokens of Independence ⸤

2.88 To indicate lateral positions other than flush left, flush right, paragraph indention, and center, use em quads (see glossary under *quad* and *spacing*) to the number desired: one quad is represented by ☐ ; two em quads by ☒ or ☐☐ ; three em quads by ☒ or ☐☐☐ ; and so forth. A quad mark to the left of the typed line tells the typesetter to indent it one em from the left margin; a quad mark to the right will indent it one em from the right margin (often used with names following material such as a foreword, or in correspondence).

☐ A Temperate Response

I. F. Stone ☐

2.89 If two or more lines in succession are to be indented an em quad or more, as in a set-off quotation, a quad sign may be drawn beside the first line with a vertical line drawn from its inner side the length of the passage to be indented. If the indentation is to be more than one em, write the number of ems inside the quad (see 2.88). (For further instruction on marking set-off quotations or extracts see 2.138–40.)

What Betsey was like . . . is told by Ebenezer:

☐ Though not strikingly beautiful, her person and manner were

infinitely engaging; her natural understanding of the first

class; her conversation and attainments beyond her age, her

station, and her instruction.

2.90 Vertical spacing in the text—spaces between lines of type, space above and below subheads and set-off quotations, and spaces showing divisions between sections of text—is measured in *points* (see glossary). In 10-point text type set *solid,* that is, with no extra space between lines, a line space equals 10 points. Additional space is frequently added between text lines to make the type page more attractive and easier to read. An extra 2 points, for example, may be added between lines of 10-point type, making the line space 12 points instead of 10. Such text is said to be set 10 on 12, or 10/12 (see also 2.138, 18.23–25). To indicate a line space in the text, write "blank line" or "line space" or, giving the point measure, "10 pt. #," "12 pt. #," and so on, in the middle of the space in the text or in the margin, with an arrow showing which two lines the space should be inserted between. Space above and below set-off quotations is usually one-half line but may be otherwise specified by the book designer. When in doubt, simply make a space mark (#) in the center of the space and leave the exact amount to the typesetter. Most typesetters have good judgment about spacing in printed material—above and below tables, equations, quotations, and so on. If the typesetter inserts either no space or widely varying amounts of space, you will have to correct it in proofs. In general, however, it is wise not to overspecify vertical spacing in the manuscript.

2.91 Vertical spacing of more than a line or two, such as at chapter openings, is measured in *picas* (see glossary). Editors, unless they are also designers, are not usually required to mark such spacing.

2.92 *Color of pencil or ink.* All editorial changes should be made in a color distinct from that used by the author for alterations. If there will be any reason to photocopy all or part of a manuscript after it has been edited, remember that the traditional blue-pencil editorial markings will be lost in many photographic processes; it is therefore best to experiment with your copying process before marking a manuscript. Many editors prefer to use a colored pencil that can be easily erased; others prefer colored ink. Whatever you use, write firmly, neatly, and legibly at all times.

2.93 Some editors use different colors to distinguish three functions: text alterations; queries to the author; and directions to the typesetter. Except in some circumstances, this distinction is not really necessary, because queries to the author are crossed out before the typesetter sees the manuscript, and directions to the typesetter are circled, indicating that they are not to be set in type. (For color-coding extracts see 2.140.)

2.94 *Emendations and type specifications.* Rules for inserting authors' corrections given in 2.34–38 apply also to the editor's emendations. For marking type specifications following a designer's layout, see 2.133–48, and 18.71 with accompanying illustrations.

EDITING TEXT

2.95 An editor will usually edit one kind of material at a time, beginning with the text, followed by the notes, tables, legends, and so on, because to edit similar matter in a manuscript in a continuous process lessens the chance of variations in style.[8] At some point, however, this other material must also be compared with the text, to avoid discrepancies. Even if notes are thoroughly edited only after all of the text has been edited, it is usually a good idea to glance at each note as its reference comes up in the text, so that verification of its relevance may be made and incorrect notes quickly spotted. Such a procedure is also appropriate for tables and figure legends.

2.96 To check spelling and meaning in editing the text, the editor must have a dictionary and other reference works close to hand. The spelling of unfamiliar names and terms should be checked, as well as some commonly misspelled familiar ones (e.g., Apennines, Pyrenees, stratagem, improvise, consensus, supersede).

2.97 *Style sheet.* No style book will provide rules covering all matters of style encountered by the editor, and no editor worth the title will apply identical rules to every book manuscript. Therefore, to ensure consistency in the style used in a particular manuscript, and to aid the editorial memory, it is helpful if not imperative to keep for each manuscript a running account of special words to be capitalized, odd spellings, compound words with or without hyphens, and the like. For easy reference this style sheet should be in rough alphabetical order, and the manuscript page number of at least the first occurrence of a word should be

8. This system is of course impractical for a long manuscript such as a book of readings or a collection of papers that goes through the publishing process in separate sections.

noted beside it. If there is any chance that the editorial mind will change late in the manuscript—about hyphenating a particular compound, for example—it is well to note the page number of each occurrence. One of the more efficient forms of style sheet is easily constructed by ruling off squares on one or two sheets of paper (some manuscripts will require more extensive lists than others) and assigning several letters of the alphabet to each square, as in the sample represented by figure 2.2. The editor should consult and add to the style sheet throughout the copyediting process, remembering that a word added from the middle or end of a manuscript may well have escaped attention in earlier pages. A final, quick rereading of the entire manuscript is desirable to catch any such slips. The style sheet should also be consulted in editing discursive notes and figure legends and in checking names on maps, words in figures, tables, and the like. For those editing electronically (2.55) it should be noted that some computer software programs now incorporate useful style-sheet functions. Remember to recheck the style sheet after the author returns the manuscript, in case any changes are necessary. A style sheet not only aids the editor's memory as editing progresses but may be indispensable in the later stages of production. Few editors can give their time exclusively to one manuscript, since they may be responsible for as many as twenty books in various stages of production. It is difficult to remember the particular style for each when checking manuscript returned from the author, galley proofs, page proofs, or index several weeks or months after the original editing. Also, another editor may have to take over at some stage of production and will need to know the style followed. Therefore the style sheet should remain in the editor's file until the book is bound.

2.98   *Watching for errors and infelicities.* In addition to regularizing details of style, the editor is expected to catch errors or infelicities of expression that mar an author's prose. Such matters include dangling or misplaced modifiers, unclear antecedents, redundancies, lack of agreement of verb with subject, faulty attempts at parallel construction, overuse of an author's pet word or phrase, unintentional repetition of words, race or gender bias, and so on.[9] The editor should also consider the

9. The thirteenth edition of this manual included split infinitives among the examples of "errors and infelicities" but tempered the inclusion by adding, in parentheses, that they are "debatable 'error.'" The item has been dropped from the fourteenth edition because the Press now regards the intelligent and discriminating use of the construction as a legitimate form of expression and nothing writers or editors need feel uneasy about. Indeed, it seems to us that in many cases clarity and naturalness of expression are best served by a judicious splitting of infinitives.

For the editor in search of guidance in avoiding sexist connotations the following sources might be suggested: Casey Miller and Kate Swift, *The Handbook of Nonsexist Writing,* and Dennis Baron, *Grammar and Gender.* Along with these and other authorities, the University of Chicago Press recommends the "revival" of the singular use of *they* and *their,* citing, as do they, its venerable use by such writers as Addison, Austen, Ches-

A B C D city-state 5 balance of power diplomacy 15 air force 16 Coprosperity Sphere 30 drillmaster 32 breechloading 36	**M N O P** macroeconomics 6 Peace of Paris 12 Napoleonic Wars 21 manpower 29 Ottoman Empire 38 map reading 50
E F G H firepower 7 esprit de corps 10 Hellenistic Age 20 great-power (adj.) 25 Hsiang-yang 39 Genghis's 40	**Q R S T** sine qua non 16 transregional 17 riverboat 23 troublemakers 25 sea power 27 shortfall 40
I J K L industrial revolution 6 Kublai Khan 11 levée en masse 20 Jürchen 25	**U V W X Y Z** war-horse 18 victuallers 31 Western Front 42 Zeitgeist 43

Fig. 2.2. Manuscript editor's style sheet

logical flow of argument and suggest moving a sentence or a paragraph, deleting irrelevant material, or adding a transitional sentence where such emendations would improve the sequence of thought. Also, special terms or little-known persons should usually be defined or identified the first time they appear in the book, and first names of persons

---

terfield, Fielding, Ruskin, Scott, and Shakespeare. For more general advice on usage see Fowler, Bernstein, and others listed at end of this chapter and in the bibliography.

should normally be given the first time they are mentioned. It is well to remember, however, that a term unfamiliar to the editor may be common in the author's field and thus need no definition for prospective readers, and first names of well-known persons (e.g., Disraeli, Shakespeare) should not be inserted by an editor. It is also incumbent on the editor to be persistently mindful of the unique relationship between the author and his or her work. Even in necessary emendations, the author's style ought to be respected and preserved, and arbitrary changes more reflective of the editor's preferences than of the requirement to rectify errors or infelicities should be resisted (see also 2.105).

2.99   *Subheads.* Subheads in the text should be checked for uniformity of style and for pertinence. Does each give an accurate indication of what is in the following text? Are they too long and can they be shortened? Are they all similar in grammatical construction? (For example, none should be a complete sentence if the rest are phrases.) Does the first sentence of text following a subhead refer to a word in the subhead without repeating it? (See 1.79.) If there is more than one level of subhead, the different levels should be indicated during editing by writing, and circling, progressions of letters or numbers in the margin. The highest level may be indicated by a circled A or 1; the next by a circled B or 2; the next by C or 3; and so on. If subheads are typed all in capitals, the editor should mark which letters should be capitalized if the heading is to be set in upper- and lowercase. No further styling of subheads, such as changing roman to italics, should be done at this time, however, since such matters of style cannot be known until the design has been prepared. Markup of this kind is ordinarily done after the edited manuscript has been returned by the author and checked again by the editor, for by then the design is usually ready (see 2.133–48).

2.100   *Cross-references.* All references in the text to tables, charts, figures, maps, appendixes, lists of references, or other parts of the book should be verified by the editor, even if the author has also done so (see 2.39–52). If the author, for example, mentions the gross national product for 1965 in the text and refers the reader to table 4, which gives figures only through 1964, the editor should query the discrepancy. Again for example, place-names on a map intended to illustrate the text must be spelled as they are in the text. When an author uses an excessive number of cross-references to specific pages, the editor should suggest eliminating most of them (see 2.43). In a text like this manual, where many cross-references are desirable, numbered paragraphs minimize the number of changes necessary from manuscript to page proof.

2.101   Some authors need to be discouraged from distracting the reader and interrupting the subject matter by frequent remarks on the structure of their work—the "This is what I did earlier in my book, this is what I am doing now, and this is what I will do later" syndrome. A clear organization of material, a good index, and, where absolutely necessary, a note or parenthetical comment giving a reference to relevant material elsewhere in the book will eliminate the need for most such remarks.

2.102 *Quotations.* Aside from adjusting quotation marks and ellipsis points to conform to house style (see 10.26–32, 10.48–63), the editor must do nothing to material an author quotes from another source. Should the author add interpolations (in square brackets) or translations, however, these may be edited for style. Misspelled words and apparent errors in transcribing a quotation (obvious omission of a word, for example) should be queried to the author. Frequent errors, or apparent errors, of this kind, including inconsistent punctuation, may indicate that the author has been careless in transcribing quoted material. The editor should then be especially firm in requesting the author to check all quotations for accuracy, including punctuation.

EDITING NOTES

2.103 In editing manuscripts with many citations, it is helpful to keep a separate alphabetical list of sources, arranged by authors' last names, and giving the chapter and note number of the first citation of each work. To provide a shortened form for subsequent citations to a work (see 15.248–62), it is often necessary to check the first, full citation, which is easy to find if the editor has noted it on the list. If the form of the shortened citation is then added to the list, all subsequent short citations to the work may be assured of consistency.

2.104 The editor must be sure that every reference to a work is given the same way. Shortened titles or abbreviations, for example, once decided upon, must be the same every time they appear. If a volume number is given with one or more references to a journal, the volume number should be given for every reference to that journal.

2.105 Before making sweeping changes affecting the style of an author's notes, the editor is often well advised to consult the author, giving reasons for wishing to make such changes and asking for the author's concurrence. Authors who have prepared notes with meticulous care, with the necessary information in each citation and consistency of style throughout, are likely to be dismayed by editorial efforts to force house style upon them. In such cases the author's style should be retained (unless the work is part of a multiauthor volume that is being edited to a uniform style). In other cases the author and editor may work out a compromise acceptable to both.[10]

10. For detailed rules about the style of notes and footnotes, and examples, see chapter 15.

2.106 Discursive material in notes is edited like the text and should be read as carefully as the text. When the notes are to be printed at the bottom of the page, the author should be asked to shorten any excessively long note, either by deleting material in it or by adding parts of it to the text. The chief reason for shortening long footnotes, apart from the reader's possible annoyance and the appearance of the printed page, is to avoid the makeup problem caused by a footnote that won't fit and must be continued on the next page. Long notes create no such problem when all notes are printed at the back of the book instead of at the foot of the page. Whichever way the notes are to be printed, however, long lists, long tables, and the like are better placed in the text or an appendix.

2.107 The editor should always check note reference numbers in the text against the notes themselves. Checking the numbers, or renumbering notes, should be a separate operation. An attempt to renumber notes while editing the text or the notes increases the risk of skipping or repeating a number. When renumbering is necessary, the old number should be crossed out and the new one inserted simultaneously in the text and before the note.

2.108 An editor's judgment is sometimes helpful to an author unsure or care-less about the use of citations. The source of any direct quotation in a scholarly text should be made clear to the reader in what the author says about it either in the text or in a note. Paraphrases of other writers' ideas should be acknowledged and sources of little-known facts given. Well-known facts, easily ascertainable from many sources, need no documentation. The editor, however, must be cautious and entirely confident before asking an author to alter documentation.

2.109 In a work containing a bibliography as well as notes, each citation in the notes should be checked against the bibliography. Any discrepancy in spelling, date of publication, and the like should be either resolved by the editor or queried for the author's attention. Since works periph-eral to the subject of the manuscript may be cited in a note but, quite properly, not listed in the bibliography, the editor should not question the omission of such items from the bibliography but should simply make certain that a source not in the bibliography is given with full bibliographical details in the note. Nor should an editor try to determine whether every entry in a bibliography is cited somewhere in the notes, even when the author titles the bibliography "Works Cited." (See also chapter 15.)

EDITING BIBLIOGRAPHIES

2.110 The editor's task in editing a bibliography or reference list is to make each entry conform to the same style: order of the items in each entry, capitalization of titles, abbreviations, punctuation.[11] Alphabetically arranged lists should be checked to see that every entry is in the right place. If the list is chronological, the dates should be checked, and so on. Discrepancies or omissions found in correlating source citations in the text or notes with the bibliography should be queried and the manuscript page number of the citation in question given so that the author can easily compare the two.

EDITING TABLES

2.111   If the author has typed the tables on pages with the text, the editor should cut them out and paste them on separate pages, making sure that the text page number is inserted on the new page containing the table and the number of the table is recorded in the margin of the text page. The text remaining after the cutting out of tables should, of course, be pasted or taped onto new sheets of standard-sized paper. An alternative, less time-consuming method is to make photocopies of the text pages containing tables, crossing out table copy on the text pages and text copy on the table pages. If the author has prepared the tables on separate pages, the editor need only check to see that the placement of each is noted in the text (see 2.47–48).

2.112   The editor will then check for uniformity of style in tables containing similar material: wording in titles, column headings, and stub entries; abbreviations; use of leaders or dashes in empty cells; and other matters. The sequence of symbols or letters referring to footnotes should be checked (see 12.50–51). Commas may need to be added in figures of four or more digits, columns brought into proper alignment, rules drawn or deleted, and so on. And sometimes the editor will find it necessary to recast an entire table to provide a clearer presentation of its material. (For various styles used in tables see chapter 12.)

PREPARING ILLUSTRATIONS AND LEGENDS

2.113   When an author fails to identify illustrations or to type legends on separate sheets, the editor must do so (see 2.49–51). The editor will often find it convenient to have a copy of the legends in the file for future reference; in some instances proofs of the illustrations may have to be checked before the proofs of the legends have been delivered.

2.114   The editor should examine the illustrations themselves or good copies of them, primarily to see that the spelling of any words in them conforms to the spelling in the text, but also to see that the correct figure is being referred to. The editor may also work with the production

11. For specific bibliographical and reference list styles see chapters 15 and 16.

department on cropping and scaling illustrations, arranging them on a page, and so on.

2.115 If a map or other illustration containing words to be set in type must be redrawn, the editor will usually provide a typed list of all such words. Place-names on a map should be arranged by category—countries, states, cities, rivers, mountains, and so forth—since each category will be set in a different type size or style. (For further suggestions on preparing illustrations and legends see chapter 11.)

PREPARING FRONT MATTER

2.116 The editor normally provides copy for the half-title page of a book, the series title, if any, and the copyright page. To prepare the copyright page, the editor needs to read the contract to identify the copyright owner and to examine any correspondence between author and publisher relating to such matters as permissions, translation, or new edition. Any oversight or inaccuracy on the copyright page is attributable to the editor, not to the author. (For the sequence and form of the preliminaries and for sample copyright pages see chapter 1.)

2.117 Often the editor will need to retype (or supply) copy for the title page, table of contents, and list of illustrations. The editor should always check the table of contents carefully to see that it lists all parts of the manuscript (including the index) and that the wording of titles matches that of the text. It may be desirable to either add or delete subheads in the table of contents.

EDITING INDEXES

2.118 Later, when the index manuscript arrives, the editor should edit and mark it for the typesetter at once. The rest of the book is now in pages, some of it perhaps even being printed, and the index must be set in type as soon as possible. If the index has been prepared in a logical fashion, the editor need only verify cross-references and check alphabetization of main entries, arrangement of subentries, sequence of page numbers (such errors as "74–74" or "85, 50, 97" obviously require consulting the pages cited), and spelling and punctuation in each entry (see also 17.134–35). If the index is excessively long or so illogically planned that it would be difficult to use, the editor must either repair the matter as quickly as possible or consult the author or whoever has prepared the index (see 17.132). If the author is to prepare the index, specific instructions given *before* he or she does so will usually, but not always, prevent such traumatic editorial experiences.

2.119 To aid the compositor, the editor should note, on the first page of the index manuscript, the page in the book on which the index is to begin, usually the recto following the last page preceding the index. To conserve space, the index may start on a verso, but it should always begin on a new page.

EDITOR AND AUTHOR

Queries on Manuscript

2.120 What to ask an author about a manuscript—and how and when to query the author—is an important part of editing. The editor usually should not query matters of house style—capitalization, spelling, and so forth. If the editor has not changed the author's pattern of capitalization, for example, but has merely tried to bring consistency to the manuscript, no mention need be made of these details. If, however, the editor has found it necessary to lowercase words consistently capitalized by the author, it might be well to explain why in the covering letter (see 2.128–30); and if there are many such editorial changes, the editor may want to send the author a copy of the style sheet (see 2.96–97). It may sometimes be more prudent, and is surely more considerate, to discuss such far-reaching style changes with the author before proceeding very far in making them. An author who has a strong attachment to certain matters of style, such as capitalization, and who might therefore resist change, would most likely prefer to discuss the matter before it is a massive accomplished fact to which the reaction might be sharp irritation, even though the reasons for the changes were presented in the editor's covering letter. If forewarned and allowed to discuss the changes, the author might consent. Should the author, after discussion, prefer to retain the original style, however, the editor ought gracefully to respect authorial wishes. In such an event, extensive editorial changes will not have to be undone, either by the author or by the editor. Time and money will have been saved, and equanimity preserved. (See also 2.126.)

2.121 The editor should avoid writing long notes explaining editorial changes. Most authors readily understand and appreciate corrections of dangling modifiers, misplaced pronouns, repeated words or phrases, misalliances between subject and verb, and the like. An editor should of course know why any such emendation has been made but need not explain it unless challenged by the author.

2.122 No query to an author should sound stupid, naive, or pedantic. Nor should a query be so phrased that it seems to reflect upon the author's scholarly ability or powers of interpretation. Humorous remarks, even when addressed to an author the editor knows will appreciate them, are generally better omitted. Every author has a right to expect conscientious, intelligent help from an editor. Unintelligent queries, as well as sloppy editing, will quite rightly make any author lose faith in an editor and may prejudice that author against the publisher as well.

2.123   The editor should call the author's attention to any discrepancies in statements of fact. For example, if a meeting is said, on page 13, to have taken place on 10 May 1896, and the same meeting is mentioned on page 87 as occurring in 1897, the editor (if sharp-eyed enough to catch it) will lightly circle each date and will write "1897? See p. 87" in the margin of page 13, and, on page 87, "1896? See p. 13." Similarly, possibly unintentional repetition of material, sometimes on widely separated pages, should be pointed out: "Repetition intentional? See p. 25." A missing quotation mark or note reference number: "Where does quote begin?" "Where is ref. to n. 87?" Or if the editor inserts the missing item where it seems to belong and wants the author to verify it: "OK?"

2.124   Some editors prefer to write queries not in the margins of the manuscript but on separate slips, or fliers, that are gummed on one end so that they can be attached to the manuscript page. The slips are detached by the editor after the author returns the edited manuscript and before it goes to the typesetter. The advantage of this method is that the margins of the manuscript remain clean; thus, in a manuscript requiring many queries or many suggestions for sentence revision, it is usually better to use separate slips (pins, *not* paper clips or staples, may be used if the slips are not gummed). The disadvantage is that the author may detach the slips, with or without answering the questions, and the editor thus has no record of what was queried. A second possible disadvantage is that, after the editor has removed the slips and sent the manuscript to the typesetter, a proofreader may ask the same question on the proofs, not knowing that the author has already given an answer.

2.125   Whatever method of querying an author is used—slips or marginal notes or, in the case of manuscripts edited on-line, queries entered electronically and manifest on the new printout—the editor should always ask the author *not* to detach slips or *not* to erase queries. The purpose of this is to avoid the possibility of the same or similar questions being raised as the editor goes through the manuscript again. When the manuscript is returned by the author, the editor, while checking the author's answers, will detach any slips or cross out any marginal queries before releasing the manuscript for typesetting.

2.126   Manuscripts requiring extensive revision—heavy rewriting, deleting, rearranging—that has not been agreed upon by the author before the editor begins work demand a more cautious approach. The editor may send a preliminary letter explaining proposed editorial changes and how they might improve the manuscript. The editor may then send one or two edited chapters and wait for the author's approval of these before proceeding with the entire manuscript.

2.127   To save time later, as the editing progresses the editor may note on a separate piece of paper any general questions, suggestions, or explanations appropriate for inclusion in the letter to the author accompanying the edited manuscript.

Covering Letter

2.128   The contents of the editor's letter to the author, sent with the manuscript or separately (but timed to reach the author no later than the manuscript itself), will depend on the nature of the manuscript, how much telephone or personal contact the editor has had with the author, and how much experience the author has had in publishing books. No form letter could ever serve the purpose, although some publishers do send, along with the letter, a standard form instructing the author how to make changes and covering other general issues.

2.129   Most covering letters should include the following points, not necessarily in this order:

1. What the editor has done to the manuscript; in brief, the reasons for doing it (e.g., "I have rephrased here and there to eliminate dangling modifiers or inadvertent repetition of words, to reduce excessive use of passive verbs, or to clarify your meaning," etc.); and what the author is expected to do now (answer all queries in the margins of the manuscript and read carefully any editorial change to make sure the meaning has not been altered). The editor may also want to advise how to make corrections on the manuscript pages, or caution the author how *not* to make them (see 2.34–38). In the absence of specific objections, the author's approval of all editorial markings is assumed. To avoid possible unpleasantness at the proof stage and to encourage a more thorough reading of the edited manuscript, some publishers ask authors to sign a statement agreeing to emendations made by the editor or decided on through consultation between author and editor.

2. A warning that now is the time for the author to make any last-minute changes, additions, or deletions in the manuscript and that, if it has not already been done, all quoted matter should now be checked for the last time. Most publishers today do not permit, without financial penalty to the author, extensive, sometimes even minor, author's alterations after type has been set (see 3.14, 3.37–41).

3. A specific date by which the editor expects the manuscript to be returned. The author should be made aware of the importance of keeping a schedule, particularly if it is the author's first book; experienced authors know, or should know, that a delay of a week on their part may result in a much longer delay in the production of the book because the book will have lost its scheduled "place in line," and the typesetter will have turned to another waiting project.

4. An approximate date for the arrival of proofs, and an inquiry about

whether the timing will cause problems for the author. Although the editor will probably not be able to give a precise date at this time, consultation with the production department should make an educated guess possible. A busy author's availability to read proofs must be considered, as well as the typesetter's schedule, when the production schedule is planned (see 3.4). To ensure the most expeditious handling of proofs, the editor should confirm the address to which the author wishes proofs sent. It goes without saying that the editor must know the author's whereabouts at all stages of the publishing process. It is the author's responsibility to inform the editor of unexpected changes of location.

5. What kind of proofs the author may expect: galleys or pages or both. If only pages are to be sent, the author should be strongly forewarned against making alterations in proofs, because of the added cost not only of resetting lines but of remaking pages and changing relevant index entries. Now is the time, too, to inquire whether the usual two sets of proofs will be sufficient; if the author has hired an indexer, for example, a third set may be required.

6. An inquiry about the index: Does the author plan to prepare it personally or have someone else prepare it, or does the author expect the publisher to provide an indexer?[12] Does the author need advice on index making? The University of Chicago Press sends reprints of the indexing chapter of this manual to its authors who request advice,[13] and the editor may supplement the reprint with suggestions about number and kind of entries, subject and name indexes, and so on, appropriate to the individual book. Although the index cannot be completed until page proofs are ready, planning about its nature and preparation should be done well in advance.

2.130 An editor must give careful thought to the style and tone of a covering letter and must never forget that it is the author's book, not the editor's. The tone should be assured, businesslike, and gracious. A well-written and informative letter accompanying a carefully edited manuscript will assure an author of the editor's ability and concern for the book and therefore make for easy cooperation between them throughout the publishing process.

Mailing an Edited Manuscript

2.131 An edited manuscript is a unique copy of that manuscript, representing a considerable investment of editorial time and thought. It must not be

---

12. As a rule, the University of Chicago Press prefers that authors prepare their own indexes. When the Press hires a freelance indexer to do it, the cost is taken out of the author's royalties.

13. The Press also sells copies of the reprint to anyone who writes for it.

lost. A manuscript sent by mail or other delivery service should be carefully wrapped with cardboard and strong wrapping paper, sealed, marked first class if sent by mail, and insured or registered. When in doubt about the reliability of delivery, the editor should retain a photocopy of the edited manuscript (see 2.92).

Checking Author's Corrections

2.132 When the manuscript comes back from the author, the editor must go through it again to see what the author has done and whether all queries have been answered. This task may be short and pleasant (the author has agreed to all suggestions, made emendations neatly and legibly, and introduced no new problems) or an editor's nightmare (the author has scribbled all over the manuscript with a pen or a dull, blurry pencil, has added material on slips clipped to the pages, has inserted new notes without renumbering, and has been thoroughly disagreeable about the editor's efforts) or somewhere in between. Returned manuscripts or printouts that are difficult to read or follow in whole or in part may require repair by the editor. In the case of a manuscript to be used in typesetting, the editor should retype heavily marked or barely legible parts or inserts and tape or paste them in place. In the case of electronic manuscripts whose editing is to be added by the typesetter, the editor should retype additions or inserts that are difficult to read, and if handwritten alterations on the printout are hard to make out, the editor, after ascertaining what they were meant to be, should carefully rewrite them in the margin or between the lines near the author's illegible versions, which should then be crossed out. Arrows may be necessary in some cases to make the replacement clear, but care should be taken not to run the arrows through text. If notes have been added or deleted, the editor should check the numbering sequence and renumber if necessary. Even if the manuscript or printout has been returned in easily readable form, the editor should look for and edit any new material the author may have added. If the editing has been done electronically, author's changes and additions, the editing of new or revised material, and any other necessary repair work are all entered directly on the disks. Illegible changes or additions made by the author must be deciphered by telephone, express mail, or some other method before the disks are revised. In cases of disagreement over wording, the author's version should now prevail, unless editor and author can reach a compromise. And the editor should refrain from further word changing unless the author can be consulted before the manuscript goes to production. The editor's next task is to mark the manuscript for the typesetter according to the book design (see 2.133–48). (This is sometimes done in conjunction with the initial editing, but more often after checking the manuscript returned from the author.)

EDITOR AND TYPESETTER

2.133   In many publishing houses, including the University of Chicago Press, the editor marks the manuscript with type specifications indicated on the designer's layout or from a list of specifications furnished by the designer (see chapter 18). Care must be exercised to follow the specifications exactly and to mark like parts alike (but see 2.135). The layout does not show all parts of a book but does give samples of all type sizes and spacing to be used in text and display matter.

2.134   In electronic typesetting, type specifications must be translated into symbols or codes that can be read by the machine; this coding is usually done by the typesetter (compare 2.56).

Type Specifications

2.135   Traditionally, each item in the opening of an article or of a preface, chapter (at least the first chapter), appendix, or other section of a book (title, chapter number, etc.) is marked for its particular type size, style, and placement; ornamental rules or other devices used in the design might also be specified. For such matters as sinkage—the vertical space from the top of the type page to the bottom of the first line of text—as well as the amount of space between article title and author's name or between chapter number, chapter title, and text, however, it is usually best to refer the typesetter to the designer's layout. Specifications for text, subheads, block quotations, and similar elements must also be given, at least at the first occurrence of each. Thereafter, handwritten "codes" added during editing identify similar elements for the typesetter.[14] This practice is still widely used among publishers. Increasingly, however, a much more abbreviated form of markup is being used that relies on the typesetter to follow directly the design layouts and detailed list of specifications provided by the publisher's design department. All the editor need do is provide, during editing, the traditional codes for elements that would not be obvious to the operator. The various levels of subheads, for instance, must be indicated for the typesetter, usually by circled alphabetical or numerical codes (A, B, C or 1, 2, 3, etc.). Extracts, or block quotations, are also coded, usually by vertical colored lines, and poetry, should there be any, must be differentiated from prose extracts. It may also be necessary, in chapter titles, subheadings, and so forth, to mark the letters to be capitalized, and if capitals and small capitals are to be used, to indicate how they are to

---

14. Such codes written by hand on the manuscript correspond to the codes used on electronic manuscripts, which are part of the electronic files; both serve the same identifying function. If a manuscript (or printout) coded by hand is to be produced electronically, the handwritten codes are translated into electronic codes.

be deployed. The following paragraphs, however, are intended to guide those who will be providing traditional markup on manuscripts.

2.136   A design often calls for the first line of a chapter to begin flush left or with a special indention or with a display initial, any of which should be marked on each chapter opening. If small caps are specified for the initial word or phrase of a chapter, the editor must indicate how much is to be set in small caps:

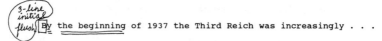

2.137   The type size, leading,[15] typeface, and type width to be used in the text proper should be written in the left margin next to the first paragraph of at least the first chapter or other division of text. In computerized typesetting, once for a whole book is enough. For example:

Here "10" is the type size (10 point); "12" is the distance in points from the base of one line to the base of the next line, technically, from *base line to base line* or *base to base* (see glossary); "Times Roman" is the name of the typeface; and "× 26" means "by 26 picas," that is, a print line 26 picas long. When the line spacing (from base to base) is greater than the point size of the typeface, the setting is said to be *leaded.* Thus 10-point type set on a 12-point line is said to have 2-point leading.

2.138   The type size, leading, and amount of indention, if any, for extracts should be placed beside the first extract (block quotation) in each chapter, or often only the first extract in a book. For example:

Here "10/10" means 10-point type with no leading, that is, 10 point solid. (For marking indentions with em quads see 2.88.)

2.139   Poetry extracts, unless the design specifies otherwise, are generally marked "center on longest line," regardless of the indention of the prose extracts. Poems with relatively long lines, however, such as blank

---

15. The term *leading* derives from older technologies, sometimes, although infrequently, still used, in which type was made of cast metal (a lead alloy), and line spaces were augmented by the addition of thin lead bars, or simply by casting lead type bars of slightly greater width (for more see glossary).

verse, are all set to the same indention, specified by the designer. It is usually sufficient to give poetry specifications once, at the first appearance. If long-lined as well as short-lined poetry is quoted, the indention of the former and the centering of the latter may be specified at least at the first appearance of each, and thereafter whenever there is a likelihood of uncertainty. Although the foregoing instructions are sometimes still useful, current practice at the University of Chicago Press, and at many other publishing houses, is simply to refer the typesetter to the carefully wrought design. In some cases, indeed, such a course is safer. The placement of a source citation following a poetry extract should be specified. "Drop one line & ctr on last letter of longest line above" is the formula used successfully by the University of Chicago Press journal editors. In some works the editor and book designer may find it more feasible to place the source citations flush right or indented one or two ems from the right. (For further discussion see 10.22–24.)

2.140 Identify *all* extracts, and any other passages with the same type specifications, by drawing a colored vertical line to the left of each one. All vertical lines indicating the same type specifications should be in the same color; the University of Chicago Press favors red for extracts. Drawing colored lines to indicate type specifications is called *color-coding*. Even when instructions are written next to the passage, draw the colored line as well, because it shows the exact beginning and end of the passage. Be sure to draw the line precisely to the bottom of the last line (see example, 2.89). Such color-coding is most easily done during editing. In material with a variety of type specifications, a different color may be used for each kind and the typesetter provided with a key to the color system. If poetry extracts appear in addition to prose extracts, the former may be distinguished either by a different color-code or by writing "poetry" or "verse" to the left of the extract color-code.

2.141 Like extracts, subheads generally need be marked for type specifications only at the first occurrence. All set-off subheads should be marked A, B, C or 1, 2, 3, etc. (circled), to indicate which level is intended (see 1.71–73). If the subheads are to be set in caps and small caps, italics, or boldface, each should be underlined accordingly at least the first time (see 2.80–82). The letter-coding, like the color-coding, alerts the typesetter to the specifications for subsequent occurrences.

      Ⓐ The Editorial Function

      Ⓑ Mechanical Editing

2.142 An italic subhead that begins a paragraph (run-in sidehead) need not be marked either with a letter or with type specifications, if it will be set in the same type size and typeface as the text.

2.143 In marking the type specifications and designating the levels of sub-heads, the editor should also do the following:

1. Check the capitalization of each subhead to see that it follows the design specifications and, if it is to be caps and lowercase or caps and small caps, that it is capitalized according to the rules for capitalizing titles (7.127–28). Run-in sideheads should have sentence capitalization.

2. Delete a period or other punctuation following a subhead set on a line by itself (use a period after a run-in sidehead).

3. At the first appearance of each level of subhead, mark the placement of the subhead (centered, flush left, etc.; see 2.86–88) and the amount of space above and below it (2.90).

4. Mark the first line of text following a subhead if the design calls for it to begin flush left or with an indention other than that used for a regular paragraph.

2.144 The first page of each section of back matter in a book should be marked with the type specifications for that section. Appendixes are often in the same type size as extracts in the text proper, but it is unnecessary to color-code them like the extracts unless several type sizes are required in the same section.

2.145 In a note section the type specifications for the subheads and for the notes themselves may be given at the beginning of the notes for the first chapter or other subsection. The editor should indicate whether note numbers are to be superior or on the line, whether each note begins with a paragraph indention or flush left, and whether any extra space is to be inserted between notes. The University of Chicago Press prefers that note numbers be set on the line, followed by a period, rather than as superscripts. An unnumbered note—a chapter source note, for example (see 15.50–51)—may be located either with the endnotes, where it precedes the numbered notes for that chapter, or at the foot of the opening page of the chapter. As a footnote, it may be typed either at the bottom of the manuscript page or on a separate following page. In the latter case, proper marginal instructions must be added for the compositor—for example, at the bottom of the opening page, "Unnumbered footnote, see following page"; on the page bearing the note, "Unnumbered footnote for bottom of opening page." (For a full description of endnotes and footnotes see chapter 15.)

2.146 A bibliography or reference list arranged alphabetically, chronologically, or by some other system is customarily set *flush and hang*. This means that the first line of each item is set flush left and all runover lines are indented under it.

2.147 An index, like a bibliography, is set flush-and-hang style. If there are no indented subentries, or if the subentries are run in (see 17.10), runover lines are indented one em; if there is one level of indented subentry, indent all runovers two ems. Mark the subentries with em quads (see 2.88), and specify the amount of indention for the runovers along with the type specifications at the beginning of the index.

2.148 An index is usually set in two columns, the width of which must be specified. If the designer has not provided specifications, you can determine the width of one column by subtracting 1 from the pica width of the print line and dividing by 2. This will give 1 pica for the space between columns. Specifications for an index of a book with a 26-pica print line might read as follows:

> *9/10 Times Roman*
> *× 12½, 2 cols.*
> *flush and hang 1 em*

Identification and Placement of Material

2.149 Before the manuscript goes to the typesetter, where it will very likely be parceled out for both typesetting and proofreading, the editor should identify each chapter and other part in the top right corner of the first page. The author's last name and the part are usually sufficient: "Jones, chap. 3," "Jones, Bibliog." At the bottom of the last page of text of a chapter or other part the editor may write "End chap. 3." At the end of the last chapter the editor should tell the typesetter what is to follow in the book (not always the same as what follows in the manuscript): "End chap. 10. Appendix A follows," for example. Each section of the front matter and the back matter should be so marked, and the last page of the last section of a book should indicate whether an index is to come: "End Bibliog., Index to follow" or, for example, "End chap. 15 & book. *No* index." All such notes to the typesetter should be circled, meaning they are not to be set in type.

2.150 In place of any material not yet received from the author, the editor should insert a sheet telling what is to come and, if possible, when (e.g., "Dedication to come," "Preface approx. 3 MS pp. to come, ca. 4/12"). Front matter often goes straight into pages even when the rest of the book is to go through the galley proof stage.

2.151 Any material that is separate from the text in the manuscript but is to be printed with the text—tables, figures, illustrations—must be identified with the author's name or the title of the work or both, and each item must be marked with the number of the manuscript page to which it refers. When figures or other illustrations are not included with the text but are to be inserted later, either the editor or the designer must specify the exact amount of vertical space to be left in the pages to accommodate each illustration.

Numbering and Pagination

2.152   Once the manuscript has been edited, the editing reviewed by the author, the whole gone over again by the editor, all elements arranged in the proper order (as described in chapter 1), type specifications marked, and the manuscript otherwise prepared for the typesetter, the manuscript should be numbered, preferably in the upper right corner, with arabic numerals starting with 1 on the half title and running consecutively to the end of the manuscript. A numbering machine may be used to simplify this process.

2.153   In addition to the numbering of the manuscript, as much of the actual pagination of the book as can be determined at this stage should also now be noted. The editor should paginate up to and including the first page of the table of contents with lowercase roman numerals, usually at the foot of the page and circled, since these numerals are not intended to be printed (expressed). Blank pages are noted also; if, for example, page ii is blank, the half-title page would be marked "p. i (p. ii blank)," or a dedication page marked "p. v (p. vi blank)." If the editor cannot determine what page an element (such as the preface) will fall on when the pages are made up, the words "recto page" or simply "recto" on the first page of the element will provide sufficient instruction for the typesetter. (Traditionally, each preliminary element following the copyright page begins on a recto; but see 1.3.) If the page number of the opening of the preface or other multipage preliminary element can be determined but not the total number of printed pages, the editor should write the folio (page number) on the first page, and the typesetter will provide the remainder of the sequence.

2.154   The portions of the book containing the text itself and all the end matter are paginated with arabic numerals. If the folio of the first page of the text section is to be expressed, as is usually the case if the text actually begins on that page, an arabic numeral 1 or some such instruction as "folio 1" or "begin arabic folios here with 1" should be written at the bottom of the page. If the folio of the first page of the text section is to be unexpressed, as in the case of a second half title or a part title, or if the design specifies unexpressed folios for all chapter openings, the numeral 1 should be circled. In either case, subsequent pagination must of course be left to the typesetter. The editor should, however, specify whether subsequent sections are to begin recto or verso.

2.155   The opening chapter, all part titles, and all chapters immediately following part titles traditionally begin on recto pages. All other chapters may usually begin either recto or verso, unless offprints of the chapters are to be provided or the design specifies all recto openings. Elements in the back matter also traditionally begin on recto pages, except that if there is, for example, more than one appendix, subsequent appendixes may begin recto or verso, whichever follows the previous appendix. As in the prelims, any page that is to be blank, such as the verso of a part title, is signaled by adding "p. 2 blank" or "verso blank" on the preceding recto.

2.156   Should the manufacturing process include the galley stage, the proofreader or editor must transfer all pagination instructions from the manuscript to the proper locations on the galley proofs.

Other Instructions

2.157   In addition to the manuscript, edited and marked with type specifications, the editor should supply on separate sheets any special information or parts needed in the production of a particular manuscript. Such material includes spine and cover copy, running heads, list of special characters, style sheet for the proofreader, and a transmittal sheet telling what is included and what is yet to come.

Spine and Cover Copy

2.158   The layout should be consulted to discover what the designer has specified for the spine of the cloth edition and what, if anything, is planned for the front cover. The editor then prepares copy accordingly.[16] Copy must also be prepared for the book jacket. Normally the editor furnishes copy only for the author's name, the title of the book, and the publisher's name (see 1.110). The marketing department generally provides promotional copy for covers (of paperback books) and jackets (of hardcover books). If the layout gives no specifications for the spine, the editor will supply copy anyway, giving the full name of the author, the main title of the book, and the publisher's name, usually in shortened form (e.g., "Chicago" instead of "The University of Chicago Press").

Running Heads

2.159   The editor must provide copy from which running heads will be set.[17] This is usually typed in two columns, one for verso, the other for recto

16. *Never* should the designer's layout be used as copy for typesetting.
17. For selection of material to be used in running heads see 1.92–98.

running heads. A running head must be included for any preliminary matter that will occupy more than one printed page, as well as for the index. Since, except in special cases provided for by the designer, a running head must be short enough to fit on a single line, usually containing the page number (folio) as well, the editor must often shorten a title to fit. To do this it is necessary to determine from the designer's layout how many characters (letters, punctuation marks, and spaces between words) are allowed for the running head. The most meaningful words in a title, considering the subject of the entire book and the significance of the chapter title within it, must be selected. (If titles must be drastically shortened for use as running heads, it is best to submit the list to the author for approval before type is set.) In shortening foreign-language titles the editor must avoid omitting a word governing the case ending of another word included in the running head. The editor might also mark the running-head copy with the type specifications and might indicate the specification for the folios. For example:

"Flush outside" means flush left on verso pages and flush right on recto pages. "O.S." means *old style* (see the glossary).

2.160   Running-head copy is usually sent with the edited manuscript to the production department and the typesetter. It may, in some cases, be sent with galley proofs when these are returned to the typesetter for page makeup.

2.161   In a work where the running head reflects what is on a given page, running heads cannot be prepared and set in type until pages have been made up. It is therefore usually the author or editor who adds these to the page proof, although it is sometimes possible to give the compositor instructions on the selection of subheads for verso and recto running heads (see 1.95).

List of Special Characters

2.162   The typesetter usually needs to know what special characters will have to be provided for a particular manuscript. Special characters normally include Greek letters, isolated mathematical or other symbols, and letters bearing diacritical marks other than the usual French accents and the German umlaut. The editor should prepare a separate list of such characters, including the number of the manuscript page where each first appears, the type size it is to be set in, and whether it is italic or roman, capital or lowercase.

Style Sheet for Proofreader

2.163 Professional proofreaders, whether the compositor's, the publisher's, or freelance, find it helpful to have a copy of the editor's style sheet (see 2.96–97). When thus advised of the editor's intentions, a proofreader need not query any of these particular points on proofs.

Transmittal Sheet

2.164 Perhaps the last thing an editor does before turning an edited manuscript over to the production department for typesetting is to prepare a transmittal sheet, listing what is being transmitted and what, if anything, is still to come. The form used by the University of Chicago Press is shown in figure 2.3. The form is filled out in triplicate, one copy remaining in the editor's file and two accompanying the manuscript to the production department, where one copy is retained and the other sent with the manuscript to the typesetter. In addition to listing the author, the editor, the correct title of the work, and such general information as the number of chapters, illustrations, and manuscript pages, the transmittal sheet also lists, in a section titled "Editor's Checklist," all possible parts of a book, followed by two blank columns, one headed "Herewith," the other "To Come." The editor checks the relevant items in the proper column and crosses out items irrelevant to the work concerned. The form also lists items not part of the manuscript itself but necessary to its production and so provided by the editor. These include layout, spine copy, running-head copy, and list of special characters. Space is also provided for instructions about the number of sets of proof needed by the author and the editor. If proofs are to be mailed directly to the author by the typesetter, the author's address and any special mailing instructions should also be included. It is often at this time also that the editor applies to the Library of Congress for the cataloging-in-publication data, which will be reproduced in the finished book (see 1.28–30).

2.165 If a manuscript goes to production piecemeal (an uneconomical practice, but sometimes necessary), a complete transmittal sheet should accompany the first batch released, indicating what is yet to come. Successive batches should each be accompanied by a partial transmittal sheet (listing only what is being transmitted) so that the editor has a record of when all parts of the manuscript were released.

UNIVERSITY OF CHICAGO PRESS
5801 S. Ellis Ave. / Chicago, Illinois 60637

AUTHOR:
TITLE:

Date:
Manuscript Editor:
House Editor:

GENERAL INFORMATION	EDITOR'S CHECKLIST	TRANSMITTAL INFORMATION		
		Here-with	To come	For printer's use
Number of chapters . . . . _____	Items to be transmitted for this publication			
Total number of MS pages . . . . _____				
Front matter . . . . _____				
Text and end matter . . . . _____				
Other matter . . . . _____	**GENERAL**			
Notes print at:	Layouts			
Foot of page . . . . _____	Spine copy (2 copies)			
End of book . . . . _____	Running-head copy			
Subheads (how many levels?) . . . . _____	List of special characters			
Reduced material . . . . _____				
Halftones	**PRELIMS**			
Print as figures on text paper . . . . _____				
Print as plates in special section(s) . . . . _____	Half title			
Text figures	Series title			
	Frontispiece			
	Title			
HANDLING OF PROOF	Copyright			
	Dedication			
Editor's Proofs	Epigraph			
Galleys_____sets	Contents			
Pages_____sets	List of illustrations			
	List of tables			
Author's Proofs	List of abbreviations			
Galleys_____sets	Foreword			
Pages_____sets	Preface			
Allow_____wks for galleys out & back	Acknowledgments			
Allow_____wks for pages out & back	Introduction			
Allow_____wks for index after last pages back				
	BODY OF BOOK			
SPECIAL INSTRUCTIONS				
	Second half title			
	Introduction			
	Part half titles			
	Text (all or part?)			
	Tables (how many?)			
	Plates (how many?)			
	Figures (how many?)			
	Legend copy			
	Footnotes			
	END MATTER			
	Appendix(es)			
	Notes			
	List of abbreviations			
	Glossary			
	Bibliography			
	Index			

Fig. 2.3. Transmittal sheet to accompany a manuscript from editor to production department and from production department to typesetter

PREPARING MANUSCRIPT FROM PRINTED MATERIAL

Using Copies of the Original

2.166 Manuscript for anthologies, collected works, and other books containing previously published material should not be retyped unless the ma-

97

terial has been substantially rewritten. If the manuscript is to be assembled from the printed material itself, the editor, compiler, or author of the volume must have *two clean sets* of the original pages to make *one* copy of the manuscript. Each page should be pasted or taped (not stapled) to a standard sheet of paper (8½ by 11 inches), so that the "manuscript" pages are of uniform size and the typesetter can follow the copy as if it were a typed manuscript. A photocopy may be made of the pasted-up pages to provide a second copy of the manuscript. (If the photocopy is clearer than the pasted-up copy, it may be used as the first copy; see 2.169.)

2.167   If footnotes on the original pages are to remain as footnotes (not endnotes) and to remain substantially unchanged, they may be left at the foot of the pasted-up pages, because to cut them apart and paste them on separate pages is to run the risk of losing some of them. If editing must be done on the notes, if an editor's notes are intermingled with the original notes, or if footnotes are to be converted to endnotes, all notes should be pasted, or typed, on separate sheets. All notes should be retyped (double-spaced) and placed in a separate section for the typesetter when the original type is very small (e.g., 8/8) or faint or when much editing of the notes is required.

2.168   Unless there is ample space to insert corrections above printed lines in the original, any corrections should be put in the margins, following the method used in correcting proofs (see 3.15). Corrections squeezed between closely set lines are usually hard to see, if not illegible.

Photocopies

2.169   When two clean copies of the original are not available for making the manuscript copy to be used by the typesetter, clear photocopies will serve the purpose, provided all words at the ends of lines are present and clearly decipherable, the image is not blurred and is neither too dark nor too light, and the copy can be written on with pencil. It is also advisable, although sometimes difficult, to avoid having the lines of type turn up at the ends, reflecting the curve of a book's page as it is being copied.

2.170   Photocopies of original illustrations are unacceptable for reproduction. The editor or compiler should make every effort to procure glossy prints of the original illustrations. Failing that, the publisher can usually have a reproduction made from the illustration in the original publication—without destroying the book or journal in which it appears.[18]

18. For a more detailed description of acceptable illustrations see chapter 11.

Source Notes

2.171 Each selection of previously published material should be accompanied either by a headnote before the text begins or by an unnumbered footnote on the first page of text giving the source of the selection (see 1.62, 15.50) and the name of the copyright owner (see chapter 4). If the title has been changed, the original title should appear in the note.

2.172 Some selections in anthologies may have been previously published in several places and in several versions. The source note should give as much of the publishing history as is necessary and, if there are several versions, should state which version is used.

2.173 Many complications may arise in seeking permissions from copyright owners and in phrasing source notes, and the compiler of an anthology may well need the advice of an expert. The matter should never be ignored or left to the last minute (see 4.63–72).

Editing

2.174 Usually only certain alterations are permissible, without explanation, in editing material previously published. Notes may be renumbered consecutively throughout a selection or a chapter in a selection. Cross-references to parts of the original work not reprinted should be deleted. Obvious typographical errors, inadvertent grammatical slips, and unintentional inconsistencies in modern works may be corrected. Single quotation marks may be changed to double quotation marks, and double to single, following American practice (see 10.26), and periods and commas may be put inside quotation marks (see 5.11–13, 5.86–87). Words set in full capitals in the text may be marked for small capitals. Other typographical oddities should not be reproduced unless they contribute to the sense of the original. An old title page, for example, should not be set in type imitating the original typeface. (If desirable, the original may be reproduced as an illustration.)

2.175 Unless the editor or compiler explains—in the preface or elsewhere—what kinds of changes have been made in the original text, all other matters of style should be retained: British or archaic spelling; excessive punctuation or lack of punctuation; capitalization in the text and notes; and style of footnotes (in some instances this may need slight modification for clarity). Any internal deletion in a selection should be indicated by ellipsis points (see 10.48–63).

2.176 The copyeditor should read all material for sense; there is always the chance that material has been pasted up out of order, that something has been omitted, that meaningless cross-references have not been deleted. Ambiguous hyphens at the ends of lines should be marked so that the typesetter will know when to keep the hyphen and when to close up the word. Discrepancies and apparently incorrect sentences should be queried, but no changes made without calling the volume editor's attention to them.

HANDLING SYMPOSIUM VOLUMES

2.177   Volumes in which each chapter is by a different author usually multiply, often magnify, the problems a publisher encounters in producing a one-author book. Even when the copyeditor does not have to deal directly with each author, to cope with a multitude of styles—not only of the writing itself but of spelling and capitalization, footnotes or references in text, bibliographies, subheads, and tables, graphs, charts, or other artwork—can be daunting. Symposia, particularly papers read before a conference of scholars learned in a highly specialized subject, usually require the most time and effort. And because the proceedings of a conference reflect the current state of research in that subject, it is highly desirable that they be published as soon after the conference as possible. A sense of urgency must be maintained through all stages of publishing the book.

Preliminary Planning

2.178   Many problems and delays may be avoided and costs reduced through careful planning by the publisher (including the copyeditor) and the volume editor or editors before the manuscript has been submitted for publication. The functions and responsibilities of each should be clearly defined and understood.[19] Some of the functions listed below, ideally the responsibility of the volume editor, may in particular cases be undertaken by the publisher.

Volume Editor's Responsibilities

2.179   The term *volume editor* as used here refers not to a member of the publisher's staff but to the scholar selected, usually by the contributors to the symposium or its sponsors, to collect the papers for the volume and to work with the publisher. The competence and availability of the volume editor can affect the publication process at every stage. Ideally, the volume editor will undertake, and carry out, the responsibilities

---

19. If there is more than one volume editor, the exact responsibilities of each must be spelled out in advance. Two or more editors attempting to perform the same functions will delay production and may easily frustrate the copyeditor with conflicting directives.

listed below, insofar as these are applicable to the project. In some cases, however, it may be necessary or desirable for the publisher to assume one or more of them.

1. Getting manuscripts, including illustrations, from all contributors well before the date set for submitting the volume to the publisher

2. Sending a publishing agreement (a legal form provided by the publisher) to each contributor (see 4.36)

3. Getting written permission from copyright owners to reproduce any material previously copyrighted: papers published elsewhere, illustrations, tables, and the like taken from another work, as well as long quotations from secondary sources, which may require permission for use (see chapter 4)

4. Editing each paper, especially those written by authors whose native language is not English, for sense and grammar and checking lists of references and other apparatus for uniformity of style

5. Sending edited or rewritten manuscripts to the contributors for their approval *before* the volume goes to the publisher

6. Editing any discussions to be included in the volume and getting any necessary approval of the editing from the discussants

7. Providing a list of contributors, with their affiliations, to be printed in the volume, or supplying an identifying note for each contributor to be printed as an unnumbered footnote on the first page of the chapter

8. Providing copy for the title page and the table of contents and writing, or providing, any necessary prefatory material

9. Sending two clear copies of the manuscript to the publisher, either complete or chapter by chapter, in a form acceptable for publication (see 2.10–33)

10. Distributing edited manuscript to the contributors (if contributors are to see edited manuscript) and *setting a strict deadline for its return*

11. Checking the edited manuscript after it has been reviewed by the contributors, making sure all of the copyeditor's queries have been answered

12. Reading the master proofs

13. Sending all contributors copies of their proofs (*if* the contributors are to see proofs), again *setting a strict deadline for the return of the proofs,* and transferring corrections from contributors' proofs to the master set before returning the master proofs to the publisher

14. Preparing the index
15. Determining whether contributors will receive offprints (reprints) and, if so, how many each contributor will receive (the publisher usually has a form for this), and providing the publisher with a list of mailing addresses to which offprints should be sent

2.180 In general, the volume editor should take responsibility for keeping the production schedule set by the publisher and for seeing that each contributor returns edited manuscript or proof by the date stipulated; one dilatory contributor will delay the entire project. The volume editor should also answer any questions and settle any complaints from individual contributors.

2.181 For some such reason as urgency of schedule, it may become necessary, or seem desirable, to omit some stage in the process of publishing a multiauthor work. The choice usually comes down to sending only edited manuscript to contributors or only proof. In either case, the omitted responsibility of the contributors—reviewing the editing or reading proof—must be assumed by the volume editor, with the consent of the contributors. Perhaps the safest choice, if all parties agree, is to send edited manuscript to the contributors and have the proofreading done by the volume editor. Such a choice is more likely to avoid unpleasantness and costly changes at the proof stage.

2.182 Since the volume editor is usually a busy professor for whom editing the proceedings of a symposium is an added chore, he or she will seek to lighten the burden. A competent secretary is of course invaluable. Notifying contributors ahead of time about what is expected of them may save time. If possible, the volume editor should inform the contributors, before they prepare their papers, of the publisher's requirements concerning manuscripts acceptable for publication, including a uniform style for listing references, and should also notify them of what they may expect to see in the way of edited manuscript or proofs, and approximately when. The volume editor must also ascertain where the contributors can be reached at all times during the publication process.

Copyeditor's Responsibilities

2.183 The publisher's copyeditor may find it necessary to perform some of the functions outlined above if the volume editor is unable or unwilling to do so. It is very important, therefore, that the exact division of responsibility for a particular volume be decided at the planning stage. The copyeditor should be fully aware of everyone's responsibilities, since the copyeditor must see that the volume goes through the publication process as quickly as possible and thus must know what is happening to all parts of the volume at all times.

2.184 The copyeditor must also edit the entire manuscript. The volume editor usually cannot be expected to bring about consistency in capitalization, spelling, abbreviations, and so forth. Rewording or substantive editing, unless clearly necessary, should be strenuously avoided, especially when contributors are not to see edited manuscript. Queries should also be kept to a minimum. The edited manuscript should be sent to the volume editor, unless other arrangements have been made in advance.

2.185 Symposium volumes often come to a copyeditor chapter by chapter and not necessarily in sequence. To keep track of matters, the copyeditor will need to prepare a schedule sheet of some kind. The left-hand column should list the chapters in the order in which they will appear in the finished volume. Columns are then provided in which to record the specific dates when (1) copy is received, (2) edited copy goes to volume editor, (3) edited copy returns from volume editor, (4) manuscript goes to typesetter, (5) proofs are received and sent to volume editor, and (6) proofs are returned from volume editor. Where pertinent, it is also helpful to note the number of illustrations and tables in each chapter. Both illustrations and tables are numbered consecutively in each chapter, not throughout the volume—that is, the first figure in each chapter is figure 1, the first table is table 1.[20] In some volumes a double-numeration system is used for tables and figures: chapter number, period, table or figure number. In chapter 2, for example, tables are numbered 2.1, 2.2, 2.3, and so on. (See 1.77.)

FOR FURTHER REFERENCE

2.186 Nearly all the works listed in the bibliography of this manual are helpful to editors and authors. Among the most generally useful are H. W. Fowler, *A Dictionary of Modern English Usage,* 2d ed., revised by Sir Ernest Gowers, for refined distinctions regarding English usage, with entertaining and informative examples; Theodore M. Bernstein, *The Careful Writer* and *Miss Thistlebottom's Hobgoblins,* for modern idiom and for avoiding jargon and other forms of bad writing; Casey Miller and Kate Swift, *The Handbook of Nonsexist Writing,* and Dennis Baron, *Grammar and Gender,* for guidance in avoiding gender bias; Wilma R. Ebbitt and David R. Ebbitt, *Index to English,* 8th ed., Porter

---

20. All illustrations and separate tables should be identified by the name of the author of the chapter as well as by the name of the volume editor and the number of the item, to avoid confusion in makeup.

G. Perrin, *Reference Handbook of Grammar and Usage,* and the survey in *Words into Type,* for grammar and syntax. Authors and editors might profitably consult such helpful writing guides as Joseph Williams, *Style,* and Strunk and White, *The Elements of Style.* For guidance in writing or editing scientific material, an excellent source is *Scientific Style and Format,* prepared by the CBE Style Manual Committee. And for help in preparing electronic manuscripts see *Chicago Guide to Preparing Electronic Manuscripts.*

3 *Proofs*

INTRODUCTION

3.1   An earlier edition of this manual, published in 1969, presupposed the tidy progression of a finished, edited manuscript through galley proof to page proof to book. Hot-metal typesetting, principally Linotype or Monotype, was the usual method of composition in the printshop. The advent of electronic and computerized typesetting equipment has altered many features of these older systems and has introduced new methods and increased capabilities. (For an account of these operations see chapter 19, especially 19.36–39. For unfamiliar terms see the glossary.)

3.2   In today's streamlined and economy-minded "printshops," proof is rarely read as carefully as it was in the days when a trained *printer's proofreader* scrutinized every word on the proofs while a *copyholder* read aloud from the manuscript. Now proofs are likely to be checked by the compositor who set the type or by a single proofreader who can only glance at the manuscript from time to time while reading rapidly through the proofs before sending them back to the compositor for correction. Eliminating typographical errors, pointing out the omission or misplacement of material, even rectifying poor page makeup and other printing lapses—all have become in varying degrees the responsibility of the publisher and the author.

3.3   Although the new technology with its different procedures and different kinds of proofs has changed many aspects of traditional book production, proofreading terms and the method of marking paper proofs in whatever form remain essentially the same. All editors and authors should therefore have a thorough knowledge of standard proofreaders' terminology and should be proficient in marking proofs correctly.

SCHEDULES

3.4   After a manuscript has been sent to the compositor for typesetting, a schedule is prepared stipulating dates for receipt and return of proofs and submission of the index manuscript and, depending on the typesetting process used, any further steps in the production process that require the publisher's attention. The final date on the schedule is the *delivery date,* the day finished books are to be delivered by the printer or binder to the publisher's warehouse. The schedule is based on various factors, chief among them the compositor's and printer's workloads: when the typesetting will be done, when the book will go on press, and finally when the bindery can finish the job. Other factors to be considered are the availability and proximity of the author (mailing time for proofs must be taken into account), the complexity of the book, and the date on which the publisher wants to issue it (*publication date,* some weeks after delivery date).

3.5   Most publishers interpret the production schedule for the author in terms of deadlines; for example, when proofs will go to the author; when the author is expected to return them to the publisher; and when the index manuscript is to be submitted. An author who cannot meet the specified deadlines should inform the editor at once. Proofs returned even a few days late may delay production of the book for weeks. A busy compositor schedules work far ahead, and when a certain time has been allotted for making up or revising pages of a book and the author's proofs have not been promptly returned, the process must be rescheduled for a later (sometimes much later) date. When the delivery date (and therefore the publication date) is put off, the marketing department is also affected, since plans for announcing, advertising, and distributing the book must be timed to reflect its actual appearance. Production schedules are therefore very important; they are not to be filed and forgotten.

FIRST PROOFS

3.6 The term *first proofs* is used here to mean the first set of proofs, either galley proofs or page proofs, sent by the compositor to the publisher and by the publisher to the author. Publishers sometimes ask authors to read both galleys and pages (galleys as first proofs, pages as second proofs), sometimes only one or the other—usually pages (because the author may need pages to make the index).

Master Proofs

3.7 Normally two copies (sets) of proofs are sent to the author, along with the edited typescript or printout. One set, called *master proofs* or *marked proofs,* carries the compositor's or proofreader's queries, if any, and is the copy to be returned to the publisher with the author's corrections marked on it. The second set is to be retained by the author for reference and, if page proofs, for indexing. The author may wish to record the corrections on this copy as well. Some publishers do not send master proofs to authors, partly for safety's sake and partly because authors sometimes correct their proofs in such a way that the typesetter has trouble deciphering their intentions. Instead, the editor transfers the proofreader's corrections and queries to another copy— the author's copy—and sends this, along with an unmarked copy, for the author to read. When the author returns proofs marked for correction, the editor then transfers the author's corrections to the master copy. Only *one* copy of proofs—the master copy with *all* corrections on it (referred to as the *corrected proofs*)—should be returned to the compositor.

Dead Manuscript

3.8 Once the typesetting has been done, the edited typescript or printout is referred to as *dead manuscript,* or *dead copy.* This dead copy is sent to the author with the first proofs, whereupon the author is expected to read proofs against the manuscript and to put corrections only on the proof sheets. No correction—no mark at all—should ever be made on the dead manuscript by the author or the editor. For the record, and to prevent repetition of questions or suggestions already made and dispensed with, the manuscript must be kept exactly as it went to the typesetter. The author must then return the corrected proofs and the dead manuscript to the publisher.[1]

PROOFREADING

Typographical Errors

3.9 The most effective—the ideal—way to catch "typos" in first proofs is for two people to read together, as printers' proofreaders used to do. One follows the proofs while the other, the copyholder, reads aloud from the manuscript. The copyholder should speak clearly and at a steady pace. In addition to reading the text, the copyholder announces, by vocal signals, such things as the beginnings of paragraphs (by saying the abbreviation *par,* pronounced "pear"); all punctuation marks (names are usually abbreviated or transformed: *com* [,], *sem* [;], *col* [:], *point* [.], *query* [?], *bang* or *screamer* [!], *quotes* ["], *close quotes* ["], *hy* [-], *poz* [']; for example, *committee's* is vocalized as "committee-poz-ess"); such typographical changes as italic *(ital)* and return to roman *(rom);* capitals and lowercase *(cap* or *caps and lc)* when there might be some question about which is used; capitals and small capitals *(cap, small caps);* and all numbers in the form of numerals *(fig,* as in "*fig twenty-seven*" [27], "*fig two thousand eighty-four*" or "*fig two-zero-eight-four*" [2084], "*fig two-com-zero-eight-four*" [2,084]). Subscripts and superscripts should also, of course, be signaled ("*cap en sub one*" [N_1], "*climate point sup 8*" [climate.^{8}]). The reader following the proof should have a good grasp of spelling in order to spot errors; regardless of education or intellectual capacity, a poor speller is a poor proofreader.

Word Division

3.10 When a word must be divided at the end of a printed line, the way it is divided has now become especially important in proofreading. In hot-

---

1. Publishers usually keep manuscripts and corrected proofs until the compositor's bill has been received in case of controversy over charges or to check errors found in the printed book. Once the finished book has been delivered, however, the University of Chicago Press returns manuscripts to the authors if they want them.

metal and strike-on composition, and in some photocomposing methods, the keyboard operator decides where a word should be divided. When copy is set electronically, however, end-of-line hyphenation is often performed by computer. Although computers can be programmed to divide words according to one system or another (hyphenation routines), and although some have extensive "exception dictionaries" stored in their data banks, not all computers are yet able to handle every problem of word division. It is therefore wise to check end-of-line hyphens carefully, not only in first proofs but in any revised proofs as well (3.41). For example, when an error in a single word is corrected, only that word is reset, but when such a correction changes the length of the line in which it occurs, that line and all the following lines in the paragraph will end differently after running through the computer again. The result may be new word divisions to be checked. To avoid what might amount to considerable charges for requesting hyphenation correction in words not included in the compositor's "routine," a list of such special words and their preferred hyphenation should be sent to the typesetter along with manuscript or disks. (For guidance in dividing words see 6.43–58.)

Coding Errors

3.11   When type is to be set by computer, the disk that drives the typesetting device is usually coded to indicate matters such as where and how to set headings, excerpts, tables, and so forth; when italics (or boldface) are to begin and end; and how much spacing to insert where needed. Mistakes in inserting code symbols may result in errors similar to those found in hot-metal composition. Such errors are usually caught and rectified before proofs are sent to a publisher, but not always.

Wrong Font and Broken Type

3.12   In photocomposition, as in hot-metal composition, a portion of text may be set in the *wrong font*—either the wrong style of type or the correct type set smaller or larger than specified in the design. When this occurs, whether because of a coding error or through some electronic aberration, the author or editor should circle the errant text and write the "wrong font" symbol in the margin of the proof (see 3.35).

3.13   Strictly speaking, *broken type* is a hazard of hot-metal composition. It means that a portion of the metal type (for a letter or several letters) is chipped or incompletely formed and therefore produces an incomplete, or "broken," image on the proof. In photocomposition, similarly incomplete letter or word impressions may also show up on proof, not because type is broken but because a piece of foreign matter (dust, a scrap of paper) has got onto the repro proofs (camera-ready copy) or film negative; this rare "error" should be marked (see 3.35, 3.57) so that the typesetter or printer can correct it by removing the obstructing object. Blurred or fuzzy type and spotty paper, which are usually caused by poor photocopying, do *not* indicate errors in photocomposition processes and should not be marked.

Sense

3.14   In addition to reading proofs for the mechanical aberrations discussed above, authors understandably want to read their works for sense. Ideally such a reading should take place after the initial word-for-word proofreading. Since all source checking and final substantive and stylistic changes should have been made on the edited manuscript (2.129), authors must refrain from rewriting in proofs in any way except to correct errors of fact (see 3.37–39).

CORRECTING PROOFS

3.15   Unlike corrections on the manuscript, corrections on proofs must always be put in the margin, left or right, next to the line of type in which the correction is to be made. A mark within the line—a caret for an addition, a line through a letter or word to be deleted—will indicate where the correction is to be made. Never should a correction or addition be written above a line of type. The typesetter responsible for making corrections scans the margins only and may not see writing buried between lines of type. Where more than one alteration is to be made in a line, corrections should be marked in the margin in the order they are to be made in the line, reading from left to right; a vertical or slant line separates one correction from the next (see fig. 3.2). Remember that in proofreading every mark in the margin requires a mark in the line, and vice versa. Guidelines (lines drawn from the point in the line where the correction is to be made to the explanation of it in the margin) are unnecessary and undesirable unless the correction cannot be put next to the line. When guidelines are used, they should never cross each other; if they must cross—as in transposing several items in an index, for example—a different color should be used for each.

3.16   Where many errors occur in a line or two, it is best to cross out the whole passage containing the errors and write it all correctly in the margin, because the typesetter will need less time to read the rewritten passage than to figure out where each of many small corrections should be made. A longer correction or addition should be typed on a separate slip and fastened to the proof by one end (with tape or a straight pin, not a paper clip or staple). A circled note in the margin reading "Insert attached," and a caret in the line to show where it goes, will alert the typesetter (don't forget to cross out a passage being replaced). A circled note on the slip itself will tell the typesetter where it belongs should the slip become detached from the proof—for example, "Insert gal. 4," "Insert p. 10." If more than one such insert must be made on a single proof (page), each should be identified by letter: Insert A, gal. 4; Insert B, gal. 4; and so forth. The note in the margin of the proof then reads: "Insert A attached," and so on. In page proofs every effort must be made to adjust spacing so that pages will not have to be remade (see 3.39). (Not only is remaking pages expensive, it also affects the index and often the placement of illustrations.)

3.17 In correcting proofs, authors and editors should use a color different from that used by the compositor's proofreader. Either a clear, sharp pencil or a pen (but not a felt-tip pen) is acceptable. Easily blurred marks from a soft lead pencil should be avoided, and handwriting must be completely legible. Do not write corrections in block letters (capitals).

3.18 Master proofs to be returned to the typesetter must never be cut apart for any reason. Material to be transposed from one galley or page to another should be so marked in the margin; for example, a paragraph on galley 4 to be moved to galley 5 would be marked "tr to gal. 5," and the place where it is to be inserted on galley 5 would be marked "tr from gal. 4."

Proofreaders' Marks

3.19 With the first set of proofs sent to the publisher, some typesetters include elaborate instructions on how to make corrections. These should be followed if possible; they will differ little from the instructions given here. Symbols and marks explained in the following paragraphs and listed in figure 3.1 are commonly understood by compositors working in English. A specimen of heavily marked proof is presented in figure 3.2, and if an instruction in the text below is not accompanied by an example, one or more may be found in the specimen.

3.20 For purposes of discussion and for easier comprehension by those unfamiliar with them, proofreaders' marks may be classified as operational signs, typographical signs, and signs clarifying certain punctuation marks to be inserted.

Proofreaders' Marks

OPERATIONAL SIGNS

ℛ	Delete
C	Close up; delete space
ℰ	Delete and close up (use only when deleting letters *within* a word)
stet	Let it stand
#	Insert space
eq #	Make space between words equal; make space between lines equal
hr #	Insert hair space
ls	Letterspace
¶	Begin new paragraph
☐	Indent type one em from left or right
⌐	Move right
⌐	Move left
⌐⌐	Center
⊓	Move up
⊔	Move down
fl	Flush left
fr	Flush right
=	Straighten type; align horizontally
‖	Align vertically
tr	Transpose
sp	Spell out

TYPOGRAPHICAL SIGNS

ital	Set in italic type
rom	Set in roman type
bf	Set in boldface type
lc	Set in lowercase
caps	Set in capital letters
sc	Set in small capitals
wf	Wrong font; set in correct type
X	Check type image; remove blemish
V	Insert here *or* make superscript
Λ	Insert here *or* make subscript

PUNCTUATION MARKS

∧	Insert comma
ᵛ ᵛ	Insert apostrophe *or* single quotation mark
⁀ ⁀	Insert quotation marks
⊙	Insert period
(set) ?	Insert question mark
;|	Insert semicolon
⁀ *or* :|	Insert colon
=	Insert hyphen
M̲	Insert em dash
N̲	Insert en dash
⫟ ⫠ *or* (|)	Insert parentheses

Fig. 3.1. Proofreaders' marks

["I don't care what kind of type you use for my
]book," said a myopic author to the publisher, but please
print the galley proofs in large type. Perhaps in the
future such a request will not sound so ridiculous]
to those familar with the printing process. today, however, type once set is not reset except to correct errors. Proofreading is an Art and a craft. All authors
should know the rudiments thereof, though no proofreader expects them to be masters of it. Watch proofreader expects them to be masters of it. Watch not only
for misspelled or incorrect works (often a most illusive
error, but also for misplace dspaces, "unclosde" quotation marks and parenthesis, and improper paragraphing; and learn to recognize the difference between an
em dash—used to separate an interjectional part of a
sentence—and an en dash used commonly between
continuing numbers, e.g., pp. 5–10; &.d. 1165 70)
and the word dividing hyphen. Whatever is underlined
in a MS. should, of course, be italicized in print. Two
lines drawn beneath letters or words indicate that these
are to be reset in small capitals, three lines indicate
full capitals To find the errors overlooked by the proofreader is the authors first problem in proof reading.
The secyond problem is to make corrections, using the
marks and symbols, devized by proffesional proofreaders, thay any trained typesetter will understand.
The third—and most difficult problem for authors
proofreading their own works is to resist the temptation to rewrite in proofs.

Manuscript editor

1. Type may be reduced in size, or enlarged photographically when a book
is printed by offset.

Fig. 3.2. Marked proof

OPERATIONAL SIGNS

3.21   The *delete* sign is used only when something is to be removed from a
line—a letter, a word or more, the whole line—without substitution. It
is *not* used when another letter, word, or line is to be inserted in place
of the deleted matter. A diagonal line through a letter to be deleted, or
a straight line through a word or more to be deleted, indicates where
the deletion is to be made. Matter to be deleted from a typeset line
should not be obliterated to the extent that the compositor cannot see
what to take out; a comma or period or single letter likely to be totally
covered by the in-line delete mark may be circled instead, so that it is
still visible. The form of the delete sign written in the margin need not
be exactly as shown in figure 3.1, but it should be made in such a way
as not to be confused with any handwritten letter, such as *d, e,* or *l.*
Where a letter is to be deleted from the middle of a word, the delete
sign may be written within close-up marks *(delete and close up),* although this is not necessary unless there might be some doubt in the
typesetter's mind, such as what to do with a word from which a hyphen
has been deleted.

> proofreader expects them to be masters of it. Watch
> proofreader expects them to be masters of it. Watch
> not only for any misspelled or all incorrect words

3.22   Too much space between letters is corrected by the *close-up* sign, used
in the line as well as in the margin. Sometimes the last letter of a word
appears at the beginning of the next word; when this happens, write the
close-up mark followed by a *space* mark in the margin and insert a
close-up mark and a vertical line indicating the space in the line.

> most elusive error) but also for misplace d spaces, "un-

3.23   The *space* mark is used to call for more space between words; a vertical
line or caret shows where the space is to be inserted. The space mark
may also be used to show where extra space (leading, or line spacing)
is needed between lines. All words in the same line should be separated
by the same amount of space. When the word spaces in a single line
are unequal, write the *equal-space* sign in the margin and insert carets
in the line to mark the difficulty. Note that spacing between words in
successive lines is not necessarily equal in justified composition (see
18.26). *Hair spaces, thin spaces,* and *letter spaces* are generally matters of design and need not concern an author unless there appears to
be some inconsistency in the setting of similar material.

> under the larger of the two sarcophagi, so that Goodman had to pry
> the end of it up with a crowbar while Phipps reached perilously

3.24   A *paragraph* sign in the margin tells the typesetter to begin a new paragraph; in the line either another paragraph sign before the first word

of the new paragraph or, more commonly, an L-shaped mark to the left and partly under the word will show the typesetter where to begin the paragraph. To run two paragraphs together, write "run in" in the margin and draw a line from the end of one paragraph to the beginning of the next.

3.25 *Indention* of a line one em from the left or right margin is indicated by a small square drawn in the left or right margin next to the line to be moved; draw another square, or a caret, next to the material itself. An indention of *two or more ems* may be indicated either by writing the desired numeral inside one square or by drawing a rectangle divided into two or more squares.

Fulton and Baumgartner slipped into their trench coats, adjusted their fedoras, and walked single file . . .

Winston F. Finston

Archibald Tucker

3.26 Use the signs for *moving* type *right* or *left* or for *centering* when a line of type is printed too far to the left or right, or when a title, an item in a table, or a letter has been set in the wrong place horizontally. Use the signs for moving type *up* or *down* when something has been set on the wrong line or is vertically out of place. All these signs are marked in the line as well as written in the margin.

3.27 To indicate that an indented line of type should start flush left, that is, at the left-hand margin, draw a *move-left* sign at the left of the first word in that line and write the abbreviation *fl* in the margin. To request that an element be made flush right, follow a similar procedure using the *move-right* sign and the abbreviation *fr.*

Toward midday the two archaeologists emerged from the dark cave and were momentarily stunned by the light.

Tadeush Moliwetski

3.28 Use the sign for *aligning horizontally*—marked in the line as well as in the margin—when one or more letters have slipped slightly above or below the line. In photocopied proofs uneven or wavy type is likely to be the fault of the copying machine (not the composition) and should be ignored in proofreading.

3.29 The sign for *vertical* alignment should be used sparingly in correcting proof; the left and right type margins are often slightly irregular in proofs from hot-metal typesetting because the type itself has not yet been locked in place for printing. In photocomposition vertical misalignment is rare. The sign should be used mainly to indicate inaccurate alignment in tabular matter.

3.30 Use the sign for *transpose* when letters, words, phrases, lines, paragraphs, or any other material must be moved from one place to another. The indication of where the transposition is to be made in the line is drawn in the same way as in editing a manuscript (see 2.68–69), but *tr* must appear in the margin in proofs so that the typesetter will see the change.

3.31 When abbreviations or numerals set in type are to be spelled out, circle them in the line and write the *spell-out* sign in the margin. Note that to spell out something in the text means that the line will be longer, possibly also making the paragraph and the page longer unless you compensate for the extra space (see 3.39). Also, the full word should be written in the margin, instead of the sign, if there is any ambiguity about spelling (see 2.84).

3.32 Use the word *stet* ("let it stand") to tell the typesetter not to take out something earlier marked for deletion. Dots under the crossed-out material show what is to remain. Where a note in the margin is also crossed out, *stet as set* will clarify what to let stand.

3.33 Areas of text, from single letters to several lines, occasionally appear much darker in proof than the surrounding text. The causes vary from one method of composition to another. In the older, hot-metal method, darker type is the result of letters sitting higher in the type line and therefore being pressed deeper into the paper during printing. The correction instruction in that case is the *push down type* sign (↓). In photocomposition, a line or so pasted in as a correction on the proof may be darker because of various mechanical and climatic conditions prevailing at the time of resetting. When such darker lines appear in photocomposition proof, *too dark* may be written in the margin.

TYPOGRAPHICAL SIGNS

3.34 Correction instructions for letters or words set in the wrong style may be given as follows: To change a capital letter to lowercase, draw a slash through the letter and write *lc* in the margin. To capitalize a lowercase letter, circle the letter or draw three short lines below it and write *cap* in the margin. Small capitals may be called for by drawing two lines under the letter and writing the marginal instruction *sc*. Italics may be indicated by drawing a single line under the word and writing *ital* in the margin. To have italicized words reset in roman type, circle the words and write *rom* in the margin. Boldface type is indicated with a wavy line under the letter or word and *bf* in the margin.

3.35 Errors characteristic of hot-metal typesetting include wrong font *(wf)*, broken type (x), and letters turned upside down (𝟿). Wrong fonts and something similar to broken type also occur in photocomposition (see 3.12, 3.13), but upside-down letters do not. In correcting photocomposition proofs, the symbol *wf* may be used to indicate wrong font, and the broken-type symbol, **x**, may be used to indicate type obstructions and other blemishes on the repro proof or film negative.

PUNCTUATION AND ACCENT MARKS

3.36   To change a punctuation mark—from a comma to a semicolon, for example—draw a vertical line through the mark or circle it and write the correct one in the margin. To supply a mark where none appears, place a caret at the spot and write the correct mark in the margin. Since a handwritten comma, apostrophe, and parenthesis may be confused one with another, a comma written in the margin should have a caret over it; an apostrophe or a quotation mark should have an inverted caret under it, indicating its superior position; a parenthesis should be made large enough not to be taken for one of the smaller marks. Parentheses may also be distinguished by drawing two short horizontal lines through each mark, as shown in figure 3.1. Hyphens and en and em dashes should be differentiated by their appropriate symbols (see fig. 3.1). A period, being small, should be circled. Semicolons, colons, question marks, and exclamation points, if written clearly, need no further identifying marks, except that a question mark that might be mistaken for a query should be followed by the circled word *set*. A letter with a missing or incorrect accent or diacritical mark should be completely crossed out and the letter and correct accent written in the margin.

PE and AA

3.37   The typesetter's job is to *follow copy* exactly. Any deviation from the manuscript found on the proofs, such as a misspelled, wrong, or missing word, is attributed to the typesetter. In times gone by, typesetter and printer were the same person or firm, and such an error is still called a *printer's error* (PE). Any change made by an author (or editor) in proofs, including filling in cross-references on page proofs, is an *author's alteration* (AA). To apportion responsibility for corrections, *PE* or *AA* (or pe, aa) should be written and circled in the margin next to each proof correction. When an editor makes a change that should not be attributed to the author, some other signal should be used, such as *EA* or a line under AA. Another way to distinguish between printer's errors and author's alterations is to use a different color for each. (Always use colors different from that used by the typesetter or compositor's proofreader for corrections or other marks on the master proofs.)

3.38   Many authors do not realize how costly alterations can be. An allowance of 5 percent stipulated by an author's contract does *not* mean 5 percent of the number of lines, or words, in a book. It means, rather, 5 percent of the initial cost of composition. Correction and alteration costs are so substantial that this percentage is easily reached and easily surpassed. The processes involved in making corrections in proofs can result in hundreds, even thousands, of dollars in alteration costs, much of which may be charged to the author. Changes made in proofs also often result in further errors—a line may be reinserted in the wrong place, for instance—and many changes will delay production and throw off schedules all along the production line. Clearly, it is extremely important for both author and publisher to keep proof corrections of any kind to a minimum.

3.39   Sometimes disaster strikes, however, and a change must be made at the last minute. Then author or editor should rewrite enough to compensate for space added or deleted by the change. Some cooperative and knowledgeable authors even compensate for typesetter's errors that might otherwise require substantial resetting. Authors should keep in mind that additions and deletions may be made more easily in galley proofs than in pages. Any addition or deletion of more than, say, one line in page proofs may throw off not only page makeup but index entries as well.

SECOND PROOFS

3.40   The term *second proofs* is used here to mean a new set of proofs sent by the typesetter to the publisher after corrections have been made on the first proofs (see 3.6). If they are page proofs and are to be sent to the author, two sets are sent, marked as were the first proofs (3.7). The first proofs, now called *foul galleys* or *foul proofs,* are sent to the author with the second proofs for comparison and checking of corrections, after which both sets should be returned to the publisher. If the author discovers and marks errors in the corrections or makes additional alterations on second proofs, printer's errors and author's alterations should again, as they were on the first proofs (see 3.6), be distinguished by the abbreviations PE and AA. Printer's errors missed in reading the first proofs and caught in the second proofs may, unless typesetter and publisher decide to the contrary, be charged as PEs. As with dead manuscript (3.8), authors and editors must make no mark whatever on foul proofs. If the second proofs are revised galleys or revised pages, they are usually checked only by the publisher.

3.41   Second proofs are not read against manuscript but are only checked against the first proofs to see that all corrections have been made and no further errors introduced. To do this most expeditiously, put the two proofs side by side and check for each correction. In some kinds of photocomposition, as in hot-metal typesetting, correction means resetting an entire line or several lines and inserting them in place of existing lines. Such an operation may result in new typographical errors or in the corrected lines being inserted in the wrong place. In proofs from these methods of composition, therefore, each reset line or lines must be proofread carefully, and the lines above and below must be checked to make sure the line has been put back in the right place. In computerized typesetting individual corrections are made without resetting whole lines. In that case, only the new wording need be read, but since the correction may change line length, end-of-line word divisions should be checked in paragraphs where corrections have been made (see 3.10). The checker of second proofs cannot always tell how corrections have been made, and therefore cannot know how much of the text must be read. Security and economy are best served in this case if the typesetter brackets all reset material, and the publisher is well advised to insist that this be done.

PAGE PROOFS

3.42   Page proofs may be either first proofs or second proofs (see 3.6, 3.40). They must be looked upon by author and editor as complete *pages* in the book or article and checked as such. Any footnote must be checked to make sure it begins on the page that carries its reference; the note itself may run over to the next page. Any table, equation, excerpt, figure, or other illustrative matter must appear where it belongs, or the correct amount of space must have been provided for its later insertion. Other matters to be checked—running heads and folios, page length, preliminary pages—are taken up in the following paragraphs. If the page proofs are the second proofs, following galley stage, the top and bottom lines of text on each page should be checked against the galleys to make sure nothing has been dropped.

Running Heads and Folios

3.43   Running heads and folios on every page must be checked, usually by the editor when page proofs are returned from the author. It is best to do this as a separate operation, not while checking the text pages. A running head may be missing altogether, the wrong running head may have been inserted through part of a chapter, or a word may suddenly turn up misspelled. Running heads and folios should be deleted by the editor from any page containing *only* a table or an illustration (see 1.98) and, of course, from all blank pages. Undivided attention is thus required to check running heads. Folios are usually accurate, but sometimes one is omitted or set in the wrong place; and in rare instances folios may somehow have got out of sequence (if this should happen, the indexer must quickly be notified of the correct pagination).

3.44 When a section of notes at the back of a book requires page numbers in the running heads (see 1.97, 15.37–40), the editor should insert the numbers or should check numbers supplied by the author.

3.45 For running heads made up of subheads or other subdivisions of a chapter, as in this manual, see 1.95. These, like all running heads, are primarily the editor's responsibility (see 2.159–61).

Adjusting Page Length

3.46 The length of the type page, specified by the book designer and carefully observed by the compositor, need concern the author or the editor only when the makeup process runs into difficulties. In regular text material it is permissible to let *facing pages* (verso and recto; pp. 68 and 69, for example) each run one line long or one line short to avoid a *widow* (short line at the end of a paragraph) at the top of a page or to fit footnotes and their references on the same page (see 19.40–42). It is also permissible—indeed necessary—to let one page run short if a subhead or only one line of an excerpt would fall at the bottom of the page. Sometimes, however, the compositor is unable to make a page come out right and will ask the author or the editor to *save a line (lose a line)* or *make a line*. To save a line, one looks for the paragraph with the shortest last line—preferably only a word or two—on the page and deletes enough characters from the paragraph to accommodate the last line at the end of the line above. To make a line is to add a phrase or substitute a longer word so that the last line of a paragraph will run over to a new line. In hot-metal composition such changes should be made as close to the end of the paragraph as possible, because all subsequent lines must be reset in consequence of the change. In computerized composition, it makes no difference where in the paragraph the change is made.

Table of Contents

3.47 Page numbers are inserted in the table of contents, usually by the editor, after all pages (except the index) have been received from the typesetter. The index will start on the first recto page after the end of any back matter preceding it. If more than one index is to be included, the page numbers for those after the first cannot be determined until index page proofs have been received. When someone other than the editor—the typesetter or the author, for example—has inserted page numbers in the table of contents, the editor should check each number against the page proofs.

3.48   The wording of chapter titles and other parts of the book in the table of contents should also be checked against the page proofs. The editor should look at each page of the proofs to make sure nothing has been omitted from the table of contents that should be in it; this is particularly important when the contents includes subheads as well as chapter titles.

3.49   Any list of illustrations, figures, or tables should be checked in the same way as the table of contents, and page numbers supplied when they are missing. Although some typesetters do supply page numbers in contents and lists in the preliminary pages, no typesetter should be expected to do so, and certainly not after corrected (proofread) page proofs have been returned by the publisher.

Preliminary Pages

3.50   Display preliminary pages (see 1.3–39) should be checked by the production department and designer for fidelity to the design specified; by the person in charge of contracts (permissions secretary or other) for information on the copyright page; and by the editor and author for typographical errors of any kind. A misspelled word in these pages—the author's name for instance—is a catastrophe in a printed book.

INDEX PROOFS

3.51   The urgency of preparing and editing indexes on schedule has been pointed out elsewhere (2.118). Indexes normally go directly to page proof. Except in rare instances, the University of Chicago Press sends neither the edited manuscript nor the proofs of an index to the author. The editor proofreads the index as soon as proofs are received; they are usually returned to the typesetter in less than twenty-four hours.

ILLUSTRATIONS

3.52   Black-and-white text figures (which for offset printing may include halftone reproductions of photographs) print along with the text and may therefore be placed anywhere in the book rather than being tipped in or grouped in unpaginated plate sections. This means that the correct amount of space, either part of a page or a full page, must be allowed for each illustration when pages are made up. Before that time comes, the designer (or if necessary, the editor) must crop and scale all illustrations (see 11.15–21) and make a record of the vertical space each will require on the page.

3.53   When first proofs are to be pages, explicit instructions about placement and size of illustrations must go to the typesetter with the manuscript. When first proofs are galleys, instructions must be sent to the typesetter with the corrected galleys, including a list of all illustrations and their finished sizes, together with the galley numbers of the passages they are to accompany, and circled notes in the appropriate galley margins: for example, "fig. 2 about here."

3.54   The designer must see that correct spaces have been left in the proofs for all illustrations and must inspect the illustrations themselves at whatever stage they first appear, usually in blueprints of the offset negatives (see 3.57), to see that they are printed right side up and have not been *flopped* (turned over, resulting in a mirror image). The editor should also check the spaces allowed for illustrations, to make sure they are correctly positioned with respect to the text references. In addition, the editor must proofread all legends and should also check the illustrations themselves when they appear to see that they are in the correct locations along with the correct legends, and that they are right side up and not flopped. If authors are to see illustrations in place, they should be reminded that any alteration at this stage means remaking the drawing, rephotographing, and restripping, with heavy expense and serious delay.

OTHER PROOFS

3.55   Page proofs are normally the last proofs seen by an author. If the book is to be printed by offset lithography, as nearly all books now are, the publisher will usually see further proofs before printing. The editor should check these to see that all corrections marked in page proofs have been made and that all material is there and in the correct order.

Reproduction Proofs

3.56   *Reproduction proofs,* or "repro" as they are usually called, are the actual camera copy from which the book will be photographed and printed. Repro represents the quality of image to be achieved in the final printing. The editor should not make any changes on repro except to correct typographical errors (and then only serious ones). Any such corrections should be indicated in the margin with a *light blue* pencil, a color the camera does not pick up. Only the faintest of blue marks should be made on the type area itself. Alternatively, corrections may be marked on a photocopy of the repro page. A list of page numbers on which such corrections have been made should go to the production department with the corrected repro. If two sets of repro are available, the art department can often make corrections by cutting letters from the second set and pasting them carefully in place on the set to be used as camera copy. Unwanted marks can be whited out at the same time. Reproduction proofs produced by photocomposition may be corrected by changing the computer file and printing out another repro page. This procedure, however, is usually reserved for more extensive changes; to save time and perhaps money, minor corrections should probably be made by the cut-and-paste method.

Blueprints

3.57   *Blueprints* ("blues"), vandykes (brown prints), and silver prints are all different forms of photographic prints made from the negatives that are to be used in offset printing. They do not show the quality of image to be attained in the final printing, but they provide a means of checking the accuracy of the contents. As with repro, the editor should check to see that all parts are in place and all previous corrections have been made. Blues should also be scanned by both editor and designer or production department for extraneous marks or type blemishes that may be caused by dirt or debris on the negative (see also 3.35). New corrections at this stage mean type must be reset by the compositor, pages made up again, and new repro made and photographed. Blueprints should be checked by the editor the moment they arrive from the printer, who is often waiting for final approval by telephone from the production department. In rare cases, authors are asked to check blues to confirm placement of illustrative material (see 3.54). The publisher and the printer must be notified at once of any error.

CASE AND JACKET, OR PAPERBACK COVER

3.58   The editor should always check proofs of the *die copy*—names, titles, and any ornaments to be stamped on the spine of a book and (sometimes) on the cover. When dies have been made, the binder submits a *sample case* for approval—an actual cover, stamped as it will be for the finished book. The production department checks the quality of the casemaking and stamping; the editor checks the accuracy and placement of the various type elements. Normally the editor also sees proof of copy for the jacket or paperback cover—front, back, spine, and (for a jacket) flaps—at some stage in their production. The author usually sees copy written for the jacket or cover but is not asked to check proofs of these.

PRESS SHEETS

3.59   *Folded and gathered sheets* (familiarly, "f and g's") are not proofs but the first printed sheets of a book (*press sheets*). By the time the publisher sees them, the book is off the press. The production department checks the quality of the presswork, and the editor runs through all pages to make sure that none are missing or out of order and that no damage has occurred to the negatives since blues were checked (3.57). Previously unnoticed typographical errors that turn up at this point must ordinarily be ignored, to await correction in a second printing of the book. The only exceptions would be errors so egregious as to cause real harm to the author or publisher if the book were issued in this form. Errors severe enough to cause misunderstanding may be put right in an errata sheet (1.107). A serious flaw in the copyright notice, a misspelling of the author's name or the book title, or a statement in the text suddenly found to be clearly libelous would qualify for correction by reprinting, but nothing less grave. Such a correction is made by reprinting all or part of the signature in which the grave error occurs—a wasteful, time-consuming, and very expensive business. The publisher's approval of the f and g's (often given initially by telephone) authorizes the binder to go ahead with binding and shipping the book.

FINISHED BOOK

3.60   When the folded and gathered sheets reach the bindery, one or two copies of the bound book from the first part of the run are sent to the publisher's production department, where the book is checked for flaws in binding or assembly. Normally neither author nor editor sees the book at this stage. When books arrive in the warehouse on the delivery date, the courteous publisher will send the author the first copy at once, by the fastest courier available. The rest of the free copies stipulated in the author's contract will be shipped from the warehouse later. Any typographical errors discovered by the author in the finished book should be recorded in case of a second printing.

FOR FURTHER REFERENCE

3.61   Some publishers have their own style manuals containing instructions for proofreading, and some typesetters send instructions with proof. Marshall Lee's *Bookmaking* (2d ed., 1979) gives lucid descriptions of the various processes used in bookmaking and explains how to deal with many of the kinds of proofs available.

4 *Rights and Permissions*

COPYRIGHT LAW AND THE LICENSING OF RIGHTS

The New Law

4.1 The foundation on which the entire publishing industry rests is the law of copyright, and a basic knowledge of it is essential for both authors and editors. For most publishing purposes the relevant law is the Copyright Act of 1976 (Public Law 94-553), which took effect on 1 January 1978. The 1976 act was a sweeping revision of prior law, superseding previous federal law and eliminating (though not retroactively) the body of state law known as common-law copyright. It did not, however, make old learning obsolete. Because prior law continues to govern most pre-1978 works in one way or another, anyone involved with publishing should understand both the old and the new regimes. Both will affect printed matter for decades to come.

4.2 Whenever a book or article, poem or lecture, database or drama comes into the world in tangible form, it is automatically covered by copyright. This is true regardless of whether the work is ever published. Whoever is the *author* (a term not synonymous with *creator,* as will be seen) controls that copyright, at the outset, and automatically possesses certain rights in the work. How these rights are owned, transferred, and administered will be the focus of this chapter.

Rights of the Copyright Owner

4.3 Copyright protects the original expression contained in a work. *Originality* for copyright purposes has a very low threshold. Only a modicum of creativity is required; the law protects such minimal intellectual effort as the selection and arrangement of entries in the telephone directory's "yellow pages." What counts is not quality or novelty, but only that the work be original with the author and not copied from some other source, even though it may duplicate someone else's equally original work. The term *expression* means the words, sounds, or images that an author uses to express an idea or describe a process, fact, or discovery. Copyright protects the expression but not the underlying conceptual or factual material.

4.4 When a work is to be published, the author normally transfers some or all of his or her rights in the work, by formal agreement, to the publisher. Two of these rights are, from the publisher's point of view, basic: the right to make copies of the work (usually, but not exclusively, by printing) and the right to distribute such copies to the public—that is, to publish the work. A third important right is the right to make what the law terms *derivative works*—that is, works based on the original work, such as translations, abridgments, dramatizations, or other adaptations. A fourth right, the right of public display, is becoming increasingly important to publishers insofar as on-line database publishing constitutes "display" of the database. Taken together, these rights (along with the right of public performance, which is not usually germane to publishing) constitute what are known as the *copyright rights* in a work. They exist from the time the work is created—that is, put in tangible form—and they belong to the author, who can sell, rent, give away, will, or transfer them in some other way, individually or as a package, to whomever the author wishes.

4.5 In addition to the foregoing rights, the law also gives the authors of certain works of fine art a so-called *moral right* against mutilation and misattribution. A dozen or more states have enacted legislation to the same effect but, generally, broader than the federal law. This moral right, however, whether federal or state, has little effect on publishers (except perhaps while in possession of original artwork) and will not be dealt with further here. The only quasi-moral right given to authors of literary works is the right to prohibit false attribution. This right, found in both state and federal law to varying degrees, prevents a publisher from crediting the author with material he or she has not written, and conversely, from failing to credit the author as the source of the work, except where the publisher is acting with the author's acquiescence.

4.6 In addition to copyright, a publishable work may have trademark protection, covering its title and, in the case of fiction, arguably the names of its characters. This right can arise under either federal law or state law or both. Book titles are harder to protect as trademarks than journal or lecture titles, because of a judicial and administrative reluctance to give trademark protection to names that are used only once. Nevertheless, it is fair to say that some book titles are clearly protectible; *Gone with the Wind* and *Winnie the Pooh* could certainly not be used without permission.

4.7 Whoever controls the copyright in a work, whether author or publisher, may not only exercise those rights directly but also empower others to exercise them. If, for example, the author of a book has transferred the whole bundle of rights to a publishing house (as is often, though not always, done), the publishing house will probably itself exercise the *basic rights* of printing and publishing the book, compensating the author by paying a percentage of the sales receipts (a *royalty*) from each copy sold. It will also be responsible for administering *subsidiary rights*. These rights (discussed in 4.39 below) usually involve exploiting markets in which the publishing house is not active. For example, foreign-language, book-club, and motion-picture rights involve specialized markets and require special expertise. For this reason, subsidiary rights are likely to be exercised by third parties under license from the publisher, although the current tendency toward large media conglomerates makes this less true than before. Part of the publisher's responsibility to the author is to see that subsidiary rights are exploited as effectively as possible. Licensing subsidiary rights also includes granting what the publishing industry calls *permissions,* a term that refers specifically to the licensing of photocopying, as for classroom use, and quoting or reproducing in a new work small parts of another work.

Duration of Copyright

4.8   Until 1 January 1978, a dual system of copyright existed in the United States. *Common-law copyright,* created by the individual states of the Union, protected works from the time of their creation until publication, however long that might be. A personal letter written in the eighteenth century but never published was protected as effectively as a 1977 doctoral thesis in the making. In neither case could the document be copied and distributed (that is, published) without the express permission of the creator of the work or his or her legal heirs. *Statutory, or federal, copyright* protected works at the moment of publication and for twenty-eight years thereafter, provided that a proper copyright notice appeared in the published work. Thereafter, copyright in the work could be renewed for another twenty-eight years if the original copyright claim had been registered with the Copyright Office (a department of the Library of Congress) and if a renewal claim was filed by the appropriate person(s) during the final year of the first term of copyright. Thus in the normal course of things federal copyright in a work was intended to last for a total of fifty-six years from the date of publication, after which time the work went into the public domain. In 1962, however, Congress, thinking ahead to the new and presumably more generous law it expected to pass someday, began to extend the length of copyright for works then in their second term, and succeeding Congresses followed suit. The result was that any work published on or after 1 January 1906, in which copyright was later validly renewed, was still protected on 1 January 1978.

4.9   The 1976 act did away with this dual system of copyright. Present law is both simpler and more complex regarding copyright duration. It is simpler in that we now have only one unified, federal system protecting all works fixed in tangible form from the moment so fixed. It is more complex in that terms of protection are different depending on authorship and that works existing before 1978 are subject to a variety of special rules. The paradigmatic copyright term, under the new law, is "life plus fifty," that is, life of the author plus fifty years. As will be seen below, however, there are many exceptions to this rule.

JOINT WORKS

4.10 Many works covered by copyright law involve the efforts of more than one author. Some of these are *joint works*. As defined by the statute, a joint work is "a work prepared by two or more authors with the intention that their contributions be merged into inseparable or interdependent parts of a unitary whole." The typical multiauthor scholarly article is an example of this, as is the Rodgers and Hammerstein type of collaborative work. The authors of a joint work are considered to be co-owners of the copyright, which runs for fifty years beyond the death of the last author to die.

4.11 Not all works in which the contributions of two or more authors are combined are joint works. Many, such as anthologies and periodicals, are considered *collective works*. Copyright in them, which covers the selection and arrangement of materials, belongs to the compiler or editor and is separate from the copyright in the various components.

WORKS MADE FOR HIRE

4.12 The new law makes special provisions for copyright in the category of *works made for hire*. These are works created by someone who is paid by another person to create them. The law regards the *employer* as the "author" of any such work and hence as the owner of the copyright. Present law defines much more stringently than previous law the conditions that must be met for a work to be considered made for hire. The work may be prepared by an employee within the scope of his or her employment, such as the editorial column in a scholarly journal, a news story in a weekly magazine, or the entry for "aardvark" written by a person on an encyclopedia's paid staff. In certain instances, someone *not* on the payroll will be treated as an "employee" for authorship purposes, if that person is acting as the agent of the party paying the bill. Determining agency is a difficult and somewhat ad hoc task, and this area of works made for hire is likely to be murky for some time to come. The third type of work made for hire is the specially ordered or commissioned work that both employer and creator agree *in writing* is to be considered a work made for hire. This sort of arrangement is available for only nine narrowly defined categories of works: contributions to collective works, such as a journal article or a paper presented at a conference or symposium; contributions to motion pictures; translations; instructional texts; tests; answer materials for tests; atlases; compilations of existing materials (e.g., anthologies); and "supplementary works" such as forewords, bibliographies, indexes, textual notes, and illustrations. It bears emphasizing that many kinds of works that could conceivably be commissioned do *not* qualify as works made for hire, no matter what agreement might be made between a writer and a publisher. Biographies and novels, for example, would not be eligible because they are not in any of the nine categories.

4.13 Since the owner of the copyright in a work made for hire is not the actual creator of the work (often, indeed, the copyright owner is a corporate entity), the law specifies a fixed term of years for the duration of copyright. This term is seventy-five years from the date of publication or one hundred years from the date of creation, whichever is the shorter.

ANONYMOUS AND PSEUDONYMOUS WORKS

4.14 As in the case of works made for hire, the regular rule for duration of copyright cannot be applied if an author publishes anonymously or under a pseudonym. Again, the law prescribes the same fixed term of copyright for these works—seventy-five years from the date of publication or one hundred years from creation, whichever is the shorter. If after publication, however, such an author's name is revealed and recorded in the documents of the Copyright Office, the regular *life plus fifty* rule (or work made for hire rule, if applicable) takes over.

PRE-1978 UNPUBLISHED WORKS

4.15 For unpublished works that were still under common-law copyright when the new law went into effect, there is a transitional rule. Such works are given the same copyright terms as post-1977 works, but with the proviso that copyright in them will last at least until 31 December 2002; if the works are published prior to that date, expiration is postponed at least until 31 December 2027. Thus, these published works have a copyright term of not less than fifty years from the date the new law went into effect, and a longer term if their authors' lives extended beyond 1977.

PRE-1978 PUBLISHED WORKS

4.16 For works published before the present law went into effect, the potential duration of copyright is seventy-five years. Copyrights still in their first term must be renewed, but the second term now runs for forty-seven years, not twenty-eight, and for works first published in 1964 or later, renewal is now automatic. For works already in their second term as of 1 January 1978, the duration of that term has been automatically extended to forty-seven years. The law retains certain benefits for those who take the trouble to file actively for renewal. The author is the person entitled to do so, if living; if not, the right passes to the author's surviving spouse and children or other heirs according to somewhat complex rules. Publishers who have obtained renewal-term rights from authors should continue to file for renewal on the author's behalf, as they have traditionally done.

THE PUBLIC DOMAIN

4.17   To enter the public domain is the ultimate fate of all copyrighted works. Most enter by age—the expiration of their copyright terms—but some enter earlier through forfeiture of copyright. (Changes in the law of copyright notice, made in March 1989, have largely eliminated forfeiture for works first published after February 1989, as will be discussed below.) Once in the public domain, a work may never again be protected and is free for all to use. The use may be direct and simple; for example, George Bernard Shaw's plays have now lost their copyrights and may be performed free of royalty. Or the public-domain works may be the compost from which new works, adaptations or other derivative works, spring in due course. In either case, the original works are public property.

Transferring Copyright Ownership

4.18   Copyright is often referred to as a "bundle" of rights. The basic components, as noted above, are the right to reproduce, the right to distribute copies of a work to the public, the right to make derivative works, and the rights to perform and display a work publicly. Each of these rights may be separately licensed or assigned. Furthermore, each of them may be carved up into smaller rights along lines of geography, time, or medium. Thus, for example, the right to publish a treatise may be carved up so that Publisher A gets North American rights while Publisher B gets United Kingdom rights. Or a French translation license may be given to Librairie C for a ten-year fixed term. Or Publisher A may receive print rights while D-NET gets electronic database rights and E-DISC gets CD-ROM rights. There is theoretically no end to the ways of subdividing a copyright, other than the limits of human ingenuity and the marketplace.

4.19   Finally, licenses may be exclusive or nonexclusive. Typically, anyone making a substantial investment will insist on exclusive rights, whereas persons making ephemeral use at low marginal cost—a typical case being classroom photocopying—need no more than nonexclusive rights. An owner or exclusive licensee of a right is presumed to have the right to sublicense others. A nonexclusive licensee is presumed not to have that right. Such a licensee is more like the holder of a "frequent flyer" coupon that is personal to the holder. Both of these presumptions may be reversed by agreement of the parties, but language to that effect must be clear and specific.

4.20   The task of a licenser of rights is to define them as narrowly as possible so that the maximum revenue may be wrung from the property. The task of a licensee is to define the license as broadly as possible so as to cover all foreseeable contingencies. Both sides, though, have a common interest in seeing that the license is clear and understandable. Disputes between licensers and licensees usually result from the use of jargon that is not mutually understood, or failure to specify when payment is due and for what, or misunderstanding of the facts and the technology concerned. Drafting a license demands and deserves care and skill, and patience between lawyers and their clients.

4.21   A license and the obligation to pay for that license are usually treated as reciprocal obligations, not interdependent ones. Thus, the failure of a licensee to pay royalties does not automatically terminate the license and turn the licensee into an infringer. It gives the licenser a contract damages claim, not a copyright infringement claim. Shrewd licensers will whenever possible reverse this presumption in their contracts, and shrewd licensees will usually resist. With luck, here as in all contract negotiations, it will not be a case of the irresistible meeting the immovable. Getting into a relationship requires the same negotiating skills as getting out of one.

4.22   Apart from contractual rights, the statute itself gives authors the right to terminate licenses and assignments of copyright under certain circumstances. The law specifically grants authors the right to terminate any post-1977 copyright arrangement after thirty-five years, and a roughly comparable termination right applies to licenses signed prior to 1978. The mechanics of termination, including the determination of who has the right to terminate, are extraordinarily complicated and are of importance to only the most lucrative of copyrights. For this reason, no more will be said here on this topic.

Copyright Notice

4.23   No aspect of copyright has caused more grief than the rules of copyright notice. These rules have been responsible for most forfeitures of copyright. Largely a trap for the unwary, they were softened somewhat in 1978 and removed almost entirely in 1989. They were not without purpose or utility, but the rules prevented the United States from joining the Berne Convention, the oldest international copyright convention, and in the end their utility was outweighed by this and other disadvantages.

4.24   Congress could not easily dispense with the rules retroactively, however, and the resulting 1989 legislation means that we now operate simultaneously under three different doctrines: (1) for works first published on or after 1 March 1989, no copyright notice is required; (2) for works first published between 1 January 1978 and 28 February 1989, copyright notice must have been used on all copies published prior to 1 March 1989, with the proviso that certain steps could be taken, Orpheus-like, to redeem deficient notice (see 4.28); and (3) for works first published prior to 1 January 1978, the copyright was almost certainly forfeited if the notice was not affixed to all copies; few excuses were or are available. Notwithstanding the liberality of the new law, continued use of notice is strongly advised to deprive infringers of any possible defense of ignorance. The rules in 4.25–26 should therefore still be followed.

CONTENT OF NOTICE

4.25   Under present law, as under the old, the notice consists of three parts: (1) either the symbol © (preferred because it also suits the requirements of the Universal Copyright Convention), the word *Copyright,* or the abbreviation *Copr.*; (2) the year of first publication; and (3) the name of the copyright owner. Many publishers also add the phrase "all rights reserved" because it affords some protection in Latin American countries that are not signatories to any worldwide copyright convention. The year of first publication is not needed for greeting cards, postcards, stationery, and certain other works not germane to the publishing industry. Where a work is in its renewal term of copyright, it is customary, but not a requirement, to include the year of renewal as well as the year of first publication. Many publishers also include the publication years of various editions of a work if the work has been revised. Technically, this is not necessary: if a revision is substantial enough to constitute a derivative work, only the publication year of the derivative work need be used. (See also 1.16–19.)

PLACEMENT

4.26   The copyright notice should be placed so as to give reasonable notice to the consumer. The old law was very specific about its location: for books, on either the title page or the page immediately following, and for journals and magazines, on the title page, the first page of text, or the front cover. Present law simply states that the notice should be so placed "as to give reasonable notice of the claim of copyright," but most publishers continue to place the notice in the traditional locations required by the old law.

UNITED STATES GOVERNMENT MATERIALS

4.27   Works published by the United States government are in the public domain. When a work consists "preponderantly" of materials created by the United States government, this must be stated in the notice. This may be done either positively (e.g., "Copyright is claimed only in the introduction, notes, appendixes, and index of the present work") or negatively (e.g., "Copyright is not claimed in 'Forest Management,' a publication of the United States government reprinted in the present volume"). Works produced by state or local governments, or by foreign governments, are not in the public domain and are not subject to this notice provision.

CORRECTING MISTAKES

4.28 Under pre-1978 law, no mechanism was available to cure the effects of defective notice: copyright was forfeited, and that was that, unless the omission of notice was accidental and occurred in a very small number of copies. For publication occurring between 1 January 1978 and 1 March 1989, a more lenient regime prevailed. A mistake in the owner's name, or a mistake by no more than a year in the date element of the notice, was largely excused. Any more serious mistake was treated as an omission of notice. Any omission of one or more of the necessary three elements would be excused if the omission was from a "relatively small" number of copies. If more extensive omission occurred, the copyright owner could still save the copyright from forfeiture by registering it (see 4.29–31) within five years after the defective publication and making a "reasonable effort" to add the notice to all copies distributed to the public after the omission was discovered.

Deposit and Registration

4.29 The law requires copyright owners to send copies of their published works to the Copyright Office for deposit and use in the Library of Congress. The copies must be sent within three months of publication. Although failure to make the required deposit does not forfeit the copyright, the copyright owner is subject to a fine for noncompliance if a specific request from the Library of Congress is ignored. For printed works, the deposit of two copies of the "best edition" is required. If, for example, both clothbound and paperback editions of a book are published simultaneously, the cloth edition must be sent. If the work is a very expensive or limited edition, relief from the requirement of depositing two copies of each book may be obtained upon application to the Library of Congress, in which case only one copy need be sent. For electronic software and databases, one copy of the "best edition" is required. When sending deposit copies to the Copyright Office, publishers usually have the copyright registered as well. In the case of printed materials, the two deposit copies also serve the requirements for

Copyright Office Registration Forms

TX	"Application for Copyright Registration for a Nondramatic Literary Work."
SE	". . . for Serials" (includes periodicals, newspapers, annuals, journals, and proceedings of societies).
VA	". . . for a Work of the Visual Arts."
PA	". . . for a Work of the Performing Arts."
SR	". . . for a Sound Recording."
GR/CP	"Adjunct Application for Copyright Registration for a Group of Contributions to Periodicals." (For a collection of works by the same author previously published with notice of copyright—used only in conjunction with one of the foregoing, such as TX.)
CA	"Application for Supplementary Copyright Registration: To Correct or Amplify Information Given in the Copyright Office Record of an Earlier Registration." (Useful for correcting errors made in the initial, basic registration.)
RE	"Application for Renewal Registration." (To register claim for renewal of copyright in works published between 1 January 1950 and 31 December 1977.)

Fig. 4.1. List of the various application forms for copyright registration. The form used for literary and scholarly works is TX.

registration. In the case of electronic software and databases, the submission of certain "identifying material" will suffice.

4.30 To register a work the author or other claimant must fill out the appropriate application form. There are several forms, tailored to different types of works. Form TX (see fig. 4.1) is the one used for books, journals, databases, and other works in the broad category called literary works. Registration requires a twenty-dollar fee. Publishers with large lists tend to keep funds on deposit at the Copyright Office for this purpose. It is important to answer all questions on the application accurately. Copyright owners have been sanctioned by courts for misleading the Copyright Office by (for example) failing to disclose that a work is based upon preexisting materials. Statements on the application do not need to be exhaustive, but they must be correct and not evasive.

4.31 Registration, it should be noted, is not necessary to "obtain" a copyright (which exists in the work from the moment it is fixed in tangible form) or to assure its validity, but responsible publishers seldom publish without registering copyright because of the added protection registration affords. Unlike the copyright notice, registration puts on public record the exact details of a copyright claim. In cases of infringement, registration is a prerequisite to bringing suit unless the work was written and first published abroad. Moreover, if registration has been made within three months of publication, or before an infringement begins, the copyright owner, instead of going through the difficulties of proving actual damages, can sue for "statutory damages" (in effect, an award of damages based on equity rather than on proof of loss) and, most significantly, is eligible to be reimbursed for attorney's fees. As noted above, registration is also necessary if a missing, defective, or erroneous notice is to be corrected.

THE PUBLISHING AGREEMENT

4.32　No publishing house may legally publish a copyrighted work unless it first acquires the basic rights to copy the work and distribute it to the public. In most instances these rights are acquired from the author by means of a contract called the *publishing agreement*.

New Books

4.33　In book publishing the publisher typically draws up the contract for a new book, to be signed by both the publisher and the author. For a joint work (see 4.10) the contract is between the publisher and all the joint authors, not just one of them. In this contract the publisher and author agree to certain things. Typically, the publisher will undertake to publish the book within a specified number of months or years after acceptance of the manuscript, and to pay the author a stipulated royalty out of the proceeds. The author, in addition to granting rights to the publisher, typically guarantees that the work is original and never before published, and that it does not violate copyright or libel anyone or otherwise expose the publisher to legal liability. The author usually agrees to correct and return proofs and to cooperate in future revisions of the work on request. Book publishing agreements are generally fairly lengthy and detailed documents and include many other points of agreement. Among the common areas of negotiation are royalty schedules; royalty advances and expense allowances; the standards for acceptance of the manuscript; what rights, beyond North American print rights, are granted to the publisher; what share of royalties the author receives for revised editions to which he or she does not contribute; and reversion of rights to the author if the book goes out of print.

4.34　In scholarly publishing, in addition to contracts with the authors of new books, several other types of agreement are in use for special kinds of works. Two of the common ones cover contributions to scholarly journals and to symposia (figs. 4.2 and 4.3).

Fig. 4.2. Agreement for publication of a journal article, currently in use by
the University of Chicago Press journals department. Here the author transfers
all copyright rights to the publisher of the journal, and the publisher transfers
back to the author the right to reprint the article in other scholarly contexts.

The University of Chicago Press

5801 S. Ellis Avenue, Chicago, Illinois 60637

Since 1891 Publishers of Scholarly Books and Journals

Telephone 312/702-7700
Fax 312/702-9756

OFFICE OF THE DIRECTOR

PUBLICATION AGREEMENT

Dear

The University of Chicago, acting through its Press, is pleased to undertake the publication of your contribution,

(the "Contribution") to be included in the volume now entitled

written/edited by   (the "Work").

As a condition of publication, it is essential that you grant us all rights, including the copyright, for the Contribution. Accordingly, the following terms of publication are submitted for your consideration:

APPROVAL AND ACCEPTANCE: We mutually agree that publication of the Contribution is contingent upon its acceptance for publication by the Press volume/manuscript editor and upon its meeting Press editorial standards. Publication is additionally contingent upon the formal and final approval for publication of the Contribution and the Work by the Board of University Publications, without whose approval no publication by us takes place.

COPYRIGHT ASSIGNMENT: Whereas the University of Chicago, acting through its Press, undertakes to publish the Contribution as above, and whereas you desire to have the Contribution so published, now, therefore, you grant and assign to the University for its exclusive use the entire copyright for the Contribution. The copyright consists of any and all rights of whatever kind or nature now or hereafter protected by the copyright laws of the United States and of all foreign countries in all forms of communication, and the University shall be the sole proprietor thereof.

WARRANTY: You warrant that the Contribution is original with you; that it contains no matter which is libelous or is otherwise unlawful or which invades individual privacy or infringes any proprietary right or any statutory copyright; and you agree to indemnify and hold the University harmless against any claim or judgment to the contrary. Further, you warrant that you have the right to assign the copyright to the University, and that no right protected by copyright to the Contribution has been previously assigned. It is understood that the copyright to the Contribution has not been registered with the United States Copyright Office, but in the event that such registration has taken place, you will promptly transfer the copyright to the University.

Fig. 4.3. Agreement, or consent, for publication of an article commissioned as a contribution to a collective work—symposium or conference papers. Other "works made for hire," such as translations, forewords, or indexes, require somewhat different forms of agreement.

PREVIOUS PUBLICATION AND PERMISSION: You warrant that the Contribution has not been published elsewhere in whole or in part (except as may be set out in a rider annexed hereto and signed by the University) and that no agreement to publish the Contribution or any part or version thereof is outstanding. Should the Contribution contain any material which requires written permission for inclusion in the Contribution, such permission shall be obtained at your own expense from the copyright proprietor and submitted for review by the University with the manuscript.

PROOFHANDLING: You will be given an opportunity to read and correct the edited manuscript and/or proofs, but if you fail to return them by the date separately agreed, production and publication may proceed without your corrections.

COMPENSATION: As total compensation for your preparation of the Contribution and the above grant and assignment of rights, the University will publish the Contribution and you will receive, upon publication, _____ free copies of the hardcover edition of the Work and _____ free copies of the paperbound edition when published by the University. You may purchase additional copies of the Work for your own use by direct order to the University of Chicago Press at 40% discount from the then prevailing list price.

If the foregoing terms are satisfactory, please sign and date this Agreement; return the University's copy to _____ immediately, retaining the Contributor's Copy for your files.

ACCEPTED AND APPROVED: FOR THE UNIVERSITY OF CHICAGO

_____   _____
                                          Morris Philipson, Director
                                          The University of Chicago Press
Date: _____

_____
Federal Tax Identification (Social Security) Number

_____
Citizenship

_____
Permanent address

_____

2/92

Journal Articles

4.35   Contributors to a journal possess at the beginning exactly the same rights in their work as authors of books. Consequently, when an article has been accepted for publication in a scholarly journal, the author is usually asked to sign a formal transfer of rights in the contribution to the publisher. In the absence of a written copyright transfer agreement, all that the publisher acquires from the agreement to publish is the privilege of printing the contribution in the context of that journal. Contributors frequently do not know this and do not understand that without broad rights the publisher cannot license anthology, database, classroom photocopying, or other uses that spread the author's message. They will sometimes balk at the breadth of the copyright transfer they are asked to make, until these legalities are explained. In the agreement currently in use at the University of Chicago Press, the publisher returns to the contributor the right to reprint the article in other scholarly works (see fig. 4.2); such a provision is fair to both sides and is to be encouraged.

Contributions to Symposia

4.36   Symposium proceedings, made up of papers by different authors, present legal situations similar to those of a scholarly journal, except that, since such papers are often specifically solicited, they can be considered a "commissioned work" that is "made for hire" (see 4.12–13), and a different form of agreement may be appropriate. The publisher of a symposium volume first negotiates a contract with the general editor or sponsor of the proposed work. At some later appropriate time either the volume editor or the publisher sends written forms to all contributors (see fig. 4.3). When these have been signed, they are returned to the publisher and filed with the contract for the volume.

PUBLISHERS' RESPONSIBILITIES

Copyright Tasks

4.37   When a publisher accepts an author's assignment of rights in a publishing contract, it normally assumes the responsibility of performing all the tasks associated with copyright. These include seeing that appropriate copyright notice is included in the published work, supplying and forwarding the deposit copies of the book to the Copyright Office, registering the copyright, and (for books published before 1978) assisting the author or the author's heirs to renew the copyright at the appropriate time.

4.38   Since the assignment of rights in most instances includes subsidiary rights as well as the basic right to publish the work, publishers also take on the tasks of licensing subsidiary rights to other publishers and granting permission to other authors and publishers who wish to use parts of the work in their own publications.

Handling Subsidiary Rights

4.39   In book publishing, subsidiary rights are usually thought of as including the following categories:

> *Foreign rights,* whereby a foreign publisher may be licensed to sell the book in its original version in that publisher's own territory or to translate the book into another language and to have standard publisher's rights in the translation (other than the right to license motion pictures).
>
> *Serial rights,* whereby a magazine or newspaper publisher may be licensed to publish the book in a series of daily, weekly, or monthly installments. *First serial rights* refers to publication before the work has come out in book form; *second serial rights* to publication afterward.
>
> *Paperback rights,* whereby a publisher is licensed to produce and sell a paperback version of the book. So-called *quality,* or *trade,* paperbacks are normally sold in bookstores, like clothbound books. *Mass-market* paperbacks are typically marketed through newsstands and supermarkets, although some find their way into bookstores. The publisher of the paperback may be either the original publisher or someone else. Some books are published only in paper, with no previously published clothbound version; these are called *original paperbacks.*
>
> *Book club rights,* whereby a book club is given the right to distribute the book to its members at a price lower than the regular trade price. Typically, copies are sold to the book club in bulk at a steep discount.
>
> *Reprint rights,* whereby another publisher is licensed to reprint the work, in whole or in part, in an anthology or some other form of collection or (usually if the work has gone out of print in English) in a cheap reprint edition.
>
> *Motion-picture rights,* whereby a movie producer or studio is given the right to make a motion picture based on the book.
>
> *Electronic rights,* whereby the book or portions of it are licensed for inclusion in an on-line database or on a compact disk (CD-ROM).

4.40   This list by no means exhausts the various forms of subsidiary rights that may be handled by the publisher, but it includes the major ones. Depending upon the administrative structure of the publishing house, and upon the importance and marketability of the book involved, various persons or departments may handle different aspects of subsidiary-rights work—a special rights and permissions department, the sales or marketing department, the acquiring editor, or even the chief executive officer. When the publisher sells or licenses rights to others, money is paid, either in a lump sum or in the form of a royalty, and these proceeds are normally split between the publisher and the author, according to whatever terms are specified in the publishing contract. In a typical book publishing agreement the author receives at least 50 percent of such income. Some publishers have tried to avoid paying the author so much by licensing at an artificially low royalty to a sister company or other affiliate, but such "sweetheart" arrangements are suspect and of doubtful legality. In general, licenses between related companies should be handled in the same way as those between unrelated companies, unless the author agrees otherwise in advance.

Granting Permission

4.41   A publisher with a relatively large backlist of books and journals, such as the University of Chicago Press, may receive dozens of letters a day requesting permission to use material from one or another publication. These requests range from whole books or journal articles to snippets of prose from a scholarly monograph. Some publishers handle these requests by themselves, others grant permission subject to the author's approval, which the requester is asked to obtain. Before any request, large or small, can be granted, however, the material requested must be checked to make sure that the publisher does indeed hold the copyright to *all* of it. And to be unequivocally sure of this the publisher needs to have had the author's full cooperation when the book or article was first published.

AUTHORS' RESPONSIBILITIES

Guarantee of Authorship

4.42   In signing a contract with a publisher an author guarantees that the work is original, that the author owns it, that no part of it has been previously published, and that no other agreement to publish it or part of it is outstanding. If a chapter or other significant part has already appeared in print—as a journal article, for example—then written permission to reprint it must be secured from the copyright owner of the other publication. This will normally be its publisher, unless the author had, for example, granted only first serial rights to that publisher. As a matter of courtesy, or where stipulated by the other publisher, notice of the original copyright and permission to reprint will be noted on the copyright page of the book, in a footnote on the first page of the reprinted material, or in a special list of acknowledgments. However, this practice is not legally required. What is required is that subsequent permissions requests for that material be referred to the original copyright owner where applicable.

Obtaining Permissions

4.43   It is the author's responsibility to request any permission required for the use of material owned by others. Most publishing agreements stipulate that any fees to be paid will be the author's responsibility. When all permissions have been received, the author should send them, or copies of them, to the publisher, who will note and comply with any special provisions contained in them. The publisher will file all permissions with the publishing contract, where they may be consulted in the event of future editions or of requests for permission to reprint from the work.

4.44   The publisher is not usually given the right to grant permission to reprint separately from the author's book any items—illustrations, charts, diagrams, poems, long prose passages, or whatever—taken from another copyrighted work or procured from a picture agency, library, or museum. Furthermore, the use of such items is often licensed for a single edition (but not a single printing). New editions, paperback reprints, serialization in periodicals, and so forth, will require renewed permissions.

4.45   In the course of writing a book or article, the author will do well to keep a record of all copyright owners whose permission may be necessary before the work is published. For a book containing many illustrations, long prose passages, or poetry, the process of obtaining permissions may take weeks, even months, to complete. For example, the author may find that an American publisher holds rights only for distribution in the United States and that European and British Commonwealth rights are held by a British publisher. The author, wishing worldwide distribution for the book *(world rights),* must then write to the British publisher requesting permission to reprint, mentioning that permission has already been obtained from the American publisher. Again, if the author of copyrighted material has died, a voluminous correspondence may ensue before anyone authorized to grant permission can be found. The author, therefore, should begin requesting permissions as soon as the manuscript is accepted for publication. Most publishers wisely decline to start setting type for a book until all of the author's permissions are in hand.[1]

4.46   To use anyone else's copyrighted work, whether published or unpublished, an author must have the copyright owner's permission, unless the intended use is a "fair use." To be on the safe side, and to meet the publisher's requirements, the author should obtain all permissions in writing. No permission is required, of course, to quote from works in the public domain—works in which copyright never existed (such as publications of the United States government) or in which copyright has expired. Although the original text of a classic reprinted in a modern edition may be in the public domain, recent translations and abridgments, as well as editorial introductions, notes, and other apparatus, are protected by copyright. Whether permission is needed or not, of course, the author should always credit any sources used.

4.47   To determine whether a work published in the United States is still in copyright, first look for the year of publication in the copyright notice. Anything that has been in publication in the United States for more than seventy-five years can safely be assumed to be in the public domain. The same cannot be assumed of foreign works, however: copyright law in the United Kingdom and many other countries has long protected works for fifty years after the death of the author, and in some countries the term may be longer. Thus, if a British author died in 1950, his works published before World War I would be in the public domain in the United States but not the United Kingdom. The practical effect of this depends on what market is to be exploited. It presents no problem within the United States, for the United States will not enforce a foreign copyright if a work is in the public domain under United States law. But the continuing existence of a foreign copyright may hinder *foreign* distribution of a work lawfully published in the United States. If the work has been in publication with notice for more than twenty-eight but less than seventy-five years, it is necessary either to assume that the copyright has been renewed, whether or not the renewal date is specified in the copyright notice, or to check the Copyright Office records for renewal, bearing in mind that renewal has become automatic for works first published in 1964 or later. If the copyright notice is absent and the work is found to have been published between 1 January 1978 and 28 February 1989, it is prudent to assume that steps necessary to cure omission have been taken (see 4.24, 4.28). Works published in the

---

1. It is possible to engage professional help in obtaining permissions for a large project. Specialists in this work are listed in the annual publication *LMP (Literary Market Place),* under "Permissions."

United States prior to 1978 without copyright notice may almost certainly be assumed to have forfeited copyright protection (see 4.24).

4.48   Unpublished works present a much greater problem. If the writer is deceased, it may be difficult to determine who controls the copyrights. Instead of being able to deal with a publishing corporation, one must deal with the author's heirs, who may not be easily identified or found. Furthermore, whether the author is living or dead, one must be careful in relying on fair use for quotation of unpublished material. As discussed in 4.54, the scope of fair use for unpublished works may be narrower than for published works.

4.49   The problem presented by unpublished works whose authors are deceased is, in a larger sense, but an example of the problem of the missing copyright owner. Another typical example is the case of the publisher that has gone out of business or, at least, is no longer doing business under a given imprint. A reasonable effort must be made to locate such copyright owner. This would require, certainly, a search of the Copyright Office records and an attempt to communicate with the copyright owner at whatever address is last stated in the file for the work concerned. If such an effort yields no results, there is minimal risk in going forward. Technically, one may still infringe a copyright under these circumstances, but it is most unlikely that any court would do more than require the payment of a reasonable permissions fee. Anyone proceeding with publication under these conditions should certainly be prepared to offer and pay a reasonable fee forthwith upon receiving any objection from the rediscovered owner.

4.50   Authors who wish to include unpublished material in their works should be aware that public regulations or private restrictions, unrelated to copyright, may limit its use. The keeper of a collection, usually a librarian or an archivist, is the best source of such information, including what permissions must be sought and from whom. It is important to bear in mind that copyright in a manuscript is different from ownership of the actual paper. Most often a library or collector will own the physical object itself but not the right to reproduce it. Thus, there may be two permissions required: one for access to the material, and one for the right to copy. It is important not to mistake one for the other.

FAIR USE: QUOTING WITHOUT PERMISSION

4.51   The doctrine of *fair use* was originally developed by judges as an equitable limit on the absolutism of copyright. Although incorporated into the new copyright law, the doctrine still does not attempt to define the exact limits of the fair use of copyrighted work. It does state, however, that in determining whether or not the use made of a work in any particular case is fair, the factors to be considered must include the following:

1. The purpose and character of the use, including whether such use is of a commercial nature or is for nonprofit educational purposes
2. The nature of the copyrighted work
3. The amount and substantiality of the portion used in relation to the copyrighted work as a whole
4. The effect of the use upon the potential market for, or value of, the copyrighted work

Essentially the doctrine excuses copying that would otherwise be infringement. For example, it allows authors to quote from other authors' work or to reproduce small amounts of graphic or pictorial material for purposes of review or criticism or to illustrate or buttress their own points. Authors invoking fair use should transcribe accurately and give credit to their sources. They should not quote out of context, making the author of the quoted passage seem to be saying something opposite to, or different from, what was intended.

4.52   Although the law lays out no boundaries or iron-bound formulas for fair use, some publishers have their own rules of thumb. It should be remembered that no such rules have validity outside the publishing house walls: courts, not publishers, adjudicate fair use. The rules exist in part to give an overworked permissions department, which often cannot tell whether or not a proposed use of a quotation is actually fair, something to use as a yardstick.

4.53   Fair use is use that is fair—simply that. Uses that are tangential in purpose to the original, such as quotation for purposes of criticism, will always be judged more leniently than those that are parallel, such as relying on quotations to prove one's point rather than putting the argument in one's own words. Use of any literary work in its entirety—a poem, an essay, a chapter of a book—is hardly ever acceptable. Use of less than the whole will be judged by whether the second author appears to be taking a free ride on the first author's labor. As a rule of thumb, one should never quote more than a few contiguous paragraphs or stanzas at a time or let the quotations, even if scattered, begin to overshadow the quoter's own material. Quotations or graphic reproductions should not be so long that they substitute for, or diminish the value of, the copyright owner's own publication. Proportion is more important than the absolute length of a quotation: to quote five hundred words from an essay of five thousand is likely to be more serious than from a work of fifty thousand.

4.54 Where the quoted work is unpublished, some recent court decisions have imposed a stricter standard. One such decision involved the unauthorized copying by the magazine *The Nation* of short passages from Gerald Ford's memoirs, which were scheduled to be excerpted a few days later in *Time*. Although only three to four hundred words were quoted, the United States Supreme Court noted that these words were of crucial importance to the text and that their publication did immediate and measurable economic damage to Ford's licensees. However, the Court went beyond this to state that lack of prior publication weighs heavily against a finding of fair use. Subsequent cases in the Second Circuit Court of Appeals took this principle beyond what most observers felt was reasonable. The Second Circuit held that extensive quotation (or paraphrase) of unpublished letters of the novelist J. D. Salinger was improper where used not for purposes of literary critique but to enliven and improve an "unauthorized" biography. On the facts, this case was not exceptional; what caused concern was the court's dogmatic approach to fair use of unpublished material. In a later case involving the founder of Scientology, L. Ron Hubbard, the court suggested that quotation from unpublished materials would be unfair *even if necessary to document serious character defects of an important public figure.* Taken together, these cases had a chilling effect on quotation from unpublished manuscripts, to the detriment of scholarship. Fortunately, Congress has now legislated that absence of prior publication is not dispositive, but merely a factor to be considered in determining fair use. Caution, but not excessive caution, should now be the watchword.

4.55 One aspect of the Salinger case that invites no argument is its equating paraphrase with copying. Traditional copyright doctrine treats extensive paraphrase as merely disguised copying. Thus, fair use analysis will be the same for both. Paraphrase of small quantities of material, on the other hand, may not even constitute copying at all, so that fair use analysis would never come into play.

4.56 With respect to pictorial and graphic materials, there is little legal precedent to navigate by. At the level of intuition, it seems that a monograph on Picasso should be free to reproduce details from a painting in order, for example, to illustrate the critic's discussion of Picasso's brushwork. Reproducing the entire image in black and white may also be reasonably necessary to illustrate the author's analysis of Picasso's techniques of composition. However, justification wears thin where a painting is reproduced in vivid color occupying a full page; the result begins to compete with large-scale reproductions of artwork that have no scholarly purpose. Likewise, reproduction on the cover would probably be seen as commercial rather than scholarly use, and therefore unjustified. As for photographs, use of them merely as illustrations would require permission, but use as described above in a scholarly treatment of photography might not.

4.57   Reproduction of charts, tables, and graphs presents a difficult judgment call. An "aggressive" approach would justify the copying of a single item on the ground that a single chart is the pictorial equivalent of a few sentences. A more "conservative" approach would argue that a graph is a picture worth a thousand words, and that reproducing it without permission is taking a free ride on the first author's work. This latter approach has the flaw of being too absolute in practice, for it is difficult under this rationale to imagine *any* fair use of such an image. Where the item in question represents a small portion of the original work and a small portion of the second work, the harm seems minimal, outweighed by the benefits of open communication. Certainly, reproduction of a graph or chart that simply presents data in a straightforward relationship, in contrast to reproduction of a graph or chart embellished with pictorial elements, should ordinarily be considered fair use.

4.58   A word of practical caution: if a use appears to be fair, the author should probably *not* ask permission. The right of fair use is a valuable one to scholarship, and it should not be allowed to decay through the failure of scholars to employ it boldly. Furthermore, excessive caution can be dangerous if the copyright owner proves uncooperative. Far from establishing good faith and protecting the author from suit or unreasonable demands, a permission request may have just the opposite effect. The act of seeking permission indicates that the author feels permission is needed, and the tacit admission may be damaging to the author's defense.

LIBRARY AND EDUCATIONAL COPYING AS FAIR USE

4.59   Fair use has been much in dispute as applied to photocopying for classroom and library use. The Copyright Act contains specific guidelines for library photocopying, and the legislative history of the act contains specific, though not official, guidelines for classroom photocopying.

4.60   The new law does attempt to define minimum fair-use limitations on machine copying by libraries, in a long section with many exemptions and caveats too complex to discuss here. In general, it allows libraries to make single copies of copyrighted works, provided each copy bears the original copyright notice and provided the copies are made for one of the purposes specifically defined in the statute, including the following:

> If the copy is made for a library's own use, because the library's own copy of the work is damaged or missing and a replacement cannot be obtained at a fair price.

If the copy is made for a patron's use and is limited to an article or small part of a larger work—or the whole of a larger work if a printed copy cannot be obtained at a fair price—and only if the copy is intended for use by the patron in "private study, scholarship, or research."

The law specifically forbids "systematic" copying by libraries. Presumably this means (1) making copies of books or periodicals as a substitute for buying them and (2) making copies for a patron without regard to the patron's intended use of the material.

4.61   The Copyright Act does not include similar guidelines for educational photocopying. But it is clear from congressional reports published at the time the law was being written that a certain limited amount of such copying was thought to constitute fair use of copyrighted material. "Brevity" and "spontaneity" are the guiding principles; the latter reflects the premise that photocopying for classroom use should be done only when insufficient time exists to obtain permission. Multiple copies should not exceed the number of students in the class. They should not substitute for anthologies or regular school purchases. The same items should not be copied from year to year or semester to semester, but once only and at the instance of a particular teacher for immediate use in the classroom. Workbooks and other consumable materials should not be copied, and the students should not be charged more than the actual copying cost. Any copy must include the copyright notice used in the original. A recent case involving Kinko's, a national chain of photocopying services, has clarified the law on at least one aspect of educational photocopying: the widespread practice of making customized anthologies for individual teachers' classes is an infringement if express permission is not received from all copyright owners. This victory has had the bittersweet effect of swamping many publishers' rights and permissions departments with more license requests than they can handle.

4.62   Indeed, the new technologies of photocopying and electronic reproduction (sometimes called *electrocopying*) present a major institutional challenge to publishers. The volume of license requests under these headings exceeds the ability of traditional techniques to process them. Publishers have traditionally processed such requests by hand, case by case, evaluating each request on its own merits and often tailoring a fee to the specific circumstances. This must and will change. Automation—the very electronic technology that they have regarded as a threat—gives publishers a powerful tool for handling requests rapidly. Coupled with the adoption of standard, publicly quoted fees, it could create a highly efficient marketplace for copying, to the mutual benefit of copyright owners and users. Such a solution has yet to be tried, but a look at the near horizon underscores both its necessity and its feasibility. A program called PubNet, an electronic clearinghouse for photocopying for interlibrary loans, provides what may be a useful model.

Requesting Permission

GENERAL REQUIREMENTS

4.63   In the dark before the dawn of this new age of automated permission processing, would-be users can help reduce delay and miscommunication by submitting their requests for permission in the best possible form. All requests for permission to reprint should be sent to the copyright holder in writing and in duplicate. The request should contain the following explicit information:

> The title of the original work and exact identification, with page numbers, of what is to be reprinted (include table or figure number, title of a poem, or for prose passages, the opening and closing phrases in addition to the page numbers). The requester should be sure to cite the original source of the material, not any subsequent reprinting of it.
>
> Information about the publication in which the author wishes to reproduce the material: title, approximate number of printed pages, form of publication (clothbound book, paperback book, or journal), publisher, probable date of publication, approximate print run, and list price (if available).
>
> The kind of rights requested. The most limited rights that a user ought to accept are "nonexclusive world rights in the English language, for one edition." The best opening gambit would be "nonexclusive world rights in all languages and for all editions, including the right to grant customary permissions requests where the licensed material is incorporated in material for which permission is requested."

In granting permission, the copyright holder will either sign and return to the author one copy of the request or will send the author the copyright owner's standard form. In either case the person responding to the request should state clearly what fee is demanded for the proposed use and what special conditions apply to the grant. The second copy of the permission form will be retained in the copyright owner's files. The requesting author should give the original to the publisher and keep a third copy for reference.

4.64   The University of Chicago Press supplies authors or editors of books requiring many permissions with a model request letter (fig. 4.4) but suggests that they write on their own personal or (when appropriate)

The University of Chicago Press

5801 Ellis Avenue, Chicago, Illinois 60637-1496
Since 1891 Publishers of Scholarly Books and Journals

Telephone: (312)702-7700
Fax: (312)702-9756

To:
Reference:
Date:

I am writing to request permission to reprint the following material from your publication:

       Author/Title/Date of publication:

       Pages as they appear in your publication:

       Other identifying information and remarks:

This material is to appear as originally published (any changes or deletions are noted on the reverse side of this letter) in the following work that the University of Chicago Press is now preparing for publication:

       Author (Editor)/Title:

       Proposed date of publication:

       Remarks:

We request nonexclusive world rights, as part of our volume only, in all languages and for all editions.

If you are the copyright holder, may I have your permission to reprint the above material in our book? If you do not indicate otherwise, we will use the usual scholarly form of acknowledgment, including publisher, author, title, etc.

If you are not the copyright holder, or if additional permission is needed for world rights from another source, please so indicate.

Thank you for your consideration of this request. A duplicate copy of this form is enclosed for your convenience.

Sincerely yours,

_____

The above request is hereby approved on the conditions specified below, and on the understanding that full credit will be given to the source.

Date: _____. Approved by: _____

Fig. 4.4. Suggestions for a letter seeking permission to reprint material in a scholarly book. Some of the information about the proposed book may be lacking when the author begins to request permissions, but as much information as possible should be supplied. Note that spaces are left so that the person addressed can use the letter itself for granting or denying the request or for referring the author elsewhere.

institutional letterhead. Every publisher would be well advised to adopt some variation of this practice, for authors are otherwise typically rudderless and at sea without it.

ILLUSTRATIONS

4.65   Permission to reproduce pictorial works—as opposed to charts, graphs, or the like that are appendages to a written text—will sometimes, but not reliably, be available from a publisher. A publisher who has used the pictorial work to illustrate text that someone is seeking to reprint may very well not have the right to sublicense use of the illustration. Even a publisher of, say, a collection of the artist's work may not have rights to the individual images. In such a case, the permission seeker must deal with the owner of the object or the artist. Formerly, it was common for the owner of such a piece to control the reproduction rights as well. But the current law has made it easy for photographers and artists to retain the reproduction rights to a piece while selling the piece itself and the right to display it. Consequently, for works produced or sold before 1978, careful inquiry may be needed to ensure that permission is requested from the right party; for works produced or sold after 1977, the artist may generally be assumed to control reproduction. The only exception to this is in the case of photographs, which are often licensed through agencies that have large inventories of images.

4.66   A permission request for an illustration should be sent to the picture agency, museum, artist, or private individual controlling reproduction rights. Again, the request should be as specific as possible regarding the identity of what is to be reproduced, the form of publication in which it will appear, and the kind of rights requested. If the author making the request knows that the illustration will also be used elsewhere than in the text proper (as on the jacket or in advertising), this fact should be noted. Any additional fee for such use is the responsibility of the publisher, however, not the author.

4.67   Fees paid for reproducing material, especially illustrations procured from a picture agency, normally cover one-time use only—in, say, the first edition of the book. If an illustration is to be used also on the jacket or in advertising, a higher fee is customary. Also, if a book is reprinted as a paperback or goes into a second edition, another fee is usually charged.

ACKNOWLEDGING SOURCES

4.68   Whether or not the use of others' material requires permission, an author should give the exact source of such material: in a note or internal reference in the text, in a source note to a table, in a credit line under an illustration. In instances where formal permission has been granted the author should, within reason, follow any special wording stipulated by the grantor. For a text passage complete in itself, such as a poem, or for a table, the full citation to the source may be followed by:

> Reprinted by permission of the publisher.

A credit line below an illustration may read, for example:

> Courtesy of the Newberry Library, Chicago, Illinois.

Examples of various kinds of credit lines may be found elsewhere in this volume, especially in chapters 11 and 12.

4.69 In a work necessitating many permissions, acknowledgments are often grouped in a special "Acknowledgments" section at the front or back of the book. Some citation to the source should still, however, be made on the page containing the relevant material.

FEES

4.70 The author is responsible for any fees charged by grantors of permission to reproduce, unless other arrangements are made, in writing, with the publisher. A publisher may agree to pay the fees and to deduct them from the author's royalties or—in rare instances—to split the fees with the author. If it appears that a book would be enhanced by illustrations not provided by the author, many publishing agreements enable the publisher to find the illustrations and (with the author's consent) pay any fees involved.

PERMISSIONS FOR AN ANTHOLOGY

4.71 A book made up entirely of other authors' copyrighted materials—stories, essays, poems, documents, selections from larger works—depends for its existence on permissions from the various copyright owners. The compiler of such a volume, therefore, should begin seeking permissions as soon as a contract for publication of the volume has been executed or a "letter of intent" has been received from the prospective publisher. Informal inquiries among copyright owners may be initiated before that time, but no sensible publisher of material to be anthologized is likely to grant permission for its use or to set fees without knowing the details of eventual publication.

4.72 Once a publication contract has been signed, the need for dispatch is obvious. Permission for a selection may be refused, or the fee charged may be so high that the compiler is forced to drop that selection and substitute another. And until all permissions have been received and all fees agreed upon, the table of contents cannot be final.

FOR FURTHER REFERENCE

4.73   The best analysis of copyright law for laymen is *The Copyright Book: A Practical Guide*, by William S. Strong (1990). Those seeking more detailed academic analysis should consult *The Fair Use Privilege in Copyright Law*, by William F. Patry, or the longer treatises on copyright by Melville Nimmer, *Cases and Materials on Copyright* and *Nimmer on Copyright;* Paul Goldstein, *Copyright: Principles, Laws, and Practice;* and Howard Abrams, *The Law of Copyright*. A useful legal treatise on publishing law generally is E. Gabriel Perle and John Taylor Williams, *Publishing Law Handbook*, 2d ed.

Part 2

Style

5 *Punctuation*

INTRODUCTION

5.1   Punctuation should be governed by its function, which is to make the author's meaning clear, to promote ease of reading, and in varying degrees to contribute to the author's style. Although there is inevitably a certain amount of subjectivity in punctuation, there are some principles that the author and editor should know, lest the subjective element become so arbitrary as to obscure the sense or make the reader's task difficult or unpleasant.

5.2   The tendency to use all the punctuation that the grammatical structure of the material suggests is referred to as close *(klōs)* punctuation. It is a practice that was more common in the past, and though it may be helpful when the writing is elaborate, it can, when misused, produce an uninviting choppiness. There is a tendency today, on the other hand, to punctuate only when necessary to prevent misreading. Most contemporary writers and editors lean toward this open style of punctuation yet preserve a measure of subjectivity and discretion.

5.3   The punctuation guidelines offered in this chapter apply largely to running text. For the special punctuation recommended in notes, bibliographies, indexes, and so on see the appropriate chapters in this manual.

TYPOGRAPHIC CONSIDERATIONS

5.4   The typographic treatment of punctuation adjacent to a variant font (italic or boldface within roman text, for instance) should be governed by both appearance and meaning. Generally, punctuation marks are printed in the same style or font of type as the word, letter, character, or symbol immediately preceding them:

Luke 4:16*a;*   **Point:** one-twelfth of a pica

compare

Luke 4:16*a*;   **Point**: one-twelfth of a pica

5.5   A question mark or exclamation point that immediately follows an italicized title and that is not part of the title should be set in roman to avoid misreading:

> When did she write *Together Again*?
> *but*
> After she wrote *What Next?*
>
> But that's not the *Pathétique*!
> *but*
> He reappears in *Forward!*

5.6   Parentheses and brackets enclosing italic material may be set in italics to avoid such common typefitting problems as overlapping ascenders or descenders or visually uneven spacing within enclosures. When the enclosed material begins and ends in italic but contains roman text in between, italic enclosures may be used. If only one end of the enclosed material is italic, however, the parentheses or brackets should be roman.

> *(express violations)*   (it was *unforeseen*)
>
> *(a)*   (see 12*b*)   *[Continued]*
>
> [it was substituted for *outrageous*]
>
> *(inappropriate* was used for *outrageous)*

PERIOD

Terminal Punctuation

5.7   A period is used to mark the end of a declarative or an imperative sentence:

> The two men faced each other in silence.
>
> Wait here.

5.8   A period should be omitted at the end of a sentence that is included within another sentence unless the included sentence is the final element and is not enclosed in parentheses or brackets (see also 5.14):

> The snow (she caught a glimpse of it as she passed the window) was now falling heavily.
>
> Gilford's reply, "He appears to be untrustworthy," was unexpected.
>
> Farnsworth had left an angry message for Isadora on the mantel (she noticed it while checking her eye shadow in the mirror).
>
> Gilford said smugly, "We never really trusted the man."

(For questions that follow introductory sentence elements see 5.23–24.)

Vertical Lists

5.9   Use a period without parentheses after numerals or letters used to enumerate items in a vertical list:

1. Strigiformes	*a.* the Bay of Pigs
2. Caprimulgiformes	*b.* the Berlin airlift

Numerals or letters enumerating items in a list within a paragraph should be enclosed in parentheses and should not be followed by a period (see 5.126).

5.10   Omit periods after items in a vertical list unless one or more of the items are complete sentences. If the vertical list completes a sentence begun in an introductory element, the final period is also omitted unless the items in the list are separated by commas or semicolons:

> The following metals were excluded from the regulation:
>
> molybdenum
> mercury
> manganese
> magnesium

> After careful investigation the committee was convinced that
>
> 1. the organization's lawyer, Watson, had consulted no one before making the decision;
> 2. the chair, Fitcheu-Braun, had never spoken to Watson;
> 3. Fitcheu-Braun was as surprised as anyone by what happened.

Note that when the items are separated by commas or, as above, semicolons, each item begins with a lowercase letter. (For further discussion of enumerated vertical lists see 5.61 and 8.75–79.)

Periods with Quotation Marks

AMERICAN STYLE

5.11   When a declarative or an imperative sentence is enclosed in quotation marks, the period ending the sentence is, in what may be called the American style, placed inside the closing quotation mark. If the quoted sentence is included within another sentence, its terminal period is omitted or replaced by a comma, as required, unless it comes at the end of the including sentence. In the latter case, a single period serves both sentences and is placed inside the closing quotation mark.

> "There is no reason to inform the president."

> "It won't be necessary to inform the president," said Emerson.

> Emerson replied nervously, "The president doesn't wish to be informed about such things."

5.12   Quoted words and phrases falling at the end of a sentence can, in the vast majority of cases, take the terminating period within the closing quotation mark without confusion or misunderstanding (see also 5.13). In those rare instances when confusion is likely, the period not only may, but perhaps should, be placed after the quotation mark.

> From then on, Gloria became increasingly annoyed by what she later referred to as Sidney's "excessive discretion."
>
> "I was dismayed," Roger confided, "by the strange exhilaration she displayed after reading 'The Metamorphosis.'"
>
> The first line of Le Beau's warning to Orlando has long been regarded as reading "Good sir, I do in friendship counsel you".
>
> Turner's memory suddenly faltered when he came to the speech beginning "Good sir, I do in friendship counsel you."

In the penultimate example above, which may be imagined as being included in a work of textual criticism, the location of the period warns against the incorrect assumption that the quoted line ends with a period. In the final example, however, which may be imagined as forming part of an account of an actor's performance, the exquisitely technical question of the position of the period is largely irrelevant and may therefore yield to "American practice."

BRITISH VERSUS AMERICAN STYLE

5.13   The British style of positioning periods and commas in relation to the closing quotation mark is based on the same logic that in the American system governs the placement of question marks and exclamation points: if they belong to the quoted material, they are placed within the closing quotation mark; if they belong to the including sentence as a whole, they are placed after the quotation mark. The British style is strongly advocated by some American language experts. In defense of nearly a century and a half of the American style, however, it may be said that it seems to have been working fairly well and has not resulted in serious miscommunication. Whereas there clearly is some risk with question marks and exclamation points, there seems little likelihood that readers will be misled concerning the period or comma. There may be some risk in such specialized material as textual criticism, but in that case authors and editors may take care to avoid the danger by alternative phrasing or by employing, in this exacting field, the exacting British system. In linguistic and philosophical works, specialized terms are regularly punctuated the British way, along with the use of single quotation marks (see 6.67, 6.74). With these qualifications, the University of Chicago Press continues to recommend the American style for periods and commas.

Periods with Parentheses or Brackets

5.14   When parentheses or brackets are used to enclose an independent sentence, the period belongs inside. When enclosed matter comes at the end of an including sentence, the period should be placed outside the parentheses or brackets:

> Florelli insisted on rewriting the paragraph. (I had encountered this intransigence on another occasion.)

> "She was determined never again to speak to him [Axelrod]."

If the enclosed matter is itself a grammatically complete sentence, its own terminal period is omitted:

> Poncifall (by this time Erika had left the room) looked dejectedly at the ring she had dropped into his hand.

> Poncifall looked at me with a desperate expression (Erika, it seems, had dropped a ring into his hand as she left the room).

Display Lines, Headings, and Legends

5.15   Omit the period after display lines, running heads, centered headings, sideheads set on separate lines, cut-in heads, column heads in tables, one-line superscriptions and legends, datelines heading communications, and signatures.

Ellipses and Abbreviations

5.16   For the use of ellipsis dots, or a series of periods, in faltering speech or to indicate omitted material in quotations see 10.39, 10.48–63. For the use of periods in abbreviations see chapter 14.

EXCLAMATION POINT

5.17   An exclamation point is used to mark an outcry or an emphatic or ironic comment. To avoid detracting from its effectiveness, however, the author should use this punctuation sparingly.

> Look out!

> Wait here!

> Your comment was certainly lacking in tact!

> The emperor, it seemed, had forgotten to notify his generals!

> Suddenly the ambassador perceived that all was lost!

5.18 A sentence that is essentially an exclamation may sometimes be cast in the form of a question. In that case the sentence may end either with an exclamation point or with a question mark, depending on the exclamatory intensity perceived or intended by the writer:

> How could you possibly believe that?
>
> How could you possibly believe that!

5.19 The use of an exclamation point as an editorial protest in quoted matter is strongly discouraged. The expression *sic* (in brackets) is preferred (see 10.66).

5.20 The exclamation point should be placed inside the quotation marks, parentheses, or brackets when it is part of the quoted or parenthetical matter; otherwise it should be placed outside. For a discussion of the conflict between exclamation point and comma in dialogue see 5.77.

> The woman cried, "Those men are beating that child!"
>
> Her husband replied—calmly—"It is no concern of mine"!
>
> Mrs. Laslow (I could have died!) repeated the whole story.
>
> Tichnick's angry reply, "I do not know the man!" took us all by surprise.
>
> "I offered to drive him to her flat, you know, but he became abusive and said, 'To hell with you, Drake!'"
>
> "Look here, Wellington, the duchess had no right to say, 'We're not at home'!"

QUESTION MARK

5.21 The question mark, or interrogation point, is used to mark a query or to express an editorial doubt:

> Who will represent the poor?
>
> The subject of the final essay was Thomas Kraftig (1610?–66), the last court jester to Baron Manfried von Katzhausen.

5.22 A question mark should be used at the end of a directly interrogative element that is part of a sentence (see also 5.27, 5.84–85):

> How can the two women be reconciled? was the question on everyone's mind.
>
> What for? he wondered.
>
> As she asked herself, How am I going to pay for this? she looked thoughtfully at John.

5.23 Whether or not a direct question should begin with a capital letter when it follows an introductory element is subjective and usually a matter for the author to decide. Generally, the more formal the question or the more attention it is intended to receive, the more usual it is to begin with a capital letter. If the question takes the form of quoted dialogue, of course, it must begin with a capital:

He wondered, what for?

Before deciding, ask yourself, will it work?

Before deciding, Farnswell asked the electrician, "Will it work?"

Pausing with his hand on the doorknob, Stetson bit his lip and wondered, What if I have been mistaken?

The question still to be decided was, Which of the two strategies would be less likely to provoke opposition?

5.24 When the question consists of a single word, such as *who, when, how,* or *why,* within a sentence, neither question mark nor capital letter need be used. In this case the word is sometimes italicized:

The question was no longer *how* but *when.*

He asked himself why.

(See also 10.38.)

5.25 A sentence essentially declarative or imperative in structure may become interrogative by the substitution of a question mark for the period:

This is your reply?   Wait here?

5.26 A request courteously disguised as a question should not be terminated by a question mark:

Will you please rush the manuscript to the publisher.

Will the audience please rise.

5.27 A question stated indirectly is not an interrogative and does not take a question mark:

Before going through with it, ask yourself whether it is worth the risk.

Plimpton was thoughtful enough to ask whether we had eaten.

How the two could be reconciled was the question on everyone's mind.

5.28 The question mark should be placed inside the quotation marks, parentheses, or brackets only when it is part of the quoted or parenthetical matter. For a discussion of the conflict between question mark and comma in dialogue see 5.77.

The ambassador asked, "Then why, sir, are these maneuvers occurring so close to our border?"

Why was Farragut trembling when he said, "I'm here to open an inquiry"?

When Crichton was introduced to the agent (had he met him before?), he turned to his host and winked.

If that was the case, why did she delay answering the governor until the morning of his departure (18 March)?

"What do you suppose he had in mind," inquired Newman, looking puzzled, "when he said, 'You are all greater fools than I thought'?"

"He looked at me for a long time," said Grant, "and then he said, 'Why have you bothered to tell me this, Peter?'"

COMMA

5.29 The comma, perhaps the most versatile of the punctuation marks, indicates the smallest interruption in continuity of thought or sentence structure. There are a few rules governing its use that have become almost obligatory. Aside from these, the use of the comma is mainly a matter of good judgment, with ease of reading the end in view.

Compound Sentences

5.30 When the clauses of a compound sentence are joined by a conjunction, a comma is usually placed before the conjunction unless the clauses are short and closely related:

> The two men quickly bolted the door, but the intruder had already entered through the window.
>
> Everyone present was startled by the news, and several senators who had been standing in the hall rushed into the room to hear the end of the announcement.
>
> Are we really interested in preserving law and order, or are we only interested in preserving our own privileges?
>
> Timothy played the guitar and Betty sang.

In contemporary writing, the comma is often omitted, but this open style should be followed only when there is little or no risk of misreading.

> Everyone present was startled by the news and several senators who had been standing in the hall rushed into the room to hear the end of the announcement.
>
> *but*
>
> Everyone present was startled by the arrival of the president, and several senators who had been standing in the hall rushed into the room to hear his announcement.

5.31   In a compound sentence composed of a series of short independent clauses, the last two of which are joined by a conjunction, commas should be placed between the clauses and before the conjunction (see also 5.57, 5.94):

> Harris presented the proposal to the governor, the governor discussed it with the senator, and the senator made an appointment with the president.

5.32   If the coordinate clauses themselves contain commas, semicolons may be used to separate them. (See the example in 5.93.)

5.33   Care should be taken to distinguish between a compound sentence (two or more independent clauses) and a sentence having a compound predicate (two or more verbs having the same subject). Preferably, the comma should not be used between the parts of a compound predicate:

> He had accompanied Sanford on his first expedition and had volunteered to remain alone at Port Royal.

> Mrs. Chapuis has been living in the building for over thirty years and is distraught over the possibility of now having to move.

> On Thursday morning Kelleher tried to see the mayor but was told the mayor was out of town.

A comma may be added, however, if misapprehension or difficult reading is considered likely without such punctuation.

Adverbial Clauses or Phrases

5.34   If a dependent clause is restrictive—that is, if it cannot be omitted without altering the meaning of the main clause—it should not be set off by commas. If it is nonrestrictive, it should be set off by commas:

> We shall agree to the proposal if you accept our conditions.

> Paul was astonished when he heard the terms.

> Charlotte and I stayed away from the piazza that afternoon because we feared that Babs might still be there.

> At last she arrived, when the food was cold.

> He didn't run, because he was afraid to move.

5.35   A dependent clause that follows the conjunction between two coordinate clauses of a compound sentence is usually followed, but not preceded, by a comma:

> Brighton examined the documents for over an hour, and had not Smedley intervened, he would undoubtedly have discovered the forgery.

In close punctuation, the dependent clause is both preceded and followed by a comma:

> In the morning, twenty angry parents assembled in Effingham's waiting room, and, if time had allowed, Effingham would have taken the occasion to depart through a back door.

In open punctuation, both commas might be omitted:

> Babs had gone to Naples with Guido, and when Baxter found out about it he flew into a rage.
> > *or even*
>
> Babs had gone to Naples with Guido and when Baxter found out about it he flew into a rage.

5.36   A dependent clause that precedes the main clause should usually be set off by a comma whether it is restrictive or nonrestrictive:

> If you accept our conditions, we shall agree to the proposal.

> Although he would have preferred to abstain, Paul voted for the proposal.

5.37   An adverbial phrase at the beginning of a sentence is frequently followed by a comma:

> After reading the note, Henrietta turned pale.

> Because of the unusual circumstances, the king sent his personal representative.

5.38   The comma is usually omitted after short introductory adverbial phrases unless misreading is likely:

> On Tuesday he tried to see the mayor.

> After breakfast the count mounted his horse.

> For thirty years the widow had refused to move.
> > *but*
>
> Before eating, the members of the committee met in the assembly room.

5.39   A comma should not be used after an introductory adverbial phrase that immediately precedes the verb it modifies:

> Out of the automobile stepped a short man in a blue suit.

> In the doorway stood a man with a summons.

5.40   An adverbial phrase or clause located between the subject and the verb should usually be set off by commas:

> Wolinski, after receiving his instructions, left immediately for Algiers.

> Morgenstern, in a manner that surprised us all, escorted the reporter to the door.

Adjectival Clauses or Phrases

5.41   An adjectival clause or phrase that follows a noun and restricts or limits the reference of the noun in a way that is essential to the meaning of the sentence should not be set off by commas; but an adjectival clause or phrase that is nonrestrictive or is purely descriptive, which could be dropped without changing the reference of the noun or the meaning of the sentence, is set off by commas:

> The report that the committee submitted was well documented.
>
> The report, which was well documented, was discussed with considerable emotion.
>
> McFetridge, sitting comfortably before the fire, slowly and ceremoniously opened his mail.
>
> The elderly woman sitting beside McFetridge was his nurse.
>
> Babs was seen entering the Villa Sorrento, where Tom was staying.

5.42 A distinction has traditionally been made between the relative pronouns *which* and *that,* the latter having long been regarded as introducing a restrictive clause, and the former, a nonrestrictive one. Although the distinction is often disregarded in contemporary writing, the careful writer and editor should bear in mind that such indifference may result in misreading or uncertainty, as in the sentence below.

> *Ambiguous:*
> The report which Marshall had tried to suppress was greeted with hilarity.
>
> *Which of the following is meant?*
> The report, which Marshall had tried to suppress, was greeted with hilarity.
> *or*
> The report that Marshall had tried to suppress was greeted with hilarity.

When the commas intended to set off a nonrestrictive clause are omitted, perhaps with the purpose of using *which* restrictively, the reader may well wonder whether the omission was inadvertent. Some uncertainty will persist.

Introductory Participial Phrases

5.43 An introductory participial phrase should be set off by a comma unless it immediately precedes the verb:

> Having forgotten to notify his generals, the king arrived on the battlefield alone.
>
> Exhausted by the morning's work, the archaeologists napped in the shade of the ancient wall.
>
> Judging from the correspondence, we may conclude that the two men never reached accord.
>
> Running along behind the wagon was the archduke himself!

Parenthetical Elements

5.44   Parenthetical elements that retain a close logical and syntactic relation to the rest of the sentence should be set off by commas; those whose relation to the rest of the sentence is more remote should be set off by dashes or parentheses (see 5.106–10, 5.123–25):

> Wilcox, it was believed, had turned the entire affair over to his partner.
>
> The Hooligan Report was, to say the least, a bombshell.
>
> The members of the commission were, generally speaking, disposed to reject innovative measures.
>
> Bardston—he is to be remembered for his outspokenness in the Wainscot affair—had asked for permission to address the assembly.
>
> The Wintermitten theory (it had already been dropped by some of its staunchest early supporters) was dealt a decisive blow by the Kringelmeyer experiments.

Interjections, Transitional Adverbs, and Similar Elements

5.45   Commas should be used to set off interjections, transitional adverbs or adverbial phrases, and similar elements that effect a distinct break in the continuity of thought (see also 5.44):

> Well, I'm afraid I was unprepared to find Virginia there.
>
> Yes, I admit that Benson's plan has gained a following.
>
> This, indeed, was exactly what Scali had feared would happen.
>
> That, after all, was more than Farnsworth could bear.
>
> On the other hand, the opposition had been conducted clumsily.
>
> All the test animals, therefore, were reexamined.
>
> Babbington, perhaps, had disclosed more than was necessary.
>
> We shall, however, take the matter up at a later date.
>
> Their credibility, consequently, has been seriously challenged.

When these elements are used in such a way that there is no real break in continuity and no call for any pause in reading, commas should be omitted:

> The storehouse was indeed empty.
>
> I therefore urge you all to remain loyal.
>
> All the test animals were therefore reexamined.
>
> Their credibility has consequently been seriously challenged.

> Wilcox was perhaps a bit too hasty in his judgment.
>
> Palmerston was in fact the chairman of the committee.

5.46   A comma is usually used after exclamatory *oh* or *ah,* but not after vocative *O:*

> Oh, what a dreadful sight!
>
> Ah, how charming!
>
> O mighty king!

So nearly have such expressions as *oh yes, oh yeah,* and *ah yes,* become irreducible units, that they are now, especially in dialogue, rendered without a comma:

> "Oh yeah? Who says?"
>
> "Ah yes," she said, arching an eyebrow. "Your mother!"

Direct Address

5.47   Use commas to set off words in direct address:

> Friends, I am not here to discuss personalities.
>
> The evidence, good people, contradicts my opponent.

In the following, *no sir* is treated almost as a single word, not as a negative followed by direct address:

> He looked at Sylvia in disbelief and said, "No sir! You're mistaken, my love!"

Sir may still, of course, be used in direct address:

> "No, sir, you must allow me to disagree!"

Display Lines

5.48   For aesthetic considerations, commas are usually omitted at the ends of display lines, such as titles, subtitles, centered headings, signatures, and datelines.

Appositives

5.49   Unless it is restrictive (see 5.50), a word, phrase, or clause that is in apposition to a noun is usually set off by commas (dashes or parentheses might also be used; see 5.108, 5.123):

The leader of the opposition, Senator Darkswain, had had an unaccountable change of heart.

Jeanne DeLor dedicated the book to her only sister, Margaret.

His second novel, a detective story with psychological and religious overtones, was said to have been influenced by the work of Dostoyevski.

My wife, Elizabeth, had written to our congressman.

The paintings by three impressionists, Monet, Sisley, and Pissarro, were arranged chronologically.

Sometimes an appositive is disguised by the conjunction *or:*

The steward, or farm manager, was an important functionary in medieval life.

A "zinc," or line engraving, will be made from the sketch.

An appositive phrase or clause may also begin with a repetition of the element being explained or amplified:

He had spent several hours discussing the strategy, a strategy that would, he hoped, eliminate the resistance.

5.50   If the appositive has a restrictive function, it is not set off by commas:

My son Michael was the first one to reply.

Walpole had borrowed the rusty bread slicer from his friend Teetering.

O'Neill's play *The Hairy Ape* was being revived.

The statement "The poor have much patience" is attributed to Count Précaire.

Coordinate Adjectives

5.51   Coordinate adjectives—that is, two or more adjectives each of which modifies the noun itself—are traditionally separated by commas:

Shelley had proved a faithful, sincere, and supportive friend.

Rocco had said that it was going to be a long, hot summer.

In the open style of punctuation, the comma between coordinate adjectives is often omitted:

She returned from her room with a small yellow parasol.

Moskowitz said over and over again that it was going to be a long dark winter.

5.52   If the first adjective modifies the idea expressed by the combination of the second adjective and the noun, no comma should be used:

He had no patience with the traditional political institutions of his country.

Blanche stood beside a tall blue spruce.

Complementary or Antithetical Elements

5.53   When two or more complementary or antithetical phrases refer to a single word following, the phrases should be separated from one another and from the following word by commas:

> This harsh, though at the same time logical, conclusion provoked resentment among those affected.

> The most provocative, if not the most important, part of the statement was saved until last.

> This road leads away from, rather than toward, your destination.

> He hopes to, and doubtless will, meet Caspar in Madrid.

5.54   An antithetical phrase beginning with *not* should usually be set off by commas if the phrase is not essential to the meaning of the modified element:

> The delegates had hoped that the mayor himself, not his assistant, would be present.

> White, not Thurgood, was the candidate to beat.

> Baum attended the lecture, not to hear what Morgan had to say, but to observe the reaction of his audience.
> > *but*
> Baum attended the lecture not so much to hear what Morgan had to say as to observe the reaction of his audience.

5.55   If an open style of punctuation is preferred, commas may be omitted between antithetical elements joined by *not . . . but* or *not only . . . but also:*

> Baum attended the lecture not to hear what Morgan had to say but to observe the reaction of his audience.

> Fournier had been appointed to the committee not only because of his experience but also because of an alliance he had formed with the chairman's cousin.

5.56   Interdependent antithetical clauses should be separated by a comma:

> The more he read about the incident, the greater became his resolve to get to the bottom of it.

> Say what you will, Senator Watson's bill leaves much to be desired.

> The higher Fisher climbed, the dizzier he felt.

Short antithetical phrases, however, should not be separated by commas:

> The more the merrier.
>
> The sooner the better.

Series and Lists

5.57 In a series consisting of three or more elements, the elements are separated by commas. When a conjunction joins the last two elements in a series, a comma is used before the conjunction (see also 5.31):

> Attending the conference were Farmer, Johnson, and Kendrick.
>
> We have a choice of copper, silver, or gold.
>
> The owner, the agent, and the tenant were having an acrimonious discussion.

5.58 When the elements in a series are very simple and are all joined by conjunctions, no commas should be used:

> I cannot remember whether the poem was written by Snodgrass or Shapiro or Brooks.

5.59 When the elements in a series are long and complex or involve internal punctuation, they should be separated by semicolons (see 5.94).

5.60 The use of *et cetera* (or *etcetera*), and especially its abbreviation, *etc.*, has long been discouraged in formal writing, although it is more acceptable in lists, tables, and parenthetical series. It is also part of the recommendation, however, that, when used, the term be set off by commas:

> The carpenter's saw, hammer, level, et cetera, were found at the bottom of the lake.
>
> The firm manufactured nuts, bolts, nails, wire, etc., at its plant on the Passaic River.

Such similar expressions as *and so on, and so forth,* which find more acceptance in formal writing, have also been customarily set off by commas:

> The carpenter's saw, hammer, level, and so forth, were found . . .

An alternative treatment for all such expressions is now also approved by the University of Chicago Press: *et cetera* and similar expressions may now be treated and punctuated like any other final element in a series.

The carpenter's saw, hammer, level, et cetera were found . . .

The carpenter's saw, hammer, level, and so forth were found . . .

Nuts, bolts, nails, wire, etc. were manufactured at the plant.

Nuts, bolts, nails, wire, and similar hardware were manufactured at the plant.

Wigs, false noses, false beards and eyelashes, costume jewelry, and other such things were scattered about the dressing room.

It is no longer obligatory to place a comma after such an expression, unless, of course, the comma is required for other grammatical reasons:

The firm's nuts, bolts, nails, wire, and so forth, formerly produced at its plant on the Passaic River, are now manufactured in Haiti.

5.61 Ordinarily, commas are not used following a series of items in a vertical list (see first list at 5.10). If the vertically listed items are phrases, especially long phrases, that grammatically complete the sentence containing them, commas may, but need not, be used. If commas are used, the last item is followed by a period:

The charges brought against Oxton included

leaving the scene of an accident involving injuries,
driving with a suspended driver's license,
driving while intoxicated.

That Is, Namely, and Similar Expressions

5.62 A comma is usually used after such expressions as *that is, namely, i.e.,* and *e.g.* The punctuation preceding such expressions should be determined by the magnitude of the break in continuity. If the break is minor, a comma should be used. If the break is greater than that signaled by a comma, a semicolon or an em dash may be used, or the expression and the element it introduces may be enclosed in parentheses:

He had put the question to several of his friends, namely, Jones, Burdick, and Fauntleroy.

The committee—that is, several of its more influential members—seemed disposed to reject the Brower Plan.

Keesler maneuvered the speaker into changing the course of the discussion; that is, he introduced a secondary issue about which the speaker had particularly strong feelings.

Bones from a variety of small animals (e.g., a squirrel, a cat, a pigeon, a muskrat) were found in the doctor's cabinet.

Mistaken Junction

5.63   A comma is sometimes necessary to prevent mistaken junction:

> To Anthony, Blake remained an enigma.
>
> Soon after, the conference was interrupted by a strange occurrence.
>
> She recognized the man who entered the room, and gasped.

Separating Identical or Similar Words

5.64   For ease of reading, it is sometimes desirable to separate two identical or closely similar words with a comma, even though the sense or grammatical construction does not require such separation:

> Let us march in, in twos.
>
> Whatever is, is good.
>   *but*
> He gave his life that that cause might prevail.

Similarly, a comma should be used to separate unrelated numbers:

> In 1992, 248 editors attended the convention.

Alternatively, revise the sentence to avoid the conjunction of unrelated numbers:

> Attending the convention in 1992 were 248 editors.

Titles, Addresses, and Dates

5.65   Although they are not necessary, commas may be used to set off a phrase indicating place of residence immediately following a person's name. If the phrase is in the middle of the sentence, it is both preceded and followed by a comma.

> She was a Farnsworth, from Texarkana, and married Andy Porkola, of Toronto.
>
> Mr. and Mrs. Osaki of Tokyo were also present.

The commas should always be omitted, however, in those cases, historical or political, in which the place-name has practically become a part of the person's name or is so closely associated with it as to render separation artificial or illogical:

> Clement of Alexandria
> Philip of Anjou

5.66 Use commas to set off words identifying a title or position following a person's name (see also 5.49):

> Merriwether Benson, former president of Acquisition Corporation, had been appointed to the commission.

5.67 Use commas to set off the individual elements in addresses and names of geographical places or political divisions:

> Please send all proofs to the author at 743 Olga Drive, Ashtabula, Ohio 44044, as soon as they arrive from the typesetter.

> The plane landed in Kampala, Uganda, that evening.

5.68 In the date style preferred by the University of Chicago Press, no commas are used to mark off the year:

> On 6 October 1924 Longo arrived in Bologna.

> The meetings were held in April 1967.

In the alternative style, however, commas must be used before and after the year:

> On October 6, 1924, Longo arrived in Bologna.

Elliptical Constructions

5.69 A comma is often used to indicate the omission, for brevity or convenience, of a word or words readily understood from the context:

> In Illinois there are seventeen such institutions; in Ohio, twenty-two; in Indiana, thirteen.

> Thousands rushed to serve him in victory; in defeat, none.

5.70 When, in spite of such omissions, the construction is clear enough without the commas (and the consequent semicolons), the simpler punctuation should be used:

> One committee member may be from Ohio, another from Pennsylvania, and a third from West Virginia.

> Ronald adored her and she him.

Quotations

5.71 Quotations—whether sentences, phrases, or words—incorporated within sentences are punctuated according to the grammatical function they perform within the sentence. Quotations serving as subjects, predicate nominatives, or predicate adjectives, for example, are not set off by commas unless they also serve as dialogue (see 5.74):

"Under no circumstances" was her rather surprising reply.

Morgenstern's favorite evasion was "If only I had the time!"

The ambassador was "not available for comment."

Spivekovski reported that Morgenstern was not only "indisposed" but also "in a bad temper."

Note that if the quotation is a sentence, it ordinarily begins with a capital letter; if it is a fragment, it does not.

5.72 As is the case with appositives generally, appositives consisting of or containing quotations are not set off by commas if they are restrictive but are set off by commas if they are nonrestrictive:

Smiling shyly, Anna talked with our friend "the neoclassical scholar."

Morgenstern, "that irascible invalid," was waiting for them at the table.

Marion observed Wilkins, the tall, sarcastic lawyer who "annoyed everyone," entering the room.

If the quotation used as an appositive is a complete sentence, its terminal punctuation is replaced by a comma if the appositive is nonrestrictive and simply omitted if the quotation is restrictive:

With yet another aphorism, "Brevity is the soul of wit," Nunbush launched himself into a long and dreary discourse.

The aphorism "Brevity is the soul of wit" was lost on Morgenstern, who went on about Durwood's faux pas until everyone was weary of it.

5.73 Quotations used as objects are not set off by commas unless they are also used as dialogue (see 5.75–77):

Fiona was amused by the "elderly bearded bathers."

Fiona and her cousin watched the "bearded bathers" enter the "choppy, chilly" water.

5.74 A quotation functioning as a predicate nominative may sometimes also be considered dialogue, in which case it is set off by a comma:

When Babs asked Morgenstern to drive her to the piazza, his reply was, "Ah my dear, if only I had the time!"

5.75 Quoted material in the form of dialogue or conversation is usually the direct object of a transitive verb denoting speaking or thinking, and although direct objects are ordinarily not set off by commas, dialogue traditionally is. The following examples illustrate the principles governing the use of commas to set off dialogue: If the quotation follows the introductory material, as in the first example, the comma is placed at the end of the introduction. If, as in the next two examples, the quotation comes first, the comma precedes the closing quotation mark. Finally, if the introductory material interrupts the quotation, as in the fourth example, a comma precedes the closing quotation mark of the first part of the quotation, and another comma comes at the end of the intervening introduction.

> Vera said calmly, "I've no idea what you mean."
>
> "Morgenstern refuses to drive us home," replied Eberly.
>
> "They're all fools," Vera told herself.
>
> "I'm afraid," suggested Croft, "that we've offended Morgenstern some-how."
>
> "I don't care if we have," thought Vera, although she said nothing.

Should the introductory material intervene between complex coordinate clauses of conversational material, it may be helpful, although not necessary, to follow the introduction with a semicolon:

> "Taking Peter by the hand, Amy tugged him along toward Virginia and made him speak to her," said Charlotte, with a crooked smile; "but Virginia was furious and abruptly turned away."

A comma may also be used in such a case.

5.76 As illustrated in two of the examples above, thought or interior dialogue, like actual dialogue, may be set off by commas. Unspoken or imagined dialogue may be similarly treated (but see also 10.42–47).

> I should have said, "Not with me, you won't!"
>
> I bet she's saying to him right now, "Morgenstern thinks he's too good for us."
>
> Barnacle heard a loud crash and told himself, "Viola's drunk again!"

5.77 Note that when a quotation preceding the introductory element is a question or an exclamation, a question mark or an exclamation point replaces the comma inside the closing quotation mark:

> "Not with me, you won't!" she said, glaring furiously.
>
> "What makes you think I meant you?" he said in an uncertain voice.

5.78 Indirect discourse should not be set off from the introductory clause:

> Morgenstern had said that they were all behaving disgracefully.

5.79 A colon should be used before a long, formal quotation. (For more on the use of other punctuation with quotation marks see under individual marks. For a detailed discussion of quotations see chapter 10.)

Maxims, Proverbs, and Other Familiar Expressions

5.80 Commas are occasionally used to set off maxims, proverbs, mottoes, and other familiar expressions. The governing principles are similar to those applicable to quotations (5.71–78).

Melchior was fond of using the motto All for one and one for all.

"A rolling stone gathers no moss" appeared to be Tom's favorite maxim.

Jasmine's favorite motto was "All work and no play . . ."

They assumed that they were obliged to follow the rule No music after midnight.

Tom was convinced that a rolling stone gathers no moss.

Tom's favorite proverb, "A rolling stone gathers no moss," was driving his wife insane.

Edna winced when Tom, predictably, said, "A rolling stone gathers no moss."

She had come to despise the proverb A rolling stone gathers no moss.

A rolling stone, it is said, gathers no moss.

It is true, Birds of a feather flock together.

5.81   Note that maxims and similar expressions are sometimes enclosed in quotation marks and sometimes not. If the maxim takes the form of dialogue, of course, it should be enclosed in quotation marks, and if there is some risk of confusion or misreading, even momentary, quotation marks may be helpful (as, perhaps, in the second example in 5.80). Otherwise, the choice is up to the author, but an effort should be made to be consistent, at least within a single work.

5.82   Note also that maxims usually begin with a capital letter unless they follow the conjunction *that,* in which case they usually begin lower-case.

5.83   Careful discrimination must sometimes be used in the treatment of appositive maxims. In the first example below, a complete thought is expressed (albeit less specifically) without the maxim, and the nonrestrictive maxim is therefore set off by a comma. In the slightly revised version in the second example, the maxim, although less obviously so, is still nonrestrictive. But in the final example the maxim is clearly restrictive and is therefore not set off by a comma.

> She made excessive use of an old saying, Politics makes strange bedfellows.
>
> You know the old saying, Politics makes strange bedfellows.
>
> Rushmore had grown weary of the maxim Less is more.

Questions

5.84   When a direct question that is included within another sentence follows the element that introduces it, the question is usually set off by a comma (see also 5.22–24). When the question comes first, however, the question mark replaces the comma.

> Suddenly he asked himself, why shouldn't I?

> What troubled Babs was, when had Anselm discovered that the key was missing?
> *but*
> Why shouldn't I? he suddenly asked himself.

5.85 An indirect question is not set off from the rest of the sentence by a comma:

> Suddenly Anselm asked himself why he shouldn't tell her.

> Babs wondered uneasily when Anselm had discovered the key was missing.

> When Anselm had discovered the key was missing was a question that weighed heavily on Babs's mind.

Use with Other Punctuation

5.86 When the context calls for a comma at the end of material enclosed in quotation marks, parentheses, or brackets, the comma should be placed inside the quotation marks but outside the parentheses or brackets (see also 5.71–77):

> See Brighton's comments on "political expedience," which may be found elsewhere in this volume.

> Here he gives a belated, though stilted (and somewhat obscure), exposition of the subject.

> Although he rejected the first proposal (he could not have done otherwise without compromising his basic position), he was careful to make it clear that he was open to further negotiations.

> "Conrad ordered [Martin], whose face was now quite flushed, to return to his post."

5.87 In close textual studies and on similar rare occasions when the inclusion of a comma inside the closing quotation mark may cause confusion, the comma may be placed outside the quotation mark (see also 5.12–13):

> Following the phrase "silently disrobing", an odd typographical error occurs.

When a comma is required after a possessive noun that ends with an apostrophe, the comma follows the apostrophe:

> Were the drawings the architects', or were they yours?

5.88 Commas should not be used with dashes except when necessary to separate quoted material from the words that identify the speaker (see 5.111–12).

SEMICOLON

5.89 Though the semicolon is less frequently employed today than in the past, it is still occasionally useful to mark a more important break in sentence flow than that marked by a comma. It should always be used between the two parts of a compound sentence (independent, or coordinate, clauses) when they are not connected by a conjunction:

> The controversial portrait had been removed from the entrance hall; in its place had been hung a realistic landscape.

Coordinate clauses may, of course, be separated into individual sentences.

5.90 The following words are considered adverbs rather than conjunctions and should therefore be preceded by a semicolon when used transitionally between clauses of a compound sentence: *then, however, thus, hence, indeed, accordingly, besides, therefore.* The adverb is usually followed by a comma, but if there is no risk of misreading, and if a pause is not desired, the comma may be omitted.

> The controversial portrait had been removed from the entrance hall; indeed, in its place had been hung a realistic landscape.

> Partridge had heard the argument before; thus, he turned his back on Fenton and reiterated his decision.

> Mildred says she intends to go to Europe this summer; however, she has made no definite plans.

> Mittelbach had forgotten his reeds; hence he was prevented from jamming with the others.

5.91 The coordinate clauses may, in this case also, be converted into separate sentences. When this is done, some editors and writers prefer not to begin the second sentence with the transitional adverb and therefore place the adverb inside the sentence. Either style is acceptable.

> The controversial portrait had been removed from the entrance hall. Indeed, in its place had been hung a realistic landscape.
> *or*
> . . . In its place, indeed, had been hung a realistic landscape.

> Partridge had heard the argument before. Thus he turned his back on Fenton and reiterated his decision.
> *or*
> . . . He thus turned . . .

> Mildred says she intends to go to Europe this summer. However, she has made no definite plans.
> *or*
> . . . She has, however, made no definite plans.

5.92 In contemporary usage, clauses introduced by the transitional adverbs *yet* and *so* are preceded by a comma:

Elizabeth was out of the office when I called, so I left a message.

Frobisher had always assured his grandson that the house would be his, yet there was no provision for this in the will.

5.93   If the clauses of a compound sentence are very long or are themselves subdivided by commas, a semicolon may be used between them even if they are joined by a conjunction:

Margaret, who had already decided that she would ask the question at the first opportunity, tried to catch the director's attention as he passed through the anteroom; but the noisy group of people accompanying the director prevented him from noticing her.

5.94   When items in a series are long and complex or involve internal punctuation, they should be separated by semicolons for the sake of clarity:

The membership of the international commission was as follows: France, 4; Germany, 5; Great Britain, 1; Italy, 3; the United States, 7.

The defendant, in an attempt to mitigate his sentence, pleaded that he had been despondent over the death of his wife; that he had lost his job under particularly humiliating circumstances; that his landlady—whom, incidentally, he had once saved from attack—had threatened to have him evicted; that he had not eaten for several days; and that he had, in this weakened condition, been unduly affected by an alcoholic beverage.

5.95   A semicolon may be used before an expression such as *that is, namely, i.e., e.g.* if the break in continuity is greater than that signaled by a comma. For comparative examples see 5.62.

5.96   The semicolon should be placed outside quotation marks or parentheses. When the matter quoted ends with a semicolon, that semicolon is dropped:

Curtis assumed that everyone in the room had read "Mr. Prokharchin"; he alluded to it several times during the discussion.

Ambassador Porkola had hoped that the committee would take up the question (several members had assured him privately that they favored such a move); but at the end of August the committee adjourned without having considered it.

COLON

Relating Clauses

5.97   The colon is used to mark a break in grammatical construction equivalent to that marked by a semicolon, but the colon emphasizes the content relation between the separated elements. The colon is used, for example, to indicate a sequence in thought between two clauses that form a single sentence or to separate one clause from a second clause that contains an illustration or amplification of the first:

> The officials had been in conference most of the night: this may account for their surly treatment of the reporters the next morning.

> Many of the policemen held additional jobs: thirteen of them, for example, doubled as cabdrivers.

In contemporary usage, however, such clauses are frequently separated by a semicolon (see 5.89) or are treated as separate sentences:

> The officials had been in conference most of the night; this may account for their surly treatment of the reporters the next morning.

> Many of the policemen held additional jobs; thirteen of them, for example, doubled as cabdrivers.

> Many of the policemen held additional jobs. Thirteen of them, for example, doubled as cabdrivers.

Introducing Statements, Quotations, or Lists

5.98   A colon is used to introduce a formal statement, an extract, or a speech in dialogue:

> The rule may be stated thus: Always . . .

> We quote from the address: "It now seems appropriate . . .

> MICHAEL: The incident has already been reported.
> TIMOTHY: Then, sir, all is lost!

5.99   A colon is commonly used to introduce a list or a series:

> Binghamton's study included the three most critical areas: McBurney Point, Rockland, and Effingham.

If the list or series is introduced by an expression such as *namely, for instance, for example,* or *that is,* a colon should not be used unless the series consists of one or more grammatically complete clauses.

> Binghamton's study included the three most critical areas, namely, McBurney Point, Rockland, and Effingham.

> For example: Morton had raised French poodles for many years; Gilbert disliked French poodles intensely; Gilbert and Morton seldom looked each other in the eye.

5.100   A colon should not be used to introduce a list that is the complement or object of an element in the introductory statement:

> Madame Mirceau had taken care to (1) make facsimiles of all the documents, (2) deliver them to the foreign minister's office, and (3) leave the country.

> The metals excluded were
>
> molybdenum
> mercury
> manganese
> magnesium
>
> Dr. Brandeis had requested wine, books, bricks, and mortar.

5.101   The terms *as follows* and *the following* require a colon if followed directly by the illustrating or enumerated items or if the introducing clause is incomplete without such items:

> The steps are as follows:
>
> 1. Tie the string to the green pole and . . .

If the introducing statement is complete, however, and is followed by one or more other complete sentences, a period may be used:

> An outline of the procedure follows. Note that care was taken to eliminate the effect of temperature variation.
>
> 1. Identical amounts of the compound were placed . . .

5.102   A colon should follow a speaker's introductory remark addressed to the chair or the audience:

> Ladies and Gentlemen:

5.103   If the material introduced by a colon consists of more than one sentence, or if it is a formal statement, a quotation, or a speech in dialogue, it should begin with a capital letter. Otherwise it may begin with a lowercase letter:

> To Henrietta, there seemed no possibility of waking from her nightmare: If she were to reveal what was in the letter, her reputation would be ruined and her marriage at an end. On the other hand, if she were to remain silent, her husband would be in mortal danger.
>
> Henrietta's distress seemed insupportable: not only had her lover abandoned her at the last moment, but she had already sent a note to her husband announcing her intention of leaving him.
>
> I wish only to state the following: Anyone found in possession of forged papers will immediately be arrested.

Use with Other Punctuation

5.104   The colon should be placed outside quotation marks or parentheses. When matter ending with a colon is quoted, that colon is dropped:

> Kego had three objections to "Filmore's Summer": it was contrived; the characters were flat; the dialogue was unrealistic.

Herschel was puzzled by one of the changes noted in the behavior of the experimental animals (rhesus monkeys): all the monkeys had become hypersensitive to sound.

DASH

5.105 There are several kinds of dashes, differing in length. There are en dashes, em dashes, and 2- and 3-em dashes (see 5.115–19). Each kind of dash has its own uses. The most commonly used is the em dash. In the following material, the em dash is referred to simply as "the dash." The other dashes are identified.

Sudden Breaks and Abrupt Changes

5.106 A dash or a pair of dashes is used to denote a sudden break in thought that causes an abrupt change in sentence structure (see also 5.44, 5.123–25, 10.39):

"Will he—can he—obtain the necessary signatures?" Mills said pointedly.

The Platonic world of the static and the Hegelian world of process—how great the contrast!

Consensus—that was the will-o'-the-wisp he doggedly pursued.

The chancellor—he had been awake half the night waiting in vain for a reply—came down to breakfast in an angry mood.

There came a time—let us say, for convenience, with Herodotus and Thucydides—when this attention to actions was conscious and deliberate.

The dash is also used in dialogue to indicate that the speech of one person has been interrupted by another:

"Well, I don't know," he began tentatively. "I thought I might—"
"Might what?" she interrupted savagely. "Might what?"

Amplifying, Explanatory, and Digressive Elements

5.107 An element added to give emphasis or explanation by expanding a phrase occurring in the main clause may be introduced by a dash. If the author prefers, a comma may also be used to set off such an element (see 5.49).

He had spent several hours carefully explaining the operation—an operation that would, he hoped, put an end to the resistance.

Marsot finally conceded that the plan was bold and unusual—bold and unusual in the sense that . . .

185

5.108 A defining or enumerating complementary element that is added to or inserted in a sentence may be set off by dashes. Such an element may also, however, be set off by commas (see 5.49); enclosed in parentheses (see 5.123); or—at the end of a sentence—introduced by a colon (see 5.97–101):

> He could forgive every insult but the last—the snub by his former office boy, Tim Warren.

> It was to the so-called battered child syndrome—a diverse array of symptoms indicating repeated physical abuse of the child—that he then began to turn his attention.

> The influence of three impressionists—Monet, Sisley, and Degas—can clearly be seen in his early development as a painter.

5.109 A dash may be used before an expression such as *that is, namely, i.e.,* or *e.g.* if the break in continuity is greater than that signaled by a comma. For comparative examples see 5.62.

5.110 In sentences having several elements as referents of a collective pronoun that is the subject of the main, summarizing clause, the summarizing clause is preceded by a dash:

> Ives, Stravinsky, and Bartók—these were the composers he most admired.

> Klingston, who first conceived the idea; Barber, who organized the fund-raising campaign; and West, who conducted the investigation—those were the women most responsible for the movement's early success.

> Broken promises, petty rivalries, and police harassment—such were the obstacles he encountered.

> Winograd, Burton, Kravitz, Johnson—all were astounded by the chair's resignation.

> Darkness, thunder, a sudden scream—nothing alarmed the child.

Sometimes the author, for a particular effect, may abandon the collective pronoun in favor of a nonspecific pronoun:

> Darkness, thunder, or lightning—it mattered little to Carrie.

Use with Other Punctuation

5.111 If the context calls for a dash where a comma would ordinarily separate two clauses, the comma should be omitted:

> Because the data had not yet been completely analyzed—the reason for this will be discussed later—the publication of the report was delayed.

5.112 A comma should be used after a dash, however, to separate quoted material from the words that identify the speaker:

"I assure you, there will never be—," Sylvia began, but Mark interrupted her.

5.113 When a parenthetical element set off by dashes itself requires a question mark or an exclamation point, such punctuation may be retained before the second dash:

> All at once Cartwright—can he have been out of his mind?—shook his fist in the ambassador's face.

> Later that night Alexandra—what an extraordinary woman she was!—rode alone to Bucharest to warn the duke.

5.114 To avoid confusion, no more than a single dash or pair of dashes should be used in a sentence.

En Dash

5.115 The en dash is half the length of an em dash and longer than a hyphen:

> em dash: —   en dash: –   hyphen: -

(In typing, a hyphen is used for an en dash, two hyphens for an em dash; in preparing a manuscript for the printer, the editor will indicate which hyphens are to be set as en dashes by marking them $\frac{1}{N}$ or $\overset{N}{\sim}$; see 2.76 and pp. 112 and 113.) The principal use of the en dash is to connect continuing, or inclusive, numbers—dates, time, or reference numbers. (The hyphen, not the en dash, is used between numbers that are not inclusive; see 5.120.)

> 1968–72   10:00 A.M.–5:00 P.M.
> May–June 1967   pp. 38–45   John 4:3–6:2
> 13 May 1965–9 June 1966
>   *but*
> from 1968 to 1972 (*never* from 1968–72)
> from May to June 1967
> between 1968 and 1970 (*never* between 1968–70)
> between 10:00 A.M. and 5:00 P.M.

When the concluding date of an expression denoting a duration of time is in the indeterminate future, the en dash alone follows the first number:

> In Professor Lach's magnum opus, *Asia in the Making of Europe* (1965–) . . .

> John Doe (1940–); *or better,* John Doe (b. 1940)

5.116 Periods or seasons extending over parts of two successive calendar years may be indicated by either an en dash or a solidus (slant line; see 5.122):

winter of 1944–45	fiscal year 1991–92	362–361 B.C.
winter 1944/45	fiscal year 1991/92	362/361 B.C.

5.117 The en dash is also used in place of a hyphen in a compound adjective when one of the elements of the adjective is an open compound (such as *New York*) or when two or more of the elements are hyphenated compounds:

> New York–London flight
> post–Civil War period
> quasi-public–quasi-judicial body
> *but*
> non-English-speaking countries
> not-to-be-forgotten moments

(For hyphenated compounds see 6.32–42 and table 6.1.)

2-Em and 3-Em Dashes

5.118 A 2-em dash is used to indicate missing letters. No space appears between the dash and the existing part of the word, but where the dash represents the end of a word, the normal word space follows it:

> We ha—— a copy in the library.
>
> H——h [Hirsch?]

(For marking the 2-em dash see 2.75.)

5.119 A 3-em dash (with space on each side) is used to denote a whole word omitted or to be supplied; it is also used in bibliographies to represent the same author named in the preceding item (see 15.66–68).

> A vessel that left the ——— in July . . .

(For marking the 3-em dash see 2.75.)

HYPHEN

5.120 The hyphen is used to separate numbers that are not inclusive, such as telephone numbers and social security numbers:

> (1-965) 386-1110, 1-965 386-1110, *or* 1-965-386-1110
> 783-45-0927

5.121 The use of the hyphen in compound words and in word division is discussed in chapter 6, especially 6.32–42, 6.43–58, and table 6.1.

SOLIDUS

5.122 Related to the dash and the hyphen in form and function is the *solidus* (/), also known as the *slash, slant,* or *virgule*. As has been noted above (5.116), the solidus is sometimes used to indicate a period extending over portions of two calendar years. It may also be used to indicate alternatives (and/or, inside/outside, free trade/protectionism) and alternative word forms or spellings (Hercules/Heracles). (For the use of the solidus in poetry in the run of text see 10.11; in fractions, 13.29–30; in abbreviations, 14.50, 14.55.)

PARENTHESES

5.123 Parentheses, like commas and dashes, may set off amplifying, explanatory, or digressive elements. If such parenthetical elements retain a close logical relation to the rest of the sentence, commas should be used. If the logical relation is more remote, dashes or parentheses should be used (see 5.8, 5.44, 5.106–10):

> The disagreement between the two men (its origins have been discussed by Westover in considerable detail) ultimately destroyed the organization.

> The final sample that we collected (under extremely difficult conditions) contained an unexpected impurity.

> The Williamsport incident (Martin still turns pale at the mention of it) was unquestionably without precedent.

> Wexford's analysis (see p. 84) was more to the point.

> He had long suspected that the inert gases (helium, neon, argon, krypton, xenon, radon) could be used to produce a similar effect.

5.124 A combination of parentheses and dashes may be used to distinguish two overlapping parenthetical elements, each of which represents a decided break in sentence continuity:

> The Whipplesworth conference—it had already been interrupted by three demonstrations (the last bordering on violence)—was adjourned without an agreement having been reached.

> He meant—I take this to be the (somewhat obscure) sense of his speech—that . . .

5.125 An expression such as *that is, namely, i.e., e.g.,* and the element it introduces, may be enclosed in parentheses if the break in continuity is greater than that signaled by a comma. (For comparative examples see 5.62.)

5.126 Use parentheses to enclose numerals or letters marking divisions or enumerations run into the text:

He had, in effect, discovered a remarkable similarity among (1) Strigiformes, (2) Caprimulgiformes, and (3) Psittaciformes.

A hyphen is used to show *(a)* the combination of two or more words into a single term representing a new idea; *(b)* the division of a word at the end of a line; *(c)* a part of a word (prefix, suffix, or root); and *(d)* the division of a word into syllables.

5.127 Commas, semicolons, colons, and dashes should be dropped before a closing parenthesis. Such punctuation, moreover, should not be used before an opening parenthesis unless the parentheses are used to mark divisions or enumerations run into the text (see 5.126). If required by the context, other nonterminal punctuation should follow the closing parenthesis. (For more regarding the use of other punctuation with parentheses, and for examples, see under individual marks: 5.14, 5.20, 5.28. For use of the single parenthesis with figures and letters in outline style see 8.79.)

BRACKETS

5.128 Brackets (sometimes called square brackets) are used to enclose editorial interpolations, corrections (but see also 10.66), explanations, translations, or comments in quoted material:

"These [the free-silver Democrats] asserted that the artificial ratio could be maintained indefinitely."

"Despite the damaging evidence that had been brought to light [by Simpson and his supporters], Fernandez continued to believe in his friend's innocence."

"As the Italian [*sic*] Dante Gabriel Ros[s]etti is reported to have said, . . ."

[This was written, it should be remembered, before Zantoni's discovery of the Driscoll manuscript.—Editor]

(For further discussion of the use of brackets with quoted material see 10.62, 10.64–68.)

5.129 Brackets should be used as parentheses within parentheses (but see also 5.124):

This thesis has been denied by at least one recognized authority (see William B. Davis, *The Second Irrawaddy Discoveries* [New York: Babbington Press, 1961], pp. 74–82).

During a prolonged visit to Australia, Glueck and an assistant (James Green, who was later to make his own study of a flightless bird [the kiwi] in New Zealand) spent several difficult months observing the survival behavior of cassowaries and emus.

(For the use of brackets in mathematics see 13.26.)

5.130 Brackets may also be used to enclose the phonetic transcription of a word:

> He attributed the light to the phenomenon called gegenschein [gā´-gən-shīn´].

5.131 Such phrases as *To be continued* and *Continued from . . .* may be placed within brackets (or parentheses) and set in italics and smaller type:

> *[Continued from page 138]*
> *[To be concluded]*

5.132 For the use of brackets with other punctuation see under individual marks.

QUOTATION MARKS

5.133 The use of quotation marks to set off direct discourse and quoted matter is explained in chapter 10, and their use with single words or phrases to signal some special usage is discussed in chapter 6. Foreign quotation marks are discussed in chapter 9. The use of quotation marks with other punctuation is treated under various marks of punctuation in this chapter.

MULTIPLE PUNCTUATION

5.134 The use of more than one mark of punctuation at the same location in a sentence (multiple punctuation) is, for the most part, limited to instances involving quotation marks, parentheses, brackets, or dashes (see 5.11–14, 5.20, 5.28, 5.77, 5.86–88, 5.111–13). An abbreviating period, however, is never omitted before a mark of sentence punctuation unless the latter is the period terminating the sentence:

> O. D., who had apparently just heard the report, came over to our table in great agitation.

> The study was funded by Mulvehill & Co.

5.135 When more than one mark of punctuation (excepting quotation marks, parentheses, brackets, and sometimes dashes) is called for at one location in a sentence, only the stronger or more necessary mark is retained. In the first sentence below, the comma yields to the question mark; in the second, the period ending the quoted sentence is omitted in deference to the question mark terminating the enclosing sentence.

> "Have you read the platform?" asked Mark.

> What had she meant when she said, "The foot now wears a different shoe"?

191

5.136   In the following interrogative sentence incorporating a quoted exclamatory sentence, the question is conveyed by the construction, and a terminal question mark following the exclamation point and the closing quotation mark is therefore unnecessary:

> Who shouted, "Up the establishment!"

A sentence that is at once interrogative and exclamatory may be so constructed that the question is implicit; in that case, only the less obvious mark of punctuation is needed:

> When will you trust me!

If neither interrogation nor exclamation is apparent from the construction of a sentence, and yet both are intended, the author may wish to end the sentence with a question mark and an exclamation point:

> That is your answer?!

So long as its use is rare, such double punctuation may occasionally be effective. Consider the range of expressiveness achieved by the following changes in punctuation:

> Go home.
> Go home!
> Go home?
> Go home?!

FOR FURTHER REFERENCE

5.137   The interested reader will find related information on punctuation theory in Perrin's *Reference Handbook of Grammar and Usage*.

6 *Spelling and Distinctive Treatment of Words*

INTRODUCTION

6.1   For general matters of spelling the University of Chicago Press recommends use of *Webster's Third New International Dictionary* and its chief abridgment, *Merriam-Webster's Collegiate Dictionary.* If two or more spellings of a word are given, the first listed is the one preferred in Press publications, and if the *Collegiate* disagrees with the *Third International* (as sometimes happens), follow the *Collegiate,* since it is revised more frequently and represents the latest lexical research.

6.2   Although the University of Chicago press uses Webster as its spelling authority, the use of such other standard dictionaries as the *American Heritage Dictionary* and the *Random House Dictionary of the English Language* is also acceptable. One source should be used consistently, of course, at least throughout a single work.

6.3   Having begun with the above advice, a chapter on spelling in a style manual may disregard most of the dozens or hundreds of questions about spelling that arise in the course of writing or editing a serious book, for the answers may be found in a standard dictionary. There are some spelling matters, however, that a dictionary does not cover or on which its guidance is obscure, and it is to these that the present chapter is addressed.

6.4   The first part of the chapter is concerned with actual questions of spelling; the second part, with related questions about distinctive treatment of words and phrases, especially the use of italics and quotation marks. The chapter ends with a tabulation of some rules for spelling compound words (table 6.1).

SPELLING

Preferences of Special Groups

BRITISH VERSUS AMERICAN SPELLING

6.5   The practice of the University of Chicago Press is generally to change British spelling to American (e.g., *colour* to *color*) in books published under its imprint and composed in the United States. This is done because American compositors, American proofreaders, and American editors are far more likely to catch inconsistencies when they are departures from normal American spellings than when they are departures from less familiar British forms. Retaining British orthography is particularly perilous when heavy editing is called for.

SPELLINGS PECULIAR TO PARTICULAR DISCIPLINES

6.6   Although University of Chicago Press practice, as noted above, is to follow Webster's first-listed form for words with variant spellings, the variant may carry special connotations within certain disciplines, and these should be respected. For example, although *archaeology* is the first spelling given for the name of that science, and the one generally preferred, some specialists in North American studies insist on the spelling *archeology* when it is used in connection with their work. So, too, many bankers, as well as students of the banking and home-loan businesses, traditionally spell the word *installment* with one *l—instalment*—an acceptable variant that editors should feel no compulsion to change.

Plurals

GENERAL RULES

6.7   The plurals of most nouns are formed by the addition of *s* or *es*. When the noun ends in soft *ch* or in *s, sh, j, x,* or *z,* the plural inflection is *es*.

      thumbs   churches   fixes   ratios   boys

Plurals of nouns ending in *y* preceded by a consonant are formed by replacing the *y* with *ies:*

babies   navies   specialties

The plurals of some nouns are formed irregularly:

women   leaves   cattle   sheep

COMPOUND NOUNS

6.8   Closed, or solid, compound nouns—that is, compound nouns written as one word—form their plurals in the usual way. Solid compounds ending with the suffix *ful* generally take the inflection at the end of that suffix, although some dictionaries give as an alternative the inflection of the root word:

bagfuls, bagsful   cupfuls, cupsful

6.9   Hyphenated and open compounds are regularly made plural by the addition of the plural inflection to the element that is subject to the change in number:

fathers-in-law	coups d'état
sergeants-at-arms	masters of art
courts-martial	
doctors of philosophy	*but* tam-o'-shanters

PLURALS IN DICTIONARIES

6.10   Standard dictionaries provide plural forms for listed nouns when those plurals are formed irregularly, including nouns with such troublesome endings as *o* and *ey*. Special cases usually not covered by dictionaries are discussed in the following paragraphs.

PROPER NOUNS

6.11   Names of persons and other proper nouns form the plural in the usual way, by adding *s* or *es:*

all the Edwards and Charleses
the Alexanders of modern times
flouting the Joneses
two Walden Ponds
rainy Sundays
three Marys

Note that the apostrophe is never used to denote the plural of a personal name: "The Schumachers left for London on Friday" (*not* "The Schumacher's . . .").

6.12   Exceptions to the general rule on adding *s* or *es* sometimes have to be made when the ending would suggest a false pronunciation. French names ending in an unpronounced *s, z,* or *x,* for example, are best left uninflected in the plural:

> the six King Georges of England and the sixteen King Louis (*not* Louises) of France
>
> the two Dumas, father and son
>
> There are Charlevoix both in Michigan and in France.

6.13   Also, when following the general rule for plurals results in what some may consider awkward formations—as, for instance, with polysyllabic Spanish names ending in sibilants—it is often best to recast the sentence to avoid the plural forms. Instead of "four El Grecos and seven Velasquezes" one could just as well write "four paintings by El Greco and seven by Velasquez."

ITALICIZED WORDS

6.14   If names of newspapers, titles of books, or other italicized names that are themselves singular in form are used in the plural, the inflectional ending is preferably set in roman:

> She bought two *Chicago Tribune*s and three *Milwaukee Journal*s.
>
> FitzGerald actually wrote three *Rubaiyat*s.

If the italicized name is itself plural, however, no additional inflectional ending is required:

> She also bought three *New York Times.*

6.15   The plural of an italicized foreign word referred to as a word also ends with a roman *s:*

> The stanza contains three *cheval*s.

The plural forms of foreign words are of course set entirely in italics:

Blume, Blumen	*rivière, rivières*
kolkhoz, kolkhozy	*halakah, halakoth*
cheval, chevaux	*spreekwijze, spreekwijzen*

LETTERS, NOUN COINAGES, NUMBERS, AND ABBREVIATIONS

6.16   So far as it can be done without confusion, single or multiple letters, hyphenated coinages, and numbers used as nouns (whether spelled out or in numerals) form the plural by adding *s* alone (see also 6.82):

*x*s and *y*s	all SOSs
the three Rs	several YMCAs and AYHs
thank-you-ma'ams	CODs and IOUs
in twos and threes	the early 1920s

Not unexpectedly, there are some exceptions to this rule. The plurals of abbreviations for *page, note,* and *line,* for example, are formed by doubling the letter: p., pp.; n., nn.; l., ll. Note also that in the plural abbreviation for *manuscript* the added *s* is a capital (MS, MSS).

6.17 Abbreviations having more than one period, such as M.D. and Ph.D., often form their plurals by the addition of an apostrophe and an *s*. Noun abbreviations with only one (terminal) period usually form their plurals by the addition of *s* before the period. (See also 14.15.)

M.A.'s and Ph.D.'s	ed., eds.
vol., vols.	yr., yrs.

If the addition of an *s* to an abbreviation forms a different abbreviation (Mr., Mrs., for example), the plural is formed irregularly:

Mr., Messrs.	Mrs., Mmes *or* Mmes.

If the word or term abbreviated is not a noun, but the abbreviation itself is referred to as a term and is hence italicized, its plural may be formed by the addition of a roman *s* before the terminal period:

The footnotes were overburdened with *ibid*s. and *ut sup*s.

The author's penchant for *viz*s. was driving Manzoni insane.

CHOICE OF PLURALS

6.18 When the dictionary followed gives two different plurals for the same word, either may be used, although the first is usually preferred. In any case, the choice should be consistent throughout the work.

memorandums, memoranda	appendixes, appendices
symposia, symposiums	millennia, millenniums

Note, however, that different senses of the same word may have different plurals. Thus a book may have two *indexes* and a mathematical expression two *indices*.

Possessives

GENERAL RULES

6.19 The possessive of singular nouns is formed by the addition of an apostrophe and an *s,* and the possessive of plural nouns (except for a few irregular plurals) by the addition of an apostrophe only:

the horse's mouth   the puppies' tails   the children's desk

There are a few exceptions to the rule for common nouns. In one notable case, tradition and euphony dictate the use of the apostrophe only:

for appearance' (conscience', righteousness', etc.) sake

In another instance, the possessive singular of such uninflected nouns as *series* and *species* is also formed with the apostrophe only, although the more usual way to express possession with such nouns is by the prepositional phrase: *of the species.*

6.20 Closely linked nouns are often considered a single unit in forming the possessive, when the entity possessed is the same for both:

my aunt and uncle's house

the skull and crossbones' symbolic meaning

When the "ownership" is separate, however, both nouns take the possessive form:

our son's and daughter's friends

6.21 Analogous to possessives, and formed like them, are expressions based on the old genitive case:

an hour's delay   in three days' time

Charles's having been there

In the last example, the genitive *Charles's* "possesses" the gerund *having*. Should the following word be a participle, or gerundive, however—that is, a verb form used as an adjective—the case is not the genitive and the apostrophe and *s* are not used:

Peter was annoyed by Carrie's reading the letter.
  but
Max was delighted to see Carrie reading the letter.

COMPOUND NOUNS

6.22 It is customary to form the possessive of all compound nouns, whether closed, open, or hyphenated, and of similar noun phrases by adding the inflection at the end of the compound or phrase:

cookbook's   doctor of philosophy's
daughter-in-law's   the mayor of Chicago's

The possessive of the plurals of compound nouns may be formed in the same way, but many of the resulting forms are awkward and might profitably be replaced by the possessive prepositional phrase with *of:*

cookbooks'
daughters-in-law's   *or*   of the daughters-in-law

To form the possessive of the plural of noun phrases, like the one illustrated above, it is best to use the construction with *of* and avoid the possessive inflection:

of the mayors of Chicago
the wives of the doctors in the amphitheater

ATTRIBUTIVE NOUNS

6.23   Among some circles there is a penchant for omitting the apostrophe from what are sometimes regarded as possessive constructions. Some business establishments and factories, for example, refer to the cafeteria for their employees as the *employees cafeteria,* and some organizations and departments have such names as *Diners Club, Actors Equity, Department of Veterans Affairs.* Actually, this might just as properly be said to constitute an attributive rather than a possessive use of nouns. A noun functions attributively if it performs an adjectival role in modifying a following noun. Below are a few examples of the attributive use of nouns:

city government	school custodian
state highways	consumer advocate

There seems little justification for restricting the attributive function to the singular noun, and such forms as the following ought also to be allowed:

carpenters union	consumers group
taxpayers meeting	environmentalists association

As in so many other matters of style, consistency is to be encouraged. Care should be taken, however, to guard against an ambiguous use of an attributive noun: *parent organization,* for example, should not be used unless intended to denote an organization from which other organizations have sprung.

PROPER NOUNS

6.24   The general rule for the possessive of nouns covers most proper nouns, including most names ending in sibilants (but see exceptions in 6.26–27 and alternatives in 6.30):

Kansas's	Texas's
Burns's poems	General Noguès's troops
Marx's theories	Jefferson Davis's home
Berlioz's opera	Dickens's novels
Ross's land	Jones's reputation
the Rosses' and the Williamses' lands	the Joneses' reputation

6.25   For names ending in silent *s, z,* or *x* (see 6.12) the possessive, unlike the plural, can generally be formed in the usual way without suggesting an incorrect pronunciation:

Josquin Des Prez's motets Margaux's bouquet
Vaucouleurs's theorems Descartes's works

6.26 Traditional exceptions to the general rule for forming the possessive are the names *Jesus* and *Moses:*

in Jesus' name   Moses' leadership

6.27 Names of more than one syllable with an unaccented ending pronounced *eez* form another category of exceptions. Many Greek and hellenized names fit this pattern. For reasons of euphony the possessive *s* is seldom added to such names:

Euripides' plays Xerxes' army
Demosthenes' orations R. S. Surtees' novels
Ramses' tomb Charles Yerkes' benefactions

6.28 Like common nouns, closely linked proper names may be treated as a unit in forming the possessive:

Fraser and Squair's French grammar

Minneapolis and Saint Paul's transportation system
but
Chicago's and New York's transportation systems

6.29 When a proper name is in italic type, its possessive ending is preferably set in roman:

the *Saturday Review*'s forty-fifth year of publication
Boris Godunov's impact on the audience

6.30 How to form the possessive of polysyllabic personal names ending with the sound of *s* or *z* probably occasions more dissension among writers and editors than any other orthographic matter open to disagreement. Some espouse the rule that the possessive of all such names should be formed by the addition of an apostrophe only. Such a rule would outlaw spellings like "Dylan Thomas's poetry," "Roy Harris's compositions," and "Maria Callas's performance" in favor of "Thomas'," "Harris'," and "Callas'," which would not commend themselves to many. Other writers and editors simply abandon the attempt to define in precise phonic or orthographic terms the class of polysyllabic names to which only the apostrophe should be attached and follow a more pragmatic rule. In essence this is, "If it ends with a *z* sound, treat it like a plural; if it ends with an *s* sound, treat it like a singular." Thus they would write "Dickens', Hopkins', Williams'," but also "Harris's, Thomas's, Callas's, Angus's, Willis's," and the like. The University of Chicago Press prefers the procedures outlined above (6.24–27). It is willing, however, to accept other ways of handling these situations if they are consistently followed throughout a manuscript.

Contractions

6.31   In the formation of contractions, the apostrophe is ordinarily placed where letters have been omitted:

> can't   isn't   wouldn't   don't   o'clock

Some contractions, like *won't,* are formed irregularly. Correct spellings for standard, or commonly used, contractions are found in most dictionaries. There are, however, a number of colloquial or dialectal contractions that are not ordinarily listed in dictionaries and whose spellings must therefore be sought in literature. A few of these contractions, or distortions, do not use apostrophes. In others, letters are omitted in more than one location. In that case it is sufficient, and perhaps more pleasing to the eye, to use only one apostrophe, although more than one may be used.

> singin'
> y'all
> meet'n
> gon' (going)
> gonna (going to)
> rhythm 'n blues (*or* rhythm 'n' blues)

Compound Words

6.32   Probably nine out of ten spelling questions that arise in writing or editing concern compound words. Should it be *selfseeking* or *self-seeking?* Is the word spelled *taxpayer, tax-payer,* or *tax payer*—closed, hyphenated, or open? Most such questions are readily answered by the dictionary. If the compound is used as a noun, the chances are good that it will appear in an unabridged dictionary, in one of the three possible spellings. If it is used as an adjective, the chances of finding it are still fair. But there will be some noun forms and a great many adjective forms for which no "authoritative" spelling can be found. It is then that general principles must be applied. Before these are outlined, however, some definitions are in order.

DEFINITIONS

6.33   An *open compound* is a combination of separate words that are so closely related as to constitute a single concept. *Examples:* settlement house, lowest common denominator, stool pigeon.

6.34   A *hyphenated compound* is a combination of words joined by one or more hyphens. *Examples:* kilowatt-hour, mass-produced, ill-favored, love-in-a-mist.

6.35 A *closed* (or *solid*) *compound* is a combination of two or more elements, originally separate words, now spelled as one word. *Examples:* henhouse, typesetting, makeup, notebook.

6.36 Not strictly compounds but often discussed with them are words bearing prefixes or suffixes. Some of these words are closed and some are hyphenated. They will also be included in this discussion.

6.37 In addition to such classification by form, compounds are also classified by function as *permanent* or *temporary*. A permanent compound is one that has been accepted into the general vocabulary of English and can (or should) be found in dictionaries. A temporary compound is a joining of words, or words and particles, for some specific purpose. A writer may employ the term *quasi-realistic,* for example, assigning it some specific meaning appropriate to the work in hand. The term *quasi-realistic* is not to be found in Webster, and probably not in other dictionaries either, and so would be considered a temporary compound. If it were to be picked up and used by other writers, it might acquire the currency and status of a permanent compound.

GENERAL PRINCIPLES

6.38 For some years now, the trend in spelling compound words has been away from the use of hyphens. There seems to be a tendency to spell compounds solid as soon as acceptance warrants their being considered permanent compounds, and otherwise to spell them open. This is a trend, not a rule, but it is sometimes helpful, when deciding how to spell some new combination, to remember that the trend exists.

6.39 A second helpful principle is this: When a temporary compound is used as an adjective before a noun, it is often hyphenated to avoid misleading the reader. The phrase *a fast sailing ship,* for example, is ambiguous. Does it refer to a ship that is now sailing fast or a sailing ship that is capable of rapid navigation? If the former construction is intended, the meaning may be made instantly apparent by hyphenating the compound adjective *fast-sailing*. If the second construction is intended—that is, if the single adjective *fast* modifies the phrase *sailing ship*—the hyphen should be omitted. The convention, in this case, is to hyphenate the compound adjective that, as a unit, modifies the noun, and to omit the hyphen when the first adjective modifies the whole noun phrase *(sailing ship)*. Such a phrase as *much loved friend,* on the other hand, offers virtually no risk of misreading and therefore does not require a hyphen for clarification.

6.40 When the compound adjective follows the noun it modifies, there is usually little or no risk of ambiguity or hesitation, and the hyphen may safely be omitted, even if the only form given in the dictionary is hyphenated.

> less-appreciated art
> able-bodied seaman
> > *but*
> an art less appreciated
> a seaman who is able bodied

Occasionally, though perhaps rarely, ambiguity may occur when the compound adjective follows the noun. For example, does "her reply was thought provoking" mean that her reply provoked thought or that it was thought (considered) provoking? Since some risk of misreading exists—or at least the possibility of distracting, perhaps humorous, secondary interpretation—the hyphenation rule should be applied here as well.

6.41   Formerly, adjectival compounds, except those beginning with an adverb ending in *ly,* were generally hyphenated before the noun they modified and open after the noun. The University of Chicago Press now takes the position that the hyphen may be omitted in all cases where there is little or no risk of ambiguity or hesitation. It also means, of course, that when ambiguity is likely, the compound adjective, whatever its position, should be hyphenated.

6.42   There are scores of other rules for spelling compound words, but many of these are almost useless because of the multitude of exceptions. Some of the more dependable rules are presented in table 6.1 at the end of this chapter. When a dependable rule is lacking, a comprehensive dictionary may offer help. Should all else fail, the writer or editor is advised to employ the tests, admittedly somewhat subjective, of ambiguity and readability.

Word Division

6.43   When type is set in *justified* lines (all lines having exactly the same length), it is inevitable that some words will be divided (broken, or hyphenated) at the ends of lines. Even in unjustified, or *ragged-right,* setting it is desirable to break some words to prevent excessive disparity in line length (see 6.57). Such divisions are made between syllables, which should be determined in doubtful cases by consulting a dictionary. Not all syllable breaks, however, are acceptable end-of-line breaks. The paragraphs that follow are intended to offer editors and proofreaders a brief guide to conservative modern practice in word division. For word division in foreign languages see chapter 9. Some computerized typesetting methods in frequent use today may render a conservative approach to word division impractical. Compromise may therefore be necessary pending the development of more sophisticated technology (see also 3.10).

GENERAL PRINCIPLES

6.44 Most words should be divided according to pronunciation (the American system, reflected in Webster), not according to derivation (the British system):

> democ-racy (*not* demo-cracy)
> knowl-edge (*not* know-ledge)
> aurif-erous (*not* auri-ferous)
> antip-odes (*still better* antipo-des; *not* anti-podes)

Consequently, words such as the following, in which the second "syllable" contains only a silent *e,* are never divided:

aimed	helped	spelled
climbed	passed	vexed

Nor are word endings such as the following, which despite occasional use in verse as disyllables are for all practical purposes monosyllables:

-ceous	-geous	-sion
-cial	-gion	-tial
-cion	-gious	-tion
-cious	-sial	-tious

And by a similar principle, final syllables in which the liquid *l* sound contains the only audible vowel sound should not be carried over to the next line:

convert-ible (*not* converti-ble)	prin-ciples (*not* princi-ples)
pos-sible (*not* possi-ble)	people (*not* peo-ple)
en-titled (*not* enti-tled)	read-able (*not* reada-ble)

6.45 Division should be made after a vowel unless the resulting break is not according to pronunciation. Where a vowel alone forms a syllable in the middle of a word, run it into the first line. Diphthongs are treated as single vowels:

> aneu-rysm (*not* an-eurysm)
> criti-cism (*not* crit-icism)
> liga-ture (*not* lig-ature)
> physi-cal (*not* phys-ical *or* physic-al)
> sepa-rate (*not* sep-arate)
> preju-dice (*not* prej-udice)

6.46 Two consonants standing between vowels are usually separated if the pronunciation warrants:

ad-van-tage	foun-dation	moun-tain
ex-ces-sive	im-por-tant	profes-sor
finan-cier	In-dian	struc-ture
fin-ger		

6.47 Words that have a misleading appearance when divided should be left unbroken if at all possible:

women   often   prayer   water   noisy

6.48 One-letter divisions are not permissible. Such words as the following must not be divided:

acre	enough	item
again	even	oboe
amen	event	onus
among	idol	unite

6.49 Two-letter divisions are permissible at the end of a line, but two-letter word endings should not be carried over to the next line if this can be avoided:

en-chant   di-pole   as-phalt
      but
losses (*not* loss-es)   stricken (*not* strick-en)
money (*not* mon-ey)   fully (*not* ful-ly)

COMPOUND WORDS

6.50 Wherever possible, hyphenated compounds should be broken only at the hyphen:

court- / martial (*not* court-mar- / tial)
poverty- / stricken (*not* pov- / erty-stricken; *much less* pover- / ty-stricken)

Words originally compounded of other words but now spelled solid should be divided at the natural breaks whenever possible:

school-master *is better than* schoolmas-ter
clearing-house *is better than* clear-inghouse
handle-bar *is better than* han-dlebar
never Passo-ver, une-ven, etc.

WORDS WITH PREFIXES

6.51 By the same principle, division after a prefix is preferred to division at any other point in the word:

dis-pleasure *is better than* displea-sure
pseudo-scientific *is better than* pseu-doscientific *or* pseudoscien-tific

THE ENDING *ING*

6.52 Most gerunds and present participles permit division before the *ing:*

| certify-ing | giv-ing | pranc-ing |

When the final consonant is doubled before the addition of *ing,* however, the added consonant is carried over:

| abhor-ring | dab-bing | run-ning |

And when the original verb ends in an *le* syllable in which the only audible vowel sound is in the liquid *l* (for example, *startle, fizzle*), one or more of the preceding consonants are carried over with *ing:*

bris-tling	fiz-zling	ruf-fling
chuck-ling	han-dling	star-tling
dwin-dling	ram-bling	twin-kling

PERSONAL NAMES

6.53 Personal names ought not to be divided if there is any way to avoid it. Since this is often a counsel of perfection, however, some guidelines are in order:

1. Try to break after a middle initial. The following breaks are in descending order of desirability:

   Frederick L. / Anderson
   Frederick L. An- / derson
   Frederick / L. Anderson
   Fred- / erick L. Anderson

2. When initials are used in place of given names, again try not to break at all, but if necessary break after the second (or last, if there are more than two):

   if necessary A. E. / Housman
   but never A. / E. Housman

3. Avoid breaking before a numeral adjective following a personal name, as in Henry V or Adlai E. Stevenson III (or 3d). If *Jr.* is set off by commas, it is permissible to break after the first comma. It should be noted, however, that the University of Chicago Press now recommends that *Jr.* and *Sr.,* like *II* and *III,* no longer be set off by commas (see 8.55).

NUMERALS

6.54 When large numbers are expressed in numerals, they should be kept intact if possible; if this cannot be done, they may be broken after a comma, but not a decimal point. Do not break after a single digit. Slant lines show permissible breaks:

| 1,365, / 000, / 000 | $24, / 126.83 | £36, / 520, / 000 |

ABBREVIATIONS

6.55   Abbreviations used with numerals should not be separated from the numerals:

345 mi.   24 kg   55 B.C.   A.D. 1066   6:35 P.M.

ENUMERATION

6.56   An enumerating letter or number, such as *(a)* or (1), even when it occurs in the middle of a sentence, preferably should not be separated from the beginning of what follows it. When such a mark occurs at the end of a line, carry it over to the next line if possible.

RAGGED-RIGHT STYLE

6.57   A good deal of typesetting nowadays is done in what is called *ragged-right* style: all lines are unjustified, so that the right-hand margin of the type column is irregular. If copy is intended for ragged-right setting, the editor should not simply mark it (for example) "Set 10/12 × 25 ragged right," or the typesetter will probably not break any words at all, in which case there are likely to be excessively long spaces at the ends of some lines. The editor (perhaps in conference with the designer) should specify a minimum line length. This will ensure that long words will be broken whereas short ones need not be.

6.58   One final point should be made about end-of-line hyphenation. The attractiveness of a page of type may be affected by the occurrence of more than a few end-of-line hyphens, and their overabundance should therefore be avoided. Moreover, no more than three succeeding lines should be allowed to end in hyphens.

O and *Oh*

6.59   The vocative *O* is capitalized, but not the interjection *oh,* unless it begins a sentence or stands alone:

> Why, O Lord, did you turn away from me?
>
> I was shocked, dismayed, and . . . oh, oh, terribly shocked!
>
> Oh! It's you!

A and *An*

6.60   Such forms as "an historical study" or "an union" are not idiomatic in American English. Before a pronounced *h,* long *u* (or *eu*), and such a word as *one,* the indefinite article should be *a:*

a hotel
a historical study
but an honor, an heir

a euphonious word
such a one
a union

Ligatures, or Digraphs

6.61 The ligatures, or digraphs, æ and œ should not be used either in Latin or Greek words or in words adopted into English from these languages:

aes   aetatis   poena
Encyclopaedia Britannica   *Oedipus tyrannus*

For most English words derived from Latin or Greek words containing æ or œ, the preferred spelling is now *e:*

coeval   ecumenical   maneuver
economy   enology   medieval
but aesthetics, archaeology

The digraph æ is needed for spelling Old English words (along with other special characters) in an Old English context:

Ælfric   Ælfred   wes hæl

And the ligature œ is needed for spelling modern French in a French context (but not for French words in an English context):

Œuvres complètes de Racine
le nœud gordien
un coup d'œil
            but
a tray of hors d'oeuvres
a circular window, or oeil-de-boeuf

DISTINCTIVE TREATMENT OF WORDS

6.62 Writers have probably always felt the need for devices to give special expression—emphasis, irony, or whatever—to the written word to achieve what gesture and vocal intonation achieve for the spoken word. One old device, the use of capital letters to lend importance to certain words, is now totally outmoded and a vehicle of satire:

When John came to the throne he lost his temper and flung himself on the floor, foaming at the mouth and biting the rushes. He was thus a Bad King.[1]

6.63 Other devices, notably the use of italics and quotation marks to achieve special effects, are not outmoded but are used less and less as time goes

1. Walter C. Sellar and Robert J. Yeatman, *1066 and All That: A Memorable History of England* (New York: E. P. Dutton, 1931), 24.

209

on, especially by mature writers who prefer to obtain their effects structurally:

> The damaging evidence was offered not by the arresting officer, not by the injured plaintiff, but by the defendant's own mother.

In the sentence above, for example, there is no need to set the words *defendant's own mother* in italics: the structure of the sentence gives them all the emphasis they need. Obviously, an effect of emphasis cannot always be achieved so easily. But writers who find themselves underlining frequently for emphasis might consider whether many of the italics are not superfluous, the emphasis being apparent from the context, or whether, if the emphasis is not apparent, it cannot be achieved more gracefully by recasting the sentence. The same reservations apply to frequent use of quotation marks to suggest irony or special usage. (Apart from these stylistic uses, of course, italics and quotation marks find purely technical uses, discussed later in the chapter, that are not to be called in question.)

Emphasis

6.64 A word or phrase may be set in italic type for emphasis if the emphasis might otherwise be lost:

> Let us dwell for a moment upon the idea of *conscious* participation.
>
> How do we learn to think in terms of *wholes?*

Seldom should as much as a sentence be set in italics for emphasis, and never a whole passage.

Foreign Words

6.65 Isolated words and phrases in a foreign language may be set in italics if they are likely to be unfamiliar to readers:

> The *grève du zèle* is not a true strike but a nitpicking obeying of work rules.
>
> *Honi soit qui mal y pense* is the motto of the Order of the Garter.
>
> What they discovered was a deed of endowment *(vakfiye).*

As with matter italicized for emphasis, a full sentence in a language other than English is only occasionally set in italics, most frequently when, as in the second example above, it is included in an English sentence. A passage of two or more sentences in another language is usually treated as a quotation and is not italicized (see 10.84).

PROPER NOUNS

6.66   Isolated foreign proper nouns are not italicized, even when cited as foreign terms:

> Moscow (in Russian, Moskva) has been the capital of the Russian national state since the late fourteenth century.

TRANSLATION APPENDED

6.67   If a definition follows a foreign word or phrase, the definition is enclosed in parentheses or quotation marks:

> The word she used was not *une poêle* (frying pan) but *un poêle* (stove).

> Volition is expressed by the infix *-ainu-,* as in the phrase *ena tuainubo,* "I would like to eat," or *ena tuainu-iai,* "I wanted to eat."

In linguistic and phonetic studies a word under discussion is often set in italics (as above) and the definition enclosed in single quotation marks, with no intervening punctuation (see also 6.74):

> French *le cheval* 'the horse' represents a replacement for Latin *equus.*

> The gap is narrow between *mead* 'a beverage' and *mead* 'a meadow'.

ETHNOLOGICAL STUDIES

6.68   Scholarly work in cultural anthropology is full of words drawn from the languages of the societies studied, and these are usually italicized only on first occurrence. In a kinship study, for example, once it is made clear that a married woman's mother-in-law's sister is her *aiku* and her father-in-law's sister is her *aiku-esu,* the terms may appear thereafter in roman type. (A glossary at the end of the work, however, is helpful.)

FAMILIAR WORDS

6.69   Familiar words and phrases in a foreign language should be set in roman type (note the lowercase style for the two German nouns):

effendi	kibitz	serape
pasha	recherché	weltschmerz
élan	mea culpa	kapellmeister
fait accompli	hacienda	a priori

The problem, of course, lies in deciding whether a word or phrase is familiar. One attempt at standardization relies on whether the term has made its way into a standard English dictionary. Such words and phrases may be regarded as having been adopted into English and as therefore not needing to be italicized. The adoption, however, does not mean that the term has necessarily become familiar to all. Words like *barranca, kiblah,* and *fazenda,* for example, at least at some times and in some places, are less familiar than *fait accompli, kibitz,* and *hacienda,* yet all are found in standard English dictionaries. Familiarity is relative; there will always be some readers for whom words familiar to the writer, and to many other readers, will remain strange. Should the less familiar words be italicized? Many words that have long resided in standard English dictionaries are unfamiliar to most of us, and that has not been regarded as a reason to italicize them. Perhaps it may be assumed that if a word or phrase can be found in a standard dictionary, the reader may have relatively easy access to its meaning, and the term therefore need not be italicized. More moderately, the decision might be based on a blend of considerations—familiarity, inclusion in a dictionary, and sympathy with the reader.

SCHOLARLY WORDS AND ABBREVIATIONS

6.70 Roman type should be used for such scholarly Latin words and abbreviations as the following:

   ibid. et al. ca. passim idem

But because of *sic*'s peculiar use in quoted matter, it seems wise to continue setting it in italics:

   They are furnished "seperate [*sic*] but equal facilities."

Special Terminology

6.71 Key terms in a discussion, terms with special meaning, and in general, terms to which the reader's attention is directed are often italicized on first use. Thereafter they are best set in roman:

   The two chief tactics of this group, *obstructionism* and *misinformation,* require careful analysis in what follows.

   What is meant by *random selection?*

In the last example, note the italic question mark. This illustrates the printer's rule that punctuation is set in the style of the immediately preceding word (but see 5.4–6 for exceptions).

TECHNICAL TERMS

6.72 A technical term, especially when accompanied by its definition, is often set in italics the first time it appears in a discussion, and in roman thereafter:

Tabular matter is copy, usually consisting of numerals, that is set in columns.

Ground and polished *thin sections* permit microscopic examination of the cellular structure of some fossils.

TECHNICAL TERMS IN SPECIAL SENSES

6.73   Often it is better to apply a standard technical term in a nonstandard way than to invent a new term. In such instances the term is often enclosed in quotation marks:

In offset printing, "proofs" of illustrations come from the darkroom, not the proof press.

the "Levalloisian" culture complex of Tanzania [application of a European term to an African site]

PHILOSOPHICAL TERMS

6.74   In works of philosophy and theology, terms having special philosophical or theological meaning are, by convention, sometimes enclosed in single quotation marks. Contrary to the usual practice, punctuation following such special terms is traditionally placed outside the closing quotation mark. (For the similar treatment of definitions in linguistic and phonetic studies see 6.67.)

If such concept is defensible, 'agrees with' must carry the sense of 'is consistent with'.

'being'   'nonbeing'   'the divine'

Quoted Phrases

6.75   Phrases quoted from another context are usually enclosed in quotation marks:

It was clear to Gulden that his unhappy staff was unhappy "in its own way" and that he would have to deal with it differently.

Bernice did not willingly "suffer the little ones" to enter her studio.

Could Werner, in this instance, be said to have been in "the pursuit of happiness"?

If the quoted phrase is very well known and is used more as a common expression than as evoking the original context, however, it may be more appropriate to drop the quotation marks:

The pursuit of happiness is a practice more often defended than defined.

Myths of paradise lost are common in folklore.

Words Used as Words

6.76   When, in running text, a word or term is referred to as the word or term itself and is not being used functionally to convey its meaning, it is commonly set in italics:

> *Correctness* and *justness* are not synonyms.
>   *but*
> Correctness and justness are not identical concepts.

> The term *critical mass* has come to be used metaphorically in many contexts.

Quotation marks are also often used for this purpose:

> "Correct" and "just" are not synonyms.

Quotation marks may be preferable when the reference is to spoken language or when the word or term is used as a quotation:

> Did she write "correct"?

> Did he say "just"?

> In Elizabethan dialogue a change from "you" to "thou" is often a studied insult.

If the word or term is presented as required or recommended for some use, either written or spoken, it may be thought of as a quotation and may therefore be enclosed in quotation marks:

> I suggest that you reply "Maybe."

> I suggest that you fill in the blank with "Not applicable."

6.77   The plurals of italicized words and terms are formed by the addition of *s* or *es* in roman type (see 6.14–15):

> three *accommodate*s   all *transfix*es

It is simpler to form the plural of an italicized word than of a word enclosed in quotation marks, but if the latter seems required or preferable, the tidiest way to show the plural is to add an apostrophe and an *s* inside the closing quotation mark:

> Tim had enough of her "maybe's."

> How many "not applicable's" did Sidney enter?

Irony

6.78   Words used in an ironic sense may be enclosed in quotation marks:

> Five villages were subjected to "pacification."

> The "debate" resulted in three cracked heads.

Slang

6.79   Words classed as slang or argot may be enclosed in quotation marks if they are foreign to the normal vocabulary of the writer:

> Alfie was accompanied by his "trouble and strife" as he strolled down the Strand.

> Had it not been for Bryce, the "copper's nark," Collins would have made his escape.

Use of *So-Called*

6.80   When the expression *so-called* is used with a word or phrase, implying that something is popularly or (sometimes) mistakenly given such-and-such a designation, the designation itself should not be enclosed in quotation marks or set in italics. *So-called* is sufficient to mark the special usage:

> The so-called shadow cabinet was thought to be responsible for some of the president's more injudicious decisions.

> A so-called right of sanctuary was offered in justification of the minister's failure to surrender the escaped felon.

Letters Used as Words or Referred to as Letters

6.81   Letters used as words or as letters demand varied treatments depending upon the kind of letter and its context.

LETTERS AS LETTERS

6.82   Individual letters and combinations of letters of the Latin (English) alphabet are italicized:

> the letter *q*   a lowercase *n*   a capital *W*
>
> The normal sign of the plural in English is a terminal *s* or *es*.
>
> He signed the document with an *X*.

In some proverbial expressions the distinction is ignored, and in that case the plural is formed by adding an apostrophe and *s* (see also 6.16):

> Mind your p's and q's.
> Dot your i's and cross your t's.

Letters used as evaluations of scholastic achievement are given in roman type and are usually capitalized:

Maitresson, who had been anticipating an A, was dumbfounded when instead he received a C.

6.83 The name of a letter, as distinct from the letter itself, is usually set in roman type:

from alpha to omega
dalet, the fourth letter of the Hebrew alphabet

an aitch   a dee   an ess

6.84 Letters standing for musical tones (which in turn are used to identify keys, chords, and so on) are usually set as roman capitals. Notice that in designations of key the terms *sharp, flat,* and *natural* are set in roman type and preceded by a hyphen (see also table 6.1 under Noun Forms). Notice also that the terms *major* and *minor* are lowercase unless part of a title (see 7.150).

middle C   G-natural
the key of G major   the key of F-sharp minor
the D-major triad   an E string

If the symbol for *sharp, flat,* or *natural* is used, there is no hyphen:

the key of F♯ minor

6.85 In technical works, various systems are used to designate pitch. Those systems that group pitches by octaves begin each ascending octave on C. In one widely used system, pitches in the octave below middle C are designated by lowercase letters: c, c♯, d, . . . , a♯, b. Octaves from middle C up are designated with lowercase letters bearing superscript numbers or primes: c^1, c^2, etc., or c', c'', etc. Lower octaves are designated, in descending order, by capital letters and capital letters with subscript numbers: C, C_1, C_2. Because of the many systems and their variants in current use, it is advisable to alert the reader to the system employed, either by indicating early in the text the symbol used for middle C, or by providing a full table. Technical works on the modern piano usually designate all pitches with capital letters and subscripts, from A_1 at the bottom of the keyboard to C_{88} at the top. Scientific works on music usually designate octaves by capital letters and subscripts beginning with C_0 (middle C = C_4). When pitches are otherwise specified, another designation system is unnecessary:

middle C   A 440   the soprano's high C

6.86 In the analysis of harmony, chords are designated by capital roman numerals indicating the degree of the scale upon which the chord is based:

> V [a chord based on the fifth, or dominant, degree of the scale]
>
> V⁷ [dominant seventh chord]

Harmonic progressions are indicated by capital roman numerals separated by en dashes: IV–I–V–I. While capital roman numerals for all chords suffice for basic descriptions of chordal movement, in more specifically technical writing, minor chords are distinguished by lowercase roman numerals, and further distinctions in chord quality and content are indicated by additional symbols and arabic numerals.

6.87 In works on musical subjects where many keys are mentioned, it is common practice to use capital letters for major keys and lowercase for minor. If this practice is followed, the words *major* and *minor* are usually omitted:

> the key of G
> the e triad: E–G-natural–B
> The second movement of Beethoven's Sonata in c, op. 13, is in the key of A-flat.

6.88 Terms indicating dynamics are given in lowercase roman type: pianissimo, piano, mezzoforte, forte, fortissimo. Abbreviations for these terms are always rendered in lowercase italics and are used without periods: *pp, p, mf, f, ff.*

LETTERS AS NAMES

6.89 A letter used in place of a name in a hypothetical statement and an initial (followed by either a period or a 2-em dash) used to stand for a name are set as roman capitals:

> If A sues B for breach of contract . . .
>
> Admiral N—— and Lady R—— were guests.
>
> Mr. D. is the one to whom your request should be addressed.

LETTERS AS SHAPES

6.90 Either roman or gothic (sans serif) letters may be used for indicating shape:

> A V-shaped valley becomes U-shaped by glaciation.
>
> an S curve   an A-frame

Sometimes a roman letter suggests a particular shape better than a gothic one:

> a steel I-beam

6.91 The spelled-out names of letters are also used as the names of particular objects, with reference to their shapes:

> an ell (of a house)
> a tee, a wye (road intersections, pipe fittings)

LETTERS INDICATING RHYME SCHEMES

6.92 Lowercase italic letters are used to indicate rhyme patterns:

> The Italian sonnet consists of an octave and a sestet: *abbaabba, cdcdcd.*
>
> The English, or Shakespearean, sonnet: *abab, cdcd, efef, gg.*

Table 6.1 Spelling Guide for Compound Words and Words with Prefixes and Suffixes

The following annotated lists are designed to be broadly representative. Recommendations are based on orthographic tradition and ease of comprehension. No list should be considered exhaustive. In doubtful cases it is advisable to consult a dictionary and, at the same time, to be alert for the likelihood of misreading.

Type	Examples	Remarks
	ADJECTIVE FORMS	
all	all-inclusive *study* all-around, all-out, all-powerful *He was* all in. *They were* all-in. allover *design* overall *plan*	Most adjectival compounds with *all* are hyphenated. A few are open, but these are hyphenated if misreading is likely. The combination with *over* is preferably closed. *See also under* Adverb Forms.
century	fourteenth-century *scholar* twenty-first-century *hopes* early-twentieth-century *poet*, mid-eighteenth-century *poet*, late-twentieth-century *poet*	Compound adjectives with *century* are hyphenated. When *early, mid,* or *late* is added to the compound, it should be followed by a hyphen. *But see under* Noun Forms.
cross	cross-referenced *entries* cross-country, cross-fertile, cross-grained crosstown *bus* crossbred, crosscut, crosshatched	Many compounds with *cross* are hyphenated; some are closed. If not listed in a dictionary, the compound should be hyphenated.
fold	tenfold *increase* twofold, multifold, 45-fold	Compounds with the suffix *fold* are closed unless they are formed with numerals.
full	full-length *mirror* full-blown, full-dress, full-fashioned, full-scale *The mirror is* full length. *The drawing was* full scale.	All compound adjectives with *full* are hyphenated before the noun and open after the noun. *See also under* Noun Forms.
half	half-baked *plan* half-blooded, half-cocked, half-timbered halfhearted *assent,* halfway *house*	Most *half* compounds are hyphenated, but a few are closed. *See also under* Noun Forms.
high, low, upper, lower, *middle,* and *mid*	*an* upper-crust *clique,* high-class *flirt,*	Most compound adjectives containing *high, low, upper,*

Table 6.1—*Continued*

Type	Examples	Remarks
	Adjective Forms—Continued	
	middle-class *voters,* high-level *achievement* high-grade, middle-aged *Am I* middle aged? *She was* upper crust. *His friends were* upper middle class. highborn, lowborn, highbrow, lowbrow, highland, lowland midlife *depression,* midweek *conference,* mid-Atlantic *tempest,* Mideast *peace*	*lower,* and *middle* are hyphenated before the noun but, unless ambiguity is likely, may be open after the noun. Some of the compounds, however, are closed. Most adjectival compounds with *mid* are closed, but a hyphen is added if the second word begins with a capital letter. *See also under* Noun Forms.
like	catlike *movements* gridlike, childlike sail-like, gull-like, basilica-like, Whitman-like, vacuum-bottle-like *but* Christlike	The suffix *like* is freely used to form new compounds. These are generally spelled closed except for words ending in *l* or *ll,* words of three or more syllables, compound words, most proper nouns, or other forms difficult to read. The exceptions are hyphenated in all positions.
over, under	overexposed, overrated, underhanded over-the-counter, under-the-table	Adjectives with the prefix *over* or *under* are closed unless they are constructions containing *the,* in which case they are hyphenated.
quasi	quasi-public *corporation* quasi-judicial, quasi-legislative, quasi-stellar	Adjectival *quasi* compounds are always hyphenated. *But see also under* Noun Forms.
self	self-reliant *child* self-sustaining, self-righteous, self-confident, self-abasing, self-conscious, unselfconscious selfless, selfish	Most adjectival compounds with *self* are hyphenated, but those formed by the addition of a suffix to *self* are closed. When the additional prefix *un* is used, the Press recommends closing the compound.
wide	statewide *referendum* worldwide, countywide	Compounds ending in *wide* are always closed unless long and cumbersome. The latter are

Table 6.1—*Continued*

Type	Examples	Remarks

Type	Examples	Remarks
	university-wide *canvass* *The canvass was* university wide.	hyphenated before the noun and open after the noun.
adjective plus a noun bearing the suffix *ed*	coarse-grained *wood,* able-bodied *sailor,* red-faced *accomplice,* straight-sided *figure,* even-handed *Willard* *The wood was* coarse grained. *He was* able bodied.	Adjectival compounds comprising an adjective followed by a noun bearing the suffix *ed* are ordinarily hyphenated when they precede the noun they modify. Following the noun, they may generally be left open.
adjective or participle plus a noun	first-floor *apartment,* living-room *windows,* hot-water *tank*	Adjectival compounds comprising an adjective or a participle followed by a noun are always hyphenated and precede the noun they modify.
adverb ending in *ly* plus a participle or adjective	poorly attired *man* highly developed, wholly involved, utterly dejected, overbearingly arrogant, ardently pursued, very ardently pursued	An adverb ending in *ly* followed by a participle or adjective is always open.
adverb other than the *ly* type plus a participle or adjective	ever faithful *groupie,* sweet smelling *flower,* high flying *kite,* late-blooming *ingenue,* *the ingenue was* late blooming, much loved *friend,* long-suffering *wife,* much-loved *music,* less-appreciated *art,* ever more resentful *neighbor,* *her* all too brief *career* *Was it* ever-eager *Bill?* *She had been* long-suffering. *Had she been too* long-suffering?	Adjectival compounds consisting of adverbs not ending in *ly* followed by participles or adjectives may be open in any position if ambiguity is unlikely. If ambiguity is likely, however, they should be hyphenated. When the adverb is itself modified by another adverb, the compound should be open unless there is a risk of misreading.
the adverbs *well, ill, better, best, little, lesser,* and *least* with an adjective or participle	well-known *crook* ill-fitting, better-prepared, best-loved, little-understood, lesser-regarded, least-desirable *He was the* lesser regarded. very ill fitting *garment* much better prepared *scholar*	Compounds with *well, ill, better, best, little, lesser,* and *least* are hyphenated before the noun, open after a noun, and open if modified by an adverb.

Table 6.1—*Continued*

Type	Examples	Remarks
	Adjective Forms—Continued	
chemical terms	sulfuric acid *bottle,* sodium chloride *solution*	Adjectival compounds consisting of chemical terms are always open.
colors	bluish green *paint* gray blue, coal black, emerald green, reddish orange, blue-green *algae,* black-and-blue *cheek* red-green *colorblindness,* black-and-white *print* *The print was* black and white. *a cheek* black and blue *His cheek was* black and blue.	Color-term compounds in which one term modifies the other are open unless they constitute a hyphenated element in an established term. If the color terms are of equal importance in the compound and do not denote a blend of colors, the compound is hyphenated. The latter compounds may be open after the noun. *See also under* Noun Forms.
foreign phrases	a priori *reasoning* postmortem, Sturm und Drang *or* sturm und drang, grand prix laissez-faire *or* laisser-faire *vient de paraître* fashion	Foreign phrases employed as adjectives are open unless hyphenated in the original language. Note also that they are not italicized unless unfamiliar.
musical terms	D-major triad, F-minor concerto, C-sharp nocturne, A-flat-major scale	Key designations with *flat, sharp, natural, major,* or *minor* are hyphenated when used as adjectives before a noun. *See also under* Noun Forms.
noun plus adjective	fuel-efficient *furnace* labor-intensive, user-friendly *The furnace is* fuel efficient.	Adjectival compounds formed from a noun followed by an adjective are usually hyphenated before the modified noun. If misreading is unlikely, they may be open after the noun.
noun plus participle	decision-making *procedures,* curiosity-evoking *mannerisms,* dust-catching *sculpture,* thought-provoking *reply,* interest-bearing *loan,* machine-made *paper* government-operated, weather-delayed, thought-depleted *The match was* weather delayed.	Adjectival compounds consisting of a noun plus a participle are usually hyphenated before the noun to prevent ambiguity. When used as a predicate adjective, however, they may be left open unless the hyphen is required to prevent misreading.

Table 6.1—*Continued*

Type	Examples	Remarks
	Adjective Forms—Continued	
	The paper was machine made. *The think tank was* thought-depleted. *The loan was* interest bearing. *Her reply was* thought-provoking.	
number plus *odd*	twenty-odd *performances,* five-hundred-odd *socks,* 360-odd *tons* *but* five hundred odd *socks*	Compounds consisting of numbers, either as words or as numerals, and *odd* are always hyphenated.
number plus *percent*	10 percent *increase,* 12 percent *profit*	Compounds consisting of a number followed by *percent,* which is not a unit of measure but an expression of ratio, are always open. *See also* number plus a unit of measure.
number plus a unit of measure	three-mile *limit,* 150-yard *skid* two-year-old *car,* sixty-five-year-old *man,* two-and-a-half-year-old *child,* six-year-old *girls,* three-meter-high *wall,* six year old girls twenty-four five-year-old *boys,* two three-ounce *bottles* *man* sixty-five years old, *child* two and a half years old, *wall* three meters high, *twenty-four boys* five years old 33 m distance 12 kg weight 3 m high wall 3 ft. high wall 1,200 lb. stone	Adjectival compounds comprising a number and a unit of measure are hyphenated before the noun. When an adjective is added after the unit of measure, the adjective and unit are joined by a hyphen. When the adjectival compound is preceded by another, modifying number, the hyphenated compound is kept separate from that number. If the compound comes after the noun, it may usually be left open, but in that case the unit is plural if the number is greater than one. When numerals are used and the units are abbreviated, as in scientific copy, hyphens are omitted even before the noun. *See also under* numbers, fractional.
numbers, fractional	two-thirds *majority,* four and one-eighth *inches,* twenty-one and one-quarter *miles,* two and three-quarters *times larger*	Spelled-out fractions used as adjectives are hyphenated. In mixed fractions, whole numbers are not joined to the fraction by hyphens. *See also under* Adverb Forms *and* Noun Forms.
numbers, whole	twenty-three *shoes,* two hundred *socks,*	Adjectival compounds consisting of spelled-out whole

223

Table 6.1—*Continued*

Type	Examples	Remarks
	Adjective Forms—Continued	
	two hundred thirty-six *aquatints*, one hundred forty-seven *old men*	numbers are hyphenated or open following the same rules that apply to whole numbers used as nouns (*q.v.*).
phrase	devil-may-care *attitude*, matter-of-fact *slaughter* up-to-date, over-the-counter	An adjectival phrase of long standing that has become a commonplace or cliché is hyphenated in any position. Other adjectival phrases are hyphenated before the noun and usually open after the noun.
	His approach was matter-of-fact. *Was the report* up-to-date? *The center fielder was* over-the-hill.	
	less-than-helpful *effort*, *effort* less than helpful, greater-than-usual *resistance*, *resistance* greater than usual	
phrase ending with a preposition	spelled-out *fraction*, burned-out *case*, unheard-of *proposal*	Adjectival compounds ending with words like *out*, *up*, and *of* are hyphenated before the noun. If misreading is unlikely, the compound may be open following the noun or when used as a predicate adjective.
	He prefers his fractions spelled out. *The proposal was* unheard of.	
proper nouns	African American *family*, French Canadian *literature*, Latin American *conference*, Native American *rights*	Adjectival compound nouns formed from the union of two proper nouns are open, hyphenated, or closed as the compound itself is open, hyphenated, or closed.
	Afro-American *scholar*, Scotch-Irish *ancestry*, Austro-Hungarian	
	Aframerican *history*	
	ADVERB FORMS	
all	*going* all out, *knowing* all along, all but *empty*, *painted* all over	Most adverbial compounds beginning with *all* are open, but those ending with an adverb formed by adding *ly* to an adjective are hyphenated.
	She entered all-importantly *and spoke* all-inclusively.	
over, under	overzealously, underhandedly	Adverbial compounds beginning with *over* or *under* are closed.

Table 6.1—*Continued*

Type	Examples	Remarks
	Adverb Forms—*Continued*	

Type	Examples	Remarks
fractions	three-fourths *completed,* one-half *empty*	Compound adverbs consisting of spelled-out fractions are always hyphenated.
other compound adverbs	*He replied* somewhat diffidently. *He* too-readily *agreed.* *He agreed* too readily.	Compound adverbs other than those already mentioned are open unless misreading is likely.

See also the adverbs used in conjunction with adjectives under Adjective Forms.

Noun Forms

Type	Examples	Remarks
ache	headache, toothache, stomachache	All compounds with *ache* are closed.
book	checkbook, notebook, pocketbook, textbook coupon book, reference book	Most compounds with *book* are closed. Consult dictionary. If not in dictionary, compound should be open.
century	nineteenth century, twenty-first century, tenth and eleventh centuries	Compound nouns naming centuries are always open. *See also under* numbers, whole, *below and* Adjective Forms.
cross	crosscurrent, crosstie, crosswalk cross-purpose, cross-pollination cross hair, cross section	Compound nouns with *cross* are closed, hyphenated, or open, as listed in a dictionary.
elect	president-elect, mayor-elect, senator-elect county assessor elect	Compounds with *elect,* meaning *newly elected,* are hyphenated unless the office title comprises two or more words.
ex	ex-president, ex-wife, ex–corporate executive former president, former wife, former county assessor	Compounds with *ex,* meaning *former,* are hyphenated; an en dash is used if the second part is an open compound. (Not recommended in formal writing; *former,* without a hyphen, is preferable.)
full	full moon, full stop, full blood, full dress *but* fullback	Nearly all compound nouns with *full* are open. *See also under* Adjective Forms.

Table 6.1—*Continued*

Type	Examples	Remarks
<td colspan="3" align="center">Noun Forms—*Continued*</td>		
general	attorney general, postmaster general, surgeon general, judge advocate general, General of the Army, general superintendent *but* governor-general	Most titles of offices that include *general* are open.
half	halfback, halftone, half-dollar, half-life, half-moon, half note, half sister	Compound nouns with *half* are closed, hyphenated, or open. If in doubt, consult dictionary. *See also under* Adjective Forms.
house	boardinghouse, boathouse, clubhouse, greenhouse, clearinghouse, farmhouse, housepainter, houseboat rest house, house rule	Most compounds with *house* are closed. Consult dictionary. If not in dictionary, compound should be open.
master	master builder, master artist, master of ceremonies, master wheel, master of arts mastermind, masterstroke, masterpiece, ringmaster toastmaster master-at-arms	Some compounds with *master* are open, some are closed, some are hyphenated.
mid	midfield, midsection, midsummer, mid Atlantic, Mid-Atlantic Range, mid-Victorian	Compound nouns with the prefix *mid* are usually closed, but if the second word is a proper noun, the compound is either open or hyphenated. When in doubt consult a dictionary. *See also under* Adjective Forms.
near	near miss, near beer, near collapse	Compounds with *near* are usually open.
over, under	oversight, undergrowth	Nouns with the prefix *over* or *under* are always closed.
quasi	quasi corporation, quasi contract, quasi scholar, quasi union	All noun compounds with the adjective *quasi* are open. *See also under* Adjective Forms.
self with noun	self-knowledge, self-restraint, self-realization, *but* unselfconsciousness	Compounds with *self* are usually hyphenated. *See also under* Adjective Forms.

Table 6.1—*Continued*

Type	Examples	Remarks
	Noun Forms—*Continued*	
self with suffix	selfhood, selfishness, selfdom, selflessness	Words formed by the addition of suffixes to the root *self* are closed.
vice	vice admiral, vice-admiral vice consul, vice-consul vice regency, vice-regency vice president, vice-president vice-king, vice-master vicegerent, viceroy, vicereine	Difference of opinion exists concerning the treatment of noun compounds with *vice*. Some authorities hyphenate compounds that others leave open. A few compounds are uniformly closed. Some are best hyphenated to prevent misreading. Consistency should be observed within a work.
colors	bluish green (*or* blue green), gray blue, emerald green, coal black, reddish orange	Compound words naming colors are all open. *See also under* Adjective Forms.
compass points	northeast, south-southwest, east by northeast	Compass points combining two directions are closed; those combining three directions are either hyphenated or, if used with the preposition *by,* open.
descriptive phrases	jack-of-all-trades, Johnny-on-the-spot, light-o'-love, stay-at-home, stick-in-the-mud flash in the pan, ball of fire, snake in the grass	Combinations of words describing a character are hyphenated or open. Most can be found in standard dictionaries.
fractions of time and similar constructions	quarter hour, half century, eighth note, quarter section, decade and a half, quarter mile, quarter of a mile half-dollar, half-life, half-moon quarterback	Fractions of time and similar constructions are open, hyphenated; or closed. Consult a dictionary. If compound is not listed, it may be open if no ambiguity results; hyphenate if ambiguous.
musical terms	key of G major, key of F-sharp, key of C-sharp minor	Key designations with *major* or *minor* are always open. Keys modified by *sharp, flat,* or *natural* are hyphenated. *See also under* Adjective Forms.
noun plus gerund	decision making, problem solving, coal mining bookkeeping, dressmaking	Some of these compounds are open, some are closed. Consult a dictionary. If not listed, the compound should be open.

Table 6.1—*Continued*

Type	Examples	Remarks
	Noun Forms—*Continued*	
noun plus noun, representing different but equal functions	scholar-poet, author-critic, soldier-statesman	All such compounds are hyphenated.
noun plus noun, single function	water ballet, water bearer, police officer, plate tectonics, decision maker policymaker, policyholder, jobholder, steamboat, torchbearer	Many of these compounds are open, but some are closed. When in doubt, consult a dictionary.
numbers, fractional	one-half, three-eighths, five-sixteenths thirty-one hundredths, three sixty-fourths four and five-sevenths	Spelled-out fractional numbers are hyphenated unless the numerator or denominator is already hyphenated. In mixed numbers, the whole number is not followed by a hyphen. *See also under* Adjective Forms.
numbers, whole	twenty-six, eighty-nine, two hundred ten, five hundred thirty-eight, one thousand two hundred six, two thousand thirty-seven	Compound nouns spelling out numbers from twenty-one through ninety-nine, whether standing alone or as part of a larger number, are hyphenated. All other numbers or parts of numbers are open. *See also under* Adjective Forms.
proper nouns	New Yorker, French Canadian, Japanese American, Latin American, Native American, African American, Afro-American, Austro-Hungarian, Austria-Hungary, Aframerican	Compound proper nouns are often open, but some are hyphenated, and a few are closed. In case of doubt, consult a dictionary; for compound personal names, a biographical dictionary. *See also under* Adjective Forms.
relationships	grandfather, grandniece great-grandson, great-great-grandmother, sister-in-law, mother-in-law fellow employee, brother officer, mother church, father figure, foster child, parent organization	*Grand*-relatives are closed; *great*-relatives and *in-laws* are hyphenated. Compound nouns expressing other relationships are open.

Table 6.1—*Continued*

PREFIXES FORMING CLOSED COMPOUNDS

Nearly all compounds formed with the prefixes listed below (the list is not exhaustive) are closed, whether they are nouns, verbs, adjectives, or adverbs. The chief exceptions are tabulated following the list.

ante	anteroom, antediluvian, antenatal
anti	anticlerical, antihero, antihypertensive
bi	bivalent, biconvex, binomial
bio	bioecology, biophysical
co	coauthor, coordinate
counter	counterclockwise, countermeasures, countercurrent, counterblow
extra	extraterrestrial, extrafine
infra	infrasonic, infrastructure
inter	interrelated, intertidal, interregnum
intra	intrazonal, intracranial
macro	macroeconomics, macrosphere, macromolecular
meta	metalanguage, metagalaxy, metaethical, metastable (*but* metanalysis)
micro	microminiaturized, microimage, micromethod
mid	midocean, midtown, midgut, midcentury (*but* mid-nineteenth century)
mini	minibus, miniskirt, minibike
multi	multifaceted, multistory, multiconductor
neo	neoclassical, neonatal, neoorthodox, neorealism, Neotropical
non	nonviolent, nonperson, nonplus, nonnegotiable, nonnative (*or* non-native)
over	overlong, overeager, overanalyzed
post	postdoctoral, postface, postwar, postparturition
pre	preempt, precognition, preconference, premalignant
pro	procathedral, procephalic
proto	protoderm, protogalaxy, protolanguage, prototypical
pseudo	pseudopregnancy, pseudoclassic, pseudoheroic
re	reedit, reunify, redigitalize, reexamine

Table 6.1—*Continued*

Prefixes Forming Closed Compounds—*Continued*

semi	semiopaque, semiconductor
socio	socioeconomic, sociopolitical
sub	subjacent, subbasement, subcrustal
super	supertanker, superhigh (frequency), superpose
supra	supranational, suprarenal, supraliminal
trans	transoceanic, transmembrane, transsocietal
ultra	ultrafiche, ultramontane, ultraorganized
un	unfunded, unchurched, uncoiffed, unneutered
under	underused, undersea, underpowered, underreport

EXCEPTIONS TO THE CLOSED STYLE FOR PREFIXED COMPOUNDS

capitalized words or numerals	anti-Semitic, mid-1944, mid-August, pre-1914, neo-Darwinian, post-Kantian *but* transatlantic	Most compounds in which the second element is a capitalized word or numeral are hyphenated.
homographs	re-cover, re-create, re-creation, un-ionized	Compounds that must be distinguished from homographs are hyphenated.
more than one word	pre-latency-period, non-English-speaking, pre–Civil War	Compounds in which the second element consists of more than one word are hyphenated. When a prefix is added to an open compound, the hyphen becomes an en dash.
prefix standing alone	over- and underused, macro- and microeconomics	When alternative prefixes are offered for one word, the prefix standing alone takes a hyphen.
repeated vowels	anti-inflammatory, anti-intellectual, co-opt, co-op, semi-independent, semi-indirect	Some compounds in which the last letter of the prefix and the first letter of the root word (especially when a vowel) are the same are hyphenated to avoid confusion.

Table 6.1—*Continued*

Exceptions to the Closed Style for Prefixed Compounds—*Continued*

misleading or puzzling forms	anti-utopian, co-edition, pro-choice, pro-democracy, pro-life, pro-regent	Compounds that might be misleading or difficult to read are hyphenated.

Final note: When you are uncertain about the spelling of a compound formed with a prefix, consult a dictionary. If the word is not listed, the following principle may be helpful: Hyphens should be used to avoid ambiguity and difficult reading, but if misreading is unlikely, the compound may be closed.

7 *Names and Terms*

INTRODUCTION

7.1   The purpose of this chapter is to help establish patterns in the use of names and of terms associated with names: names of persons and places, of events and movements, of governmental bodies and their actions, and of certain things and classifications, as well as titles of literary and artistic works. Which of these should always be capitalized? What titles are commonly set in italics? These and similar questions must be resolved before any reasonable editorial consistency can be attained in a book or journal.

Capitalization

7.2   Modern publishers of works in the English language, American perhaps more than British, usually discourage excessive use of capital letters in text. Proper nouns are still conventionally capitalized,[1] but many words derived from or associated with them may be lowercased with no loss of clarity or significance. Questions and differences of opinion arise over what constitutes a proper noun, other than the name of a person or a place. It is with this realm of uncertainty that the following rules attempt to deal. They reflect the tendency toward the use of fewer capitals, toward what is called a *down* (lowercase) style as opposed to an *up* (uppercase, i.e., capital letter) style.

7.3   Although the pattern of capitalization chosen for the various categories illustrated in this chapter may prove adaptable to most publications, any such pattern may require modification in some specialized works. Experienced editors realize that no set of rules in the area of capitalization can be universally applied. Particular authors may have particular and valid reasons for capitalizing certain terms normally lowercased in other works. When authors do have reason to depart from the usual patterns, however, they should so inform their publishers by providing a list of the terms involved. If an editor can find no valid reason for an author's departure from convention, there should be a consultation between editor and author, and agreement or compromise reached, before the editor undertakes to prepare the manuscript for publication.

7.4   Most authors, however, do not feel strongly about capitalization, and many are oblivious to inconsistencies in their manuscripts. The manuscript editor must therefore establish a logical, acceptable style and regularize any departures from it (see 2.96). The following categories and lists are meant to provide a helpful pattern for editors to follow. The editor, understanding the nature of the work, must use discretion, judgment, and intuition in deciding when to follow the pattern and when to depart from it.

Names and Titles

7.5   Names of some things and titles of some works are conventionally set in italic type. Other titles, chiefly of shorter works or parts of larger works, are set in roman type and enclosed in quotation marks. Still others are capitalized but neither italicized nor quoted. Like the conventions of capitalization, these conventions may also be altered in certain situations. For example, the author of a critical study in literature or music containing many references to short stories or essays as well as book-length works or to both long and short poems or musical compositions is well advised to give *all* titles in italics. (See 7.126–54.)

---

1. To *capitalize* a word means to capitalize only the initial letter. A word or phrase printed all in capital letters, LIKE THIS, is said to be set in *full caps*.

PERSONAL NAMES

7.6   Names and initials of persons are capitalized:

C. K. Scott-Moncrieff	R. W. B. Lewis
W. Theodore Watts-Dunton	C. V. Wedgwood
John F. Kennedy	LBJ

The space between initials should be the same as the space between initial and name (*not* R.W.B. Lewis), except when initials are used alone, without periods (see 14.4).

7.7   For most names, the University of Chicago Press uses the spelling in *Webster's New Biographical Dictionary*. Additional authorities include the biographical-names sections of such dictionaries as *Webster's New Collegiate Dictionary,* as well as *Who's Who* and *Who's Who in America*. Some variation will be found among the authorities, and selection must sometimes be made, but the choice should in each case be followed consistently throughout a single work.

English Names with Particles

7.8   Many names of French, Spanish, Portuguese, Italian, German, and Dutch derivation include particles: *de, du, la, l', della, von, van, van der, ten,* and so forth. For names of this type borne by people in English-speaking countries, practice with regard to capitalizing the particles varies widely, and competent authority should be consulted in doubtful cases.[2] Generally the surname retains the particle when used alone:

Eugen D'Albert; D'Albert
Lee De Forest; De Forest
Walter de la Mare; de la Mare
Daphne du Maurier; du Maurier
Eva Le Gallienne; Le Gallienne
Abraham Ten Broeck; Ten Broeck
Martin Van Buren; Van Buren
Wernher von Braun; von Braun
Alexander de Seversky; de Seversky
Eamon De Valera; De Valera

Non-English Names

FRENCH NAMES

7.9   In French practice, the articles *le, la,* and *les,* as well as the contractions *du (de le)* and *des (de les),* are capitalized whether or not a first

---

2. For alphabetizing names with particles see 17.106.

name or title precedes (in many family names, of course, they are run in—Desmoulins, Lafayette):

François, duc de La Rochefoucauld; La Rochefoucauld
Philippe Du Puy de Clinchamps; Du Puy de Clinchamps

The preposition *de* (or *d'*) itself is always lowercased and is often dropped when the surname is used alone:

Alexis de Tocqueville; Tocqueville
Alfred de Musset; Musset
but
Charles de Gaulle; de Gaulle
Jean d'Alembert; d'Alembert
Comte de Grasse; Admiral de Grasse; de Grasse

French given names are sometimes hyphenated. When initials for these are used, the hyphen is retained, along with the usual periods:

Jacques-Louis David
J.-L. David

ITALIAN, PORTUGUESE, GERMAN, AND DUTCH NAMES

7.10   Particles in Italian, Portuguese, German, and Dutch names are lowercased and are usually dropped when the surname is used alone in the original language. In English, writers have shown little consistency in their treatment of such names. The frequent older practice was to retain and capitalize the particle when the surname was used alone. Consequently, for some names the form with the particle is the only familiar one and must necessarily be used. For other names the native practice should be followed:

Giovanni da Verrazano; Verrazano
Luca della Robbia; *in English contexts,* della Robbia
Vasco da Gama; *in English contexts,* da Gama
Heinrich Friedrich Karl vom und zum Stein; Stein
Alexander von Humboldt; Humboldt
Maximilian von Spee; Spee
Friedrich von Steuben; *in English contexts often* von (*or* Von) Steuben
Ludwig van Beethoven; Beethoven
Vincent van Gogh; *in English usually* van Gogh
Bernard ter Haar; ter Haar
Jacobus Hendricus van't Hoff; *in English contexts* van't Hoff
Wouter Van Twiller; Van Twiller

SPANISH NAMES

7.11   Many Spanish surnames are composed of both the father's and the mother's family names, in that order, sometimes joined by *y* (and). These names are often shortened to a single name (usually but not always the first of the two). It is never incorrect to use both names, but tradition or the person's own preference sometimes dictates the use of only one:

José Ortega y Gasset; Ortega y Gasset *or* Ortega
Pascual Ortiz Rubio; Ortiz Rubio *or* Ortiz
Federico García Lorca; García Lorca

Many Spanish names are compounded with an article, a preposition, or both, as are many French names:

Tomás de Torquemada; Torquemada
Manuel de Falla; *in English contexts,* de Falla
Bartolomé de Las Casas; Las Casas

(For more on Spanish names see 17.110–12.)

ARABIC NAMES

7.12   Surnames of Arabic origin often are prefixed by such elements as *Abu* ("father of"), *Abd (Abdul, Abdel), ibn* ("son of"), *al,* or *el.* These are part of the surname and should not be dropped when the surname is used alone (for alphabetizing Arabic names see 17.114–15):

Syed Abu Zafar Navdi; Abu Zafar Navdi
Aziz ibn Saud; Ibn Saud

Names of rulers of older times, however, are often shortened to the first name rather than the last:

Harun al-Rashid *or* Harun ar-Rashid; Harun

(See also 9.94.)

CHINESE NAMES

7.13   In Chinese practice, the family name comes before the given name, which usually has two elements. As romanized in the Wade-Giles system, the family name and the first element of the given name are capitalized, and the given name is hyphenated: Chiang Kai-shek, Pai Ch'ung-hsi. Chinese may be referred to by family name alone: Chiang, Pai. Ancient Chinese names often have only two elements, which may not be separated: Li Po, Tu Fu, Lao Tsu. The pinyin romanization system, generally used since the late 1970s for Chinese names in material in the English language, employs no hyphens or apostrophes and spells given names as one word (see 9.95–98; 17.116–18).

RUSSIAN NAMES

7.14   Russian family names, as well as middle names (patronymics), sometimes but not always take different endings for male and female members of the family. For example, Lenin's real name was Vladimir Ilyich Ulyanov; his sister was Maria Ilyinichna Ulyanova. Often in text only the given name and patronymic are used; in the index, of course, the name should be listed under the family name, whether this appears in the text or not.

HUNGARIAN NAMES

7.15   In Hungarian practice the family name precedes the given name—Molnár Ferenc—but (as with this playwright) the names are often inverted to normal English order when used in a non-Hungarian context: Ferenc Molnár.

Titles and Offices

7.16   Civil, military, religious, and professional titles and titles of nobility are capitalized when they immediately precede a personal name, as part of the name:

President Buchanan	Cardinal Newman
General Eisenhower	Prince Charles

The title is also capitalized if it refers to more than one name (compare 7.43):

Mayors Cermak and Walker   Doctors Joseph and Hershall

When such titles are used in apposition to a name they are not part of the name and so are lowercased:

the emperor Maximilian (i.e., the emperor who was Maximilian)
French president François Mitterrand (*better:* President François Mitterrand of France)

7.17   In formal usage, such as acknowledgments and lists of contributors, titles following a personal name are usually capitalized. A title used alone, in place of a personal name, is capitalized in such contexts as toasts or formal introductions:

The translators wish to acknowledge their indebtedness to C. R. Dodwell, Fellow and Librarian of Trinity College, Cambridge.

Ladies and gentlemen, the President of the United States.

Titles used in place of names in direct address are capitalized:

I would have done it, Captain, but the ship was sinking.
Only yesterday, Professor, you said . . .

7.18   In text, titles following a personal name or used alone in place of a name (other than in direct address) are, with few exceptions, lowercased. The lists in the sections that follow show various titles and words related to them as they might appear in text sentences. The lists are not exhaustive, but they will at least offer patterns for those titles and offices not included.

CIVIL TITLES AND OFFICES

7.19 One of the exceptions referred to above is the title *Speaker* (of the House), which is customarily capitalized when used alone or after a personal name to avoid ambiguity. Note also that a member of the House of Representatives is commonly referred to as *congressman* or *congresswoman,* although *representative* may also be used to avoid gender distinction, and *representative from* may be used before the name of a state and after the name of the representative.

> the president of the United States; the president; the presidency; President George Washington; President Washington; President and Mrs. Washington; George Washington, president of the United States; the Washington administration; Vice President Garner; John Nance Garner, vice president of the United States

> the secretary of state; the secretary; Secretary of State George C. Marshall; Secretary of State Marshall; George Catlett Marshall, secretary of state

> the senator; the senator from Ohio; Senator Howard M. Metzenbaum; Senator Metzenbaum; Howard M. Metzenbaum, senator from Ohio

> the state senator; the senator; Olga Parker, Ohio state senator; state senator Parker (see also 7.16)

> the congressman from Oregon; the congresswoman from Ohio; the representative from New Mexico; Congressman Olin Paprowski; Congresswoman Deborah Baron; Congresswoman Baron; Representative Paprowski; Deborah Baron, representative from Ohio; Olin Paprowski, congressman from Idaho

> Speaker of the House of Representatives; the Speaker; Thomas P. O'Neill, Speaker of the House; Congressman O'Neill

> the mayor of New York; the mayor; Mayor Dinkins; David N. Dinkins, mayor of New York

> the chief justice of the United States; the chief justice; Chief Justice Warren; Earl Warren, chief justice of the United States

> the justice; Justice Stevens *or* Mr. Justice Stevens; John Paul Stevens, associate justice

> the ambassador; the ambassador to Great Britain *or* the ambassador to the Court of Saint James's; the American ambassador; the American embassy; Ambassador Brewster; Kingman Brewster, ambassador to Great Britain

> the governor; the governor of Illinois; Governor Stevenson; Adlai E. Stevenson, governor of the state of Illinois

> the prime minister; the prime minister of England; Frederick Lord North, prime minister of England; Lord North; the North ministry

a member of Parliament; Geoffrey Windermere, member of Parliament (*or* M.P.)

foreign minister; foreign minister of Great Britain; the British foreign minister; George Canning, foreign minister of Great Britain; the foreign office

the emperor; the kaiser; Emperor William (*or* Wilhelm) II of Germany; William II, emperor of Germany; Kaiser Wilhelm

Chancellor Adolf Hitler; the chancellor; the führer

MILITARY TITLES AND OFFICES

7.20   Two exceptions to the "down" style in this category are *General of the Army* and *Fleet Admiral,* which are capitalized to avoid ambiguity. Note also that *commander in chief* is not hyphenated.

the general; commander in chief; General Ulysses S. Grant, commander in chief of the Union army; General Grant

the General of the Army; Omar N. Bradley, General of the Army; General Bradley, chairman of the Joint Chiefs of Staff; General Bradley; General of the Army Omar N. Bradley

the British general; General Sir Guy Carleton, British commander in New York City; Sir Guy; General Carleton; General Emerson T. Barrel, retired

the admiral; commander of the Pacific Fleet; Fleet Admiral; Chester W. Nimitz, Fleet Admiral; Admiral Nimitz, commander of the Pacific Fleet; Admiral Nimitz

the captain; the company commander; Captain Gagliardi, the company commander

the sergeant; a noncommissioned officer (NCO); Sergeant Carleton C. Singer

the warrant officer; Warrant Officer Carmichael; Mr. Carmichael

the chief petty officer; the chief; Chief Petty Officer Tannenbaum

the private; Private T. C. Alhambra

RELIGIOUS TITLES AND OFFICES

7.21   the pope; the papacy; Pope John Paul II

the cardinal; the sacred college of cardinals; Jerome Cardinal Sikorski *or, less formally,* Cardinal Jerome Sikorski

the archbishop; Archbishop Makarios III

the archbishop of Canterbury; Frederick Temple, archbishop of Canterbury

the rabbi; Rabbi Stephen Wise

the bishop; bishopric; diocese; the Reverend Gerald Francis Burrill, bishop of Chicago *(Anglican);* Bishop Burrill; the bishop of Chicago; the Most

Reverend John A. Donovan, bishop of Toledo *(Roman Catholic);* Bishop Donovan; the bishop of Toledo; the Catholic bishop of Toledo

the minister; the Reverend James Neal, minister of Third Presbyterian Church; Mr. *(or* Dr.) Neal; Rev. James Neal (see 14.7)

the rector; the Reverend George Smith, rector of Saint David's Church *(Anglican);* Father Smith *or* Mr. Smith *or* the Reverend Mr. Smith *(not* Reverend Smith)

John Flynn, O.F.M.; Nadine Solonski, D.D.; Leroy Ohlmstead, Th.D.

the mother superior of the Ursuline convent; Mother Superior *(direct address)*

the patriarch; the patriarch of Constantinople; the patriarchate

PROFESSIONAL TITLES

7.22   Among professional titles, named academic professorships and fellowships are usually capitalized wherever they appear, especially if they are accompanied by a personal name.

the professor; Professor T. Peter Norsag; Mary M. Warren, Alfred R. Wellman Distinguished Service Professor; Professor Warren; Arthur M. Trouville, Wellington Kingsley Professor Emeritus; a professor emeritus; Margaret J. O'Neal, professor emerita; Marcello Sonata, professor of music

the chair of the department; Farland P. Whithermaster, chair of the Department of Chemistry

the president; the president's office; President Serafina; Olga Serafina, president of Causwell University; President and Dr. Serafina; Alfred Beamish, president of Hostwell Corporation; Mr. Beamish; president of the corporation; Vice President George Nakamura; George Nakamura, vice president of the corporation

Fulbright scholar

TITLES OF NOBILITY

7.23   the queen; the queen of England; Queen Elizabeth; Elizabeth II, queen of England

the emperor; Emperor Charles V; the emperor Charles V; the Holy Roman Emperor Charles V; the Holy Roman Emperor

the earl; the earl of Shaftesbury; Anthony Ashley Cooper, third earl of Shaftesbury

the baronet; Sir Humphrey Blimp, Bart.; Sir Humphrey

the duke; Prince Philip, duke of Edinburgh *(often capitalized in this honorary title)* the dowager queen; Dowager Queen Mary

the count; Count (*or* Graf) Helmuth von Moltke; Count von Moltke

the duc de Guise; François de Lorraine, duc de Guise; the second duc de Guise; the duke

7.24   For the sake of clarity, or perhaps unbreakable tradition, some British titles are capitalized when used without a personal name:

Prince of Wales	Dame of Sark
Queen Mother	*but*
Princess Royal	prince consort

British usage favors a more liberal use of capitals for titles than that recommended above.

Academic Years

7.25   Terms designating academic years are lowercased:

freshman   sophomore   junior   senior

Academic Degrees and Honors

7.26   The names of academic degrees and honors should be capitalized when following a personal name, whether abbreviated or written in full:

Clyde M. Haverstick, Doctor of Law
Joseph Hershall, M.D.
Lee Wallek, Fellow of the Royal Academy

But when academic degrees are referred to in such general terms as *doctorate, doctor's degree, bachelor's degree, master of science,* they are not capitalized.

Honorific Titles

7.27   Honorific titles and forms of address should be capitalized in any context:

Her (His) Majesty	Your Grace	Excellency
His (Her) Royal Highness	His Eminence	Your Honor
but		
my lord	sir	madam

Temporary, Role-Denoting Epithets

7.28   Role-denoting ad hoc epithets such as *citizen, schoolboy, housewife, defendant, historian,* and the like are sometimes capitalized in newspaper and magazine writing, but this is a practice to be avoided. Such temporary, ad hoc epithets are not titles and are not parts of, or replacements for, the name but rather elements in apposition to the name, and as such they should be lowercased. The article *the* usually precedes the epithet. Temporary epithets are not to be confused with commonly accepted epithets for particular persons, which are discussed in 7.29:

> the schoolboy Stephen Cavanagh (*not* Schoolboy Cavanagh)
> the historian Arthur Schlesinger Jr. (*not* Historian Schlesinger)

Commonly Accepted Epithets

7.29   A characterizing word or phrase that has become a commonly accepted epithet used as part of, or a substitute for, the name of some person is capitalized and not enclosed in quotation marks:

> the Great Emancipator   the Sun King
> the Wizard of Menlo Park   the Young Pretender
> Stonewall Jackson   the Great Commoner
> the Autocrat of the Breakfast Table   the Iron Duke
> Babe Ruth   the Swedish Nightingale

When such an epithet is used within the full name, it is usually enclosed in quotation marks. When it is used following the full name, it is usually enclosed in quotation marks and preceded by a comma or, if it appears in the middle of a sentence, is set off by a pair of commas:

> George Herman "Babe" Ruth
> Jenny Lind, "the Swedish Nightingale"
> Huey Long, "the Kingfish," dominated Louisiana politics . . .

Note that an initial *the,* even if part of the epithet, is not capitalized. (See also 7.28.)

Fictitious Names

7.30   Names used for fictitious or unidentified persons and names used as personifications are capitalized

> John Doe   John Barleycorn   Johnny Reb
> Jane Doe   John Bull   Uncle Sam

except when used in such expressions as

by george   every man jack

Kinship Names

7.31   Kinship names are lowercased when preceded by modifiers. When used before a proper name or alone, in place of the name, they are usually capitalized:

His father died at the age of ninety-three.
My brother and sister live in California.
the Grimké sisters
Happy birthday, Uncle Ed.
I know that Mother's middle name is Marie.
Please, Dad, let's go.

Personification

7.32   The personification of abstractions—giving them the attributes of persons—is not a common device in today's prose writing. When it is used, the personified noun is usually capitalized:

Nature's handmaid, Art . . .
In the springtime nature is at its best.
Then Spring—with her warm showers—arrived.
The icy blasts of winter had departed.
Like Milton, he bade Melancholy be gone.
He had suffered from melancholy all his life.

Where there is doubt, the word should be lowercased:

It was a battle between head and heart; reason finally won.

NATIONALITIES, TRIBES, AND OTHER GROUPS OF PEOPLE

7.33   The names of specific racial, linguistic, tribal, religious, and other groupings of people are capitalized:

Aborigine	Caucasian
African American	Chicana/Chicano
Afro-American	Highlander (of Scotland)
American Indian	Hispanic
Arab	Indo-European
Asian	Latina/Latino

Magyar	Native American[3]
Malay	Negro
Mongol	Nordic
Mormon	Romany
Muslim	

7.34 Designations based only on color, size, habitat, customs, or local usage are often lowercased (but see 7.35). Some designations that are capitalized when referring to specific peoples (as in 7.33) are lowercased when applied more generally.

aborigine	highlander
black	white

7.35 The term *Black* is now often capitalized as the widely accepted name of the dark-skinned group or groups of people originating in Africa. (*African American* has also been gaining broad acceptance among these groups.) Similarly, *White* is often capitalized as the preferred term for light-skinned people, for some reason long known as Caucasians. *Red, Yellow,* and *Brown,* however, are no longer commonly used to designate ethnic groups. *Native American, Asian,* and *Latina/Latino* or *Latin American* are preferred and used more widely.

PLACE-NAMES

Geographical and Related Terms

7.36 Geographical terms commonly accepted as proper names are capitalized. Other descriptive or identifying geographical terms that either are not taken to apply to one geographical entity only or have not become commonly regarded as proper names for these entities are not capitalized. Cultural or climatic terms derived from geographical proper names are generally lowercased. Terms designating longitude and latitude, even when singular in application, such as *prime meridian* and *equator,* are also regularly lowercased, as are compass directions when not part of a proper name such as *Northwest Passage. North, South, East,* and *West* are often capitalized on a map, and *N, S, E,* and *W* generally are. The term *tropic* (circle) is lowercased even when used in such names as *tropic of Cancer* and *tropic of Capricorn,* but when used in plural form to refer to the zone between these two tropics, it becomes a capitalized proper name, *Tropics,* synonymous with *Torrid Zone.*

---

3. Both words are capitalized when referring to an American Indian; when the reference is to any native-born American, *native* is lowercased: native American.

Antarctica, Antarctic Circle, subantarctic; the Arctic, Arctic Circle, arctic climate, Arctic waters

Central America, Central American; central Europe (but see 7.38)

the Continent (Europe), continental Europe, the European continent, Continental customs

the East, the Orient, oriental culture (*but* an Oriental), Eastern culture; eastern Europe (but see 7.38); Middle East(ern); Near East(ern); Eastern (Western) Hemisphere; the East, eastern, easterner, eastern seaboard (U.S.); east, eastern, eastward (direction)

the equator, equatorial climate; equatorial Africa; Equatorial Current; meridian, prime meridian; thirty-eighth parallel; international date line

North Africa; East (West) Africa; northern, southern, central, or eastern Africa

North (South) American continent

North Atlantic, northern Atlantic

Northern (Southern) Hemisphere

North (South) Pole, the Pole, North Polar ice cap, polar regions; polar climate; Northwest Passage; northwest (direction)

the South, southern, southerner (but see 7.38), the Southwest (U.S.); the south of France (the Midi); south, southern, southeastern, southwestern (directions)

Southeast Asia; central Asia (*but in certain contexts*[4] Central Asia)

South (North) Temperate Zone

tropic of Cancer, tropic of Capricorn; Neotropics, Neotropic(al); the Tropics; tropical, subtropical; the Torrid Zone

Upper Michigan, the Upper Peninsula, northern Michigan; Upper Egypt; Upper Rhine

the West, Occident, occidental culture (*but* an Occidental), Western world, western Europe (but see 7.38), westerner; Western Hemisphere; the West, West Coast, Northwest, Pacific Northwest, Far West, Middle West, Midwest (U.S.); west, western, westerner, westward (direction)

7.37   When a capitalized geographical term comprising more than one word is used as an adjective before a noun, the term should not be hyphenated, since there is no risk of misreading:

Middle Eastern journey
North Atlantic fog
Torrid Zone lassitude
Gulf of Mexico oil spill

---

4. For example, in reference to a division of Imperial Russia (also Russian Central Asia) and of the former Soviet Union (also Soviet Central Asia).

7.38   In works dealing with the years following World War II it is customary to capitalize *Western Europe* and *Eastern Europe* when referring to the political rather than simply geographical divisions of the Continent. Similarly, *Central Europe* is capitalized when referring to the political divisions of World War I. In American Civil War contexts, *Southern(er)* and *Northern(er)* are capitalized.

7.39   Popular and legendary names of places are usually capitalized and are not enclosed in quotation marks:

> Albion
> Back Bay (Boston)
> the Badger State
> Badlands (South Dakota)
> Bay Area (San Francisco)
> Benelux countries
> Cathay
> the Channel (English Channel)
> City of Brotherly Love
> Deep South (U.S.); Old South; antebellum South
> the Delta (region in state of Mississippi)
> Eastern Shore (of Chesapeake Bay)
> Eternal City
> Fertile Crescent
> Foggy Bottom
> Holy City
> the Keys (Florida)
> Lake District
> Land of the Rising Sun
> Left Bank (Paris)
> the Levant
> the Loop (Chicago)
> Near North (Chicago)
> New World; Old World
> Old Dominion (Virginia)
> Panhandle
> the Piedmont
> Promised Land
> Skid Row
> South Seas
> the States (U.S.)
> Sun Belt
> Tenderloin (San Francisco)
> Third World *or* third world
> Twin Cities
> Utopia *or* utopia[5]
> the Village (New York or Montréal)
> West Side (New York or Chicago)
> Wild West

5. *Utopia* is capitalized in reference to the imaginary country described by Thomas More. When used as a generic name for an ideal state, it is usually lowercased.

Political Divisions

7.40   Words such as *empire, state, county, city, kingdom, colony, territory,* and so forth, which designate political divisions of the world, are capitalized when they are used as an accepted part of the proper name. When not used as an accepted part of the proper name, or when used alone, such terms are usually lowercased.

> Roman Empire; the empire under Augustus; the empire
> Washington State; the state of Washington
> State of Illinois; the state of Illinois
> New England states; Middle Atlantic states
> Hennepin County; the county of Hennepin
> county Cork (Irish usage)
> New York City; the city of New York
> the City[6] (old London)
> Massachusetts Bay Colony; the colony at Massachusetts Bay
> the British colonies; the thirteen colonies
> the Province of Ontario; Kiangsi Province; the province
> the Union of Soviet Socialist Republics; the Soviet Union; the USSR
> the Union of South Africa; the Union
> the Union (U.S.)
> Northwest Territory
> Indiana Territory; the territory of Indiana
> the Western Reserve
> Evanston Township; the town of Evanston
> Eleventh Congressional District; his congressional district
> Kweneng District; the district
> Fifth Ward; the ward; ward politics
> Sixth Precinct; the precinct
> the Commonwealth
> the Dominion of Canada; the dominion *or* the Dominion
> the Republic of France; the French republic; the republic *or* the Republic;
>   the Fifth Republic
> the Republic (U.S.)

Socioeconomic Classes or Groups

7.41   Terms denoting socioeconomic classes or groups are generally lowercased. Terms of more than one word are hyphenated when used as adjectives before nouns.

> middle class
> working class
> white-collar worker
> the homeless
> street people

6. The *City,* meaning the financial center—the old city—of London, is always capitalized.

the working poor
working-class parents
upper-middle-class families

Topographical Names

7.42   Names of mountains, rivers, oceans, islands, and so forth are capitalized. A generic term such as *lake, mountain, river,* or *valley* is also
capitalized when used as part of the name, whether or not it is capitalized in the gazetteer or atlas. All doubtful spellings in atlases or gazet-
teers should be checked against such an authority as *Webster's New
Geographical Dictionary.*

> Bering Strait
> Black Forest
> Cape Sable
> Continental Divide
> Great Barrier Reef
> Himalaya Mountains; the Himalayas
> Iberian Peninsula; the peninsula
> Indian Ocean
> Kaskaskia River (*but* the river Elbe)
> Mozambique Channel
> Nile Delta
> Silver Lake
> the Sea of Azov
> South China Sea
> Walden Pond
> Windward Islands; the Windwards

7.43   The University of Chicago Press now recommends that when a generic
term is used in the plural either before or after more than one proper
name, the term should be capitalized if, in the singular form and in the
same position, it would be recognized as a part of each name. Formerly
such plural terms were capitalized only when preceding the proper
names.

> Lakes Erie and Huron
> Mounts Everest and Rainier
> the Adirondack and Catskill Mountains
> the Hudson and Mississippi Rivers
> > *but*
> the rivers Hudson and Mississippi

7.44   When a generic term is used descriptively rather than as part of the
name, or when it is used alone, it is lowercased:

> the valley of the Mississippi
> the Hudson River valley
> the French coast (*but* the West Coast [U.S.])

> the California desert
> the Kansas prairie
> the Indian peninsula (*but* the Malay Peninsula)
> along the Pacific coast (*but* Pacific Coast *if the region is meant*)

7.45   When a foreign term forms part of a geographic name in English, the meaning of the foreign term should be observed:

> Rio Grande (*not* Rio Grande River)
> Sierra Nevada (*not* Sierra Nevada Mountains *or* the Sierras, *although the latter is often used in informal speech*)
> Mauna Loa (*not* Mount Mauna Loa *or* Mauna Loa Mountain)
> Fujiyama (*also* Fuji, Fujinoyama, *or* Fuji-san) *or* Mount Fuji (*not* Mount Fujiyama *or* Fujiyama Mountain)

Structures and Public Places

7.46   Names of buildings, architecturally or historically significant houses, thoroughfares, monuments, and the like are capitalized. An introductory *the*, even if part of the name, is not capitalized in running text.

> the White House
> the Capitol (national; distinguish between *capital*, a city, and *capitol*, a building)
> the Mall (Washington, D.C.; London)
> Statue of Liberty[7]
> Washington Monument
> Jefferson Memorial
> Robie House
> Chrysler Building
> the Breakers
> the Midway (Chicago)
> the Pyramids (*but* the Egyptian pyramids)
> the Sphinx
> Leaning Tower of Pisa
> Stone of Scone

7.47   Such terms as *avenue, boulevard, bridge, building, church, fountain, hotel, park, room, square, street,* or *theater* are capitalized when part of an official or formal name. When the plural form is used before or following more than one name and constitutes, albeit in the singular, part of each name, the term is capitalized (see 7.43). Standing alone, however, such terms are lowercased.

> Adler Planetarium; the planetarium
> Buckingham Palace

---

7. Regarded as a monument, not a piece of sculpture, and therefore not italicized. For names of statues and other works of art see 7.154.

> Carnegie and Euclid Avenues
> the Eiffel Tower
> Empire State Building; the Empire State
> the Empire State and Chrysler Buildings
> Fifth Avenue (*by New Yorkers sometimes called* the Avenue)
> Fifty-seventh Street
> First Congregational Church; the church
> Golden Gate Bridge
> 4146 Grand Avenue
> Lincoln Park; the park
> the Outer Drive; the drive (*by Chicagoans sometimes called* the Drive)
> the Oval Office; the president's office
> the Persian Room (*of a hotel; but* room 16)
> Philharmonic Hall in Lincoln Center for the Performing Arts; the hall; the center
> Phoenix Theatre (*in this case not* Theater); the theater
> Piccadilly Circus
> U.S. Route 66; U.S. Routes 1 and 2; Routes 1 and 2; Maine Route 3; a state route; Interstate 80; an interstate highway
> Spassky Gate
> Times Square
> Westminster Abbey
> > *but*
> the ducal palace
> the Lateran palace
> a temple of Venus
> Winchester cathedral

7.48 Titles of foreign structures, streets, and so forth given in the original language are not italicized (see also 9.21):

> Bibliothèque Nationale
> Bois de Boulogne
> Champs-Elysées
> Palacio Nacional
> Palais Royal
> Piazza delle Terme
> Puente de Segovia
> 18, rue de Provence
> Via Nazionale

WORDS DERIVED FROM PROPER NAMES

7.49 Nouns, adjectives, and verbs derived from personal, national, or geographical names are often lowercased when used with a specialized meaning. According to some authorities, however, certain of these terms ought to be capitalized. Authors and editors must decide for themselves, but whatever choice is made should be followed consistently throughout a work.

DOWN STYLE

anglicize
arabic numerals
arctic boots
bohemian
brussels sprouts
china (ceramic ware)
diesel engine
dutch oven
frankfurter
french fries, dressing, windows
herculean
homeric
india ink
italicize
japan (varnish)
jeremiad
lombardy poplar

macadam road
manila envelope
mecca
morocco (leather)
paris green
pasteurize
pharisaic
philistine
plaster of paris
quixotic
roman numerals
roman type
russian dressing
scotch whisky
sienna (pigment)
venetian blinds
vulcanize

UP STYLE

Arabic numerals
Dutch oven
French fries
French windows
Homeric

Lombardy poplar
Paris green
Roman numerals
Russian dressing
Scotch whisky

(See also 7.108.)

NAMES OF ORGANIZATIONS

Governmental and Judicial Bodies

7.50 Full names, and often the shortened names, of legislative, deliberative, administrative, and judicial bodies, departments, bureaus, and offices are capitalized. Adjectives derived from them are usually lowercased, as are paraphrastic designations, except abbreviations.

LEGISLATIVE AND DELIBERATIVE

7.51 United Nations Security Council; UN Security Council; the Security Council; the council

United States Congress; the Ninety-seventh Congress; Congress; Cong.; congressional

Senate (U.S.); the upper house of Congress

House of Representatives; the House; the lower house of Congress

Committee on Foreign Affairs; Foreign Affairs Committee; Fulbright committee; the committee

General Assembly of Illinois; Illinois legislature; assembly; state legislature; state senate
Chicago City Council; city council; council
Parliament; parliamentary; an early parliament; both houses of Parliament
House of Commons; the Commons
the Crown (British monarchy); Crown lands
Cortes (Spain)
Curia Regis; the great council (England)
Duma (Russia)
States General *or* Estates General (France)
Reichstag (Germany)

ADMINISTRATIVE

7.52   Department of State; State Department; the department
National Labor Relations Board; the board; NLRB
Bureau of the Census; Census Bureau; the bureau; the census of 1960
Agency for International Development; AID; the agency
Peace Corps
Chicago Board of Education; the board of education; the board

JUDICIAL

7.53   United States Supreme Court; the Supreme Court; the Court[8]
Arizona Supreme Court; state supreme court
United States Court of Appeals for the Second Circuit; court of appeals; circuit court; the court
Circuit Court of Cook County; county court; circuit court
Municipal Court of Chicago; municipal court
District Court for the Southern District of New York; district court
Juvenile Division of the County Department of the Circuit Court of Cook County
Court of King's Bench; the court
Star Chamber

7.54   Generic terms designating courts are frequently used in place of a full name. They are lowercased even when they refer to a specific court:

traffic court   family court   juvenile court

7.55   Each state has its own system for denominating its courts. Sometimes capitalization other than that suggested above is desirable for clarity. For example, in New York and Maryland the highest state court is not the supreme court but the court of appeals:

New York Court of Appeals; the Court of Appeals (capitalized to distinguish it from the U.S. court); the court

___

8. The word *court* when used alone is capitalized only in references to the U.S. Supreme Court.

7.56   Not usually capitalized are the following:

> administration; Eisenhower administration
> brain trust
> cabinet (*but* Kitchen Cabinet in the Jackson administration)
> church and state
> city hall (i.e., the municipal government)
> civil service
> court (royal)
> electoral college
> executive, legislative, or judicial branch
> federal (government, agency, court, powers, etc.)
> government
> ministry
> monarchy
> parlement (*but* Parlement of Paris)
> post office
> state (powers, laws, etc.; state's attorney)
> witenagemot

Political and Economic Organizations and Alliances

7.57   A disconcerting variety is encountered, even among authoritative sources, in the capitalization of names of political and economic organizations and alliances and of their adherents. Writers and editors might profitably become aware of such inconsistencies, choose carefully among alternatives, and follow their choices with as much consistency as possible. But readers should not become downcast if perceived inconsistencies occur, since as anyone working extensively with such terms must soon recognize, extremely subtle and perhaps irreconcilable differences exist. Along with the quest for uniformity, an enlightened tolerance should be practiced. In this spirit, the Press offers the following discussion.

7.58   One principle on which a choice between capitalizing and lowercasing is made is whether the term is used in a restricted, official way or in a more generic, less official way. When one has in mind an actual follower of the Bolshevist cause in early-twentieth-century Russia, for instance, the term should be capitalized: "They had been identified by the state police as Bolshevists." If one refers less historically to someone considered to be of a radical and generally "bolshevist" inclination, however, lowercase should be chosen: "The man is a bolshevist." Such terms as *party, movement, platform, bloc,* and the like have usually been lowercased when used with organizational terms. The Press now recognizes, however, that many writers and editors prefer to capitalize *party* if the name of the party itself is capitalized. Although lowercasing in this instance is still acceptable, capitalization is also correct and in fact may be recommended. When *party* is used alone, however, in reference to a capitalized group, it is still generally lowercased.[9] In the following examples, choices listed after a semicolon are assumed to be used in a generic rather than a specific or historical sense.

> Bolshevik, Bolshevist, Bolshevik movement, Bolshevism; bolshevism, bolshevist
> Communist Party, the party, Communist(s), Communist bloc, Communism; communism, communist
> Common Market
> Democratic Party *or* party, Democrat(s), democracy; democrat (a general advocate of democracy)
> Entente Cordiale, the Entente
> Fascist Party, Fascist(s), Fascista (*pl.* Fascisti); fascism, fascist
> Federalist Party, Federalist(s) (U.S. history); federalist
> Free-Soil Party, Free-Soiler(s)
> Hanseatic League, Hansa
> Holy Alliance
> Know-Nothing Party, Know-Nothing(s)
> Labour Party, Labourites favor the interests of labor[10]
> Loyalist(s) (American Revolution, Spanish civil war, etc.)
> Marxism-Leninism, Marxist-Leninist; marxism, marxist
> Nazi Party, Nazism, Nazi(s); nazi
> North Atlantic Treaty Organization, NATO
> Populist Party, Populism, Populist; populism, populist
> Progressive Party, Progressive movement, Progressive(s); progressive
> Quadruple Alliance
> Republican Party, Republican platform, Republican(s); republicanism, republican
> Tammany Hall, Tammany

7.59 Another consideration in choosing between capitalization and lowercasing is whether the organization referred to is "recognized." Appellations of political groups other than recognized parties are usually lowercased:

> independent(s)
> labor bloc
> mugwump(s)
> opposition[11]
> right wing; right-winger; leftist (*but usually* the Right; the Left)

9. In certain contexts—for example, a work on the Communist Party—where *party* is used in place of the full name and other parties may also be mentioned, the word *party* may be capitalized in references to the Communist Party to avoid ambiguity.

10. In capitalized British names, British spelling is retained. If *Labourite* is used in reference to a person who votes for the Labour Party and, as is sometimes the case, is therefore not capitalized, American spelling should be used in a work published in the United States: *laborite.*

11. Often capitalized in British contexts, meaning the party out of power.

Institutions and Companies

7.60   Full titles of institutions and companies and their departments and divisions are capitalized. In some cases, especially when they might otherwise be mistaken, shortened versions of those titles, even solitary generic terms, are also capitalized. Otherwise, such generic terms as *school, company,* and *press* are lowercased when used alone:

> the University of Chicago;[12] the Law School; the Department of History; the university; the history department
> the Universities of Chicago and California; Harvard and Northwestern Universities
> the University of Chicago Press; the Press; the university press
> Iowa Falls High School; the high school
> the Library of Congress (*not* Congressional Library); the Manuscripts Division; the library
> Smithsonian Institution (*not* Institute); the Smithsonian
> Metropolitan Museum of Art; the Met; the museum
> Hudson's Bay Company; the company
> General Foods Corporation; General Foods; the corporation
> Illinois Central Railroad; the Illinois Central; the railroad; Amtrak
> the Board of Regents of the University of California; the Board of Regents; the board
> New York Philharmonic
> New York Stock Exchange; stock exchange
> Washington National Symphony; the National Symphony; the orchestra

Associations and Conferences

7.61   Full official names of associations, societies, unions, meetings, and conferences are capitalized. A *the* preceding a name is lowercased in textual matter, even when it is part of the official title. Such generic terms as *society, union,* or *conference* are lowercased when used alone:

> Boy Scouts of America; Boy Scouts; a Boy Scout; a Scout
> Congress of Industrial Organizations; CIO; the union
> Fifty-second Annual Meeting of the American Historical Association; the annual meeting of the association
> Green Bay Packers; the Packers; the team
> Independent Order of Odd Fellows; IOOF; an Odd Fellow
> Industrial Workers of the World; IWW; Wobblies
> Ku Klux Klan; KKK; the Klan
> League of Women Voters; the league
> New-York Historical Society;[13] the society
> Republican National Convention; the national convention; the convention
> Textile Workers Union of America; the union

12. The word *the* at the beginning of such titles is capitalized only when the official corporate name of the institution is called for: © 1992 by The University of Chicago.
13. Note that a hyphen is used in the official name.

Union League Club; the club
Young Men's Christian Association; YMCA

7.62   A substantive title given to a conference is enclosed in quotation marks:

"Systematic Investigation of the African Later Tertiary and Quaternary," a
   symposium held at Burg Wartenstein, Austria, July–August 1965
   but
the 1965 International Conference on Family Planning Programs

HISTORICAL AND CULTURAL TERMS

Periods

7.63   A numerical designation of a period is lowercased unless it is part of a
proper name:

eighteenth century
the seventeen hundreds
the twenties
quattrocento (fifteenth century)
Eighteenth Dynasty (*but* Sung dynasty)
the period of the Fourth Republic

(For numerical designations in numerals see 8.40.)

7.64   Some names applied to historical or cultural periods are capitalized,
either by tradition or to avoid ambiguity. Such appellations are not enclosed in quotation marks:

Age of Louis XIV
Age of Reason
Augustan Age *or* Age of Augustus
Bronze Age
Christian Era
Dark Ages
Enlightenment
Era of Good Feelings
Gilded Age
Grand Siècle
Ice Age
Jazz Age
Mauve Decade
Middle Ages; High Middle Ages; late Middle Ages
Old Regime; *l'ancien régime* (*or* the ancien régime)
Pleistocene
Progressive Era
Reformation; Counter Reformation
Renaissance; High Renaissance
Restoration
Roaring Twenties

(See also 7.111.)

7.65 Most period designations, however, are lowercased except for proper nouns and adjectives (but see 7.68):

> antiquity; ancient Greece; imperial Rome
> baroque period
> classical period
> colonial period (U.S.)
> fin de siècle
> golden age
> Hellenistic period
> Romanesque period
> romantic period
> Victorian era

7.66 Names of cultural periods recognized by archaeologists and anthropologists and based upon characteristic technology are capitalized:

> Stone Age; Old Stone Age   Bronze Age
> Neolithic, Paleolithic times   Iron Age

(For geological periods see 7.111.)

7.67 Analogous latter-day designations, often capitalized in popular writing, are best lowercased:

> age of steam   nuclear age   space age

Events

7.68 Appellations of historical, political, economic, and cultural events, plans, and so forth, are generally capitalized. Titles of exhibitions should, in addition, be italicized:

> Battle of the Books
> Boston Tea Party
> Civil Rights movement (often lowercased)
> Fall of Rome
> Great Depression; the depression
> Great Society
> Industrial Revolution (often lowercased)
> Kentucky Derby
> New Deal
> New York World's Fair
> Prohibition
> Reconstruction (U.S.)
> Reign of Terror
> South Sea Bubble
> War on Poverty
> the Baltimore Museum of Art's exhibition *American Prints, 1870–1950*;
>   the museum's exhibition of American prints
>   *but*
> baby boom

cold war
Dreyfus affair
dust bowl
gold rush; California gold rush
green revolution
panic of 1837
westward movement
XYZ affair

(For wars, battles, and conquests see 7.97; for religious events, 7.92; for acts and treaties, 7.70.)

Cultural Movements and Styles

7.69   Nouns and adjectives designating philosophical, literary, musical, and artistic movements, styles, and schools and their adherents are capitalized if they are derived from proper nouns. Others are usually lowercased unless, in certain contexts, capitalization is needed to distinguish the name of a movement or group from the same word in its general sense (Cynic, cynic). Capitalization of German nouns is usually retained, but lowercase may be used in English-language contexts. This classification of names and terms is one most dependent on editorial discretion. In any given work a particular term must be consistently treated. The following list illustrates commonly acceptable style; terms lowercased here may sometimes require capitalization:

abstract expressionism
Aristotelian
baroque
camp
Cartesian
Chicago school of architecture
classical
concrete poetry
cubism
Cynic(ism)
dada(ism)
deconstruction
Doric
Epicurean
existentialism
fauvism
Gothic
Gregorian chant; plainsong
Hellenism
Hudson River school
humanism
idealism
imagism
impressionism

jazz
mannerism
miracle plays
modernism
mystic(ism)
naturalism
neoclassic(ism)
Neoplatonism
New Criticism
nominalism
op art
Peripatetic
philosophe
Physiocrat
pop art
postimpressionism
postmodernism
Pre-Raphaelite
realism
rococo
Romanesque
romantic(ism)
Scholastics; Schoolmen
Scholasticism
scientific rationalism
Sophist(s)
Stoic(ism)
structural(ism)
Sturm und Drang *or* sturm und drang
surrealism
symbolism
theater of the absurd
transcendentalism

(For religious movements and schools of thought see 7.84.)

Acts, Treaties, and Government Programs

7.70   Full formal or accepted titles of pacts, plans, policies, treaties, acts, laws, and similar documents or agreements, together with names of programs resulting from them, are usually capitalized and set in roman type without quotation marks. Incomplete names are usually lowercased:

> Mayflower Compact; the compact
> Constitution of the United States; United States (*or* U.S.) Constitution; the Constitution (usually capitalized when referring to the U.S. Constitution); Article 6; the article
> Illinois Constitution; the state constitution; the constitution
> Fifteenth Amendment (to the U.S. Constitution); the amendment; the Smith amendment

Bill of Rights (first ten amendments to the U.S. Constitution; also the English act of 1689)
due process clause (*sometimes* Due Process Clause)
Articles of Confederation
Declaration of Independence
Wilmot Proviso
Monroe Doctrine; the doctrine
Open Door policy (*sometimes* open door policy)
Peace of Utrecht
Treaty of Versailles; the Versailles treaty; the treaty at Versailles
Pact of Paris (*or frequently, but less correctly,* Kellogg-Briand Pact); the pact
Hawley-Smoot Tariff Act; the tariff act; the act
Atomic Energy Act *or* McMahon Act; the act
Federal Housing Act of 1961; the act of 1961; the 1961 act
Marshall Plan; the plan
Social Security (*or* social security)
Medicare; Medicaid (*or* medicare; medicaid)
Reform Bills; Reform Bill of 1832 (England); the 1832 bill
Corn Laws (England) (*sometimes* corn laws)
New Economic Policy (USSR); NEP
Second Five-Year Plan; five-year plans

When the published text of a bill or law is referred to or cited as a source, the title is italicized (see 15.347–57, 16.161–66).

7.71   Descriptive references to pending legislation are lowercased:

The anti-injunction bill was introduced on Tuesday.
A gun-control law is being considered.

Legal Cases

7.72   The names of legal cases (plaintiff and defendant) are usually italicized; *v.* (versus) may be roman or italic, provided that use is consistent:

Miranda v. *Arizona*
Green v. *Department of Public Welfare*
West Coast Hotel Co. v. *Parrish*

In discussion, a case name may be shortened:

the *Miranda* case
Miranda

Where the person rather than the case is meant, the name should of course be in roman type:

Escobedo's case, trial

(For information on acceptable legal style, see *The University of Chicago Manual of Legal Citation,* edited by the staff of the *University of*

Chicago Law Review and the University of Chicago Legal Forum, and *A Uniform System of Citation,* published by the Harvard Law Review Association.)

Awards

7.73   Names of awards and prizes are capitalized, but some terms used with the names are not:

> Nobel Prize in physics; Nobel Peace Prize; Nobel Prize winners; Nobel laureate; Nobel Prize–winning statesman
> Pulitzer Prize in fiction
> Academy Award; Oscar; Emmy Award
> International Music Scholarship
> Heywood Broun Memorial Award
> Laetare Medal
> Guggenheim Fellowship (*but* Guggenheim grant)
> National Merit scholarships

CALENDAR AND TIME DESIGNATIONS

Seasons, Months, and Days of the Week

7.74   Names of days of the week and months of the year are capitalized. The four seasons are lowercased (unless personified; see 7.32).

Tuesday	spring	the vernal (spring) equinox
November	fall	winter solstice

(For centuries and decades see 7.63.)

Holidays and Holy Days

7.75   The names of religious holidays and seasons are capitalized:

Ash Wednesday	Maundy Thursday
Christmas Eve	Michaelmas
Easter Day or Easter Sunday	Passover
Good Friday	Pentecost
Halloween; All Hallows' Eve	Ramadan (Ramaḍān)
Hanukkah	Twelfth Night
Holy Week	Yom Kippur
Lent	Yuletide

The names of most secular holidays and other specially designated days are also capitalized:

All Fools' Day, April Fools' Day	National Book Week
Arbor Day	New Year's Day
Fourth of July; the Fourth;	Thanksgiving Day
Independence Day	V-E Day
Labor Day	Washington's Birthday
Mother's Day	

       but

D day

Mere descriptive appellations like *election day* or *inauguration day* are lowercased.

Time and Time Zones

7.76 When spelled out, designations of time and time zones are lowercased, except for proper nouns. Abbreviations are capitalized:

Greenwich mean time (GMT)	central daylight time (CDT)
daylight saving time (DST)	eastern standard time (EST)

RELIGIOUS NAMES AND TERMS

7.77 In few areas is an author more tempted to overcapitalize or an editor more loath to urge a lowercase style than in religion. That this is probably due to unanalyzed acceptance of the pious customs of an earlier age, to an unconscious feeling about words as in themselves numinous, or to fear of offending religious persons is suggested by the fact that overcapitalization is seldom seen in texts on the religions of antiquity or more recent localized, relatively unsophisticated religions. It is in the contexts of Christianity, Judaism, Islam, Buddhism, and Hinduism that we go too far. The editors of the University of Chicago Press urge a spare, *down* style in this field as in others: capitalize what are clearly proper nouns and adjectives, and lowercase everything else except to avoid ambiguity. The following paragraphs offer practical guidance on the present state of capitalization in religious contexts. (For religious titles and offices see 7.21.)

God, Deities, and Revered Persons

7.78 The names of deities, whether monotheistic or polytheistic, are, like all proper nouns, capitalized:

Allah (Allāh)	Astarte
El	Dagon

God	Diana
Jehovah	Pan
Yahveh (Yahweh)	Shiva (Śiva)
Itzamna	Vishnu (Viṣṇuḥ, Viṣṇu)

THE ONE GOD

7.79   Other references to deity as the one supreme God, including references to the persons of the Christian Trinity, are capitalized:

Adonai	Most High
the Almighty	the Omnipotent
Christ	the Paraclete
the Father	Prince of Peace
the First Cause	Providence
God sent his Son	the Savior (Jesus Christ)
Holy Ghost; Holy Spirit	Son of God
the Holy One	Son of man
King of Kings	the Supreme Being
Lamb of God	the Supreme Shepherd
the Logos	the Third Person (of the Trinity)
the Lord, our Lord	the Word
Messiah (Jesus Christ)	

7.80   Pronouns referring to the foregoing are today preferably not capitalized:

God in his (or her) mercy	Allah in his mercy
Jesus and his disciples	Yahveh and his commandments

Nor are most derivatives, whether adjectives or nouns, capitalized:

Allah's oneness
(God's) fatherhood, kingship, omnipotence
(Jesus') sonship
messianic hope
godlike; godly
christological
    but
Christology; Christlike; Christian

REVERED PERSONS

7.81   Appellations of revered persons such as prophets, apostles, and saints are often capitalized:

the Apostle to the Gentiles	Messiah (Jewish)
the Baptist	Mother of God
the Beloved Apostle	our Lady
the Blessed Virgin	the prophet Muhammad; the Prophet
Buddha	Queen of Heaven
Christ child	Saint Mark the Evangelist

the Divine Doctor
the Fathers; church fathers; the
 patriarchs
the Lawgiver

the Twelve; the Twelve Apostles; the
 apostles
the apostle Thomas; Thomas the
 Apostle
the Virgin (Mary)
Virgin and child

PLATONIC IDEAS

7.82 Words for transcendent ideas in the Platonic sense, especially when used in a religious context, are often capitalized:

Good; Beauty; Truth; One

Religious Bodies

BROAD GROUPS AND SYSTEMS

7.83 Names of religions, denominations or churches, and communions and their members, as well as derived adjectives, are capitalized:

Anglicanism; an Anglican; the Anglican Church; the Anglican Communion
the Baptist Church
Buddhism; a Buddhist; Buddhist ideas
Catholicism; the Church Catholic; the Catholic Church
Church of Christ, Scientist; Christian Science; a Christian Scientist
the Church of England, of Scotland, of Sweden, etc.
Druidism; Druid (both, however, are sometimes lowercased)
Hinduism
Islam; Islamic; Muslim
Judaism; Orthodox Judaism; Reform Judaism; an Orthodox Jew
the Methodist Church; Methodism; Methodist
Mormonism; Mormon; the Mormon Church; Church of Jesus Christ of
  Latter-day Saints (Utah); Latter Day Saints (Missouri)
Orthodoxy; the Orthodox Church; the (Greek, Russian, Serbian, etc.) Or-
  thodox Church; Eastern Church
Protestantism; Protestant
the Reformed Church in America; the Reformed Church
Roman Catholicism; a Roman Catholic; the Roman Catholic Church
Shiism; Shia; Shiite; Shiitic
Shinto; Shintoism; Shintoist; Shintoistic
Sunnism; Sunni; Sunnite
Taoism; Taoist; Taoistic *or* Daoism; Daoist; Daoistic
Vedanta
    but
the mother church of the area
church fathers
the church
church and state

267

SECTS, MOVEMENTS, AND ORDERS

7.84   The names of religious sects and movements and of religious orders are similarly capitalized:[14]

> Ajivikas (Ājīvikas)
> Arianism; the Arian heresy
> Christian Brothers
> Dissenters
> Essene; the Essenes
> Fundamentalism
> a Gentile; gentile laws
> Gnosticism; a Gnostic; the Gnostic heresy, gospels
> High Church (*or* high church) movement, party
> Hussites
> Jehovah's Witnesses
> Monophysitism; Monophysite; Monophysite or Monophysitic churches
> Nonconformists
> Order of Preachers; the Dominican order; the order; a Dominican
> Puritans
> Satanism; Satanist; Satan (*but* the devil, devil worship)
> Society of Jesus; a Jesuit; Jesuit teaching; jesuit, jesuitical (*derogatory*)
> Sufi; Sufism
> Theosophy; Theosophist; Theosophical Society
> Zen; Zen Buddhism

LOCAL GROUPS

7.85   The names of smaller organized religious communities, congregations, or jurisdictions and the buildings in which they meet are usually capitalized:

> Abbey of Mont Saint-Michel
> Al Shaheed Mosque
> Archdiocese of Chicago
> Bethany Evangelical Lutheran Church
> Church of the Redeemer
> Congregation Anshe Mizrach
> Grace Presbyterian Church
> Holy See
> Midwest Baptist Conference
> Missouri Synod
> Nichiren Buddhist Temple
> Our Lady of Sorrows Basilica
> Saint Andrew's Greek Orthodox Church
> Saint Joseph the Worker Church
> Saint Leonard's House

14. Many of these terms are used either specifically, that is, to name specific sects, movements, and orders, or generically, to refer generally to the appearance elsewhere of certain traits characteristic, or thought to be characteristic, of specific groups; for example, *Puritan* and *puritan*, *Fundamentalist* and *fundamentalist*.

Saint Mary's Cathedral, Salisbury (*but* Salisbury cathedral)
Sinai Temple

Note that in the foregoing examples *church* is capitalized when it is part of the official name of an organized body of Christians or of a building (the Church of England, Saint Matthew's Church) but lowercased when generic or merely descriptive (a Presbyterian church or a Catholic church). When standing alone, *Church* is often capitalized when it refers to the whole body of Christians, worldwide or throughout time, but lowercased when it refers to a division of the universal Church or to the church as an institution. Terms like *cathedral, congregation, meeting* (Quaker), *mosque, synagogue,* and *temple* likewise are capitalized only when part of an official name.

COUNCILS, SYNODS, AND MEETINGS

7.86   The accepted names of historic councils and synods and the official names of modern counterparts are capitalized:

Council of Chalcedon; Fourth General Council
Council of Nicaea
General Convention (Episcopal Church)
Second Vatican Council; Vatican II
Synod of Whitby

Religious Writings

THE BIBLE

7.87   Capitalize names—and use roman type—for the Judeo-Christian Bible and its versions and editions:

Authorized or King James (*not* Saint James) Version
Bible; biblical
Breeches Bible
Codex Sinaiticus
Complutensian Polyglot Bible
Douay (Rheims-Douay) Version
Gospels (*but* the gospel)
Hebrew Bible
Holy Bible
Holy Writ
New English Bible
New Jerusalem Bible
Peshitta
Psalter (*but* a psalter)
Revised Standard Version
Scripture(s) (i.e., the Bible); scriptural
Septuagint
Vinegar Bible
Vulgate

Also the books of the Bible (for abbreviations of the books of the Bible see 14.34):

Genesis
Chronicles
Job; Book of Job
Psalms; Psalm 22 (*but* a psalm); Twenty-third Psalm
Ezekiel
2 Maccabees
the Rest of Esther
John; the Gospel of John; the Fourth Gospel
Acts; the Acts; Acts of the Apostles
Romans; the Epistle to the Romans
3 John
Revelation (*not* Revelations); the Revelation of Saint John the Divine; the Apocalypse

And various divisions and sections of the Bible:

Old Testament; New Testament
Apocrypha
the Law *or* the Teachings; the Prophets; the Writings
Pentateuch *or* Torah
Hagiographa *or* Ketuvim
the Gospels; the Epistles
the synoptic Gospels
the pastoral Epistles

OTHER SACRED WORKS

7.88 Other sacred or highly revered works are similarly treated:

Bhagavad Gita	Sunnah
Book of the Dead	Sutra (Sūtra)
Dead Sea Scrolls	Talmud
Mishnah	Tripitaka
Qur'an (Qur'ān, Quran, Koran)	Upanishads (Upaniṣads)
Rig-Veda (Ṛgveda)	Vedas

ADJECTIVES

7.89 Adjectives derived from the names of sacred books are generally lower-cased (apocryphal, biblical, scriptural, talmudic), but a few retain the initial capital (Koranic, Qur'anic, etc., Mishnaic, Pentateuchal, Vedic).

SHORTER RELIGIOUS WRITINGS AND UTTERANCES

7.90 Various scriptural selections of special importance bear names that are usually capitalized:

the Decalogue; Ten Commandments
the Beatitudes
Sermon on the Mount
the Miserere
the Shema
 but
the parable of the unjust steward

So also many special prayers and canticles (mostly of scriptural origin) used devotionally:

Gloria Patri (*but* the doxology)
Kaddish (*or* kaddish)
the Litany (Anglican)
the Litany of the Saints
the Lord's Prayer; the Our Father
Nunc Dimittis
Salat al-fajr (Salāt al-fajr)
Te Deum

CREEDS AND CONFESSIONS

7.91 Names of particular creeds and confessions are also capitalized:

Apostles' Creed; the creed Nicene Creed
Augsburg Confession the Thirty-nine Articles
Luther's Ninety-five Theses Westminster Confession

Events and Concepts

7.92 Biblical and other religious events and religious concepts of major theological importance are often capitalized:

the Atonement the Fall
the Creation Hegira (Muhammad's)
the Crucifixion the New Covenant
Dharma (*or* dharma) Passion of Christ
the Diaspora (of the Jews) Redemption
the Exodus (from Egypt) the Resurrection

Religious Services

EUCHARISTIC RITE

7.93 References to the eucharistic sacrament are capitalized:

the Divine Liturgy Holy Communion
the Eucharist the Liturgy of the Lord's Supper

The terms *Mass, High Mass,* and *Low Mass* are often capitalized when referring to the celebration in general. In reference to individual celebrations, however, lowercase is frequently used:

The High Mass is a sung mass.
There is a high mass at noon.
The full ceremony of a solemn High Mass
Three masses are offered daily.

Terms for the elements of the Holy Communion are capitalized in contexts where the doctrine of the real presence is assumed:

Body and Blood of Christ	Precious Blood
the Divine Species	the Sacrament

OTHER SERVICES

7.94 Names of other rites and services are usually not capitalized in run of text:

prime, terce, sext, etc.	sun dance
morning prayer; matins	confirmation
evening prayer; evensong	vespers, vesper service
bar mitzvah; bas mitzvah	khutbah *(khuṭba)*
seder	green corn ceremony

(See also 7.75.)

Objects of Religious Use or Significance

7.95 Objects of religious use or significance are preferably given lowercase treatment:

ark	relic of the true cross
chalice and paten	rosary
mandala *(maṇḍala)*	sanctuary
mezuzah	shofar
phylacteries	stations of the cross

MILITARY TERMS

Forces and Groups of Participants

7.96 Full titles of armies, navies, air forces, fleets, regiments, battalions, companies, corps, and so forth are capitalized. The words *army, navy,* and so forth are lowercased when standing alone or used collectively in the plural or when they are not part of an official title:

Afrika Korps (German, World War II)
Allied armies
Allied Expeditionary Force; the AEF
the Allies (World Wars I and II); Allied forces
Army Corps of Engineers
Army of Northern Virginia
Army of the Potomac; the army
Axis powers (World War II)
Central Powers (World War I)
Combined Chiefs of Staff (World War II)
Continental navy (American Revolution)
Eighth Air Force
Fifth Army; the Fifth; the army
First Battalion, 178th Infantry; the battalion; the 178th
French foreign legion
Highland Light Infantry
Joint Chiefs of Staff (U.S.)
King's Own Yorkshire Light Infantry
Luftwaffe
National Guard; the guard
Pacific Fleet (U.S., World War II)
Red Army; Russian army
Rough Riders
Royal Air Force; British air force
Royal Army Educational Corps
Royal Artillery; the British army
Royal Horse Guards
Royal Navy; the British navy
Royal Scots Fusiliers; the fusiliers
Seventh Fleet; the fleet
Task Force Fifty-eight; the task force
Thirty-third Infantry Division; the division; the infantry
Union army (American Civil War)
United States Army; the army; the American army; the armed forces
United States Coast Guard; the Coast Guard
United States Marine Corps; the Marine Corps; the U.S. Marines; the
marines
United States Signal Corps; the Signal Corps

Wars, Battles, Campaigns, and Theaters of War

7.97   Full titles of wars are capitalized. The words *war* and *battle* are lower-cased when used alone (*battle* is often lowercased also when used with the name of the spot where the battle took place).

American Civil War;[15] the Civil War; the war
American Revolution; American War of Independence; the Revolution; the Revolutionary War; the American and French Revolutions

15. "The earlier official title, War of the Rebellion, has been dropped, out of deference to Southern wishes; and the cumbrous title 'The War between the States' is grossly inac-

Battle of Bunker Hill *or* battle of Bunker Hill; the battle at Bunker Hill
Battle of the Bulge
Conquest of Mexico; the conquest
Crusades; the Sixth Crusade; a crusader
European theater of operations (World War II); ETO
French Revolution; the Revolution; revolutionary France
Great Sioux War; Sioux war; Indian wars
Korean War
Maginot line
Mexican border campaign
Mexican Revolution; the revolution
Napoleonic Wars
Norman Conquest; the conquest of England; the conquest
Operation Overlord
revolution(s) of 1848
Russian Revolution; the revolution
Seven Years' War
Shays's Rebellion
Spanish-American War
Spanish civil war
Third Battle of Ypres *or* third battle of Ypres
Vicksburg campaign
Vietnam War
War of Jenkins' Ear
western front (World War I)
western theater of war (American Civil War)
Whiskey Rebellion
World War I (*or* 1); the First World War; the Great War; the war; the two
  world wars
World War II (*or* 2); the Second World War

Military Awards and Citations

7.98   Specific names of medals and awards are capitalized:

Distinguished Flying Cross
Distinguished Service Order; DSO
Medal of Honor; congressional medal
Purple Heart
Silver Star
Victoria Cross
  but
croix de guerre

---

curate. 'The War for Southern Independence' suggested by the historian Channing is well
enough; but why change 'The American Civil War,' which it was? During the war it was
generally called 'The Second American Revolution' or 'The War for Separation' in the
South" (Samuel Eliot Morison, *The Oxford History of the American People* [New York:
Oxford University Press, 1965], 614n).

SHIPS, TRAINS, AIRCRAFT, AND SPACECRAFT

7.99   Names of specific ships, submarines, aircraft, spacecraft, and artificial satellites are italicized, but not such abbreviations as *SS* or *HMS*[16] preceding them:

Bonhomme Richard	CSS *Shenandoah*
HMS *Frolic*	SS *United States*
USS *SC-530*	*Pioneer 11*
Graf Zeppelin	*Voyager 2*
Spirit of Saint Louis	*Uhuru*
Sputnik II	*IUE*
Mariner 4	*SMM*

7.100   Designations of class or make, names of trains, and names of space programs are capitalized but not italicized:

Spitfire	Ford Mustang
DC-10	Nike
Boeing 747	Project Apollo
Airflo Desoto	Concorde
Broadway Limited	Train à Grande Vitesse

Designations of generic classes or types of vessels, aircraft, and so on, however, are neither capitalized nor italicized:

submarine
aircraft carrier
space shuttle
schooner
subway
jetliner
   but
U-boat (from the German *Unterseeboot*)

SCIENTIFIC TERMINOLOGY

Scientific Names of Plants and Animals

7.101   Although the rules for the naming (taxonomy) of plants and animals are complex, the discussion and examples in the following paragraphs should help the inexperienced copyeditor avoid the most dangerous pitfalls in this field. (For technical assistance and a bibliography of scientific references see CBE, *Scientific Style and Format.*)

---

16. Such terms as *ship, schooner, frigate,* and *aircraft carrier* should not, of course, be used with these abbreviations.

GENUS AND SPECIES

7.102 Whether in lists or in running text, the generic and specific (Latin) names of plants and animals are set in italic type. The genus name is capitalized, the species name lowercased (even though it may be a proper adjective):

> Many specific names, such as *Rosa caroliniana* and *Styrax californica*, reflect the locale of the first specimens described.
> The Pleistocene saber-toothed cats all belonged to the genus *Smilodon*.
> In Europe the pike, *Esox lucius*, is valued for food as well as sport.

After the first use the genus name may be abbreviated:

> The "quaking" of the aspen, *Populus tremuloides*, is due to the construction of the petiole. An analogous phenomenon noted in the cottonwood, *P. deltoides*, is similarly effected.

7.103 Subspecies names, when used, follow the specific name and are also set in italic type:

> *Trogon collaris puella*
> *Noctilio labialis labialis* (also written *Noctilio l. labialis*)

In systematic work the name of the person (or persons) who proposed a generic, specific, or subspecific name is sometimes added in roman type, the name often being abbreviated:

> *Molossus coibensis* J. A. Allen
> *Diaemus youngii cypselinus* Thomas
> *Felis leo* Scop.
> *Quercus alba* L.
> *Euchistenes hartii* (Thomas)

Use of parentheses in the last example means that Thomas described the species *hartii* but referred it to a different genus.

7.104 Other designations following generic, specific, or subspecific names are also set in roman type:

> *Viola* sp.   *Rosa rugosa* var.

The designation *sp.* (species) means that in this case the species is unknown or unspecified (plural, *spp.*). The abbreviation *var.* denotes a variety of the species, in this case of *Rosa rugosa*.

HIGHER DIVISIONS

7.105 Divisions higher than genus—phylum, class, order, and family—are capitalized and set in roman type:

> Chordata [phylum]   Monotremata [order]
> Chondrichthyes [class]   Hominidae [family]

So also are intermediate groupings:

> Ruminantia [suborder]
> Felinae [subfamily]
> Selachii [term used of various groups of cartilaginous fishes]

ENGLISH DERIVATIVES

7.106   English derivatives of scientific names are lowercased:

> amoeba, amoebas [from *Amoeba*]
> mastodon [like the foregoing, identical with the generic name]
> carnivore [from the order Carnivora]
> felid [from the family Felidae]

Vernacular Names of Plants and Animals

7.107   Common names of plants and animals are capitalized in a bewildering variety of ways, even in lists and catalogs having professional status. It is often appropriate to follow the style of an "official" list, and authors doing so should let their editors know what list they are following.

7.108   In the absence of such a list the University of Chicago Press recommends a *down* style for names of wild plants and animals, capitalizing only proper nouns and adjectives used with their original reference, or suggests consulting a standard dictionary:

> Dutchman's-breeches   Cooper's hawk
> mayapple   Canada thistle
> black-eyed Susan   Virginia creeper
> New England aster   jack-in-the-pulpit
> Michaelmas daisy   Rocky Mountain sheep
> rhesus monkey   black bass

7.109   The same principles may usually be followed for breeds of domestic animals and horticultural varieties of plants, especially the older ones:

> white leghorn (*or* Leghorn) fowl
> Rhode Island red
> Hereford cattle
> Poland China swine
> English setter
> golden retriever
> King Charles spaniel
> brahma fowl (*but* Brahman *or* Brahma cattle)
> boysenberry
> rambler rose
> Thoroughbred (*or* thoroughbred) horse

7.110   Many domestic breeds and varieties, however, have been given special names, sometimes fanciful, that must be respected. This is particularly

277

true of horticultural varieties of plants that may be patented or may possess names registered as trademarks:

Queen of the Market aster   Golden Bantam corn
Peace rose   Hale Haven peach

Geological Terms

7.111 Names of geological eras, periods, epochs, series, and episodes are capitalized (but not the words *era, period, epoch,* etc., which are often omitted):

Cenozoic era
Tertiary period
Pliocene epoch
Lower Jurassic
Pennsylvanian (*or* Upper Carboniferous)

Modifiers such as *early, middle,* or *late,* used merely descriptively, are usually lowercased:

the early Pliocene
late Pleistocene times

The term *Ice Age* is capitalized in reference to the Recent or Pleistocene glacial epochs but lowercased when used in a general sense. Glacial and interglacial stages are lowercased:

the Ice Age, or Pleistocene; *but* an ice age
Illinoian (*European,* Riss) stage
second interglacial stage *or* II interglacial

(For prehistoric cultural periods see 7.66. For technical assistance and bibliography see U.S. Geological Survey, *Suggestions to Authors.*)

Astronomical Terms

7.112 The names of asteroids, planets and their satellites, stars, and constellations are capitalized:

Big Dipper   85 Pegasi
North Star; Pole Star   Scorpius
Cassiopeia's Chair   Saturn
Aldebaran   Ursa Major
α Centauri (*or* Alpha Centauri)   Phobos

(For artificial satellites see 7.99.)

7.113 Names of other unique celestial objects are usually capitalized except for generic astronomical terms forming part of the name:

> the Milky Way
> the Magellanic Clouds
> the Crab Nebula
> the Galaxy (i.e., the Milky Way; *but* a galaxy, our galaxy)
> the Southern Cross
> the Coalsacks
> Halley's comet *or* comet Halley
>   *but*
> the solar system

7.114 Objects listed in well-known catalogs are designated by the catalog name, usually abbreviated, and a number:

> NGC 6165   Bond 619   Lalande 5761   Lynds 1251 *or* L1251

7.115 The names *earth, sun,* and *moon* are often lowercased, but when used as the names of specific bodies in the solar system they are properly capitalized, as are the names *Mercury, Venus, Mars,* and the rest. When *Earth* is used in this way, it is not preceded by an article. *Sun* and *Moon,* however, even when capitalized, are preceded by the definite article.

> From their extraordinary vantage point, the two astronauts looked back in awe at Earth (*but* the earth).
>
> The precious atmosphere of Earth!
>
> On that day, Earth passed between the Sun and the Moon.

7.116 Terms merely descriptive in nature applied to unique celestial objects or phenomena are not capitalized:

> the gegenschein   the rings of Saturn
> aurora borealis   sun dog

Medical Terms

7.117 The names of diseases, syndromes, signs, symptoms, diagnostic procedures, anatomical parts, and the like should be lowercased, except for proper names forming part of the term (for x rays see 7.123):

> Hodgkin's disease   syndrome of Weber   trapezius
> infectious granuloma finger-nose test   medulla oblongata
> Ménière's syndrome   femur   islands of Langerhans

Acronyms, however, are usually capitalized:

> CAT scan (computerized axial tomography)

7.118 Names of infectious organisms are treated like other taxonomic terms (see 7.101–6), but the names of diseases or pathological conditions based upon such names are lowercased and set in roman type:

In streptococcemia, or streptococcal infection, microorganisms of the genus *Streptococcus* are present in the blood.

The disease trichinosis is characterized by infestation by trichinae, small parasitic nematodes. It is commonly caused by eating underdone pork containing *Trichinella spiralis*.

Pharmaceuticals

7.119   Generic names of pharmaceuticals should be used so far as possible and given lowercase treatment. Proprietary names (trade names or brands), if used at all, should be capitalized and enclosed within parentheses after the first use of the generic term:

The patient was kept tranquilized with meprobamate (Miltown).

Physical and Chemical Terms

LAWS, PRINCIPLES, AND THE LIKE

7.120   Only proper names attached to the names of laws, theorems, principles, and the like are capitalized:

big bang theory
Boyle's law
Avogadro's theorem
Planck's constant
(Einstein's) general theory of relativity
the second law of thermodynamics
Newton's first law

CHEMICAL NAMES AND SYMBOLS

7.121   Names of chemical elements and compounds are lowercased when written out; the chemical symbols, however, are capitalized and set without periods (for a list of symbols for the elements see 14.54):

sulfuric acid; H_2SO_4 tungsten carbide; WC
sodium chloride; NaCl   ozone; O_3

The numeral giving the number of atoms in a molecule is placed in the inferior position after the symbol for the element, as in the examples above.

7.122   The *mass number*, formerly placed in the superior position to the right of the element symbol, is now according to international agreement placed in the superior position to the left of the symbol: ^{238}U, ^{14}C. In work intended for a nonprofessional audience, however, the mass number is still often placed in the old position (U^{238}, C^{14}). Such locutions as

uranium 238; U-238   carbon 14; C-14

are also seen in popular writing and need not be changed.

RADIATIONS

7.123 The style recommended by the University of Chicago Press for the terms for various electromagnetic radiations may be illustrated by the following:

x rays *(noun)*
x-ray *(verb or adjective)*

beta rays *(noun)*
beta-ray *(adjective)*
β-ray *(noun or adjective)*

gamma rays *(noun)*
gamma-ray *(adjective)*
γ-ray *(noun or adjective)*

cosmic rays *(noun)*
cosmic-ray *(adjective)*

ultraviolet rays *(noun)*
ultraviolet-ray *(adjective)*

Variations of style for *x ray* are often encountered, and the Press acknowledges and will accept these too, so long as a style is followed consistently throughout the work:

X ray, X-ray, x-ray *(noun)*
x-ray, X-ray *(verb or adjective)*

METRIC UNITS: METER/METRE, LITER/LITRE

7.124 Although the spellings *meter* and *liter* are still widely followed in the United States, the spellings *metre* and *litre* are used in other English-speaking countries and in France. In the United States some businesses, government agencies, and professional organizations have also adopted the latter spellings. The University of Chicago Press accepts either orthography, so long as spelling is consistent within a work. (For more on the units of measure used in the metric system—or, more correctly, the International System—and for the abbreviations of those units, see 14.41–49.)

TRADEMARKS

7.125   Dictionaries indicate registered trademark names. A reasonable effort should be made to capitalize such names:

> Anacin, Bufferin, Excedrin (*but* aspirin *or* buffered aspirin)
> Coca-Cola (*but* cola drink)
> Dacron (*but* polyester)
> Frigidaire (*but* refrigerator)
> Gold Medal flour
> Kleenex (*but* cleansing *or* facial tissue)
> Levi's
> Orlon
> Ping-Pong (*but* table tennis)
> Pyrex dishes
> Vaseline (*but* petroleum jelly)
> Xerox (*but* photocopier)

The symbols ® and TM, which often accompany registered trademark names on product packaging and in advertisements, need not be used in running text.

TITLES OF WORKS

General Rules

7.126   The following rules concerning capitalization, spelling, punctuation, italics, and quotation marks apply to titles mentioned in text.[17] (For various styles of capitalization in notes and bibliographies see chapters 15 and 16; for capitalization in foreign titles see 9.4–6.) The rules govern titles of all publications (books, journals, newspapers, magazines, pamphlets, reports, etc.); of short works (poems, stories, articles); of divisions of long works (parts, chapters, sections); of unpublished lectures, papers, and documents; of plays and radio and television programs; and of musical and graphic works.

CAPITALIZATION

7.127   In regular title capitalization, also known as headline style, the first and last words and all nouns, pronouns, adjectives, verbs, adverbs, and subordinating conjunctions (*if, because, as, that,* etc.) are capitalized. Articles *(a, an, the),* coordinating conjunctions *(and, but, or, for, nor),*

---

17. In many publishing houses there is a custom of typing book titles in full capitals instead of underlining them (which takes twice as long). This is a useful, time-saving device, but typists should remember that it must be reserved for reports, interdepartmental memorandums, letters to authors or other publishers, and the like. Never should titles in copy intended for publication be so typed.

and prepositions, regardless of length, are lowercased unless they are the first or last word of the title or subtitle. The *to* in infinitives is also lowercased. Long titles of works published in earlier centuries may retain the original capitalization, except that any word in full capitals should carry only an initial capital. No word in a quoted title should ever be set in full capitals, regardless of how it appears on the title page of the book itself, unless it is an acronym, such as WAC, UNICEF, or FORTRAN.

7.128   Capitalizing hyphenated and open compounds in titles may be simplified by application of the following rule: First elements are always capitalized; subsequent elements are capitalized unless they are articles, prepositions, coordinating conjunctions, or such modifiers as *flat, sharp,* and *natural* following musical key symbols; second elements attached by hyphens to prefixes are not capitalized unless they are proper nouns or proper adjectives. If a compound (other than one with a hyphenated prefix) comes at the end of the title, its final element, whatever part of speech it may be, is always capitalized (see 7.127).

> Twentieth-Century Literature
> Out-of-Fashion Initiatives
> Run-of-the-Mill Responses
> Spanish-Speaking People
> Medium-Sized Libraries
> Under-the-Counter Transactions
> E-flat Concerto
> Non-Christian Religions
> Strategies for Re-establishment
> Self-Sustaining Reactions
> Anti-intellectual Pursuits
> Spurning the Order of the Garter
> Investigating Quasi Corporations
> A Run-in with Authorities
> Avoiding a Run-In

Note that although modern practice tends toward deleting traditional hyphens (*reestablish, toolmaker*) hyphenated spellings in the original title should be retained (see 7.129). Only capitalization and punctuation may be altered. Note also that, as illustrated in the example "E-flat Concerto" above, musical key symbols modified by *flat, sharp,* or *natural* are treated as single words (see 7.150).

7.129   Retain the spelling of the original title, but change & to *and;* and except perhaps in non-English titles, spell out names of centuries (*12th Century* becomes *Twelfth Century)* and other numbers usually spelled out in text.

PUNCTUATION

7.130   In running text or in bibliographies, it is sometimes necessary, for clarity, to add to or alter the punctuation of titles as they appear on title pages. Title pages are usually designed to require a minimum of punctuation. Commas are sometimes omitted from the ends of lines, and punctuation may be omitted between titles and subtitles. In citations, commas required for clarity should be inserted, and a colon (not a semicolon or a dash) should be added between title and subtitle. If there is a dash within the original title or subtitle, it should be retained. The dash does not affect the capitalization status of the word that follows it. Dates not grammatically related to the rest of the title should be set off with commas.

7.131   The following examples illustrate modern title punctuation and capitalization:

> *Disease, Pain, and Sacrifice: Toward a Psychology of Suffering*
> *Melodrama Unveiled: American Theater and Culture, 1800–1850*
> *Browning's Roman Murder Story: A Reading of "The Ring and the Book"*
> *The Labour Party in Perspective—and Twelve Years Later*
> *Thought and Letters in Western Europe, A.D. 500–900*
> "Foreign Aid Re-examined"
> "The Take-off into Self-Sustained Growth"
> Sonata in B-flat Major
> "Digression concerning Madness"
> *Learning to Look*
> *Noble-Gas Compounds*
> "What to Listen For"

7.132   Old-fashioned titles connected by *or* are usually treated as follows:

> *England's Monitor; or, The History of the Separation*
> *or*
> *England's Monitor, or The History of the Separation*

(For rules of capitalization governing titles in foreign languages see 9.4–6.)

Books and Periodicals

7.133   Titles and subtitles of published books, pamphlets, proceedings and collections, periodicals, and newspapers and sections of newspapers published separately *(New York Times Book Review)* are set in italics when they are mentioned in the text or notes. Such titles issued in microfilm are also italicized. In works where titles are otherwise treated in references (see 16.23–24), titles mentioned in the text are nevertheless italicized and usually capitalized according to the rules outlined above (7.127–28).

7.134   A title that is cited in full in the notes, bibliography, or list of references may be shortened in the text. In the shortened title, the words chosen must be in the same form and order as in the full title (for fuller discussion of shortened titles see 15.252).

7.135   An initial article, such as *A, An,* or *The,* in a title may prove awkward in running text, especially if it follows a possessive noun or possessive pronoun. If such an opening article will not gracefully fit, it should be dropped:

> Had she read Faulkner's *Fable*? (*But* Faulkner's novel *A Fable* was first on the list of required readings.)

> His *Rise of the West* won the National Book Award.

An initial article should also be omitted if an adjective or another article precedes it:

> That dreadful *Old Curiosity Shop* character, Quilp . . .

> An *Oxford Universal Dictionary* definition . . .

An initial article that does not offend the syntax may be retained as part of the title (except in newspaper titles):

> In *The Old Curiosity Shop,* Dickens . . .
> *or*
> In the *Old Curiosity Shop,* Dickens . . .

7.136   When newspapers and periodicals are mentioned in the text, an initial *The,* omitted in note citations, is set in roman type and, unless it begins a sentence, is lowercased. In foreign language titles, however, the equivalent is retained:

> She reads the *Sun-Times* every morning.
> On the ship she read *Le Monde.*
> The *New York Times* and the *Christian Science Monitor* are among the most widely respected newspapers.
> His book is reviewed in the *American Historical Review.*

7.137   A title should not be used as the object of a preposition such as *on* or *about,* as in the designation of a topic.

> *Illogical:*
> In his well-known book on *Modern English Usage,* Fowler provides an excellent article on the use and abuse of italics for emphasis.

> *Logical:*
> In his well-known book on English usage, Fowler . . .
> *or*
> In his well-known *Dictionary of Modern English Usage* . . .

7.138 A title is a singular noun and must therefore take a singular verb:

> *The Counterfeiters* is perhaps Gide's best-known work.
>
> *Ends and Means* marks a new turn in Aldous Huxley's thought.

ARTICLES AND PARTS OF A BOOK

7.139 Titles of articles and features in periodicals and newspapers, chapter titles and part titles, titles of short stories, essays, and individual selections in books are set in roman type and enclosed in quotation marks:

> "A Defense of Shelley's Poetry," by Kathleen Raine in the *Southern Review*
> Caldwell's "Country Full of Swedes"
> "Talk of the Town" in last week's *New Yorker*
> "Wordsworth in the Tropics," from Huxley's *Collected Essays*
> "Maternal Behavior and Attitudes," chapter 14 of *Human Development*

In literary studies referring to many writings, both long and short, it is sometimes expedient to give all titles in italics.

7.140 In passing references and in cross-references within a book, such common titles as *foreword, preface, introduction, contents, appendix, glossary, bibliography, part, index* are set in roman type, without quotation marks, and lowercased:

> In his preface to . . .
> The editor's preface gives an excellent summary.
> Allan Nevins wrote the foreword to . . .
> The table of contents lists all the subheadings.
> The bibliographical essay is incomplete.
> The book contains a glossary, a subject index, and an index of names.
> Full citations are listed in the bibliography.
> Further examples will be found in the appendix.

7.141 The word *chapter* is lowercased and spelled out in text; it may be abbreviated in parenthetical references: (chap. 3). Chapter numbers in text references are given in arabic numerals, even when the actual chapter numbers are spelled out or given in roman numerals.

SERIES AND EDITIONS

7.142 Titles of book series and editions are capitalized and set in roman type without quotation marks. The words *series* and *edition* are lowercased when they are not part of the title:

> Chicago History of American Civilization series
>
> Modern Library edition
>
> Phoenix Books

Poems and Plays

7.143   Titles of long poems that have been published separately and titles of poetry collections are italicized. Titles of short poems are set in roman type and quoted:

> *Paradise Lost*
> "The Love Song of J. Alfred Prufrock," from *Prufrock and Other Observations*

In literary studies where many poems are mentioned, it may be helpful to set all the titles alike, in italics.

7.144   When a poem is referred to by its first line rather than a title, capitalization should follow the poem, not the rules for capitalizing titles:

> "Shall I compare thee to a Summer's day?"

7.145   Titles of plays are italicized, regardless of the length of the play or whether it is published separately or in a collection:

> Shaw's *Arms and the Man*, in volume 2 of his *Plays: Pleasant and Unpleasant*

7.146   Words denoting parts of poems and plays are usually lowercased and set in roman type, with arabic numerals:

> canto 2   act 3
> stanza 4   scene 5

Unpublished Works

7.147   Titles of dissertations and theses, manuscripts in collections, lectures and papers read at meetings, and photocopies of typescripts are set in roman type and quoted. Titles of book-length manuscripts that are under contract to be published may be italicized, but the fact that they are not yet published, or that they are "forthcoming," should be noted. Names of depositories, archives, and the like and names of manuscript collections are capitalized and set in roman type without quotation marks. Such words as *diary, journal,* and *memorandum* are set in roman type, not quoted, and usually lowercased in text references:

> In a master's thesis, "Charles Valentin Alkan and His Pianoforte Works," . . .
> In *Hierarchies and Declivities*, a forthcoming book, Harold Ingleside maintains . . .
> "A Canal Boat Journey, 1857," an anonymous manuscript in the Library of Congress Manuscripts Division, . . .
> Papers of the Continental Congress in the National Archives

Motion Pictures and Television and Radio Programs

7.148   Titles of motion pictures are italicized. Titles of television and radio programs are set in roman type and quoted unless they are continuing series, in which case they are italicized.

> the movie *Moonstruck*
> PBS's *Sesame Street*
> the following episode of *Hill Street Blues,* "Death on the Hill," . . .
> National Public Radio's *All Things Considered*

When a continuing series on radio or television, such as PBS's *Masterpiece Theater,* presents a limited series—for example, the dramatization of a novel in several episodes—the title of the limited series is italicized as well as that of the ongoing series, and the titles of individual episodes are given in quoted roman:

> *Masterpiece Theater, The Fortunes of War,* "Casualties"

Numerals denoting movie sequels are part of the title and are italicized:

> *Project A* and *Project A II*
> *The Exorcist II: The Heretic*
> *The Godfather Part 2*

Musical Compositions

7.149   Titles of operas, oratorios, motets, tone poems, and other long musical compositions are italicized. Titles of songs and short compositions, as well as vocal pieces cited by their incipits (that is, their opening words) are usually set in roman type and quoted:

Harold in Italy	"Jesu Joy of Man's Desiring"
Don Giovanni	"Wohin" from *Die schöne Müllerin*
Death and Transfiguration	"Strange Fruit"
Elijah	"La ci darem la mano"

As with other such arbitrary distinctions (see 7.139, 7.143), where many titles of musical compositions are mentioned in a critical study, all may be italicized regardless of individual length.

7.150   Many musical compositions have no distinctive titles but are identified by their musical form (symphony, concerto, sonata, prelude, nocturne, andante, scherzo, etc.), often plus a number or a key designation, or both. When used as the title of a work the name of the form and the key are usually capitalized and set in roman type. If the key is modified by the term *flat, sharp,* or *natural,* the modifying term is lowercased and the key phrase is hyphenated:

Symphony in B Major	Sonata in E-flat
Fantasy in C Minor	Adagio from the Fifth Symphony

Allegretto for Orchestra   D Minor Violin Concerto
Italian Suite no. 3   B-flat Nocturne

When elements from the title are used in an informal reference, however, those elements are, except for the key designation and proper nouns or adjectives, lowercased:

the B minor symphony
the third Italian suite

(For lowercase letters indicating minor keys see 6.87.)

7.151 If numbers are included in the designation of a musical composition, the terms *op.* (opus; plural *opp.* or *opera*) and *no.* (number; plural *nos.*) are usually lowercased, but both are sometimes capitalized; either style is acceptable if used consistently. An abbreviation designating a catalog of a particular composer's works is always capitalized; for example, BWV (Bach-Werke-Verzeichnis) for Bach, D. (Deutsch) for Schubert, K. (Köchel) for Mozart. When a number, or an opus or catalog number, is used restrictively—that is, when it serves to identify the work—it is not set off by commas. If the work is otherwise identified—for example, by a restrictive phrase designating the key—the number is then merely in apposition, offering additional information about the identified work, and is therefore set off by commas.

Sonata op. 45 was composed . . .
Sonata in E Major, op. 45, was composed . . .

A composition number is usually restrictive and is therefore not set off with commas. When the number is spelled out it is capitalized.

Hungarian Rhapsody no. 12; the Twelfth Hungarian Rhapsody
Symphony no. 9; the Ninth Symphony

When both an opus and a composition number are used, either restrictively or nonrestrictively, they are separated by a comma:

Sonata op. 31, no. 3, was first performed . . .
Sonata in E-flat, op. 31, no. 3, was first performed . . .

If the key is given after the composition number, it is considered part of the title and is not set off by commas:

Symphony no. 5 in C Minor

Should the designation be so worded as to be in apposition to the title, however, it is set off by commas:

Beethoven's Symphony no. 5, the C Minor Symphony, . . .

A catalog number is treated as an opus number:

Mozart's Fantasy in C Minor, K. 475, is regarded . . .
Mozart's Fantasy K. 475 is regarded . . .

7.152   When the name of a traditional musical form is used in the title of a composition, it is set in italic or quoted in roman type:

>   Zackmeyer's *August Concerto,* like his "Blue Sonata," is . . .

7.153   Descriptive titles bestowed on works by their composers, by critics or music historians, or by the public may, in the usual way with titles, be italicized if the work is long, quoted in roman if short:

>   Air with Variations ("The Harmonious Blacksmith") from Handel's Suite no. 5 in E
>   Bach's Prelude and Fugue in E-flat ("Saint Anne")
>   *Messiah* or the *Messiah* (not *The Messiah*)
>   Piano Sonata no. 2 *(Concord, Mass., 1840–60);* the *Concord* Sonata, by Charles Ives
>   Piano Concerto no. 5 *(Emperor);* the *Emperor* Concerto, by Beethoven
>   String Quartet in D Minor *(Death and the Maiden); Death and the Maiden* Quartet (but the song "Death and the Maiden")
>   Symphony no. 41 *(Jupiter);* the *Jupiter* Symphony
>   *William Tell* Overture

Alternatively, all such additional titles may be treated as "nicknames" and given in quoted roman:

>   Piano Concerto no. 5 ("Emperor")
>   Quartet in D Minor ("Death and the Maiden")

Paintings and Sculpture

7.154   Titles of paintings, drawings, statues, and other works of art are italicized:

>   Grant Wood's *American Gothic*
>   El Greco's *View of Toledo*
>   Hogarth's series of drawings *The Rake's Progress*
>   Rembrandt's etching *Christ Presented to the People*
>   Rodin's *The Thinker*
>   Newman, *Onement III*
>   Rothko, *Orange Yellow Orange*
>   Knöbel, *Double Counter in the Right Corner*
>   Buckley, *Untitled*
>   Fatsburn, *Opus 26*
>   Penk, *T3 (R)*
>   Fetting, *Dancers III*

Traditional but "unofficial" titles of works of art are sometimes rendered in capitalized roman:

>   Victory of Samothrace
>   Apollo Belvedere
>   Mona Lisa

Notices

7.155 Specific wording of common short signs or notices should be capitalized in running text, but there is usually no need to enclose them in quotation marks:

> He has a No Smoking sign in his car.
> The door was marked Authorized Personnel Only.

Mottoes

7.156 Mottoes may well be treated the same way:

> Over the door was the astonishing motto Less Is Less!

Computer Terms

7.157 Many computer terms are familiar English words or word combinations with specific new meanings. A few such terms follow:

> access *(verb)*
> bit
> byte
> database (*often* data base)
> debug
> format; formatting; formatter
> hard copy; hard code; hardwired
> input *(verb)*
> log on *(verb); logging on (noun)*
> on-line; off-line (*sometimes* online; offline)
> program; programming; programmer
> realtime (*or* real time)

7.158 Names of hardware (machines), assigned by the manufacturers, are often given in full capitals as acronyms; sometimes with initial capital only, as a person's name:

> IBM PS/2   Amdahl

7.159 Software (languages, programs, systems, packages) terms indicating specific units are set in full capitals if they are acronyms; otherwise they are spelled according to their trade or market names:

LANGUAGES

APL	FORTRAN
BASIC	Assembler
C++	Pascal
COBOL	

PROGRAMS, PACKAGES, SYSTEMS

> PENTA
> SPSS *or* Statistical Package for the Social Sciences
> Microsoft Word
> WordPerfect
> WordStar
> XyWrite III Plus

7.160 Terms from programming languages (function names, names of routines, commands) are spelled according to the syntactic rules of each language:

printf	mov
SIN	GOTO 400

FOR FURTHER REFERENCE

7.161 The most readily available and generally accurate sources for the spelling and capitalization of personal names are *Webster's New Biographical Dictionary, Who's Who, Who's Who in America, Dictionary of American Biography, Dictionary of Canadian Biography,* and *Dictionary of National Biography* (British). For geographical names, see *Webster's New Geographical Dictionary* and the *Cambridge World Gazetteer.* For astronomical and for medical terms see Hopkins, *Glossary of Astronomy and Astrophysics,* and *Stedman's Medical Dictionary.* For computer terms, *Computer Dictionary* from Microsoft Press defines a large number of microcomputing terms as well as general terms. Oxford's *Dictionary of Computing,* which defines many of the major algorithms and theorems omitted from the Microsoft book, is better suited for work in academic computer science.

8 *Numbers*

INTRODUCTION

8.1   It is difficult if not impossible to be entirely consistent in the treatment of numbers in textual matter. As soon as one thinks one has arrived at a simple rule for handling some category of numbers, exceptions begin to appear, and one realizes that the rule has to be made more complicated. This chapter summarizes some of the conventions observed by the University of Chicago Press in handling numbers, especially in making the choice between spelling them out and using numerals. Following a short explanation of the general rules, brief discussions of various special categories of number use are offered, many of them involving exceptions to the general rules. Detailed discussions of some of these categories, as well as of others not treated here, appear elsewhere in this volume; for these consult the index.

GENERAL PRINCIPLES

8.2   Several factors work together to govern the choice between spelling out and using numerals for any particular number. Among them are whether the number is large or small, whether it is an approximation or an exact quantity, what kind of entity it enumerates, and what kind of text it appears in—scientific or technological on the one hand, humanistic on the other.

Numerals or Words

8.3   According to Press style the following are spelled out in ordinary text (for scientific or technical style see 8.11–22, 8.67):

> Whole numbers from one through one hundred: note that the numbers twenty-one through twenty-nine, thirty-one through thirty-nine, and so on are hyphenated, whether used alone or as part of a larger number, should the larger number for some reason (see 8.9) be spelled out (e.g., one hundred eighty-six)

> Any of the whole numbers above followed by *hundred, thousand, hundred thousand, million,* and so on.

For all other numbers numerals are used.[1]

> Thirty leading Republicans from eleven states urged the governor to declare his candidacy.

> The property is held on a ninety-nine-year lease.

> His son is twenty-four years old.

> The first edition ran to 2,670 pages in three volumes, with 160 copperplate engravings.

> The entire length of 4,066 feet is divided into twelve spans of paired parabolic ribs.

> The three new parking lots will provide space for 540 more cars.

If a number between one thousand and ten thousand can be expressed in terms of hundreds, that style is preferred to numerals:

> In response to the question, he wrote an essay of fifteen hundred words.

When spelled-out numbers would cluster thickly in a sentence or paragraph, however, it is often better to use numerals:

> The ages of the eight members of the city council are 69, 64, 58, 54 (two members), 47, 45, and 35.

> Only six communities in the county number one thousand or more in population: Arbington, 4,500; Bearknap, 4,500; Wahlmah, 4,000; Painwell, 3,200; Wayward, 2,100; and Sauercreek, 1,000.

Ordinals

8.4   The general rule stated above applies to ordinal as well as cardinal numbers:

1. It should be noted, perhaps, that newspaper style, as well as that of some general publishers and scholarly journals, decrees that only the numbers from one through nine and such multiples as one hundred or nine thousand are to be spelled out.

> He found himself in 125th position out of 360.
>
> Roberts stole second base in the top half of the eighth inning.
>
> The 122d and 123d days of the strike were marked by renewed violence.

Note that the ordinals *second* and *third* may be represented by *d* alone. If *nd* and *rd* are preferred, however, they should be used consistently.

> The 122nd and 123rd days . . .

Round Numbers

8.5 Round numbers—that is, approximations used in place of exact numbers—generally fit the category of numbers that are spelled out according to the general rule:

> Her essay summarizes two thousand years of Christian history.
>
> Local officials announced that some forty thousand persons had attended the Allegan County Fair.

8.6 In addition to these, round numbers that are even hundred thousands are usually spelled out:

> The population of the seaport is now over two hundred thousand.

8.7 Very large numbers may be expressed in numerals followed by *million, billion,* and so forth:

> By the end of the fourteenth century the population of Britain had probably reached 2.3 million.
>
> A figure of 4.5 billion years is often given as the age of the solar system.
>
> The galaxy contained more than 3 billion (*or* three billion) stars.

(See also 8.25.)

Consistency

8.8 Numbers applicable to the same category should be treated alike within the same context, whether a paragraph or a series of paragraphs; do not use numerals for some and spell out others. If according to rule you must use numerals for one of the numbers in a given category, then for consistency's sake use numerals for them all:

> There are 25 graduate students in the philosophy department, 56 in the classics department, and 117 in the romance languages department, making a total of 198 students in the three departments.

In the past ten years fifteen new buildings have been erected. In one block a 103-story office building rises between two old apartment houses only 3 and 4 stories high.

The population of Gary, Indiana, grew from 10,000 to 175,000 in only thirty years.

Note that, as in the foregoing examples, numbers in the same context but representing different categories may be treated differently.

First Word in Sentence

8.9   At the beginning of a sentence any number that would ordinarily be set in numerals is spelled out, regardless of any inconsistency this may create:

One hundred ten men and 103 women will receive advanced degrees this quarter.

Twenty-seven percent of the cost was guaranteed.

Nineteen seventy-six was the year of the nation's bicentennial celebration.

Forty-one thousand casualties were sustained in the assault.

8.10   If spelling out a number that begins a sentence is impracticable or cumbersome, the sentence should be recast so that it does not begin with a number:

The nation celebrated its bicentennial in 1976.

The year 1976 was marked by the nation's bicentennial celebration.

SPECIAL CASES

Physical Quantities

SCIENTIFIC USAGE

8.11   In mathematical, statistical, technical, or scientific text, physical quantities such as distances, lengths, areas, volumes, masses, pressures, and so on are expressed in numerals, whether whole numbers or fractions (see also 14.41–49):

45 miles	240 volts
3⅓ cubic feet	45 pounds
21 hectares	6.5 meters *or* metres
10 picas	30 cubic centimeters *or* centimetres
10°C, 10.5°C *or* 10 °C, 10.5 °C	an 8-point table with 6-point heads
10° (of arc), 10.5° *or* 10°30′	

NONSCIENTIFIC USAGE

8.12   In ordinary text such quantities should be treated according to the rules governing the spelling out of numbers:

> The temperature dropped twenty degrees in less than an hour.
>
> The train approached at a speed of seventy-five miles an hour.
>
> Some students live more than fifteen kilometers from the school.
>
> Type the entries on three-by-five-inch index cards.

8.13   Included under the nonscientific-usage rule are common fractions:

> More than two-thirds of the registered voters stayed away from the polls on election day.
>
> Furious, Babs walked three and one-half miles through the snow to Margaret's house.

8.14   Quantities consisting of both whole numbers and fractions, however, are often cumbersome to write out and should be expressed in numerals:

> All manuscripts are to be typed on $8^1/_2$-by-11-inch paper.

Whenever possible, case fractions (also called piece, or split, fractions) should be requested in running text (e.g., $8^1/_2$, as in the example above, rather than 8 1/2).

ABBREVIATIONS

8.15   If an abbreviation is used for the unit of measure, the quantity should always be expressed by a numeral (see also chapter 14):

3 mi	12 V	50 lb	35 mm
55 mph	7 hr *or* 7 h	13 g	137 km

When a relation between two or more similar measurements is expressed, the abbreviation is often, although not always, repeated:

26 mm × 45 mm	2 ft. × 6 ft. × 9 ft.
26 × 45 mm	2 × 6 × 9 ft.

SYMBOLS

8.16   If a symbol is used instead of an abbreviation, the quantity is also expressed by a numeral:

> $3^1/_2''$ $36°30'$ N $9'$

When a relation between two or more similar measurements is expressed, the symbol is often, although not always, repeated:

3″ × 5″	30°–50°
3 × 5″	30–50°

Percentages and Decimal Fractions

8.17 Percentages and decimal fractions (including academic grades) are set in numerals in humanistic as well as scientific copy (but see 8.9):

> For these purposes pi will be considered equal to 3.14.
>
> Grades of 3.8 and 95 are identical.
>
> Only 45 percent of the electorate voted.

PERCENTAGES

8.18 In scientific and statistical copy use the symbol % for a percentage; in humanistic copy, the word *percent:*

> Of the cultures tested, fewer than 23% yielded positive results.
>
> The five-year credit will carry interest of 3 percent.
>
> Between 20 and 23% yielded positive results.
>
> The positive responses had increased from 10% to 18%.
>
> Marvin's profit had decreased from 40 percent to 35 percent.
>
> The likelihood had improved by 5 to 9 percent.

Note that there is no space between the numeral and the symbol %, but a word space is added before the spelled-out form.

DECIMAL FRACTIONS

8.19 In scientific contexts decimal fractions of less than 1.00 are set with an initial zero if the quantity expressed is capable of equaling or exceeding 1.00:

> a mean of 0.73   the ratio 0.85

8.20 If the quantity never exceeds 1.00, as in probabilities, levels of significance, correlation coefficients, factor loadings, and so forth, no zero is used:

> $p < .05$ $R = .10$

8.21 When decimal fractions appear in humanistic contexts, the distinction above is seldom observed:

> The average number of children born to college graduates dropped from 2.3 to .95 per couple.

> Last season Mendoza batted .327.
>
> On retirement Boyer destroyed his .38 police special and his .22-caliber single-shot rifle.

8.22 In older British practice the decimal point was a raised dot (3·14159); that style is sometimes still used by conservative writers. In Continental practice the decimal point is represented by a comma (3,14159).

Money

UNITED STATES CURRENCY

8.23 Isolated references to amounts of money in United States currency are spelled out or expressed in numerals in accord with the general rules (8.2–10). If the number is spelled out, so is the unit of currency, and if numerals are used, the symbol $ or ¢ is used:

> The fare has been raised to twenty-five cents (*or* 25¢ *or* $.25).
>
> The committee raised a total of $325.
>
> Hundreds of collectors paid five dollars each to attend the annual event.

8.24 Fractional amounts over one dollar are set in figures like other decimal fractions. Whole-dollar amounts are set with zeros after the decimal point when they appear in the same context with fractional amounts— and only then:

> In a very short time the price of gold rose from the controlled $35 an ounce to $375.
>
> Articles bought for $6.00 were sold for $6.75.
>
> The agent received $5.50, $33.75, and $175.00 for the three sales.

8.25 Like other very large round numbers, sums of money that it would be cumbersome to express in numerals or to spell out in full may be expressed in units of millions or billions, accompanied by numerals and a dollar sign:

> A price of $3 million was agreed upon by both firms.
>
> Teenage consumers account for an annual market of some $15 billion.
>
> The military establishment was slated to receive an additional $7.3 billion over the previous year's appropriation.

BRITISH CURRENCY

8.26 Since the decimalization of British currency in 1971, sums of money in pounds and pence are handled similarly to those in dollars and cents:

> To anyone used to paying fifty pence, three pounds seemed a steep price.

The property had been sold for £35,375.

Receipts for the three days' sales were £175.64, £225.36, and £207.00.

The eventual cost of the program is estimated to be £7.8 million.

It is important to bear in mind that in British usage a billion is equal to a million million, not a thousand million as in American usage. When writing about British sums for American readers, it may therefore be preferable to use the term *thousand million* or *million million,* whichever fits the case, instead of *billion,* or else to remind the reader, perhaps in a note, of the difference.

8.27   Before decimalization of the currency, three monetary units were in use: the pound, the shilling (one-twentieth of a pound), and the penny (one-twelfth of a shilling):

four pence	nineteen shillings	twenty pounds
£123	£52 million	£1,346 million

In fractional sums the abbreviations for shillings (s.) and pence (d.) followed the figures they applied to:

£14 19s. 6d. (*but sometimes simply* £14.19.6)

8.28   For some purposes, mainly professional fees and prices of luxury items, sums of money were expressed in guineas (a unit of value equal to twenty-one shillings or, in modern currency, £1.05):

thirty guineas   342 guineas (gns.)

OTHER CURRENCIES

8.29   Sums of money in other currencies are generally handled similarly to those in United States or decimalized British currency. Note, however, that if an abbreviation rather than a symbol is used for the monetary unit (as *Fr* for *francs* and *DM* for *deutsche Marks*), space is left between the abbreviation and the figure:

Fr 342.46   DM 45 million

8.30   If a distinction has to be made between sums of money in two currencies employing the same symbol for the monetary unit, a prefix or suffix is used, without intervening space (see also "Symbols" in 14.55):

In Canada the current quotation was $2.69 (U.S.$2.47) a pound.

8.31   An author or editor having to deal with names and abbreviations of monetary units in currencies other than American or British may find it helpful to consult the table "Foreign Money" in the United States Government Printing Office *Style Manual.*

Parts of a Book

8.32 Numbers referring to parts of a book, periodical, or manuscript—volumes, chapters and other divisions, pages, plates and text figures, tables, and so on—are usually set as numerals. Except for the preliminary pages of a book, which are still traditionally numbered in lowercase roman numerals, the University of Chicago Press prefers that all such numbers be set as arabic numerals:

> See *Modern Philology* 52 (1954): 100–109.
>
> Plate 7 and figures 23–29 appear in chapter 6.
>
> The preface of the book will be found on pages vii–xiv and the introduction on pages 3–46.
>
> (pp. 426–29) (see vol. 3, introd.) (fol. 8r)

Dates

8.33 Numbers used for dates—the day of the month and the year itself—constitute an important group of exceptions to the general rule on spelling out exact numbers.

THE YEAR ALONE

8.34 Years are expressed in numerals, whatever their magnitude, unless they stand at the beginning of a sentence (see 8.9):

> Octavian was born in 63 B.C., became emperor in 27 B.C., and died in A.D. 14.

THE YEAR ABBREVIATED

8.35 In informal contexts the full number of a particular year is sometimes abbreviated:

> the class of '84   the spirit of '76
>
> He told them he was born in '07.

THE DAY OF THE MONTH

8.36 The University of Chicago Press prefers that in all text, including notes and bibliographies, exact dates be written in the sequence day-month-year, without internal punctuation:

> *Newsweek,* 27 April 1981, 27.
>
> On 4 February 1945 Roosevelt, Stalin, and Churchill met at the Black Sea resort town of Yalta.

The Press will also accept the alternative sequence month-day-year if it is preferred by the author and used consistently. In this sequence, the year must be set off by commas; that is, unless the date is immediately followed by such other punctuation as a period, semicolon, or dash, a comma follows as well as precedes the year:

> The events of April 18, 1775, have long been celebrated in song and story.

8.37   After an exact date has been used, an elliptical reference to another date in the same month is spelled out:

> On 5 November the national elections took place. By the morning of the sixth, returns for all but a few precincts were in.

8.38   Although the day of the month is actually an ordinal (and so pronounced in speaking), the American practice is to write it as a cardinal number: 18 April or April 18, *not* 18th April or April 18th.

MONTH AND YEAR

8.39   When a period of time is identified by the month and year, no internal punctuation is necessary or appropriate:

> The events of August 1945 were decisive to the outcome of the war.

CENTURIES AND DECADES

8.40   Spell out (in lowercase letters) references to particular centuries. Decades may be either spelled out or expressed in numerals with apostrophes.

> the twentieth century   during the eighties and nineties
> the fifth century   the '80s and '90s

If decades are identified by their century, numerals are used:

> the 1880s and 1890s (*preferred to* the 1880s and '90s)

Note that no apostrophe is needed between the year and the *s*. The first two decades of a century cannot be represented in the forms illustrated above, because these decades offer no expressions equivalent to "the twenties and thirties" and so on, or to "the '20s and '30s." The decades may, however, be expressed in either of the following ways:

> the first decade of the nineteenth century
>
> the second decade of the twentieth century
>   *or*
> the years 1800–1809
>
> the years 1910–19

ERAS

8.41   Numerals are used for years followed or preceded by era designations, and words are used for centuries. The abbreviations for eras, or systems of chronology, are conventionally set in small caps. Among the most frequently used era designations are A.D. (*anno Domini,* "in the year of the Lord"); A.H. (*anno Hegirae,* "in the year of [Muhammad's] Hegira," or *anno Hebraico,* "in the Hebrew year"); A.U.C. (*ab urbe condita,* "from the founding of the city" [Rome, in 753 B.C.]); B.C. ("before Christ"); C.E. and B.C.E. ("of the common era" and "before the common era"—equivalent to A.D. and B.C.); B.P. ("before the present"). Note that the abbreviations A.D. and A.H. properly precede the year number, whereas the others follow it. (For abbreviations of other systems of chronology see 14.27.)

> Greek philosophy reached its highest development in the fourth century B.C.
>
> Britain was invaded successfully in 55 B.C. and A.D. 1066.
>
> Mubarak published his survey at Cairo in A.H. 1306 (A.D. 1886).
>
> After 621 B.C.E. worship was permitted only at Jerusalem.
>
> Radiocarbon dating indicates that the campsite was in use by about 13,500 B.P.

In the last example note the use of the comma in a year number of more than four digits (see 8.65).

8.42   Because of the literal meaning of A.D., conservative usage formerly rejected such an expression as "the second century A.D." in favor of "the second century of the Christian Era" or "the second century after Christ." Recognizing, however, that A.D. has taken on a purely conventional significance, most scholars and scholarly editors have long since withdrawn their objections to the locution.

ALL-NUMERAL DATES AND OTHER BRIEF FORMS

8.43   Although the all-numeral style of writing dates (5/10/92 or 5-10-92) finds no place in formal writing, it sometimes falls to the lot of scholars to interpret dates so written. Accordingly, something should perhaps be said about them here. The trouble is that Americans on the one hand and the British (as well as many Canadians) on the other use different conventions of abbreviation, resulting in dates that often look alike but mean quite different things on different sides of the Atlantic. For example, to an American 5/10/92 might stand for the tenth day of May in the year 1992, but to the English it means the fifth day of October. The lesson, of course, is to be sure you know which convention a writer is using when you decipher a date that could be interpreted either way.

When correctly deciphered, dates given in all-numeral style should be converted to expressions containing the name of the month:

> 10 May 1992 *or* May 10, 1992
> 5 October 1992 *or* October 5, 1992

8.44 One way of getting around the ambiguity of all-figure dates is to use a lowercase roman numeral for the month, as many Continentals do. Thus 10 May 1992 is written 10.v.92. The periods not only separate the figures but, in the Continental convention, make ordinals of the figures they follow: that is, *tenth* and *fifth*. This style commends itself to many scholars and editors for dating memorandums and informal communications.

8.45 Another system, less elegant but equally unambiguous, is one employed by the military. In this the order day-month-year is preserved, but the name of the month is abbreviated to three letters where necessary, without a period. Thus 31 December 1991 appears as 31 Dec 91 (army style) or 31 DEC 91 (navy style).

8.46 Still another system of all-numeral dating, one recommended by the International Standards Organization (ISO), is used in work with computers, which are usually programmed to read and accept dates only in this form. In this system ten keystrokes are always used, and the sequence is year-month-day, separated by hyphens. Thus 10 May 1992 appears as 1992-05-10.

Time of Day

8.47 Times of day in even, half, and quarter hours are usually spelled out in text matter:

> The directors expected the meeting to continue until half past three.
>
> First-year students must be in their rooms by midnight on weekdays.
>
> He left the office at a quarter of four.
>
> The family always ate dinner at seven o'clock.

But numerals are used (with zeros for even hours) when the exact moment of time is to be emphasized:

> The program is televised at 2:30 in the afternoon.
>
> If we don't eat dinner, we can catch the 6:20 train.
>
> The county will return to standard time tomorrow morning at 2:00.

(In Britain a period rather than a colon is used between hour and minutes—2.30.)

8.48   As with the abbreviations for era designations (8.41), abbreviations for divisions of the day (A.M., P.M.) are usually set in small caps. Numerals are used with these abbreviations, but not with *o'clock.*

> at 4:00 P.M. *or* 4 P.M.
> 4:32 P.M.
> 11:30 A.M.
> eight o'clock
> midnight

8.49   In the twenty-four-hour system of expressing time, no punctuation is used between the hours and minutes:

> General quarters sounded at 0415.
>
> Visiting hours are from 0930 to 1100 and from 1800 to 2030.

8.50   A variation of the twenty-four-hour system that is especially useful in scientific and technical works can show hours, minutes, seconds, and decimal fractions of seconds and is compatible with the ISO dating system (8.46). The hours, minutes, and seconds are separated by colons:

> 09:27:08.6 (27 minutes, 8.6 seconds after 9 A.M.)
>
> 12:08:31 (8 minutes, 31 seconds after 12 noon)
>
> 16:09:41.3 (9 minutes, 41.3 seconds after 4 P.M.)

The time series may be appended, following a hyphen, at the end of the date series:

> 1992-05-10-16:09:41.3

Names

MONARCHS AND SUCH

8.51   Sovereigns and popes with the same names are differentiated by numerals, traditionally roman:

> Elizabeth II   John XXIII

In Continental practice the numeral is sometimes followed by a period or a superscript abbreviation indicating that the number is an ordinal (Wilhelm II., François Ier). These should be edited out in an English context.

VEHICLES AND SUCH

8.52   Sometimes similarly treated are such things as yachts, racing cars, and spacecraft:

America IV   Bluebird III   Voyager II

Earlier spacecraft generally carried roman numerals, but current custom is to use arabic (see examples at 7.99).

PERSONAL NAMES

8.53 Roman numerals are also used to differentiate male members of the same family with identical names. Two different conventions govern the use of such numbers. According to the older custom the system works as follows: If Robert Allen Smith's son or grandson is given the same name, the latter adds *Jr.* to the name (a nephew or grandnephew would use *II*). If later a third member of the family is given the name, he adds *III*. The first, or eldest, of the name is sometimes, though not regularly, referred to as Senior *(Sr.):* Kingsley Wade Watchmore Sr. On the death of the eldest, Robert Allen Smith Jr. drops the *Jr.,* and Robert Allen Smith III (if a grandson) becomes Robert Allen Smith Jr. Exceptionally, within this system, if the original or some subsequent bearer of the name is a famous person, a younger namesake often keeps the suffix:

Douglas Fairbanks Jr.   Adlai E. Stevenson III

8.54 Perhaps under the influence of these exceptions, a newer custom has grown up in some American families given to using the same names in successive generations. In these families same-name males sometimes keep their suffixes throughout life and go to the grave, like emperors and popes, with *III* or *IV* or *V* still attached to their names.

8.55 Traditionally, *Jr.* and *Sr.* have been set off with commas, whereas *I, II, III, IV,* and so on have not. This tradition is still widely followed, and the University of Chicago Press recognizes and accepts it; but the Press now also accepts, and in fact recommends, that the commas be omitted in both cases. In either style, of course, consistency should be observed.

Charles William DeLor Jr. ran for Congress.
Charles William DeLor, Jr., ran for Congress.
Charles William DeLor III ran for Congress.

Governmental Designations

GOVERNMENTS

8.56 Particular dynasties, governments, and governing bodies in a succession are usually designated by ordinal numbers, spelled out if one hundred or less, preceding the noun:

Eighteenth Dynasty	Third Reich
Fifth Republic	Second International
Second Continental Congress	Ninety-seventh Congress

The 107th Congress will be elected in the year 2000.

POLITICAL DIVISIONS

8.57 Spell out in ordinal form numerals of one hundred or less designating political divisions:

Fifth Ward	Fourteenth Precinct
Court of Appeals for the	Second Congressional District
Tenth Circuit	Ninth Naval District

MILITARY UNITS

8.58 Similarly, spell out in ordinal form numerals of one hundred or less designating military subdivisions:

Fifth Army	Seventy-seventh Regiment
Second Infantry Division	323d Fighter Wing
Third Battalion, 122d Artillery	Twelfth Armored Division

Organizations

CHURCHES AND SUCH

8.59 Numerals designating religious organizations or houses of worship are generally spelled out in ordinal form before the name:

First Baptist Church   Seventh-Day Adventists

Twenty-first Church of Christ, Scientist

UNIONS AND LODGES

8.60 Numerals designating local branches of labor unions and of fraternal lodges are usually expressed in arabic numerals after the name:

Typographical Union no. 16

American Legion, Department of Illinois, Crispus Attucks Post no. 1268

Amalgamated Meat Cutters and Butcher Workmen of North America, Local 15

Addresses and Thoroughfares

HIGHWAYS

8.61 State, federal, and interstate highways are designated by arabic numerals:

U.S. Route 41 (U.S. 41)   Interstate 90 (I-90)   Illinois 12

NUMBERED STREETS

8.62   It is preferable, except where space is at a premium, to spell out the names of numbered streets of one hundred or less:

Fifth Avenue   Twenty-third Street

The address "1212 Fifth Street" is easier to read than "1212—5th Street," a device sometimes employed in typing addresses.

BUILDING NUMBERS

8.63   Address numbers are written in arabic numerals before the name of the street in both British and American addresses (the older British practice of using a comma after the building number has been generally abandoned there):

5801 Ellis Avenue, Chicago, Illinois 60637

126 Buckingham Palace Road, London SW1W 9SD

When a building's name is its address, the number is often spelled out:

One Thousand Lake Shore Drive   One Park Avenue

FORMS AND USES OF NUMBERS

Plurals of Numbers

8.64   The plurals of spelled-out numbers are formed like the plurals of other nouns:

The contestants were in their twenties and thirties.

The family was at sixes and sevens.

The plurals of numerals are formed by adding *s* alone:

Among the scores were two 240s and three 238s.

The bonds offered were convertible $4^1/_2$s.

Jazz forms developed in the 1920s became popular in the 1930s.

Use of the Comma

NONSCIENTIFIC COPY

8.65   In most numbers of one thousand or more, commas should be used between groups of three digits, counting from the right:

309

32,987   1,512   1,000,000

Exceptions to this rule are page numbers, addresses, numbers of chapters of fraternal organizations and the like, decimal fractions of less than one (but see 8.67), and year numbers of four digits, which are written in numerals without commas. (Years with five or more digits use the comma—for an example see 8.41.)

8.66   British practice is similar to American in marking off groups of three digits with commas. In Continental practice, however, periods or spaces are often used: 93.000.000; 93 000 000. Except in quoted matter or in scientific work (see below), numbers like these should be edited to conform to American standards.

SCIENTIFIC COPY

8.67   In the international measurement system, generally used within the world's scientific community (see 14.41–53), long numerals are commonly avoided by the use of special units of measure and by the use of multiples and powers of ten. When long numerals do occur, however, the digits are usually marked off in groups of three by spaces, starting from the decimal point and going both to the left and (unlike the common usage) to the right:

3 426 869   0.000 007

Spacing is optional in numbers consisting of four digits left or right of a decimal point unless they are in a column with numbers having five or more digits. When the four digits left of the decimal point are closed up, no comma is used either.

8300 *or* 8 300   0.0259 *or* 0.025 9

For the decimal point, the international system permits either the dot (the British and American practice) or, since it is not used to set off groups of three digits, the comma (the continental European practice):

46 738.07 *or* 46 738,07

Inclusive Numbers

8.68   Inclusive, or continuous, numbers may be represented by the pair of numbers that indicate the beginning and ending of the series. If such numbers are joined by an en dash, they must not be preceded by a preposition:

167–72   *not*   from 167–72

1898–1903   *not*   from 1898–1903

The beginning and ending numbers of the series may also be related by a pair of prepositions *(from/to),* but then the dash is omitted:

> from 167 to 172
> from 1898 to 1903

The limits of inclusive numbers are sometimes preceded by the preposition *between* and separated by the conjunction *and:*

> between 167 and 172
> between 1898 and 1903

If such a coupling is used, however, the two numbers might be regarded as boundaries for the series of numbers running between them, and not as part of the series. Such a construction should not, therefore, be used indiscriminately as a substitute for "167–72," "from 167 to 172," and so forth. If inclusiveness is meant, it might be better to use some such wording as "from the beginning of 1898 to the end of 1903."

As illustrated in the examples above, inclusive numbers linked by prepositions are given in full, whereas those separated by an en dash may be abbreviated by omitting certain repeated digits. The University of Chicago Press now accepts two systems of abbreviation. The two systems, which are discussed below, are modified for application to inclusive numbers that represent years (8.71) and to numbers whose digits are grouped by commas (8.73).

ABBREVIATION SYSTEMS

8.69　The first of these abbreviation systems for inclusive numbers employs the principles outlined in the following (the examples may be thought of as representing page numbers, serial numbers, or other numbers not using commas):

FIRST NUMBER	SECOND NUMBER	EXAMPLES
Less than 100	Use all digits	3–10, 71–72, 96–117
100 or multiple of 100	Use all digits	100–104, 600–613, 1100–1123
101 through 109 (in multiples of 100)	Use changed part only, omitting unneeded zeros	107–8, 505–17, 1002–6
110 through 199 (in multiples of 100)	Use two digits, or more if needed	321–25, 415–532, 1536–38, 1496–504, 14325–28, 11564–78, 13792–803

To avoid ambiguity, inclusive roman numerals are given in full:

> xxv–xxviii　　cvi–cix

8.70   The second system of abbreviating inclusive numbers now accepted by the Press is a greatly simplified version of the first (8.69). In this version the second number includes only the changed part of the first number:

3–10	600–13	1002–6	1496–504
71–2	1100–23	321–5	14325–8
96–117	107–8	415–532	11564–78
100–4	505–17	1536–42	13729–803

INCLUSIVE YEARS

8.71   The following examples illustrate the style for inclusive years. Note that when the century changes or when the sequence is B.C. or B.P. (that is, diminishing numbers), all digits are repeated. (Diminishing numbers are given in full because an abbreviated second number may be read as the complete year: 327–321 B.C. is not 327–21 B.C.)

the war of 1914–18	the years 1597–1601 and 1701–4
the winter of 1900–1901	fiscal year 1975–76 (*or* 1975/76)
A.D. 325–27	327–321 B.C.
A.D. 300–325	115 B.C.–A.D. 216

8.72   When inclusive dates occur in titles, it is usual to repeat all the digits:

An English Mission to Muscovy, 1589–1591

In references to published works in whose titles inclusive dates are abbreviated, however, the abbreviation should be retained:

Clarkson's Antagonism, 1946–51

INCLUSIVE NUMBERS WITH COMMAS

8.73   Inclusive numbers whose digits are separated into groups of three by commas are often given in full, but they may also be abbreviated. In the latter case, however, for ease of reading, abbreviation is restricted to changes in the hundreds digit and below. If a change occurs in any digit to the left of a comma, all digits must be repeated.

6,000–18		
12,473–9	*or* 12,473–479	*or* 12,473–79
13,248–57	*or* 13,248–257	
1,247,689–705		
17,847–18,128		

ROMAN NUMERALS

8.74   Table 8.1 shows the formation of roman numerals with their arabic equivalents. The general principle is that a smaller letter before a larger

Table 8.1 Roman and Arabic Numerals

Arabic	Roman	Arabic	Roman	Arabic	Roman
1	I	16	XVI	90	XC
2	II	17	XVII	100	C
3	III	18	XVIII	200	CC
4	IV	19	XIX	300	CCC
5	V	20	XX	400	CD
6	VI	21	XXI	500	D
7	VII	22	XXII	600	DC
8	VIII	23	XXIII	700	DCC
9	IX	24	XXIV	800	DCCC
10	X	30	XXX	900	CM
11	XI	40	XL	1,000	M
12	XII	50	L	2,000	MM
13	XIII	60	LX	3,000	MMM
14	XIV	70	LXX	4,000	$M\overline{V}$
15	XV	80	LXXX	5,000	$\overline{V}$ (or ↀ)

one subtracts from its value, and a smaller letter after a larger one adds to it; a bar over a letter multiplies its value by one thousand. Roman numerals may also be written in lowercase letters (i, ii, iii, iv, etc.), and in older practice a final *i* was often made like a *j* (vij, viij). Also, in early printed works, IↃ is sometimes seen for D, CIↃ for M, and IIII for IV. The University of Chicago Press now uses arabic numerals in many situations where roman numerals formerly were common, as in references to volume numbers of books and journals or chapters of books (8.32).

ENUMERATIONS

Run-in Style

8.75 Enumerations that are run into the text may be indicated by numerals or italic letters in parentheses. In a simple series with little or no punctuation within each item, separation by commas is sufficient. Otherwise, semicolons are used:

> This was determined by a chi-square test using as observed frequencies *(a)* the occurrence of one class and *(b)* the total occurrence of all classes among the neighbors of the subject classes.

> Data are available on three different groups of counsel: (1) the public defender of Cook County, (2) the member attorneys of the Chicago Bar Association's Defense of Prisoners Committee, and (3) all other attorneys.

> Specifically, the committee set down fundamental principles, which in its opinion were so well established that they were no longer open to controversy: (1) the commerce power was complete, except as constitutionally

313

limited; (2) the power included the authority absolutely to prohibit specified persons and things from interstate transit; (3) the only limitation upon this authority, as far as the Keating-Owen bill was concerned, was the Fifth Amendment, which protected against arbitrary interference with private rights; and (4) this authority might be exercised in the interest of the public welfare as well as in the direct interest of commerce.

Outline Style

8.76 For long enumerations it is preferable to begin each item on a line by itself, in what is known as *outline style*. The numerals are aligned on the periods that follow them, and are either set flush with the text or indented. In either case runover lines are best aligned with the first word following the numeral.

> The inadequacy of the methods proposed for the solution of both histological and mounting problems is emphasized by the number and variety of the published procedures, which fall into the following groups:
>
> 1. Slightly modified classical histological techniques with fluid fixation, wax embedding, and aqueous mounting of the section or the emulsion
> 2. Sandwich technique with separate processing of tissue and photographic film after exposure
> 3. Protective coating of tissue to prevent leaching during application of stripping film or liquid emulsion
> 4. Freeze substitution of tissue with or without embedding followed by film application
> 5. Vacuum freeze-drying of tissue blocks followed by embedding
> 6. Mounting of frozen sections on emulsion, using heat or adhesive liquids

Note that in the example above, each item begins with a capital letter and ends without punctuation. If, as is also the case above, the enumerated items are syntactically part of the sentence, the items may also begin lowercase and carry appropriate end punctuation (see example in 5.10).

8.77 Items in a vertical list need not be enumerated if they are not referred to by number or letter. Should some of the items run over to the next line, paragraph style may be used for clarity, the runovers may be indented (flush-and-hang style), or extra space may be added between items. If the items do not run over but are nearly line length, they may be separated with extra space. The use of bullets (heavy dots •) in place of enumeration is sometimes resorted to, but these may be considered cumbersome, especially in a scholarly work. Sometimes em dashes are used in place of bullets.

8.78 When referring to an item in an enumeration by letter or number only, enclose the letter or numeral in parentheses, whatever the style of the enumeration itself; if a category name is used, however, open style is preferable:

> From *(a)*, *(b)*, and *(d)* it is apparent . . .

> Methods 4, 5, and 6 all require special laboratory equipment.

Note that when letters are used they are frequently italicized.

8.79   Enumerations in which items are subdivided call for a more elaborate form of outline style. The following example illustrates the form favored by the University of Chicago Press. Note that the numerals or letters denoting the top three levels are set off by periods and those for the lower levels by single or double parentheses:

> I. Historical introduction
> II. Dentition in various groups of vertebrates
>   A. Reptilia
>   1. Histology and development of reptilian teeth
>   2. Survey of forms
>   B. Mammalia
>   1. Histology and development of mammalian teeth
>   2. Survey of forms
>   *a)* Primates
>   (1) Lemuroidea
>   (2) Anthropoidea
>   *(a)* Platyrrhini
>   *(b)* Catarrhini
>   i) Cercopithecidae
>   ii) Pongidae
>   *b)* Carnivora
>   (1) Creodonta
>   (2) Fissipedia
>   *(a)* Ailuroidea
>   *(b)* Arctoidea
>   (3) Pinnipedia
>   *c)* Etc. . . .

In the foregoing example, note that roman numerals are aligned on the following period or parenthesis. Any runover lines would be aligned as in the example in 8.76.

FOR FURTHER REFERENCE

8.80   For special uses of numbers not covered in this chapter, the reader is referred to the United States Government Printing Office *Style Manual*.

9   *Foreign Languages in Type*

INTRODUCTION

9.1   This chapter is intended as an aid to authors and editors in solving some of the problems that arise in preparing foreign language copy for setting in type. Some of the suggestions are addressed primarily to authors (such as the recommendations on choice of transliteration systems), others primarily to manuscript editors (such as the hints on what kinds of capitalization one is likely to encounter in various languages). It should be emphasized that the chapter does not pretend to constitute a style manual for any of the languages treated. Nor does it pretend to be comprehensive: only the languages likely to be met in the course of general editing are covered at all, and some of these are covered more completely than others, depending partly upon their relative importance in scholarly work and partly upon the complexity of the problems they raise.

9.2   The problems one encounters with foreign language copy differ according to whether the copy was originally written with the same alphabet as English, whether it has been transliterated or romanized, or whether it is to be set in the alphabet of the original. The organization of the chapter reflects these three categories.

LANGUAGES USING THE LATIN ALPHABET

9.3   With languages using an alphabet basically similar to that of English (the *Latin* alphabet), editorial questions arise mainly from differing systems of capitalization, punctuation, and syllabication (word division). But since some of these languages supplement the basic Latin alphabet with additional letters or use a variety of accents and diacritics on the familiar letters, there is the mechanical problem of making sure that the typesetter can reproduce these special characters.

General Principles

CAPITALIZATION

9.4   The chief problem concerning capitalization is what to do with titles of books and articles in bibliographies, notes, and run of text. Here the

University of Chicago Press recommends following a simple rule: In any language but English, capitalize only the words that would be capitalized in normal prose. For all the languages in question this means capitalizing the first word of the title and of the subtitle and all proper nouns;[1] in addition, it means capitalizing proper adjectives in Dutch and common nouns in German. The rule can easily be extended to the names of foreign journals and even of institutions, although in practice these are often capitalized in the same way as their English counterparts. See examples of foreign language titles in 15.118–19 and 15.227–29.

9.5 In English, capitalization is applied to more classes of words than in any other Western language. Consequently, it is always surprising to English-speaking persons learning their first foreign language—say, French—to discover that the equivalents of *I* and *American* and *Tuesday* are spelled with no capitals. The remarks under "Capitalization" in the sections that follow are an attempt to mitigate some of the manuscript editor's surprises—to suggest some of the more obvious ways in which various languages differ from English in their use of capitals.

9.6 Except where it is stated to the contrary, the language in question is assumed to use lowercase type for all adjectives (except adjectives used as proper nouns), all pronouns, the names of the months, and the days of the week. In addition, it can be assumed that capitals are used much more sparingly than in English for names of offices, institutions, places, organizations, and so on. (For the capitalization of foreign personal names, see 7.9–15.)

PUNCTUATION

9.7 Punctuation in foreign languages using the Latin alphabet is in some ways even more "foreign" to the English-speaking editor than foreign capitalization. The remarks under "Punctuation" in the sections below are an attempt to point out some of the more obvious departures from what is familiar to us. These remarks apply, of course, to foreign punctuation in a foreign language context, that is, in an article or book in that language. (See, for example, the passage in 9.49.) They also apply to quotations in a foreign language used in an English language context,

1. The rule for French titles followed by the *French Review, PMLA,* and *Romanic Review,* and recommended by the University of Chicago Department of Romance Languages and Literatures, is as follows: Always capitalize the first word and any proper nouns in the title; if the first word is an article, capitalize the first substantive and any intervening adjective(s); if the first word is neither an article nor an adjective, lowercase all following words. Thus: *Le Rouge et le noir; L'Illusion comique; Les Fausses Vérités; A la recherche du temps perdu; Dans le labyrinthe.* The Press accepts this rule for studies in French literature but for general use (especially when works in several languages are cited) prefers the simpler rule stated in the text.

except that when run in with English text the foreign language quotation is usually enclosed in American-style quotation marks:

> "Anche il primo incontro di Henry James con l'Italia, nel 1869," writes Franco Piazza, "riflette il tradizionale atteggiamento americano del tempo."

9.8   A fragment of text or dialogue composed by the author and used in an American English context is usually punctuated American fashion:

> "Por qué estás aquí todavía?" cried Juana, looking furiously at Pablo, whose face suddenly turned white.
> Marcus, alarmed, tried to calm them both. "It doesn't matter," he said. "It's nada!"

compare with

> —¿Por qué estás aquí todavía?—preguntó Juana.

WORD DIVISION

9.9   Anyone who has ever read a book in English that was composed and printed in a non-English-speaking country knows how easy it is to err in word division when working with a language not one's own. Condensed rules for dividing words in the Latin alphabet foreign languages most frequently met in book and journal work are given below.

SPECIAL CHARACTERS

9.10   English is one of very few languages that can be set without accents, diacritics, or special alphabetic characters for native words. Whenever passages in a foreign language occur in a book, or foreign titles in reference lists or notes, the manuscript editor should scan them carefully for special characters, especially unusual ones. The ordinary umlauted (as in German) and accented (as in French and Spanish) lowercase vowels are readily available in most type fonts, but anything more unusual, including many accented capital letters, should be listed or circled on a copy of table 9.1 for the information of the typesetter (see 2.162).

9.11   Diacritical marks most commonly used in European and Asian languages written in the Latin alphabet are the acute accent (é), grave accent (è), diaeresis or umlaut (ü), circumflex (ê), tilde (ñ), cedilla (ç), macron (ē), and breve (ĕ).

African Languages

9.12   African languages, other than the Arabic of the northern African countries, use the Latin alphabet and follow the American English style of

Table 9.1 Special Characters in the Latin Alphabet

Á	á	Ğ	ğ	Ǫ	ǫ
À	à	Ḥ	ḥ	Œ	œ
Ä	ä	Í	í	Ṛ	ṛ
Â	â	Ì	ì	Ṝ	ṝ
Ā	ā	Ï	ï	Ř	ř
Ā	ā	Î	î	Ś	ś
Ă	ă	Ī	ī	Ṣ	ṣ
Å	å	Ĭ	ĭ	Š	š
Ą	ą	İ	ı	Ş	ş
Æ	æ	Ƙ	ƙ		ß
Ǣ	ǣ	Ł	ł	Ṭ	ṭ
Б ʼВ	б	Ḷ	ḷ	Ť	ťʼ
Ć	ć	Ḹ	ḹ	Ţ	ţ
Ç	ç	Ṃ	ṃ	þ	þ
Č	č	Ń	ń	Ù	ù
Ḍ	ḍ	Ñ	ñ	Ü	ü
Ď	ďʼ	Ň	ň	Ű	ű
Đ ʼD	ḍ ɖ	Ṇ	ṇ	Û	û
Đ	ð	Ṅ	ṅ	Ū	ū
É	é	Ŋ	ŋ	Ũ	ũ
È	è	Ó	ó	Ú	ú
Ë	ë	Ò	ò	Ų	ų
Ê	ê	Ö	ö	Ů	ů
Ē	ē	Ő	ő	Ý	ý
Ĕ	ĕ	Ô	ô	Ź	ź
Ě	ě	Ō	õ	Ż	ż
Ė	ė	Ō	ō	Ž	ž
Ę	ę	Ŏ	ŏ	Ʒ	ʒ
Ğ	ğ	Ø	ø		

capitalization and punctuation. Of the two most widely spoken languages, Swahili uses no additional letters or diacritics. Hausa adds a symbol for the nasal *n* (Ŋ ŋ) and other special characters: Ɓ 'B ɓ , Đ 'D ɗ ɗ, Ƙ ƙ, Ọ ọ. Hausa, spoken by about fifteen million people and used in trade in western Africa, provides the phonetic base for transcribing other languages, for example, Kriol.

Czech

CAPITALIZATION

9.13 See 9.4–6.

SPECIAL CHARACTERS

9.14 Czech, a Slavic language, is written in the Latin alphabet but uses many diacritical marks to indicate sounds not represented by this alphabet.

Á á, Č č, Ď ď, É é, Ě ě, Í í, Ň ň, Ó ó, Ř ř, Š š, Ť ť, Ů ů, Ú ú, Ý ý, Ž ž

Danish

CAPITALIZATION

9.15 See 9.4–6. The polite personal pronouns *De, Dem, Deres,* and the familiar *I* are capitalized in Danish. Formerly, common nouns were capitalized as in German.

SPECIAL CHARACTERS

9.16 Danish has three additional alphabetic letters, and special characters are required for these:

Å å, Æ æ, Ø ø

Dutch

CAPITALIZATION

9.17 See 9.4–6. When the pronouns *U, Uw,* and *Gij* appear in personal correspondence, they are capitalized. Proper adjectives are capitalized as in English. When a word beginning with the diphthong *ij* is capitalized, both letters are capitals: *IJsland.* When a single letter begins a sentence, it is set lowercase, but the next word is capitalized: *'k Heb niet. . . .* (For the capitalization of particles with personal names see 7.10.)

9.18   Dutch requires no special characters outside the ordinary Latin alphabet.

Finnish

9.19   See 9.4–6.

9.20   Finnish requires two umlauted vowels:

Ä ä, Ö ö

French

9.21   See 9.4–6. Generic names denoting roadways, squares, and the like are lowercased, whether used alone or with a specific name as part of an address:

le boulevard Saint-Germain	13, rue des Beaux-Arts
la place de l'Opéra	le carrefour de Buci

In names of most political, military, religious, or other institutions, only the first substantive is capitalized. Note, however, that in the names of specific churches, the generic term is lowercased.

l'Académie française	le Conservatoire de musique
l'Assemblée nationale	la Légion d'honneur
l'Eglise catholique (*but* l'église de Saint-Eustache)	

If such names are hyphenated (and French makes frequent use of hyphens), both elements are capitalized:

la Comédie-Française

Names of buildings are generally capitalized:

l'Hôtel des Invalides   le Palais du Louvre

Names of members of religious groups are lowercased:

un chrétien   des juifs   une carmélite   un protestant

In most geographical names, the substantive is lowercased and the modifying word capitalized:

la mer Rouge   le pic du Midi   le massif Central

Adjectives formed from proper nouns are usually lowercased:

une imagination baudelairienne

PUNCTUATION

9.22   Small angle marks called *guillemets* («») are used for quotation marks and are placed on the lower part of the type body (but see 9.8). A small amount of space is added between the guillemets and the quoted material. Note that in French such tags as *écrit-il* or *dit-il* are often introduced without additional guillemets.

> A vrai dire, Abélard n'avoue pas un tel rationalisme: «je ne veux pas être si philosophe, écrit-il, que je résiste à Paul, ni si aristotélicien que je me sépare du Christ», ou encore: «Vois combien il est présomptueux de discuter par la raison ce qui dépasse l'homme et de ne pas s'arrêter avant d'avoir éclairé toutes ses paroles par le sens ou la raison humaine.»[2]

9.23   Punctuation belonging to the quoted matter is placed inside the closing guillemets:

«Va-t'en!» m'a-t-il dit.

Punctuation belonging to the including sentence is placed outside, and a period belonging to the quotation is dropped:

D'où vient l'expression «sur le tapis»?

Est-ce Louis XV qui a dit: «Après moi, le déluge»?

When the end punctuation of the simultaneously terminating quotation and including sentence is identical, the mark outside the closing guillemets is dropped:

Qui a dit: «Où sont les neiges d'antan?»

9.24   If a quotation in text (that is, not a block quotation) is more than one paragraph long, guillemets are placed at the beginning of each additional paragraph and closing guillemets at the end of the last.

9.25   Guillemets are also used for quotations within quotations. When the second quotation runs over to additional lines, each runover line begins with opening guillemets. If the two quotations end simultaneously, however, only one pair of terminating guillemets is used:

2. Emile Bréhier, *Histoire de la philosophie,* vol. 1, fasc. 3 (Paris: Presses Universitaires de France, 1931), 517.

Raoul suggéra à sa sœur: «Tu connais sans doute la parole «De «l'abondance du cœur la bouche parle.»

9.26 In quoted conversation, the guillemets are frequently replaced by dashes. The dash is used before each successive speech but is not repeated at the end of the speech, even when followed by other matter. A space is added after the dash:

— Vous viendrez aussitôt que possible? a-t-il demandé.
— Tout de suite.
— Bien. Bonne chance!

If a quotation is used in dialogue, guillemets set off the quotation.

9.27 Three closely spaced periods—suspension points—are frequently used to indicate interruptions or sudden breaks in thought. A space is used after, but not before, such points:

«Ce n'est pas que je n'aime plus l'Algérie... mon Dieu! un ciel! des arbres!... et le reste!... Toutefois, sept ans de discipline....»

WORD DIVISION

9.28 The fundamental principle of French word division is to divide as far as possible after a vowel, avoiding consonantal ending of syllables except where *n* nasalizes a preceding vowel:

a-che-ter	ba-lan-cer (*not* bal-anc-er)
in-di-vi-si-bi-li-té	ta-bleau (*not* tab-leau)

9.29 Two adjacent and different consonants of which the second is *l* or *r* (but not the combinations *rl* and *lr*) are both carried over to the following syllable. Otherwise, different consonants are divided:

é-cri-vain	par-ler	plas-tic
qua-tre	Mal-raux	ob-jet

9.30 In groups of three adjacent consonants the first goes with the preceding syllable; the others are carried over:

es-prit   res-plendir

9.31 There are as many syllables as there are vowels or diphthongs, even if some vowels are not sounded:

fui-te   guer-re   sor-tent

A mute *e* following a vowel, however, does not form a syllable:

é-taient   re-çue

9.32 When preceding and blending in pronunciation with other vowels, *i, y, o, ou,* and *u* do not form syllables:

bien	é-tions	loin
é-cuel-le	fouet-ter	yeux

Nor should division be made after an apostrophe:

jus-qu'à demain

SPECIAL CHARACTERS

9.33   French as sometimes set employs the following special characters:

À à, Â â, Ç ç, É é, È è, Ê ê, Ë ë, Î î, Ï ï, Ô ô, Œ œ, Ù ù, Û û, Ü ü

Note, however, that French may be set without accents on capital letters,[3] and if necessary the ligature *Œ œ* may be set as separate characters *(OE oe)*. This leaves as the essential minimum *C c* with cedilla and the lowercase accented vowels, characters that are found in many English and American fonts.

German

CAPITALIZATION

9.34   See 9.4–6. The most striking feature of German capitalization is that all nouns and words used as nouns are capitalized:

ein Haus   Weltanschauung   das Sein

Although proper adjectives are generally lowercased, those derived from personal names, and used with their original signification, are capitalized:

die deutsche Literatur   die Platonischen Dialoge

The pronouns *Sie, Ihr,* and *Ihnen,* as polite second-person forms, are capitalized. As third-person pronouns they are lowercased. Also, in correspondence such forms as *Du, Dein, Ihr,* and *Euch* are capitalized.

PUNCTUATION

9.35   The apostrophe is used to note the colloquial omission of *e:*

wie geht's   was gibt's   hab' ich

---

3. French printers vary in practice, some retaining accents on all capitals (except the preposition *à*, which never carries the accent when capitalized), some retaining accents only on *I* and *E* (or using an accent on *I* even when omitting one from *E*), some omitting them altogether. English and American publishers reflect all these practices.

The apostrophe is also used to note the omission of the genitive ending *s* after proper names ending in *s, ß, x,* or *Z:*

Jaspers' Philosophie   Leibniz' Meinung

9.36   In German, quotations take split-level pairs of primes, („"), split-level inverted quotation marks („ "), or guillemets («»)—sometimes inverted (»«). (See also 9.8.)

> Adam Smith hat sehr wohl gesehen, daß in „Wirklichkeit die Verschiedenheit der natürlichen Anlagen zwischen den Individuen weit geringer ist als wir glauben."

Punctuation is placed inside or outside closing quotation marks according to whether it belongs to the quotation or the including sentence.

WORD DIVISION

9.37   The fundamental principle of German word division is to divide after a vowel as far as possible:

Fa-brik   hü-ten   Bu-ße

9.38   If two or more consonants stand between vowels, the word is usually divided before the last of those consonants:

Karp-fen	Klir-ren	Ver-wand-te
Klemp-ner	Rit-ter	Was-ser

9.39   The consonant groups *ch, sch, ph, st,* and *th* are separated only when the letters belong to different syllables:

Hä-scher	Philoso-phie	Morgen-stern
Häus-chen	Klapp-hut	Reichs-tag

9.40   If *ck* must be divided, it is separated into *k-k:*

Deckel—Dek-kel

9.41   In non-German words combinations of *b, d, g, k, p,* and *t* with *l* or *r* are carried over:

Hy-drant   Me-trum   Pu-bli-kum

9.42   Compound words are first separated into their component elements, and within each element the foregoing rules apply:

Für-sten-schloß   In-ter-esse   Tür-an-gel

SPECIAL CHARACTERS

9.43   German is almost never set in the old Fraktur type nowadays. For setting in roman type, one special character (ß) is needed, plus the umlauted vowels:

Ä ä, Ö ö, Ü ü

It is acceptable to set ß as *ss* and umlauted capitals as *Ae, Oe,* and *Ue,* but lowercase umlauted letters should not be so set.

Hungarian

CAPITALIZATION

9.44   See 9.4–6.

SPECIAL CHARACTERS

9.45   Hungarian requires several varieties of accented vowels:

Á á, É é, Í í, Ó ó, Ö ö,Ő ő, Ú ú, Ü ü,Ű ű

Italian

CAPITALIZATION

9.46   See 9.4–6. In Italian, titles preceding a proper name are normally lowercased:

il commendatore Ugo Emiliano   la signora Rossi

The formal second-person pronouns *Ella, Lei,* and *Loro* are capitalized.

PUNCTUATION

9.47   A series of closely spaced dots is used to indicate a sudden break in thought or an interruption in faltering speech. If other punctuation precedes the series, three periods are used; otherwise, four are used:

«Piano!... Ho sentito muovere di là.... C'è qualcuno.... Dev'essere la.... cosa dell'ingegnere....»

9.48   The apostrophe is used to indicate the omission of a letter. Space should be added after an apostrophe that follows a vowel. No space is used after an apostrophe that follows a consonant:

po' duro   de' malevoli   l'onda   all'aura

9.49   Italian quotation marks are often identical to French guillemets, but marks in the form " „ are also used—and with increasing frequency.

Anche il primo incontro di Henry James con l'Italia, nel 1869, riflette il tradizionale atteggiamento americano del tempo. Le lettere che scrive a casa mentre dal Gottardo, attraverso Milano, Verona, Padova, Venezia,

Mantova, Firenze, scende a Roma, parlano con insistenza della «meraviglia profonda», dell' «estasi e della passione» che lo invadono via ch'egli viene a contatto con «l'atmosfera italiana», «la melodiosa lingua d'Italia», lo «Spirito del Sud», finché la sera della sua prima giornata romana, trascorsa «vagando come ubriaco per le strade, in preda a una gioia delirante», scrive al fratello William: «Finalmente — per la prima volta — io vivo!»[4]

In dialogue, however, dashes, followed by a space, are used instead of guillemets. Each successive speech is introduced by a dash, and if other matter follows the speech in the same paragraph, another dash is used at the end of the speech (compare with French practice, 9.26).

— Avremo la neve, — annunziò la vecchia.
— E domani? — chiese Alfredo, voltandosi di scatto dalla finestra.

WORD DIVISION

9.50 The fundamental principle of Italian word division is to divide after a vowel, and to let each syllable, insofar as possible, begin with a consonant. Where there is only one consonant in intervocalic position, place it with the following vowel:

a-cro-po-li	mi-se-ra-bi-le	ta-vo-li-no

9.51 Certain consonant groups must also be placed with the following vowel. These are *ch, gh, gli, gn, qu, sc,* and *r* or *l* preceded by any consonant other than themselves:

a-qua-rio	na-sce	ri-flet-te-re
fi-glio	pa-dre	so-gna-re
la-ghi	rau-che	u-sci-re

9.52 Consonants, however, must be divided when (1) double (repeated), (2) in the group *cqu,* or (3) in a group beginning with *l, m, n,* or *r:*

ac-qua	cam-po	par-te
af-fre-schi	com-pra	poz-zo
cal-do	den-tro	sen-to

9.53 Vowel combinations are not divided:

miei	pia-ga	pie-no	tuo

9.54 Division is traditionally avoided immediately after an apostrophe:

dal-l'accusa	quel-l'uomo
del-l'or-ga-no	un'ar-te

4. Franca Piazza, *Città e paesaggi di Toscana visti da Henry James* (Florence: G. Barbèra, 1961), 7–8.

SPECIAL CHARACTERS

9.55 In Italian, the grave accent on uppercase vowels is usually optional, but in stressed final syllables it must be retained to avoid confusion:

CANTÒ (he sang)   CANTO (I sing)

Latin

CAPITALIZATION

9.56 Editors around the world tend to capitalize Latin according to the principles of their own languages. In English-speaking countries, however, titles of ancient and medieval books and shorter pieces are capitalized not as English titles but as English prose; that is, only the first word, proper nouns, and proper adjectives are capitalized:

> *De bello Gallico*   *De viris illustribus*   *Cur Deus homo?*

Renaissance and modern works with Latin titles are usually capitalized in the English fashion:

> *Novum Organum*   *Religio Medici*

WORD DIVISION

9.57 A Latin word has as many syllables as it has vowels or diphthongs *(ae, au, ei, eu, oe, ui):*

o-pe-re   gra-ti-a   na-tu-ra   o-pus

9.58 When a single consonant occurs between two vowels, divide before the consonant, except *x:*

Cae-sar   me-ri-di-es   lex-is

9.59 The combinations *ch, ph, th, gu,* and *qu* are treated as single consonants and never separated:

e-chī-nus   lin-gua
co-phi-nus   a-qua

9.60 When two or more consonants are grouped together, the word is divided before the last consonant except that the following consonant groups are never broken: *chl, chr, phl, phr, thl, thr, bl, br, cl, cr, dl, dr, gl, gr, pl, pr, tl,* and *tr.*

om-nis   cunc-tus   pan-chrēs-tus
scrip-tus   pa-tris   ex-em-pla

9.61   Compound words are first separated into their component elements; within each element the foregoing rules apply:

ab-rum-po   ad-est   red-e-o   trans-i-go

SPECIAL CHARACTERS

9.62   Latin requires no special characters for setting ordinary copy. Elementary texts, however, usually mark the long vowels, and so all five vowels with the macron would be needed for setting such works. Also, authors occasionally mark short quantities, and so vowels with the breve may be useful as well. The entire series for elementary Latin is thus:

Ā ā, Ă ă, Ē ē, Ĕ ĕ, Ī ī, Ĭ ĭ, Ō ō, Ŏ ŏ, Ū ū, Ŭ ŭ

Norwegian

CAPITALIZATION

9.63   See 9.4–6. As in Danish, the polite personal pronouns *De, Dem,* and *Deres* are capitalized. Formerly, common nouns were capitalized as in German.

SPECIAL CHARACTERS

9.64   Norwegian requires the same special characters as Danish:

Å å, Æ æ, Ø ø

Polish

CAPITALIZATION

9.65   See 9.4–6.

WORD DIVISION

9.66   Division of Polish words is similar to that of transliterated Russian (see 9.117–25).

SPECIAL CHARACTERS

9.67   Polish requires the following special characters:

Ą ą, Ć ć, Ę ę, Ł ł, Ń ń, Ó ó, Ś ś, Ź ź, Ż ż

Since Ł and ł are likely to confuse the typesetter, the editor should note in the margin "canceled el" or "slashed el" or some such description.

Portuguese

CAPITALIZATION

9.68   See 9.4–6.

SPECIAL CHARACTERS

9.69   Portuguese employs three special characters:

Ã ã, Ç ç, Õ õ

In addition, however, Portuguese makes extensive use of accents: all five vowels with both the acute and the grave are needed, plus *a, e,* and *o* with the circumflex. The vowels *i* and *u* sometimes appear with the diaeresis *(ï, ü),* but the same letters with the grave may be substituted. If display lines are to be set in full or small capitals, accented characters must be available, but for text work accented capitals may be dispensed with.

Spanish

CAPITALIZATION

9.70   See 9.4–6. Titles preceding names are lowercased in Spanish: *el señor Jaime López.* When a question or an exclamation occurs within a sentence, its first word is lowercased (see example in 9.73).

PUNCTUATION

9.71   Guillemets are used for quotation marks, and in a quotation enclosed by guillemets, dashes may be used to set off words identifying the speaker (but see 9.8). If dashes are used, the opening dash is preceded by a space; the closing dash, unless followed by punctuation, is followed by a space. Neither dash is separated from the words identifying the speaker. Note that the period follows the closing guillemets.

> El demonio, el activo demonio cuyo poder había quebrantado Hernán Cortés con espada y con lanza, gozaba utilizando al hijo como instrumento de sus infernales designios. «Vino el negocio a tanto —comenta Suárez—, que ya andaban muchos tomados por el diablo». Los frailes, desde los púlpitos, lanzaban catilinarias y aconsejaban a los padres sobre la forma en que debían salvaguardar el honor de sus familiares.[5]

5. Fernando Benítez, *Los primeros Mexicanos: La vida criolla en el siglo XVI,* 3d ed. (Mexico, D.F.: Ediciones ERA, 1962), 181.

In dialogue, dashes introduce each successive speech. If other matter follows the quoted speech in the same paragraph, a dash or a comma should be added at the end of the speech.

—Esto es el arca de Noé, afirmó el estanciero.
—¿Por qué estas aquí todavía? —preguntó Juana alarmada.

9.72 Three closely spaced periods are used to indicate a sudden break in thought or an interruption in faltering speech:

Hemos comenzadola vida juntos... quizá la terminaremos juntos también...

9.73 In Spanish an additional question mark or exclamation point precedes, in inverted form, a question or an exclamation:

¿Qué pasa, amigo?

Por favor, señor ¿donde está la biblioteca municipal?

Alguien viene. ¡Vámonos!

WORD DIVISION

9.74 The fundamental principle of Spanish word division is to divide after a vowel or group of vowels. Two or more adjacent vowels may not be divided:

au-tor	fue-go	re-cla-mo
bue-no	mu-jer	se-ño-ri-ta
cam-biáis	ne-ga-ti-va	tie-ne
ca-ra-co-les	pre-fe-rir	viu-da

9.75 A single vowel may not stand alone at the end of a line:

acei-te (*not* a-ceite)	ene-ro (*not* e-nero)
áti-co (*not* á-tico)	uni-dad (*not* u-nidad)

9.76 Some two- and three-syllable words may be divided, while others may not:

aho-ra	cie-go	leer
ao-jo	creer	lí-nea
aún	ellos	oa-sis
au-to	eo-lio	oí-do
baúl	ideas	oír

9.77 A single intervocalic consonant goes with the following vowel, except that compound words are usually divided according to derivation:

ave-ri-güéis	mal-es-tar	semi-es-fe-ra
des-igual	nos-otros	sub-or-di-nar
fle-xi-bi-li-dad	re-ba-ño	(*but* bien-aven-tu-ra-
in-útil	re-unión	do)

9.78 Spanish *ch, ll,* and *rr* are considered single characters:

    ci-ga-rri-llo   mu-cha-cho

9.79 Two adjacent consonants may usually be separated:

ac-cio-nis-ta	al-cal-de	efec-to
ad-ver-ten-cia	an-cho	is-la

The following pairs, however, containing *l* or *r,* are inseparable except rarely in compounds: *bl, cl, fl, gl, pl,* and *br, cr, dr, fr, gr, pr, tr:*

ci-fra	ma-dre	re-gla
co-pla	ne-gro	se-cre-to
im-po-si-ble	no-ble	te-cla
le-pra	pa-tria	(*but* sub-lu-nar, sub-ra-
li-bro	re-fle-jo	yar)

9.80 Groups of three consonants not ending with one of the inseparable pairs listed above always have an *s* in the middle. They are divided after the second consonant, since an *s* is always disjoined from a following consonant:

cons-pi-rar	ins-tan-te	obs-cu-ro
cons-ta	in-ters-ti-cio	obs-tan-te

SPECIAL CHARACTERS

9.81 Spanish employs one special character:

    Ñ ñ

In addition, however, all five vowels with the acute accent are needed, plus *u* with the diaeresis *(ü).* As with Portuguese, accented capitals can probably be safely dispensed with for ordinary text work.

Swedish

CAPITALIZATION

9.82 See 9.4–6. In Swedish the second-person pronouns *Ni, Eder,* and *Er* are capitalized in correspondence.

SPECIAL CHARACTERS

9.83 Swedish requires the following special characters:

    Å å, Ä ä, Ö ö

Turkish

CAPITALIZATION

9.84   See 9.4–6. In Turkish the names of months and days of the week are capitalized.

SPECIAL CHARACTERS

9.85   Turkish requires the following special characters:

Â â, Ç ç, Ğ ğ (or Ğ ğ), İ, ı, Ö ö, Ş ş, Û û, Ü ü

Note that there are dotted and undotted varieties of both the capital and the lowercase *i*. A dotted lowercase *i* retains its dot when capitalized.

TRANSLITERATED AND ROMANIZED LANGUAGES

9.86   In general work it is usual to *transliterate* or *romanize* such languages as Arabic, Aramaic, Chinese, Hebrew, Hindi, Japanese, Korean, Persian, Russian, Urdu, and others not written in Latin characters. A comprehensive resource for this is a publication issued by the Library of Congress, titled *ALA-LC Romanization Tables: Transliteration Schemes for Non-Roman Scripts.*

Arabic

9.87   In transcribing Arabic—or Aramaic, Hebrew, Persian, Ottoman Turkish, Urdu, and so forth—the author should use a system employing as few diacritics as possible, except in linguistic or highly specialized studies. If the hamza (ʾ) and the ʿayn (ʿ) are used, they may be represented in typescript by an apostrophe and a superscript *c*. A single opening quotation mark—an option on most computer keyboards—may be substituted for the superscript *c,* as long as that character is readily distinguishable from an apostrophe in the printout, and as long as it is clear that it is not, in fact, being used as an opening single quotation mark.

TRANSLITERATION

9.88   There is no universally accepted form for the transliteration of Arabic. One very detailed system is that included in the *ALA-LC Romanization Tables*. Another is that followed by the *International Journal of Middle East Studies,* published by Cambridge University Press.

9.89 For transliterated Arabic materials to be set in type, sorts for the hamza and ʿayn should be obtained in the appropriate sizes. If necessary, a Greek smooth breathing (ʾ) may be used for the hamza and a rough breathing (ʿ) for the ayn. Sometimes an apostrophe (ʾ) and an opening single quotation mark (ʿ) are used for these two signs.

SPELLING

9.90 Having selected a system of transliteration, the author should stick to it with as few exceptions as possible. Isolated references in text to well-known persons or places should employ the forms familiar to English-speaking readers: *Avicenna,* not *Ibn Sina; Mecca,* not *Makkah; Faiyum,* not *Madinat al-Fayyum* or some other variant.

9.91 In particular, the definite article, *al,* should always be joined to the noun with a hyphen: *al-Islam.* And although in speech the sound of the *l* ending the article is suppressed before the sounds *d, n, r, s, sh, t,* and *z,* the preferred scholarly practice is to write the article-noun combination without indication of the elision:

al-Nafud (*not* an-Nafud)   Bahr al-Safi (*not* Bahr as-Safi)

CAPITALIZATION

9.92 Problems with Arabic capitalization occur only in transliterations, since the Arabic alphabet does not distinguish between capital and lowercase letter forms as the Latin and Cyrillic alphabets do. Hence practice in capitalizing transliterated Arabic varies widely. For transliterated titles of books and articles in Arabic the preference of the University of Chicago Press is to capitalize only the first word and proper nouns:

ʿAbd al-Rahman al-Jabarti, *ʿAjaʾib al-athar fi al-tarajim wa al-akhbar* (The marvelous remains in biography and history) (Cairo, A.H. 1297 [A.D. 1879]).

9.93 The same system may appropriately be used for the names of journals and organizations. Note that the article in Arabic is never capitalized except at the beginning of a sentence or at the beginning of a book or article title.

PERSONAL NAMES

9.94 In alphabetizing Arabic personal names the article is ignored and the person is listed under the capital letter of the last name. Thus, Ishaq al-Husayni is listed as al-Husayni, Ishaq, and alphabetized with the *H*s. (For other Press preferences in citing Arabic names see 7.12, 17.114–15.)

Chinese and Japanese

ROMANIZATION

9.95   *Chinese.* The romanization system called *pinyin,* introduced by the Chinese in the 1950s, has now largely supplanted the older Wade-Giles romanization system and the place-name spellings of the *Postal Atlas of China.* Many individual scholars, however, long familiar with Wade-Giles or other older systems, have not switched to pinyin in their books, and some use pinyin only sporadically (resulting in index problems). To encourage consistent spelling throughout a book, one sensible practice for scholarly publications is to use Wade-Giles in books about the pre-1949 period and pinyin in those about the period after 1949.

9.96   Even where pinyin is adopted as the primary romanization system, exceptions and modifications are possible. Place-names long familiar in the Western world, names listed in *Webster's New Geographical Dictionary,* generally retain their old spelling. A modification recommended by some writers is to use the old spelling for the names of persons no longer living and pinyin for the names of those still alive. Another is to spell names in pinyin followed by the old spellings in parentheses. Whatever system or modification is used, names must be spelled consistently throughout a book. Copyeditors must be wary of altering spellings without the advice of an expert; the complexities of the Chinese language, with its dialects and nuances, preclude any simple formula for its romanization. Table 9.2 is included as an aid for those familiar enough with the Wade-Giles system to find a conversion table useful, not as a tool for the novice.[6]

9.97   In an attempt to reproduce sounds more accurately, pinyin spellings often differ markedly from the older ones, and personal names are usually spelled without apostrophes or hyphens; an apostrophe is sometimes used, however, to avoid ambiguity when syllables are run together (as in Chang'an to distinguish it from Chan'gan.

9.98   Some names frequently encountered:

DYNASTIES

Wade-Giles	*pinyin*	*Wade-Giles*	*pinyin*
Chou	Zhou	Sung	Song
Ch'in	Qin	Yüan	Yuan
T'ang	Tang	Ch'ing	Qing

6. A useful and comprehensive reference book on the conversion to pinyin is *Reform of the Chinese Written Language* (Peking: Foreign Languages Press, 1958). For the older, modified Wade-Giles system, see "List of Syllabic Headings," pp. xviii–xxi, in the revised American edition of Robert H. Mathews's *Chinese-English Dictionary,* published for Harvard-Yenching Institute, 1943.

PERSONAL NAMES

Wade-Giles	pinyin	Wade-Giles	pinyin
Mao Tse-tung	Mao Zedong	Hua Kuo-feng	Hua Guofeng
Teng Hsiao-p'ing	Deng Xiaoping	Lin Piao	Lin Biao
Lu Hsun	Lu Xun	Fang Li-chih	Fang Lizhi

But Mao Tse-tung, Chou En-lai, Sun Yat-sen, Chiang Kai-shek are usually written in Wade-Giles.

GEOGRAPHICAL NAMES

Wade-Giles	pinyin	Postal Atlas
Kuang-tung	Guangdong	Kwangtung
Su-chou	Suzhou	Soochow
Ta-lien	Dalian	Dairen
Pei-ching (Pei-p'ing)	Beijing	Peking (Peiping)
Shang-hai	Shanghai	Shanghai

9.99 *Japanese.* Japanese is usually romanized following the system used in *Kenkyusha's New English-Japanese Dictionary.* This system places an apostrophe after *n* at the end of a syllable that is followed by a vowel or *y: Gen'e, San'yo.* A macron is used over a long vowel in all Japanese words except well-known place-names (Kyoto, Tokyo, Hokkaido) and words that have entered the English language and are thus not italicized (shogun, daimyo). Hyphens should be used sparingly: *Meiji jidai shi no shinkenkyū.*

CAPITALIZATION AND ITALICS

9.100 Capital letters do not exist in Japanese or Chinese, but they are introduced in the usual cases in romanized versions of these languages (see 7.2–4). Personal names and place-names are capitalized, but in hyphenated names, only the first element is capitalized (see examples below). Common nouns and other words used in an English sentence are lowercased and set in italics as foreign words (see 6.65). Names of institutions, schools of thought, religions, and so forth are usually set in roman if they are capitalized, in italics if they are lowercased (the Wade-Giles romanization system is used for the Chinese in the following examples):

> Tung-lin Academy; Tung-lin movement

> Buddhism, Taoism, *feng shui* and other forms of magic . . .

> Under the Ming dynasty the postal service was administered by the Board of War *(ping-pu)* through a central office in Peking *(hui-t'ung kuan).*

> The heirs of the Seiyūkai and Minseitō are the Liberal and Progressive parties of Japan.

> It was Genrō Saionji (the genrō were the elder statesmen of Japan) who said . . . [note that *genrō* is both singular and plural]

Table 9.2 Conversion of Chinese Romanization

Wade-Giles to Pinyin

Wade-Giles	Pinyin	Wade-Giles	Pinyin	Wade-Giles	Pinyin	Wade-Giles	Pinyin	Wade-Giles	Pinyin	Wade-Giles	Pinyin
a	a	ch'ün	qun	ka	ga	mao	mao	po	bo	tou	dou
ai	ai	chung	zhong	k'a	ka	mei	mei	p'o	po	t'ou	tou
an	an	ch'ung	chong	kai	gai	men	men	pou	bou	tsa	za
ang	ang			k'ai	kai	meng	meng	p'ou	pou	ts'a	ca
ao	ao			kan	gan	mi	mi	pu	bu	tsai	zai
		en	en	k'an	kan	miao	miao	p'u	pu	ts'ai	cai
		erh	er	kang	gang	mieh	mie			tsan	zan
				k'ang	kang	mien	mian			ts'an	can
				kao	gao	min	min	sa	sa	tsang	zang
cha	zha			k'ao	kao	ming	ming	sai	sai	ts'ang	cang
ch'a	cha	fa	fa	kei	gei	miu	miu	san	san	tsao	zao
chai	zhai	fan	fan	k'ei	kei	mo	mo	sang	sang	ts'ao	cao
ch'ai	chai	fang	fang	ken	gen	mou	mou	sao	sao	tse	ze
chan	zhan	fei	fei	k'en	ken	mu	mu	se	se	ts'e	ce
ch'an	chan	fen	fen	keng	geng			sen	sen	tsei	zei
chang	zhang	feng	feng	k'eng	keng			seng	seng	tsen	zen
ch'ang	chang	fo	fo			na	na	sha	sha	ts'en	cen
chao	zhao	fou	fou	ko	ge	nai	nai	shai	shai	tseng	zeng
ch'ao	chao	fu	fu	k'o	ke	nan	nan	shan	shan	ts'eng	ceng
che	zhe			kou	gou	nang	nang	shang	shang	tso	zuo
ch'e	che			k'ou	kou	nao	nao	shao	shao	ts'o	cuo
chen	zhen	ha	ha	ku	gu	nei	nei	she	she	tsou	zou
ch'en	chen	hai	hai	k'u	ku	nen	nen	shen	shen	ts'ou	cou
cheng	zheng	han	han	kua	gua	neng	neng	sheng	sheng	tsu	zu
ch'eng	cheng	hang	hang	k'ua	kua	ni	ni	shih	shi	ts'u	cu
chi	ji	hao	hao	kuai	guai	niang	niang	shou	shou	tsuan	zuan
ch'i	qi	hei	hei	k'uai	kuai	niao	niao	shu	shu	ts'uan	cuan
chia	jia	hen	hen	kuan	guan	nieh	nie	shua	shua	tsui	zui
ch'ia	qia	heng	heng	k'uan	kuan	nien	nian	shuai	shuai	ts'ui	cui
chiang	jiang	ho	he	kuang	guang	nin	nin	shuan	shuan	tsun	zun
ch'iang	qiang	hou	hou	k'uang	kuang	ning	ning	shuang	shuang	ts'un	cun
chiao	jiao	hsi	xi	kuei	gui	niu	niu	shui	shui	tsung	zong
chieh	jie	hsia	xia	k'uei	kui	no	nuo	shun	shun	ts'ung	cong
ch'ieh	qie	hsiang	xiang	kun	gun	nou	nou	shuo	shuo	tu	du
chien	jian	hsiao	xiao	k'un	kun	nu	nu	so	suo	t'u	tu
ch'ien	qian	hsieh	xie	kung	gong	nü	nü	sou	sou	tuan	duan
chih	zhi	hsien	xian	k'ung	kong	nuan	nuan	ssu	si	t'uan	tuan
ch'ih	chi	hsin	xin	kuo	guo	nüeh	nüe	su	su	tui	dui
chin	jin	hsing	xing	k'uo	kuo	nung	nong	suan	suan	t'ui	tui
ch'in	qin	hsiu	xiu					sui	sui	tun	dun
ching	jing	hsiung	xiong	la	la	o	e	sun	sun	t'un	tun
ch'ing	qing	hsü	xu	lai	lai	ou	ou	sung	song	tung	dong
chiu	jiu	hsüan	xuan	lan	lan					t'ung	tong
ch'iu	qiu	hsüeh	xue	lang	lang					tzu	zi
chiung	jiong	hsün	xun	lao	lao	pa	ba	ta	da	tz'u	ci
ch'iung	qiong	hu	hu	le	le	p'a	pa	t'a	ta		
cho	zhuo	hua	hua	lei	lei	pai	bai	tai	dai		
ch'o	chuo	huai	huai	leng	leng	p'ai	pai	t'ai	tai	wa	wa
chou	zhou	huan	huan	li	li	pan	ban	tan	dan	wai	wai
ch'ou	chou	huang	huang	lia	lia	p'an	pan	t'an	tan	wan	wan
chu	zhu	hui	hui	liang	liang	pang	bang	tang	dang	wang	wang
ch'u	chu	hun	hun	liao	liao	p'ang	pang	t'ang	tang	wei	wei
chü	ju	hung	hong	lieh	lie	pao	bao	tao	dao	wen	wen
ch'ü	qu	huo	huo	lien	lian	p'ao	pao	t'ao	tao	weng	weng
chua	zhua			lin	lin	pei	bei	te	de	wo	wo
ch'ua	chua			ling	ling	p'ei	pei	t'e	te	wu	wu
chuai	zhuai	i	yi	liu	liu	pen	ben	teng	deng		
ch'uai	chuai			lo	luo	p'en	pen	t'eng	teng		
chuan	zhuan			lou	lou	peng	beng	ti	di	ya	ya
ch'uan	chuan	jan	ran	lu	lu	p'eng	peng	t'i	ti	yai	yai
chüan	juan	jang	rang	lü	lü	pi	bi	tiao	diao	yang	yang
ch'üan	quan	jao	rao	luan	luan	p'i	pi	t'iao	tiao	yao	yao
chuang	zhuang	je	re	lüan	lüan	piao	biao	tieh	die	yeh	ye
ch'uang	chuang	jen	ren	lüeh	lüe	p'iao	piao	t'ieh	tie	yen	yan
chüeh	jue	jeng	reng	lun	lun	pieh	bie	tien	dian	yin	yin
ch'üeh	que	jih	ri	lung	long	p'ieh	pie	t'ien	tian	ying	ying
chui	zhui	jo	ruo			pien	bian	ting	ding	yu	you
ch'ui	chui	jou	rou			p'ien	pian	t'ing	ting	yü	yu
chun	zhun	ju	ru	ma	ma	pin	bin	tiu	diu	yüan	yuan
ch'un	chun	juan	ruan	mai	mai	p'in	pin	to	duo	yüeh	yue
chün	jun	jui	rui	man	man	ping	bing	t'o	tuo	yün	yun
		jun	run	mang	mang	p'ing	ping			yung	yong
		jung	rong								

Table 9.2—*Continued*

Pinyin to Wade-Giles

Pinyin	Wade-Giles
a	a
ai	ai
an	an
ang	ang
ao	ao
ba	pa
bai	pai
ban	pan
bang	pang
bao	pao
bei	pei
ben	pen
beng	peng
bi	pi
bian	pien
biao	piao
bie	pieh
bin	pin
bing	ping
bo	po
bou	pou
bu	pu
ca	ts'a
cai	ts'ai
can	ts'an
cang	ts'ang
cao	ts'ao
ce	ts'e
cen	ts'en
ceng	ts'eng
cha	ch'a
chai	ch'ai
chan	ch'an
chang	ch'ang
chao	ch'ao
che	ch'e
chen	ch'en
cheng	ch'eng
chi	ch'ih
chong	ch'ung
chou	ch'ou
chu	ch'u
chua	ch'ua
chuai	ch'uai
chuan	ch'uan
chuang	ch'uang
chui	ch'ui
chun	ch'un
chuo	ch'o
ci	tz'u
cong	ts'ung
cou	ts'ou
cu	ts'u
cuan	ts'uan
cui	ts'ui
cun	ts'un
cuo	ts'o
da	ta
dai	tai
dan	tan
dang	tang
dao	tao
de	te
deng	teng
di	ti
dian	tien
diao	tiao
die	tieh
ding	ting
diu	tiu
dong	tung
dou	tou
du	tu
duan	tuan
dui	tui
dun	tun
duo	to
e	o
en	en
er	erh
fa	fa
fan	fan
fang	fang
fei	fei
fen	fen
feng	feng
fo	fo
fou	fou
fu	fu
ga	ka
gai	kai
gan	kan
gang	kang
gao	kao
ge	ko
gei	kei
gen	ken
geng	keng
gong	kung
gou	kou
gu	ku
gua	kua
guai	kuai
guan	kuan
guang	kuang
gui	kuei
gun	kun
guo	kuo
ha	ha
hai	hai
han	han
hang	hang
hao	hao
he	ho
hei	hei
hen	hen
heng	heng
hong	hung
hou	hou
hu	hu
hua	hua
huai	huai
huan	huan
huang	huang
hui	hui
hun	hun
huo	huo
ji	chi
jia	chia
jian	chien
jiang	chiang
jiao	chiao
jie	chieh
jin	chin
jing	ching
jiong	chiung
jiu	chiu
ju	chü
juan	chüan
jue	chüeh
jun	chün
ka	k'a
kai	k'ai
kan	k'an
kang	k'ang
kao	k'ao
ke	k'o
kei	k'ei
ken	k'en
keng	k'eng
kong	k'ung
kou	k'ou
ku	k'u
kua	k'ua
kuai	k'uai
kuan	k'uan
kuang	k'uang
kui	k'uei
kun	k'un
kuo	k'uo
la	la
lai	lai
lan	lan
lang	lang
lao	lao
le	le
lei	lei
leng	leng
li	li
lia	lia
lian	lien
liang	liang
liao	liao
lie	lieh
lin	lin
ling	ling
liu	liu
long	lung
lou	lou
lu	lu
lü	lü
luan	luan
lüan	lüan
lüe	lüeh
lun	lun
luo	lo
ma	ma
mai	mai
man	man
mang	mang
mao	mao
mei	mei
men	men
meng	meng
mi	mi
mian	mien
miao	miao
mie	mieh
min	min
ming	ming
miu	miu
mo	mo
mou	mou
mu	mu
na	na
nai	nai
nan	nan
nang	nang
nao	nao
nei	nei
nen	nen
neng	neng
ni	ni
nian	nien
niang	niang
niao	niao
nie	nieh
nin	nin
ning	ning
niu	niu
nong	nung
nou	nou
nu	nu
nü	nü
nuan	nuan
nüe	nüeh
nuo	no
ou	ou
pa	p'a
pai	p'ai
pan	p'an
pang	p'ang
pao	p'ao
pei	p'ei
pen	p'en
peng	p'eng
pi	p'i
pian	p'ien
piao	p'iao
pie	p'ieh
pin	p'in
ping	p'ing
po	p'o
pou	p'ou
pu	p'u
qi	ch'i
qia	ch'ia
qian	ch'ien
qiang	ch'iang
qiao	ch'iao
qie	ch'ieh
qin	ch'in
qing	ch'ing
qiong	ch'iung
qiu	ch'iu
qu	ch'ü
que	ch'üeh
qun	ch'ün
ran	jan
rang	jang
rao	jao
re	je
ren	jen
reng	jeng
ri	jih
rong	jung
rou	jou
ru	ju
ruan	juan
rui	jui
run	jun
ruo	jo
sa	sa
sai	sai
san	san
sang	sang
sao	sao
se	se
sen	sen
seng	seng
sha	sha
shai	shai
shan	shan
shang	shang
shao	shao
she	she
shen	shen
sheng	sheng
shi	shih
shou	shou
shu	shu
shua	shua
shuai	shuai
shuan	shuan
shuang	shuang
shui	shui
shun	shun
shuo	shuo
si	ssu
song	sung
sou	sou
su	su
suan	suan
sui	sui
sun	sun
suo	so
ta	t'a
tai	t'ai
tan	t'an
tang	t'ang
tao	t'ao
te	t'e
teng	t'eng
ti	t'i
tian	t'ien
tiao	t'iao
tie	t'ieh
ting	t'ing
tong	t'ung
tou	t'ou
tu	t'u
tuan	t'uan
tui	t'ui
tun	t'un
tuo	t'o
wa	wa
wai	wai
wan	wan
wang	wang
wei	wei
wen	wen
weng	weng
wo	wo
wu	wu
xi	hsi
xia	hsia
xian	hsien
xiang	hsiang
xiao	hsiao
xie	hsieh
xin	hsin
xing	hsing
xiong	hsiung
xiu	hsiu
xu	hsü
xuan	hsüan
xue	hsüeh
xun	hsün
ya	ya
yai	yai
yan	yen
yang	yang
yao	yao
ye	yeh
yi	i
yin	yin
ying	ying
yong	yung
you	yu
yu	yü
yuan	yüan
yue	yüeh
yun	yün
za	tsa
zai	tsai
zan	tsan
zang	tsang
zao	tsao
ze	tse
zei	tsei
zen	tsen
zeng	tseng
zha	cha
zhai	chai
zhan	chan
zhang	chang
zhao	chao
zhe	che
zhen	chen
zheng	cheng
zhi	chih
zhong	chung
zhou	chou
zhu	chu
zhua	chua
zhuai	chuai
zhuan	chuan
zhuang	chuang
zhui	chui
zhun	chun
zhuo	cho
zi	tzu
zong	tsung
zou	tsou
zu	tsu
zuan	tsuan
zui	tsui
zun	tsun
zuo	tso

Source: *People's Republic of China: Administrative Atlas* (Washington, D.C.: Central Intelligence Agency, 1975), 46–47.

9.101 Titles of books and periodicals are set in italics, and titles of articles are set in roman and enclosed in quotation marks:

> Ch'en Shih-ch'i, *Ming-tai kuan shou-kung-yeh ti yen-chiu* (Studies on government-operated handicrafts during the Ming dynasty) . . .

> Fang Hao, "Liu-lo yü hsi p'u ti chung-kuo wen-hsien" (The lost Chinese historical literature in Spain and Portugal), *Hsüeh-shu chi-k'an* . . .

> Okamoto Yoshitomo, *Jūrokuseiki Nichi-Ō kōtsūchi no kenkyū* (Study of the intercourse between Japan and Europe during the sixteenth century) . . .

> Akiyama Kenzō, "Goresu wa Ryūkyūjin de aru" (The Gores are the Ryukyuans), *Shigaku-Zasshi* . . .

The first word of a romanized title is always capitalized, and proper nouns (especially in Japanese) often are.

9.102 Chinese and Japanese characters, although difficult for the printer, are necessary in references to works that can only be found, even in Western libraries, if one knows the characters for the author's name and the title of the work. In general, their use should be confined to bibliographies and glossaries; in running text they disrupt the type line and should be avoided. When characters are used in a bibliography, they follow the romanized version of the item they represent (asterisks here show where the characters should be placed):

> Fang Hao * *. "Liu-lo yü hsi p'u ti chung-kuo wen-hsien" * * * * * * * * * * (The lost Chinese historical literature in Spain and Portugal), *Hsüeh-shu chi-k'an* * * * * 1 (1953): 161–79.

Hebrew

9.103 Hebrew is read from right to left.[7] In its most ancient form the Hebrew alphabet contained only consonants, the vowel sounds being entrusted to the memory of the reader. Later, some consonants came to be used to indicate vowel length and quality. The most commonly used were wāw (ו) for *ō* and *ū*, yōd (י) for *ē* and *ī*, and hē (ה) for word-final *ā*, *ē*, and *e;* much rarer is the use of 'alef (א) for word-internal *ā* (see table 9.3). Consonants so used are referred to as *matres lectionis,* "mothers of reading" (sing., *mater lectionis*). Later still, distinct vowel signs, consisting of a system of dots and short lines, were invented and added to certain texts. The most widely used system, the Tiberian, was devised for vocalizing traditional texts such as the Hebrew Bible. The system is still in use today when, primarily for educational purposes,

---

7. This section on Hebrew is a free adaptation, after consultation of other sources, of the material on Hebrew presented in the United States Government Printing Office *Style Manual.*

modern Hebrew texts are vocalized. Such explicit vocalization is rare in modern Hebrew, although the use of *matres lectionis* without the accompanying vowel signs is a nearly universal convention. For example, in the word דברים (*dᵊbārīm* in traditional transliteration or *dvarim* according to modern conventions) the *yōd* is a *mater lectionis* for *ī*; in the vocalized form of the word the *yōd* is maintained and the vowel *ḥīrīq* is added: דְּבָרִים.

9.104   With one exception (known as the *furtive patah*), the vowel signs have the effect of adding a vowel after the consonant. A furtive patah, however—that is, a patah beneath a final gutteral consonant such as ḥet (ה)—transfers the vowel sound to the front of the consonant.

TRANSLITERATION

9.105   The transliteration, as well as the pronunciation, of the twenty-two Hebrew consonants is presented in the first part of table 9.3. The vowel signs are listed in the second part of the table (the long dash stands for the Hebrew consonant). Note that the consonants bēt/vēt, kaf/khaf, pē/ fē, and śiñ/shīn have two sounds each, distinguished by a dot. Three other consonants (gīmel, dalet, and tāw) once had two pronunciations. Today these differences are no longer observed, although the graphic rules are still taught as a part of Hebrew grammar. Note also that five consonants (kaf, mēm, nūn, pē, and ṣadē) have a so-called final form, shown immediately to the right of their regular forms. The final form of the letter is used when it is the last letter of a word.

9.106   In transliteration, the underdot is used beneath *h* to indicate a pronunciation similar to the *ch* in German *Buch*. The dot is used beneath *s* to denote a sound approaching *ts*, which letters are in fact often used in place of *ṣ*.

9.107   In transliteration, especially of names, the macrons over vowels and the dots under consonants, as well as ʾ and ʿ, are often omitted, and ʿ is often printed as ʻ. For *f*, *ph* is often used. For *ś* an ordinary *s* is often found. For *sh*, *š* is sometimes used, especially in scholarly works. There are other special transliteration practices to be found in scholarly works. Author and editor should compile a list of these before editing begins on a particular work.

CAPITALIZATION, PUNCTUATION, AND ITALICS

9.108   In Hebrew no distinction is made between capital and lowercase letters, and there are no italics. In transliterations of Hebrew, capitalization and the use of italics may follow the style usual in many other foreign languages: The first word and all proper nouns are capitalized in sentences

Table 9.3 Hebrew Alphabet and Transliteration

Hebrew Letter		Name	Trans-literation	Pronunciation	Numeral Value
א		'alef *or* alef	' *or* ᵓ	originally a glottal stop; now silent	1
ב		bēt	b	*b* in *book*	2
ב		vēt	v *or* ḇ	*v* in *vest*	
ג		gīmel	g	*g* in *go*	3
ג		gīmel	g̱	no longer observed; originally aspirated *g*	
ד		dalet	d	*d* in *dark*	4
ד		dalet	ḏ	no longer observed; originally like *th* in *there*	
ה		hē	h	*h* in *hill;* silent at the end of word	5
ו		wāw *or* vāv	w *or* v	originally *w;* now *v*	6
ז		zayin	z	*z* in *zero*	7
ח		ḥēt	ḥ	*ch* in German *Buch*	8
ט		ṭēt	ṭ	*t* in *top*	9
י		yōd	y	*y* in *yes*	10
כ	ך	kaf	k	*k* in *kind*	20
כ	ך	khaf	kh	*ch* in German *Buch*	
ל		lamed	l	*l* in *light*	30
מ	ם	mēm	m	*m* in *mount*	40
נ	ן	nūn	n	*n* in *near*	50
ס		sameḥ *or* samekh	s	*s* in *salt*	60
ע		'ayin *or* ayin	' *or* ᶜ	originally a laryngeal-voiced spirant; now silent	70
פ		pē	p	*p* in *past*	80
פ	ף	fē	f *or* p̱	*f* in *fast*	
צ	ץ	ṣadē *or* tzade	ṣ *or* ts	*ts* in *nets*	90
ק		qōf	q	*k* in *kind*	100
ר		rēsh	r	*r* as in French uvular or Italian trilled	200
שׂ		śīn	ś	*s* in *sew*	300
שׁ		shīn	sh	*sh* in *show*	
ת		tāw	t	*t* in *toe*	400
ת		tāw	ṯ	no longer observed; originally like *th* in *thin*	

Vowel Signs

Long

ָ	qāmaṣ *or* qāmats	ā	*a* in *palm*
יֵ *or* ֵ	ṣēre *or* tsēre	ē	*ei* in *vein*
יִ	ḥīrīq gādōl	ī	*i* in *machine*
וֹ *or* ֹ	ḥōlām	ō	*o* in *no*
וּ	shūrūq	ū	*oo* in *moon*

Short

ַ	pattāḥ	a	*a* in *part*
ֶ	sᵊgōl	e	*e* in *bed*

Table 9.3—*Continued*

Hebrew Letter	Name	Trans- literation	Pronunciation	Numeral Value
ִ	ḥīrīq qāṭān	i	*i* in *big*	
ָ	qāmaṣ qāṭān *or* qāmats qāṭān	o	*o* in *soft*	
ֻ	qubbūṣ *or* qubbūts	u	*u* in *full*	
ְ	shᵊwā	ə	slight schwa sound, as *a* in *medal;* or silent	
ֳ	composite shᵊwā[1]	ă	*a* in *about*	
ֱ		ĕ	*i* in *fit*	
ֲ		ŏ	*o* in *obtain*	

1. The composite shᵊwā consists of a qāmaṣ, a pattāḥ, or a sᵊgōl followed by a shᵊwā. The names of the composite shᵊwās are ḥāṭāf pattāḥ, ḥāṭāf sᵊgōl, and ḥāṭāf qāmaṣ qāṭān.

and in titles of books and articles. Book titles are italicized, and the titles of articles and chapters are enclosed in quotation marks. Punctuation may follow that practiced in American English.

WORD DIVISION

9.109 In modern Hebrew, words may be divided between syllables of three or more letters. When a double consonant occurs at the point of division, one consonant goes with each division:

> Rosh Ha-shana Suk-koth
> Yom Kip-pur Sim-ḥath Torah

Russian

TRANSLITERATION

9.110 There are many systems for transliterating Russian, the most important of which are summarized in table 9.4. Journals of Slavic studies generally prefer a "linguistic" system making free use of diacritics, since such a system more nearly reflects the nature of the Cyrillic alphabet (one symbol to one sound). But for a book or article reaching a more general audience, a system without diacritics or ligatures is desirable. The preference of the University of Chicago Press, for general use, is the system of the United States Board on Geographic Names. Regardless of the system of transliteration, however, well-known Russian names should be given in the form that has become familiar to English-speaking readers: that is, the spellings in *Webster's New Biographical Dictionary* and the *Columbia Lippincott Gazetteer* or *Webster's New Geographical Dictionary* should prevail:

Table 9.4 Transliteration of Russian

Cyrillic Alphabet		U.S. Board on Geographic Names	Library of Congress	"Linguistic" System
Upright	Cursive			
А а	*А а*	a		
Б б	*Б б*	b		
В в	*В в*	v		
Г г	*Г г*	g		
Д д	*Д д*	d		
Е е	*Е е*	ye,[1] e	e	e
Ё ё[2]	*Ё ё*	yë,[1] ë	ë	e, ë
Ж ж	*Ж ж*	zh		ž
З з	*З з*	z		
И и	*И и*	i		
Й й	*Й й*	y	ĭ	j
К к	*К к*	k		
Л л	*Л л*	l		
М м	*М м*	m		
Н н	*Н н*	n		
О о	*О о*	o		
П п	*П п*	p		
Р р	*Р р*	r		
С с	*С с*	s		
Т т	*Т т*	t		
У у	*У у*	u		
Ф ф	*Ф ф*	f		
Х х	*Х х*	kh		x, ch
Ц ц	*Ц ц*	ts	t͡s	c
Ч ч	*Ч ч*	ch		č
Ш ш	*Ш ш*	sh		š
Щ щ	*Щ щ*	shch		šč
Ъ ъ[3]	*Ъ ъ*	"	"	"
Ы ы[3]	*Ы ы*	y		
Ь ь[3]	*Ь ь*	'	'	'
Э э	*Э э*	e	ė	è
Ю ю	*Ю ю*	yu	i͡u	ju
Я я	*Я я*	ya	i͡a	ja

Note: The Library of Congress and "linguistic" systems employ the same characters as the U.S. Board system except where noted.

1. Initially and after a vowel or ъ or ь.
2. Not considered a separate letter.
3. Does not occur initially.

Tchaikovsky   Moscow
Chekhov   Nizhni Novgorod (Gorki)
Catherine the Great   Dnieper

CAPITALIZATION

9.111 Conventions of capitalization in the Cyrillic original are much like those of French and should be preserved in transliteration. Pronouns, days of the week, months, and most proper adjectives are lowercased.

Geographical designations are capitalized when they apply to formal political units or formal institutions but otherwise are lowercased:

Tverskaya guberniya   Moskovskiy universitet
tverskoe zemstvo   russkiy kompozitor

9.112 Titles of books and articles and the names of periodicals are lowercased except for the first word and proper nouns:

N. A. Kuryakin, *Lenin i Trotskiy.*

O. I. Skorokhodova, *Kak ya vosprinimayu i predstavlyayu okruzhayushchiy mir* [How I perceive and imagine the external world] (Moscow: Izd. Akad. Pedag. Nauk, 1954).

9.113 In the Cyrillic originals of these citations the author's name and the title are both set in ordinary type (called in Russian *pryamoy,* "upright"); the author's name, however, is letterspaced. The Cyrillic *kursiv* is used more sparingly than our italic—never for book titles.

PUNCTUATION

9.114 Russian resembles French in its use of guillemets for quotations and of dashes for dialogue:

«Bozhe, bozhe, bozhe!» govorit Boris.
— S kem ya rabotayu?
— S tovarishchem.
— Kak my rabotaem?
— S interesom.

Quotation marks of the German type (see 9.36) are sometimes used instead (but see 9.8).

9.115 Suspension points are also used in Russian as in French:

Ya... vy... my tol'ko chto priyekhali.

In Russian, however, an exclamation point or a question mark takes the place of one dot:

Mitya!.. Gde vy byli?..

9.116 A dash is sometimes inserted, without space, between subject and complement when the equivalent of *is* or *are* is omitted:

Moskva—stolitsa Rossii.

A dash is also used in place of a verb omitted because it would be identical to the preceding verb. In this case the dash is preceded and followed by space.

Ivan i Sonya poyedut v Moskvu poyezdom, Lëv i Lyuba — avtobusom.

WORD DIVISION

9.117   Transliterated Russian should be divided according to the rules governing word division in the Cyrillic original. Adapted from the transliteration system of the United States Board on Geographic Names, the rules are as outlined below.

9.118   Combinations representing single Cyrillic letters should never be divided: *ye, yë, zh, kh, ts, ch, sh, shch, yu, ya.*

9.119   Combinations of a vowel plus short *i* (transliterated *y*) should never be divided: *ay, ey, yey,* etc.

9.120   The following consonant combinations may not be broken:

$$
\left. \begin{array}{l} b \text{ or } p \\ g \text{ or } k \\ f \text{ or } v \end{array} \right\} \text{ plus } l \text{ or } r, \text{ namely} \left\{ \begin{array}{ll} bl, pl, & br, pr \\ gl, kl & gr, kr \\ fl, vl & fr, vr \end{array} \right.
$$

also

dv, dr   tv, tr   sk, skv, skr   st, stv, str   zhd   ml

9.121   Words may be divided after prefixes, but generally the prefixes themselves should not be divided:

bes-poryadok	za-dat'	na-zhat'	obo-gnat'
pere-stroika	pred-lozhit'	pro-vesti	

9.122   Words may be divided after a vowel or diphthong before a single (Cyrillic) consonant

Si-bir'   voy-na   Gorba-chev   da-zhe

or before a consonant combination (see 9.120)

puteshe-stvennik   khi-trit'   pro-stak   ru-brika

9.123   Division may be made between single consonants or between consonants and consonant combinations:

ubor-ku	mol-cha	mor-skoy
chudes-nym	sred-stvo	

9.124   Division may be made between single vowels or between a single vowel and a diphthong:

ma-yak	nochna-ya	oke-an
ori-entirovat'	svo-yëm	

9.125   Compound words are preferably divided between parts:

radio-priyëmnik   gor-sovet   kino-teatr

South Asian Languages

9.126   Transliteration of the principal South Asian languages requires some or all of the following special characters:

Ā ā, Æ æ, Ǽ ǽ, Ē ē, Ī ī, Ō ō, Ū ū, Ḍ ḍ, Ḥ ḥ, Ḷ ḷ, Ḹ ḹ, M m, N n, Ṅ ṅ,
Ñ ñ, Ṛ ṛ, Ṝ ṝ, Ṣ ṣ, Ś ś

EDITING AND COMPOSING CLASSICAL GREEK

9.127   The following information is intended to aid editors who do not read Greek, as well as proofreaders and typesetters, in handling terms and quotations in classical Greek that appear in English works.

9.128   The first thing necessary for setting Greek is a font of Greek type. If a book contains any Greek at all, the publisher should make certain well ahead of copy deadline that the typesetter can set the Greek words in the required sizes, with accents and breathing marks. (Greek is usually set one point size smaller than the text to prevent its overwhelming the roman type.) If this turns out to be impossible, (1) the publisher or typesetter will have to have the passages set elsewhere and inserted in the English pages, (2) the Greek copy will have to be killed or translated into English, or (3) it will have to be transliterated into the Latin alphabet—something that should be done only if the Greek consists of isolated words and phrases or of short passages.

Transliteration

9.129   Table 9.5 shows the usual way to transliterate Greek letters. Omit all Greek accents. Use the macron to distinguish long vowels eta and omega (*ē* and *ō*) from short vowels epsilon and omicron (*e* and *o*). Transliterate the iota subscript by an *i* on the line, following the vowel with which it is associated (ἀνθρώπῳ, *anthrōpōi*). The rough breathing is transliterated by *h,* which precedes a vowel or diphthong and follows the letter rho (as in the English word *rhythm*). The smooth breathing is ignored, since it represents merely the absence of the *h*-sound. Transliterated Greek words or phrases are usually italicized, unless the same words occur frequently.

Breathings

9.130   When Greek is written or set in Greek characters, every initial vowel or diphthong and the letter rho standing at the beginning of a Greek

Table 9.5 Greek Alphabet and Transliteration

Name of Letter	Greek Alphabet		Transliteration
Alpha	A	α	a
Beta	B	β	b
Gamma	Γ	γ	g
Delta	Δ	δ ∂^1	d
Epsilon	E	ε	e
Zeta	Z	ζ	z
Eta	H	η	ē
Theta	Θ	θ ϑ^1	th
Iota	I	ι	i
Kappa	K	κ	k
Lambda	Λ	λ	l
Mu	M	μ	m
Nu	N	ν	n
Xi	Ξ	ξ	x
Omicron	O	o	o
Pi	Π	π	p
Rho	P	ρ	r; *initially,* rh; *double,* rrh
Sigma	Σ	σ ς^2	s
Tau	T	τ	t
Upsilon	Υ	υ	u; *often* y, *exc. after* a, e, ē, i
Phi	Φ	φ φ^1	ph
Chi	X	χ	kh
Psi	Ψ	ψ	ps
Omega	Ω	ω	ō

1. Old-style character. Usually used in mathematical formulas; should not be combined with other fonts.
2. Final letter.

word must be marked either with the rough breathing (ʻ), to indicate the sound *h,* or with the smooth breathing (ʼ), to indicate absence of the sound *h.* (Thus ἕν, meaning "one," is pronounced *hen,* while ἐν, meaning "in," is pronounced *en.*) Initial rho and upsilon always receive the rough breathing.

9.131 The breathing mark is placed directly over the initial lowercase vowel (over the second vowel of a diphthong); it is placed to the left of capital letters.

αὖτε, ἕτεραι, Ἕλλην, ἥβη, Ἶρις, ὑπέχω, ὠκνς, ῥᾴδιος

9.132   Typesetters sometimes become confused and set a single quotation mark in place of a breathing mark before a capital letter; the single quotation mark cannot function as a breathing because it is the wrong size and does not sit close enough to the letter.

Accents

9.133   There are three Greek accent marks: acute (´), circumflex (ˆ), and grave (`). Use of the circumflex is restricted to the two final syllables of a word. The grave accent can occur only on the last syllable, and it is used then only in this circumstance: an acute accent on the final syllable is changed to grave when the word directly precedes another accented word in the same clause. Like the breathings, the accents are placed over the lowercase vowels, over the second vowel of a diphthong, and to the left of capital vowels.

9.134   With two exceptions, *all* Greek words are marked with accents—usually one, very occasionally two (see below). The two exceptions to this rule are (1) a group of monosyllabic words called proclitics, which are closely connected with the words following them (the proclitics are the forms of the definite article ὁ, ἡ, οἱ, αἱ; the prepositions εἰς, ἐν, ἐκ [ἐξ]; the conjunctions εἰ, ὡς; and the adverb οὐ [οὐκ, οὐχ]); and (2) enclitics, short words pronounced as if part of the word preceding them. Enclitics usually lose their accents altogether (Ἀρταξερξής τε) and in certain circumstances the word preceding them actually gains a second accent (φοβεῖταί τίς). The diaeresis is used in Greek, as in French *(naïve),* to indicate that two successive vowels do not form a diphthong but are to be voiced separately.

9.135   Vowels complete with breathing marks and accents, in all combinations, are an integral part of every Greek font. Each font should, for example, be able to provide, for lowercase eta, η, ή, ῆ, ῂ, ἠ, ἡ, ἤ, ἢ, ἦ, ἧ, ῄ, ῇ, ῃ, and, for uppercase eta, Ἠ, Ἡ, Ἤ, Ἢ, Ἦ, Ἧ, Ἠ, Ἡ.

Punctuation

9.136   In Greek the period and comma are the same as in English; the colon and semicolon are both represented by a raised dot (·); the Greek interrogation point is the same as the English semicolon (;). The English apostrophe (') is used as an elision mark when the final vowel of one word is elided before a second word beginning with a vowel. In English texts, quotations set in Greek, of whatever length, should not be enclosed in quotation marks.

Table 9.6 Greek Numerals

1	α'	24	$\kappa\delta'$
2	β'	30	λ'
3	γ'	40	μ'
4	δ'	50	ν'
5	ε'	60	ξ'
6	ς'	70	o'
7	ζ'	80	π'
8	η'	90	ϱ'
9	θ'	100	ρ'
10	ι'	200	σ'
11	$\iota\alpha'$	300	τ'
12	$\iota\beta'$	400	υ'
13	$\iota\gamma'$	500	ϕ'
14	$\iota\delta'$	600	χ'
15	$\iota\varepsilon'$	700	ψ'
16	$\iota\varsigma'$	800	ω'
17	$\iota\zeta'$	900	$\mathcal{A}'$
18	$\iota\eta'$	1,000	$,\alpha$
19	$\iota\theta'$	2,000	$,\beta$
20	κ'	3,000	$,\gamma$
21	$\kappa\alpha'$	4,000	$,\delta$
22	$\kappa\beta'$	5,000	$,\epsilon$
23	$\kappa\gamma'$		

Numbers

9.137   Numbers, when not written out, are represented in ordinary Greek text by the letters of the alphabet, supplemented by three obsolete Greek letters, $\varsigma' = 6$, $\varrho' = 90$, $\mathcal{A}' = 900$. The diacritical mark resembling an acute accent distinguishes the letters as numerals and is added to a sign standing alone or to the last sign in a series, $111 = \rho\iota\alpha'$. For thousands, the foregoing signs are used with a different diacritical mark: $,\alpha = 1,000$, $,\alpha\rho\iota\alpha' = 1,111$, $,\beta\sigma\kappa\beta' = 2,222$. The entire series of Greek numerals is shown in table 9.6.

Word Division

9.138   In Greek, word division follows rules that are straightforward and fairly easy to apply.

9.139   When a single consonant occurs between two vowels, divide before the consonant:

ἔ-χω   ἐ-γώ   ἐ-σπέ-ρα

9.140   If a consonant is doubled, or if a mute is followed by its corresponding aspirate, divide after the first consonant:

Ἐλ-λάς   ὤμ-μαι   ἄϊσ-σω   ὀρ-ρωδία
ἀπ-φύς   Ἀτ-θίς   Βακ-χίς   ἔγ-χος

9.141   If the combination of two or more consonants begins with a liquid (λ, ρ) or a nasal (μ, ν), divide after the liquid or nasal:

ἄλ-σος   ἀρ-γός   ἄμ-φω   ἄν-θος

(But before μν: μέ-μνημαι)

9.142   The division comes before all other combinations of two or more consonants:

πρᾶ-γμα   ἀ-κμή   ἄ-φνω   ἔ-τνος   ἄ-στρον

9.143   Compound words are divided into their original parts; within each part the rules given above apply. The most common type of compound word begins with a preposition:

ἀμφ-   ἀν-   ἀπ-   ὑπ-   ἐξ-έβαλον
ἀφ-   ἐφ-   ὑφ-   κατ-   καθ-ίστημι

OLD ENGLISH AND MIDDLE ENGLISH

9.144   Several Old English or Middle English letters not used in modern English are considered "special characters" by typesetters. These occur in both lowercase and capital forms.

ð   Ð   Called edh or eth and pronounced like *th* in *them.*

þ   þ   Called thorn and pronounced like *th* in *three.*

ʒ   ʒ   Called yogh; occurs in Middle English sometimes for *y* as in *year,* sometimes for *gh* as in *light.*

æ   Æ   Ligature; should not be printed as two letters in Old English names and text (Ælfric).

Since a typesetter may easily mistake a thorn for a *p* and a yogh for a *g* or even a 3, the copyeditor should flag each occurrence either by writing the names of the characters in the margin when there are few or by color-coding (underlining or circling with a colored pencil) when there are many. In electronic manuscripts such characters may require special coding.

9.145   Two characters occasionally found in Old English texts are ⁊ for *and* (ampersand) and ƿ (wyn) for *w,* but the modern ampersand and *w* may be substituted for these.

FOR FURTHER REFERENCE

9.146   Many questions about setting foreign language copy that are not considered in this manual are answered in the United States Government Printing Office *Style Manual.* Also very helpful is *ALA-LC Romanization Tables,* issued by the Library of Congress.

10 Quotations

INTRODUCTION

10.1   This chapter offers rules and suggestions for incorporating quoted matter in text. The use of quotation marks for purposes other than direct quotation is described in chapter 6. Rules for citing, in footnotes or endnotes, the sources of quotations are to be found in chapter 15. Chapter 2 explains how to type block quotations in preparing a typescript for publication (2.20) and describes the manuscript editor's responsibilities regarding quoted material (2.102). In chapter 5 there is a discussion of the use of punctuation in quotations.

10.2   Almost every serious study depends in part on works that have preceded it. Ideally, authors of works of original scholarship present their arguments in their own words, illustrating and amplifying the text with quotations judiciously chosen from the works of others. In selecting quotations, authors should consider their readers. Is direct quotation desirable, or would a paraphrase be more effective? Will the reader who, for lack of time or inclination, chooses to skip over long or frequent direct quotations miss any significant point? This is not to denigrate the use of quotations, however, but only to caution against their overuse or misuse. "Quoting other writers and citing the places where their words are to be found are by now such common practices that it is pardonable to look upon the habit as natural, not to say instinctive. It is of course nothing of the kind, but a very sophisticated act, peculiar to a civilization that uses printed books, believes in evidence, and makes a point of assigning credit or blame in a detailed, verifiable way."[1]

Credit and Permission

10.3   Whether authors paraphrase or quote from sources directly, they should give credit to words and ideas taken from others. In most instances a

---

1. Jacques Barzun and Henry F. Graff, *The Modern Researcher,* 5th ed. (New York: Harcourt Brace Jovanovich, 1992), 273.

note² or a parenthetical reference in the text keyed to the bibliography or list of sources is sufficient acknowledgment. If an author quotes at length, or uses many short passages, from a copyrighted work or from certain manuscript materials, written permission must be obtained from the owner of the copyright or of the literary rights (see chapter 4).

What Not to Quote

10.4 Commonly known facts, available in numerous sources, should not be enclosed in quotation marks or given a source citation unless the wording is taken directly from another work. Also not to be treated as quotations are proverbial, biblical, and well-known literary expressions used as part of the author's text:

> On 14 April 1865, a few days after Lee's surrender, Lincoln was assassinated. [No note necessary]
>
> No one can convince the young that practice makes perfect.
>
> If reading maketh a full man, Henry is half empty.

ACCURACY

10.5 It is impossible to overemphasize the importance of meticulous accuracy in quoting from the works of others. Authors should check every direct quotation against the original, if possible, or against a first, careful transcription of the passage. (Authors who take notes carelessly are in for trouble later if they no longer have access to the sources.)

10.6 Checking quotations is an operation to be performed *on the final typescript,* not left until type has been set (see 2.129, point 2). Resetting type to rectify an author's sins of transcription is an extremely costly process, and is chargeable to the author. Thus, rigorous attention to accuracy in the typescript (or final disk) saves time at the proof stage, avoids excessive alteration costs, and lessens the chance of further errors being introduced in proofs.

PERMISSIBLE CHANGES

10.7 Direct quotations must reproduce *exactly* not only the wording but the spelling, capitalization, and internal punctuation of the original, except that single quotation marks may be changed to double, and double to

---

2. Throughout this chapter the word *note* refers to a note at the foot of the page or at the back of a book, at the end of an article or in parentheses in the text—wherever such documentation appears in a printed work (see chapter 15).

single, as the situation prescribes (see 10.26, 10.28), and commas or periods appearing outside the closing quotation mark may be moved inside. A few other changes are permissible to make the passage fit smoothly into the syntax and typography of the work in which it is quoted.

1. The initial letter may be changed to a capital or a lowercase letter (see 10.13–16, 10.62).

2. The final period may be omitted or changed to a comma as required, and punctuation marks may be omitted where ellipsis points are used (see 5.11, 5.71–73, 10.13, 10.52, 10.55, 10.59).

3. Original notes and note reference marks in a short quotation from a scholarly work are generally omitted unless the omission would significantly affect the meaning of the quotation or the author's purpose in quoting it. If a note is included, the quotation should be set off as an extract, with the note given in smaller type at the end. Should the author prefer, the note may be paraphrased or summarized in the accompanying text. Authors may, on the other hand, add note references of their own within quotations.

4. In a passage quoted from a modern book, journal, or newspaper, an obvious typographical error may be silently corrected, but in a passage from an older work or from a manuscript source, any idiosyncrasy of spelling should generally be preserved, although in some cases the author may consider it desirable to modernize spelling and punctuation for the sake of clarity. The reader should be informed of any such alterations, either in a note or, in a book containing many such quotations, by an explanation in the preface or elsewhere.

10.8 Typographical style, particularly of display type, may be changed to agree with the style of the work in which the quotation occurs. In a quotation from a play, for example, the names of speakers might be changed from the small caps of the original to italic and moved from a centered to a flush left position, or vice versa; stage directions might be changed from roman to italic. A word or words in full caps in the text of the original may be set in small caps, if these are available, to maintain the effect; if small caps are not available, the full caps should be reproduced in the quotation. In other words, those elements of typography that are not an author's doing but the publisher's or the printer's need not, and often should not, be reproduced exactly. (For changing typography when citing titles of works see 7.127, 15.103; for typography and other design considerations of plays see 18.62–66.)

RELATION TO TEXT

10.9   Quotations may be incorporated in two ways: run in—that is, integrated into the text in the same type size as the text and enclosed in quotation marks (see example in 10.12)—or set off from the text, without quotation marks. Quotations of the latter sort may be set in smaller type, or with all lines indented from the left, or with unjustified lines (if text lines are justified), or with less space between lines than the text—or some combination of these typographical devices may be specified by the book designer (see one example in 10.14). Quotations set off from the text are called *block quotations, extracts,* or *excerpts.*

Run In or Set Off

10.10   Whether to run in or set off a quotation is commonly determined by its length. In general, quoted matter that runs to ten or more typed lines or that involves more than one paragraph is set off from the text; shorter quotations are usually run into the text. Before arbitrarily following this rule, however, author (and editor) should consider the nature of the material, the number of quotations, and the appearance of the printed page. Many quotations of varying lengths—some over ten typed lines—may be less distracting to the reader if they are all run in, regardless of length, provided they are skillfully integrated with the text. On the other hand, where the quotations are being compared or otherwise used as entities in themselves it is best to set them all off from the text, even quotations of one or two lines. In other words, compared quotations in the text should be typographically comparable.

10.11   Quotations of two or more lines of poetry are usually set off from the text (see 10.22). If more than one line is run into the text, a solidus (/), with equal space on either side, marks the end of one line and the beginning of another:

> Andrew Marvell's praise of John Milton, "Thou hast not missed one thought that could be fit, / And all that was improper dost omit" ("On *Paradise Lost*"), might well serve as our motto.

Syntax

10.12   The skill with which fragmentary quotations are incorporated into a text reflects an author's awareness of syntax, verb tenses, personal pronouns, and so forth. Only so much of the source as is necessary should be quoted, and the incorporating sentence should be phrased in such a way that the quoted words fit logically and grammatically into it. A master of the felicitous quotation, Ronald S. Crane, provides many illustrations in his two-volume *The Idea of the Humanities* (Chicago: University of Chicago Press, 1967). Among them:

> In short, there has been "almost a continual improvement" in all branches of human knowledge; and since this improvement has taken place not merely in the speculative sciences but likewise in those other forms of learning, such as politics, morality, and religion, "which apparently have a more immediate influence upon the welfare of civil life, and man's comfortable subsistence in it," it seems to follow, "as a corollary, plainly deducible from a proposition already demonstrated," that human happiness has also increased. (1:281)

Initial Capital or Lowercase

10.13   A quotation used as an essential syntactic part of a sentence—the object of a preposition or of an infinitive, for example, or a noun clause introduced by a conjunction such as *that, if,* or *whether*—may begin with a lowercase letter even though the original is a complete sentence beginning with a capital.[3] It is preferable in scholarly works and essential in legal works and textual criticism, however, to retain the capital or to bracket the change (see 10.16).

> Benjamin Franklin admonishes us to "plough deep while sluggards sleep."

> With another aphorism, he reminded his readers that "experience keeps a dear school, but fools will learn in no other"—an observation as true today as then.
>
> *or*
>
> Benjamin Franklin admonishes us to "Plough deep . . ."

When the quotation has a more remote syntactic relation to the rest of the sentence—when it is merely modified by the rest of the sentence, as in the first example below, or when it is used as discourse, as in the second, or an appositive, as in the last two—the initial capital is always retained. Note also the punctuation in the examples (see 5.71–79):

> As Franklin advised, "Plough deep while sluggards sleep."

> Franklin advised, "Plough deep . . ."

> With another aphorism, "Experience keeps a dear school, but fools will learn in no other," he puts his finger on a common weakness of mankind.

> His aphorism "Experience keeps a dear school, but fools will learn in no other" is a cogent warning to people of all ages.

If a borrowed fragment of poetry is used out of context as an expressive phrase in a sentence, an initial capital letter may be lowercased:

3. For altering capitalization other than the initial letter of a quotation see 10.62.

> Whether "to be, or not to be" was a major consideration or not, Sir Thomas hastily drew his sword.

10.14 Although the initial capital of a block quotation may be lowercased if the syntax of the introductory text encourages it, it is also acceptable, perhaps preferable, especially in scholarly and legal works and works of textual criticism, to retain the capital, as in the following example involving a quotation from Aristotle's *Politics* in the Jowett translation (Modern Library) (see also 10.16):

> In discussing the reasons for political disturbances, Aristotle observes that
>
> > Revolutions also break out when opposite parties, e.g. the rich and the people, are equally balanced, and there is little or no middle class; for, if either party were manifestly superior, the other would not risk an attack upon them. And, for this reason, those who are eminent in virtue usually do not stir up insurrections, always a minority. Such are the beginnings and causes of the disturbances and revolutions to which every form of government is liable. (*Politics* 5.4)
>
> > *Also acceptable*
>
> In discussing the reasons for political disturbances, Aristotle observes that
>
> > revolutions also break out . . .

Another possibility, of course, is to omit the *that* in the introduction and substitute a colon, in which case the initial capital remains above suspicion.

10.15 If a quotation that is only part of a sentence in the original forms a complete sentence as quoted, an initial lowercase letter may be changed to a capital where the structure of the text suggests it. To use the second sentence in the preceding quotation from Aristotle:

> As Aristotle remarked, "Those who are eminent in virtue usually do not stir up insurrections, always a minority."
>
> > *but*
>
> Aristotle's observation that "those who are eminent in virtue usually do not stir up insurrections, always a minority" might serve as a subject for debate.

10.16 In legal works and textual criticism, and usually in scholarly works, any change in capitalization should be indicated by brackets (see also 10.62):

> [r]evolutions . . .
>
> [T]hose . . .

Introductory Phrases and Punctuation

10.17 A formal introductory phrase, such as *thus* or *the following,* is usually followed by a colon:

> The role of the author has been variously described. Henry Fielding, at the beginning of his *History of Tom Jones,* defines it thus: "An author ought to consider himself, not as a gentleman who gives a private or eleemosynary treat, but rather as one who keeps a public ordinary, at which all persons are welcome for their money."

> Of the Ten Commandments, he had already broken the following:

>> Thou shalt not take the name of the Lord thy God in vain.
>> Honor thy father and thy mother.
>> Thou shalt not bear false witness against thy neighbor.

10.18   Such introductory phrases as

> Professor Jones writes:

> She said (stated, observed, etc.):

are often awkward and redundant. A sensitive writer will avoid them.

10.19   A quotation consisting of more than one complete sentence is often introduced by a colon if the text preceding the quotation is not a complete sentence but a phrase like

> As the president of the council suggested:

> And again:

A comma is also acceptable in such a case, however, and if the quotation is only one sentence, a comma is preferable. If the introductory text is a complete sentence, either a colon or the normal terminal punctuation may be used:

> The president of the council suggested an alternative.

> What, you might ask, was the alternative?

> The president's suggestion provoked an acrimonious response:

(See also 5.71–79.)

Paragraphing Block Quotations

10.20   A block quotation should reflect the paragraphing of the original. If the quotation includes the beginning of the opening paragraph, it should start with a paragraph indention. If the first part of the paragraph is omitted, the opening line ordinarily begins flush left (not indented) and need not be preceded by ellipsis dots. Should ellipsis dots be used, however, they are indented as representing the opening of the paragraph (see 10.58). If the author has begun the opening paragraph flush left and the editor cannot determine whether the first part of the paragraph has been omitted, the flush-left beginning may be retained. In quotations of more than one paragraph, the original paragraphing is retained, and indented ellipsis dots (three) are used where necessary to indicate omission of the first part of a paragraph.

Block Quotations Beginning in Text

10.21 A long quotation may begin with a few words or a sentence run into the text; the rest of the quotation is then set off as an extract. This device should be used only if a few words of text intervene between the quoted matter in the text and its continuation:

> "There is no safe trusting to dictionaries and definitions," observes Charles Lamb.
>
> We should more willingly fall in with this popular language, if we did not find *brutality* sometimes awkwardly coupled with *valour* in the same vocabulary. The comic writers . . . have contributed not a little to mislead us upon this point. To see a hectoring fellow exposed and beaten upon the stage, has something in it wonderfully diverting. ("Popular Fallacies," *Essays of Elia*)
>
> "In short," says Crane, summarizing Gordon's philosophy,
>
> there has been "almost a continual improvement" in all branches of human knowledge; . . .

An alternative permissible in most instances is to set off the entire quotation, putting the intervening words of text in brackets as an interpolation:

> In short [says Crane, summarizing Gordon's philosophy], there has been . . .

Poetry

10.22 Quotations from poetry are often centered on the page, but they may also be set at a small uniform indention from the left. Poetry should be set line for line, and with the same indention pattern and the same spacing between stanzas as in the original:[4]

> Sure there was wine
> Before my sighs did drie it: there was corn
>   Before my tears did drown it.
> Is the yeare onely lost to me?
>   Have I no bayes to crown it?
> No flowers, no garlands gay? all blasted?
>   All wasted?
>   (George Herbert, "The Collar")

---

4. For lines of poetry run into the text see 10.11. For examples of typography and other design considerations see 18.59–61.

If the quotation does not begin with a full line, placement should ap-proximate that of the original:

> there was corn
> Before my tears did drown it.

10.23 In a work containing quotations from poems with lines too long to be centered on the page, such as Walt Whitman's "Song of Myself," all poetic quotations may be set with a uniform, short indention—two or three picas from the left, for example—with any runover lines being further indented:

> My tongue, every atom of my blood, form'd from this soil, this air,
> Born here of parents born here from parents the same, and their parents
> the same,
> I, now thirty-seven years old in perfect health begin,
> Hoping to cease not till death.

Uniform indention is also usually specified where all or most quotations in a work consist of blank verse (as in studies of Shakespeare).

> I have full cause of weeping, but this heart
> Shall break into a hundred thousand flaws
> Or ere I'll weep. O fool! I shall go mad.

10.24 Quotation marks at the beginning of a line of poetry are often aligned with the first letter of the line above:

> He holds him with his skinny hand,
> "There was a ship," quoth he.
> "Hold off! unhand me, grey-beard loon!"
> Eftsoons his hand dropt he.
>
> (Coleridge, *Rime of the Ancient Mariner*)

In older practice, sometimes followed today and actually preferred by the University of Chicago Press, such quotation marks were *cleared*, that is, placed outside the alignment of the poem:

> He holds him with his skinny hand,
> "There was a ship," quoth he.
> "Hold off! unhand me, grey-beard loon!"
> Eftsoons his hand dropt he.

Paragraphing Following a Block Quotation

10.25 If, following an extract or block quotation, whether of prose or poetry, the resuming text is a continuation of the paragraph that introduces the quotation, the resuming text should begin flush left. If the resuming text is a new paragraph, it should be given regular paragraph indention.

QUOTATION MARKS

Double and Single

10.26 Quoted words, phrases, and sentences run into the text are enclosed in double quotation marks. (Note that in the fields of linguistics and philosophy single marks are used in certain contexts to enclose individual words or letters; see 6.67, 6.74.) Single quotation marks enclose quotations within quotations; double marks, quotations within these; and so on:

> "Don't be absurd!" said Henry. "To say that 'I mean what I say' is the same as 'I say what I mean' is to be as confused as Alice at the Mad Hatter's tea party. You remember what the Hatter said to her: 'Not the same thing a bit! Why you might just as well say that "I see what I eat" is the same thing as "I eat what I see"!'"

British practice is often, though not always, the reverse: single marks are used first, then double, and so on.

10.27 The placement of terminal punctuation in a sentence ending with two or more sets of closing quotation marks follows a principle similar to that governing such placement in a sentence ending with a single set of quotation marks. Question marks and exclamation points are located just within the set of quotation marks ending the element to which such terminal punctuation belongs. In the example above, the exclamation point belongs to the speech of the Mad Hatter and therefore is placed within the closing (single) quotation mark ending that speech. Had the exclamation point belonged to the speech *quoted by* the Mad Hatter, it would belong inside the first set of quotation marks: "I eat what I see!'" Had it belonged to Henry's speech, it should have gone just before Henry's closing quotation mark: "I eat what I see"'!" And finally, had it belonged to the narrator quoting Henry quoting all the rest, it should have been placed outside all of the closing quotation marks: "I eat what I see"'"! A period—and, for multiple quotations ending before the end of the including sentence, a comma—is, by convention (see 5.11–13 and 5.86–87), placed inside the first set of closing quotation marks: "I eat what I see."'"

In Block Quotations

10.28 Material set off from the text as a block quotation is not enclosed in quotation marks. Quoted matter within the block quotation is of course set off with double quotation marks; quotations within these quotations, with single quotation marks; and so on (see 10.26). When a quotation that is run into the text in the typescript is converted to a block quotation, the quotation marks enclosing it are dropped, and interior quotation marks are changed accordingly:

> The narrator then breaks in: "Imagine Bart's surprise, dear reader, when Emma turned to him and said, contemptuously, 'What "promise"?' "

> The narrator then breaks in:
>> Imagine Bart's surprise, dear reader, when Emma turned to him and said, contemptuously, "What 'promise'?"

Similarly, if a quotation set off from the text in the typescript is run into the text, initial and final quotation marks must be added and internal quotation marks changed accordingly. (For the placement of terminal punctuation with respect to these quotation marks see 5.28.)

With More Than One Paragraph

10.29 If a passage consisting of more than one paragraph from the same source is quoted and is not set off as an excerpt, quotation marks are used at the beginning of each paragraph and at the end of the last paragraph. That is, quotation marks are not used at the *end* of any paragraph in the quotation except the last one. (This practice is also followed in presenting the dialogue of a single speaker that extends over more than one paragraph.) If the quoted passage contains an interior quotation that also runs for more than one paragraph, a single quotation mark is used at the interior quotation's beginning, before each new paragraph (inside the double quotation mark), and at its conclusion. If its conclusion coincides with the conclusion of the including quotation, the single quotation mark precedes the double one.

10.30 Poetry quotations, when not treated as excerpts, take quotation marks at the beginning of the quotation, at the beginning of each stanza, and at the end of the quotation.

10.31 A quotation of a letter carries quotation marks before the first line (usually the salutation) and after the last line (usually the signature) as well as at the beginning of each new paragraph within the letter.

10.32 Note that the usual practice of setting these kinds of material as block quotations obviates the use of quotation marks.

With Display Type

10.33 Quotation marks are not used with epigraphs (quotations used as ornaments to the text rather than as part of the text itself) or before a display initial beginning a chapter or section:

Oh, what a tangled web we weave,
When first we practice to deceive!
—Sir Walter Scott

It is a truth universally acknowledged, that a single man in possession of a good fortune must be in want of a wife.
—Jane Austen, *Pride and Prejudice*

O F THE MAKING OF MANY BOOKS there is no end," declared an ancient Hebrew sage, who had himself magnificently aggravated the situation he was decrying.

(For more on the stylistic treatment of epigraphs see 1.38–39; for typographic treatment, 18.48.)

Rules and Familiar Expressions

10.34 Rules, maxims, mottoes, and other familiar expressions are sometimes enclosed in quotation marks and sometimes not. In either case, however, it may be necessary to set them off from the rest of the including sentence with a comma. (For examples see 5.80–83.)

Questions

10.35 Unless they constitute dialogue, questions introduced within sentences are ordinarily not enclosed in quotation marks. Direct questions are frequently set off from the rest of the sentence by a comma, but if the question comes first, the comma yields to the question mark. Indirect questions never require a comma. (For examples see 5.22–24, 5.27, 5.84–85.)

SPEECH, DIALOGUE, AND CONVERSATION

Direct Discourse

QUOTATION MARKS AND PARAGRAPHS

10.36 Direct discourse or dialogue is traditionally enclosed in quotation marks. A change in speaker is usually indicated by a new paragraph. If one speech occupies more than a paragraph, the rule for repeating quotation marks with succeeding paragraphs applies (see 10.29).

> "Ransomed? What's that?"
> "I don't know. But that's what they do. I've seen it in books; and so of course that's what we've got to do."

"But how can we do it if we don't know what it is?"

"Why, blame it all, we've *got* to do it. Don't I tell you it's in the books? Do you want to go to doing different from what's in the books, and get things all muddled up?"

(Mark Twain, *The Adventures of Huckleberry Finn*)

10.37 Authors sometimes prefer to run an exchange of dialogue together within a single paragraph, choosing to make the paragraphing depend more on the narrative than on a change of speaker:

Hearing this, Po-ch'in reflected a while. He then said, "Elder, for generations this humble family has never kept a vegetarian diet. We could, I suppose, find some bamboo shoots and wood ears and prepare some dried vegetables and bean cakes, but they would all be cooked with the fat of deer or tigers. Even our pots and pans are grease-soaked! What am I to do? I must ask the elder's pardon." "Don't fret," said Tripitaka. "Enjoy the food yourself. Even if I were not to eat for three or four days, I could bear the hunger. But I dare not break the dietary commandment." "Suppose you starve to death," said Po-ch'in, "what then?" "I am indebted to the Heavenly kindness of the Guardian," said Tripitaka, "for saving me from the packs of tigers and wolves. Starving to death is better than being food for a tiger." (Yu, trans., *Journey to the West*, 1:292)

SINGLE-WORD SPEECH

10.38 Words such as *yes, no, where, how,* and *why* are quoted in direct discourse but not when indirect discourse is intended:

Without hesitation, she answered, "No!"

"Why?" he asked.

He asked himself, "Why?"

He had expected her to say yes.

He asked himself why.

Did he say where?

"There!" she replied.

FALTERING SPEECH

10.39 Authors and editors are not always consistent in the way they use ellipses and dashes in interrupted speech, but an attempt should be made to establish a distinction. Ellipsis points suggest faltering or fragmented speech accompanied by confusion, insecurity, distress, or uncertainty, and they should be reserved for that purpose. The dash, on the other hand, suggests some decisiveness and should be reserved for interruptions, abrupt changes in thought, or impatient fractures of grammar.

"I . . . I . . . that is, we . . . yes, *we* have made an awful blunder!"

"The binoculars . . . where the devil did I put them?"

"The ship . . . oh my God! . . . it's sinking!" cried Henrietta.

Felicia sat down suddenly, almost as though she had fallen into her chair, and said, "I don't understand. We were beginning . . . I had thought . . ."

"But . . . but . . . ," said Tom.

Notice that three ellipsis points are used between the speech fragments. If other punctuation, such as an exclamation point or a question mark, occurs at the end of the fragment, it is retained before the three points, as in the third example. Note also that in the last example a comma is used after the closing series of dots to separate the speech from the words identifying the speaker. For examples of the use of dashes to denote sudden breaks or changes in thought or interruptions in dialogue see 5.106.

ALTERNATIVES TO QUOTATION MARKS

10.40   As widely as quotation marks are used in dialogue throughout English-language narrative, alternatives are occasionally seen. One such alternative (commonly used in French) employs the dash to set speech off. Although inconsistency occurs in the deployment of dashes in passages of conversation, the general idea seems to be that the dash should indicate only the opening of a speech and not its conclusion or its interruption by descriptive material or material identifying the speaker. Another alternative, albeit infrequent, employs nothing at all but the prose itself. Neither quotation mark nor dash nor any other punctuation signals conversation. It is left to the author to make dialogue "sound" like dialogue, and to the reader to have the ear to hear it.

DRAMA AND DISCUSSION

10.41   When the name of the speaker introduces the speech, as in the script of a play or the transcription of a discussion, the dialogue is not set off by quotation marks:

> *R. Roister Doister.* Except I have her to my wife, I shall run mad.
> *M. Merygreeke.* Nay, "unwise" perhaps, but I warrant you for "mad."
> *R. Roister.* I am utterly dead unless I have my desire.
> *M. Mery.* Where be the bellows that blew this sudden fire?

> DR. LEVENE: Mr. Chairman, we have heard the revolutionary notion today, first of all, that the smooth muscle cell can behave like the fibroblast to synthesize collagen, and, second, that it does the job of a macrophage: it takes up fat. . . .
> DR. TAYLOR: I wish to inquire as to how those proposing the smooth muscle theory reconcile their thoughts with the concept that was given considerable support by the late Dr. Lyman Guff and also by Dr. McMillan; . . .

In the examples above, periods or colons are used to separate the speaker and the speech. Other styles are also used, depending in part on the design. For a discussion of the various ways of setting up dialogue in plays and similar materials see 18.64–65.

Indirect and Interior Discourse

INDIRECT DISCOURSE

10.42 Indirect discourse paraphrases dialogue; it does not reproduce it. For this reason indirect discourse is not enclosed in quotation marks:

> Eberly said that Morgenstern had refused to drive them home.
>
> Croft suggested that perhaps they had somehow offended Morgenstern.
>
> Vera calmly replied that she had no idea what they were talking about.

INTERIOR DISCOURSE

10.43 Thought, imagined dialogue, and other interior discourse, presented in more or less conventional syntax, is often, but not always, enclosed in quotation marks. Alternatives to enclosure in quotation marks include the use of italics or plain roman type. The choice—in fiction especially, but in other writing as well—should be the author's, but consistency ought to be observed within a single work.

> "I don't care if we have offended Morgenstern," thought Vera. "Besides," she told herself, "they're all fools!"
>
> "I should have said, 'What business is it of yours!'" thought Tom.
>
> I suppose he's telling her right now, "Morgenstern is not to be trusted."
>
> Francine blushed and turned away. I could die! she told herself.
>
> Edgar looked at her in despair and thought, *Now what have I done?*

10.44 Interior discourse that is given indirectly, that is, paraphrased, should of course be set in unenclosed roman:

> Vera told herself that she didn't care if they had offended Morgenstern.
>
> She had decided, anyway, that they were all fools.
>
> I should have said I wouldn't be available.

STREAM OF CONSCIOUSNESS AND INTERIOR MONOLOGUE

10.45 *Stream of consciousness* is a narrative device widely used in contemporary fiction. A similar technique, of much older origin, is the interior monologue. Lucid definitions of these techniques are provided in *Benét's Reader's Encyclopedia:*

> In general, . . . "stream of consciousness" is . . . the description of mental life at the borderline of conscious thought and is characterized by the devices of association, reiteration of word- or symbol-motifs, apparent incoherence, and the reduction or elimination of normal syntax and punctuation to simulate the free flow of the character's mental processes. "Interior monologue" refers to a presentation of thoughts more consciously controlled and on a level closer to direct verbalization.[5]

Stream of consciousness is traditionally presented without quotation marks. Perhaps because interior monologue is more closely related to stream of consciousness than to brief and occasional snatches of interior discourse, it also is usually presented without quotation marks, although they are sometimes used.

10.46 Interior monologue differs from the brief interior discourse described above (10.43) in that it is more sustained, extending over several sentences or several paragraphs. If both interior monologue and brief bits of interior discourse are employed in the same work, both should be treated in the same way, that is, all in quotation marks or all without.

10.47 Needless to say, interior monologue sometimes obtrudes into stream of consciousness. It is, in fact, often difficult to distinguish one from the other or to detect the point at which they merge. In any case, when they occur conjoined, both are presented without quotation marks:

> Reading two pages apiece of seven books every night, eh? I was young. You bowed to yourself in the mirror, stepping forward to applause earnestly, striking face. Hurray for the God-damned idiot! Hray! No-one saw: tell no-one. Books you were going to write with letters for titles. Have you read his F? O yes, but I prefer Q. Yes, but W is wonderful. O yes, W. Remember your epiphanies on green oval leaves, deeply deep, copies to be sent if you died to all the great libraries of the world, including Alexandria? Someone was to read them there after a few thousand years, a mahamanvantara. Pico della Mirandola like. Ay, very like a whale. When one reads these strange pages of one long gone one feels that one is at one with one who once . . . (James Joyce, *Ulysses*)

ELLIPSES

10.48 An ellipsis, or elision—the omission of a word, phrase, line, paragraph, or more from a quoted passage—must be indicated by ellipsis points or dots (also called suspension points), never by asterisks (stars). The ellipsis points are printed on the line like periods, not above it like multiplication dots in mathematics. They are usually separated from each other and from the text and any contiguous punctuation by 3-to-em spaces (see glossary under *spacing*). The number of dots and the

5. *Benét's Reader's Encyclopedia*, 3d ed. (New York: Harper and Row, 1987), 939–40.

spacing between them and the preceding and following words should be checked carefully for consistency by the manuscript editor.

10.49 Two common methods of using ellipsis points are described here. The University of Chicago Press prefers the second one but will allow the first if the author has used it consistently.

10.50 The first method is, briefly, to use three dots for any omission, regardless of whether it comes in the middle of a sentence or between sentences:

> For instance, consider the rule about ellipses in broken quotations—that when a quoted sentence ends with a period, this period should be printed close up, followed by three dots to show ellipsis . . . In my opinion those publishers and journals who have decided to forget about this nicety and now invariably use three dots . . . must be congratulated on their common sense. (Eleanor Harman, "A Reconsideration of Manuscript Editing," *Scholarly Publishing* 7 [January 1976]: 151)

10.51 The second method distinguishes between omissions within a sentence and omissions between sentences. This method is described in the following paragraphs.

Within a Sentence

10.52 Three dots indicate an omission within a quoted sentence or fragment of a sentence. Thus an omission in the sentence

> The glottal stop, which is common in this family of languages, is marked by an apostrophe.

could be shortened to

> The glottal stop . . . is marked by an apostrophe.

Note that, in addition to the relative clause, the commas that set it off are omitted.

10.53 Other punctuation may be used on either side of the three ellipsis dots if it helps the sense or better shows what has been omitted. Consider the following passage (Dan. 3:4–6) in original and cut versions:

> Then a herald cried aloud, To you it is commanded, O people, nations, and languages, that at what time ye hear the sound of the cornet, flute, harp, sackbut, psaltery, dulcimer, and all kinds of music, ye fall down and worship the golden image that Nebuchadnezzar the king hath set up: and whoso falleth not down and worshippeth shall the same hour be cast into the midst of a burning fiery furnace.

> To you it is commanded . . . that at what time ye hear the sound of the cornet, flute, . . . and all kinds of music, ye fall down and worship the

> golden image . . . . : and whoso falleth not down and worshippeth shall . . .
> be cast into . . . a burning fiery furnace.

Between Sentences

10.54 Procedures for indicating omissions between sentences, including portions of those enclosing sentences and extending to whole paragraphs, may be illustrated by using portions of the following complete passage from Emerson's "Politics"; from a brief, imaginary source; and, later, from a portion of *Walden* by Thoreau:

> The spirit of our American radicalism is destructive and aimless: it is not loving, it has no ulterior and divine ends; but is destructive only out of hatred and selfishness. On the other side, the conservative party, composed of the most moderate, able, and cultivated part of the population, is timid, and merely defensive of property. It vindicates no right, it aspires to no real good, it brands no crime, it proposes no generous policy, it does not build, nor write, nor cherish the arts, nor foster religion, nor establish schools, nor encourage science, nor emancipate the slave, nor befriend the poor, or the Indian, or the immigrant. From neither party, when in power, has the world any benefit to expect in science, art, or humanity, at all commensurate with the resources of the nation. (Emerson, "Politics")

10.55 When the last part of a quoted sentence is omitted and what remains is still grammatically complete, four dots—a period followed by three ellipsis dots—are used to indicate the omission. If the sentence ends with a question mark or an exclamation point, that punctuation, of course, replaces the period and is followed by the three ellipsis dots. Note that there is no space between the period or other terminal punctuation and the preceding word, even though that word does not end the original sentence:

> The spirit of our American radicalism is destructive and aimless. . . . the conservative party . . . is timid, and merely defensive of property.

> Whether her criticism is valid or not, shall I capitulate to her? . . . And shall I be subject to her ridicule the rest of my life! . . . I would rather cut off my ears.

When what remains is not grammatically complete, the period is omitted:

> American radicalism . . . the conservative party . . . From neither party . . . has the world any benefit. . . .

If the beginning of the opening sentence of a quotation is deleted, ellipsis dots are usually not necessary and are ordinarily omitted (see 10.61):

> the conservative party . . . is timid, and merely defensive of property. . . .

10.56   Omission of the beginning of a later sentence in the quotation is indicated by four dots—the period ending the preceding sentence and three dots indicating the omission:

> The spirit of our American radicalism is destructive and aimless: it is not loving, it has no ulterior and divine ends; but is destructive only out of hatred and selfishness. . . . the conservative party . . .

10.57   The omission of a whole sentence or more from within a quotation is indicated by the usual three ellipsis dots; if the omission is preceded by a grammatically complete sentence, the three dots are preceded by a period:

> The spirit of our American radicalism is destructive and aimless. . . . the conservative party . . . is timid, and merely defensive of property. . . . From neither party, when in power, has the world any benefit to expect in science, art, or humanity, at all commensurate with the resources of the nation.

10.58   If one or more paragraphs are omitted from within a quotation, the omission is indicated by the usual three ellipsis dots run in at the end of the quoted paragraph preceding the omission. If that paragraph ends with a grammatically complete sentence, a closing period precedes the three dots, even if something has been deleted from that sentence or, indeed, if more material from the end of that paragraph has been omitted. It is also used, of course, when the preceding paragraph is quoted in full.

> When I was four years old . . . I was brought from Boston to this my native town, through these very woods and this field, to the pond. It is one of the oldest scenes stamped on my memory. . . .
> Before yet any woodchuck or squirrel had run across the road, or the sun had got above the shrub oaks, while all the dew was on, though the farmers warned me against it—I would advise you to do all your work if possible while the dew is on—I began to level the ranks of haughty weeds in my bean-field and throw dust upon their heads. . . . (Thoreau, *Walden*)

If a paragraph in the quotation, other than the first paragraph, begins with a sentence that does not open the paragraph in the original, the sentence should be preceded by three dots following the usual paragraph indention. It is thus possible on occasion to use ellipsis points at the end of one paragraph and at the beginning of the next in a block quotation:

> In summarizing the action of a drama, the writer should use the present tense. In summarizing a poem, story, or novel, he should also use the present, though he may use the past if it seems more natural to do so. . . .
> . . . whichever tense the writer chooses he should use throughout. Shifting from one tense to another gives the appearance of uncertainty and irresolution. (Strunk and White, *Elements of Style,* 3d ed., 31)

10.59 Three dots—no period—are used at the end of a quoted sentence that is deliberately and grammatically incomplete:

> Everyone knows that the Declaration of Independence begins with the sentence "When, in the course of human events . . ." But how many people can recite more than the first few lines of the document?

In the example below, however, the fragment is presented not as part of a sentence but rather as a "beginning." It is therefore not necessary to indicate its fragmentary nature by ellipsis dots.

> Please look at the quotation beginning "The spirit of our American radicalism" and tell me how you would shorten it.

(For the use of the dash in interrupted speech see 5.106.)

Full Lines Omitted in Poetry

10.60 The omission of one full line or several consecutive lines of verse is indicated by one line of em-spaced dots approximately the length of the line above it (or of the missing line, if that is determinable).

> I will arise and go now, and go to Innisfree,
> .   .   .   .
> And live alone in the bee-loud glade.
> (W. B. Yeats, "The Lake Isle of Innisfree")

> Heard melodies are sweet, but those unheard
>   Are sweeter; therefore, ye soft pipes, play on;
> .   .   .   .
>   Pipe to the spirit ditties of no tone.
> (John Keats, "Ode on a Grecian Urn")

When Ellipsis Points Are Not Used

10.61 Readers will understand that a quoted phrase, sentence, or longer passage, unless it is the beginning or end of a work, will have been preceded and followed by additional material in the source. It is therefore seldom necessary to use ellipsis points in the following situations:

1. Before or after an obviously incomplete sentence separately quoted:

> Rhuigbach had devised what she referred to as an "unorthodox method of elucidating the ineffable," but Northfeather declared the idea "an empty pretense."

2. Before or after a run-in quotation of a complete sentence or several sentences:

Midway through his essay, after having observed that "Wiznowski's theorem was no extraordinary breakthrough," Canatelli apologized for what he called his "earlier enthusiasm."

3. Before a block quotation, whether it begins with a grammatically complete sentence or not:

Briggs continues the discussion of Roebuck as follows:

> His great-grandfather had founded the Carron Iron Works in Scotland and was given a place of honor in Smiles's *Industrial Biography.* He himself was a friend of John Brown, the Sheffield steel king. He had little sympathy with the doctrines of the Manchester School, particularly with the views of foreign policy which they expressed, but he had been a vigorous Benthamite in his youth and a close personal friend of John Stuart Mill, the first friend the precocious young Mill ever had. (Asa Briggs, *Victorian People,* rev. ed. [Chicago: University of Chicago Press, 1972])

Briggs has noted that Roebuck

> had little sympathy with the doctrines of the Manchester School, particularly with . . .

4. After a block quotation ending with a grammatically complete sentence (see first example under no. 3 above).

If ellipsis dots are considered necessary, however, three should precede and three should follow the quoted matter, along with a period if the last sentence is grammatically complete or if the quotation completes a sentence begun in the text.

Capitalization Following Ellipses

10.62 In a quotation from a modern work, the first word of a sentence following four dots may be capitalized even though it is not the first word of the sentence in the original. For example, the opening of the extract from Emerson's "Politics" (see 10.54) may be changed as follows:

> The spirit of our American radicalism is destructive. . . . The conservative party . . .

But in scholarly works usually and in legal works and textual criticism always, an original lowercase letter following four dots either should not be capitalized or should be capitalized in brackets (see 10.16) so that the reader attempting to locate the quotation in its source will not be misled.

> . . . destructive. . . . [T]he conservative party . . .

In a quotation from an older work where many words are capitalized, it is also best to make no such changes:

> Let such Imps of Ill-nature . . . rail on. . . . to my gentle Readers of an-
> other Cast, I would willingly apologize.

Instead of introducing a capital, it may be desirable in some cases to add a connective in brackets:

> The spirit of our American radicalism is destructive and aimless . . . [and] the conservative party . . . is timid, and merely defensive of property.

(For capitalizing the *first* word of a quotation see 10.13–16.)

Faithful Elision

10.63 In making elisions in quoted material, the author should take great care to avoid altering the meaning of the original.

MISSING OR ILLEGIBLE WORDS

10.64 Words or parts of words missing or illegible in the original are custom-arily indicated by 1- or 2-em spaces, with or without brackets, rather than ellipsis dots. Interpolations are enclosed in brackets (for a discussion of interpolations of missing letters or words see 10.65):

> Although the Genl.'s victory in the Supreme has sa[ved him] from the mor-tification of being ejected by our late   it has not from the vexation of being pursued by   [He] is now trying the skill of his lawyer in framing a new a[ppeal] and means to carry the Genl. over the whole ground [again.] (Madison to Joseph Jones, 24 October 1780, *Papers of James Madison,* 2:147)

> I have great marvel that ye will so soon incline to every man his device and [counsel and   ] specially in matters of small impor[tance   ] yea, and as [it is] reported [unto me   ] causes as meseemeth th[at   ] nothing to [   ]ne gentlewomen. (Thomas Cromwell to Lord Lisle, 1 September 1533, *Lisle Letters,* ed. Byrne, 1:552–53)

A line of dots may be used, however, to indicate missing or illegible lines in a manuscript.

INTERPOLATIONS AND ALTERATIONS

10.65 Insertions may be made in quoted material to clarify an ambiguity, to provide a missing word or letters, or to give the original foreign word or phrase where an English translation does not convey the exact sense. Any such interpolations are enclosed in brackets (not parentheses). When an interpolated word takes the place of a word in the original, ellipsis points are omitted:

> Marcellus, doubtless in anxious suspense, asks Barnardo, "What, has this thing [the ghost of Hamlet's father] appear'd again tonight?"

> "Well," said she, "if Mr. L[owel]l won't go, then neither will I."

> James "preferred to subvert the religion and laws of his people" rather than to "follow the character and reasons of his state [*indolis rationesque sui Regni*]."

> Even in its romantic origins, Jebb tells us, satire "is the only [form] which has a continuous development extending from the vigorous age of the Commonwealth into the second century of the Empire."

(See also the interpolations in the example in 10.64.) Contempt, scorn, or doubt may sometimes be expressed by [!] or [?], although such interpolations are usually best left unmade.

Sic

10.66   *Sic* ("so," "thus," "in this manner") may be inserted in brackets following a word misspelled or wrongly used in the original. (Note that *sic* is a complete word, not an abbreviation, and therefore takes no period; it is customarily set in italics.) Overuse of this device, however, is to be discouraged. In most books it is unnecessary to call attention to every variant spelling, every oddity of expression, in quoted material. An exclamation point should ordinarily not be used after *sic;* the insertion of *sic* alone is enough to call attention to the error in the source. While not really necessary, it would be permissible to use *sic* in the following sentence from Thoreau's *Walden:*

> Or on a Sunday afternoon, if I chanced to be at home, I heard the cronching [*sic*] of the snow made by the step of a long-headed farmer, who from far through the woods sought my house, to have a social "crack."

Italics Added

10.67   When it is desirable to call attention to a certain word or words in material being quoted, such words may be set in italics (underlined in manuscript). The reader should be told when this has been done, either in the note giving the source of the quotation, in parentheses directly following the quotation, or in brackets following the italicized passage in the quotation. One or the other system should be used throughout a book. "Italics mine," "italics added," "emphasis added" are all acceptable phrases, but choose one and stick with it.[6]

6. Note that an explanation such as "Underlined words do not appear in the second edition" makes sense in the manuscript but not in print, where the words in question are set in italics, not underlined. Hence in a manuscript intended for publication the explanation should read, "Words in italics do not appear in the second edition."

10.68   Occasionally it may be desirable to point out that italics in a quotation are *not* the present author's doing but were indeed in the original. Here the usual phrase is "italics in original" or, better, using the name of the quoted author, "Tocqueville's italics" or "Tocqueville's emphasis."

CITING SOURCES IN TEXT

In Running Text

10.69   In a scholarly work the source of a direct quotation is often given in a note, but in many cases it may be given in the text, in whole or in part and enclosed in parentheses. Such text references present some editorial problems in placement and punctuation, and these will be dealt with in the following discussion.

10.70   In a work containing no notes or bibliography and only a few quoted passages, a source may be given in full in parentheses following the quotation, or it may be worked into the text, with publication facts in parentheses:

> The programs of today reflect the demands of a musically more sophisticated audience. "The age is fortunately nearly past when eighteenth-century composers were subject in concert programs to a kind of 'type-casting' in which a few Scarlatti pieces, or a little Couperin on the part of the more adventurous, a Mozart sonata or a Bach organ fugue were served up as well-styled appetizers to be unregretted by late-comers and to act as finger warmers and curtain raisers to the 'really expressive' music of the nineteenth century" (Ralph Kirkpatrick, *Domenico Scarlatti* [Princeton: Princeton University Press, 1953], 280).

> At the beginning of the introduction to her well-known book *Mythology* (Boston: Little, Brown, 1942) Edith Hamilton observes that "the real interest of the myths is that they lead us back to a time when the world was young and people had a connection with the earth, with trees and seas and flowers and hills, unlike anything we ourselves can feel."

10.71   If another passage is quoted from the same source on the next page or two of text and there is no intervening quotation from a different source, "ibid." may be used in the parenthetical reference: for example, (ibid., 282). If a different source has been cited or more than two or three pages have elapsed, a short citation should be given: (Kirkpatrick, *Scarlatti,* 282).

10.72   In works using frequent quotations from a single source, each needing its own location, particularly in literary studies, it is usually preferable to give such locating page or line numbers, act and scene, book, part, or the like in parentheses following each quotation instead of in the notes (see 15.45, point 3).

10.73   Even when citations are given in the text, the full citation may be confined to a note at the first mention of the source. The text citations would then be in abbreviated form. If only one edition of the work is used, the note may include the statement that all subsequent quotations from that source are from the edition cited. If more than one edition of a work has been used, however, this fact must be mentioned in the note and the edition specified each time in the text citation.

10.74   If part designations are explained in the note, it is unnecessary to include their abbreviations in the text references. For example, if the note says "References are to act, scene, and line," the text reference following a passage may read simply (1.2.14–15), meaning act 1, scene 2, lines 14–15,[7] or similarly, following appropriate explanation in a note, (3:22–23), meaning volume 3, pages 22–23, (12.45–50) *or* (12:45–50), meaning book 12, lines 45–50, (2.8.14), meaning book 2, canto 8, stanza 14. *Ibid.* should not be used for subsequent text references to act, scene, and so forth, because repeating the part numbers generally takes less space.

10.75   Where a number of sources are used this way, it is well to devise an abbreviation for each and, instead of giving full citations and explanations in the notes, to compile a list of abbreviations to be placed at the front or back of the book (or article) (see 1.54, 15.24–25, 15.261). In a study of Shakespeare's comedies, for example, one might refer to a passage from *A Midsummer Night's Dream* and abbreviate the identification in the text: (*MND* 2.2.1–8).

10.76   If the quotation comes in the middle of the text sentence, the source is given after the closing quotation mark, and the rest of the text sentence follows. If, as in the example below, the quoted matter ends with a period in its original context, the period is suppressed here, as it is whenever one sentence is included in the middle of another (see 5.8), unless the quoted sentence is set off as a block quotation, as are the examples in paragraph 10.52. Also in the example, the citation may be considered part of the introductory adverbial phrase, and the comma setting off the phrase therefore follows the citation:

> With his "Nothing will come of nothing; speak again" (1.1.92), the exasperated Lear tries to draw from his youngest daughter a verbal expression of filial devotion.

10.77   When the quoted passage falls at the end of a sentence and, in its original context, ends with a period, the period is preferably suspended and placed at the end of the citation, outside the closing parenthesis.

---

7. If roman numerals are preferred for act numbers, the citation would read: (I, 2, 14–15) or, using roman numerals for both act and scene: (I, ii, 14–15) or (I.ii.14–15).

> Lear, trying to draw from his youngest daughter an expression of filial devotion, says with some exasperation, "Nothing will come of nothing; speak again" (1.1.92).

This rule holds even when the quotation is more than one sentence:

> It has been three-quarters of a century since Henry Adams said: "Fifty years ago, science took for granted that the rate of acceleration could not last. The world forgets quickly, but even today the habit remains of founding statistics on the faith that consumption will continue nearly stationary" (*Education*, 493).

10.78 When a quotation comes at the end of a sentence and is itself a question or an exclamation, demanding its own final punctuation, that punctuation is retained as part of the quotation, and a period is added after the closing parenthesis:

> And finally, in the frenzy of grief that kills him, Lear pitifully rails, "Why should a dog, a horse, a rat, have life, / And thou no breath at all?" (5.3.306).

10.79 An alternative method of punctuating quotations and their sources at the ends of sentences is to put the punctuation mark concluding the whole sentence inside the final quotation mark and use no punctuation following the source citation:

> Lear says with some exasperation, "Nothing will come of nothing; speak again." (1.1.92)

> And finally . . . Lear pitifully rails, "Why should a dog, a horse, a rat have life, / And thou no breath at all?" (5.3.306)

10.80 One or the other of the two methods (10.77–78, 10.79) must be used consistently throughout a book or an issue of a journal.

Following Block Quotations

10.81 The source of a set-off, or block, quotation is usually given in parentheses (not brackets) at the end of the quotation and in the same type size. It is best put after the final punctuation mark so that it will not be read as part of the quotation. If the reference begins with a word or abbreviation, the first letter is usually capitalized: (Vol. 3). No punctuation is used following the source.

10.82 A citation following a prose quotation is placed right after the final punctuation mark.

> From Joseph Addison in *The Spectator:*

> I shall endeavour to enliven morality with wit, and to temper wit with morality. . . . The mind that lies fallow but a single day sprouts up in follies

that are only to be killed by a constant and assiduous culture. (No. 10, 12 March 1710/11)

From W[illiam] D[ean] Howells, *Literary Friends and Acquaintance* (New York: Harper, 1900):

Then and always he [Walt Whitman] gave me the sense of a sweet and true soul. . . . The apostle of the rough, the uncouth, was the gentlest person; his barbaric yawp, translated into the terms of social encounter, was an address of singular quiet, delivered in a voice of winning and endearing friendliness. (P. 75)

10.83 Citations following poetry quotations should be dropped to the line below the last line of the quotation and centered on the last letter of the longest line of the quotation. The citation may also be set flush right or indented uniformly from the right margin (placement is often specified by the designer).

From Milton's *Paradise Lost* (reference is to book and lines):

So glistered the dire Snake, and into fraud
Led Eve, our credulous mother, to the Tree
Of Prohibition, root of all our woe.
(9.643–45)

From Alexander Pope, *The Rape of the Lock* (reference is to canto and lines):

The meeting points the sacred hair dissever
From the fair head, forever, and forever!
(3.153–54)

From Shakespeare's *Love's Labour's Lost* (reference is to act, scene, and lines):

For wisdom's sake, a word that all men love;
Or for love's sake, a word that loves all men.
(4.3.354–55)

From Edmund Spenser, *The Faerie Queene* (reference is to book, canto, and stanza):

Who will not mercie unto others shew,
How can he mercy ever hope to have?
(6.1.42)

FOREIGN LANGUAGE QUOTATIONS

10.84 Quotations in a foreign language that are incorporated into an American English text are not italicized (for isolated words and phrases see 6.65) and, for the most part, are punctuated as in the original, except that ellipsis points follow American style and short quotations run in with

English language text are usually enclosed in American-style quotation marks (see 9.7).

Original Language or Translation

10.85 Whether an author should provide translations of quoted passages depends on the linguistic abilities of the anticipated readers. As a general rule, in a literary study of, say, Racine, quotations from Racine's plays should be given in the original French only. Similarly, in a work to be read by classicists, Latin or Greek sources[8] may be quoted freely in the original. In a scholarly work where there is a possibility that not all readers will be able to grasp the original, both the original and a translation may be given. In this case either the original is put in the text and the translation in a note, or the translation is given in the text and the original in the note. It is also acceptable to put both in the text. If both versions are given in the text, whether run in or set off as block quotations, the second version is usually enclosed in square brackets. When the second version is given in a note, the square brackets are omitted. In all cases, quotation marks, if appropriate, are used to enclose only the first version, whether that is the original or the translation. In works where quotations are used for their content alone, not for their style, only the English translation need appear, with of course the proper attribution.

Author's Translation

10.86 Passages in a foreign language may be translated by the person quoting them if no acceptable English translation of the source has been published or if the person quoting finds it expedient to provide a new translation; in this case "my translation" should be added either in parentheses following the translation or in the note identifying the source. If translations of this sort are numerous, a general notice may be given in the preface (if by the author) or foreword (if by a translator); for example: "Unless otherwise noted, all translations are my own." Where a published translation is used, the title of the translation, the translator's name, and the bibliographical details should be given in a note or in the bibliography, and the relevant page number of the translation should be used in identifying the quotation.

10.87 Finally, never *re*translate from a foreign language a passage from a book originally published in English! Find the original and use it.

8. Most typesetters charge extra for setting Greek, Cyrillic, or other non-Latin alphabets. Authors who quote from works in languages using these alphabets and who do not wish to transliterate the passages should so advise their publishers.

11 *Illustrations, Captions, and Legends*

ILLUSTRATIONS

Definitions

11.1   The term *illustration* refers to a variety of materials such as line drawings, paintings, photographs, charts, graphs, and maps. Tables, since they are set in type rather than reproduced from artwork, are not considered illustrations. They are separately listed in the preliminary pages and separately numbered—and in this manual they are separately discussed in a chapter of their own (see chapter 12). Although each type of illustration requires slightly different treatment, peculiar to its own kind, some general remarks can be made about the preparation of all these materials for reproduction. First, however, a few definitions and distinctions are in order.

LINE AND CONTINUOUS-TONE COPY

11.2   Artwork containing only blacks and whites, with no shading—a pen-and-ink drawing, for instance, or a bar chart—is known as *line copy.* Artwork that does contain shading—a painting, a wash drawing, or a photograph—is known as *continuous-tone copy* or, less accurately, *halftone copy.* Mechanically the two kinds of copy are handled differently for reproduction, and authors and editors should keep the distinction in mind.

11.3   Both kinds of copy must be photographed by the publisher's supplier before they can be reproduced. Line copy is shot directly, whereas continuous-tone copy—say, a photograph—is shot through a *screen* that breaks the image up into hundreds of tiny dots of varying size (for a fuller discussion see 19.49–53). The resulting *halftone* is actually a printed reproduction of these dots (visible under a magnifying glass), which the naked eye sees as tones of gray shading into one another.

TEXT FIGURES AND PLATES

11.4   Illustrations in a book may print along with the text, in which case they are called *text figures,* or they may be printed separately, on either regular text paper or coated paper, and grouped in one or more sections containing nothing but illustrations, in which case they are called *plates.* These sections of plates are often called *galleries.* Galleries are usually not counted in the page-numbering sequence of the book. A section of text figures may sometimes be numbered with the text, provided all the illustrations have been fully settled on before paging begins, but even then it is not uncommon to exclude these pages from the numbering sequence.

OFFSET LITHOGRAPHY

11.5   The printing method now used for nearly all books, whether illustrated or not, and whether the illustrations are line art or halftones, is *offset lithography* (see 19.3–8). Illustrations that appear in separate sections on coated paper are also almost always printed by offset rather than by the nearly obsolete letterpress or gravure methods. In the following paragraphs procedures for handling all illustration copy for offset lithography will be discussed.

Artwork for Offset Reproduction

PLACEMENT AND NUMBERING

11.6   An illustration should be placed as close as possible to the first text reference to it. The illustration may precede the reference only if it is on the same page as the reference; otherwise it should follow. To show placement the author or editor writes (for example) "fig. 1 here" or simply "fig. 1" in the margin of the manuscript at the best place for the illustration, circling the words so they will not be set by mistake. The editor must later see that these directions are transferred to the galley proofs, if these are seen by the editor, as a guide to the printer in making up the pages.

11.7   If there are many illustrations, they should be numbered, and text references to them should be by the numbers: "figure 1 shows . . . ," "see figure 2," "(fig. 3)." *Never* should a figure be referred to as "the figure opposite" or "the photograph reproduced on this page." The exigencies of page makeup may well rule out that placement—and then the reference will have to be rewritten in proof. The examples given illustrate some of the conventions observed at the University of Chicago Press: *figure* (or *plate*—see the later discussion) is set in lowercase roman, and the number is an arabic numeral. The word *figure* is spelled out except in simple parenthetical references.

11.8   In a book where line and halftone illustrations are mixed and distributed through the text, they should be numbered continuously throughout, beginning with figure 1. There are exceptions, of course. Maps, unless they are used to illustrate specific points, are usually separately numbered (map 1, map 2, etc.) or not numbered at all. (Tables, we have seen, are always numbered separately, not being considered illustrations.) Also, in a book with chapters by different authors—such as conference papers or a symposium—numeration of figures customarily starts over with each chapter.

11.9   In scientific and technical books, heavily illustrated books, and books with chapters by different authors, a *double numeration* system is often employed. In this system an illustration number consists of the number of the chapter in which the figure appears plus the number of the figure within that chapter. For example, figure 9.3 is the third figure in chapter 9. Should a chapter in such a book contain only one illustration of a kind, the double numeration system would still apply: figure 6.1, map 6.1. Such a system makes finding an illustration easier by directing the reader first to the chapter.

PHYSICAL HANDLING

11.10   For a book containing a large number of illustrations, physically handling the art copy and photographs after they come to the publisher's
office—sorting, identifying, and marking them—is often a job of some
magnitude, and one that frequently falls to the lot of the manuscript
editor in charge of the project. Some cautions must be observed in
handling copy for illustrations:

> Never use staples on a photograph or piece of artwork.
>
> Never use paper clips either, unless they are padded with several
> thicknesses of paper to prevent scratching or indentation.
>
> Except for crop marks on photographs, make no marks on the illus-
> tration; for annotation, use a tissue overlay or a gummed label at-
> tached to the back, or write very gently with pencil on the back (see
> 2.49–50).
>
> When writing on the back of a photograph or piece of artwork, use
> nothing harder than the softest of lead pencils, being careful not to
> mar the print surface. Since much modern photographic print paper
> will not accept pencil markings, a self-sticking label or a piece of
> plastic tape of the kind that can be written on may be stuck to the
> back of the print to bear the identification. Most preferable is the
> kind of tape that can be removed when no longer needed. *Never* use
> a ballpoint pen. Do not use a grease pencil or a felt-tip marker
> either, for the marks may transfer to another photograph.

11.11   When a package of illustrations arrives, a number of editorial tasks
should be done immediately. Before the package is opened, or at least
before the contents are spread out, the editor's desk or (preferably) a
large table should be totally cleared of papers. Few things are more
frustrating than to mislay a small bit of illustration copy by letting it
slip in among other papers on the working surface. The chief things to
do then are the following:

> Inventory everything received, first arranging items in sequence and
> then checking them off individually on a list provided by the author.
> If the author has not provided such a list, you will have to make
> one. It is important at this point to note any missing items: later no
> one will believe you did not lose them yourself.
>
> Turn each illustration over and make sure it is completely identified
> on the back. The minimum is author, short title, and chapter and
> figure numbers. For a volume of conference papers, include the
> name of the author of the particular chapter as well as the chapter
> number.
>
> If any of the necessary identifying information is missing, supply it
> by using one of the methods outlined in 2.49–50.

If the author has not supplied separate legend copy, transcribe or paste onto separate sheets any legends that are attached to the illustrations and number the legends for later editing. The typesetter cannot set from anything attached to illustrations.

If legend copy has to be removed from an illustration, it is a good idea to make some brief record of the subject on the back of the piece, in addition to the purely formal identification data there.

It is very easy for the printer to get some kinds of illustrations wrong side up if they are not marked—tissue sections and photomicrographs of all kinds are notorious in this regard. The editor should consequently mark *TOP* in the margin or on the back of any illustration subject to this kind of mistake.

MARKUP

11.12   In a large publishing house editors seldom have occasion to mark illustration copy for reproduction, but in a house too small to boast a production department, art and photo markup is a normal editorial task. What follows is only a sketch of what is typically involved in simple markup, not a set of directions. Unless one is thoroughly conversant with art and photo markup for the particular process and materials being used, one should seek advice from a trained production person or from a supplier before doing any markup.

11.13   For black-and-white copy (and this is all we are considering in this chapter) the chief things to communicate to the offset camera operator are (1) whether or not the negative is to be screened (for halftone reproduction) and, if it is, what grade of screen is to be used; and (2) what the dimensions of the finished reproduction should be.

11.14   For (1), the editor might write, "Make halftone, 133-line screen, crop as shown" or "Make line neg, size as shown." Such directions are best written in the margin of any piece of illustration copy, but for a photograph they may be written on the back, where there is more room.

CROPPING

11.15   For (2), the editor must decide how much of the illustration is to be used (photographs, particularly, are commonly *cropped* in reproduction—that is, only part of the image appears on the printed page). A pair of L-shaped pieces of cardboard can be used to frame the area of interest and to help the editor see what the picture will look like as cropped (see fig. 11.1). The person doing the cropping should make sure that any verticals in the picture—the corner of a building, for instance, or the trunks of trees—appear to be vertical when the photograph is cropped. Photographs shot by nonprofessionals are often faulty

Fig. 11.1. Two L-shaped pieces of cardboard used as an aid in cropping photographs

in this regard. A horizon in the picture should be horizontal, but other horizontals, such as stair edges or building cornices, often quite correctly appear slanted because of the effect of perspective. When correcting verticals, pick a vertical near the center of the image to judge by, not one near the edge, since it is common in photography for verticals to converge as they rise, the more so the farther they are from the center.

11.16 When the area to be used has been decided upon, small *crop marks* are placed in the margin to show what area the camera operator is to include—all of the photograph or only part of it. Ordinary soft pencil is best for marking on artwork. For marking in the margin on the glossy front of photographs, a pencil designed for writing on glass or plastic and offering little risk of smearing or transferring to other materials is recommended (an excellent example is the Stabilo red pencil). The

← —————————— *27 picas* —————————— →

Fig. 11.2. Crop marks and reduction notation on a photograph

marks are not permanent and can be removed later with a tissue. (In the unlikely event that smearing or transfer should occur with such a pencil, the marks may similarly be wiped off without harm to the photograph.) One of the dimensions of the finished reproduction, usually the width, is then written between the appropriate crop marks. (This is recommended for the nonprofessional in preference to such directions as "reduce 2 : 1" or "reduce 50%" that professionals often use; for an example of such marking see fig. 11.2.)

SCALING

11.17 When a photograph or a piece of artwork is to be reduced to fit a particular space, it must be *scaled;* that is, finished dimensions must be computed from the dimensions of the cropped original. There are many ways of doing this, all based on the fact that when an illustration is reduced or enlarged, all dimensions shrink or gain in the same proportion. That is, when the long side of an eight-by-ten-inch photograph is reduced to five inches, the short side automatically reduces to four inches. There are three common methods of scaling, one mechanical (or visual), the others arithmetical.

11.18 First method (see fig. 11.3): When the photograph has been cropped, lay a piece of tracing paper over it and draw—lightly!—a rectangle the

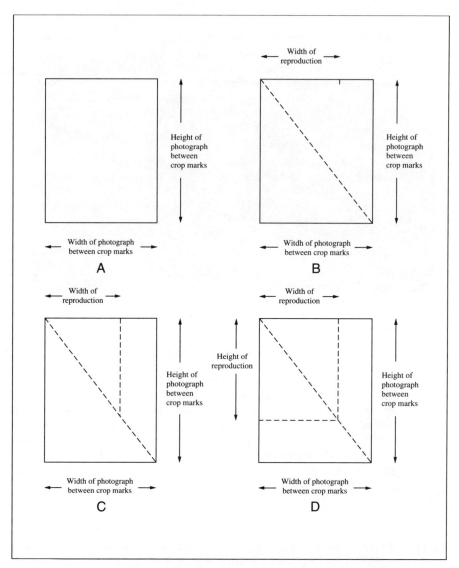

Fig. 11.3. Scaling a photograph by means of an overlay and a diagonal

size of the usable area of the photograph *(A).* Next *(B),* mark on the top line the width you want the reproduction to be and draw a diagonal line across the rectangle. Then *(C)* drop a vertical line from the mark you made to the diagonal line, using a drafter's triangle or a rectangular piece of cardboard. Finally *(D),* run another line, parallel to the top and bottom of the rectangle, from the point where your vertical line hits the diagonal to the left side of the rectangle. You now have a small rectangle inside the large one; this inner rectangle represents, and may be measured as, the finished halftone. *Picas* rather than inches are used to measure illustrations because the type area of a printed page is always measured in picas. The pica, moreover, is much smaller than an inch (approximately 6 picas per inch), and rough fractions are therefore less troublesome. To make sure that enough space will be left for the illustration, pica measurements are rounded *up* to the next half pica; for example, a measurement of slightly more than 22 picas (say 22⅛) is rounded up to 22½.

11.19   Second method: Measure between crop marks the height and width of the image *in picas* to the nearest half pica. Substitute these two figures ("original width" and "original height") in the following equation:

reduced height = (original height × reduced width) ÷ original width.

Now determine from the page specifications how wide the finished halftone must be and substitute this figure in the equation ("reduced width"). Finally, perform the computation (a pocket calculator is a great help) to obtain the height of the finished product. For example, the usable area of the original photograph measures 35.5 picas wide by 55 picas high, and the halftone is to drop into a type column that is 15 picas wide. Substituting these figures in the equation gives

reduced height = (55 × 15) ÷ 35.5 = 23.239, rounded up to the nearest half pica, 23½.

If you count on a height of 23½ picas for the finished halftone, you will be close enough. To this add a little white space, say half a line above and half a line below (if the illustration is to go in the middle of the column), plus enough space for the caption and legend, to figure how big a "hole" to leave in the column for the illustration.

11.20   The third method is a variation of the second. The required width of the printed halftone, determined from the page specifications, is divided by the original width of the photograph, yielding the percentage of reduction. The calculated percentage, in decimal-fraction form, is then multiplied by the original height of the photograph, resulting in the required height of the printed halftone. Using, for example, the same dimensions as in the example above (11.19),

percentage reduction = 15 ÷ 35.5 = 0.4225, or 42.25%
reduced height = 55 × 0.4225 = 23.238, rounded up to 23½ picas.

11.21   A *proportion wheel* may also be used to determine percentages and proportions, but the above method (11.20), with the assistance of a pocket calculator, permits quick and accurate scaling of a sizable batch of illustrations.

Corrections on Art Copy

11.22 Unless drawings have been made especially for reproduction after consultation between author, editor, designer, and production controller, they often require changes, major or minor, before they can be reproduced. Changes are of two sorts: (1) those necessary to ready the artwork physically for reproduction—strengthening weak lines, redrawing fuzzy line copy, whiting out unwanted marks in the background, and so on—and (2) editorial changes—bringing spelling and capitalization of labels into conformity with other drawings and with the text, attaining consistency in the use of symbols and wording, improving clarity, and so on. All names on a map that is to be redrawn and any words appearing in other kinds of illustrations must be typed as a separate list for typesetting. In a publishing house with a production department, a designer or production controller is responsible for seeing that artwork corrections are made, an editor for editorial changes. In a small house, the editor is responsible for all.

11.23 Corrections on artwork, unless they are so gross and simple that an unskilled and shaky hand is not likely to spoil the drawing, should be left to an artist. The directions to the artist are written not on the drawing or photograph itself, but on a flap of tracing paper *(overlay)* taped to the back of the piece and folded down over the face. On this the editor marks what is to be done, writing with the least possible pressure. When the corrections have been made, the editor removes the overlay before sending the *camera-ready copy* to the printer.

CAPTIONS AND LEGENDS

11.24 Most text figures and plates require some sort of explanatory material to make them understandable to the reader. This is supplied by a *caption* or a *legend*—two terms often confused or considered synonymous, but at the University of Chicago Press distinguished one from the other. A caption is a title or headline, but unlike many newspaper headlines, the caption is never a grammatically complete sentence, even when extending, as it sometimes does, to more than one line. Formerly placed above the illustration, the caption is now generally placed below. A legend is an explanation consisting of one or more sentences. (On a map, the legend is the key to the symbols used—something quite different from what is described here.) The following is an example of a traditional caption and legend for a halftone plate:

Colinton Parish Church as It Appeared in Walker's Time

This photograph shows the church as it appeared before 1908, when it was extensively enlarged and reconstructed. It had changed little from the time of Walker's ministry until then. The coffin-shaped object in the foreground is an eighteenth-century mortsafe, a block of cast iron placed over a newly made grave to discourage "resurrectionists" from digging up the body for sale to anatomists. (Courtesy of the Reverend W. B. Johnston, B.D., minister of Colinton.)

The traditional separation of caption and legend is more often ignored than followed in contemporary practice. The two are now commonly run together, and in that case the caption ends with a period.

> Plate 1
> A Group of Artifacts from Site 3. In all these objects the high degree of finish and the aesthetic appeal are notable. *A, C, E,* flint points, and *B,* obsidian bird point, all approximately natural size; *D,* grain-storage jar of grayish clay decorated in black ($\times$ 1/20); *F,* votive figure of red clay, undecorated ($\times$ 1/5).

11.25 Text figures frequently carry legends only, captions being omitted, especially in scientific writing, where such figures are used in profusion:

> Fig. 1. Clearly visible here are the giant transparent vacuole *V* and its septa *S* wrapped around the end of the resorbing bone.

Editorial Conventions and Typography

11.26 Type specifications for captions and legends are best left to the designer. A few editorial conventions probably ought to be observed, however, and these are discussed in the paragraphs that follow.

NUMERATION

11.27 The University of Chicago Press recommends the use of arabic numerals with plates as well as text figures. Further, if halftone illustrations print with the text, it is preferable to number them with the text figures, not separately as if they were plates. In a book containing numbered figures, each figure should bear its own number. Especially painful to a careful editor, and perhaps disconcerting to the reader, is an additional figure stuck in at the last moment and given a designation such as figure 43A. If the figure *must* be included and no nearby figure can be killed, and if it is too late or too expensive to renumber the rest of the figures, this may have to be done. (If it is done, the sequence would be 43, 43A, 44, and so on.) It should be noted, however, that very commonly in scientific works, and occasionally in other fields as well, a single illustration of a complex subject consists of several parts, each part being designated by a letter, such as A, B, C, and so on. Although the illustration with all its parts has but a single number (fig. 3.12, for instance), text references to the various parts will include the part letter ("as shown in fig. 3.12A," "note that in fig. 3.12F . . ."). In contrast to the aforementioned case, where figure 43 and figure 43A are separate illustrations and may have little to do with each other, in this case the author regards all parts alphabetically designated as constituting a single figure, and a reference such as "see fig. 3.12F" means "see part F of fig. 3.12."

11.28   If a book is illustrated wholly with photographs, reproduced either as plates or as text illustrations, the author and editor might consider whether they need to be numbered at all. The criterion is text reference. If the illustrations are not referred to in the text or are referred to in such a way that they can easily be identified without numbers, numbers are useless and should be eliminated. In such a case, however, illustrations and legends must still be assigned temporary numbers (not to be used in the printed book) to identify them and to make sure they will be matched up properly in printing. The number should be attached to, or very lightly written on, the back of the art copy (see 2.49). For letterpress illustrations, the number should be transferred to the engraver's proof when it comes in. The same number should be written on the typed legend copy (circled so that it will not be set) and transferred to the legend proof when it comes in.

ABBREVIATING *FIGURE* AND *PLATE*

11.29   The label *Figure* is commonly abbreviated ("Fig.") and a period is placed after the figure number when a caption or legend follows. If no captions or legends are used with the figures in a book, the editor may appropriately decide to spell out the label—"Figure 1"—especially when there are only a few figures, and in that case no period follows the number. *Plate* is usually spelled out, but it may be abbreviated— "Pl. 1, Pl. 2," etc.—if many small plates occur close together.

PUNCTUATION AND CAPITALIZATION

11.30   As demonstrated above (11.24), a period is not used after a caption set by itself but is used if the caption and legend are run together. Captions may be given headline capitalization (7.127) or may be capitalized sentence style. Legends are punctuated and capitalized in the same manner as regular text.

> Fig. 7. Wall Drawing of Huntsman
>
> Fig. 13. Idealized random distribution curve
>
> Fig. 21. Augustus addressing his troops. This portrayal of the emperor deliberately harks back to old times. The details on the breastplate depict incidents from early Roman history, and the artistic style imitates fifth-century work.

Fig. 2. Photomicrographs of mouse-radius rudiments. *A*, left radius cultivated for 3 days in PTE; *B*, right radius similarly cultivated; *C*, left radius
cultivated for 2 days in PTE.

IDENTIFYING PARTS OF AN ILLUSTRATION

11.31 Such terms as *top, bottom, left, right, above, below, left to right,* or
clockwise from left are frequently used in legends to identify individual
subjects in an illustration or parts of a composite. These are set in
italics, and Press preference is that they precede the phrase identifying
the object or person:

> Fig. 4. *Above left,* William Livingston; *right,* Henry Brockholst Living-
> ston; *below left,* John Jay; *right,* Sarah Livingston Jay.

If a list follows the introductory tag, a colon rather than a comma is
preferred:

> *Left to right:* Dean Acheson, Harry Hopkins, President Roosevelt, Harold
> Ickes.

11.32 Letters of the Latin alphabet, abbreviations, and symbols are all used
as keys for identifying parts of a figure. When such a key is referred to
in a legend, the form used there should reflect as closely as possible the
form used in the figure itself. If capital letters are used in the figure,
capitals should be used in the legend, and so on. The typeface used in
the legend for the key should, however, always be italic, whatever is
employed in the figure.

> Fig. 5. Four types of Hawaiian fishhooks: *a,* barbed hook of tortoise shell;
> *b,* trolling hook with pearl shell lure and point of human bone; *c,* octopus
> lure with cowrie shell, stone sinker, and large bone hook; *d,* barbed hook
> of human thigh bone.

> Fig. 6. Facial traits of *(A) Propithecus verreauxi verreauxi* and *(B) Lemur
> catta,* which vary from one individual to the next; *ea,* ear; *ca,* cap; *cpl,*
> capline; *br,* brow.

When symbols are used in a figure, use of the same symbols in the
legend requires the least effort of the reader:

> Fig. 7. Dependence of half-life on atomic weight for elements in the
> radium-uranium region: $\bigcirc$ = even α-emitters; $\bullet$ = odd α-emitters; $\square$ =
> isotopes capable of K-capture or β-decay.

If the symbols are not available in type or in the appropriate size of
type, they must be described:

> Fig. 8. Dependence of half-life on atomic weight for elements in the
> radium-uranium region: *open circles,* even alpha-emitters; *solid circles,*

odd alpha-emitters; *open squares,* isotopes capable of *K*-capture or beta-decay.

In the last example, note also that in a scientific context the names of the Greek letters may usually be substituted for the letters themselves.

GIVING DIMENSIONS OF ORIGINAL

11.33   When a legend provides the dimensions of an original work of art, it is customary to list them in the following sequence: height, width, and (if applicable) depth.

> Oil on canvas. 45 cm × 38 cm
>
> Bronze, 49 in. × 22 in. × 16 in.

Note that either a period or a comma may follow the description of the medium, but the choice must be consistent within a work.

Credit Lines

11.34   For most illustrative matter used in a book or a journal article a *credit line*—a brief statement of the source of the illustration—is either necessary or appropriate. The only significant exception is an illustration (chart, graph, drawing, photograph, etc.) of the author's own creation.

PERMISSIONS

11.35   Illustrative material under copyright, whether published or unpublished, usually requires permission from the copyright owner before it can be reproduced. It is the author's responsibility, not the publisher's, to determine what is under copyright and to obtain permission to reproduce it. An author working with a publisher, however, should always consult the publisher about the form in which to request permission (see 4.43–58).

PLACEMENT

11.36   The credit line may appear in any one of several locations and in various forms. Set in very small type, a short credit line may run parallel to the lower edge of the illustration or even to one of the vertical edges, especially if the illustration is a photograph. It may run at the end of the legend, often in parentheses and sometimes in a different style of type, or the pertinent facts may be worked into the legend copy. If most or all of the illustrations are from a single source, that fact may be stated in the preface or acknowledgments or on the copyright page. Finally, in a heavily illustrated book, especially one in which it is desirable to keep the illustrated pages uncluttered, what are called *box credits* may be resorted to. This is a lumping together of all the picture credits for a volume on one page or a series of pages in the front or the back of the book. Picture agencies, incidentally, may demand a higher fee for the use of an illustration if box credits are employed.

FORM

11.37 The form of the credit line itself varies according to its placement and according to the type and copyright status of the illustration. For material under copyright, the copyright owner may demand a certain form of credit line, but apart from this contingency, credit lines of a given type (say, those for charts reproduced from published works) should follow a consistent pattern. If the credit appears alone, end punctuation is omitted. If it follows a caption or a legend, however, the credit line customarily ends with a period. The discussion and examples that follow offer some simple and workable patterns for credit lines of various types. In all of them the assumption is that the credit line will run at the end of the legend.

PREVIOUSLY PUBLISHED MATERIAL

11.38 An illustration reproduced from a source protected by copyright always requires formal permission from the copyright owner, unless *fair use* applies (see 4.56–57). There is no fixed style for such credit lines, but they should be consistent and for a source of book length should include a page number, figure number, or the like. A short form is appropriate if the work from which the illustration has been taken is listed in the bibliography (see 15.248–52). The person who grants permission to reproduce the illustration may, however, specify a certain form of credit line including the full facts of publication and even a copyright notice (see 1.16–17, 15.151).

> [*a kinship diagram*]
> Reprinted, by permission, from Wagner, *Curse of Souw,* 82.
>
> [*a portrait engraving*]
> From a drawing by J. Webber for Cook's *Voyage to the Pacific Ocean, 1776–1780,* reprinted, by permission of the author, from Edwin H. Bryan Jr., *Ancient Hawaiian Life* (Honolulu, 1938), 10.
>
> [*a photograph of a lemur*]
> Reprinted, by permission, from Jolly, *Lemur Behavior,* pl. 6. Photograph by C. H. Fraser Rowell. © 1966 by The University of Chicago.

(For an extended discussion of the form for citing sources see chapter 15.)

11.39 Illustrations may be reproduced from published works without seeking permission if the work is in the public domain (see 4.17). Even though permission is not required, it is good policy to use a credit line, however—out of deference to the reader if not the creator of the material.

> Illustration by Joseph Pennell for Henry James, *English Hours* (Boston, 1905), facing p. 82.

> Reprinted from John D. Shortridge, *Italian Harpsichord Building in the Sixteenth and Seventeenth Centuries,* U.S. National Museum Bulletin 225 (Washington, D.C., n.d.).

ORIGINAL MATERIAL

11.40 Although illustrations that are the author's own do not need credit lines, this does not mean that credit lines should *not* be used if there is some reason for them. If, for example, all but a few of the illustrations in a book are from one source and this source is acknowledged in the preliminaries, it would be appropriate to place under a photograph taken by the author a line reading:

> Photograph by the author
> *or*
> Photo by author

Somewhat different is the case of material commissioned by the author, usually maps, photographs, or drawings. Ordinarily such material is produced under a "work made for hire" contract (see 4.12–13), which may or may not specify that credit be given. Whether credit is required or not, however, professional courtesy dictates mention of the creator of the material either in the preliminaries or below each piece, where the credit line might read:

> Map by Robert Williams

> Photograph by Eleanor Warren

> Drawing by Joseph E. Alderfer

If a map or drawing is signed and the signature reproduced, nothing further is needed.

11.41 For material that the author has obtained free of charge and without restrictions on its use, a credit line is seldom legally required but is usually appended nonetheless. In such credit lines it is appropriate to use the word *courtesy:*

> Photograph courtesy of Ford Motor Company
> *or*
> Courtesy Ford Motor Company

If the name of the photographer is well known or if the supplier of the print requests it, the photographer's name may be given also:

> Photograph by Henri Cartier-Bresson, courtesy of the Museum of Modern Art.

11.42   Agency material—photographs and reproductions of prints, drawings, paintings, and the like obtained from a commercial agency—usually requires a credit line. The contract or bill of sale will specify what is expected. Typical credits might be

> Woodcut from Historical Pictures Service, Chicago
>
> Photograph from Wide World Photos

11.43   Sometimes an author does not directly pick up and reproduce another's material but nonetheless is indebted to that person. The author may, for example, use data from a table in another book to construct a chart, or revise another's graph with fresh data, or redraw a figure with or without significant changes. In such situations, although the author's material is technically original, a credit line is in order. There is no set form. Thus for a chart based on a table in another book the credit line might read:

> Data from John F. Witte, *Democracy, Authority, and Alienation in Work* (Chicago: University of Chicago Press, 1980), table 10.

If the book is fully listed elsewhere, the citation could be

> Data from Witte, *Democracy, Authority, and Alienation in Work,* table 10.
> *or*
> Data from Witte 1980, table 10.

Other typical credit lines are

> [*a graph*] Adapted from Pauly 1980, fig. 4.1.
>
> [*a map*] Redrawn from Day, *Guide to Fossil Man,* fig. 32.

LIST OF ILLUSTRATIONS

11.44   A task that often falls to the manuscript editor (but is more properly done by the author) is preparing the list of illustrations. Not every illustrated book requires such a list. The criterion is, Are the illustrations of interest apart from the text they illustrate? For a scientific monograph on interstellar particles, illustrated largely by graphs, the answer is obviously no. For a book on Roman architecture, illustrated by photographs of ancient buildings, the answer is obviously yes. For some other illustrated books, the answer may not be so easy to give, and the

ILLUSTRATIONS

Plates

Hermetic Silence, from Achilles Bocchius's *Symbolicarum quaestionum . . .* (1555)	*frontispiece*
The Wisdom of Thomas Acquinas, fresco by Andrea da Firenze	*facing page* 50
Justice and Peace, fresco by Ambrogio Lorenzetti (detail)	81
The Zodiac, from Robert Fludd's *Ars memoriae*	336
The De Witt sketch of the Swan Theater	337

Figures

1. The Human Image on a Memory *Locus*	*page* 111
2. The Ladder of Ascent and Descent, from Ramon Lull's *Liber de ascensu et descensu intellectus* (Valencia, 1512)	180
3. Memory Theater, or Repository, from J. Willis's *Mnemonica* (1618)	209
4. Suggested plan of the Globe Theater	358

Fig. 11.4. A somewhat complicated list of illustrations for a scholarly book (see also figs. 1.12 and 1.13)

author and editor must decide whether the list of illustrations is worth the space it will take.

Preparing the List

11.45 The list of illustrations follows the table of contents, normally on a new recto page, and is headed simply Illustrations. The titles of the illustrations listed are capitalized in sentence style or headline style in agreement with the style used in the list of tables and so forth. If illustrations are of more than one type, they are listed by category—plates, figures, maps, and so forth—and by number if numbers are used in the text (see 11.28, also fig. 11.4). For figures and maps that print with the text (and hence have folios assigned to them, whether or not the folios are expressed on the page), page numbers are given (*000* or ■■■ in the copy as first prepared). For plates and for maps printed separately, another type of location is given. If plates are to be inserted in groups of four or more pages at one location, each group is listed under the tag *Following page 000* when copy is prepared. If they are to be inserted in the text two pages at a time (each page of plates accordingly lying opposite a text page), the location is given as *facing page 000*. The editor changes the zeros to real numbers once page proofs are out and page numbers are known.

Editing Captions

11.46 It should be remembered that the list of illustrations is a *list,* not a reprinting of the captions and legends. If the captions are short and adequately identify the subjects of the pictures, they may do double duty in the list of illustrations. Long captions, however, should be shortened, and discursive legends should never be used here.

CHECKING ILLUSTRATIONS IN PROOFS

11.47 In offset printing, page proofs may carry line art in place, but halftones usually do not appear until a later stage, when the camera-ready proofs prepared by the compositor and checked by the editor are sent to the printer for platemaking. At the page proof stage all that can be seen of the halftones are the empty spaces ("holes") or ruled boxes ("windows") into which they will eventually be "dropped." Captions and legends may be in place on the page proofs, or they may instead appear together on separate proofs or not appear at all. Whatever is present on the proofs—line art, captions, legends, halftone holes—should be inspected for accuracy, size, and proper location. When at last the corrected camera-ready proof goes to the printer, it becomes the responsibility of the offset platemaker, guided by adequate instructions from the author and editor, to drop the illustrations into the right holes, and the next stage the editor sees might be printed sheets or even bound books. For many editors this requires too great an act of faith, and so they demand a further stage of "proof"—photographic prints made from the negatives from which plates will be made—for all pages or for those with illustrations. Various kinds of prints are made—among them, blueprints ("blues"), silver prints, and vandykes—but all have the same function. At the University of Chicago Press such prints are mandatory for any illustrated book printed by the offset process (see also 3.55, 3.57).

11.48 When illustrations, captions, and legends appear, whether at the page proof stage or, in the case of halftones, at the blueprint stage, the author and editor should make sure that the illustrations are (1) in correct sequence, (2) in appropriate places, (3) not upside down or sideways (sometimes hard to detect in a photomicrograph), (4) not "flopped" (that is, not a mirror image of what should appear), (5) accompanied

by the correct captions and legends, and (6) correctly listed in the preliminaries (if a list of illustrations is included).

FOR FURTHER REFERENCE

11.49 The reader who wants to know more about the mechanical processes
involved in the reproduction of illustrations may consult the lucidly
written and beautifully illustrated *Bookmaking,* by Marshall Lee, and
Graphic Designer's Production Handbook, by Norman Sanders. *Illustrating Science,* published by the Council of Biology Editors (CBE),
and Frances W. Zweifel's *Handbook of Biological Illustration* discuss
preparation of various kinds of illustrative materials and have relevance
for other areas of science as well as biology. *Envisioning Information*
and *The Visual Display of Quantitative Information,* both by Edward
Tufte, are excellent and extensively illustrated guides to the presentation of quantitative data and other information in graphic form. A clear
and comprehensive discussion of the appropriateness and effective employment of expository cartography may be found in Mark Monmonier's *Mapping It Out: Expository Cartography for the Humanities and
Social Sciences.*

12 *Tables*

INTRODUCTION

12.1 Tables offer a useful means of presenting large amounts of detailed information in small space. A simple table can give information that would require several paragraphs to present textually and can do so with greater clarity. Tabular presentation is often not simply the best but the only way to arrange large numbers of individual, similar facts. Whenever the bulk of information to be conveyed threatens to bog down a textual presentation, an author should give serious consideration to use of a table.

12.2 References to tables, like discussions of them, should do more than simply describe the table or repeat the facts presented in it. If discussion is not necessary, then a simple cross-reference may suffice: "See table 14."

12.3 This chapter, like most others in this manual, is addressed to both authors and editors. The first section, "Planning and Constructing Statistical Tables," is intended primarily for authors who have never compiled a table from raw data and are uncertain how to begin; other readers may wish to skip this section and go on to the next. The final sections of the chapter, beginning with "Editing Tables" (12.62), will probably be of more interest to editors than to authors.

PLANNING AND CONSTRUCTING STATISTICAL TABLES

12.4 Although other kinds exist (see 12.57–61), most tables are constructed to present information in numerical form—percentages, tallies of occurrences, amounts of money, and the like—and are known as statistical tables. As a simple example, say that a scholar has completed a survey on smoking among American adults, incorporating information on the respondents' date of birth, sex, income, social background, and so forth, and wishes to present some of the data in tabular form. The survey has produced responses from 7,308 individuals—3,362 males and 3,946 females, all eighteen years old or over.

12.5 In any one table a single category of data is always the center of attention. The table is constructed to illustrate the variations in that category (the dependent variable) with respect to some other set or sets of data (independent variables). Here the dependent variable would be whether or not the respondent smoked, and the independent variable could be any of several other categories of facts concerning the respondent, for example, the person's sex. Classifying responses according to these two

Table 12.1
Smokers and Nonsmokers, by Sex

	Smoke	Don't Smoke	Total
Males	1,258	2,104	3,362
Females	1,194	2,752	3,946
Total	2,452	4,856	7,308

variables might then result in the simple array shown in table 12.1. (Our survey, needless to say, is imaginary, and all the data shown are entirely hypothetical.)

12.6   An array of raw data like this is relatively useless, however: for comparison the data must be presented in terms of percentages. This has been done in table 12.2. In any statistical table employing percentages (or other proportional figures) the compiler should always give the finite number—the *database,* or *N*—from which the percentages are derived. Here *N* is given in a separate column, but other arrangements are also appropriate.

Table 12.2
Smokers and Nonsmokers, by Sex

	N	Smoke	Don't Smoke
Males	3,362	37.4%	62.6%
Females	3,946	30.3%	69.7%
Total	7,308	33.6%	66.4%

12.7   Table 12.2 represents an extremely simple statistical situation: both the independent variable (sex) and the dependent variable (smoke/don't smoke) are *dichotomies*—entities that divide into two mutually exclusive categories. When either variable consists of more than two categories, tabular presentation necessarily becomes more complex.

12.8   Say the researcher wishes to present the data in terms of age rather than sex. For this purpose birth dates would be grouped by years or spans of years to represent respondents' ages at the time of the survey, and these groups would be divided according to the smoke/don't smoke dichotomy. The results could be presented as in table 12.3. Here age is broken down into four categories, the first three consisting of fifteen-year spans, but smaller groupings could be used.

Table 12.3
Smoking among American Adults, by Age

Age	N	Smoke (%)	Don't Smoke (%)
18-32	1,722	30.6	69.4
33-47	2,012	37.1	62.9
48-62	1,928	35.2	64.8
63+	1,646	30.5	69.5
Total	7,308		

Table 12.4
Smoking among American Adults, by Age and Sex

Age and Sex	N	Smoke (%)	Don't Smoke (%)
Males			
18-32	792	30.0	70.0
33-47	926	44.9	55.1
48-62	886	34.5	65.5
63+	758	39.3	60.7
Total (males)	3,362		
Females			
18-32	930	31.0	69.0
33-47	1,086	30.4	69.6
48-62	1,042	35.7	64.3
63+	888	23.0	77.0
Total (females)	3,946		
Total (both)	7,308		

12.9   If the author wishes to present the data by both age and sex, the responses would be subdivided once more. The data might then be presented as in table 12.4.

12.10   In addition, let us say that respondents were asked other questions about smoking—whether they had quit smoking or had ever tried to quit and (if they smoked at all) whether they smoked cigarettes. Presenting these data in meaningful ways would involve expanding the tabular display and making it more complicated.

12.11   Take the data on quitting smoking. If these statistics are to be presented in connection with age and sex as the independent variables, they might be arranged as in table 12.5. Here each half of the basic smoke/don't smoke dichotomy has been further split according to whether the respondent has quit smoking or has tried to quit. The *N* for each age group also must be split between smokers and nonsmokers. Note that each column of *N*s applies to the two columns immediately to the right of it.

12.12   Finally, let us say, our author wants to present the data on cigarette smoking in connection with an element of social background—whether the respondent came from a rural, small-town, or big-city environment—as well as age and sex. (The question eliciting this response would of course have to be a definite one, such as "Which of these categories comes closest to the type of place you were living in when you were sixteen years old?" followed by a listing of various kinds of locales.) Responses are first sorted by age and sex, as for table 12.4, and then by background of the respondent, with "Don't know" answers

Table 12.5
Smoking History of American Adults, by Age and Sex

	Smoke			Don't Smoke		
	<u>N</u>	Have Tried to Quit (%)	Never Tried to Quit (%)	<u>N</u>	Never Smoked Regularly (%)	Quit Success-fully (%)
Males						
18-32	238	15.1	84.9	554	93.9	6.1
33-47	416	28.8	71.2	510	72.2	27.8
48-62	306	60.1	39.9	580	46.6	53.4
63+	298	88.6	11.4	460	38.7	61.3
Total (males)	1,258	48.0	52.0	2,104	63.5	36.5
Females						
18-32	288	18.8	81.2	642	40.3	59.7
33-47	330	28.5	71.5	756	68.5	31.5
48-62	372	62.4	37.6	670	50.4	49.6
63+	204	89.2	10.8	684	41.8	58.2
Total (females)	1,194	47.1	52.9	2,752	62.6	37.4
Total (both)	2,452	47.6	52.4	4,856	45.2	54.8

omitted. The twenty-four groups created by dividing the responses in this manner constitute the database for the final dichotomy into those who smoke cigarettes and, by elimination, everybody else (table 12.6). As before, the total in each category is expressed as a percentage of N. Here it is impractical to show Ns in columns of their own, and so another device has been adopted: the N for each category, as the note explains, is shown in parentheses below and slightly to the right of the percentage figure. Other arrangements are possible, but this one is preferred by most people who work with statistics.

ARRANGEMENT OF THE ELEMENTS

12.13 The conventions governing the arrangement of the various elements of a statistical table, though not immutable, are pretty well agreed upon by those who make frequent use of tables. Consequently, it is wise to follow existing fashions rather than try to set new ones in the basics of tabular presentation.

12.14 One style that has changed since the twelfth edition of this manual in 1969 is the use of vertical rules in tabular matter. So costly had the handwork required for setting these rules become that most publishers at length regarded their inclusion as no longer justified. Together with

Table 12.6

Smoking among Adult Americans, by Type of Background, Urban or Rural

	Country (%)	Town or Small City (%)	Big City and Suburbs (%)
Males			
18–32	26.5 (98)	29.6 (294)	29.9 (398)
33–47	34.6 (153)	41.2 (306)	43.0 (460)
48–62	28.6 (220)	31.4 (385)	34.1 (270)
63+	34.8 (273)	35.1 (279)	36.5 (189)
Total (males)	31.8 (744)	34.2 (1,264)	36.3 (1,317)
Females			
18–32	28.4 (116)	31.0 (348)	31.5 (463)
33–47	27.9 (179)	30.6 (359)	31.1 (540)
48–62	27.7 (260)	35.8 (450)	42.3 (319)
63+	21.5 (329)	23.1 (325)	25.8 (213)
Total (females)	25.6 (884)	30.6 (1,482)	32.8 (1,535)
Total (both)	28.4 (1,628)	32.2 (2,746)	34.4 (2,852)

Note: Figures in parentheses are base Ns for the adjacent percentages. Total N = 7,226 (3,325 males, 3,901 females). Respondents (82) who did not know where they were living at age 16 have been excluded from the database.

nearly all scholarly and commercial publishers, the University of Chicago Press abandoned vertical rules as a standard feature of tables in the books and journals it published. More than two decades of this austerity have demonstrated that banishing vertical rules has not decreased the clarity of well-organized tables and that it has, on the other hand, increased their attractiveness. Should vertical rules nevertheless be considered necessary, perhaps for very complicated tables, there are now computer typesetting programs that are capable of supplying the rules economically.

12.15 Anyone preparing a set of tables for publication in a particular journal should inquire about the journal's preferences (or requirements) regarding spacing, centering or flushing of elements, ruling, and so forth before typing final copy. The typing suggestions that follow will result in a simple, flush-left style for most elements of a table or, alternatively, a style in which table number, title, and sometimes headings are centered (for additional instruction on typing tables see 2.23–26; for discussion and examples of a centered style see 12.65 and tables 12.12 and 12.13). Copy prepared along these lines is acceptable to most publishers of scholarly books, but not necessarily to all journal publishers. Like all copy intended for publication in typeset form, tables should be double-spaced in typing.

Table Number

12.16 Every table should be given a number and should be cited in the text by that number, either directly or parenthetically:

> The wide-ranging nature of the committee's discussions can
>
> be judged from the topics enumerated in table 14.
>
> Topics covered by the worker-management committee in three
>
> years of deliberations fell into five general categories
>
> (table 14).

12.17 Tables are numbered in the order in which they are to appear in the text—which should also be the order in which they are first mentioned. Arabic numerals are used, and each table is given a number, even though there may be only a few tables in the work. Tables intended to be compared should be given separate numbers (14, 15, 16, *not* 14a, 14b, 14c).

12.18 Numeration of tables normally continues straight through the text. One exception is a book consisting of individual contributions by different authors. There numeration starts over with each chapter or paper. Another exception is a book, often a textbook or a reference work like this manual, in which text sections, figures, and tables are given double numbers reflecting their locations in the book (see 1.77).

12.19 Tables in an appendix to a book are usually numbered separately from the text (A.1, A.2, A.3, etc.), and if there is more than one appendix, numeration starts over in each (A.1, A.2, . . . , B.1, B.2, . . . , C.1, C.2, . . . , etc.).

12.20 The table number ("Table 14," for example) may be placed on a line by itself, either flush left or centered, depending on the style followed. It is also acceptable to place table number and table title on the same line, in which case the number should be flush left with additional space (more than normal word space) left between number and title.

Title

12.21 The title, or caption, set above the body of the table, should identify the table briefly. It should not furnish background information or describe the results illustrated by the table. For example,

```
Effect of DMSO on Arthritic Rats and Nonarthritic Rats

after 20, 60, and 90 Days of Treatment
```

should be pared down to something like

```
Effect of DMSO on Rats
```

The column headings 20, 60, and 90 days and the cross rows for arthritic and nonarthritic rats will give the results. Also, the kind of editorial comment implied by a title like

```
High Degree of Recidivism among Reform School Parolees
```

should be eliminated.

```
Recidivism among Reform School Parolees
```

is sufficient. A table should merely give facts; discussion and comment are reserved for the text.

12.22 Grammatically, the title should be substantival in form. Relative clauses should be avoided in favor of participles.
Not

```
Number of Families That Subscribe to Weekly News Magazines
```

but rather

```
Families Subscribing to Weekly News Magazines
```

12.23 A minor point of usage: in conservative practice, *percent* (*per centum*, by the hundred) is still not considered a noun, although colloquially it is commonly so used. Accordingly, a title reading

```
Percent of Cases Diagnosed Correctly
```

should preferably be made to read

```
Percentage [or Proportion] of Cases Diagnosed Correctly
```

Within the table, the symbol % can stand for either *percent* or *percentage*.

12.24 The table title may carry a subheading, usually enclosed in parentheses:

```
Investment in Automotive Vehicles since 1900

(in Thousands of Dollars)
```

```
Effect of Age on Accumulation of PAH by Kidney Slices of

Female Rats

(M = 200   g PAH/cc; t = 15 min)
```

The number of individuals in a group under consideration (for example, $N = 253$) may be treated as a subheading if it applies to the whole table.

12.25 The table title and subheading (if any) are typed on separate lines, flush left or centered, below or following the table number (see 12.20). Capitalization may be headline style (as in the foregoing examples) or sentence style (first word and proper nouns and proper adjectives only). Never type a title in full caps.

Column Headings

12.26 A table must have at least two columns and usually has more. The columns carry *headings* (or *heads*—the terms are synonymous) at the top, brief indications of the material in the columns. These were formerly called *boxheadings* or *boxheads,* from the fact that in a fully ruled table they were enclosed in rectangles of rules, or *boxes.* The term is occasionally still heard.

12.27 Like the table title, the column headings are substantival in form, and the same grammatical strictures apply to them. If the first column of a table (the *stub,* discussed below) carries a heading, it should be singular in number. The other headings may be singular or plural according to sense.

12.28 Column heads may carry subheadings when they are needed, usually to indicate the unit of measurement employed in the column below. Subheadings are normally enclosed in parentheses, and abbreviations, if used consistently throughout a series of tables, are acceptable: ($), (lb), (%), (mi), ($\times$ 100 km), and so on. If the columns of a table must be numbered for purposes of text reference, arabic numerals are set in parentheses.

12.29 When tabular matter demands two or more levels of headings, *decked heads* must be used. A decked head consists of a *spanner head* and the two or more column heads to which it applies. A horizontal rule (called a *spanner rule*) is set between spanner and column heads to show what columns the spanner applies to (see tables 12.5 and 12.7). Decked heads should seldom exceed two levels, since larger ones are hard to follow down the columns of an unruled table.

12.30 Excessive decking of the heads can sometimes be avoided by using a *cut-in head*—a head that cuts across the statistical columns of the table and applies to all the tabular matter lying below it. For an example of cut-in heads, see table 12.7.

12.31 In typing column heads, leave at least two spaces between the widest lines in adjacent headings. The width of the column headings generally determines the total width of a table, so they should be kept as brief as possible. Use either headline- or sentence-style capitalization, and type successive lines consistently either flush left or centered. Spanner and cut-in heads, however, must be centered above the columns they pertain to. The column head with the most lines defines the vertical space available for all the heads. In typing, it is simplest to align the last lines of all the other heads horizontally with the last line of the longest one. Any subheads are typed on the line below this one. Rules running the full width of the table are customarily typed or drawn above and below

Table 12.7
Elections in Gotefrith Province, 1900–1910

Party	1900		1906		1910	
	% of vote	Seats Won	% of Vote	Seats Won	% of Vote	Seats Won
			Provincial Assembly			
Conservative	35.6	47	26.0	37	30.9	52
Socialist	12.4	18	27.1	44	24.8	39
Christian Democrat	49.2	85	41.2	68	39.2	59
Other	2.8	0	5.7	1[a]	5.1	0
Total	100.0	150	100.0	150	100.0	150
			National Assembly			
Conservative	32.6	4	23.8	3	28.3	3
Socialist	13.5	1	27.3	3	24.1	2
Christian Democrat	52.1	7	42.8	6	46.4	8
Other	1.8	0	6.1	0	1.2	0
Total	100.0	12	100.0	12	100.0	13[b]

Source: Erewhon National Yearbooks for the years cited.

[a]This one seat was won by a Radical Socialist, who became a member of the Conservative coalition.

[b]Reapportionment in 1910 gave Gotefrith an additional seat in the National Assembly.

the column heads and any spanners used. The rule below a spanner head is exactly as wide as the column headings spanned, and the rules above and below a cut-in head are exactly as wide as the column heads they apply to (usually just the statistical columns, but sometimes the first column as well).

The Stub

12.32   The left-hand column of a table is known as the *stub*. It is a vertical listing of categories or individuals about which information is given in the other columns. It generally carries a heading, though sometimes the table title makes clear what is in the stub. There is no hard and fast rule about placing one type of variable (dependent or independent) in the stub and the other in the column headings, but once the choice is made, it should be applied consistently to all the tables in the same series.

12.33   Consistency within the stub is also important. Items that are logically similar should be treated similarly: Authors, Publishers, Printers, *not* Authors, Publishing concerns, Operates printshop. In a series of tables, the same item should always bear the same name in the stub: the United States, for instance, should not appear as USA in one table and United States in another.

12.34   Items in the stub may form a straight sequential list (as all the states of the Union listed alphabetically) or a classified one (as the states listed by geographic regions). In the latter instance the categories are given as subheadings within the stub. Subheadings may be typed flush left and the items that follow indented two spaces (as in table 12.4). If there are two or more levels of subheads, successive levels are indented successively (see fig. 12.1).

12.35   Stub items are not ordinarily numbered unless they need to be referred to in the text by number, and ditto marks must never be used. Runover lines are indented two spaces more than the maximum regular indention.

12.36   If the word *Total* appears at the foot of the column, it is usually indented two spaces more than the greatest indention above it, and if there are subtotals and a grand total, the grand total is given a further indention (see fig. 12.2).

12.37   Leaders (spaced periods following a stub item) should *not* be added by the author; if they are needed in a complicated table to connect stub items and the rows they apply to, they will be supplied by the publisher.

```
Amphibians
  Frogs and toads
  Caudates
    Newts
    Salamanders
  Caecilians
Reptiles
  Crocodilians
```

Fig. 12.1. Part of a stub in which successive levels of subheadings are indented successively

```
Imports
  Olive oil
  Magnesium
  Petroleum
  Tungsten
    Subtotal
    Total
```

Fig. 12.2. Segment of stub showing indention of subtotal and total headings

12.38 Capitalization of items in the stub of a table is invariably sentence style, and no periods are used at the ends of items.

The Body

12.39 The *body* of a table comprises the vertical columns, typically consisting of figures, to the right of the stub and below the column headings. These columns constitute the real substance of the table, the array of information that the rest of the table merely supports and clarifies. They should accordingly be arranged in as clear and orderly a fashion as can be achieved.

416

12.40 Whenever possible, avoid mixing different kinds of information in one column. For instance, place amounts of money in one column, percentages in another, and information expressed in words in another. If a column heading does not apply to one of the items in the stub, that *cell* (as the intersection is called) should be left blank: it is unnecessary to insert *N.A.,* for "not applicable" or "not available." If there is no datum for a particular cell, insert a dash (two hyphens on the typewriter) or three or more leaders. If the quantity in a cell is zero, however, 0 should be typed.

ALIGNMENT

12.41 Attention should be given to the horizontal and vertical alignment of the information in the columns. Horizontally, each cell aligns with the item in the stub to which it applies. If the stub item occupies more than one line and the column entry one line, align on the last line of the stub item. If both contain more than one line, align first lines. It sometimes happens, as in the tabular listing in 14.47, that single-line items in later columns must align with the last line of an item in a preceding column.

12.42 Vertically, align a column of figures on the decimal points or commas (figures of 1,000 or more should have commas). Dollar signs and percentage signs are aligned, and in a column containing all the same kinds of figures such signs are used only at the top of the column and after any horizontal rule cutting across it. If the table title or column head shows what unit the figures are, the signs are omitted. Mathematical operational signs ($+$, $-$, $<$, $=$, etc.) are aligned if they precede quantities in a column of figures. If all figures in a column begin with a zero to the left of the decimal point, all the zeros (in conservative practice, all but the first and last) may be omitted. When possible, all decimal fractions in a column ought to be carried to the same number of places, but adding zeros may give a false impression of precision.

12.43 In a column consisting of information expressed in words, appearance governs vertical alignment. If all the items are short, they may be centered in the column. Longer items generally look best if they are flush left.

TOTALS, SUBTOTALS, AVERAGES, AND MEANS

12.44 When a table includes totals at the feet of some or all of the columns, either a horizontal rule or a blank line is placed above the totals. If a rule is used, it cuts across the body columns but not the stub, or it may be interrupted between columns. Subtotals, averages, and means are similarly treated, and if the table continues below these figures, another rule or blank line separates them from the continuation.

12.45 Totals at the feet of columns of percentages present special problems. They may be included or not, according to how useful they are to the presentation. When the percentages in the column are based on different Ns, a final percentage based on the total N may be elucidating, and if so it should be included (see table 12.2 and others in that series). When the percentages in a column are all based on the same N (as in table 12.7), the total may also be given, to show that nothing has been left out, or the total may be omitted as unnecessary. If the total is given, the actual total (which may be 99.9% or 100.2% or some other figure) should be given, not a pro forma 100.0%. Discrepancies due to rounding often cause such a total to be slightly more or slightly less than 100%. If totals are off for this reason, a note explaining why should be appended to the table in which the discrepancy first occurs. It need not be repeated in other tables of a series.

Footnotes

12.46 Footnotes to a table are of four general kinds and should appear in this order: (1) source notes, (2) other general notes, (3) notes on specific parts of the table, and (4) notes on level of probability. The footnotes are typed below the body of the table, double-spaced and flush left. An extra blank line should be left between notes.

SOURCE NOTES

12.47 If the table is reproduced without change from another source, proper credit should be given in an unnumbered source note, introduced by the word *Source* or *Sources,* generally set in italic or in caps and small caps.

> Source: Reprinted, by permission of the publisher, from
>
> Ana-Maria Rizzuto, "Freud, God, the Devil, and the Theory of
>
> Object Representation," International Review of Psycho-
>
> Analysis 31 (1976): 165.

If data for a table are not the author's own but are taken from another source, that must also be acknowledged in a source note:

> Source: Data from Michael H. Day, Guide to Fossil Man, 3d
>
> ed. (Chicago: University of Chicago Press, 1977), 291–304.

12.48   Other unnumbered notes, applying to the table as a whole, follow and are introduced by the word *Note(s),* usually set in italic or in caps and small caps. These might include remarks on the reliability of the data presented or on how they were gathered or handled; when practical, such notes should be gathered into one paragraph.

> <u>Note</u>: Since data were not available for all items on all
>
> individuals, there is some disparity in the totals. This
>
> table may be compared with table 14, which presents similar
>
> data for Cincinnati, Ohio.

SPECIFIC NOTES

12.49   For notes on specific parts of a table, superior letters, beginning with *a* in each table, are usually employed as reference marks. They may be used on the column headings, on the stub items, and in the body of the table, but not on the table number or title. Any note applying to the number or title would be a general note and should be so treated. The reference marks are placed on the table in whatever order the reader will find easiest to follow, normally beginning at the upper left and extending across the table and downward, row by row. The same mark may be used on two or more elements if the corresponding note applies to them.

PROBABILITY-LEVEL NOTES

12.50   If a table contains values for which levels of probability are given, a fourth type of note is used, following the other specific notes. By convention, asterisks are used for these notes, both on the value in the body of the table and before the note at the foot. A single asterisk is used for the lowest level of probability, two for the next higher, and so on, with the specific levels given in the notes below:

> $*\underline{p} < .05.$ $**\underline{p} < .01.$ $***\underline{p} < .001.$

These short notes may be set on the same line.

NOTE REFERENCE MARKS

12.51   For a table consisting only of words, superior numbers may be used as reference marks (though even here letters are quite usual); for a table that includes mathematical or chemical equations, a series of arbitrary symbols may be used, because of the danger of mistaking letters or figures for exponents. The series is as follows:

* (asterisk or star), † (dagger), ‡ (double dagger), § (section mark), ‖ (parallels), # (number sign)

When more symbols are needed, these may be doubled and tripled in the same sequence:

, ††, ‡‡, §§, ‖‖, ##, *, †††, ‡‡‡, §§§, ‖‖‖, ###

12.52 The reference marks—letters, numbers, or symbols—for each note to a table are conventionally placed in superior position before the notes themselves, not on the line as numbers generally are in textual notes.

ESTIMATING SIZE AND CORRECTING ODD SHAPES

Dimensions

12.53 In planning a table an author should pay attention to its physical dimensions, making sure that they do not exceed the limits imposed by the printed page. If a table is intended for journal publication, the editor can supply the maximum dimensions of tables for that journal, expressed in terms of typewriter characters for width and a certain number of lines for depth.

12.54 For book publication a maximum width of about 85 characters and a maximum depth of about 60 lines are safe limits for vertical 8-point tables in a book measuring 6 inches by 9 inches. In other words, if a table is typed the ordinary way, in elite type, double-spaced, on $8^{1}/_{2}$-by-11-inch paper, with 1-inch margins, a full-page table in typescript will make a half-page table when set the ordinary way. In counting characters for width, one must allow at least two characters for space between column headings, with no overlapping, and indentions in the stub must be at least two characters. In counting lines for the depth of the table, one must include the table number and title and all blank lines in the count; any horizontal rules count as one line each. For a *broadside* table (one that runs the long way of the page, as does table 12.14), safe maximums are 135 characters in width and 45 lines in depth. Both vertical and broadside tables can continue on another page, of course: depth alone—the number of lines in the table—is seldom a serious problem in fitting a table onto the printed page.

12.55 The significant factor is the width of the table, and this is controlled by the number of columns and the width of the material in each column. If a table is too wide to run vertically, the editor or designer may elect to run it broadside (some journals, however, will not accept broadside tables). If it is too wide to be accommodated as a broadside, it may be run vertically across two facing pages or set in smaller type—perhaps 7- or 6-point instead of 8-point—or both. But this is the limit. There are no further remedies for a table that is too wide except to print it separately on a large sheet of paper and bind it into the book as a fold-out insert. This is an extremely expensive operation, and something no publisher is likely to do except for a very important table in a very important book.

Shape

12.56 The shape of a table, as well as its overall size, is something else an author should keep in mind while drafting tables. No publisher is happy to see a long, narrow table, two or three columns wide and half a page or more deep, or a shallow, wide one that must be printed broadside. Both waste a great deal of expensive space on the printed page. The remedy for a long, skinny table is to *double it up*—run the table in two halves side by side, with the column heads repeated over the second half (see table 12.8). For a wide, shallow table the remedy is applied the other way round—divide the table between columns as close to the table's center as possible and run one half above the other, with the stub items repeated for the lower half (see table 12.9). Another possible solution is to turn the table around, making column heads of the stub items and stub items of the column heads (see table 12.10); if the table turns out to be too long and narrow that way, it can then be doubled up. Table 12.11 shows how three similar tables may be combined into one, or how one very wide, shallow table may be transformed into a more compact, three-tiered table.

SPECIAL TYPES OF TABLES

12.57 Statistical tables and enumerations are the commonest types of tabular matter employed in scholarly work, but there are many other kinds as well. Some of these are illustrated below.

Table 12.8
Relative Contents of Odd Isotopes for Heavy Elements

Element	Z	γ	Element	Z	γ
Sm	62	1.48	W	74	0.505
Gd	64	0.691	Os	76	0.811
Dy	66	0.930	Pt	78	1.160
Eb	68	0.759	Hg	80	0.500
Yb	70	0.601	Pb	82	0.550
Hf	72	0.440			

Table 12.9
Economic Profile of Five Communities, 1988

	Population	Personal Income ($)			Number of Businesses	
		Highest	Lowest	Median	Small	Large
Ashbyville	45,000	250,800	5,000	18,000	121	2
Clayton	18,500	45,320	4,000	15,000	32	0
Morland	65,700	450,000	8,000	21,000	231	3
Onaway	51,000	280,000	7,000	22,000	189	2
Warrington	18,000	75,000	18,500	25,000	28	0

	Business Failures		Individuals on Welfare	Homeless Individuals
	Small Businesses	Large Businesses		
Ashbyville	14	0	450	97
Clayton	8	0	489	59
Morland	12	1	521	82
Onaway	8	0	124	10
Warrington	1	0	18	0

Table 12.10
Economic Profile of Five Communities, 1988

	Ashbyville	Clayton	Morland	Onaway	Warrington
Population	45,000	18,500	65,700	51,000	18,000
Personal income ($)					
Highest	250,800	45,320	450,000	280,000	75,000
Lowest	5,000	4,000	8,000	7,000	18,500
Median	18,000	15,000	21,000	22,000	25,000
Number of businesses					
Small	121	32	231	189	28
Large	2	0	3	2	0
Business failures					
Small businesses	14	8	12	8	1
Large businesses	0	0	1	0	0
Individuals on welfare	450	489	521	124	18
Homeless individuals	97	59	82	10	0

Matrix

12.58   A matrix is a tabular structure designed to show mutual or reciprocal relationships within a group of individuals, whether human beings, animals (as in table 12.12), concepts, or whatever. In a matrix the column headings and the stub items are identical, and there may or may not be totals for the vertical columns and horizontal rows. A matrix works best with an absolute minimum of ruling.

Table 12.11
Indexes of Class Organization via Trade Unions

	1900	1910	1920	1930	1940	1950	1960	1970	1975
			A. Unionized Manual Workers/Manual Workers						
Denmark	13.9	16.2	37.0	33.8	44.3	54.4	64.3	72.1	77.7
Norway	—	—	—	—	—	—	—	65.3	64.5
Sweden[a]	8.7	12.2	32.4	41.7	64.3	75.2	83.4	89.6	92.3
Germany[b]	5.7	13.8	45.2	25.8	—	35.8	39.8	40.4	44.4
France	—	11.0[c]	38.0	9.5	45.0[d]	23.0[e]	17.3[f]	31.0[g]	31.0[h]
			B. Manual Workers in the Largest Federation/Manual Workers Unionized						
Denmark	76.8	81.0	73.0	72.6	93.3	96.3	95.6	98.5	98.5
Norway	23.9	100.0[i]	100.0	100.0	100.0	100.0	100.0	97.2	97.4
Sweden[j]	100.0	99.4	92.5	95.6	97.5	98.5	98.8	98.6	99.0
Germany[k]	80.2	82.8	85.8	85.4	—	100.0	96.5	98.5	98.5
France	—	36.4[l]	—	—	—	—	—	64.5[m]	71.0[n]
			C. Manual Workers in the Largest Federation/Manual Workers[o]						
Denmark	10.7	13.1	27.0	24.5	41.3	52.4	61.5	71.0	76.5
Norway	—	—	—	—	—	—	—	63.5	62.8
Sweden	8.7	12.1	30.0	39.9	63.0	74.1	82.4	88.3	91.4
Germany	4.6	11.4	38.8	22.0	—	35.8	38.4	39.8	43.7
France	—	4.0	—	—	—	—	—	20.0	22.0

Sources: For Danish, Swedish, and German union density and Danish pre-1950, Norwegian pre-1970, and Swedish and German pre-1960 concentration, the source is Bain and Price (1980). For recent concentration in Denmark, Norway, and Germany, Visser (1983). For France: Mitchell and Stearns (1971:68) for 1906; Sellier (1976) as cited by Adam (1983:45) for 1920, 1930, 1936, 1954, and 1962; Adam (1983:46) for 1970 and 1978.

[a] Until 1950 obtained by dividing LO and SAC members as given by Bain and Price (1980) by the number of manual workers as given by Przeworski et al. (1978). The 1950 figure derived in the same way would have been 77.8.

[b] Until 1933 these numbers slightly underestimate the total, since they do not include minor and ephemeral unions.

[c] 1906.

[d] 1936.

[e] 1954.

[f] 1962.

[g] Survey response.

[h] 1978 survey response.

[i] Slightly overstated.

[j] Members of LO divided by members of LO and SAC. These numbers are slightly overstated because LO includes some nonmanual workers.

[k] Until 1933 these numbers slightly overstate the degree of concentration because they do not include minor and peripheral unions.

[l] 1906.

[m] Survey response.

[n] 1978 survey response.

[o] Obtained by multiplying A and B.

Table 12.12
Observations of Mutual Grooming by Age and Sex Classes

	ANIMALS GROOMED					
ANIMALS GROOMING	Silver-backed male	Black-backed male	Female	Juvenile	Infant	TOTAL
Silver-backed male	0	0	0	0	3	3
Black-backed male	0	0	0	0	0	0
Female	0	1	5	13	76	95
Juvenile	1	1	9	10	12	33
Infant	0	0	2	0	1	3
TOTAL	1	2	16	23	92	134

Table in Words

12.59 A very complex discussion can often be simplified and lucidly illustrated by a "visual aid" such as table 12.13. Alignment of the items in such a table is discussed in 12.41 and 12.43.

Table 12.13
Role-Style Differentiae in the Lewin, Lippitt, and White "Group Atmosphere" Studies

Authoritarian	Democratic	Laissez-faire
All determination of policy by leader	All policies a matter of group discussion and decision, encouraged and assisted by the leader	Complete freedom for group or individual decision, with a minimum of leader participation
Techniques and activity steps dictated by the authority, one at a time, so that future steps were uncertain to a large degree	Activity perspective gained during discussion period. General steps to group goal sketched, and when technical advice was needed the leader suggested two or more alternative procedures from which choice could be made	Various materials supplied by leader, who made it clear that he would supply information when asked. He took no other part in work discussion
Leader usually dictated the task and companion of each member	Members were free to work with whomever they chose, and division of tasks was left to the group	Complete nonparticipation of the leader
Leader tended to be "personal" in his praise and criticism of each member's work; remained aloof from active group participation except when demonstrating	Leader was "objective" in his praise and criticism and tried to be a regular group member in spirit without doing too much work	Leader did not comment on member activities unless questioned, did not attempt to appraise or regulate the course of events

Genealogical Table

12.60   A pedigree (not illustrated here) is a simple table showing the ancestry of one individual—human being or purebred animal—in a branching array of names. No attempt is made to avoid repetition: if the same individual appears twice among the eight great-grandparents or sixteen great-great-grandparents, the name is simply repeated. A genealogical table like table 12.14 is considerably more complex. Such a table attempts to show important relationships within a family or several families by means of branching and connecting lines. If possible, names are not repeated. Equals signs show marriages or liaisons, and usually all children are listed or noted. A good genealogical table takes careful planning so that it shows the intended relationships without crossing lines and stays within a reproducible shape and size.

Genetic Table

12.61   Somewhat analogous to pedigrees and genealogical tables are the genetic tables designed to show the results of crossbreeding in plants or animals according to Mendelian principles (see table 12.15). Here multiplication signs indicate the crosses, and symbols and abbreviations show the genetic makeup of the individual.

EDITING TABLES

12.62   Editing a series of tables may involve regularizing capitalization, spelling, and punctuation; adding or deleting rules; verifying column totals and footnote symbols; making sure the table and text do not contradict one another; and so on. Often the tables require little more than markup for typesetting. If the author is unfamiliar with the principles of good tabular presentation, however, the manuscript editor may have to intervene more extensively, showing the author, for example, how the table might be recast to make it more accessible or to make it fit on the page. The commonest errors are probably inconsistency—as, for example, when a given variable is listed in the column headings in one table and in the stub in another—and constructing sprawling or misshapen tables that are difficult or impossible to reproduce in type. Often a table that is technically acceptable may still be improved in appearance and made to occupy less space with no loss of content or impact. The editor may wish to review the entire set of tables with this in mind before turning to the job of markup. The editor will also want to check all tables for relevance and freedom from duplication. Tables are expensive to set, and if any can be eliminated or combined, this should be suggested to the author.

Table 12.14
The Family of Galla Placidia Augusta

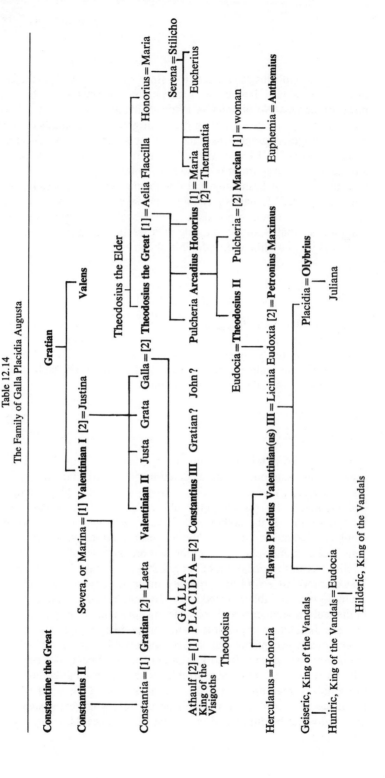

NOTE: Stemmata are simplified. Emperors are shown in boldface type.

Table 12.15
Mendelian Cross: Cocker Spaniel and Basenji

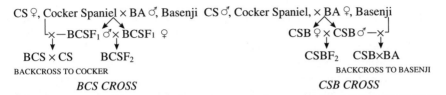

Note: The basic plan was to repeat each of the two crosses with four matings and obtain two litters from each mating. Because of deaths among the cocker spaniel females, replication was completed only three times in the BCS cross.

12.63 It is mainly in bookwork that an editor or designer has any latitude concerning the type format of a set of tables. Every journal that accepts tables (not all do) has its own style for them, as for other editorial elements, and this style is seldom departed from. In books, tables are usually set in the same typeface as the body of the book—and in a book containing a great many tables a typeface that works well for tabular setting (like Times Roman) is often chosen for the whole book. Most tables are set in 8-point type, with footnotes (and sometimes column headings) in 7-point.

Table Numbers, Titles, and Headings

12.64 The table number and title may be set in the same size type as the body of the table or in a contrasting size. A subtitle may be set off with a colon or by the use of a contrasting type (as italic with a roman title). All headings—column heads, spanners, and cut-in heads—are treated alike as to type size and style, usually 8-point roman, but 7-point can be used if space must be conserved. Apart from these conventions, there are a good many options open to the designer or editor in the treatment of these elements (the same treatment is usually given to both the title and the table headings).

12.65 In alignment, the choice is between flush style (normally flush left) and centered style. If flush-left style is adopted, the table number and the title are aligned with the left edge of the table, and each column heading is aligned on the left margin of the space allotted to it. (As noted earlier, spanner heads and cut-in heads must be centered over the columns they apply to, even when flush style is used for the column heads.) If centered style is used, the table number and title are centered, one above the other, over the whole table, and each column head is centered within its column. With centered style, column heads of different lengths (running to varying numbers of lines) usually "float" within the vertical space given them, whereas with flush style the last lines ordinarily align across the page, but there is no set rule for this.

12.66   In type style, roman is usual, and there are two main options for titles and column headings: caps and small caps or caps and lowercase. Both work well. Caps and small caps are more formal, caps and lowercase more informal and more modern. The word TABLE may be set in full caps, but titles and headings should never be: full caps take up too much room and are hard to read. For some kinds of tables italic or boldface may work for titles; but both are hard to read in large doses and difficult to handle aesthetically, so it is better not to use them for column heads. The expression *N,* which appears frequently in headings, must always be set either as an italic capital or as a roman small capital (*N* or ɴ) unless it refers to a subgroup, when italic lowercase is used.

12.67   In capitalizing titles and headings, one can choose between the traditional headline style (Popular Support for Educational Reform in the Late Twentieth Century) and the more "contemporary" sentence style (Popular support for educational reform in the late twentieth century). The former works with any type style, but the latter looks best with caps and lowercase.

The Stub and the Body

12.68   Fewer options are open in the design of the stub and body of a table. Both are set in the same size and style of type, normally 8-point roman caps and lowercase. Capitalization is sentence style in both.

12.69   In the stub, subheads are sometimes set in italic and may be centered in the column or set flush left. The style in which the manuscript is typed need not be followed in typesetting if an alternative is preferable. In flush-left style, stub items are usually indented one em under the subhead. Runovers in stub items are indented one em from where the item begins; subtotals and totals are each indented one further em.

12.70   With two or more levels of subheads in the stub, it is often better not to rely solely on indention for distinguishing levels, or the stub may grow disproportionately wide. The top level may be centered and the second level flush left, or different type may be used (small caps, italic, roman) and everything kept flush left. Another solution is to use cut-in heads for the top-level subheads (in this case the rules above and below the cut-in heads extend across the stub as well as the body of the table). When stub items are long, space can often be saved by not indenting the runovers; extra space must then be left between items.

12.71   Watch for the alignment of stub items with the rows they govern and the vertical alignment of the elements within the columns. These considerations are discussed (from the author's point of view) in earlier sections of this chapter (12.41–43). If leaders seem necessary to make alignment clear, they may be used after stub items. Leaders may also be used in empty cells, but centered em dashes are now more usual.

Footnotes

12.72 Footnotes are normally set one size smaller than the body of a table (e.g., 7-point with an 8-point table). Long notes run the full width of the table, but short notes may be set two or more to the line. Notes may be set paragraph style or flush left, and in the latter case a point or two of leading should be used between notes. The words *Source(s)* and *Note(s)* are traditionally distinguished typographically from the note that follows, either by caps and small caps or by italic caps and lowercase (SOURCE; *Source*).

12.73 As noted earlier (12.52), reference marks on specific notes are conventionally set in superior position, and the series starts over for each table. (Occasionally an inexperienced author will integrate table notes and text notes. If this happens, the editor must separate them.)

Rules

12.74 Some of the ruling in a table is functional, but much of it is aesthetic. The rule below a spanner head is functional: it makes clear just which columns of the table are governed by the head. It is also possible to show the relation by adding space to the right and left of the columns affected, but it is easier to accomplish with a rule. A rule is generally needed between the column heads and the body of the table. A rule above a row of totals is traditional, but a blank line works just as well, with another blank line below the totals if the table continues. The full-width rules at the top and bottom of a table are also traditional, but aesthetically they are harder to dispense with than internal rules. Individual tables in a series often vary greatly in size, shape, and configuration, and the only thing tying them together visually is the pair of rules at top and bottom of each. The rules in a conventional table are usually half-point rules, but any size consistent with the design of a book can be used, especially for rules that are nonfunctional.

Copyfitting Large Tables

12.75 An important part of an editor's job is to foresee production problems and solve them before the tables get as far as the typesetting stage. The commonest problem is size—the table that is too big for the space available. Tables are generally set to fit within the *type page* area (see 19.44) of the publication. If the outer (fore-edge) margin is fairly wide, a pica or two is often stolen from it to accommodate a wide vertical table, but the inner (back) margin is usually too narrow to permit encroachment. For a full-page table, the area usually occupied by the running head at the top of the page may be utilized (running heads are not set on pages with full-page tables), and when necessary, the deep bottom (tail) margin may be encroached upon. Some of the ways of handling very wide tables have been discussed in connection with compiling tables (12.54–55), as have techniques for dealing with tables that are oddly shaped (12.56).

WIDE TABLES

12.76 If a table looks too wide, the first thing to do is measure its width in characters. Count every character in the widest stub item, including spaces, and in the columns or column headings, whichever is wider, and allow two characters for each space between columns. If the total is 100 and your type page allows 85 characters for a table, some squeezing is in order. (If you do not know the allowable width in characters, you can multiply the width of the type page in picas by three for the equivalent in typewriter or computer characters: most 8-point faces set about three characters per pica.)

12.77 The requisite number of characters may sometimes be reduced by running some of the stub items over to additional lines, by dividing words in the column headings, or by introducing abbreviations. A few characters of excess width may be accommodated by setting column heads one size smaller. Consider, also, whether the stub can be narrowed by any of the devices discussed above (12.70). The type in the column headings can be set on edge, so they read up the page rather than across, but this is undesirable if any other solution is available, because vertical heads are hard to read and hard to set. Table 12.16 demonstrates a method of avoiding long, clumsy column heads by using numbers and relegating the text of the heads to a general note.

12.78 If the number of characters across a table greatly exceeds the available width of the type page, the table will have to run broadside, or vertically on facing pages, as described earlier (12.55). Measuring for this kind of placement can be done the same way, but with different limits on the allowable space. Remember that in a broadside table the headings must read *up* the page, not down, whether the table occurs on a verso page or a recto.

Table 12.16 Timing of Socialist Entry into Elections and of Suffrage Reforms

Country	(1)	(2)	(3)	(4)	(5)	(6)	(7)
Austria	1889	1897	1907	—	1919	—	—
Belgium	1885[a]	1894	1894	45.7	1948	38.4	22.2
Denmark	1878[a]	1884	1849	28.1[b]	1915	24.6	23.9
Finland	1899	1907	1906	22.0	1906	—	22.0
France	1879	1893	1876	36.5[c]	1946	33.9	24.9
Germany	1867	1871	1871	25.5	1919	34.2[d]	34.0[d]
Italy	1892[a]	—	1913	—	1945	—	—
Netherlands	1878	1888	1917	—	1917	—	—
Norway	1887	1903	1898	34.1	1913	27.7	28.8
Spain	1879	1910	1907	—	1933	—	—
Sweden	1889	1896	1907	28.9	1921	35.0	37.0
Switzerland	1887	1897	1848	—	—	—	—
United Kingdom	1893[a]	1892[e]	1918	—	1928	—	—

Note: Column headings are as follows: (1) Socialist Party formed; (2) first candidates elected to Parliament; (3) universal male suffrage; (4) workers as a proportion of the electorate in the first elections after universal male suffrage; (5) universal suffrage; (6) workers as a proportion of the electorate in the last election before extension of franchise to women; and (7) workers as a proportion of the electorate in the first election after the extension.

[a]Major socialist or workers parties existed earlier and dissolved or were repressed.
[b]In 1884, approximate.
[c]In 1902.
[d]Under different borders.
[e]Keir Hardie elected.

LONG TABLES

12.79   A very long table of normal width is easier to deal with, because it can be continued on successive pages. There are some conventions for setting continued tables, however, that should be observed.

12.80   Continued lines are used as needed, the one at the foot of a page reading, perhaps,

> *Continued on next page*

and the one at the top of the next page reading, for example,

> Table 14—*Continued*

12.81   For a vertical table the column heads are repeated on each page, but the title is not. For a broadside table the column headings are repeated only on the verso page, and the columns of the table jump over the back margins (the gutter) to continue on the recto. *Continued* lines are then placed only where they are needed.

12.82   In a continued table containing columns of figures representing money, with totals at the end, it is usual to strike subtotals at the foot of every page except the last. These subtotals appear below a rule or a blank line opposite a stub entry *Carried forward*. At the head of the next page they are repeated opposite a stub entry *Brought forward*. The subtotals and forwarding notations are ordinarily added by the typesetter, but the author and the editor should check them at the proof stage.

12.83 Footnotes in a continued table must be divided up according to what they refer to. Source notes and other general notes are placed at the foot of the first page or two-page spread. Specific notes are preferably placed on the pages to which they apply, or if need be they can be gathered at the end of the whole table.

12.84 In marking up a long table for typesetting, the editor should circle (meaning "do not set") the repeated column headings on all manuscript pages but the first, since the page breaks will probably not come at these points. A note to the typesetter should explain what headings and continued lines are wanted on the runover parts of the table.

13 Mathematics in Type

INTRODUCTION

13.1   Mathematics has long been known in the printing trade as *difficult,* or *penalty,* copy because it is slower, more difficult, and more expensive to set in type than any other kind of copy normally occurring in books and journals. The uninformed author, by exercising poor judgment in selecting notation and by ignoring precepts of good manuscript preparation, can add enormously to the cost of setting mathematical material. Book and journal editors are continually faced with this problem and may occasionally have to reject a manuscript for such nonmathematical considerations.

13.2   This chapter will describe some of the common problems that arise in setting technical material and will suggest ways in which these problems can be solved or circumvented. It is intended for authors unfamiliar with techniques of typesetting and for copyeditors not blessed with a mathematical background. For more on typesetting and printing in general see chapter 19.

COMPOSITION

13.3   The advent of sophisticated phototypesetting systems, including both photomechanical and CRT systems, has revolutionized the setting of mathematical copy in recent years. Many expressions and arrangements of expressions that formerly were impossible or very difficult to set are now relatively easy to achieve. Not every manuscript involving mathematical expressions is composed by such an advanced system, however, and authors and editors should have some idea what to expect of the particular typesetting system employed for the manuscript in hand.

13.4   Typesetting systems can be thought of as existing on four levels of sophistication in mathematical capabilities. Least sophisticated are the systems designed for setting nontechnical matter. These include hot-metal systems (now infrequently used) and photomechanical composition systems (also called filmset systems) that are equipped only with "reader" fonts—fonts intended for ordinary book and job work. Also included at this level of sophistication is the ordinary office typewriter. Mathematical copy of an elementary sort can be set with such a system if it is to be printed by offset lithography (as almost everything is nowadays), but only with a good deal of handwork on the reproduction proofs or the typescript. In typewriter work of this sort, superior and inferior expressions necessarily appear in the same type size as the expressions to which they are attached.

13.5   On the second level of sophistication are math typewriters and computerized word processors equipped with math programs. An example of the math typewriter is the IBM Selectric machine equipped with an assortment of type elements capable of typing many of the symbols and alphabets used in mathematics, as well as an element for typing straight matter. A mathematics element makes available almost all commonly used symbols, but oversize characters, like large summation and integral signs, as well as any esoteric characters, must be drawn in on the typescript. Typewriter composition is not as efficient as typesetting—a book page of math printed from copy prepared on the typewriter will contain scarcely more than half as much material as a similar typeset page—but, when costs must be kept down, it offers an attractive alternative to the more sophisticated (and expensive) methods described in 13.6–8. Rapidly replacing the math typewriter are computer systems designed specifically for mathematical and tabular work. One such system currently in use is the UNIX platform with its math composition programs TEX and TROFF. This and other systems offer nearly the same range and variety of symbols and nearly the same level of sophistication in formatting as that offered by the most advanced typesetting systems. Printouts from these computer systems are aesthetically superior to those from math typewriters but still inferior to proof prepared by top-of-the-line typesetting systems. Some typesetting companies can enhance the resolution of output from computer files, although the procedure is more costly than using the original printout as camera-ready copy. The enhancement is nevertheless much less expensive than the typesetting methods discussed in the following paragraphs.

13.6 On the third level is the classic hot-metal Four-Line Mathematics system of the Monotype Corporation. This system produces elegant work using a very wide range of symbols and alphabets. A good deal of the makeup can be done by the operator at the keyboard, but most displayed equations must be set twice to get the spacing right. Rules and very large (more than 14-point) braces, brackets, summation signs, integrals, and so on must be inserted by hand. Corrections are relatively easy to make in the metal type because the Monotype system produces individual pieces of type that can be picked out by hand "on the stone" and replaced by the correct characters. The chief disadvantages of Monotype are that fewer and fewer typesetting houses offer it, and that the production of new, unlisted characters is extremely expensive and time consuming.

13.7 Photomechanical typesetting systems have largely taken over mathematical setting at this level of sophistication. These systems use film negatives of type characters to produce a positive photographic image on paper. This is used as a "repro proof," or camera-ready copy, for printing by the offset method (see 19.5–6, 19.47). Photomechanical typesetting generally requires the mathematical copy be set twice to get alignment and spacing correct. Corrections are made by resetting all or part of an equation and pasting the correct version over the incorrect one. Film negatives of new characters are fairly easy to produce, although there may be a delay of a few weeks before they are available.

13.8 On the fourth level of sophistication are the CRT typesetters, electronic typesetting machines that, from information stored digitally in a computer, generate type characters on the face of a cathode-ray tube, from which they are transferred photographically to a paper printout. Systems employing electronic typesetters are only as sophisticated as the computer programs used to drive them, but some of these are very sophisticated indeed. For example, the PENTA mathematics program is capable of making a wide variety of decisions regarding spacing and alignment and can handle characters of any size. Equations need be keyboarded only once. New characters, provided suitable copy is available, can be converted to digital form and added to the type font with little trouble.

13.9   Most mathematics composition is expensive. Older systems were expensive, and the advent of electronic setting has made little difference in the cost of setting a page of complicated mathematics. More operator and computer time, both of which are costly, are required for mathematical than for almost any other kind of composition. Difficult notational expressions, which will be discussed later, should be converted to simpler forms whenever possible, and authors should consider expressing some proofs conceptually, when that can be done without diminishing argument or communication, rather than computationally, in fully notational form.

THE PROBLEM OF SIGNS AND SYMBOLS

13.10   Whatever the mode of composition employed, setting high-level mathematics is bound to present some problems with signs and symbols, problems that the author and editor should face as early as possible. Typesetters who specialize in mathematics have fonts containing all the traditional characters needed for this kind of work, and many of the more specialized ones, but no fonts contain all the possible variants. The number of special signs and symbols is almost limitless, and new ones are constantly being introduced. Typesetters are understandably reluctant to make available every new character, since many of them will be used only rarely, and generating a totally new character always requires additional time and expense, even though the process is more easily accomplished by the more advanced electronic system.

The List of Symbols and Special Characters

13.11   Before editing begins it may be advisable, depending on the typesetter and the publisher's knowledge of the typesetter's resources, to prepare a list of all mathematical symbols and special characters in the manuscript. This is preferably done by the author but may also be done by the editor. The page numbers of first and last occurrences of unusual or new characters should be indicated in such a list, along with an estimate of how many times each is used.

13.12   If such a list is made, a copy should be given to the production controller, who will check with the typesetter to make sure the necessary characters are available. If some are not, the author may be asked to use some more accessible forms, but if that is impossible the typesetter must be asked to obtain or generate the characters needed.

Substitutions for Easier Composition

13.13 It may also be advisable for the editor to suggest to the author other substitutions that facilitate composition. A number of "embellished," or accented, characters are readily available, including, for example, *à, ä, ā, ă, ã, â, é, è*. Embellishments under an ordinary italic letter may be troublesome to set—*a̱ a̤, a̲, g̲*—as may embellished characters from other alphabets such as roman or Greek. Frequently some easily set character may be substituted, such as a character with the embellishment at one side or the other: *a*↑, *a*↓, *a'*, *a''*, *'a*, *"a*, *a**, *a*†, *a#*, and so forth. It is important to confer with the typesetter before making final choices.

13.14 Mathematicians often employ notation in handwriting to make distinctions between characters that are otherwise distinguished in type. One of these devices is "blackboard bold," in which part of the letter is doubled when it stands for what would be boldface in type, as $\mathbb{R}$ for **R**. An author should not ask for letters of this kind in type but should specify boldface, sans serif, or something else. Blackboard bold should be confined to the classroom.

Unusual Type Sizes

13.15 Most mathematics work is set in 10-point type, the size in which the greatest number of mathematical symbols are available. If a book is planned for a type size other than 10 point, or if it includes reduced matter (such as extracts or footnotes) containing mathematical expressions, the editor should, at an early stage, check on the availability of the special characters and symbols involved. Although odd sizes of type present no problem in filmset or electronic composition, they frequently do in hot metal, and they should ordinarily be avoided. What would be a footnote can be incorporated in the text, either parenthetically or as a "Remark." The latter device is now widely accepted by mathematicians and warmly appreciated by editors. Bibliographic footnotes can be eliminated by citing the author and date of the work (see 16.3–31) and including a reference list at the end of the book or article.

MANUSCRIPT PREPARATION

13.16 The author who is preparing a manuscript for a specific publisher should obtain from the publisher either a style sheet or, perhaps, another book that can be followed generally for style. The more care given to manuscript preparation, the fewer problems there will be in processing the manuscript—and the more likely it is that the manuscript will be accepted for publication. No manuscript has ever been accepted simply because it was clean and well prepared, but some have been rejected because they were sloppy and poorly prepared.

13.17 In general, the more of the manuscript that can be prepared on a typewriter or computer the better. If the manuscript is prepared on a typewriter, however, even on a math typewriter, it may not be possible for the author to type all the copy. Some signs and symbols, especially the Greek, German, script, and sans serif characters, and newer or more esoteric symbols, may have to be drawn by hand. Neatness is very important here, for a poorly prepared manuscript with special characters drawn in an illegible hand can become, after the addition of editorial changes and typographical instructions, a nightmare for compositor, proofreader, and editor. Also, in checking proofs, the author will be faced with a great many errors to correct—and perhaps heavy alterations charges.

13.18 Manuscript for mathematical papers and books should be double-spaced on 8½-by-11-inch white paper, with 1¼-inch margins for text and 2-inch margins for display work. If handwritten equations or symbols are to be inserted in the typescript, generous space should be allowed for them. Since marginal notes to the typesetter nearly always have to be added by the editor, ample margins are particularly important in mathematics.

Style and General Usage

13.19 Obviously the author and editor will give careful attention to matters of style, usage, sense, meaning, clarity, accuracy, and consistency. For example, 0.2×10^5 should not be used in one place and 0.02×10^6 in another unless there is a reason. Decimal fractions in text should be preceded by a zero—0.25, not .25—except for quantities (such as probabilities) that never exceed unity.

13.20 All copy, including the equations, should be in good sentence form and should "read" as clearly and grammatically as any other kind of copy. The signs are substitutes for words: $A + B < C$ reads "A plus B is less than C."

13.21 Qualifying expressions should be couched in a consistent style. That preferred by the University of Chicago Press is as illustrated:

Therefore $a + b = c$, where $a = 2$.

(When the equation is displayed, "Therefore" and the qualifying clause are often in the text, not the display.)

PUNCTUATION

13.22   Without punctuation in mathematical copy, it may be difficult to tell where one sentence ends and another begins, especially when there is heavy use of signs and symbols. Punctuation often must be added after displayed equations. This press prefers to see mathematical copy punctuated, but it accepts copy without punctuation, so long as the author avoids ambiguity.

13.23   In elisions, if commas or operational signs are required they should come after each term and after the three ellipsis dots if a final term follows them. For example:

$$x_1, x_2, \ldots, x_n \qquad \text{not} \qquad x_1, x_2, \ldots x_n$$
$$x_1 + x_2 + \cdots + x_n \qquad \text{not} \qquad x_1 + x_2 + \cdots x_n$$
$$y = 0, 1, 2, \ldots \qquad \text{not} \qquad y = 0, 1, 2 \ldots$$

In the second example above note that centered ellipsis dots have been used between operational signs, for appearance' sake. Centered dots may also be used in an expression like

$$a_1 a_2 \cdots a_n$$

for the same reason. It is never incorrect to use on-the-line ellipsis dots, however, and they are always used in nonmathematical text.

NUMERATION

13.24   Sections, theorems, definitions, lemmas, equations, and the like may be numbered, and if the numeration system is not too cumbersome, this offers a convenient and space-saving method of cross-referring. The system preferred by most mathematicians is double numeration: that is, chapter number followed, for example, by equation number, starting with number 1 for the equations in each chapter.

13.25   There is little point in numbering all displayed equations. Usually only those that are referred to elsewhere should be numbered. All numbered equations should be displayed. For example:

Wrong
Hence it is apparent that $abc = xyz$. $\hfill (1.1)$

Right
Hence it is apparent that
$$abc = xyz. \hfill (1.1)$$

The displayed equation is either centered on the line or given a standard indention from the left margin (as in this chapter). The equation number, enclosed in parentheses to avoid misreading, is usually placed flush right, but it is not uncommon for it to be placed flush left. In cross-

Therefore $F_x^n \subset G \cap B_n$ and $F_x^n \cap B_m = \emptyset$ for $n \neq m$, since $b \in G$.

(null set)   *("element of")*

The temperature function is

$$u(x, t) = \frac{2}{L} \sum_1^\infty \exp\left(-\frac{u^2 \pi^2 k t}{L^2}\right) \sin \frac{n\pi x}{L} \int_0^L f(x') \sin \frac{n\pi x'}{L} \, dx'. \qquad (3.1)$$

An $m \times n$ matrix $\underset{\sim}{A}$ over a field F is a rectangular array of mn elements $a_j^{\,i}$ in F, arranged in m rows and n columns:

$$\underset{\sim}{A} = \begin{bmatrix} a_1^{\,1} & a_2^{\,1} & \cdots & a_n^{\,1} \\ a_1^{\,2} & a_2^{\,2} & \cdots & a_n^{\,2} \\ \cdot & \cdot & \cdots & \cdot \\ a_1^{\,m} & a_2^{\,m} & \cdots & a_n^{\,m} \end{bmatrix}.$$

("greater than")

The modulus of the correlation coefficient of X_1 and X_2 is

(rho) $\rho = |\langle X_1, X_2 \rangle| / \|X_1\| \, \|X_2\|$ for $\|X_1\| > 0$, $1 = 1, 2.$

(angle brackets)   *(ell)*   *(ell)*

Hence

$$\frac{\partial F}{\partial x} = \lim_{\Delta x \to 0} \frac{\Delta F}{\Delta x} = \lim_{\Delta x \to 0} \frac{1}{\Delta x} \left\{ \int_{a,b}^{x+\Delta x, y} P \, dx + Q \, dy \right.$$

$$\left. - \int_{a,b}^{x,y} P \, dx + Q \, dy \right\} + P + Q.$$

From equation (2.4), where $M = [(a + b - 1)/(k + 1)]$, we obtain

(alpha)   *(lc Gr. mu)*

$$\alpha_\nu(a + b) = (-1)^\nu \sum' \frac{(i_1 + \cdots + i_M)!}{i_1! \cdots i_M!} \prod_{h=1}^M (-1)^{i_h} \binom{a + b - kh - 1}{h}^{i_h},$$

the sum being extended over all sets $(i_1, \cdots, i_M)$.

To summarize our findings:

(lc Gr. eta)

$$v^*(z, t_n) \geq H_{\delta_1} [v(x) + o(1)] - 2\eta \geq v(z) + o(1) + \eta^{1/2} o(1).$$

(lc oh)   *(lc oh)*   *(cap oh)*

Fig. 13.1. An example of a well-prepared page of mathematical copy with suggested marking for clarity. This page is not intended to make mathematical sense, but merely to illustrate good preparation of mathematical copy.

Therefore $F_z{}^n \subseteq G \cap B_n$ and $F_z{}^n \cap B_m = \emptyset$ for $n \neq m$, since $b \in G$. The temperature function is

$$u(x, t) = \frac{2}{L} \sum_1^\infty \exp\left(-\frac{u^2 \pi^2 kt}{L^2}\right) \sin \frac{n\pi x}{L}$$

$$\times \int_0^L f(x') \sin \frac{n\pi x'}{L} \, dx' . \qquad (3.1)$$

An $m \times n$ matrix $\mathbf{A}$ over a field F is a rectangular array of mn elements $a_j{}^i$ in F, arranged in m rows and n columns:

$$\mathbf{A} = \begin{bmatrix} a_1{}^1 & a_2{}^1 & \cdots & a_n{}^1 \\ a_1{}^2 & a_2{}^2 & \cdots & a_n{}^2 \\ \cdot & \cdot & \cdots & \cdot \\ a_1{}^m & a_2{}^m & \cdots & a_n{}^m \end{bmatrix} .$$

The modulus of the correlation coefficient of X_1 and X_2 is

$$\rho = |\langle X_1, X_2 \rangle| / \|X_1\| \, \|X_2\| \quad \text{for} \quad \|X_l\| > 0 , \quad l = 1, 2 .$$

Hence

$$\frac{\partial F}{\partial x} = \lim_{\Delta x \to 0} \frac{\Delta F}{\Delta x} = \lim_{\Delta x \to 0} \frac{1}{\Delta x} \left\{ \int_{a,b}^{x+\Delta x, y} P \, dx + Q \, dy \right.$$

$$\left. - \int_{a,b}^{x,y} P \, dx + Q \, dy \right\} + P + Q .$$

From equation (2.4), where $M = [(a + b - 1)/(k + 1)]$, we obtain

$$a_\nu(a + b) = (-1)^\nu \sum{}' \frac{(i_1 + \ldots + i_M)!}{i_1! \ldots i_M!}$$

$$\times \prod_{h=1}^M (-1)^{i_h} \left(\frac{a + b - kh - 1}{h}\right)^{i_h} ,$$

the sum being extended over all sets $(i_1, \ldots, i_M)$.

To summarize our findings:

$$v^*(z, t_n) \geq H_{\delta_1}[v(x) + o(1)] - 2\eta \geq v(z) + o(1) + \eta^{1/2} O(1).$$

Fig. 13.2. The page of manuscript shown in figure 13.1 set in type

references, equation numbers are enclosed in parentheses to match the marginal enumerations (see figs. 13.1 and 13.2).

SIGNS OF AGGREGATION, OR FENCES

13.26   The preferred order for enclosures is as follows:

$$\{ [(\{ [(\quad)] \})] \}$$

These signs of aggregation, or "fences," may be supplemented with double brackets when needed:

$$[\![\{ [([\![\{ [(\quad)] \}]\!])] \}]\!]$$

Angle brackets, bars, and double bars often carry special mathematical significance and should not be used to supplement the usual series shown above.

13.27   Note that when using fences in mathematics, one starts with parentheses and works from the inside out,

$$[(x + y)^2 z],$$

just the opposite of the practice in ordinary text, where one works from the outside in.

Difficult Expressions

13.28   "Difficult" terms and equations may occur both in displayed work and in text ("in line"). Such expressions in line require the lines of type to be spread apart to accommodate them. This makes for an unsightly text and, when the setting is in hot metal, an expensive one, because of the handwork involved. Some mathematical journals do not allow any difficult expressions in line, and a few go so far as to disallow any equations whatever in line. As examples of difficult expressions, the terms $\sum_{n=0}^{\infty}$ and $\prod_{n=0}^{\infty}$ require leading above and below the line, but $\Sigma_{n=0}^{\infty}$ and $\Pi_{n=0}^{\infty}$ can be substituted without any change of meaning.

FRACTIONS

13.29   If an equation like $\dfrac{x}{a} + \dfrac{y}{b} = 1$ occurs in line rather than displayed, it is advisable to use the solidus (/): $x/a + y/b = 1$. The use of the solidus can make it much easier for the compositor to set some fractions: for subscripts and superscripts, solidus fractions should always be used.

for   use

$$\frac{\dfrac{x}{a} + \dfrac{y}{4}}{a} \qquad \frac{x}{a} + \frac{y}{4/a} \text{ or } x/a + ay/4$$

$$\frac{\dfrac{A}{B}}{\sqrt{A - \dfrac{B}{C}}} \qquad \frac{A/B}{(A - B/C)^{1/2}} \text{ or } (A/B)/(A - B/C)^{1/2}$$

$$(x^2 + y^2)^{\frac{a^2 + b^2}{2ab}} \qquad (x^2 + y^2)^{(a^2 + b^2)/2ab}$$

$$\int_0^{\frac{a}{b}} \qquad \int_0^{a/b}$$

$$\prod_{\frac{a}{b}}^{\infty} \qquad \prod_{a/b}^{\infty}$$

Note that parentheses must often be added to preserve meaning when converting fractions to the solidus form.

13.30   Some difficult equations involving fractions should always be displayed; for example:

$$a = \frac{\sum\limits_{k=1}^{n} x_k m_k}{\sum\limits_{k=1}^{n} x_m}.$$

But here again the form of the same equation employing the solidus instead of the horizontal fraction rule may well be used to save space on the page:

$$a = \sum_{k=1}^{n} x_k m_k \left/ \sum_{k=1}^{n} x_m \right. .$$

SCALARS, VECTORS, AND TENSORS

13.31   Three basic quantities, scalars, vectors, and tensors, are often encountered in mathematical copy, as well as in physics. A *scalar* is a quantity having magnitude without direction; a *vector* has both magnitude and direction; and a *tensor* may be regarded as a complex vector that is dependent on several vector variables and denotes a position within multiple coordinate systems. Typographical conventions for these quantities have been established by the International Organization for Standardization (ISO). According to these conventions, scalars are best set in lightface italics ($a \div b = c$, for instance, or *V* for volume, *I* for electric current, *m* for mass); vectors are set in boldface italic (***a, AB, eb***); and tensors are set in lightface italics sans serif (T, T:S). Provision is made for consistent alternate representation of these quantities, and if further information and guidance are desired, these may be obtained from ISO publications (for instance, *General Principles concerning Quantities, Units, and Symbols*).

OVERBARS

13.32 In hot-metal composition bars over groups of letters, such as those used with the radical sign and with averages, are often avoided because they usually involve costly handwork. With filmset or electronic composition, however, overbars cause no trouble in display work, but it is advisable to avoid them in running text, where they may interfere with characters in the line above. Alternatives to the overbar include the following:

for	use		
$\sqrt{xy}$	$\sqrt{(xy)}$	or	$(xy)^{1/2}$
$\dfrac{1}{\sqrt{xy}}$	$1/\sqrt{(xy)}$	or	$(xy)^{-1/2}$
$\sqrt{x + y}$	$\sqrt{(x + y)}$	or	$(x + y)^{1/2}$
$\sqrt{\dfrac{x}{y}}$	$\sqrt{(x/y)}$	or	$(x/y)^{1/2}$
$\sqrt{\dfrac{x + y - z}{a - b + c}}$	$\sqrt{[(x + y - z)/(a - b + c)]}$		
	or		
	$[(x + y - z)/(a - b + c)]^{1/2}$		
$\overline{mv}$	$\langle mv \rangle_{\text{av}}$		

Note that in the alternative expressions it is particularly important to use aggregation signs in the element that would otherwise have been covered by the overbar.

EXPONENTS

13.33   If an exponential expression, particularly in text, is very complex, it
may be worthwhile to rewrite it in a simpler form. An exponential
function such as

$$e^{\frac{2\pi i \Sigma n_j}{\sqrt{(x^2 + y^2)}}}$$

can be set in line as "exp $[2\pi i \Sigma n_j / \sqrt{(x^2 + y^2)}]$." For other expressions
with complicated exponents, make a simple substitution. For example,

$$A^{\frac{2\pi i \Sigma n_j}{\sqrt{(x^2 + y^2)}}}$$

can be set in line as "A^α, where $\alpha = 2\pi i \Sigma n_j / \sqrt{(x^2 + y^2)}$." The same
device may be used for complicated limits to integrals.

Breaking Displayed Equations

13.34   When long equations occur in line they should ordinarily be changed
to the displayed form because of the probability that they will break
badly at the end of a line. Even in displayed form, however, some long
equations may not fit on one line. Rules for breaking displayed equations are complicated, but a few practical guidelines may be offered
here concerning breaks at operational signs.[1] Mathematicians recognize
two kinds of operational signs: those referred to as *verbs,* and those
referred to as *conjunctions.* Examples of each follow:

Verbs: $= \quad \neq \quad < \quad > \quad \leq \quad \geq \quad \supset \quad \subset \quad \ni \quad \notin \quad \cong \quad \not\cong$

Conjunctions: $+ \quad - \quad \times \quad \mp \quad \cup \quad \cap$

Displayed equations may be broken before a verb operator; they may
also be broken before a conjunction that follows an aggregation (see
13.26). If displayed equations are centered, runover lines are aligned
on the verb operators, but if a runover line begins with a conjunction,
the conjunction must be lined up to the right of the verb in the line
above.

$$
\begin{aligned}
(x + r_t) = N_{\delta_2} \, [x(v) + r(p)] + 4_\eta \\
\geq x(r_t) + R(z) + \eta^{1/2} O(p) - H(t_n + r) \\
+ N(v + z) - O(z - 1).
\end{aligned}
$$

---

1. For more extensive guidance in breaking equations, both in-line and displayed, see
Ellen Swanson, *Mathematics into Type,* 3.2–4.

If displayed equations are not centered, the runover lines may be set either flush right (as below) or a standard indention from the right margin, allowing space for an equation number. If the equation takes more than two lines, however, it is common practice to align runover lines on verb operators.

$$\|T_a f - f\| = \sup_s \|T_s^{s+a} f(s + a) - f(s)\|$$
$$- \sup_{s \leq A} \|T_s^{s+a} f(s + a) - f(s)\| + 2 \sup_{s \geq A} \|f(s)\|.$$

$$X,Y (s,\ t) = \int_{-\infty}^{\infty} \dots \int_{-\infty}^{\infty} e^{i(sx+ty)}\ dF_{x,y}(x,\ y)$$
$$= \int_{-\infty}^{\infty} e^{ity} \left[\int_{-\infty}^{\infty} e^{isx}\ dF_{x|y}(x) \right] dF_y(y)$$
$$= \int_{-\infty}^{\infty} e^{ity} x | y(s|y)\ dF_y(y).$$

In unbroken equations or portions of equations, operational signs are followed and preceded by equal space; an operational sign that begins an additional line of a broken equation is followed by a space.

13.35 Fractions and expressions enclosed in aggregation signs or following radical signs should not be broken unless it is absolutely necessary.

Matrices and Determinants

13.36 Matrices and determinants are composed of mathematical terms displayed in rectangular arrangements of rows and columns and enclosed left and right by large fences. Matrices are enclosed by square brackets, determinants by straight vertical lines.

Matrix

$$\begin{bmatrix} a_1^1 & a_2^1 \dots & a_n^1 \\ a_1^2 & a_2^2 \dots & a_y^2 \\ . & . \quad \dots & \\ a_1^m & a_2^m \dots & a_n^3 \end{bmatrix}$$

Determinant

$$\begin{vmatrix} a_1 & b_1 \dots & h_1 \\ . & . \quad \dots & . \\ . & . \quad \dots & . \\ . & . \quad \dots & . \\ a_j & b_j \dots & h_y \end{vmatrix}$$

Although such column matrices as

$$\begin{bmatrix} a \\ b \\ c \end{bmatrix}$$

may be set in line as "col. (a, b, c)," most matrices and determinants must be set as displays (see fig. 13.2). If such a display begins close to the bottom of a page, it may not fit on the page. Since matrices and determinants must not be broken, it may be necessary to treat the display as a figure and assign it a number. It may then be reproduced in full on the following page.

Illustrations

13.37 Most of the illustrations used in mathematics are line drawings (rather than halftones), usually charts and graphs. These should be numbered sequentially (preferably, in a book, by double numeration, like equations; see 13.24). If the illustrations include letters, signs, or symbols corresponding to those in the text, the lettering in the illustration should approximate that in the text. It can be confusing, for example, if points A, B, and C appear in the text in italic type and in an illustration in roman.

13.38 Some mathematical material is too difficult, if not impossible, to set wholly in type and may have to be produced by a combination of type and artwork:

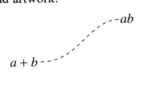

MARKING MATHEMATICAL COPY

13.39 The paragraphs that follow describe markup procedures for mathematical copy prepared on older typewriters that cannot produce such frequently needed variants as italic and boldface characters. Manuscripts prepared in this way often require considerable markup and detailed instructions to the compositor. Predominantly, however, mathematical copy is now prepared on complex and very versatile word processors or computers that can set not only italic and boldface material but many other difficult mathematical symbols and signs as well. To the extent that a manuscript shows such characters, symbols, and signs as they should appear, the compositor may simply be instructed to follow the author's copy. Any unusual characters not achieved, of course, must be marked or identified. Authors should be advised, however, that the advantage gained by the use of advanced equipment may be lost if the manuscript is printed out on a low-tech, draft-quality printer with a tired ribbon. Authors should be urged to supply the highest quality printout possible, keeping in mind that their equations may be intelligible to them only because they are familiar with their own work, not because the copy is readable.

Italic Type

13.40   Unless a compositor experienced in setting mathematics is to be used, the editor should either underline all copy to be set in italic or give general instructions to the compositor to set all letters used as mathematical terms in italic unless they are marked otherwise. The general instructions to the compositor should also specify italic type for letters used in subscripts and superscripts.

Letters in Other Type Styles

ABBREVIATIONS

13.41   Abbreviations such as log (logarithm), max (maximum), exp (exponential function), tan (tangent), cos (cosine), cosh (hyperbolic cosine), lim (limit), arg (argument), cov (covariance), diag (diagonal), ln (natural logarithm), and var (variance) are set in roman:

$$\sin x \qquad \log_a x \qquad \langle mv \rangle_{av} \qquad y_{min}$$

These need not be marked for an experienced compositor. Abbreviations for geometric points, units of measurement, and chemical elements, which are also set in roman type, are marked only where ambiguity could occur.

SINGLE LETTERS

13.42   Special marking must be used, however, when single letters used as variables are to be set in any typeface other than italic. Although it is rather uncommon, a mathematics book may require the use of some letters in roman, usually to indicate properties different from those expressed by the same letters in italic. Underlining is the standard method of indicating italic, but it can be used instead, with covering instructions to the compositor, to indicate letters that are to be in a roman face. If, however, the editor does not use general instructions but underlines all letters to be set italic, then letters not underlined will be set, as intended, in roman type. Double underlining is used to indicate small capitals. Wavy underlining is used to indicate boldface type, normally used for vectors and matrices. (The author should clearly identify all vectors, to distinguish them from their components, which are set in lightface italic. The editor will find it difficult to make the distinction.) Color-codes are often used to indicate other typefaces. For example, red underlining or circling can be used to indicate German, blue to indicate script, green to indicate sans serif, and so forth. The covering instructions to the compositor must explain clearly the marking and coding system used. If a photocopy must be made of the edited manuscript for estimating by the typesetter or for querying the author, color-coding should be avoided. (See also 13.31.)

USING CORRECT TERMINOLOGY

13.43 The copyeditor and typesetter are often misled by authors who confuse German with script, specifying the latter when they mean the former. Boldface and sans serif are also frequently mislabeled. Examples of each are shown below:

German	Script	Boldface	Sans Serif
𝔄𝔅ℭ𝔇	𝒜ℬ𝒞𝒟	**ABCD**	ABCD

Note that to a typesetter the term *gothic* means a somewhat heavy sans serif face, like that illustrated above, *not* German or Old English. Standard terminology for typefaces used in mathematical setting is given in table 13.3, at the end of the chapter.

Definitions, Theorems, Lemmas, and the Like

13.44 For definitions, theorems, propositions, corollaries, lemmas, assumptions, and rules, it is common practice to set the head in caps and small caps and the text—including mathematical expressions, except numerals such as 0 (zero)—in italic. Enumerations of these enunciations, unlike those for equations, are not enclosed in parentheses, and in cross-references the numbers are also unenclosed.

> DEFINITION 1.1. *The graph of an equation consists of all the points whose coordinates satisfy the given equation.*
> THEOREM 2.2. *Two nonvertical lines are parallel if and only if their slopes are equal.*
> LEMMA 3.3. *K is unbounded if and only if $A = B$.*
> ASSUMPTION. *Time t is finite and always greater than* 0.
> RULE 4.4. *The length of a vertical segment joining two points is the ordinate of the upper point minus the ordinate of the lower.*

Note that, in the assumption above, the expression t is preceded by an identifying word so as to avoid beginning the sentence with a lowercase letter. Some mathematicians and editors would also object to beginning lemma 3.3 with the expression $K,$ even though it is a capital letter, preferring to write *"The quantity K. . . ."*

13.45 The text of proof, examples, remarks, demonstrations, and solutions is usually set in roman, with only variables in italics. The heads, however, are set in caps and small caps.

> PROOF. Let $A = B$. Hence $C = D$.
> SOLUTION. If $y = 0$, then $x = 5$.

Marking for Clarity

13.46 What may seem perfectly clear to the author can be bewildering to anyone who is not a mathematician. The author must take particular care to clarify ambiguous expressions.

13.47 It is not advisable, however, for either the author or the editor to mark the copy excessively. Provided that inferior and superior characters have been marked in a few places by the symbols $\vee$ and $\wedge$ (see example below), and new characters or symbols identified when they first appear, a trained compositor will have no difficulty with well-prepared copy. If the spatial relationship of terms is not clearly shown in typed or handwritten expressions, the terms should be marked so that there can be no doubt in the mind of the compositor. For example, in the expression

$$x_{t1}^{k}$$

it may not be clear in the manuscript whether this means

$$X_{t1}^{k} \text{ or } X_{t1}^{k} \text{ or } X_{t_1}^{k}.$$

The expression should therefore be marked in one of the following ways for complete clarity:

$$X\overset{k}{_{t1}} \quad \text{or} \quad X\overset{k}{_{t1}} \quad \text{or} \quad X\overset{k}{_{t/1}}$$

13.48 The examples above show the subscripts and superscripts aligned, the setting generally preferred by authors for elegance and clarity. In filmset or electronic composition this can generally be achieved without extra work or expense, but in hot metal the aligning may require considerable handwork, particularly if subscripts and superscripts occur together frequently throughout a book.

13.49 Figure 13.1 shows a page of manuscript as marked initially by the author and then by the editor before being sent to the typesetter. Figure 13.2 shows the same page set in type. The author's marks merely identify ambiguous symbols. The editor's marking was done for a compositor experienced in mathematical setting; for an inexperienced compositor the marking must be more elaborate.

13.50 In the manuscript certain letters, numbers, and symbols can easily be misread, especially when Greek, German, script, and sans serif letters are handwritten rather than typed. Some of the handwritten and typed characters that cause the most difficulty are shown in table 13.1.

13.51 These and other signs and symbols that could be misread by the compositor should be clearly identified either by marginal notations or otherwise. (For lists of symbols and special characters commonly used in mathematics see tables 13.2 and 13.3.) Illegible handwriting and unidentifiable signs and symbols can reduce composition speed and result in time-consuming and costly corrections.

FOR FURTHER REFERENCE

13.52 Readers who want to explore the problems of mathematical typesetting more fully are referred to *Mathematics into Type,* by Ellen Swanson (1987), published by the American Mathematical Society. Other AMS publications that are helpful for authors of mathematical materials include *A Manual for Authors of Mathematical Papers* (1990) and Steenrod et al., *How to Write Mathematics* (1983). *Guidelines for Preparing Electronic Manuscripts: AMS-T$_E$X* (1991) and *Guidelines for Preparing Electronic Manuscripts: AMS-LATEX* (1991) are intended for authors whose papers or longer works are to be published by the society. Translators of Russian mathematical works will find assistance in yet another AMS publication, S. H. Gould's *A Manual for Translators of Mathematical Russian* (1991). For a comprehensive treatment of international standards for typographical representation of mathematical quantities see ISO, *General Principles concerning Quantities, Units, and Symbols.*

Table 13.1 Ambiguous Mathematical Symbols

Hand-written Symbols and Letters[a]	Symbols Set in Type[b]	Marginal Notation to Operator[c]	Remarks and Suggestions for Manuscript Preparation
a	*a*	lc "aye"	In typescript, leave single space before and after
∝	α	lc Gr. alpha	∝ and all operational signs (=, ≤, ∈, ∩, ⊂,
∝	∝	variation	etc.)
∞	∞	infinity	
B	*B*	cap "bee"	
β	β	lc Gr. beta	
χ	χ	lc Gr. chi	Carelessly written χ also easily misread as
X	*X*	cap "ex"	numeral 4
x	*x*	lc "ex"	
×	×	"times" or "mult"	Leave single space before and after × and all other conjunction signs (+, −, ÷, etc.) Do not add space when such signs as −, +, or ± are adjectives (−3, ±1, etc.).
δ, ∂	δ	lc Gr. delta	
∂	∂	partial differential	Simpler to use printer's term "round dee"
d	*d*	lc "dee"	
ϵ	ϵ	lc Gr. epsilon	
E	∈	"element of"	
η	η	lc Gr. eta	
n	*n*	lc "en"	
γ	γ	lc Gr. gamma	
τ	τ	lc Gr. tau	
r	*r*	lc "are"	
t	*t*	lc "tee"	
ι	ι	lc Gr. iota	Author should avoid using ι and i together
i	*i*	lc "eye"	because of similarity in print
κ	κ	lc Gr. kappa	
k	*k*	lc "kay"	
K	*K*	cap Gr. kappa	
K	*K*	cap "kay"	
ℓ	*l*	lc "ell"	Typed *l* and 1 identical; note "ell" but leave
1	1	numeral 1	numeral unmarked[d]
ν	ν	lc Gr. nu	Avoid using ν and v together because of
v	*v*	lc "vee"	similarity in print

[a]Symbols and letters commonly mistaken for each other are arranged in groups.
[b]Letters in mathematical expressions will automatically be set in italics unless marked otherwise.
[c]Only if symbols, letters, or numbers are badly written is it necessary to identify them for the compositor.
[d]Computers and some math typewriters have a special symbol for "ell."

Table 13.1—*Continued*

Hand-written Symbols and Letters[a]	Symbols Set in Type[b]	Marginal Notation to Operator[c]	Remarks and Suggestions for Manuscript Preparation
O	O	cap "oh"	Zero usually unmarked; degree sign (if typed as lc "oh") and Greek letters identified in margin
	o	lc "oh"	
	0	zero	
	O	cap Gr. omicron	
	o	lc Gr. omicron	
	°	degree sign	
Λ	Λ	cap Gr. lambda	
	$\wedge$	matrix symbol	
	ϕ, φ	lc Gr. phi	Preference for form φ should be specified by author; ϕ more commonly used
	$\varnothing$	empty set or null set	
	Π	product	
	Π	cap Gr. pi	
	π	lc Gr. pi	
	ρ	lc Gr. rho	
	p	lc "pee"	
	θ, ϑ	lc Gr. theta	Preference for form ϑ should be specified by author; θ more commonly used
	Θ	cap Gr. theta	
	U	cap "you"	
	$\cup, \cup$	union symbol	
	υ	lc Gr. upsilon	
	μ	lc Gr. mu	
	u	lc "you"	
	ω	lc Gr. omega	
	w	lc "doubleyou"	
	Z	cap "zee"	
	z	lc "zee"	
	2	numeral 2	
	$'$	prime	Type apostrophe for prime; raise superscript one-half space above line
	$_1$	superscript 1	In handwritten formulas, take care to distinguish comma from subscript 1 and
	,	comma	prime from superscript 1
	$_1$	subscript 1	
	—	em dash	Type two hyphens for em dash; no space on either side
	–	minus sign	To indicate subtraction, leave single space on each side of sign; omit space after sign if negative quantity is represented
	·	multiplication dot	Type period one-half space above line for multiplication dot, allowing single space on each side; do *not* show space around a center dot in a chemical formula ($CO_3 \cdot H_2$)

Table 13.2 Standard Signs and Symbols

N.B. Remember that verb operator signs are abbreviations for inflected verbs: that is, for example, the sign > stands for *is* or *are greater than*, not simply *greater than*. The necessary verbs are not always indicated in the table below.

+	Plus	~	Difference
−	Minus	∽	Difference
×	Multiplied by	⧣	Equal and parallel
÷	Divided by	≐	Approaches a limit
=	Equal to	≝ (m)	Is measured by
±	Plus or minus	⊥	Perpendicular to
∓	Minus or plus	⊥s	Perpendiculars
±	Plus or equal to	‖	Parallel
++	Double plus	‖s	Parallels
⌒	Difference between	∦	Not parallel
−:	Difference excess	∠	Angle
≡	Identical with, congruent	⦟	Angle
≢	Not identical with	⦞	Angle
≠	Not equal to	∠s	Angles
≈	Nearly equal to	L	Right angle
≅	Equals approximately	⩵	Equal angles
≊	Equals approximately	△	Triangle
≥	Equal to or greater than	△s	Triangles
≤	Equal to or less than	/	Rising diagonal
<	Less than	\	Falling diagonal
⌐	Less than	∥/	Parallel rising diagonal
>	Greater than	∖∖	Parallel falling diagonal
⌐	Greater than	///	Rising parallels
≷	Greater than or less than	\\\	Falling parallels
≮	Not less than	‖‖	Triple vertical
≯	Not greater than	≡	Quadruple parallels
≤	Less than or equal to	⌒	Arc
≤	Less than or equal to	⌣	Arc
≦	Less than or equal to	⟁	Sector
≤	Less than or equal to	⌒	Segment
≶	Less than or greater than	○	Circle
≥	Greater than or equal to	⊙s	Circles
≥	Greater than or equal to	◯	Ellipse
≧	Greater than or equal to	⌀	Diameter
≥	Greater than or equal to	□	Square
≎	Equivalent to	□s	Squares
≢	Not equivalent to	▭	Rectangle
≢	Not equivalent to	▭s	Rectangles
⊂	Included in	⊞	Cube
⊃	Excluded from	▱	Rhomboid

Table 13.2—*Continued*

Symbol	Meaning	Symbol	Meaning
⑤	Rhomboids	⌒	Horizontal integral
⬠	Pentagon	˘	Mathmodifier
⬡	Hexagon	ᶜ	Mathmodifier
∴	Hence, therefore	∿	Cycle sine
∵	Because	ӿ	Quantic
·	Multiplied by	/	Single bond
:	Ratio	|	Single bond
::	Proportion	\	Single bond
÷	Geometrical proportion	|	Single bond
′	Minute	|	Single bond (punched to right)
″	Second	⦵	Double bond
°	Degree	‖	Double bond
⍭	Dotted minute	⫽	Double bond
⍮	Dotted second	‖	Double bond
⍩	Dotted degree	⋮	Triple bond
″	Canceled second	↔	Reaction goes both right and left
‴	Triple prime	↕	Reaction goes both up and down
√	Square root	⇋	Equilibrium reaction beginning at right
∛	Cube root	⇌	Equilibrium reaction beginning at left
∜	Fourth root	⇌	Reversible reaction beginning at left
ⁿ√	nth root	⇋	Reaction begins at right and is completed to left
∠	Horizontal radical	⇋	Reaction begins at right and is completed to right
Σ	Summation	⇌	Reaction begins at left and is completed to right
Π	Product sign	⇌	Reaction begins at left and is completed to left
π	Pi (3.1416)	⇋	Reversible reaction beginning at right
∪	Union sign	↕	Reversible
∩	Intersection sign	⇑	Elimination
!	Factorial sign	⇓	Absorption
∅	Empty set; null set	⇅	Exchange
∈	Is an element of	↯	Electrolysis
∉	Is not an element of	C	Ring opening
e	Base (2.718) of natural logarithms	↷	Repositioning
e	Charge of the electron	○	Ring cycle
Δ	Delta	↗	Reversible reaction
∇	Nabla; del	↘	Reversible reaction
∝	Variation		
∞	Infinity		
㎡	Mills		
⊢	Assertion sign		
h	Planck's constant		
ℏ	h/2π		
k	Boltzmann's constant		
c̄	Mean value of c		
∂	Partial differential		
∂	Partial differential		
∫	Integral		
∮	Contour integral		

Table 13.3 Representative Samples of Ten-Point Monotype Typefaces
Commonly Used for Mathematics

ROMAN LOWERCASE   a b c . . . z æ œ ff fi fl ffi ffl

ROMAN SMALL CAPS   A B C . . . Z Æ Œ &

ROMAN CAPS   A B C . . . Z Æ Œ &

ROMAN FIGURES AND FRACTIONS   1 2 3 4 5 6 7 8 9 0

½ ⅓ ⅔ ¼ ¾ ⅙ ⅛ ⅜ ⅝ ⅞

ROMAN PUNCTUATION   . , ; : - ' ! ? ([

ITALIC LOWERCASE AND ACCENTS   (as with corresponding roman type)

ITALIC CAPS   *A B C . . . Z Æ Œ &*

ITALIC NUMERALS   *1 2 3 4 5 6 7 8 9 0*

GERMAN   𝔄 𝔅 ℭ 𝔇 𝔈 𝔉 𝔊 ℌ ℑ 𝔍 𝔎 𝔏 𝔐 𝔑 𝔒 𝔓 𝔔 ℜ 𝔖 𝔗 𝔘 𝔙 𝔚 𝔛 𝔜 ℨ

a b c d e f g h i j k l m n o p q r s t u v w x y z

GERMAN BOLD   𝕬 𝕭 𝕮 𝕯 𝕰 𝕱 𝕲 𝕳 𝕴 𝕵 𝕶 𝕷 𝕸 𝕹 𝕺 𝕻 𝕼 𝕽 𝕾 𝕿 𝖀 𝖁 𝖂 𝖃 𝖄 𝖅

a b c d e f g h i j k l m n o p q r s t u v w x y z

GREEK   Α Β Γ Δ Ε Ζ Η Θ Ι Κ Λ Μ Ν Ξ Ο Π Ρ Σ Τ Υ Φ Χ Ψ Ω

α β γ δ ε ζ η θ ι κ λ μ ν ξ ο π ρ σ τ υ φ χ ψ ω   ϝ ∂ ϑ ς ϕ

GREEK BOLD   **Α Β Γ Δ Ε Ζ Η Θ Ι Κ Λ Μ Ν Ξ Ο Π Ρ Σ Τ Υ Φ Χ Ψ Ω**

α β γ δ ε ζ η θ ι κ λ μ ν ξ ο π ρ σ τ υ φ χ ψ ω   ϱ

SUPERIOR AND INFERIOR GREEK LOWERCASE

H$^{\alpha\beta\gamma\delta\epsilon\zeta\eta\theta\iota\kappa\lambda\mu\nu\xi o\pi\rho\sigma\tau\upsilon\phi\chi\psi\omega \quad \digamma\partial\varphi\varsigma\phi}$

H$_{\alpha\beta\gamma\delta\epsilon\zeta\eta\theta\iota\kappa\lambda\mu\nu\xi o\pi\rho\sigma\tau\upsilon\phi\chi\psi\omega \quad \digamma\partial\varphi\varsigma\phi}$

HEBREW   א ב ג ד ה ו ז ח ט י כ ל מ נ ס ע פ צ ק ר ש ת

Table 13.3—*Continued*

RUSSIAN	А Б В Г Д Е Ж З И Й К Л М Н О П Р С Т У Ф Х Ц Ч Ш Щ Ъ Ы Ь Ѣ Э Ю Я
CENTURY EXPANDED	A B C D E F G H I J K L M N O P Q R S T U V W X Y Z a b c d e f g h i j k l m n o p q r s t u v w x y z
CENTURY EXPANDED ITALIC	*A B C D E F G H I J K L M N O P Q R S T U V W X Y Z* *a b c d e f g h i j k l m n o p q r s t u v w x y z*
GOTHIC SANS SERIF	**A B C D E F G H I J K L M N O P Q R S T U V W X Y Z**
SCRIPT	𝒜ℬ𝒞𝒟ℰℱℊℋℐ𝒥𝒦ℒℳ𝒩ℴ𝒫𝒬ℛ𝒮𝒯𝒰𝒱𝒲𝒳𝒴𝒵
SUPERIOR CHARACTERS	$A^{ABC}\ A^{abc}\ A^{\alpha\beta\gamma}\ A^{123}$
INFERIOR CHARACTERS	(a stock similar to the superior characters) $B_{DEF}\ B_{def}\ B_{\delta\epsilon\zeta}\ B_{456}$
SYMBOLS	$+\ -\ \times\ \div\ =\ \pm\ \mp\ /\ \parallel\ <\ >\ \leq\ \geq\ \equiv\ \neq\ \neq\ \doteq\ \sim$ $\simeq\ \to\ \surd\ (\,)\ \{\,\}\ [\,]\ \infty\ \propto\ °\ '\ ''$ $\vert\vert\ (\,)\ \{\,\}\ [\,]\ /\ \surd\ \int\ \$\ [\![\,]\!]\ \langle\,\rangle$
SUPERIOR SYMBOLS	$A^{+\ -\ =\ \times\ \div\ \pm\ <\ >\ \leqq\ \geqq\ \surd\ \odot\ \infty\ /\ (\,)\ \{\,\}\ [\,]\ 1/2\ 1/4\ \int,\,.}$ $A^{'\ \parallel\ \perp}$
INFERIOR SYMBOLS	$B_{+\ -\ =\ \times\ \div\ \pm\ <\ >\ \leqq\ \geqq\ \surd\ \odot\ \infty\ /\ (\,)\ \{\,\}\ [\,]\ 1/2\ 1/4\ \int\ \parallel}$ $B_{.\ ,\ ;\ :\ '\ \parallel\ \perp}$
SPLIT FRACTIONS	$\frac{1234567890}{1234567890}$
MISCELLANEOUS	¤ ₢ ! ° '' % @ ¶ ∮ ☾ ⚠ ∠ ☉ ◎ ⊕ Ⓢ ⊖ ⊖ ⊛ ⇁ ⊥ ⊿ ※ ⊙ °(6 pt.) †(6 pt.) ✱ † ‡ § $ # ᵈ ʰ ˢ ᵐᵍ ᴹ ⋛ ⋕ ⧣ ≺ ≼ ≽ ↔ ⇆ ⇄ ⇌ ♂ ⚤ ♀ ⊀

14 *Abbreviations*

INTRODUCTION

14.1 For several centuries the use of abbreviations and symbols in formal, general writing has become less and less frequent, whereas during the past few decades the use of both has been on the increase in technical writing of all kinds. In the main this chapter is concerned with abbreviations and symbols in general writing—authors and editors of technical material in a fast-changing field usually know and can follow the fashions of that field—but the chapter does offer some guidance in technical work, especially to the generalist editor confronted with special-interest copy to prepare for typesetting. Outside the area of science and technology, abbreviations and symbols appear most frequently in tabular matter, notes, bibliographies, and lists. For rules concerning the formation of the plurals of various abbreviations see 6.16–17.

14.2 It is often an open question whether or not periods should be used with particular abbreviations. The trend now is strongly away from the use of periods with all kinds of abbreviations that have carried them in the past. In the Press's view this is to the good: anything that reduces the fussiness of typography makes for easier reading. In the examples that follow, however, the periods have sometimes been left where they have traditionally appeared. It is simple enough for users of this manual to omit periods if that is the style they wish to adopt. One caution: omitting periods after abbreviations that spell words (for example, *in., a., no.*) may be confusing in some contexts. Another caution if periods are used: In many abbreviations with internal periods (A.D., A.M., N.Y., Litt.D., N.Dak., S.Sgt., M.Sgt., M.P.E., U.S.) there is no space between the elements. Other abbreviations with internal periods (Atty. Gen., Brig. Gen., Dist. Atty., Gov. Gen., Lt. Col., Sgt. Maj.) customarily separate the elements with a word space. When in doubt, consult an authoritative list of abbreviations, perhaps in one of the standard dictionaries. Initials of personal names are also regularly followed by word spaces (E. F. Benson, R. G. T. Wundermacher).

14.3 Despite the long-continued trend in general writing to get along without abbreviations, a few words are almost never spelled out. Among these are *Mr., Mrs., Messrs.,* and *Dr.* (and, of course, *Ms.,* which has no spelled-out form) before a name, abbreviations for affiliations or scholarly degrees after a name *(Litt.D., M.P., Ph.D.),* and abbreviations such as A.M. and P.M., A.D. and B.C. A symbol or figure beginning a sentence, on the other hand, is nearly always spelled out; if it cannot be, the sentence is recast:

> Alpha particles are . . . (*not* α particles are . . .)
>
> Eighteen forty-five was . . . (*not* 1845 was . . .)

(For other advice on the use of numerals in run of text see chapter 8.)

NAMES AND TITLES

Personal Names and Titles

14.4 Normally, abbreviations should not be used for given names:

> Benjamin (*not* Benj.) Harrison
> William (*not* Wm.) Warfield

A signature, however, should be transcribed as the person wrote it:

> Benj. Franklin   Geo. D. Fuller   Ch. Virolleaud

Some names contain a middle initial that does not stand for a name, and some given names consist only of initials. A purist would omit the period after these initials. For convenience and consistency it is recommended that all initials given with a name be followed by a period:

> Charles C. Thomas   Harry S. Truman   P. J. Carter

When persons are referred to by the initials of their given and family names—some American presidents, for instance, or the subject of a biography—no periods are used and there is no space between initials:

> JFK (John Fitzgerald Kennedy)   SM (Stanley Morison)
> FDR (Franklin Delano Roosevelt)

When persons are referred to in informal writing or in dialogue by the initials of their given names only, both periods and space separate the initials:

> With a patronizing smile, R. J. took the document from his briefcase and held it above his head.
> "What are you doing, R. J.!" shrieked Phyllis.

TITLES BEFORE NAMES

14.5 When a civil or military title is used with the surname alone, the title must be spelled out:

> General Washington   Senator Borah
> Lieutenant Colonel Smith   Alderman Farley

With full names, most such titles may be abbreviated:

> Brig. Gen. Thornton W. Bluster
> Col. William M. Rich
> Sen. Howard M. Metzenbaum

The following is a list of abbreviations for a number of civil and military titles (but see 14.2):

Adj. Gen.	A1c., *or* A/1C, air-	Asst. Prof.
Adm. *or* ADM	man, first class	Brig. Gen.
A1d.	Assoc. Prof.	Bvt., brevet

Capt.	Lt. Gov.	S1c., seaman, first
Col.	Lt. (jg) *or* LTJG,	class
Comdr.	lieutenant, junior	2d Lt.
Cpl.	grade	Sen.
CWO, chief warrant	Maj.	Sfc. *or* SFC, sergeant,
officer	Maj. Gen.	first class
Ens. *or* ENS	MP, military police	Sgt.
Fr., Father	M.Sgt.	Sp3c., specialist, third
1st Lt.	Pfc. *or* PFC, private,	class
1st Sgt.	first class	Sr., Sister
Gen.	PO, petty officer	S.Sgt., Staff sergeant
Gov.	Pres.	Supt.
Insp. Gen.	Prof.	T2g., technician, sec-
Judge Adv. Gen.	Pvt.	ond grade
Lt.	Q.M. Gen. *or* QMG	T.Sgt., technical ser-
Lt. Col.	Q.M. Sgt.	geant
Lt. Comdr.	Rear Adm.	Vice Adm.
Lt. Gen.	Rep., representative	WO, warrant officer

(Within the armed services briefer forms of abbreviation are commonly used, but these have little currency in the civilian world.)

14.6   Always abbreviated, whether with the full name or the surname, are such social titles as the following:

Mr.   Mrs.   Messrs.   Ms.   M.   MM.   Mme   Mlle   Dr.

14.7   The titles *Reverend* and *Honorable* are spelled out if preceded by *the:*

the Reverend Henry L. Brown; the Reverend Mr. (*or* Dr.) Brown

the Very Reverend Robert C. Wilson; the Right Reverend David O. Carlson; the Right Reverend Monsignor Thomas L. Bennett; the Honorable Frank R. Hawkins

In other instances with the full name the title may be abbreviated :

Rev. Henry L. Brown; Very Rev. Robert C. Wilson; Rt. Rev. David O. Carlson; Rt. Rev. Msgr. Thomas L. Bennett; Hon. Frank R. Hawkins

TITLES, DEGREES, AFFILIATIONS, AND
SO FORTH AFTER NAMES

14.8   The abbreviations *Jr., Sr., II, III* and so forth after a person's name are part of that name and so are retained in connection with any titles or honorifics:

Mrs. James Jefferson Sr., widow of the governor
Dexter Harrison III, LL.D.   Rev. Oliver C. Jones Jr.

Note that these abbreviations are used only with the full name—never, for example, Mr. Kelly Jr. (See also 8.53–55.)

14.9   The abbreviation *Esq.* is never used when any other title is given, either before or after the name:

> Anthony Wright, Esq. (*not* Mr. Anthony Wright, Esq. *or* Anthony Wright, Esq., M.A.)

14.10   *Mr., Mrs., Ms.,* and *Dr.* are also dropped if another title is used:

> Leroy S. Wells, Ph.D.   Jane Roudebush, M.D.

14.11   The following list includes frequently used abbreviations for academic degrees and professional and honorary designations:

> A.B., Artium Baccalaureus (Bachelor of Arts)
> A.M., Artium Magister (Master of Arts)
> B.A., Bachelor of Arts
> B.D., Bachelor of Divinity
> B.F.A., Bachelor of Fine Arts
> B.S., Bachelor of Science
> D.B., Divinitatis Baccalaureus (Bachelor of Divinity)
> D.D., Divinitatis Doctor (Doctor of Divinity)
> D.D.S., Doctor of Dental Surgery
> D.O., Doctor of Osteopathy
> D.V.M., Doctor of Veterinary Medicine
> Esq., Esquire
> F.A.I.A., Fellow of the American Institute of Architects
> F.R.S., Fellow of the Royal Society
> J.D., Juris Doctor (Doctor of Law)
> J.P., Justice of the Peace
> L.H.D., Litterarum Humaniorum Doctor (Doctor of Humanities)
> Litt.D., Litterarum Doctor (Doctor of Letters)
> LL.B., Legum Baccalaureus (Bachelor of Laws)
> LL.D., Legum Doctor (Doctor of Laws)
> M.A., Master of Arts
> M.D., Medicinae Doctor (Doctor of Medicine)
> M.F.A., Master of Fine Arts
> M.P., Member of Parliament
> M.S., Master of Science
> Ph.B., Philosophiae Baccalaureus (Bachelor of Philosophy)
> Ph.D., Philosophiae Doctor (Doctor of Philosophy)
> Ph.G., Graduate in Pharmacy
> S.B., Scientiae Baccalaureus (Bachelor of Science)
> S.M., Scientiae Magister (Master of Science)
> S.T.B., Sacrae Theologiae Baccalaureus (Bachelor of Sacred Theology)

Company Names

14.12   The following abbreviations are frequently used as parts of firm names:

> Bro.,   Bros.,   Co.,   Corp.,   Inc.,   Ltd.,   &

In straight text it is best to give a firm name in its full form, but *Inc.* or *Ltd.* is usually dropped:

A. G. Becker and Company   Kyle Publishing Company

14.13   In notes, bibliographies, lists, and so on the abbreviations listed above may be freely (if consistently) used:

Macmillan Co.   Norfolk & Western Railroad
Ginn & Co.   Great Lakes Dredge & Dock Co.

(For the further abbreviation of publishers' names in bibliographies and notes, see 15.160–61.)

14.14   In closely set tabular matter further abbreviation is often used (*RR, Ry, Assoc., Mfg.,* etc.).

Agencies and Organizations

14.15   Both in run of text (preferably after one spelled-out use) and in tabular matter, notes, and so forth, the names of government agencies, network broadcasting companies, associations, fraternal and service organizations, unions, and other groups are often abbreviated. Such abbreviations or acronyms are usually set in full caps with no periods. The use of small capitals, especially for acronyms, is followed by some publishers, but the University of Chicago Press favors the use of full capitals.

AAAS	GTE	NEH	TVA
AFL-CIO	HMO	NFL	UN
AMA	NAACP	NIMH	VA
FTC	NAFTA	NSF	YMCA
GATT	NBC	OPEC	YWHA

Uncertainty often arises concerning the proper choice of the indefinite article before an abbreviation. A workable solution may be based on the way such an abbreviation is read. The assumption is that it is read either as a series of letters or as a neologism, or coined word. Rarely is the abbreviation read as though all of the words were spelled out. If, as is usually the case, it is treated as a series of letters, the choice of the article depends on the pronunciation of the first letter:

an NAACP position (*contrast* a National Association for the Advancement of Colored People . . .)
a TVA power station

If the abbreviation is widely pronounced as though it were a word, the article is determined by the pronunciation of the word:

a NATO meeting
a LOOM parade *but* an NFL team

(For guidance in forming the plurals of abbreviations see 6.16. For alphabetizing see 17.97.)

Names with *Saint*

14.16   *Saint* is often abbreviated (*St.*, pl. *SS.*) before the name of a Christian saint, but many prefer to spell the word out in text, abbreviating only where space is at a premium:

> Saint Ignatius Loyola
> Saint Michael the Archangel
> the Church of Saints Constantine and Helena
> Saint Paul's Cathedral

Saint is usually omitted before the names of apostles, evangelists, and church fathers:

> Matthew, Mark, Luke, Paul, Peter, Bartholomew, Augustine, Ambrose, Jerome, etc.

When *Saint* forms part of a personal name, the bearer's usage is followed:

> Augustus Saint-Gaudens   Ruth St. Denis
> Muriel St. Clare Byrne

GEOGRAPHICAL TERMS

States

14.17   The names of states, territories, and possessions of the United States should always be given in full when standing alone. When they follow the name of a city or some other geographical term, it is preferable to spell them out except in lists, tabular matter, notes, bibliographies, indexes, and mailing addresses. In such instances, except in the case of mailing addresses, the first of the two forms of abbreviation listed is preferred; the two-letter form is specified by the United States government for use with zip code addresses in mailing and is often useful in other contexts:

Ala.	AL	Del.	DE	Iowa	IA
Alaska	AK	D.C.	DC	Kans.	KS
Amer. Samoa	AS	Fla.	FL	Ky.	KY
Ariz.	AZ	Ga.	GA	La.	LA
Ark.	AR	Guam	GU	Maine	ME
Calif.	CA	Hawaii	HI	Md.	MD
C.Z.	CZ	Idaho	ID	Mass.	MA
Colo.	CO	Ill.	IL	Mich.	MI
Conn.	CT	Ind.	IN	Minn.	MN

Miss.	MS	N.Dak.	ND	Tex.	TX
Mo.	MO	Ohio	OH	Utah	UT
Mont.	MT	Okla.	OK	Vt.	VT
Nebr.	NE	Oreg. *or* Ore.	OR	Va.	VA
Nev.	NV	Pa.	PA	V.I.	VI
N.H.	NH	P.R.	PR	Wash.	WA
N.J.	NJ	R.I.	RI	W.Va.	WV
N.Mex.	NM	S.C.	SC	Wis. *or* Wisc.	WI
N.Y.	NY	S.Dak.	SD	Wyo.	WY
N.C.	NC	Tenn.	TN		

Names with *Fort, Saint,* and So Forth

14.18 Prefixes of most geographic names should not be abbreviated in text:

Fort Wayne	Mount Airy	South Orange
Saint Cloud	San Diego	Port Arthur

Many editors make an exception for names beginning with *Saint* (St. Louis, St. Lawrence), and where space must be saved any such prefixes (except *San, Santa,* etc.) may be abbreviated (*Ft., Pt., Mt., S.* [*South*], etc.).

Names of Countries

14.19 The names of countries, except for the Soviet Union, which is often abbreviated *USSR,* are spelled out in text. In tabular and other tightly set matter they may be abbreviated as necessary (see also 14.2):

U.S. U.K. (*or* G.B.) Fr. Ger. Swed. It.

14.20 As an adjective, *U.S.* has gained currency in serious prose, although it is still not used in the most formal writing:

U.S. courts   U.S. dollars   U.S. involvement in Asia

Addresses

14.21 With a few exceptions, abbreviations should not be used in addresses in running text. (In letter writing, which this manual does not deal with, the two-letter state abbreviations are recommended as most efficient for both the recipient's address and the return address; see 14.17.) The following terms should be spelled out:

Avenue, Boulevard, Building, Court, Drive, Lane, Parkway, Place, Road, Square, Street, Terrace; North, South, East, West

Exceptions are the abbreviations

NW, NE, SE, and SW,

used in some city addresses after the street name. State names are spelled out in addresses. (For the use of numerals in addresses see 8.62–63. For state abbreviations in mailing addresses see 14.17.)

14.22 Addresses may be abbreviated in such closely set matter as lists or tables, especially state names and the words mentioned above as spelled out in text:

Ave., Blvd., Bldg., Ct., Dr., La. *or* Ln., Pkwy., Pl., Rd., Sq., St., Terr.; N., S., E., W. *(before street name)*

Points of the Compass

14.23 When abbreviation of the points of the compass is called for (seldom in formal text), the following system may be used:

Cardinal: N, E, S, W; *intercardinal:* NE, SE, SW, NW
Others: NNE, ENE, ESE, etc.; N by E, NE by N, NE by E, etc.

Latitude and Longitude

14.24 When standing alone, and in nontechnical running text, the words *latitude* and *longitude* are never abbreviated:

the polar latitudes
the zone from ten to forty degrees north latitude
from 10°30′ north latitude to 10°30′ south latitude
longitude 90° west

14.25 In technical work and in tabulations of coordinates, one of the following systems is used:

lat. 42°15′30″ N	long. 89°17′45″ W
lat. 42-15-30 N	long. 89-17-45 W
lat. 42°15.5′ N	long. 89°17.75′ W
lat. 42°15′.5 N	long. 89°17′.75 W

In any of these systems periods may be omitted after *lat* and *long*, or the designations may be dropped altogether, since *E, W, N,* or *S* identifies the coordinate:

The chart showed shoal water at 19°29.65′ N, 107°45.36′ W.

DESIGNATIONS OF TIME

14.26 Note that units of time are treated in a later section of this chapter (see 14.40) and that numerical designations of dates and time of day are treated in 8.43–50.

Systems of Chronology

14.27 Accepted abbreviations for various systems of chronology are used in text or other matter, normally in small caps. The first four abbreviations listed below usually precede the year number; the others follow it. (For further explanation and examples see 8.41–42.)

A.D.	*anno Domini* (in the year of [our] Lord)
A.H.	*anno Hegirae* (in the year of the Hegira); *anno Hebraico* (in the Hebrew year)
A.M.	*anno mundi* (in the year of the world)
A.S.	*anno salutis* (in the year of salvation)
A.U.C.	*ab urbe condita* (from the founding of the city [Rome, in 753 B.C.])
B.C.	before Christ
B.C.E.	before the common era
B.P.	before the present
C.E.	common era
M.Y.B.P.	million years before the present

Months

14.28 Names of the months are always spelled out in text, whether alone or in dates. In chronologies, notes, tabular matter, and so on they may be abbreviated according to one of the following systems, preferably the first. The second is used mainly in indexes of periodical literature.

> Jan. Feb. Mar. Apr. May June July Aug.
> Sept. Oct. Nov. Dec.
>
> Ja F Mr Ap My Je Jl Ag S O N D

Days of the Week

14.29 Like those of the months, the names of the days of the week should be spelled out in text but may be abbreviated in other situations according to one of the following systems. The second is used only in very closely set catalogs and the like.

Sun. Mon. Tues. Wed. Thurs. Fri. Sat.

Su M Tu W Th F Sa

Time of Day

14.30 The part of the day to which clock time applies is indicated, in regular text as well as tabular and similar matter, by the usual abbreviations:

A.M., *ante meridiem* (before noon)
M., *meridies* (noon)
P.M., *post meridiem* (after noon)

These abbreviations are usually set, as above, in small capitals with no space added between them. This is the common American printed style and the preference of the University of Chicago Press. British practice is to use lowercase letters with periods—a.m., m., p.m.—an alternative that is accepted here also. Another acceptable alternative is the use of small capitals without periods: AM, M, PM. In typed material and in typesetting systems where small capitals are not available, full capitals may be used. (For the use of numerals with these abbreviations, see 8.48.)

14.31 The abbreviations for periods of the day should not be used with *morning, noon, afternoon, evening,* or *night,* nor should they be used with *o'clock.*

10:45 A.M.   eight o'clock in the evening
10:45 in the morning

SCHOLARSHIP

14.32 Abbreviations have a very long history of use in scholarship, and general principles concerning their use are widely agreed upon:

To the greatest extent possible, abbreviations should be kept out of running text, except in technical matter.

General abbreviations such as *etc., e.g.,* and *i.e.* are preferably confined to parenthetical references.

Purely scholarly abbreviations such as *ibid., cf.,* and *s.v.* are preferably used only in notes and other forms of scholarly apparatus.

14.33 The following is a list of abbreviations that may be encountered in editing general scholarly text:

abbr., abbreviated, -ion
ab init., *ab initio,* from the beginning

abl., ablative
abr., abridged; abridgment
acc., accusative
act., active
add., addendum
ad inf., *ad infinitum,* to infinity
ad init., *ad initium,* at the beginning
ad int., *ad interim,* in the meantime
adj., adjective
ad lib., *ad libitum,* at will
ad loc., *ad locum,* at the place
adv., adverb
aet., *aetatis,* aged
AFr., Anglo-French
AN, Anglo-Norman
anon., anonymous
app., appendix
art., article
AS, Anglo-Saxon
b., born; brother
bibl., *bibliotheca,* library
bibliog., bibliography, -er, -ical
biog., biography, -er, -ical
biol., biology, -ical, -ist
bk., block; book
c., chapter (in law citations); *circa*
ca., *circa,* about, approximately
Cantab., *Cantabrigiensis,* of Cambridge
cf., *confer,* compare
chap., chapter
Cia, *Compañia,* Company (no period)
Cie, *Compagnie,* Company (no period)
col., column
colloq., colloquial, -ly, -ism
comp., compiler (*pl.* comps.); compiled by
compar., comparative
con., *contra,* against
conj., conjunction; conjugation
cons., consonant
constr., construction
cont., continued
contr., contraction
copr., cop., *or* ©, copyright
cp., compare
d., died; daughter
dat., dative
def., definite, definition
dept., department
deriv., derivative
d.h., *das heißt,* namely
d.i., *das ist,* that is
dial., dialect

dict., dictionary
dim., diminutive
dist., district
div., division; divorced
do., ditto (the same)
doz., dozen
dram. pers., *dramatis personae*
Dr. u. Vrl., *Druck und Verlag,* printer and publisher
D.V., *Deo volente,* God willing
ea., each
ed., editor (*pl.* eds.); edition; edited by
EE, Early English
e.g., *exempli gratia,* for example
encyc., encyclopedia
Eng., English
eng., engin., engineering
engr., engineer; engraved, engraving
eq., equation (*pl.* eqq. *or* eqs.)
esp., especially
et al., *et alii,* and others
etc., *et cetera,* and so forth
et seq., *et sequentes,* and the following
ex., example (*pl.* exx. *or* exs.)
f. *or* fem., feminine; female
f., and following (*pl.* ff.)
fasc., fascicle
fig., figure
fl., *floruit,* flourished
fol., folio
Fr., French
fr., from
fut., future
f.v., *folio verso,* on the back of the page
Gael., Gaelic
gen., genitive; genus
geog., geography, -er, -ical
geol., geology, -ist, -ical
geom., geometry, -ical
Ger. *or* G., German
ger., gerund
Gk., Greek
hist., history, -ian, -ical
HQ *or* hdqrs., headquarters
ibid., *ibidem,* in the same place
id., *idem,* the same
IE, Indo-European
i.e., *id est,* that is
imper., imperative
incl., inclusive; including; includes
indef., indefinite
indic., indicative
inf., *infra,* below

infin., infinitive
infra dig., *infra dignitatem,* undignified
in pr., *in principio,* in the beginning
inst., instant, this month; institute, institution
instr., instrumental
interj., interjection
intrans., intransitive
introd. *or* intro., introduction
I.Q. *or* IQ, intelligence quotient
irreg., irregular
It., Italian
L., Latin; left (in stage directions)
l., left; line (*pl.* ll.) *(best not abbreviated)*
lang., language
Lat., Latin
lit., literally
loc., locative
loc. cit., *loco citato,* in the place cited
loq., *loquitur,* he or she speaks
m., married; male; measure (*pl.* mm.)
m. *or* masc., masculine
marg., margin, -al
math., mathematics, -ical
ME, Middle English
med., median; medical; medieval; medium
memo, memorandum
mgr., manager
MHG, Middle High German
mimeo., mimeograph
misc., miscellaneous
MM, Maelzel's metronome *(tempo indication)*
m.m., *mutatis mutandis,* necessary changes being made
Mod. E., Modern English
MS (*pl.* MSS), *manuscriptum (-a),* manuscript(s)
mus., museum; music, -al
n., *natus,* born; note, footnote (*pl.* nn.); noun
nat., national; natural
N.B., *nota bene,* take careful note
n.d., no date
neg., negative
neut., neuter
no., number (*pl.* nos.)
nom., nominative
non obs., *non obstante,* notwithstanding
non seq., *non sequitur,* it does not follow
n.p., no place; no publisher; no page
N.S., New Style (dates)
n.s., new series
ob., *obiit,* died
obs., obsolete
OE, Old English
OFr, Old French

OHG, Old High German
ON, Old Norse
op. cit., *opere citato,* in the work cited
O.S., Old Style (dates)
o.s., old series
Oxon., *Oxoniensis,* of Oxford
p., page (*pl.* pp.); past
par., paragraph
part., participle
pass., *passim,* throughout; passive
path., pathology, -ist, -ical
perf., perfect; perforated
perh., perhaps
pers., person, personal
pl., plate; plural
p.p., past participle
PPS, *post postscriptum,* a later postscript
prep., preposition
pres., present
pron., pronoun
pro tem., *pro tempore,* for the time being
prox., *proximo,* next month
PS, *postscriptum,* postscript
pt., part
pub., publication, publisher, published by
Q.E.D., *quod erat demonstrandum,* which was to be demonstrated
quart., quarterly
q.v., *quod vide,* which see
R., *rex,* king; *regina,* queen; right (in stage directions)
r., right; reigned; recto
refl., reflexive
repr., reprint, reprinted
rev., review; revised, revision
R.I.P., *requiescat in pace,* may he or she rest in peace
s., son; substantive
S.A., South America
s.a., *sine anno,* without year; *sub anno,* under the year
sc., scene; *scilicet,* namely; *sculpsit,* carved by
s.d., *sine die,* without setting a day for reconvening
sec., section; *secundum,* according to
ser., series
sing. *or* sg., singular
s.l., *sine loco,* without place
sociol., sociology, -ical
Sp., Spanish
st., stanza
subj., subject; subjective; subjunctive
subst., substantive, -al
sup., *supra,* above
superl., superlative
supp. *or* suppl., supplement
s.v., *sub verbo, sub voce,* under the word (*pl.* s.vv.)

syn., synonym, -ous
theol., theology, -ian, -ical
trans., transitive; translated, -or
treas., treasurer
ult., *ultimatus,* ultimate, last; *ultimo,* last month
univ., university
usw., *und so weiter,* and so forth
ut sup., *ut supra,* as above
v., verse (*pl.* vv.); verso; versus; *vide,* see
v. *or* vb., verb
v.i., verb intransitive
viz., *videlicet,* namely
voc., vocative
vol., volume
vs. *or* v., versus
v.t., verb transitive
yr., year; your

BIBLE

Books and Psalms

14.34 In text, references to whole books of the Bible and whole psalms are spelled out:

> The opening chapters of Ephesians constitute Paul's most compelling sermon on love.

> Jeremiah, chapters 42–44, records the flight of the Jews to Egypt when Jerusalem fell in 586 B.C.

> As Falstaff lay dying, he apparently sought comfort in reciting the Twenty-third Psalm.

Exact references to scriptural passages, whether used in text, in parenthetical citations, or in notes, employ abbreviations for the names of most books of the Bible (see 15.294 for the form of such citations). The first of the following lists gives the books of the Bible as they appear in the Authorized (King James) Version, along with the usual abbreviations. Protestant scholars generally use these names and abbreviations in citing Scripture in later English-language versions also.

OLD TESTAMENT

Genesis	Gen.	1 Samuel	1 Sam.
Exodus	Exod.	2 Samuel	2 Sam.
Leviticus	Lev.	1 Kings	1 Kings
Numbers	Num.	2 Kings	2 Kings
Deuteronomy	Deut.	1 Chronicles	1 Chron.
Joshua	Josh.	2 Chronicles	2 Chron.
Judges	Judg.	Ezra	Ezra
Ruth	Ruth	Nehemiah	Neh.

Esther	Esther	Joel	Joel
Job	Job	Amos	Amos
Psalms	Ps. (*pl.* Pss.)	Obadiah	Obad.
Proverbs	Prov.	Jonah	Jon.
Ecclesiastes	Eccles.	Micah	Mic.
Song of Solomon	Song of Sol.	Nahum	Nah.
Isaiah	Isa.	Habakkuk	Hab.
Jeremiah	Jer.	Zephaniah	Zeph.
Lamentations	Lam.	Haggai	Hag.
Ezekiel	Ezek.	Zechariah	Zech.
Daniel	Dan.	Malachi	Mal.
Hosea	Hos.		

APOCRYPHA

1 Esdras	1 Esd.
2 Esdras	2 Esd.
Tobit	Tob.
Judith	Jth.
The Rest of Esther	Rest of Esther
The Wisdom of Solomon	Wisd. of Sol.
Ecclesiasticus	Ecclus.
Baruch	Bar.
The Song of the Three Holy Children	Song of Three Children
Susanna	Sus.
Bel and the Dragon	Bel and Dragon
Prayer of Manasses (*or* Manasseh)	Pr. of Man.
1 Maccabees	1 Macc.
2 Maccabees	2 Macc.

NEW TESTAMENT

Matthew	Matt.	1 Timothy	1 Tim.
Mark	Mark	2 Timothy	2 Tim.
Luke	Luke	Titus	Titus
John	John	Philemon	Philem.
Acts of the Apostles	Acts	Hebrews	Heb.
Romans	Rom.	James	James
1 Corinthians	1 Cor.	1 Peter	1 Pet.
2 Corinthians	2 Cor.	2 Peter	2 Pet.
Galatians	Gal.	1 John	1 John
Ephesians	Eph.	2 John	2 John
Philippians	Phil.	3 John	3 John
Colossians	Col.	Jude	Jude
1 Thessalonians	1 Thess.	Revelation	Rev.
2 Thessalonians	2 Thess.	*or* Apocalypse	Apoc.

Roman Catholic versions of the Bible include the Apocrypha within the canon of the Old Testament, and so the sequence of books is somewhat different. The following is a list of the books as they appear in the New American Bible, with the abbreviations used by the scholars who prepared that version. The very brief forms should be useful in any scriptural studies.

OLD TESTAMENT

Genesis	Gn	Proverbs	Prv
Exodus	Ex	Ecclesiastes	Eccl
Leviticus	Lv	Song of Songs	Sg (Song)
Numbers	Nm	Wisdom	Wis
Deuteronomy	Dt	Sirach	Sir
Joshua	Jos	Isaiah	Is
Judges	Jgs	Jeremiah	Jer
Ruth	Ru	Lamentations	Lam
1 Samuel	1 Sm	Baruch	Bar
2 Samuel	2 Sm	Ezekiel	Ez
1 Kings	1 Kgs	Daniel	Dn
2 Kings	2 Kgs	Hosea	Hos
1 Chronicles	1 Chr	Joel	Jl
2 Chronicles	2 Chr	Amos	Am
Ezra	Ezr	Obadiah	Ob
Nehemiah	Neh	Jonah	Jon
Tobit	Tb	Micah	Mi
Judith	Jdt	Nahum	Na
Esther	Est	Habakkuk	Hb
1 Maccabees	1 Mc	Zephaniah	Zep
2 Maccabees	2 Mc	Haggai	Hg
Job	Jb	Zechariah	Zec
Psalms	Ps(s)	Malachi	Mal

NEW TESTAMENT

Matthew	Mt	1 Timothy	1 Tm
Mark	Mk	2 Timothy	2 Tm
Luke	Lk	Titus	Ti
John	Jn	Philemon	Phlm
Acts of the Apostles	Acts	Hebrews	Heb
Romans	Rom	James	Jas
1 Corinthians	1 Cor	1 Peter	1 Pt
2 Corinthians	2 Cor	2 Peter	2 Pt
Galatians	Gal	1 John	1 Jn
Ephesians	Eph	2 John	2 Jn
Philippians	Phil	3 John	3 Jn
Colossians	Col	Jude	Jude
1 Thessalonians	1 Thes	Revelation	Rv
2 Thessalonians	2 Thes		

The titles of the books that constitute the Jewish Scriptures may all be found among the books of the Old Testament in the lists above and may be abbreviated according to either of the two systems shown.

Versions and Sections

14.35 In the field of biblical scholarship, it is customary to refer to various versions and sections of the Bible by abbreviations:

Syr.	Syriac
MT	Masoretic text
LXX	Septuagint
Vulg.	Vulgate
AV	Authorized (King James) Version
DV	Douay Version
RV	Revised Version
RV m	Revised Version, margin
ERV	English Revised Version
ERV m	English Revised Version, margin
ARV	American Revised Version
ARV m	American Revised Version, margin
RSV	Revised Standard Version
EV	English version(s)
AT	American Translation
NAB	New American Bible
NEB	New English Bible
NJB	New Jerusalem Bible
OT	Old Testament
Apoc.	Apocrypha
NT	New Testament

MEASURE

14.36   Abbreviations of units of measure are identical in the singular and plural.

English Measure

14.37   Abbreviations for the English units of measure find very little use in straight text except for technical work. On the rare occasions in which they are used in scientific copy they are usually set without periods. Like other abbreviations, these are most useful in tabular work. (For the use of numerals with abbreviations see 8.15.)

LENGTH, AREA, AND VOLUME

14.38

LENGTH		AREA		VOLUME	
in. *or* "	inch	sq. in.	square inch	cu. in.	cubic inch
ft. *or* '	foot	sq. ft.	square foot	cu. ft.	cubic foot
yd.	yard	sq. yd.	square yard	cu. yd.	cubic yard
rd.	rod	sq. rd.	square rod		
mi.	mile	sq. mi.	square mile		

Sometimes exponents are used with the common abbreviations to designate area or volume:

The area of the floor to be covered is 425 ft.^{2}.
The volume of the tank was estimated to be 638 ft.^{3}.

WEIGHT AND CAPACITY

14.39 The complicated English system of measures is further complicated in the case of weight and mass by having three systems to deal with: *avoirdupois* (the common system), *troy* (used mainly by jewelers), and *apothecaries' measure*. There is little chance of confusion between systems, however, and the abbreviations are similar. If need be, an abbreviation can be referred to the appropriate system in this way: *lb. av., lb. t., lb. ap.* Also, the systems of capacity measure used in the United States and in parts of the British Commonwealth differ, but the names of the units are the same, and abbreviations seldom have to be distinguished.

WEIGHT OR MASS		DRY MEASURE		LIQUID MEASURE	
gr.	grain	pt.	pint	min. *or* ♏	minim
s. *or* ℈	scruple	qt.	quart	fl. dr. *or* f.ʒ	fluid dram
dr. *or* ʒ	dram	pk.	peck	fl. oz. *or* f. ℥	fluid ounce
dwt.	pennyweight	bu.	bushel	gi.	gill
oz. *or* ℥	ounce			pt.	pint
lb. *or* #				qt.	quart
(av. only)	pound			gal.	gallon
cwt.	hundredweight			bbl.	barrel
tn.	ton				

TIME

14.40 English abbreviations for the standard units of time are given here. (For other abbreviations concerned with time, see 14.26–31. For a discussion of time of day see 8.47–50.)

sec.	second	h. *or* hr.	hour	mo.	month
min.	minute	d. *or* day	day	yr.	year

In the international system of measure, which is discussed in the following paragraphs, the abbreviations (often referred to as "symbols") for *second, minute, hour,* and *day* are *s, min, h,* and *d*—without periods. These abbreviations are used for both singular and plural.

International Measure

14.41 The International System of Units (*Système international d'unités*, abbreviated internationally as SI) is a modernized and expanded version of the metric system. It is in general use among the world's scientists, and its employment in other fields is also nearly worldwide. In the

United States its implementation, although progressing slowly, is now an officially recognized goal.

14.42   As the system is currently used, there are seven fundamental SI units, termed "base units":

QUANTITY	UNIT	ABBREVIATION
length	meter/metre[2]	m
mass[1]	kilogram	kg
time	second	s
electric current	ampere	A
thermodynamic temperature	kelvin	K
amount of substance	mole	mol
luminance intensity	candela	cd

14.43   Although not included among the base units, the *liter* is widely used in the international system as a fundamental measure of volume or capacity. One liter is the equivalent of one cubic decimeter or 1,000 cubic centimeters. The abbreviation for liter is *l*.

14.44   All SI units are written in lowercase style except *Celsius* (as in "degrees Celsius"), which, like *Fahrenheit,* is capitalized. Abbreviations, or symbols, for the units are also lowercased, with the exception of two classes: certain SI prefixes (see 14.45) that must be distinguished from similar but lowercased abbreviations, and abbreviations for terms derived from such proper names as André Ampère, Heinrich Hertz, James Joule, and Alessandro Volta (see 14.48). No periods are used with the abbreviations in the international system, and the same abbreviations are used for both singular and plural.

14.45   In addition to the base units of the system, a host of derived units, which stem from the base units, are employed. One class of these is formed by adding a prefix, representing a power of ten, to the base unit. For example, a *kilometer* is equal to 1,000 meters, and a *millise-*

---

1. Although *weight* and *mass* are generally measured in the same units, the distinction between them must be observed in the fields of science and technology, and although this distinction is less of a concern in nontechnical fields, care should nevertheless be taken not to use one term when the other is meant. *Mass* is the amount of matter in an object; it may also be regarded as the object's resistance to movement or acceleration. *Weight,* on the other hand, is the gravitational force acting on the object. The weight of an object varies with its distance from the center of the earth, or from any other great astronomical body. Mass is constant at any distance from such a body but increases as the velocity of the object approaches that of light.

2. For a discussion of the variant spellings of *meter* and *liter* see 7.124.

cond is 0.001 (that is, 1/1,000) second. The prefixes in current use are as follows:

PREFIXES

Factor	Prefix	Symbol	Factor	Prefix	Symbol
10^{24}	yotta	Y	10^{-1}	deci	d
10^{21}	zetta	Z	10^{-2}	centi	c
10^{18}	exa	E	10^{-3}	milli	m
10^{15}	peta	P	10^{-6}	micro	μ
10^{12}	tera	T	10^{-9}	nano	n
10^{9}	giga	G	10^{-12}	pico	p
10^{6}	mega	M	10^{-15}	femto	f
10^{3}	kilo	k	10^{-18}	atto	a
10^{2}	hecto	h	10^{-21}	zepto	z
10^{1}	deka (*or* deca)	da	10^{-24}	yocto	y

14.46   Although, for historical reasons, the kilogram rather than the gram was chosen as the base unit, prefixes are applied to the term *gram* instead of the official base unit: megagram (Mg), milligram (mg), nanogram (ng), and so forth.

14.47   Another class of derived units consists of powers of base units and of base units in algebraic relationships. Some of the more familiar of these are the following:

QUANTITY	UNIT	SYMBOL
area	square meter	m^2
volume	cubic meter	m^3
velocity	meter per second	m/s *or* $m \cdot s^{-1}$
acceleration	meter per second squared	m/s^2 *or* $m \cdot s^{-2}$
density	kilogram per cubic meter	kg/m^3 *or* $kg \cdot m^{-3}$
luminance	candela per square meter	cd/m^2 *or* $cd \cdot m^{-2}$
heat capacity	joule per kelvin	J/K *or* $J \cdot K^{-1}$
dynamic viscosity	pascal second	$Pa \cdot s$

Note the raised dot, or multiplier sign, used in some of the symbols above.

14.48   Many derived SI units have names of their own:

QUANTITY	UNIT	SYMBOL	EQUIVALENT
frequency	hertz	Hz	cycles per second
force	newton	N	kilogram-meters per second squared
pressure	pascal	Pa	newtons per square meter
energy	joule	J	newton-meter
power	watt	W	joules per second

quantity of electricity	coulomb	C	ampere-second
electric potential	volt	V	watts per ampere
capacitance	farad	F	coulombs per volt
electrical resistance	ohm	Ω	volts per ampere
electrical conductance	siemens	S	amperes per volt
magnetic flux	weber	Wb	volt-second
inductance	henry (*pl.* henries)	H	webers per ampere
absorbed dose	gray	Gy	joules per kilogram
activity (of radio-nuclides)	becquerel	Bq	cycles per second

Note that a Greek omega is used as the symbol for *ohm*. If a Greek font is not available, the full three-letter term may be used in place of the symbol. In expressions consisting of abbreviations or symbols, the word may be treated as an abbreviation and, because derived from a proper name, capitalized. Thus 10 kilo-ohms, or 10,000 ohms, may be represented as 10 kOhm.

USE OF NUMERALS WITH SI UNITS

14.49   In the international system it is considered preferable to use only numbers between 0.1 and 1,000 in expressing the quantity of any SI unit. Thus the quantity 12,000 meters is expressed as 12 km, not 12,000 m. So too, 0.003 cubic centimeter is preferably written 3 mm³, not 0.003 cm³. A word space is used between the numeral and the abbreviation.

SCIENCE AND TECHNOLOGY

Units Other Than SI Units

14.50   The International System of Units (14.41–49) has not yet displaced many older units and modes of expression used in all branches of science. A number of disciplines accept the SI units and usages only insofar as they retain some elements of older scientific vocabulary, and others accept the system but supplement it with units and practices of their own. What follows is a list of units of measure and their abbreviations, as well as other common abbreviations, used in various branches of the physical and biological sciences or by engineers and technicians. A few of these units are identical with units of the international system, many are compatible with the system, and some are unrelated to it.

A, ampere
Å, angstrom (unit for wavelength: 10^{-10} m *or* 0.1 nm)
ac, alternating current
AF, audiofrequency
Ah, ampere-hour
AM, amplitude modulation
atm, standard atmosphere (unit of pressure: 101.325 kPa)
at mass, atomic mass (*replaces* atomic weight)
av *or* avdp, avoirdupois
bar, bar (unit of pressure: 100 kPa)
°Bé, degrees Baumé
BHP, brake horsepower
BP, boiling point
Bq, becquerel
Btu, British thermal unit
°C, degrees Celsius (*replaces* centigrade)
C, coulomb
C/kg, coulomb per kilogram (*replaces* roentgen)
Cal, large calorie, *or* kilocalorie
cal, small calorie
cm³, cubic centimeter
CP, candlepower
cps *or* c/s, cycles per second
cu, cubic
dB, decibel
dc, direct current
d.f. *or* DOF, degrees of freedom
dyn, dyne (10^{-5} N)
EMF, electromotive force
erg, erg (10^{-7} J)
eV, electron volt
°F, degrees Fahrenheit
FM, frequency modulation
ft lb *or* ft lbf, foot-pound force
GeV, billion (10^9) electron volts
Gy, gray (*replaces* rad)
ha, hectare (10^4 m²)
hp, horsepower
Hz, hertz
K, kelvin (unit of absolute temperature)
kb, kilobar
kc, kilocycle
kHz, kilohertz
km/h, kilometers per hour
kn, knot (nautical mile per hour)
kW, kilowatt
kWh, kilowatt-hour
l, liter
LS, least squares
Mc, megacycle
mc, millicurie
MeV, million electron volts

ml, milliliter
MP, melting point
MPG, miles per gallon
MPH, miles per hour
MS, mean square
N *or* n, number (database)
neg, negative
NM *or* naut mi, nautical mile (1,852 m)
NS *or* n.s., not significant
p, probability
pF, picofarad (*replaces* micromicrofarad)
pH, measure of acidity or alkalinity
pos, positive
R *or* r, correlation
°R, degrees Réaumur
RF, radio frequency
rms, root mean square
rpm *or* r/min, revolutions per minute
SD *or* s.d., standard deviation
SE *or* s.e., standard error
sp gr, specific gravity
sq, square
SS, sum of squares
std, standard
STP, standard temperature and pressure
STPA, standard temperature and pressure, absolute
Sv, sievert (*replaces* rem)
t, tonne *or* metric ton (10^3 kg)
temp, temperature

Astronomy

14.51 Astronomers and astrophysicists employ the international system of measure but supplement it with special terminology and abbreviations. Some of these are detailed in the paragraphs that follow.

CELESTIAL COORDINATES

14.52 *Right ascension,* abbreviated R.A. or α, is given in hours, minutes, and seconds of sidereal time, and *declination,* abbreviated δ, is given in degrees, minutes, and seconds of arc north (marked + or left unmarked) or south (marked $-$) of the celestial equator:

$14^h6^m7^s$ $-49°8'22''$

If decimal fractions of the basic units are employed, they are indicated as shown:

$14^h6^m7\overset{s}{.}2$ $+34\overset{°}{.}26$

OTHER UNITS AND ABBREVIATIONS

14.53 Some other units and abbreviations used in astronomy are the following:

AU	astronomical unit (mean earth-sun distance)
lt-yr	light-year (distance light travels in a year: 9.46×10^{12} km)
pc	parsec (parallax second: 3.084×10^{13} km), kpc (1,000 pc), Mpc (10^6 pc)
UT *or* UTC	universal time

Chemical Elements

14.54 The symbols for the chemical elements are one-, two-, or three-letter abbreviations of their official or Latin names (e.g., lead = *plumbum*). They are used in text as well as in equations, formulas, and tabular matter. These abbreviations are never set with periods. (For the use of mass and molecular numbers with names of the elements see 7.122.)

actinium	Ac	gallium	Ga
aluminum	Al	germanium	Ge
americium	Am	gold	Au
antimony	Sb	hafnium	Hf
argon	Ar	helium	He
arsenic	As	holmium	Ho
astatine	At	hydrogen	H
barium	Ba	indium	In
berkelium	Bk	iodine	I
beryllium	Be	iridium	Ir
bismuth	Bi	iron	Fe
boron	B	krypton	Kr
bromine	Br	lanthanum	La
cadmium	Cd	lawrencium	Lr
calcium	Ca	lead	Pb
californium	Cf	lithium	Li
carbon	C	lutetium	Lu
cerium	Ce	magnesium	Mg
cesium	Cs	manganese	Mn
chlorine	Cl	mendelevium	Md
chromium	Cr	mercury	Hg
cobalt	Co	molybdenum	Mo
copper	Cu	neodymium	Nd
curium	Cm	neon	Ne
dysprosium	Dy	neptunium	Np
einsteinium	Es	nickel	Ni
erbium	Er	niobium	Nb
europium	Eu	nitrogen	N
fermium	Fm	nobelium	No
fluorine	F	osmium	Os
francium	Fr	oxygen	O
gadolinium	Gd	palladium	Pd

phosphorus	P	sulfur	S
platinum	Pt	tantalum	Ta
plutonium	Pu	technetium	Tc
polonium	Po	tellurium	Te
potassium	K	terbium	Tb
praseodymium	Pr	thallium	Tl
promethium	Pm	thorium	Th
protactinium	Pa	thulium	Tm
radium	Ra	tin	Sn
radon	Rn	titanium	Ti
rhenium	Re	tungsten	W
rhodium	Rh	unnilhexium	Unh
rubidium	Rb	unnilpentium	Unp
ruthenium	Ru	unnilquandium	Unq
samarium	Sm	uranium	U
scandium	Sc	vanadium	V
selenium	Se	xenon	Xe
silicon	Si	ytterbium	Yb
silver	Ag	yttrium	Y
sodium	Na	Zinc	Zn
strontium	Sr	Zirconium	Zr

COMMERCIAL COPY

14.55 Copy concerned with commerce, especially tabular matter, makes frequent use of many of the abbreviations and symbols given here.

GENERAL ABBREVIATIONS

acct.	account	doz.	dozen
agt.	agent	dr.	debit, debtor
a/v, a.v., *or* AV	ad valorem	ea.	each
bal.	balance	f.o.b. *or* FOB	free on board
bbl.	barrel	gro.	gross
bdl.	bundle	mdse.	merchandise
bu.	bushel	mfg.	manufacturing
c. *or* ct.	cent	mfr.	manufacturer
c.l. *or* CL	carload	p.	penny, pence
c/o	in care of	pd.	paid
COD	cash on delivery	pk.	peck
cr.	credit, -or	pkg.	package
cwt.	hundredweight	s.	shilling
d.	pence	std.	standard
dol.	dollar	ult.	*ultimo* (last month)

SYMBOLS

℔ *or* /	per	©	copyright
#	number; pound	Mex$	Mexican peso
%	percent	Can$	Canadian dollar
@	at	£	pound
$	dollar	I£	Israeli pound
¢	cent	¥	yen

485

CONSTITUTIONS AND BYLAWS

14.56 In quoting from constitutions, bylaws, and the like, the words *section* and *article* are spelled out the first time they are used and abbreviated thereafter. Caps and small caps are traditionally employed for these words:

> SECTION 1. The name of the association . . .
> SEC. 2. The object of the association . . .
>
> ARTICLE 234. It shall be the duty of . . .
> ART. 235. It shall be the duty of . . .

FOR FURTHER REFERENCE

14.57 *Webster's New Collegiate Dictionary* and the *American Heritage Dictionary* include a great many abbreviations from all fields—in strict letter-by-letter alphabetical order.

15 *Documentation 1*
Notes and Bibliographies

INTRODUCTION

15.1 Almost every work that is neither fiction nor an account based on personal experience relies in part on secondary sources (other publications on the same or related subjects) or on primary sources (manuscript collections, archives, contemporary accounts, diaries, books, personal interviews, and so on). Ethics, as well as the laws of copyright, requires authors to identify their sources, particularly when quoting directly from them. Conventions and practices for thus documenting a text have long varied from discipline to discipline, from publisher to publisher, and from journal to journal. Increasingly, however, the old distinctions are becoming blurred as scholars cross disciplinary lines and as publishers, more than ever concerned about the balance sheet, urge conciseness and practicality over scholarly indulgence in documentation.

15.2 Two basic documentation systems, each favored by different groups of scholars, will be presented in this manual. One of these systems, often referred to as the documentary-note or humanities style and still favored by many in literature, history, and the arts, provides bibliographic citations in notes. Documentary notes of this sort may or may not be accompanied by a bibliography. The other system, long used by those in the physical and natural sciences and now gaining adherents in the social sciences and humanities, is known as the author-date system. Sources are cited in the text, usually in parentheses, by author's last name and the date of publication. These short author-date citations are then amplified in a list of references, where full bibliographic information is given. The author-date system of citation will be presented in the next chapter. The advantages of the author-date system are its brevity and clarity. Its use for the more esoteric source citations, however, is somewhat cumbersome. The humanities system is not so succinct as the author-date style, but it does offer its own forms of condensation, and it is probably more accommodating to a book with many esoteric sources.

15.3 A third method, somewhat related to the author-date system, but in the Press's opinion much less satisfactory, employs a numbered list of references cited in the text by number. The reference numbers in the text are placed in parentheses (12) or square brackets [12] or, in some medical publications, are set as superior figures (^{12}). The list of references or works cited is arranged either alphabetically by authors' last names or in order of the first appearance of each source in the text. The chief disadvantage of this system is that additions or deletions cannot be

---

In the preparation of this chapter, some material has been adapted from *A Manual for Writers of Term Papers, Theses, and Dissertations,* by Kate L. Turabian, revised and expanded for the fifth edition by Bonnie Birtwistle Honigsblum, © 1987 by The University of Chicago.

made without changing numbers in both text references and list. The author-date system, on the other hand, permits additions or deletions up to the moment the manuscript is set in type and has the added advantage that readers familiar with the sources will not have to turn to the list of works cited each time a reference is given in the text.

Notes

15.4   Notes documenting the text, and corresponding to reference numbers in the text, are properly called *footnotes* when they are printed at the foot of the page and *notes* or *endnotes* (sometimes *backnotes*) when they are printed at the back of the book, at the end of a chapter, or at the end of an article in a journal.

15.5   In book manuscripts using the note system of documentation, the University of Chicago Press, generally for economic but sometimes also for aesthetic reasons, prefers that authors use endnotes rather than footnotes. (For guidelines on preparing notes see 2.21–22.)

NOTE NUMBERS

15.6   Notes should be numbered consecutively, beginning with 1, throughout each chapter or article. Although in scholarly books this sometimes results in three-digit numbers, it is far more practical than the old-fashioned system of numbering footnotes beginning with 1 on each page, which required resetting numbers in proof.

15.7   If any notes are added or deleted in the typescript, the following numbers throughout the chapter or article must be changed, including the numbered references in the text and any cross-references to notes. Such evidence of incompletely digested revision as a note numbered 4a is unprofessional. If the book has already been typeset, material to be added to the notes should be inserted at the end of an existing note, or in parentheses in the text. At the page-proof stage, however, strenuous effort should be made to add nothing that would alter the length of the type page.

15.8   *Note reference numbers.* The superior numerals used for note reference numbers in the text should follow any punctuation marks except the dash, which they precede. The numbers should also be placed outside closing parentheses.

"This," George Templeton Strong wrote approvingly, "is what our tailors can do."[1]

(In an earlier book he had said quite the opposite.)[2]

This was obvious in the Shotwell series[3]—and it must be remembered that Shotwell was a student of Robinson.

15.9   Wherever possible a note number should come at the end of a sentence, or at least at the end of a clause. Numbers set between the subject and verb or between other related words in a sentence are distracting to the reader.

15.10   Preferably, the note number *follows* a quotation, whether the quotation is short and run into the text or long and set off from the text. Occasionally it may be inserted after an author's name or after text introducing the quotation.

15.11   Placing note reference numbers at the end of, or within, a line of display type (such as a chapter title or a subheading) is discouraged, not only for aesthetic reasons, but also because it may suggest negligence in organization. A note applicable to an entire chapter or article should be unnumbered and should precede the numbered notes (see 15.50–52). A reference number that appears at the end of a subhead should be moved to an appropriate location in the text.

15.12   The use of more than one note reference at a single text location (such as [5,6]) should be rigorously avoided. Instead, the notes referred to should be combined into a single note. A change in subject matter within such a note is sufficiently indicated by separate paragraphing.

15.13   *Multiple citation of a single note.* A note that is applicable to more than one location in the text may be cited, or cross-referenced, as follows:

> 18. See note 3 above.

15.14   *Notes to tables and other illustrative material.* Notes to tables, charts, graphs, or other illustrative material are numbered independently of the text notes. Symbols or letters, sometimes numbers, indicate notes to such material (see 12.51), and the notes are printed below the table or illustration, not at the foot of the text page or at the end of the book or article.

EXTENSIVE VERSUS EXCESSIVE DOCUMENTATION

15.15   Although a few scholarly works may require extensive or even preponderant annotation, most benefit from a more sparing documentation. In most instances authors can, by careful planning, avoid the pitfalls of excessive documentation without compromising their obligations to scholarship.

15.16   *Reducing the length and number of notes.* The author may reconsider a lengthy discursive note amplifying the text. Is all of it essential? Can some or all of it be included in the text rather than in a note?

15.17 *Several citations in one paragraph.* The number of note references in a paragraph might be reduced by grouping several citations in one note instead of devoting a separate note to each. For example, a sentence such as the following requires only one footnote, not five:

> Only when we gather the work of several men—Walter Sutton's explications of some of Whitman's shorter poems; Paul Fussell's careful study of structure in "Cradle"; S. K. Coffman's close readings of "Crossing Brooklyn Ferry" and "Passage to India"; and the attempts of Thomas I. Rountree and John Lovell, dealing with "Song of Myself" and "Passage to India," respectively, to elucidate the strategy in "indirection"—do we begin to get a sense of both the extent and specificity of Whitman's forms.[1]

> 1. Sutton, "The Analysis of Free Verse Form, Illustrated by a Reading of Whitman," *Journal of Aesthetics and Art Criticism* 18 (December 1959): 241–54; Fussell, "Whitman's Curious Warble: Reminiscence and Reconciliation," in *The Presence of Whitman,* ed. R. W. B. Lewis, 28–51; Coffman, "'Crossing Brooklyn Ferry': Note on the Catalog Technique in Whitman's Poetry," *Modern Philology* 51 (May 1954): 225–32, and "Form and Meaning in Whitman's 'Passage to India,'" *PMLA* 70 (June 1955): 337–49; Rountree, "Whitman's Indirect Expression and Its Application to 'Song of Myself,'" *PMLA* 73 (December 1958): 549–55; and Lovell, "Appreciating Whitman: 'Passage to India,'" *Modern Language Quarterly* 21 (June 1960): 131–41.

15.18 *Several short quotations in one paragraph.* A paragraph containing several short quotations may carry one note reference at the end of the paragraph or following the last of the quotations. The corresponding note must, of course, list the citations in order of their appearance in the paragraph. Here, in deference to the reader, the author must be judicious. One note listing four references when there are, say, six unidentified quotations in the paragraph is confusing. Ordinarily, one note reference should not apply to material in more than one paragraph (except, of course, to a single quotation of more than one paragraph).

15.19 *Parenthetical references to works by several authors.* In a discussion of several works, each by a different author, the note for the first quotation or reference might give the full documentation for all of the works in such a way as to enable subsequent references to be reduced to parenthetical page citations in the text:

> 1. Unless otherwise stated, the poetry of Wallace Stevens is quoted from *The Collected Poems* (New York: Alfred A. Knopf, 1954), that of Marianne Moore from *The Complete Poems* (New York: Viking Press, 1967), and that of Robert Frost from *The Poetry of Robert Frost,* ed. Edward Connery Lathem (New York: Holt, Rinehart, and Winston, 1969).

Page numbers for all quotations from Stevens, Moore, and Frost may then be given in the text rather than in the notes. For example:

> Frost found the indefinite pronoun a useful device: "Something there is that doesn't love a wall" (p. 33).

15.20 *Tables, lists, and similar entities.* Complicated tabular material, lists, and other entities that are not part of the text should be put in an appendix at the back of the book rather than in the footnotes. The footnotes may read simply:

> 2. For a list of institutions involved see appendix A.

If endnotes are used instead of footnotes, simple tables, lists, and so forth, may be included in the notes rather than set up as separate appendixes.

15.21 *Use and overuse of ibid.* When a number of successive references are made to a single work, without intervention of a reference to a different work, all but the first, full reference may be shortened by the use of *ibid.* (see 15.253–54). The use of ibid., which, incidentally, is ordinarily set in roman type (see 6.70), should not be so extensive, however, as to produce a string or "garland" of ibids. A series of notes consisting of nothing more than ibids. and page or line references may exasperate the reader. The reader's convenience is better served if the successive page or line references are placed in parentheses in the text.

15.22 Should a reference to a different work intervene in such a succession of references to a single work, the first reference following the intervention should be given in a note containing a short citation of the original work (see 15.248–61).

> As he engages Blassingham's notion, Fermator at first expresses, with some annoyance, the opinion that it is without practical application,[1] but while tracing the idea's development by other commentators, he seems to begin gradually, tentatively, to change his mind (38–45). Although never quite adopting the view that much will come of the idea, Fermator at one point does acknowledge that it might be worth someone's while to pursue the "remote" possibility of the concept's being put to some, perhaps minor, industrial use (61). Later, however, he again becomes skeptical and denies the concept any relevance "in the world of practical affairs" (206).
>
> At the same time that he is disposing of Blassingham's idea, Fermator displays interest in a proposal offered in an article published by his brother-in-law, Charles Gimperson.[2] Growing more and more enthusiastic as he discusses it, Fermator goes so far as to remark that the idea not only has a certain freshness, but that indeed it has immeasurable practical implications.[3] So captivated is Fermator by Gimperson's idea that he takes the trouble to provide colorful sketches of some of the more important consequences he foresees (241–53).
>
> Ultimately, however, a very odd thing happens. Near the end of his book (288), Fermator permits himself the following enigmatic observation: "When all is said and done, however, Gimperson's idea may prove to be of less importance than Blassingham's."
>
> 1. August Wellington Fermator, *Industrial Development in the Late Twentieth Century* (Colefax, Md.: Colefax University Press, 1990), 24.
> 2. Charles Gimperson, "A Suggestion for Combining Seemingly Oppos-

ing Processes," *Industrial Waste Management Review* 9 (April 1989): 12–13.

   3. Fermator, *Industrial Development,* 231.

15.23 *Clarity of reference.* When several citations are combined into one note, as described in the paragraphs above, care should be taken in both the placing of the note reference number in the text and the arrangement of the citations within the note that no ambiguity arises concerning the various references. Similarly, the reference number to a note containing a single citation or a single discussion should be close enough to the relevant material in the text that the reference is clear.

15.24 *Using abbreviations for frequently cited works.* Citations of works frequently mentioned throughout a chapter, article, or book may be made parenthetically in the text by employing abbreviations, with full citations provided in a note at the first mention.

> He wrote to his close friend Gorham Munson: "The more I think about my *Bridge* poem the more thrilling its symbolical possibilities become, and since my reading of you and [Waldo] Frank (I recently bought *City Block*) I begin to feel myself directly connected with Whitman. I feel myself in currents that are positively awesome in their extent and possibilities" (*L*, 128).[1] This confession that *The Bridge* and Whitman were, from the outset, inextricably mixed . . .

>   1. Quotations from Hart Crane's works are cited in the text with the abbreviations listed below. When lines are sufficiently located, as by the titles of short poems or sections of longer poems, no citation appears.
>   *L: The Letters of Hart Crane, 1916–1932,* ed. Brom Weber (Berkeley and Los Angeles: University of California Press, 1965).
>   *CP: The Complete Poems and Selected Letters and Prose,* ed. Brom Weber (Garden City, N.Y.: Doubleday, Anchor Books, 1966).

Subsequent text appearance:

> Crane himself explained, in "General Aims and Theories" (written sometime in 1924–26): "When I started writing 'Faust & Helen' it was my intention to embody in modern terms . . . a contemporary approximation to an ancient human culture. . . . And in so doing I found that I was really building a bridge between so-called classic experience and many divergent realities of our seething, confused cosmos of today, which has no formulated mythology yet for classic reference or for religious exploitation" (*CP*, 217).

15.25 *Lists of abbreviations.* Where many abbreviations of titles, manuscript collections, personal names, or other entities—say, ten or more—are used throughout a book or merely throughout the notes, they are best listed alphabetically in a separate section preceding the endnotes. If the list occupies half a page or less, the abbreviations may be placed between the heading "Notes" and the beginning of the notes themselves (fig. 15.1). A longer list is usually given the heading "Abbreviations"—set in a style parallel to "Notes"—and placed on a page, or

---

Notes

In citing works in the notes, short titles have generally been used. Works frequently cited have been identified by the following abbreviations:

Ac. Sc. Archives de l'Académie des sciences.

A.P. *Archives parlementaires de 1787 à 1860, première série (1787 à 1799).* Edited by M. J. Mavidal and M. E. Laurent. 2d ed. 82 vols. Paris, 1879–1913.

Best. Theodore Besterman, ed. *Voltaire's Correspondence.* 107 vols. Geneva, 1953–65.

B. Inst. Bibliothèque de l'Institut de France.

B.N., nouv. acqu. Bibliothèque Nationale. Fonds français, nouvelles acquisitions.

Corresp. inéd. Charles Henry, ed. *Correspondance inédite de Condorcet et de Turgot (1770–1779).* Paris, 1883.

HMAS *Histoire de l'Académie royale des sciences. Avec les mémoires de mathématique et de physique . . . tirés des registres de cette académie (1699–1790).* 92 vols. Paris, 1702–97. Each volume comprises two separately paginated parts, referred to as *Hist.* and *Mém.,* respectively.

Inéd. Lespinasse Charles Henry, ed. *Lettres inédites de Mlle de Lespinasse.* Paris, 1887.

O.C. A. Condorcet-O'Connor and F. Arago, eds. *Oeuvres de Condorcet.* 12 vols. Paris, 1847–49.

Preface

1. Peter Gay, *The Enlightenment: An Interpretation,* 2 vols. (New York, 1966–69), 2:319. I have suggested some criticisms of Gay's treatment of this theme in a review of the second volume of his work, *American Historical Review* 85 (1970): 1410–14.

2. Georges Gusdorf, *Introduction aux sciences humaines: Essai critique sur leurs origines et leur développement* (Strasbourg and Paris, 1960), 105–331.

Fig. 15.1. A short list of abbreviations preceding endnotes

pages, preceding the note section (fig. 15.2). Where abbreviations are used in footnotes rather than endnotes, the list of abbreviations may be printed at the end of the preliminary pages or at the end of the text.

15.26 *Shortened citations.* In order to reduce the bulk of documentation in scholarly works, subsequent citations to sources already given in full should be shortened whenever possible. A detailed discussion of the shortening process is presented in 15.248–61, after the components and varieties of full documentation for book and periodical literature have been covered. Other references, such as those to public documents, require somewhat different methods of shortening, and guidance

Abbreviations

ALHUA	Archives of Labor History and Urban Affairs, Wayne State University, Detroit, Michigan
DFP	*Detroit Free Press*
DLN	*Detroit Labor News*
DN	*Detroit News*
DT	*Detroit Times*
EG	Eugene Gressman
EG Papers	Eugene Gressman Papers, Michigan Historical Collections, Ann Arbor, Michigan
EGK	Edward G. Kemp
EGK Papers	Edward G. Kemp Papers, Michigan Historical Collections
EGK-BHC	Edward G. Kemp Papers, Burton Historical Collection, Detroit, Michigan
EMB	Eleanor M. Bumgardner
EMB Papers	Eleanor M. Bumgardner Papers, Michigan Historical Collections
FDR	Franklin D. Roosevelt
FDRL	Franklin D. Roosevelt Library, Hyde Park, New York
FM	Frank Murphy
FM Papers	Frank Murphy Papers, Michigan Historical Collections
GM	George Murphy
GM Papers	George Murphy Papers, Michigan Historical Collections
HM	Harold Murphy
HM Papers	Harold Murphy Papers, Michigan Historical Collections
HSB	Norman H. Hill Scrapbooks, Michigan Historical Collections
IM	Irene Murphy
IM Papers	Irene Murphy Papers, Michigan Historical Collections
JAF	James A. Farley
JRH	Joseph Ralston Hayden

Fig. 15.2. First page of a list of abbreviations including personal names as well as manuscript collections and newspaper titles, all of which are used extensively in the note section that follows. The abbreviations for newspaper titles are italicized; other abbreviations are roman.

for these will be offered where necessary in the discussion of such material.

THE CONTENT OF NOTES

15.27 *Citations.* In a work with no bibliography or with only a discursive bibliographical essay or other nonalphabetical arrangement of sources, a note—either endnote or footnote—documenting the first reference to a source should include full bibliographical details (see 15.77). Subsequent citations to the same source may use a short form (15.248).

15.28 In a work with many references cited in footnotes, repetition of the full citation at first appearance in each chapter is often helpful, but not essential. With endnotes a full citation of the same source in each chapter is unnecessary and perhaps even undesirable because the notes are all together and the reader can find other references to a given work much more readily than if they were scattered throughout the book in footnotes.

15.29 When endnotes or footnotes are extensive or when references to a particular source are far apart, a cross-reference to the note giving the full citation will aid the reader:

> 95. Miller, *Quest,* 81 (see chap. 1, n. 4).

15.30 *Order of items.* When a note contains not only the source of material in the text but related substantive material as well, the source comes first. The additional material may start a new sentence or may be separated from the source by a semicolon, depending on the nature of the material. (For more on substantive notes see 15.53.)

15.31 Several references documenting a single fact in the text should be separated by semicolons, the last one followed by a period (see example in 15.17).

15.32 *Quotations.* When a note includes a quotation, the source may be given following the terminal punctuation of the quotation, as follows:

> 1. One estimate of the size of the reading public at this time was that of Sydney Smith: "Readers are fourfold in number compared with what they were before the beginning of the French war. . . . There are four or five hundred thousand readers more than there were thirty years ago, among the lower orders." *Letters,* ed. Nowell C. Smith (New York: Oxford University Press, 1953), 1:341, 343.

An acceptable alternative is to give the source in parentheses after the quotation and before the final period. In that case, the period is transferred from the end of the quotation to the end of the citation, following the closing parenthesis, and square brackets within the parentheses enclose the facts of publication.

". . . among the lower orders" (*Letters,* ed. Nowell C. Smith [New York: Oxford University Press, 1953], 1:341, 343).

Consistency should be observed in this, as in other matters, throughout the book.

15.33 A long quotation in the midst or at the end of an endnote (but not in a footnote) may be treated as a block quotation, or extract, is treated in the text (see 10.9). A similarly long quotation standing by itself as an endnote, however, or a long quotation that comes at the beginning of an endnote, should be set full measure and enclosed in quotation marks to avoid "floating" note numbers.

15.34 *See also and cf.* Authors should keep in mind the distinction between *see* or *see also* and *cf.* (*confer,* "compare"). These expressions are not italicized in notes (except *cf.* in legal style) and are capitalized only when they begin a sentence.

ENDNOTES

15.35 *Placement.* Endnotes are best placed at the back of a book, in a section entitled "Notes," after any appendix material and before a bibliography. Notes may be placed at the end of a chapter in a volume that has a different author for each chapter, such as collections of essays, symposium papers, or reports. (Notes must be printed with their respective papers when offprints are to be supplied.) Most readers, however, consider notes at the end of a chapter harder to find than notes printed together at the end of a book, with running heads to assist in their location.

15.36 *Arrangement.* Endnotes are arranged by chapter in the note section. The chapter number or title or both must be given—usually as an A-level subhead (see 1.71). Book designers' specifications will differ, of course, but one way to print notes is illustrated in figure 15.3.

15.37 *Running heads.* To facilitate location of specific notes, each page of the note section, except the opening page, should carry a running head indicating the inclusive text pages on which the references to the notes on that page appear (see fig. 15.3). Page numbers in these running heads must be inserted, after all pages have been made up, by either the author or the editor; they must never be left to the typesetter.

15.38 To determine what text page numbers to use in the running head for a particular page of the note section, find the numbers of the first and last notes beginning on that page (disregarding a runover from a previous page) and locate the references to these notes in the text. The numbers of the first and last pages on which these references appear are the numbers to use in the running head for that note page.

46. Here I have been very influenced by the work of Paul Johnston. See his "Politics of Public Work" (Ph.D. diss., University of California, Berkeley, 1988).

47. See Burawoy, "Should We Give Up on Socialism? Reflections on Bowles and Gintis' *Democracy and Capitalism*," *Socialist Review* 89:1 (1989): 59–76. For Sam Bowles and Herb Gintis's reply, see "Democratic Demands and Radical Rights," *Socialist Review* 89:4 (1989): 57–72.

48. That jokes are such a pervasive form of communication is itself testimony to the gulf between appearances and reality. Jokes are the most effective way of capturing the double existence of workers: the opposition between ideological and real experiences. In capitalism, ideology is more diffuse and enjoined to reality more smoothly, so jokes are not so central to the discourse of daily life. See, for example, the preponderance of jokes about socialism in Steven Lukes and Itzhak Galnoor, *No Laughing Matter* (London: Routledge and Kegan Paul, 1985).

Chapter Six: The Radiant Future

1. I say *mankind* advisedly, since much of the anticommunist agitation has gone along with an equally vehement endorsement of the patriarchal family.

2. It has become a cliché to criticize Lenin for his neglect of individual rights. One of his earliest and most eloquent critics was Rosa Luxemburg, who argued that there can be no radical democracy without the protection of bourgeois rights. See Rosa Luxemburg, "The Russian Revolution" (1918), in *Rosa Luxemburg Speaks*, ed. Alice Waters (New York: Pathfinder, 1970). For more contemporary criticisms, see A. J. Polan, *Lenin and the End of Politics* (Berkeley: University of California Press, 1984), and Steven Lukes, *Marxism and Morality* (Oxford: Oxford University Press, 1985).

3. For an excellent description and analysis of the miners' strikes in the Ukraine, see Theodore Friedgut and Lewis Siegelbaum, "Perestroika from Below: The Soviet Miners' Strike and Its Aftermath," *New Left Review* 181 (May–June 1990): 5–32.

4. See László Bruszt, "1989: The Negotiated Revolution in Hungary," *Social Research* 57 (1990): 365–87. Ellen Comisso argues that the difference between Poland's and Hungary's negotiated transitions lay in the presence of Solidarity—an established alternative to the Communist party which was absent in Hungary. "It is this that perhaps explains why the PUWP [Polish United Workers' Party] stood firm for so long in the face of mass opposition while the Hungarian party, confronted with the demands of a few thousand intellectuals, conceded virtually everything" (Comisso, "Crisis in Socialism or Crisis of Socialism," *World Politics* 42 [1990]: 570).

5. Many writers believe that the socialist economy is inherently unreformable. János Kornai, for example, argues that the root of the problem lies in soft budget constraints, and that any attempt to harden them without changing ownership relations is doomed to failure. See Kornai, *The Economics of Short-*

Fig. 15.3. A page of endnotes, showing how notes are divided by chapter and how the running head gives the location of the references to the notes on this page

15.39   There is an alternative that will eliminate the need to wait for page proof before making up the running heads for the note section. Instead of inclusive text page numbers, chapter numbers are used in running heads—for example, "Notes to Chapter 12." If notes for one chapter start at the top of the page or continue over the entire page, that chapter number is used in the running head. If notes for one chapter end and the notes for another chapter begin on the page, the running head should reflect the new chapter only. If notes for more than one new chapter begin on either of two facing pages (verso or recto), the verso running head should carry the number of the first new chapter beginning on that page; the recto running head, the number of the last chapter beginning on the two-page spread (see fig. 15.4). It will also be necessary, of course, to use the chapter number as a running head in the text itself (e.g., "Chapter 12") on at least one page of all two-page spreads, that is, on either all versos or all rectos.

15.40   The combined use of chapter numbers in running heads and note numbers on the pages should make location just as easy as the use of inclusive page numbers. The great advantage is that the running heads may be added by the typesetter during page makeup. The author and editor should, of course, check running heads at the page-proof stage to make sure that all are correct.

FOOTNOTES

15.41   *Page makeup.* Computer elements, both hardware and software, can now often be programmed by professional compositors to cope adequately, expeditiously, and economically with the scholar's predilection for notes at the bottom of the page, and the decades-long resistance to notes in this location is now undergoing some relaxation.

15.42   *Minimizing the problems.* When the publisher and the author have agreed on the use of footnotes, the author can minimize the problems that will arise in page makeup by limiting both the number of footnotes per page and the length of individual notes. Good bookmaking still requires that the type pages, including the footnotes, all be the same length and that each footnote appear on the same page as the reference to it, although the final note on a page may run over to the next page. Thus, a manuscript peppered with footnote references, two or more of which might fall in the last line of text on the printed page, may well be a typesetter's nightmare. Similarly, several long footnotes, the references to which fall close together toward the end of a page, present a sometimes insoluble problem in any kind of page makeup.

15.43   *Appearance.* In addition to the typesetter's problems in reproducing heavy documentation as footnotes, there is the matter of appearance. A page of type containing more footnote material than text not only is unpleasant to the eye but may discourage all but the most determined reader. In those few scholarly works where footnotes necessarily outweigh the text, publisher and typesetter must understand and cope with the difficulties. In the great majority of cases, however, careful employment of the measures discussed above (15.15–26) ought to ensure a more sensible balance between text and notes and a more attractive presentation of material.

ENDNOTES VERSUS FOOTNOTES

15.44 An advantage of endnotes over footnotes is that the length of each note is not a great concern, since notes and text need not be juggled about to make them fit on the same printed page. The author may therefore include in the notes such things as lists, poems, and discursive adjuncts to the text. It is desirable, however, that the note section not overbalance the text.

15.45 When preparing endnotes, which the reader must find at the end of the text rather than at the bottom of the page, the author accustomed to using footnotes will need to keep certain differences in mind:
1. Material necessary for understanding the argument should be included in the text rather than placed in the note, where the incurious may miss it.
2. The name of the author and the title of the work ought to be included in the first note citation to it, even if one or both have been mentioned in the text. Such repetition is unnecessary in a footnote.
3. In endnotes it is even more important than in footnotes to avoid "garlands of ibids." by placing page and line numbers for a single identified work in parentheses in the text (see 15.21–22). It is also helpful to avoid repeated note references to frequently cited works by using abbreviations in parenthetical text citations (see 15.24–25).

DUAL SYSTEM OF NOTES

15.46 *Endnotes plus footnotes.* In a heavily documented work it is sometimes helpful to separate substantive notes from those largely devoted to citing sources. In such a system the citation notes should be numbered and set as endnotes. The substantive notes, indicated by symbols beginning with an asterisk for the first note on each printed page (sequence of symbols: * † ‡ §; see also 12.51), are set as footnotes. Before electing a dual system such as both footnotes and endnotes, an author should consider the less cumbersome and more economical combination of author-date references for all source citations with endnotes to accom-

See Donald L. Martin, "The Economics of Jury Conscription," *Journal of Political Economy 80* (July/August 1972): 680–702.

9. For elaboration of this analysis, see Buchanan and Tullock, *The Calculus of Consent.*

10. For a detailed discussion of the uniformity requirement for taxation under the United States Constitution, as interpreted historically by the courts, and with especial emphasis on the asymmetry between the taxing and spending sides of the budget in this respect, see David Tuerck, "Constitutional Asymmetry," *Papers on Non-Market Decision Making*, 2 (1967). (This journal is now *Public Choice*.) Or, more comprehensively, see Tuerck, "Uniformity in Taxation, Discrimination in Benefits: An Essay in Law and Economics" (Ph. D. diss., University of Virginia, 1966).

CHAPTER SEVEN

1. For a general paper which covers material similar in many respects to that treated here, see W. H. Riker, "Public Safety as a Public Good," in *Is Law Dead?* ed. E. V. Rostow (New York: Simon and Schuster, 1971), pp. 379–85.

2. The analysis applies only to "law" which does, in fact, lend itself to the "publicness" description. In technical terms, "law" which involves the elimination of general external diseconomies or the creation of general external economies is the subject of analysis, not "law" which attempts to regulate individual behavior that may be unrelated to the extent of external effects. For example, a law that requires me to vaccinate my dog against rabies clearly qualifies because, in so doing, I am exerting external economies on all others in the community. By contrast, a law that might prevent me from purchasing the services of a prostitute could hardly be brought within the "publicness" description.

My use of "law" in this respect is similar to that employed by Rousseau. See Rousseau, *The Social Contract*, p. 399.

3. For a general discussion, see Paul Craig Roberts, *Alienation and the Soviet Economy* (Albuquerque: University of New Mexico Press, 1973), chap. 3; idem, "An Organizational Model of the Market," *Public Choice* 10 (Spring 1971): 81–92.

4. See Thomas R. Ireland, "Public Order as a Public Good," typescript (Chicago: Loyola University, 1968). Ireland's discussion is one of the few that seems to be based on a recognition of the central points made here.

5. This argument may appear to be related to the analysis of direct regulation and effluent charges as policy alternatives in dealing with pollution, but on closer examination the two arguments are quite distinct. The pollution analogue concerns collective decisions on the quantity of clean-up (the public good) and the means of sharing the costs. Direct regulation does embody a determinate cost-sharing scheme, imposing differentially higher costs on those whose liberty of action is more highly valued. This is the equivalent of the adoption of any quantity of behavioral restrictiveness or law, as discussed in the text. The levy of effluent charges provides an alternative means of attaining chosen targets, along with alternative means of sharing costs. But effluent charges are not analogous to modifications or adjustments in the distribution of tax prices so as to produce more widespread agreement on preferred quantities in the orthodox public-goods model.

Fig. 15.4. Endnotes with chapter numbers indicated in running heads

6. For extended discussion, see Buchanan and Tullock, *The Calculus of Consent*, especially chap. 10.

7. For a development of this approach, see H. Aaron and M. McGuire, "Public Goods and Income Distribution," *Econometrica* 38 (November 1970): 907–20; M. McGuire and H. Aaron, "Efficiency and Equity in the Optimal Supply of a Public Good," *Review of Economics and Statistics* 51 (February 1969): 31–39. See also William H. Breit, "Income Redistribution and Efficiency Norms" (Paper presented at Urban Institute Conference on Income Redistribution, 1972, forthcoming in conference proceedings volume).

8. For an application with disturbing racial overtones, see Andrew Hacker, "Getting Used to Mugging," *New York Review of Books*, 19 April 1973.

9. An alternative, but related, explanation of observed order is based on the hypothesis that individuals follow rules not because these are formally enacted as law or because of the acceptance of ethical precepts but simply because they are rules which exist. The origin of rules, in this view, is essentially evolutionary in an unpredictable sense. This hypothesis is supported by F. A. Hayek. See his *Law, Legislation, and Liberty*, vol. I, *Rules and Order*. Hayek cites, in elaboration of the specific hypothesis of "man as rule follower," a book by R. S. Peters, *The Concept of Motivation* (London, 1959).

10. An excellent example of this interrelationship is provided in the testimony of Jeb Magruder before the Senate Watergate Committee in June 1973. Magruder justified the departures from formal legal requirements by the Nixon supporters on the grounds that the antiwar militants of the late 1960s and early 1970s had been repeatedly observed to violate formal laws without being subjected to the penalties which were presumably attached to such violations.

11. For a specific discussion of this effect in an externality setting, see my "Externality in Tax Response," *Southern Economic Journal* 32 (July 1966): 35–42.

12. For related discussion, see my "A Behavioral Theory of Pollution," *Western Economic Journal* 6 (December 1968): 347–58; and my "Public Goods and Public Bads," in *Financing the Metropolis*, ed. John P. Crecine, vol. 4, Urban Affairs Annual Review (Beverly Hills: Sage Publications, 1970), pp. 51–72. Also see, James M. Buchanan and Marilyn Flowers, "An Analytical Setting for a Taxpayers' Revolution," *Western Economic Journal* 7 (December 1969): 349–59.

13. For a general discussion that introduces several helpful examples, see Thomas C. Schelling, "The Ecology of Micromotives," *Public Interest* 25 (Fall 1971): 59–98. Also see his "Hockey Helmets, Concealed Weapons, and Daylight Saving," Discussion Paper No. 9, Public Policy Program (John F. Kennedy School of Government, Harvard University, July 1972). For a discussion applied to ethical standards, see my "Ethical Rules, Expected Values, and Large Numbers."

CHAPTER EIGHT

1. As witness the infamous gun-trap judgment in Iowa. For a general discussion of state laws, see Richard A. Posner, "Killing or Wounding to Protect a Property Interest," *Journal of Law and Economics* 14 (April 1971): 201–32.

modate further documentary, amplifying, or explanatory requirements (see chapter 16).

15.47 *Editor's or translator's notes plus author's notes.* Notes supplied by an editor, translator, or compiler in a work having notes by the author must be differentiated from the author's notes. When the added notes are numbered, they may be distinguished by placing "Ed." or "Trans." after the period ending the note or by enclosing the entire note, except for the note number, in square brackets. In either case such notes should be numbered in sequence with those of the author. The identifying tags (Ed., Trans., Comp.) may be italicized, set in caps and small caps, distinguished in some other way, or simply set in roman upper- and lowercase.

> 14. The argument offered by Marvin Witchhazel has been roundly criticized by a number of authorities, including Bosworth, Stonehedge, and Crawford.
> 15. Millicent Cliff was Norton Westermont's first cousin, although to the very last she denied it. *Ed.*

> 7. Such an explanation was also suggested by Dinstoki (*Exploration of Events,* 211–13).
> 8. [Hayes was reported to have been in the same building at the time La Mott denounced the committee. Trans.]

15.48 Another way of distinguishing notes added by an editor or translator from those of the author is to use symbols (the asterisk and so on) for the former and numbers for the latter. Both sets of notes may be printed as footnotes, in which case each set is grouped separately, one set (usually the symbol-keyed notes) above the other. As an alternative, the added, symbol-keyed notes may be printed as footnotes, and the numbered author's notes as endnotes.

15.49 It should be remembered, however, that whatever method is chosen must be used consistently throughout the work.

UNNUMBERED NOTES

15.50 In anthologies, books of readings, and other collections of previously published material, or in otherwise new publications that contain one or more previously published chapters, the source of each reprinted chapter or piece may be given in an unnumbered note and inserted, before any numbered notes, either on the first page of that chapter or preceding the endnotes for the chapter. For material still in copyright from a previous publication the note should include mention of permission from the copyright owner to reprint; it may also include a copyright notice (and must do so when the copyright owner asks for one). A note containing a copyright notice is usually best treated as an unnumbered footnote on the first page of the chapter or article, even when the rest of the notes are endnotes. Such notes are referred to as *source notes,* samples of which follow:

> Reprinted with permission of the Macmillan Company and Geoffrey Bles, Ltd., from *A Guide to Communist Jargon,* by R. N. Carew Hunt. © 1957 by R. N. Carew Hunt.

> From Ali al-Giritli, *Tarikh al-sinaʿa fi Misr* (The history of industry in Egypt) (Cairo, [1952]), 40–51, 97–104, 141–50; reproduced by kind permission of the author.

> From Maxim Gorky, *Days with Lenin* (New York, 1932), 3–7, 11–57, by permission of International Publishers Co., Inc.

> Reprinted from *Journal of Social Activism* 14 (fall 1989): 112–34.

> Reprinted, with changes, from *The Metropolis in Modern Life,* ed. Robert Moore Fisher (New York: Doubleday & Co., 1955), 125–48, by permission of the author and the publisher. © 1955 by The Trustees of Columbia University in the City of New York.

> Reprinted from *Geographic Reports,* Series GEO, no. 1, August 1951, 1–3. Washington, D.C.: U.S. Department of Commerce, Bureau of the Census.

(For source notes with tables see 12.47.)

15.51 In symposia and other multiauthor works the background or affiliations of the authors of the chapters may be identified in unnumbered notes similarly placed. Such identifying notes are unnecessary in books containing a list of contributors that includes the authors' affiliations (see 1.56). Special acknowledgments may also be given in an unnumbered note.

> Philip B. Kurland is professor of law, University of Chicago.

> Ramiro Delgado García, M.D., is president, Interdisciplinary Committee, Division of Population Studies, Colombian Association of Medical Schools; vice president, Colombian Association for the Scientific Study of Population; and executive secretary, University Committee for Population Research, Universidad del Valle, Colombia. This paper represents the personal opinions of the author and has not been officially endorsed by the institutions of which he is a member.

> This paper was supported in part by grant AM-04855, National Institutes of Health, and in part by grant 5-M01-FR-0047-04, United States Public Health Service.

> The author gratefully acknowledges the assistance of Dr. Oscar J. Blunk of the National Cyanide Laboratory in the preparation of this chapter.

When endnotes are used in multiauthor works, unnumbered identification or acknowledgment notes, like source notes, may be inserted before note 1 for each chapter. Where the author-date system is used instead of endnotes, each such note becomes a footnote on the opening page of the chapter.

15.52 In some works—translations and editions of the classics, for example, or works intended for a wider readership than the academic community—it may be desirable not to have note numbers in the text. In that case, notes may be keyed to the text by line, page, or page and line numbers, usually followed by the word or phrase being explained in the note. Such notes may be located at the foot of the page, as in figures 15.5 and 15.6, where the notes are keyed to the text above them by line numbers. (In figure 15.5 the bracket stands between the word or phrase from the text and a variant word or phrase found in another manuscript version of the piece. In figure 15.6 the bracket stands between the words from the text and their meanings or explanations.) Notes may also be placed at the back of the book and keyed to the text by page number and, if the lines of the text are numbered, by line number (figs. 15.7, 15.8). The page (or page and line) number is then followed by the word or phrase being elucidated or by a citation. Figure 15.9 illustrates endnotes keyed only to the page and word or phrase, because the text lines are not numbered.

SUBSTANTIVE NOTES

15.53 Substantive, or discursive, notes consist of explanations or amplifications of the discussion in the text. When it is desirable to cite the source of material included in the substantive note, the reference may be given in parentheses or worked into a sentence much as sources are sometimes worked into running text, or it may be given separately at the end of the material. If the source has been cited in full elsewhere in the work, it may be shortened in the substantive note (see 15.248); otherwise, a full reference must be given. When a full reference is presented in parentheses, brackets are used to enclose the publication facts (see 15.151).

> 1. Although the matter has been thoroughly and excellently discussed elsewhere (Manuel Moyado, *Turbulent Confabulations* [Memphis, Tenn.: Warburton, 1992], 96–123), it seems appropriate here to offer corroborating evidence.
> 2. Detailed evidence of the great increase in the array of goods and services bought as income increases is shown in S. J. Prais and H. S. Houthaker, *The Analysis of Family Budgets* (Cambridge: Cambridge University Press, 1955), 52.
> 3. Ernst Cassirer takes important notice of this in *Language and Myth* (59–62) and offers a searching analysis of man's regard for things on which his power of inspirited action may crucially depend.
> 4. In 1962 the premium income received by all voluntary health insurance organizations in the United States was $6.3 billion, while the benefits paid out were $7.1 billion. Health Insurance Institute, *Source Book of Health Insurance Data* (New York: Health Insurance Institute, 1963), 36, 46.

O sweete soule Phillis w'haue liu'd and lou'd for a great while,   45
(If that a man may keepe any mortal ioy for a great while)
Like louing Turtles and Turtledoues for a great while:
One loue, one liking, one sence, one soule for a great while,
Therfore one deaths wound, one graue, one funeral only
Should haue ioyned in one both loue and louer Amintas.   50
    O good God what a griefe is this that death to remember?
For such grace, gesture, face, feature, beautie, behauiour,
Neuer afore was seene, is neuer againe to be lookt for.
O frowning fortune, ô death and desteny dismal:
Thus be the poplar trees that spred their tops to the heauens,   55
Of their flouring leaues despoil'd in an houre, in a moment:
Thus be the sweete violets that gaue such grace to the garden,
Of their purpled roabe despoyld in an houre, in a moment.
    O how oft did I roare and crie with an horrible howling,
When for want of breath Phillis lay feintily gasping?   60
O how oft did I wish that Phœbus would fro my Phillis
Driue this feuer away: or send his sonne from Olympus,
Who, when lady Venus by a chaunce was prickt with a
    bramble,
Healed her hand with his oyles, and fine knacks kept for a
    purpose.
Or that I could perceiue Podalyrius order in healing,   65
Or that I could obtaine Medæas exquisite ointments,
And baths most precious, which old men freshly renewed.
Or that I were as wise, as was that craftie Prometheus,
Who made pictures liue with fire that he stole from Olympus.
Thus did I cal and crie, but no body came to Amintas,   70
Then did I raile and raue, but nought did I get by my railing,   [C₄ᵛ]
Whilst that I cald and cry'd, and rag'd, and rau'd as a mad
    man,

45 for] *omit* C E   62 this] that D
49 Therfore] Thefore A   64 his] *omit* E   purpose.] purpose:
58 roabe] roabes B C D E   C E; purpose? D
59 roare and crie] cry, and   70 Amintas,] Amintas. C E;
roare D   Amintas: D

Fig. 15.5. Footnotes showing textual variants and keyed to line numbers

Florimell. What's that?   115
Celadon. Such an Ovall face, clear skin, hazle eyes, thick
   brown Eye-browes, and Hair as you have for all the
   world.
Flavia. But I can assure you she has nothing of all this.
Celadon. Hold thy peace Envy; nay I can be constant an'   120
   I set on't.
Florimell. 'Tis true she tells you.
Celadon. I, I, you may slander your self as you please;
   then you have, ———— let me see.
Florimell. I'll swear you shan'not see. ————   125
Celadon. A turn'd up Nose: that gives an air to your face:
   Oh, I find I am more and more in love with you! a
   full neather-lip, an out-mouth, that makes mine
   water at it: the bottom of your cheeks a little bulb,
   and two dimples when you smile: for your stature 'tis   130
   well, and for your wit 'twas given you by one that
   knew it had been thrown away upon an ill face; come
   you are handsome, there's no denying it.
Florimell. Can you settle your spirits to see an ugly face,
   and not be frighted, I could find in my heart to life   135
   up my Masque and disabuse you.
Celadon. I defie your Masque, would you would try the
   experiment.
Florimell. No, I won'not; for your ignorance is the
   Mother of your devotion to me.   140
Celadon. Since you will not take the pains to convert me
   I'll make bold to keep my faith: a miserable man I am
   sure you have made me.
Flavia. This is pleasant.
Celadon. It may be so to you but it is not for me; for   145
   ought I see, I am going to be the most constant *Maud-*
   lin.

   116 *Ovall face*] probably a description of Nell Gwyn. See
the illustration facing p. 31; one incongruous detail, the
turned-up nose, may have been included as a joke, like the
ironic description of King George in the person of the Emperor of Lilliput (*Gulliver's Travels,* I, ii).
   128 *out-mouth*] i.e., having full lips.
   129 *blub*] swelling.   134 *Can*] if you can.

Fig. 15.6. Footnotes annotating text and keyed to line numbers

24:2 *Batorrendão* Unidentified. Roo de la Faille (7) reads this as *Batoe Rendang* and says that it is a pun of sorts on *Batoe,* an island group on the equator, off the west central coast of Sumatra.

24:6 *shahbandar* From the Persian *shah* (king) and *bandar* (seaport). Title of an officer at native ports all over the India seas, who was the chief authority with whom foreign traders and shipmasters had to transact. The *shahbandars* had multiple duties, for they functioned as harbormasters, customs officers, protectors of immigrants, and superintendents of trade. At the time the Portuguese held sway in Malacca, there were four *shahbandars* assigned to four different quarters of the city, inhabited by people of different races or religions. See Richard Winstedt, *The Malays,* 6th ed. (London: Routledge & Kegan Paul, 1961), 76.

24:10 *Campalator* Unidentified. Roo de la Faille (8) says that this name does not appear to be correct and that Pinto might have taken it from the Malay *kam-pong-ke-palar.*

24:12 *amborrajas* From the Malay *hamba-raja,* meaning "servant of the king." Marsden points out that these were Malay and not Battak officers (304).

25:14 *bailéu* From the Malay, meaning "audience hall" or "magistrate's tribunal." The word was given secondary meanings by the Portuguese writers, who used it variously in the sense of tribune, veranda, porch, lean-to, public banquet hall, or a raised fighting platform on a ship.

25:15 *skull of a cow* Roo de la Faille (8) sees in the cow's head with gilded horns a symbolic reference to the ancient kindgom of Menangkabow, which was held in deep veneration by all the states of Sumatra.

25:26 *prayer* Marsden, writing in 1783, says that it is very difficult to find traces of what can be called religion among the Battak. "They have some idea of a powerful Being, disposed to benevolence, and of another, the worker of ill to mankind, but they pay no worship to either. . . . Their only ceremonies that wear the appearance of religion are those used on taking an oath, in their prognostications, and at their funeral rites" (309).

25:37 *Turbão* Unidentified. Roo de la Faille (8) sees a possible connection between *Turbão* and the Malay *Batoe-poer-wa-Boewana,* but does not explain why. My thanks to Ms. Vera Rubinstein of Holland for her help in translating Roo de la Faille's article from the Dutch.

Fig. 15.7. Endnotes identified by page and line number, with key phrases in italics

Bibliographies

15.54 A list of books and other references used by an author in a scholarly work may be titled Bibliography, Select or Selected Bibliography, or, if it includes only works referred to in the text, Works Cited, Literature Cited, or References; other appropriate titles are not ruled out.

15.55 A bibliographical list is best placed at the end of the book, before the index. Lists are sometimes placed at the ends of the chapters to which they apply, particularly in textbooks and in multiauthor books when there are to be offprints.

15.56 A bibliography appended to a scholarly work rarely includes all works available in the field. When it is desirable, in the author's opinion, to mention the principle of selection, a note may precede the list (see fig.

p. 79   *l. 23*   Friedrich Nietzsche, *Ecce Homo,* in *On the Genealogy of Morals and Ecce Homo,* p. 258.

p. 83   *l. 14*   Friedrich Nietzsche, *The Gay Science,* trans. Walter Kaufmann (New York: Vintage Books, 1974), p. 274.

p. 83   *l. 31*   On this, see Lawrence J. Hatab, *Nietzsche and Eternal Recurrence: The Redemption of Time and Becoming* (Washington: University Press of America, 1978), pp. 93–116; Martin Heidegger, *Nietzsche,* vol. 2: *The Eternal Recurrence of the Same,* trans. David Farrell Krell (San Francisco: Harper and Row, 1984); and Richard Schacht, *Nietzsche* (London: Routledge & Kegan Paul, 1983), pp. 253–66.

p. 84   *l. 18*   *The Twilight of the Idols,* in *A Nietzsche Reader,* trans. R. J. Hollingdale (Harmondsworth: Penguin, 1977), p. 163.

p. 84   *l. 26*   Ibid., p. 164.

p. 85   *l. 16*   Friedrich Nietzsche, *The Case of Wagner,* in *The Birth of Tragedy and The Case of Wagner,* trans. Walter Kaufmann (New York: Vintage Books, 1967), pp. 158–59.

p. 85   *l. 26*   Ibid., p. 59.

p. 85   *l. 29*   *The Gay Science,* p. 89.

p. 86   *l. 9*   Ibid., p. 319.

p. 86   *l. 19*   Ibid.

p. 86   *l. 37*   Ibid.

p. 87   *l. 31*   *The Will to Power,* p. 387.

p. 88   *l. 11*   Ibid., p. 388.

Fig. 15.8. Bibliographical citations in endnotes identified by page and line number

15.10). Similarly, a list of abbreviations used in text and bibliography may precede the entries, just as an abbreviation list may accompany a note section (see figs. 15.1, 15.2). It is not necessary to list standard abbreviations of journal titles.

15.57   Note systems of documentation do not in themselves require bibliographies, because full bibliographical details can be given in a note accompanying the first reference to a work. In a work containing many citations in notes, however, a bibliography in addition to the notes is a most useful device for the reader and an economical one for the author and publisher: the reader not only can locate each source readily but can also see at a glance the sources the author has relied on or has selected as most germane to the subject. When the book does include many citations in notes, full particulars for each source need appear only in the bibliography; citations in the notes may thus be considerably shortened or abbreviated. Various forms such a bibliography may take are (1) a straight alphabetical list; (2) a list divided into sections according to kinds of material, subject matter, or other appropriate categories; (3) an annotated bibliography; (4) a bibliographical essay. Author's preference, nature of the material, and convenience to the reader should dictate the form to be used.

Morten Vilhelm Brandt (1854–1921) in memory of his wife (née Rovsing). It is given to women "of liberal persuasion with a slightly conservative tendency."

89 *Politiken*   One of the two largest Copenhagen morning dailies; associated with the Liberal Party.

89 *Mr. Hasager*   Niels Hasager (1888–1969) had been employed at *Politiken* since 1918 and was known for his English sympathies.

89 *the German envoy, Renthe-Finck*   Cecil Renthe-Finck (1885–1964) had been the German minister to Denmark since 1936.

91 *the tenth of April*   Denmark was invaded by German troops early in the morning of 9 April 1940.

91 *Heretica*   The leading literary periodical of postwar Denmark, published 1948–53.

92 *General von Lettow-Vorbeck*   Paul Emil von Lettow Vorbeck (1870–1964).

92 *Let the saga of the past*   Not identified.

93 *"nothing left remarkable beneath the visiting moon"*   *Antony and Cleopatra* IV, 15, 67.

94 *Nis Kock's book*   The Danish title is *Sønderjyder vender hjem fra Østafrika* (Copenhagen, 1938). English translation by Eleanor Arkwright: *Blockade and Jungle* (London, 1940).

97 *Professor Horn*   Carl Horn (1874–1943) was the stepfather of Ilse Hess, née Pröhl. He was director of the Academy of Art in Bremen.

109 *Carlyle said*   Perhaps quoting from memory, Karen Blixen has partially obscured Carlyle's meaning. The passage in Carlyle is as follows: "The sword indeed: but where will you get your sword! Every new opinion, at its starting, is precisely in a *minority of one* .... One man alone of the whole world believes it; there is one man against all men. That *he* take a sword, and try to propagate with that, will do little for him. You must first get your sword!" (from "The Hero as Prophet," in *On Heroes, Hero-Worship, and the Heroic in History* [London, 1897], p. 61).

111 *Abd el Rhaman*   'Abd al Rahmān ibn 'Abd Allāh (dates unknown), governer of Andalusia, invaded Gaul in 732 and was defeated at Poitiers.

112 *Louise of Schaumburg-Lippe*   Louise of Denmark (1875–1906),

Fig. 15.9. Endnotes keyed to page numbers only. Terms elucidated are in italic type. The running head identifies the range of pages covered by the notes.

SELECTED BIBLIOGRAPHY

I list here only the writings that have been of use in the making of this book. This bibliography is by no means a complete record of all the works and sources I have consulted. It indicates the substance and range of reading upon which I have formed my ideas, and I intend it to serve as a convenience for those who wish to pursue the study of humor, comic literature, the history of comic processes, the British novel, and the particular writers and fictions that are the subjects of this inquiry. (Unless there is a standard edition or only one widely available edition of the complete works of the novelists I study, I have not listed their complete works.)

1. THE THEORY, PSYCHOLOGY, AND HISTORY OF THE COMIC

Auden, W. H. "Notes on the Comic." In *Comedy: Meaning and Form,* edited by Robert Corrigan, 61–72. San Francisco: Chandler, 1965.
Bakhtin, Mikhail. *Rabelais and His World.* Translated from the Russian by Helene Iswolsky. Cambridge, Mass.: M.I.T. Press, 1968.

. . . .

2. JANE AUSTEN AND *EMMA*

Austen, Jane. *The Novels of Jane Austen.* Edited by R. W. Chapman. 5 vols. 3d ed. London: Oxford University Press, 1932–34.
———. *Jane Austen's Letters to Her Sister Cassandra and Others.* Edited by R. W. Chapman. 2d ed. London: Oxford University Press, 1952.
———. *Minor Works.* Edited by R. W. Chapman. Vol. 6 of *The Novels of Jane Austen.* London: Oxford University Press, 1954.
———. *"Emma": An Authoritative Text, Backgrounds, Reviews, and Criticism.* Edited by Stephen M. Parrish. Includes commentary and criticism by Sir Walter Scott, George Henry Lewes, Richard Simpson, Henry James, A. C. Bradley, Reginald Ferrar, Virginia Woolf, E. M. Forster, Mary Lascelles, Arnold Kettle, Wayne Booth, G. Armour Craig, A. Walton Litz, W. A. Craik, and W. J. Harvey. New York: W. W. Norton, 1972.

Fig. 15.10. Bibliography divided into sections according to subjects reflecting the organization of the text. The example shows part of the first two of ten sections and the author's note explaining the principle of selection.

TYPES OF BIBLIOGRAPHIES

15.58 *One alphabetical list.* The bibliography arranged in a single alphabetical list is the most common and usually the best form for a work with or without notes to the text. All sources to be included—books, articles, papers—are alphabetically arranged, by the last names of the authors, in a single list. Such an arrangement usually offers the simplest means of locating all references.

15.59 *Division into sections.* A long bibliography may be broken into sections if such division into categories would really make it more useful to the reader (sometimes division merely makes finding a given item more difficult). For example, in a work using manuscript sources as well as printed works, the two kinds of sources may be put in separate sections, the manuscripts arranged either by depository or by name of collection. In a work with many references to newspapers, the newspapers may be separated from the rest of the bibliography and listed together, each with its run of relevant dates. In a lengthy bibliography listing many printed sources, books are sometimes separated from articles (see fig. 15.11). The University of Chicago Press, however, discourages such a separation and recommends that books and articles be grouped together. Some bibliographies may be classified by subject if the distinctions are clear (see fig. 15.10). In a study of the work of one person, it is usually best to list works *by* that person separately from works *about* him or her (see fig. 15.12). Note that a list of works by one person is usually arranged in chronological order (by date of publication or, if unpublished, date of composition) rather than in alphabetical order. In a book about one person, such a list sometimes constitutes the entire bibliography. Division of references according to the chapter or part in which they are cited may be feasible, particularly if each cites references not used in the other chapters or parts. Whatever the arrangement of a bibliography, no source should be listed more than once; if the need for more than one listing for the same work arises, the arrangement is probably faulty.

15.60 When a bibliography is divided into sections, a headnote sometimes states that fact and lists the titles of the sections.

15.61 *Annotations.* When a bibliography is intended to direct the reader to other works for further reading and study, an annotated bibliography is useful. This is a list of books (sometimes articles as well) in alphabetical order with comments appended to some or all of the entries. The comments may be run in (see fig. 15.13) or set on separate lines (see the bibliography at the end of this manual). A long annotated bibliography is sometimes also divided into separate lists with subject headings (see 15.59).

Select Bibliography

Books

Abelard, Peter. *Peter Abelard's Ethics*. Edited and translated by D. E. Luscombe. Oxford: Clarendon Press, 1971.

Adkins, Arthur W. H. *Merit and Responsibility: A Study in Greek Values*. Oxford: Clarendon Press, 1960.

Anscombe, G. E. M. *Intention*. 2d ed. Oxford: Blackwell, 1963.

Atkinson, Ronald. *Sexual Morality*. London: Hutchinson, 1965.

Austin, J. L. *Philosophical Papers*. Oxford: Clarendon Press, 1961.

The Babylonian Talmud. Translated into English . . . under the editorship of Rabbi Dr. I. Epstein. London: Soncino Press, 1948–52.

Baier, Kurt. *The Moral Point of View: A Rational Basis of Ethics*. Ithaca: Cornell University Press, 1958.

Baxter, Richard. *A Christian Directory, or A Sum of Practical Theology and Cases of Conscience: The Practical Works of Richard Baxter.* Edited by W. Orme. 23 vols. London: Duncan, 1830. References are to part, chapter, and (where appropriate) direction and question, to which a reference to the volume and page of the *Practical Works (P. W.)* is added.

Beck, Lewis White. *A Commentary on Kant's Critique of Practical Reason*. Chicago: University of Chicago Press, 1960.

———. *Early German Philosophy*. Cambridge: Harvard University Press, Belknap Press, 1969.

———. *Studies in the Philosophy of Kant*. Indianapolis: Bobbs-Merrill, 1965.

. . . .

Articles

Anscombe, G. E. M. "Modern Moral Philosophy." *Philosophy* 33 (1958): 1–19.

———. "Thought and Action in Aristotle." In *New Essays on Plato and Aristotle,* edited by Renford Bambrough, 143–58. London: Routledge and Kegan Paul, 1965.

———. "Contraception and Chastity." *Human World,* no. 7 (May 1972): 9–30.

Fig. 15.11. Part of a bibliography of printed sources divided into books and articles.

Publications by Joseph J. Schwab

"A Further Study of the Effect of Temperature on Crossing-Over." *American Naturalist* 69 (1935): 187–92.

With Edna Bailey and Anita D. E. Laton. *Suggestions for Teaching Selected Material from the Field of Genetics.* Bureau of Educational Reserach in Science, Monograph 1. New York: Columbia University, Teachers College, 1939.

"A Study of the Effects of a Random Group of Genes on Shape of Spermatheca in *Drosophila melanogaster.*" *Genetics* 25 (1940): 157–77.

"Deriving the Objectives and Content of the College Curriculum." In *New Frontiers in Collegiate Education: Proceedings of the Institute for Administrative Officers of Higher Education,* vol. 13, edited by John Dale Russell, 35–52. Chicago: University of Chicago Press, 1941.

"The Role of Biology in General Education: The Problem of Value." *Bios* 12 (1941): 87–97.

"The Fight for Education." *Atlantic Monthly* 169 (1942): 727–31.

"The Science Programs in the College of the University of Chicago." In *Science and General Education,* edited by Earl McGrath, 38–58. Dubuque, Iowa: William C. Brown Co., 1947.

. . . .

"On Reviving Liberal Education." In *The Philosophy of the Curriculum,* edited by Sidney Hook et al., 37–48. Buffalo, N.Y.: Prometheus Books, 1975.

"Education and the State: Learning Community." In *The Great Ideas Today, 1976,* 234–71. Chicago: Encyclopaedia Britannica, 1976.

"Freedom and the Scope of Liberal Education." In *The President as Educational Leader,* 610–88. Washington, D.C.: Association of American Colleges, 1976.

"Teaching and Learning." *The Center Magazine* 9, no. 6 (November–December 1976): 36–45.

Fig. 15.12 The beginning and end of a list of one author's works, arranged in chronological order by date of publication. Such a list may be entitled "Works by ——" and include unpublished as well as published material.

15.62 *Bibliographical essay.* An informal way to provide information for further reading is a bibliographical essay, in which the author treats the literature of the field discursively, giving the facts of publication in parentheses following each title. The material may be arranged in one continuous essay or it may be divided by chapter or by subject category with or without subheads marking the divisions (see fig. 15.14). Often called Suggested Reading, this kind of bibliography is best suited to books intended for the general reader—books with few or no text references to specific sources and no notes dependent on an alphabetical list of references. Such a bibliographical essay may be used in addition to an alphabetical bibliography or a reference list, in which case it

Bibliography

· ·

Sorokin, Boris. "Lev Tolstoj in Pre-Revolutionary Russian Criticism." Doctoral dissertation, University of Chicago, 1973. Survey of major prerevolutionary criticism and extensive bibliography.

Zhilina, E. N. *Lev Nikolaevich Tolstoi, 1828–1910.* Leningrad, 1960. A bibliographical aid; includes selective secondary literature on individual works.

II. *Reminiscences and Biographies*

Alexandre, Aimée. *Le mythe de Tolstoi.* Paris, 1960.

Asquith, Cynthia. *Married to Tolstoy.* London, 1960. A defense of Tolstoy's wife in her difficulties with Tolstoy.

Biryukov, P. *Lev Nikolaevich Tolstoy.* 4 vols. Moscow, 1911–23. Still perhaps the best biography of Tolstoy.

Brodsky, N. A., et al., eds. *L. N. Tolstoi v vospominaniyakh sovremennikov.* 2 vols. Moscow, 1955. There is also a 1960 edition, ed. S. N. Golubov et al., with some additional material. These are very important volumes. The English edition is considerably abbreviated and awkwardly translated by the Moscow Foreign Publishing House. The 1960 Soviet volume adds some items and drops others, especially of recently published separate books of reminiscences, such as Bulgakov's and Goldenweizer's.

Bulgakov, Valentin. *The Last Year of Leo Tolstoy.* Translated by Ann Dunnigan. Introduction by George Steiner. New York, 1971. Fascinating account (by Tolstoy's male secretary) of Tolstoy's last year and his torturous relations with his wife.

———. *O Tolstom, vospominaniya i rasskazy.* Tula, 1964. Supplementary to his *Poslednii god,* but written after the events, the account does not have the sharply vivid sense of the diary. Often a record of objects in the room and other inconsequential matters.

Bunin, Ivan. *Osvobozhdenie Tolstogo.* Paris, 1937. Draws upon personal recollections, as well as the diary, letters, and reminiscences of others. Beautifully written.

Dole, Nathan Haskell. *The Life of Count Lyof N. Tolstoi.* New York, 1911.

Fig. 15.13. Excerpts from an annotated bibliography. Note that not every entry bears an annotation.

Suggested Readings

The most thorough bibliography of American religion is Nelson R. Burr, *A Critical Bibliography of Religion in America,* 2 vols. (Princeton, 1961). More recent and more selective is the same author's contribution to the Goldentree Bibliographies in American History, called *Religion in American Life* (New York, 1971). Specialized lists of writings on Catholicism are John Paul Cadden, *The Historiography of the American Catholic Church, 1745–1943* (Washington, 1944); . . . On books on American Judaism, see Moses Rischin, *An Inventory of American Jewish History* (Cambridge, 1954). The old standby in this general field, still useful, is Peter G. Mode, *Source Book and Bibliographical Guide for American Church History* (Menasha, Wis., 1921).

The sections in all the above works listing books and articles and theses that deal historically with religious thought and theology are instructive, partly by reason of their brevity. . . .

For a study of religion with neatly balanced attention to Catholicism and Judaism as well as Protestantism, Winthrop S. Hudson, *Religion in America,* rev. ed. (New York, 1973), serves well and provides useful bibliographical guides. The most encyclopedic work by a single author is Sydney E. Ahlstrom's mammoth and remarkably detailed book, *A Religious History of the American People* (New Haven, 1972).

. . . .

The more strictly theological heritage of Edwards, down to the last Edwardian, is surveyed in Frank Hugh Foster, *A Genetic History of the New England Theology* (Chicago, 1907). The rival theology of Unitarianism, of course, had its own tradition going back in America to Edwards's own day, as is shown by Conrad Wright, *The Beginnings of Unitarianism in America* (Boston, 1955), covering 1735–1805.

FROM EMERSON TO JAMES

The more theologically inclined thinkers who are treated in this second "Interlude" have been studied in great detail, but the full range and variety of religious thought during Emerson's lifetime and down to the beginnings of pragmatism have yet to be surveyed in a reliable volume. The theology of Emerson and the Transcendentalists, of the Princeton and Mercersburg theologians, and of Bushnell is woven into the history of Continental and British theological movements by Claude Welch, *Protestant Thought in the Nineteenth Century,* vol. 1 (New Haven, 1972), which also reckons with other Americans such as Lyman Beecher, Brownson, Channing, Dwight, Edwards, Finney, Hopkins, James, Parker, Schmucker, and, at some length, Taylor.

Fig. 15.14. Excerpts from a bibliographical essay addressed to the general reader

should come first. If the works discussed in the essay are included in full in the bibliography or reference list, they may be given as shortened or author-date citations in the essay as well as in the text itself. An essay may also be used in a book with footnotes or endnotes, but one must remember that essay and notes are not interdependent: a work cited in a note and discussed in the essay must be given with full bibliographical details in both places.

15.63   A discursive essay, an annotated list, or a combination of the two is often used to explain the contents, relevance, or value of specific bodies of material, such as manuscript collections (see figs. 15.15, 15.16).

ARRANGEMENT OF ENTRIES

15.64   The most practical and useful way to arrange entries in a bibliography is in alphabetical order, by author. There is rarely any reason to number the items (see 15.3). Authors who wish to list sources in order of their importance to the work at hand rather than alphabetically should consider whether the reader will need to find a specific source quickly; if so, an alphabetically arranged, annotated bibliography would serve both purposes.

15.65   *Alphabetizing.* Rules for alphabetizing an index (chapter 17) obtain also in a bibliographical list. Special problems may be solved by observing the following principles:
   1. A single-author entry comes before a multiauthor entry beginning with the same name.

> Fontanelle, Eric C. *Preparing for the Postwar Period.* Columbus, Ohio: W. C. Cartwright and Daughters, 1944.
> ———. *What Really Happened When the War Ended.* Cleveland: Chagrin Valley Press, 1952.
> Fontanelle, Eric C., and Valerie Mandible. "Iron Despair: Postwar Bewilderment." *World Spectator,* 6 April 1951.

   2. Original works usually precede works edited, compiled, or translated by the same person. Works by the same person may be arranged either chronologically by date of publication or alphabetically by title (discounting an initial article). Compiled, edited, or translated works are grouped, in that order, following the authored works (see also 16.28).

> CHRONOLOGICAL ORDER:
> McKeon, Richard. *The Philosophy of Spinoza: The Unity of His Thought.* New York: Longmans, Green, 1928.
> ———. "Aristotle's Conception of the Development and the Nature of Scientific Method." *Journal of the History of Ideas* 8 (1947): 3–44.
> ———. "Rhetoric and Poetic in the Philosophy of Aristotle." In *Aristotle's*

Bibliography

. . . .

MANUSCRIPT SOURCES

1. Private Papers
France
Larras MSS. Archives. Ministère de la Guerre. Section d'Afrique, Paris. The papers of General Larras, who served with the French military mission in Morocco from 1898 to 1905. He was responsible for preparing many of the maps of Morocco later utilized during the first stages of pacification. The papers relate principally to the period of his service in Morocco.
Mangin MSS. Archives Nationales, Paris. The papers and reports of General Charles Mangin, the hero of the battle of Sidi Bou Outhman and deliverer of Marrakech. In its essentials, it duplicates the holdings of the Ministère de la Guerre, Section d'Afrique, although there are additional papers. Only a portion deals with Mangin's Moroccan career.

. . . .

Great Britain
Satow Papers. Public Record Office, London. PRO 30/33. Includes the correspondence of Sir Ernest Satow from his mission to Morocco in 1893 and his correspondence with Sir James Macleod, H.M. Consul at Fez, 1893–1916. Of subsidiary interest only.
Nicolson Papers. Public Record Office, London. F.O. 800/336–381. Miscellaneous papers of Sir Arthur Nicolson, H.M. Minister at Tangier from 1894 to 1904. Of little interest.

. . . .

2. Official Papers
France
Archives de l'Alliance Israélite Universelle, Paris. Valuable chiefly for the annual reports of the official inspectors sent to survey the works of the Alliance in Morocco.
Archives de l'Ancien Gouvernement Général de l'Algérie, Aix-en-Provence. Série H. Affaires Musulmans et Sahariennes. Little of value on central Morocco. Of great importance for French penetration into eastern Morocco.

Fig. 15.15. Excerpts from a long bibliography, showing entries for manuscript collections with annotations explaining their relevance to the author's subject

. . . .

British Archives

The shift from a fifty- to a thirty-year rule has opened extensive British records to scholars, though it must be noted that many documents and whole files are being kept closed until 1990, 2015, and even later. Most important for this project have been the voluminous papers of the Foreign Office at the Public Record Office; also used have been cabinet papers, prime minister's papers, the records of such cabinet committees as the Committee on Imperial Defence and the Committee on Foreign Policy, and the papers of Lord Halifax, Sir Nevile Henderson, Sir John Simon, Sir Alexander Cadogan, Sir Archibald Clark Kerr, and Viscount Runciman in the FO 800 series.

At Cambridge University I have used the Baldwin and Templewood papers; at the Beaverbrook Library the Lloyd George papers; at the London School of Economics the Dalton papers; at King's College the Ismay papers; and at the Scottish Record Office the Lothian muniments.

Other Archives

The Soviet archives are closed. Some French archives have been made available to certain scholars, but there has been as yet no general opening similar to the American or British. Publications of documents from Soviet and French, as well as other, archives are listed in the bibliography.

No effort has been made to make this bibliography exhaustive. Only works actually cited in this book are included, together with a *small* selection of other works whose general ideas, organizing concepts, or supplementary details were of real significance in shaping the account. The bibliographies listed in section I and many of the secondary works in section IV provide additional listings.

I. Bibliographies, Guides, Archive Inventories, and Other Reference Works

American Historical Association, Committee for the Study of War Documents, and National Archives and Records Service. *Guides to German Records Microfilmed at Alexandria, Va*. Washington: National Archives, 1958–.
Bauer, Yehuda, ed. *Guide to Unpublished Materials of the Holocaust Period*. Vol. 3. Jerusalem: Hebrew University, 1975.

Fig. 15.16. A small segment of a scholarly bibliography with discursive accounts of archival material preceding a list of printed works arranged by category

"*Poetics*" *and English Literature,* edited by Elder Olson, 201–36. Chicago: University of Chicago Press, 1965.

———. "The Hellenistic and Roman Foundations of the Tradition of Aristotle in the West." *Review of Metaphysics* 32 (1979): 677–715.

———, ed. *The Basic Works of Aristotle.* New York: Random House, 1941.

ALPHABETICAL ORDER:

McKeon, Richard. "Aristotle's Conception of the Development and the Nature of the Scientific Method." *Journal of the History of Ideas* 8 (1947): 3–44.

———. "The Hellenistic and Roman Foundations of the Tradition of Aristotle in the West." *Review of Metaphysics* 32 (1979): 677–715.

———. *The Philosophy of Spinoza: The Unity of His Thought.* New York: Longmans, Green, 1928.

———. "Rhetoric and Poetic in the Philosophy of Aristotle." In *Aristotle's* "*Poetics*" *and English Literature,* edited by Elder Olson, 201–36. Chicago: University of Chicago Press, 1965.

———, ed. *The Basic Works of Aristotle.* New York: Random House, 1941.

The last entry in both lists illustrates placement of edited works *after* original works. In most bibliographies, however, this particular work would appear under the author's name:

Aristotle. *The Basic Works of Aristotle.* Edited by Richard McKeon. New York: Random House, 1941.

15.66 *Three-em dash for repeated names.* As may be observed in the preceding examples, for successive works by the same author a 3-em dash is used in place of the author's name after the first appearance. The 3-em dash is also used in place of the name of an editor, compiler, or translator for successive entries. If an additional author, editor, compiler, or translator is added, however, the originally listed person's name must be repeated.

Sorokin, Pitirim A. *Social and Cultural Dynamics.* Vol. 4, *Basic Problems, Principles, and Methods.* New York: Bedminster Press, 1941.

———. *Sociocultural Causality, Space, Time.* Durham, N.C.: Duke University Press, 1943.

Sorokin, Pitirim A., and Robert K. Merton. "Social Time: A Methodological and Functional Analysis." *American Journal of Sociology* 42 (1937): 615–29.

15.67 A single 3-em dash is also used to signify several authors, editors, compilers, or translators, provided they are listed in the same order.

West, Donald J., and D. P. Farrington. *Who Becomes Delinquent?* London: Heinemann, 1973.

———. *The Delinquent Way of Life.* London: Heinemann, 1977.

Merchison, Alfred A., John T. Pironi, and Kego Goshi. *Lost Text and Interpolations in* Macbeth. Iowa City: Town Crier Press, 1972.

————. *Absence of Bounds in the Character of Hamlet.* Iowa City: Town and Gown, 1986.

————, eds. *Doctoral Theses and the Future of Literary Criticism.* Chicago: Willberg and Sorenson, 1978.

————. *Surfeit and Sufficiency in Critical Directions.* Chicago: Willberg and Sorensen, 1993.

Merchison, Alfred A., Kego Goshi, and John T. Pironi, eds. *Recent Retrogressions.* Iowa City: Town Crier Press, 1989.

15.68 A dash may also be used for institutional or corporate authors. It takes the place of as much of the name as is the same. In the second entry below, the dash stands for "U.S. Senate." In the third entry, it stands for "U.S. Senate. Committee on Public Lands."

U.S. Senate. Committee on Foreign Relations. *Investigations of Mexican Affairs.* 2 vols. 66th Cong., 2d sess., 1919–20.

————. Committee on Public Lands. *Leasing of Oil Lands.* 65th Cong., 1st sess., 1917.

————. *Leases upon Naval Oil Reserves.* 68th Cong., 1st sess., 1924.

COMPARISON WITH AUTHOR-DATE REFERENCE LIST

15.69 Before setting forth in detail the components and style of bibliography entries and note citations, it might be helpful to preview in general the differences between bibliographies and reference lists. The principal differences may readily be seen in the following examples, which include both book and journal article entries.

HUMANITIES STYLE:

Smith, John Q. *Urban Turmoil: The Politics of Hope.* New City: Polis Publishing Co., 1986.

Wise, Penelope. "Money Today: Two Cents for a Dollar." *No Profit Review* 2 (1987): 123–42.

AUTHOR-DATE STYLE:

Smith, J. Q. 1986. *Urban turmoil: The politics of hope.* New City: Polis.
    or
Smith, J. Q. 1986. *Urban turmoil.* New City: Polis.

Wise, P. 1987. Money today: Two cents for a dollar. *No Profit Rev.* 2:123–42.
    or
Wise, P. 1987. Money today. *No Profit Rev.* 2:123–42.
    or
Wise, P. 1987. *No Profit Rev.* 2:123–42.

15.70 The similarities, of course, are obvious. Both systems offer the same information: author's name; title of work; and facts of publication—city, publisher, and date. In both systems, moreover, the authors' names are inverted so that alphabetical arrangement and location of individual entries may be facilitated.

15.71 It should also be noted that in both styles arabic numerals are used for volume numbers, even when roman numerals are used in the work itself. Thus, III and CXXXVIII become 3 and 138.

15.72 In both systems the major components are separated by periods, and colons separate titles from subtitles, cities from publishers, and volumes from pages. In both systems only two type styles are used, roman and italic. In some publications other typefaces are used—for example, caps and small caps for authors' names or boldface for the volume numbers of journals. These refinements raise cost, however, without increasing clarity, and the University of Chicago Press discourages their use.

15.73 The differences between the two systems are as follows:

1. The humanities style ordinarily spells out the author's given name, generally following the listing on the title page of a book or the opening page of the article. In the author-date system, often only the initials are given. This is not a rigid distinction, however; given names are sometimes spelled out in the author-date system, and initials only may be used in the humanities style. It should be borne in mind, however, that many readers and librarians prefer the more helpful practice of including the full given names of authors.

2. Reflecting the arrangement in the author-date text citation (see 15.2), the author-date reference list entry places the date immediately after the author's name. In the humanities style, where this arrangement is not necessary, the date is placed after the publisher of a book and after the volume number of a journal.

3. In the humanities style, all titles are given title, or headline, capitalization (see 7.127, 15.104). Author-date entries, on the other hand, employ a "down," or sentence, style—capitalizing only the first word of the main title and the subtitle and all proper nouns and proper adjectives—for the titles of books and articles; journal titles, however, are given title capitalization.

4. The full titles of books and articles are provided in humanities-style entries. Although this may also be done in author-date entries, the subtitle is often omitted, and sometimes the entire title of the article is omitted.

5. Quotation marks enclose titles of articles (as well as of chapters and short poems, etc.) in the humanities style, but not in the author-date style.

6. Another difference is that in the author-date system names of publishers and of journals are more likely to be abbreviated.

Such abbreviation is sometimes also used, though less frequently, in the humanities style.

15.74 There are many acceptable alternatives to and combinations of these basic styles. The main criteria of acceptability are clarity, consistency, and usefulness.

CONTENT OF DOCUMENTARY NOTES AND BIBLIOGRAPHIES

15.75 Documentary notes and bibliographies are intended to provide much the same information—full bibliographic details—although in somewhat different form. The first time a work is cited in a note, the reference is usually complete, much as it would be in a bibliography. In subsequent citations, however, the information is curtailed, and a short form of reference is given (usually only the author's last name, a shortened version of the title, and a page reference, if applicable; sometimes only the author's last name and the page reference). When the work contains an alphabetical bibliography as well as documentary notes, the initial citation itself may be given in short form. For fuller discussion of shortened note references, see 15.248–61.

15.76 Among the differences between citations in notes and bibliography entries, aside from the possibility of shortened forms in the notes, are the following:

1. In bibliography entries the names of authors are inverted, that is, last name first, because the entries are arranged alphabetically by authors' last names. In note citations, where alphabetical arrangement is not used, authors' names are given in normal order.

2. In bibliography entries the various components of information are separated by periods. In notes the separation is by commas, except for the publication facts, which are enclosed in parentheses, with no preceding punctuation but with a comma separating the closing parenthesis from the page or volume number.

1. Charles R. Simpson, *SoHo: The Artist in the City* (Chicago: University of Chicago Press, 1981), 231.

Simpson, Charles R. *SoHo: The Artist in the City.* Chicago: University of Chicago Press, 1981.

BOOKS

Information to Be Included

15.77   The following information should be included, where applicable, in both full documentary notes and bibliography entries. The order in which this information is listed is, by and large, the order in which it should appear. Variations in content and order are necessary for certain types of publications, but these will be discussed under the individual entries.

> Author: full name of author or authors; full name of editor or editors if no single author is listed (editor's name may be given after title); or name of institution responsible for the writing of the book
> Title: full title of the book, including subtitle if there is one
> Editor, compiler, or translator, if any, and if in addition to listed author (may be located in author's position if no author is listed)
> Edition, if not the first
> Volumes, total number if multivolume work is referred to as a whole
> Volume number of multivolume work, if single volume is cited
> Title of individual volume, if applicable
> Series title, if applicable, and volume number within series
> Facts of publication: city, publisher, and date
> Page number(s); or volume and page number(s), if applicable

15.78   In sum, the full reference in a note and in a bibliography entry must include enough information to enable the interested reader to find the work in a library, though the form of the note need not correspond precisely to that of the library catalog card.

15.79   Although the Press hopes that authors who use a note system of documentation for their books will follow the style outlined in this chapter, logical variations should be allowed provided consistency is maintained and the publisher is informed of the author's preferences before the manuscript is edited for publication.

15.80   Designations for volume, part, number, page, edition, and so on *in languages other than English* may be translated into their English equivalents in notes and bibliographies. Editors without a reasonably good knowledge of the language, however, should be wary of attempting to translate unfamiliar terms and should instead keep the author's original. An editor with a guidebook grasp of terminology might triumphantly translate "zweite Auflage" into "2d ed." only to discover, in another note, a phrase such as "Herausgegeben von Heribert Jussen, im Auftrag und mit Förderung des Deutschen Instituts für wissenschaftliche Pädagogik." Although daunted by the longer phrase, and wisely leaving it alone, the editor might justifiably translate the obvious ones.

Author's Name

15.81 Authors' names in notes and bibliographies should be spelled as they appear on the title pages of their books, except that the first names may be presented in full in place of initials (see also 16.22). Degrees or affiliations following names on the title page should normally be omitted (except "M.D." for authors of medical works). Several references to the same author in one bibliography should follow the same style. For example, an author listed as "Jones, Mary L." should not in another entry (as coauthor or editor) appear as "M. L. Jones." Use one or the other for both.

15.82 When an omitted portion of an author's first name is supplied in the note citation or bibliography entry, the part of the name not included on the title page may be enclosed in square brackets—G[eoffrey] A. Cranfield—but this is not necessary. In the following example, the author's name might have been given as "Crane, R[onald] S.," since "R. S." appears on the title page; but for most scholarly purposes, this is a needless refinement.

> Crane, Ronald S. *The Idea of the Humanities and Other Essays Critical and Historical.* 2 vols. Chicago: University of Chicago Press, 1967.

Full given names should not be supplied, however, for authors who always use initials only: T. S. Eliot, J. B. S. Haldane, O. Henry [pseud.], E. E. Cummings, P. D. James, F. R. Leavis, C. S. Lewis, G. E. Moore, J. D. Salinger, C. P. Snow, J. M. Synge, A. J. P. Taylor, C. V. Wedgewood, H. G. Wells. (Note that space is added between initials, following the guidelines in 7.6.)

> Eliot, T. S. *Four Quartets.* London: Faber and Faber, 1944.

ONE AUTHOR

15.83 In a documentary note, the author's name is presented in the normal order, given name first. The name itself is followed by a comma.

> 1. Emery Blackfoot, *Chance Encounters* (Boston: Serendipity Press, 1987).

In the bibliography, however, where entries are arranged alphabetically by authors' last names, the name is inverted, last name first. A comma follows the family name, and a period separates the name from the next element, the title.

> Blackfoot, Emery. *Chance Encounters*. Boston: Serendipity Press, 1987.

15.84   In a few languages, such as Hungarian, the family name is normally given first, followed, without comma, by the given name:

> Bartók Béla

In English-language publications this order is usually reversed, to conform with English usage. In bibliographies the name is reinverted, and a comma is used:

> Bartók, Béla

TWO AUTHORS

15.85   When a work has two authors, their names are listed in the order in which they appear on the title page. In a note the names are given in their natural order, first name first.

> 2. Liam P. Unwin and Joseph Galloway, *Peace in Ireland* (Boston: Stronghope Press, 1990).

In the bibliography the name of the first author is inverted, the second is given in its natural order, and the conjunction joining the two names is preceded by a comma:

> Unwin, Liam P., and Joseph Galloway. *Peace in Ireland*. Boston: Stronghope Press, 1990.

When both authors have the same family name, the name is usually repeated:

> 3. Arthur Weinberg and Lila Weinberg, *Clarence Darrow: A Sentimental Rebel* (New York: Putnam's Sons, 1980).

> Weinberg, Arthur, and Lila Weinberg. *Clarence Darrow: A Sentimental Rebel*. New York: Putnam's Sons, 1980.

THREE AUTHORS

15.86   In the case of three authors, the names are listed in the order shown on the title page:

> 4. P. D. Brett, S. W. Johnson, and C. R. T. Bach, *Mastering String Quartets* (San Francisco: Amati Press, 1989).
> 5. Jane S. Merk, Ida J. Fogg, and Charles A. Snowe, *Astrology for the Beginning Meteorologist* (Chicago: Darkweather and Clere, 1987).

For the bibliography entry, only the first author's name is inverted. In the interest of clarity and ease of reading, especially when many initials are involved, the names may be separated by semicolons, although commas may also suffice. Either practice must be followed consistently.

> Brett, P. D.; S. W. Johnson; and C. R. T. Bach. *Mastering String Quartets.* San Francisco: Amati Press, 1989.
> *or*
> Brett, P. D., S. W. Johnson, and C. R. T. Bach. *Mastering String Quartets.* San Francisco: Amati Press, 1989.
> Merk, Jane S., Ida J. Fogg, and Charles A. Snowe. *Astrology for the Beginning Meteorologist.* Chicago: Darkweather and Clere, 1987.

MORE THAN THREE AUTHORS

15.87 For works having more than three authors, a note citation should give the name of the first-listed author followed by "et al." or "and others" without intervening punctuation:

> 6. Charlotte Marcus et al., *Investigations into the Phenomenon of Limited-Field Criticism* (Boston: Broadview Press, 1990).
> 7. Wanda Ketchum and others, *Battering Husbands, Cornered Wives* (Cincinnati: Justice and Daughters, 1990).

15.88 In the bibliography entry, the usual practice is to list all the authors. The name of the first author is inverted. It is also acceptable, if the author wishes, to list only the first author, followed by "et al." or "and others."

> Marcus, Charlotte, Jerome Waterman, Thomas Gomez, and Elizabeth DeLor. *Investigations into the Phenomenon of Limited-Field Criticism.* Boston: Broadview Press, 1990.
> *or*
> Ketchum, Wanda, and others. *Battering Husbands, Cornered Wives.* Cincinnati: Justice and Daughters, 1990.

AUTHOR'S NAME IN TITLE

15.89 When the author's name appears in the title of a cited work, such as an autobiography, a collection of letters, or an edition of the complete works, the note citation may begin with the title, whereas the bibliography entry, for ease of location, should begin with the author's name, even though it is also in the title:

> 8. *The Education of Henry Adams: An Autobiography* (Boston: Houghton Mifflin, 1918), 163–65.
> 9. *The Letters of George Meredith,* ed. C. L. Cline, 3 vols. (Oxford: Clarendon Press, 1970), 1:125.
> 10. *The Complete Poems of Elizabeth DeLor* (Chicago: Seraphim, 1991), 67–68.

Adams, Henry. *The Education of Henry Adams: An Autobiography.* Boston: Houghton Mifflin, 1918.
Meredith, George. *The Letters of George Meredith.* Edited by C. L. Cline. 3 vols. Oxford: Clarendon Press, 1970.
DeLor, Elizabeth. *The Complete Poems of Elizabeth DeLor.* Chicago: Seraphim, 1991.

If the editor or compiler, however, is of primary interest to the discussion, that name may be given first (see also 15.99):

9. C. L. Cline, ed., *The Letters of George Meredith,* 3 vols. (Oxford: Clarendon Press, 1970), 1:125.

Cline, C. L., ed. *The Letters of George Meredith.* 3 vols. Oxford: Clarendon Press, 1970.

ANONYMOUS WORKS

15.90 If the authorship of a work is known but not revealed on the title page, the name is given in brackets:

11. [Jane Doe], *The Burden of Anonymity* (Nowhere: Nonesuch Press, 1948).

[Doe, Jane]. *The Burden of Anonymity.* Nowhere: Nonesuch Press, 1948.

If the identity of the author is merely surmised, a question mark follows the name before the closing bracket:

12. [Jane Doe?], *The Burden . . .*

[Doe, Jane?]. *The Burden . . .*

15.91 If the name of the author is unascertainable, both the note citation and the bibliography entry should begin with the title of the work. The use of *Anonymous* or *Anon.* is to be avoided.

13. *The Burden of Anonymity* (Nowhere: Nonesuch Press, 1948).

The Burden of Anonymity. Nowhere: Nonesuch Press, 1948.

In alphabetizing the entry in the bibliography, the initial article is discounted. The article may be transposed to the end of the title, preceded by a comma:

Burden of Anonymity, The.

DESCRIPTIVE PHRASE AS "AUTHOR"

15.92 When a descriptive phrase appears in place of the author's name on the title page, that phrase is used for the author in both note and bibliography:

14. A Cotton Manufacturer, *An Inquiry into the Causes of the Present Long-Continued Depression in the Cotton Trade, with Suggestions for Its Improvement* (Bury, 1869).

Cotton Manufacturer. *An Inquiry into the Causes . . .*

Once again, the article is discounted in alphabetizing the entry and may, in this case, be omitted.

PSEUDONYM

15.93 A pseudonym is generally treated in both note and bibliography as if it were the author's name, unless the sense of the text demands the real name. The author's real name, if known, may follow the pseudonym in brackets, although this is not necessary if the pseudonym is well known.

15. George Eliot, *Middlemarch,* Norton Critical Editions (New York: W. W. Norton, 1977).
16. John Le Carré [David John Moore Cornwell], *The Quest for Karla* (New York: Knopf, 1982).
or
16. John Le Carré, *The Quest for Karla* (New York: Knopf, 1982).

Eliot, George. *Middlemarch.* Norton Critical Editions. New York: W. W. Norton, 1977.
Le Carré, John [David John Moore Cornwell]. *The Quest for Karla.* New York: Knopf, 1982.
or
Le Carré, John. *The Quest for Karla.* New York: Knopf, 1982.

15.94 If the author's real name is better known than the pseudonym, the former should be used in both note citation and bibliography. The pseudonym, enclosed in brackets, may be included but is not essential. If used, the pseudonym is followed, after a comma, by the abbreviation *pseud.*

17. Charlotte Brontë [Currer Bell, pseud.], *Jane Eyre* (London, 1847).
or simply
17. Charlotte Brontë, *Jane Eyre* (London, 1847).

Brontë, Charlotte [Currer Bell, pseud.]. *Jane Eyre.* London, 1847.
or
Brontë, Charlotte. *Jane Eyre.* London, 1847.

15.95 If the author's real name is not known, the pseudonym may be followed by *pseud.* in brackets:

18. Jack Quester [pseud.], *Searching for the Real Shakespeare* (London: Grieff Publications, 1946).

Quester, Jack [pseud.]. *Searching for the Real Shakespeare.* London: Grieff Publications, 1946.

EDITOR, TRANSLATOR, OR COMPILER

15.96   The name of the editor, translator, or compiler takes the place of the author when no author appears on the title page. In both note and bibliography, the abbreviation *ed./eds., comp./comps.,* or *trans.* follows the name and is preceded by a comma.

> 19. Anthony B. Tortelli, ed., *Sociology Approaching the Twenty-first Century* (Los Angeles: Peter and Sons, 1991).
> 20. Peter Gianakakos and William Poweska, trans., *Studies of Transformation in Eastern Europe* (Buffalo, N.Y.: Touser and Blinken, 1991).
> 21. Manuel Santos, comp., *The Collected Works of Henrietta Kahn* (Boston: I. J. Filbert, 1989).

> Tortelli, Anthony B., ed. *Sociology Approaching the Twenty-first Century.* Los Angeles: Peter and Sons, 1991.
> Gianakakos, Peter, and William Poweska, trans. *Studies of Transformation in Eastern Europe.* Buffalo, N.Y.: Touser and Blinken, 1991.
> Santos, Manuel, comp. *The Collected Works of Henrietta Kahn.* Boston: I. J. Filbert, 1989.

EDITOR, TRANSLATOR, OR COMPILER WITH AN AUTHOR

15.97   The edited, translated, or compiled work of one author is normally listed with that author's name appearing first. The editor, translator, or compiler is listed after the title. In the note citation, the name of the editor, translator, or compiler is separated from the title by a comma and is preceded by the abbreviation *ed.* (here meaning *edited by* and thus never *eds.*), *trans.* (*translated by*), or *comp.* (*compiled by*):

> 22. John Stuart Mill, *Autobiography and Literary Essays,* ed. John M. Robson and Jack Stillinger (Toronto: University of Toronto Press, 1980), 15.
> 23. Julio Cortázar, *Cronopios and Famas,* trans. Paul Blackburn (New York: Random House, Pantheon Books, 1969).

15.98   In the bibliography, the name of the editor, translator, or compiler is separated from the title by a period and is preceded by the expression *Edited by, Translated by,* or *Compiled by.* The abbreviation *Ed. (Edited by), Trans. (Translated by),* or *Comp. (Compiled by)* may also be used.

> Mill, John Stuart. *Autobiography and Literary Essays.* Edited by John M. Robinson and Jack Stillinger. Toronto: University of Toronto Press, 1980.
> Cortázar, Julio. *Cronopios and Famas.* Translated by Paul Blackburn. New York: Random House, Pantheon Books, 1969.
> *or*
> Cortázar, Julio. *Cronopios and Famas.* Trans. Paul Blackburn . . .

When matters are more complicated, the information may need to be spelled out:

24. *Chaucer Life-Records,* edited by Martin M. Crow and Clair C. Olson from materials compiled by John M. Manly and Edith Rickert, with the assistance of Lilian J. Redstone and others (London: Oxford University Press, 1966), 372–74.

Chaucer Life-Records. Edited by Martin M. Crow and Clair C. Olson from materials compiled by John M. Manly and Edith Rickert, with the assistance of Lilian J. Redstone and others. London: Oxford University Press, 1966.

Note that since these compiled life records cannot be attributed to an author or group of authors, the title is given first.

15.99 When the editor, translator, or compiler is more important to the discussion than the author, however, that name comes first and the name of the author follows the title. In both note and bibliography, the author's name is separated from the title by a comma and is preceded by the word *by:*

25. T. S. Eliot, ed., *Literary Essays,* by Ezra Pound (New York: New Directions, 1953).

Eliot, T. S., ed. *Literary Essays,* by Ezra Pound. New York: New Directions, 1953.

15.100 Amplifications of the editor's or translator's role indicated by such phrases as "Edited and with an Introduction [Notes] by" or "Translated with a Foreword by" are usually simplified to *Ed.* or *Edited by, Trans.* or *Translated by.* For example, for a book whose title page reads

The Red Notebook of Charles Darwin
Edited with an Introduction and Notes
by Sandra Herbert

the listing should be rendered as follows:

26. Sandra Herbert, ed., *The Red Notebook of Charles Darwin* (Ithaca, N.Y.: Cornell University Press, 1980).
or
26. *The Red Notebook of Charles Darwin,* ed. Sandra Herbert (Ithaca, N.Y.: Cornell University Press, 1980).

Darwin, Charles. *The Red Notebook of Charles Darwin.* Edited by Sandra Herbert. Ithaca, N.Y.: Cornell University Press, 1980.

AUTHORS OF FOREWORDS AND INTRODUCTIONS

15.101 Authors of forewords or introductions to books by other authors should be omitted from the note citation and the bibliography entry unless the foreword or introduction is the item cited. In that case the author of the foreword or introduction is given first, and the name of the author of the work itself follows the title, from which it is separated by a comma and the word *by.*

27. Mark Harris, introduction to *With the Procession,* by Henry Fuller (Chicago: University of Chicago Press, 1965).

28. Nodj Namsorg, foreword to *The Psychodynamics of Chronic Stress,* by Salvador Mensana (New York: Isadore O'Mally and Son, 1990).

Harris, Mark. Introduction to *With the Procession,* by Henry B. Fuller. Chicago: University of Chicago Press, 1986.

Namsorg, Nodj. Foreword to *The Psychodynamics of Chronic Stress,* by Salvador Mensana. New York: Isadore O'Mally and Son, 1990.

ORGANIZATION, ASSOCIATION, OR CORPORATION AS "AUTHOR"

15.102 If a publication issued by an organization carries no personal author's name on the title page, the organization is listed as the author, even if its name is repeated in the title or in the series title or as the publisher:

29. International Monetary Fund, *Surveys of African Economies,* vol. 7, *Algeria, Mali, Morocco, and Tunisia* (Washington, D.C.: International Monetary Fund, 1977).

International Monetary Fund. *Surveys of African Economies.* Vol. 7, *Algeria, Mali, Morocco, and Tunisia.* Washington, D.C.: International Monetary Fund, 1977.

Titles

15.103 Compiling documentary notes and bibliography entries raises questions about the extent of editing acceptable when applying the rules of style to the titles of printed works. Because capitalization, punctuation, and the use of italics on the title page of a book or the opening page of a chapter or an article in a periodical are generally matters determined by the publisher rather than the author, scholars agree that these may be changed within limits so long as the author's spelling is not altered.

TITLE, OR HEADLINE, CAPITALIZATION

15.104 In the humanities style of documentation all words in the title are capitalized except prepositions (regardless of length), articles *(the, a, an),* and coordinating conjunctions *(and, but, or, for, nor),* unless they are the first or last word in the title or subtitle. The *to* in infinitives is also lowercased. In hyphenated compounds the second and subsequent elements are capitalized unless they are articles, prepositions, coordinating conjunctions, or such modifiers as *flat, sharp,* and *natural* following musical key symbols; second elements attached to prefixes are not capitalized unless they are proper nouns or proper adjectives (see also 7.128). Words printed in full capitals on the title page are regularly changed to upper and lowercase. All of this is referred to as regular title, or headline, capitalization. Foreign words or foreign titles included in English titles are capitalized as are English titles:

> Horace. *Satires, Epistles, and Ars Poetica.*
> Phlumatsoff. *Sporting with les Jeunesse Dorée.*

SPELLING, PUNCTUATION, AND OTHER MATTERS OF STYLE

15.105 The spelling in the original title should be retained, except that an ampersand should be spelled out. Abbreviations may be either spelled out or left as they are. Names of centuries and other numbers are usually spelled out, although the numerals may be retained if desired.

15.106 Since punctuation is often omitted from title pages, it may be necessary to add this to citations in notes or bibliographies. Series commas, commas setting off dates, and colons between title and subtitle are frequently omitted at the ends of lines on title pages and must therefore be added.

15.107 *Italic titles.* Titles of books are set in italic type. Titles of other book-length works, long poems, or plays included in a book title may be either enclosed in quotation marks or set in contrasting roman type (see 15.112).

15.108 *Series commas.* Although often omitted from the ends of lines on the title page for aesthetic reasons, series commas are restored or, in some cases, added in note and bibliography citations:

> 1. Mark Cavanagh, *Color, Harmony, and Rhythm in Early Twentieth-Century American Music* (Chicago: Arcane Publications, 1989).

> Cavanagh, Mark. *Color, Harmony, and Rhythm in Early Twentieth-Century American Music.* Chicago: Arcane Publications, 1989.

15.109 *Subtitles.* A colon is used to separate the main title from the subtitle. A regular word space follows the colon:

> 2. Patrick Skelton, *Skating on Thin Ice: A Study of Honesty in Political Campaigning* (Cleveland: Cicero Publications, 1988).

> Skelton, Patrick. *Skating on Thin Ice: A Study of Honesty in Political Campaigning.* Cleveland: Cicero Publications, 1988.

Notice that in italic titles the colon is also italic.

15.110 *Dates in titles.* When not introduced by prepositions (for example, from 1920 to 1945), dates in a title are set off with commas:

> 3. Betty Jeanne DeLor, *Diplomacy in Latin America, 1981–1990* (New York: Hemisphere Press, 1991).

> DeLor, Betty Jeanne. *Diplomacy in Latin America, 1981–1990.* New York: Hemisphere Press, 1991.

15.111 *Numbers in titles.* Names of centuries are usually spelled out; thus 12th Century becomes Twelfth Century. Other numbers may be spelled out, following the rules set forth in chapter 8, or left as numerals:

> 4. Stephen Christopher, *Sighting 200 Species in My 17th Year* (Chicago: Ornithology Press, 1990).
> *or*
> 4. Stephen Christopher, *Sighting Two Hundred Species in My Seventeenth Year* . . .

> Christopher, Stephen. *Sighting Two Hundred Species in My Seventeenth Year.* Chicago: Ornithology Press, 1990.

15.112 *Titles and names within titles.* Titles of both long and short works appearing in italicized titles are usually also given in italics and set off with quotation marks:

> 5. Olga E. Porkola, *On First Reading "Ode on a Grecian Urn" and Other Such Romantic Rhapsodies* (Cleveland: Nilo Mikksonen, 1967).
> 6. Jack Plainreader, *The Month I Nodded and Plodded through "Finnegans Wake"* (Stamford, Conn.: John Kocinak, 1988).

> Porkola, Olga E. *On First Reading "Ode on a Grecian Urn" and Other Such Romantic Rhapsodies.* Cleveland: Nilo Mikksonen, 1967.
> Plainreader, Jack. *The Month I Nodded and Plodded through "Finnegans Wake."* Stamford, Conn.: John Kocinak, 1988.

As an alternative, titles of long or book-length works, which would ordinarily be italicized, may be set in roman type without quotation marks when included within another italicized title:

> Plainreader, Jack. *The Month I Nodded and Plodded through* Finnegans Wake. Stamford, Conn.: John Kocinak, 1988.

If used, of course, this alternative must be followed consistently, and titles of shorter works should be retained in italics and quotation marks, as in example note 5 above.

15.113 In quoted titles, titles of long works are given in italics and titles of short works are enclosed in single quotation marks:

> Skelton, Nicole. "Remembering My Mother Reading *Hamlet.*" In *Recollections of Childhood.* Chicago: Namsorg Press, 1990.

> Margolis, Evian. "Making a Movie of Joyce's 'The Dead.'" In *From Printed Page to Silver Screen.* Los Angeles: Cinema Press, 1990.

15.114 When incorporated within book titles, the names of ships, aircraft, or spacecraft, which are ordinarily given in italics, are italicized and enclosed in quotation marks or, alternatively, set in roman type:

> 7. Irmgard Finnery, *The Brief Glories of the "Akron" and the "Macon"* (Akron, Ohio: Dirigible Press, 1983).
> *or*

7. Irmgard Finnery, *The Brief Glories of the* Akron *and the* Macon (Akron, Ohio: Dirigible Press, 1983).

15.115 *Quotations within titles.* A quotation used within an italicized title is normally enclosed in quotation marks:

> Gerontion, Thomas. *Feeling like an "Old Man in a Dry Month."* London: Fibber and Fibber, 1972.

A quotation appearing within a quoted title is enclosed in single quotation marks:

> 8. Fargus Witmore, "When I Asked for a Definite Answer, She Said, 'Perhaps.'" In *Tales of the Indecisive.* Detroit: Odo Publishers, 1976.

If the quotation is well known and constitutes the whole title (main title or subtitle), it need not be enclosed in quotation marks:

> 9. Joseph Hershal, *To Be, or Not to Be: Dilemmas of Emerging Self-Awareness* (Chicago: Enigma Press, 1989).

15.116 *Titles ending with question marks or exclamation points.* When a title or subtitle ends with a question mark or an exclamation mark, the regular documentary punctuation is omitted:

> 10. Irma Tweeksbury, *If Only We Had Known! Confessions of a Regretter* (New Orleans: Ash Press, 1949).

> Tweeksbury, Irma. *If Only We Had Known! Confessions of a Regretter.* New Orleans: Ash Press, 1949.
> Velasquez, Fernando. *What Could We Have Done?* Toledo, Ohio: I. M. Heartsick, 1950.

OLDER TITLES

15.117 Titles of works published in earlier centuries may retain their original punctuation, spelling, and capitalization (except whole words in capital letters, which should be given an initial capital only):

> 11. William Baldwin, *A Treatise of morall philosophy Contaynynge the sayings of the wyse* (London, 1579).

> Baldwin, William. *A Treatise of morall philosophy Contaynynge the sayings of the wyse.* London, 1579.

These titles, which are sometimes excessively long, may be shortened by omitting various phrases, but the omissions must be indicated by three ellipsis dots within the title and four, including the period, at the end:

> Ray, John. *Observations Topographical, Moral, and Physiological: Made in a Journey Through part of the Low-Countries, Germany, Italy, and France: with A Catalogue of Plants not Native of England . . . Where-*

unto is added A brief Account of Francis Willughby, Esq., his Voyage through a great part of Spain. [London], 1673.

[Beverley, Robert]. *The History and Present State of Virginia . . . by a Native of the Place.* London, 1705.

Escalante, Bernardino. *A Discourse of the Navigation which the Portugales doe make to the Realmes and Provinces of the East Partes of the Worlde.* . . . Translated by John Frampton. London, 1579.

TITLES IN LANGUAGES OTHER THAN ENGLISH

15.118   Titles of works in languages other than English are treated the same as English titles except that capitalization follows the conventions of the language of the work (see chapter 9):

12. Henry Cesbron, *Histoire critique de l'hystérie* (Paris: Asselin et Houzeau, 1909).

13. Wilhelm Gundert, *Japanische Religionsgeschichte: Die Religionen der Japaner und Koreaner in geschichtlichem Abriss dargestellt* (Stuttgart: Gundert Verlag, 1943).

14. G. Martellotti et al., *La litteratura italiana: Storia e testi,* vol. 7 (Milan: Riccardo Ricciardi, 1955).

Cesbron, Henry. *Histoire critique de l'hystérie.* Paris: Asselin et Houzeau, 1909.

Gundert, Wilhelm. *Japanische Religionsgeschichte: Die Religionen der Japaner und Koreaner in geschichtlichem Abriss dargestellt.* Stuttgart: Gundert Verlag, 1943.

Martellotti, G., et al. *La letteratura italiana: Storia e testi.* Vol. 7. Milan: Riccardo Ricciardi, 1955.

When it is desirable to provide readers with a translation of a title, the translation follows the title and is enclosed in parentheses (sometimes in square brackets). The translation is set in roman type, without quotation marks, and only the first word (of title and subtitle) and proper nouns and adjectives are capitalized. When a summary in another language is provided, that fact is also included in parentheses:

15. Natan Gross, Itamar Yaoz-Kest, and Rinah Klinov, eds., *Ha-Shoah be-Shirah ha-Ivrit: Mivhar* (The Holocaust in Hebrew poetry: An anthology) (Ha-Kibbutz ha-Me'uhad, 1974).

16. Henryk Wereszyncki, *Koniec sojuszu trzech cesarzy* (The end of the Three Emperors' League; summary in German) (Warsaw: PWN, 1977).

Gross, Natan, Itamar Yaoz-Kest, and Rinah Klinov, eds. *Ha-Shoah be-Shirah ha-Ivrit: Mivhar* (The Holocaust in Hebrew poetry: An anthology). Ha-Kibbutz ha-Me'uhad, 1974.

Wereszyncki, Henryk. *Koniec sojuszu trzech cesarzy* (The end of the Three Emperors' League; summary in German). Warsaw: PWN, 1977.

15.119   If a title is given only in translation, the translation is treated as the title, but the original language must be specified:

17. N. M. Pirumova, *The Zemstvo Liberal Movement: Its Social Roots and Evolution to the Beginning of the Twentieth Century* (in Russian) (Moscow: Izdatel'stvo "Nauka," 1977).

Pirumova, N. M. *The Zemstvo Liberal Movement: Its Social Roots and Evolution to the Beginning of the Twentieth Century* (in Russian). Moscow: Izdatel'stvo "Nauka," 1977.

Chapters or Other Titled Parts of a Book

GENERAL

15.120 When a chapter or other titled part of a book is cited, that title is given in quotation marks and roman type before the title of the book itself. In note citations, the two titles are separated by a comma and the word *in* or *of*. For the bibliography entry, the titles are separated by a period, and *In* is capitalized.

1. Brendan Phibbs, "Herrlisheim: Diary of a Battle," in *The Other Side of Time: A Combat Surgeon in World War II* (Boston: Little, Brown, 1987), 117–63.

Phibbs, Brendan. "Herrlisheim: Diary of a Battle." In *The Other Side of Time: A Combat Surgeon in World War II*. Boston: Little, Brown, 1987.

15.121 The particular chapter or part may be specified by number with the term abbreviated. (The full terms may also be used if the practice is followed consistently.)

2. William H. McNeill, "The Era of Middle Eastern Dominance to 500 B.C.," pt. 1 of *The Rise of the West* (Chicago: University of Chicago Press, 1963).
3. Virgil Thomson, "Cage and the Collage of Noises," chap. 8 in *American Music since 1910* (New York: Holt, Rinehart and Winston, 1971).

McNeill, William H. "The Era of Middle Eastern Dominance to 500 B.C." Pt. 1 of *The Rise of the West*. Chicago: University of Chicago Press, 1963.
Thomson, Virgil. "Cage and the Collage of Noises." Chap. 8 in *American Music since 1910*. New York: Holt, Rinehart and Winston, 1971.

PART OF AN EDITED OR TRANSLATED WORK

15.122 If a cited chapter or contribution is part of an edited or translated work, the identification of the editor or translator follows the title of the book and, in both note and bibliography, is preceded by a comma and lowercase *ed.* or *edited by, trans.* or *translated by*. Note that when, as here, the chapter or other part of the edited or translated work is the primary reference, the identification of the editor or translator is not separated from the title of the work as a whole by a period in the bibliography but is joined to it by a comma (compare 15.98).

> 4. Ernest Kaiser, "The Literature of Harlem," in *Harlem: A Community in Transition,* ed. J. H. Clarke (New York: Citadel Press, 1964).

> Kaiser, Ernest. "The Literature of Harlem." In *Harlem: A Community in Transition,* edited by J. H. Clarke. New York: Citadel Press, 1964.

15.123 Inclusive page numbers may be indicated if desired. In the note citation, these are given last, after the publication facts. In the bibliography, they follow the editor's name.

> 5. David Ogilvy, "The Creative Chef," in *The Creative Organization,* ed. Gary A. Steiner (Chicago: University of Chicago Press, 1965), 199–213.

> Ogilvy, David. "The Creative Chef." In *The Creative Organization,* edited by Gary A. Steiner, 199–213. Chicago: University of Chicago Press, 1965.

CHAPTER ORIGINALLY PUBLISHED ELSEWHERE

15.124 When it is desirable to indicate that a chapter was originally published as an article in a journal or a chapter in another book, this may be done in the bibliography entry. It is not necessary to cite the original publication in the note.

> Fromson, Orlando. "Progressives in the Late Twentieth Century." In *To Left and Right: Cycles in American Politics,* edited by Wilmer F. Turner. Boston: Lighthouse Press, 1990. First published in *North American Political Review* 18 (fall 1988): 627–42.

> Wallowitz, Kazimir. "The Series Paintings of Monet." In *Claude Monet and Light: New Perspectives,* edited by Wallingford Moribundi. Boston: Tetzel and Schumacher, 1989. Originally published in Kazimir Wallowitz, *Varieties of Impressionism* (Boston: Revere Publications, 1987).

The citation of the original publication is in the nature of an annotation, and therefore its form is more like that of a citation in a note; that is, the elements are not separated by periods, and the facts of publication, if the original source is a book, are enclosed in parentheses.

PLAY OR LONG POEM

15.125 If the cited part of a book is a large entity in itself, such as a play or a long poem, its title is italicized:

> 6. Thomas Bernhard, *A Party for Boris,* in *Histrionics: Three Plays,* trans. Peter K. Jansen and Kenneth Northcott (Chicago: University of Chicago Press, 1990).
> 7. John Milton, *Paradise Lost,* in *Complete Poetical Works,* ed. Douglas Bush, Cambridge Edition (Boston: Houghton Mifflin, 1965).

> Bernhard, Thomas. *A Party for Boris.* In *Histrionics: Three Plays,* translated by Peter K. Jansen and Kenneth Northcott. Chicago: University of Chicago Press, 1990.

> Milton, John. *Paradise Lost.* In *Complete Poetical Works,* edited by Douglas Bush. Cambridge Edition. Boston: Houghton Mifflin, 1965.

Letters, Memoranda, and Similar Communications in Published Collections

15.126 A reference to a letter, memorandum, or similar communication in a published collection begins with the names of the sender and the recipient, in that order. In a note, last names only may be given if the identity is clear from the text. The names are followed by the date and sometimes the place where the communication was prepared. Finally, the citation of the published collection itself is given in the usual form. The word "letter" is unnecessary, but other forms of communication (telegram, memorandum) are specified. The letter may be located by page or, if the letters are numbered, by letter number.

> 1. Adams to Charles Milnes Gaskell, London, 30 March 1868, *Letters of Henry Adams, 1858–1891,* ed. Worthington Chauncey Ford (Boston: Houghton Mifflin, 1930), 141.
> 2. EBW to Harold Ross, memorandum, 2 May 1946, *Letters of E. B. White,* ed. Dorothy Lobrano Guth (New York: Harper and Row, 1976), 273.
> 3. Paulina Jackson to John Pepys Junior, 3 October 1676, *The Letters of Samuel Pepys and His Family Circle,* ed. Helen Truesdell Heath (Oxford: Clarendon Press, 1955), no. 42.
> 4. Secretary of State to the Special Commissioners, 27 May 1914, *Papers Relating to the Foreign Relations of the United States, 1914* (Washington, D.C., 1928), 509–10.
> 5. Minister of Foreign Relations of Mexico to the American Ambassador, memorandum, 27 November 1925, Ministerio de Relaciones Exteriores, *Correspondencia oficial cambiada entre los gobiernos de México y los Estados Unidos con motivo de las dos leyes reglamentarias de la fracción primera del Articulo 27 de la Constitución Mexicana* (Mexico City, 1926).

15.127 If a number of letters or other communications are cited from a single source, the source itself is entered in the bibliography, rather than the individual communications:

> Adams, Henry. *Letters of Henry Adams, 1858–1891.* Edited by Worthington Chauncey Ford. Boston: Houghton Mifflin, 1930.

> U. S. Department of State. *Papers Relating to the Foreign Relations of the United States, 1914.* Washington, D.C., 1928.

> Mexico. Ministerio de Relaciones Exteriores. *Correspondencia oficial cambiada entre los gobiernos de México y los Estados Unidos con motivo de las dos leyes reglamentarias de la fracción primera del Articulo 27 de la Constitución Mexicana.* Mexico City, 1926.

15.128 If only one item from a collection is mentioned, however, it may be listed in the bibliography as in the note, with the usual changes in style:

> Adams, Henry. Letter to Charles Milnes Gaskell. London, 30 March 1868. In *Letters of Henry Adams, 1858–1891,* edited by Worthington Chauncey Ford, 141. Boston: Houghton Mifflin, 1930.
>
> White, E. B. Memorandum to Harold Ross, 2 May 1946. In *Letters of E. B. White,* ed. Dorothy Lobrano Guth, 273. New York: Harper and Row, 1976.
>
> Paulina Jackson. Letter to John Pepys Junior, 3 October 1676. *The Letters of Samuel Pepys and His Family Circle,* ed. Helen Truesdell Heath, no. 42. Oxford: Clarendon Press, 1955.
>
> Secretary of State. Letter to the Special Commissioners, 27 May 1914. *Papers Relating to the Foreign Relations of the United States, 1914,* 509–10. Washington, D.C., 1928.
>
> Minister of Foreign Relations of Mexico. Memorandum to the American Ambassador, 27 November 1925. Ministerio de Relaciones Exteriores. *Correspondencia oficial cambiada entre los gobiernos de México y los Estados Unidos con motivo de las dos leyes reglamentarias de la fracción primera del Artículo 27 de la Constitución Mexicana.* Mexico City, 1926.

Preface, Foreword, Introduction, and Similar Parts of a Book

15.129 If the reference is to some such part of a book as the preface, foreword, or introduction, that term (lowercased unless following a period) is added before the title of the book.

> 1. James B. Jacobs, introduction to *Drunk Driving: An American Dilemma* (Chicago: University of Chicago Press, 1989).
>
> Jacobs, James B. Introduction to *Drunk Driving: An American Dilemma.* Chicago: University of Chicago Press, 1989.

15.130 If the author of the cited preface, foreword, or introduction is someone other than the author of the book, that name should begin the entry, and the name of the author of the book itself should follow the book title. The author's name is introduced by a comma and the word *by.*

> 2. Franklin E. Zimring, foreword to *Drunk Driving: An American Dilemma,* by James B. Jacobs (Chicago: University of Chicago Press, 1989).
>
> Zimring, Franklin E. Foreword to *Drunk Driving: An American Dilemma,* by James B. Jacobs. Chicago: University of Chicago Press, 1989.

15.131 It may sometimes be desirable, in citing a book by one author, to note that the book contains a foreword or some other part by another author:

> 3. Dag Hammarskjöld, *Markings,* with a foreword by W. H. Auden (New York: Knopf, 1964).

> Hammarskjöld, Dag. *Markings.* With a foreword by W. H. Auden. New York: Knopf, 1964.

Edition

SUBSEQUENT EDITIONS

15.132 When an edition other than the first is used, the number or description of the edition follows the title in the listing. The number of an edition and its date of publication may be found in the copyright notice of the book (see 15.170–72). A new edition may be called "Revised Edition" (no number), "Second Edition, Revised and Enlarged," or some other variant. In bibliography entries or notes these are commonly abbreviated: *rev. ed.; 2d ed., rev. and enl.* (or just *2d ed.*); and so on. Such terms and their abbreviations should be given in English even though the book is in a foreign language.

> 1. John N. Hazard, *The Soviet System of Government,* 5th ed. (Chicago: University of Chicago Press, 1980), 25.
> 2. Halsey Stevens, *The Life and Music of Béla Bartók,* rev. ed. (New York: Oxford University Press, 1964), 128–29.
> 3. Charles Dickens, *The Life and Adventures of Martin Chuzzlewit,* New Oxford Illustrated Dickens (London: Oxford University Press, 1951), 733; all subsequent citations are to this edition.
> 4. M. Weber, H. M. de Burlet, and O. Abel, *Die Säugetiere,* 2d ed., 2 vols. (Jena: Gustav Fischer, 1928).

> Hazard, John N. *The Soviet System of Government.* 5th ed. Chicago: University of Chicago Press, 1980.
> Stevens, Halsey. *The Life and Music of Béla Bartók.* Rev. ed. New York: Oxford University Press, 1964.
> Dickens, Charles. *The Life and Adventures of Martin Chuzzlewit.* New Oxford Illustrated Dickens. London: Oxford University Press, 1951.
> Weber, M.; H. M. de Burlet; and O. Abel. *Die Säugetiere.* 2d ed. 2 vols. Jena: Gustav Fischer, 1928.

Although the edition terminology appearing in the published work should, to avoid confusion, be reproduced in the citation, the University of Chicago Press recommends that a uniform and simplified edition designation be used in all future publications (see 1.20–22).

MODERN EDITIONS OF THE CLASSICS

15.133 When classics are referred to by page number, the edition used must be specified. For well-known editions, only the name of the edition and the date of the volume are necessary:

5. Horace, *Satires, Epistles, and Ars Poetica,* Loeb Classical Library (1932), 146.

Horace. *Satires, Epistles, and Ars Poetica.* Loeb Classical Library. 1932.

15.134 Editor, place of publication, and publisher should be added for less well known editions:

6. Maimonides, *The Code of Maimonides, Book 5: The Book of Holiness,* trans. and ed. Louis I. Rabinowitz and Philip Grossman, Yale Judaica Series (New Haven: Yale University Press, 1965), 98.

Maimonides. *The Code of Maimonides. Book 5: The Book of Holiness.* Translated and edited by Louis I. Rabinowitz and Philip Grossman. Yale Judaica Series. New Haven: Yale University Press, 1965.

REPRINT EDITIONS

15.135 Reprint editions are discussed under "Facts of Publication," 15.178–82.

Multivolume Works

CITING THE WORK AS A WHOLE

15.136 When a multivolume work is cited as a whole, the total number of volumes is usually indicated after the title of the work:

1. Muriel St. Clare Byrne, ed., *The Lisle Letters,* 6 vols. (Chicago: University of Chicago Press, 1981).

Byrne, Muriel St. Clare, ed. *The Lisle Letters.* 6 vols. Chicago: University of Chicago Press, 1981.

If the volumes have been published over several years, the publication date should include the beginning and concluding years:

2. Caeli Love Peterspring and Ian Mills Michaelson, eds., *The Flowering of Harmonious Internationalism,* 4 vols. (Chicago: Marmer, 1990–93).

Peterspring, Caeli Love, and Ian Mills Michaelson, eds. *The Flowering of Harmonious Internationalism.* 4 vols. Chicago: Marmer, 1990–93.

In both note and bibliography entries *volumes* is abbreviated; in the note citation, the number of volumes is preceded by a comma; in the bibliography, it is preceded by a period.

CITING A PARTICULAR VOLUME

15.137 *Volume number and volume title.* If a particular volume is cited, the volume number and often the individual volume title, if there is one, are given in addition to the general title. If the volume title is given, it may either precede or follow the general title. In either case the page reference follows the publication facts in the notes. It is not necessary when citing a particular volume to give the total number of volumes.

> 3. William Farmwinkle, *Humor of the American Midwest,* vol. 2 of *Survey of American Humor* (Boston: Plenum Press, 1983), 132.
> *or*
> 3. William Farmwinkle, *Survey of American Humor,* vol. 2, *Humor of the American Midwest* (Boston: Plenum Press, 1983), 132.

> Farmwinkle, William. *Humor of the American Midwest.* Vol. 2 of *Survey of American Humor.* Boston: Plenum Press, 1983.
> *or*
> Farmwinkle, William. *Survey of American Humor.* Vol. 2, *Humor of the American Midwest.* Boston: Plenum Press, 1983.

Note that in the bibliography entries a period separates the two titles, and the abbreviation of *volume* is capitalized.

15.138 *General title only.* If the particular volume cited has no title of its own, it is distinguished by the volume number only. In a reference to such a volume as a whole, the volume number follows the general title and precedes the publication facts.

> 4. Edward Banicek, *A History of India,* vol. 2 (Philadelphia: Ross and Kittredge, 1988).

> Banicek, Edward. *A History of India.* Vol. 2. Philadelphia: Ross and Kittredge, 1988.

15.139 If a note citation refers to specific pages of such a volume, both volume and page numbers are given at the end of the citation, following the publication facts. The volume and page numbers are preceded by a comma and separated by a colon. The abbreviation *vol.* is omitted. (See also 15.196–98, 15.257.)

> 5. Edward Banicek, *A History of India* (Philadelphia: Ross and Kittredge, 1988), 2:143–55.

If the volume has a title but the title is not included in the citation, the entry is treated as though the volume had no title.

> 6. William Farmwinkle, *Survey of American Humor* (Boston: Plenum Press, 1983), 2:132.

> Farmwinkle, William. *Survey of American Humor.* Vol. 2. Boston: Plenum Press, 1983.

15.140 *Chapters and other parts of individual volumes.* References to chapters and other parts of individual volumes of multivolume works are made in the same way as references to parts of single-volume works (see also 15.120–23):

7. Edward Banicek, "Pakistanian Independence," in *A History of India* (Philadelphia: Ross and Kittredge, 1988), 2:213–31.

8. William Farmwinkle, preface to *Survey of American Humor* (Boston: Plenum Press, 1983), 1:xi.

9. Rachel Ravencrest, foreword to *A History of India,* by Edward Banicek (Philadelphia: Ross and Kittredge, 1988), 1:ix–xii.

Banicek, Edward. "Pakistanian Independence." In *A History of India.* Vol. 2. Philadelphia: Ross and Kittredge, 1988.

Farmwinkle, William. Preface to *Survey of American Humor.* Vol. 1. Boston: Plenum Press, 1983.

Ravencrest, Rachel. Foreword to *A History of India,* by Edward Banicek. Vol. 1. Philadelphia: Ross and Kittredge, 1988.

15.141 *Author's name in general title.* When the author's name is part of the general title of a multivolume work, the name introduces the note citation only if the individual volume title precedes the general title:

10. William Makepeace Thackeray, *The English Humorists of the Eighteenth Century,* vol. 13 of *The Complete Works of William Makepeace Thackeray* (Boston, 1889), 113–330.
   but
10. *The Complete Works of William Makepeace Thackeray,* vol. 13, *The English Humorists of the Eighteenth Century* (Boston, 1889), 111–330.

Bibliography entries in both cases would begin with the author's name:

Thackeray, William Makepeace. *The English Humorists of the Eighteenth Century.* Vol. 13 of *The Complete Works of William Makepeace Thackeray.* Boston, 1889.
   or
Thackeray, William Makepeace. *The Complete Works of William Makepeace Thackeray.* Vol. 13, *The English Humorists of the Eighteenth Century.* Boston, 1889.

15.142 *One volume in two or more books.* Occasionally, when a single volume of a multivolume work is very extensive, the volume may be published as two or more books. In that case, reference to one of the books must contain the book number as well as the volume number:

11. Margaret Skelton, *A Critical History of Modern Dance,* vol. 2, bk. 1 (Chicago: Terpsichore Press, 1988).

Skelton, Margaret. *A Critical History of Modern Dance.* Vol. 2, bk. 1. Chicago: Terpsichore Press, 1988.

When a page citation is added to the note, it follows the publication facts:

11. Margaret Skelton, *A Critical History of Modern Dance,* vol. 2, bk. 1 (Chicago: Terpsichore Press, 1988), 118–20.

If the book has its own title, this may be added:

> 12. Donald F. Lach, *Asia in the Making of Europe,* vol. 2, bk. 2, *The Literary Arts* (Chicago: University of Chicago Press, 1977).
> *or*
> 12. Donald F. Lach, *The Literary Arts,* vol. 2, bk. 2 of *Asia in the Making of Europe* (Chicago: University of Chicago Press, 1977).

> Lach, Donald F. *Asia in the Making of Europe.* Vol. 2, bk. 2, *The Literary Arts.* Chicago: University of Chicago Press, 1977.
> *or*
> Lach, Donald F. *The Literary Arts.* Vol. 2, bk. 2 of *Asia in the Making of Europe.* Chicago: University of Chicago Press, 1977.

GENERAL EDITORS AND VOLUME EDITORS OR AUTHORS

15.143 Some multivolume works have both a general editor and individual editors or authors for each volume. In citations of individual volumes of such works, the editor's or author's name follows that part for which he or she is responsible.

> 13. *The Letters of Edmund Tancredi,* ed. William Tismont, vol. 2, *The War Years,* ed. Arthur Soma (San Francisco: Idlewink Press, 1989), 195.
> *or*
> 13. Edmund Tancredi, *The War Years,* ed. Arthur Soma, vol. 2 of *The Letters of Edmund Tancredi,* ed. William Tismont (San Francisco: Idlewink Press, 1989), 195.

> Tancredi, Edmund. *The Letters of Edmund Tancredi.* Edited by William Tismont. Vol. 2, *The War Years,* edited by Arthur Soma. San Francisco: Idlewink Press, 1989.
> *or*
> Tancredi, Edmund. *The War Years.* Edited by Arthur Soma. Vol. 2 of *The Letters of Edmund Tancredi,* edited by William Tismont. San Francisco: Idlewink Press, 1989.

> 14. Gordon N. Ray, ed., *An Introduction to Literature,* vol. 2, *The Nature of Drama,* by Hubert Hefner (Boston: Houghton Mifflin, 1959), 47–49.
> *or*
> 14. Hubert Hefner, *The Nature of Drama,* vol. 2 of *An Introduction to Literature,* ed. Gordon N. Ray (Boston: Houghton Mifflin, 1959), 47–49.

> Ray, Gordon N., ed. *An Introduction to Literature.* Vol. 2, *The Nature of Drama,* by Hubert Hefner. Boston: Houghton Mifflin, 1959.
> *or*
> Hefner, Hubert. *The Nature of Drama.* Vol. 2 of *An Introduction to Literature,* edited by Gordon N. Ray. Boston: Houghton Mifflin, 1959.

Note that in the bibliography entries for such works, the last-mentioned title and editor (or author) are separated not by a period but by a comma. The purpose of this is to clarify the role of the last-named person in the preparation of the part of the work cited.

Series

15.144 A series is a sequence of publications related in subject matter and developed under the supervision of an editor or group of editors well grounded in that subject matter. The titles of series may indicate the publishing agency (Smithsonian Miscellaneous Collections), the general subject of the series (Nature of Human Society), or both (Chicago History of American Civilization; Logan Museum Publications in Anthropology). Its name is capitalized as a title, set in roman type, and not enclosed in quotation marks or parentheses. Many series do not have numbered volumes; others have both volume numbers and subsidiary numbers. Any such number should follow the series title in the reference, separated from it by a comma if the title is complete without the number (Middle American Research Records, vol. 1, no. 14), no comma if the number is part of the title (Bureau of American Ethnology Bulletin 143). The name of the series editor may be included but is usually omitted. If the publisher's name appears in the series title, or as the author, it need not be repeated in the facts of publication (see 15.151). Ambiguous series titles should be avoided (Current Report no. 4; Bulletin no. 143; Research Records, no. 5); the responsible agency should appear somewhere in the listing.

15.145 Series titles are included for illustrative purposes in all of the following examples, but if the works can be located without them, or if they are given in bibliography listings, series titles may be omitted from notes to save space.

> 1. Helen Caldwell, *The Brazilian Othello of Machado de Assis: A Study of "Dom Casmurro,"* Perspectives in Criticism, vol. 6 (Berkeley and Los Angeles: University of California Press, 1960), 134.
>
> 2. Theta Holmes Wolf, *The Effects of Praise and Competition on the Persisting Behavior of Kindergarten Children*, Child Welfare Monograph Series, no. 15 (Minneapolis: University of Minnesota Press, 1938), 33–38.
>
> 3. Pierre Biays, *Les marges de l'œkoumène dans l'est du Canada: Partie orientale du Bouclier canadien et île de Terre-Neuve*, Travaux et documents du Centre d'études nordiques (Quebec: Presses de l'Université Laval, 1964), 112–14.
>
> 4. Julian H. Steward, ed., *Handbook of South American Indians*, Smithsonian Institution, Bureau of American Ethnology Bulletin 143 (Washington, D.C., 1949), 10.
>
> 5. Joachim Hopp, *Untersuchungen zur Geschichte der letzten Attaliden*, Vestigia, Beiträge zur alten Geschichte, no. 25 (Munich: C. H. Beck'sche Verlag, 1977), 115–20.
>
> 6. Robert Wauchope, *A Tentative Sequence of Pre-Classic Ceramics in Middle America*, Middle American Research Records, vol. 1, no. 14 (New Orleans: Tulane University, 1950), 10.

7. Arthur H. R. Fairchild, *Shakespeare and the Arts of Design,* University of Missouri Studies, vol. 12 (Columbia, 1937), 104, 109.

Caldwell, Helen. *The Brazilian Othello of Machado de Assis: A Study of "Dom Casmurro."* Perspectives in Criticism, vol. 6. Berkeley and Los Angeles: University of California Press, 1960.

Wolf, Theta Holmes. *The Effects of Praise and Competition on the Persisting Behavior of Kindergarten Children.* Child Welfare Monograph Series, no. 15. Minneapolis: University of Minnesota Press, 1938.

Biays, Pierre. *Les marges de l'œkoumène dans l'est du Canada: Partie orientale du Bouclier canadien et île de Terre-Neuve.* Travaux et documents du Centre d'études nordiques. Quebec: Presses de l'Université Laval, 1964.

Steward, Julian H., ed. *Handbook of South American Indians.* Smithsonian Institution, Bureau of American Ethnology Bulletin 143. Washington, D.C., 1949.

Hopp, Joachim. *Untersuchungen zur Geschichte der letzten Attaliden.* Vestigia, Beiträge zur alten Geschichte, no. 25. Munich: C. H. Beck'sche Verlag, 1977.

Wauchope, Robert. *A Tentative Sequence of Pre-Classic Ceramics in Middle America.* Middle American Research Records, vol. 1, no. 14. New Orleans: Tulane University, 1950.

Fairchild, Arthur H. R. *Shakespeare and the Arts of Design.* University of Missouri Studies, vol. 12. Columbia, 1937.

SERIES EDITOR

15.146 If a series editor's name is included in the citation, it is placed after the series title, following a comma and the abbreviation *ed.* (meaning *edited by*):

8. Charles Issawi, *The Economic History of Turkey, 1800–1914,* Publications of the Center for Middle Eastern Studies, ed. Richard L. Chambers, no. 13 (Chicago: University of Chicago Press, 1980).

Issawi, Charles. *The Economic History of Turkey, 1800–1914.* Publications of the Center for Middle Eastern Studies, ed. Richard L. Chambers, no. 13. Chicago: University of Chicago Press, 1980.

If the series number is part of the series title, as in example note 4 above, the series editor's name would follow that number and, in this case, be preceded by the abbreviation *ser. ed.*

MULTIVOLUME WORK WITHIN A SERIES

15.147 If a work within a series consists of more than one volume, the number of volumes or (if the reference is to a particular volume) the volume number is placed after the title of the work:

9. Broderick Mummerston, *An Introduction to Inca Sports and Rituals,* 2 vols., Ancient American Culture Series (Houston: H. D. Dobbs, 1990).

10. Broderick Mummerston, *An Introduction to Inca Sports and Rituals,* vol. 1, Ancient American Culture Series (Houston: H. D. Dobbs, 1990).

Mummerston, Broderick. *An Introduction to Inca Sports and Rituals.* 2 vols. Ancient American Culture Series. Houston: H. D. Dobbs, 1990.
Mummerston, Broderick. *An Introduction to Inca Sports and Rituals.* Vol. 1. Ancient American Culture Series. Houston: H. D. Dobbs, 1990.

15.148 If each volume of a multivolume work in a series has its own title, either the volume title or the general title may come first:

11. Ralph Wattle, *Economic Aspects of Professional Sports in America,* vol. 2, *Player Salaries and Bargaining Power,* Trends in American Economy, no. 11 (Boston: Flummery Press, 1989).
or
11. Ralph Wattle, *Player Salaries and Bargaining Power,* vol. 2 of *Economic Aspects of Professional Sports in America,* Trends in American Economy, no. 11 (Boston: Flummery Press, 1989).

Wattle, Ralph. *Economic Aspects of Professional Sports in America.* Vol. 2, *Player Salaries and Bargaining Power.* Trends in American Economy, no. 11. Boston: Flummery Press, 1989.
or
Wattle, Ralph. *Player Salaries and Bargaining Power.* Vol. 2 of *Economic Aspects of Professional Sports in America.* Trends in American Economy, no. 11. Boston: Flummery Press, 1989.

SUBSEQUENT SERIES NUMBERING

15.149 Some series have been going on so long that, like some journals, their volumes have begun to be numbered over again in a new series (*n.s.*), sometimes designated by a number or letter (*2d ser., 3d ser., ser. b,* etc.). Books in the old or original series are identified as such by the abbreviation *o.s.* or *1st ser.* Note that a comma separates the series identifier from the volume number.

12. Charles R. Boxer, ed., *South China in the Sixteenth Century,* Hakluyt Society Publications, 2d ser., vol. 106 (London, 1953).
13. Helen C. Palmatary, *The Pottery of Marajó Island, Brazil,* Transactions of the American Philosophical Society, n.s., 39, pt. 3 (Philadelphia, 1950).
14. Everett Truewit, *Discerning the Evanescent,* Studies in Fugitive Phenomena, o.s., 17 (Camden, N.J.: Flieger, 1951).

Boxer, Charles R., ed. *South China in the Sixteenth Century.* Hakluyt Society Publications, 2d ser., vol. 106. London, 1953.
Palmatary, Helen C. *The Pottery of Marajó Island, Brazil.* Transactions of the American Philosophical Society, n.s., 39, pt. 3. Philadelphia, 1950.
Truewit, Everett. *Discerning the Evanescent.* Studies in Fugitive Phenomena, o.s., 17. Camden, N.J.: Flieger, 1951.

15.150 Names of reprint series (Midway Reprints), paperback series (Phoenix Fiction), microfiche or text-fiche series (Chicago Visual Library), and others indicating publishing or production methods are properly part of the publication facts (see 15.151, 15.168), not series titles reflecting subject categories.

Facts of Publication

FULL FACTS

15.151 Traditionally the facts of publication of a book include the place (city), the publisher, and the date (year). All three are usually included in full note references and bibliography entries. In note references, the facts of publication are enclosed in parentheses and are placed, without intervening punctuation, after the title and such other descriptive material as the identification of editors, translators, series, or number of volumes. If a full citation is introduced in parentheses in a discursive note, or in running text, brackets are used to set off the facts of publication (see example at 15.53). In the bibliography entry the publication facts are also placed after the title and other descriptive material, but they are not enclosed in parentheses; they are preceded by a period. In both note and bibliography citation, a colon follows the place-name (regular word space after the colon), and a comma follows the name of the publisher.

> 1. Olga Porkola, *Contemporary Finnish Design and Architecture* (Cleveland: Cuyahoga Press, 1990).
> 2. Itzka Schmutki, *Struggles against Oppression in Eastern Europe,* 2 vols., trans. Peter Foldes (Boston: Revere Publications, 1991).

> Porkola, Olga. *Contemporary Finnish Design and Architecture.* Cleveland: Cuyahoga Press, 1990.
> Schmutki, Itzka. *Struggles against Oppression in Eastern Europe.* 2 vols. Translated by Peter Foldes. Boston: Revere Publications, 1991.

ALTERNATIVE FORMS

15.152 Although the use of full publication facts is preferred in listings of modern works, alternatives are acceptable in certain cases. One alternative is the inclusion of place and date only (no publisher's name); another, date only (no place or publisher's name).

15.153 The use of place and date only is the practice of many academic journals and of authors who follow a particular journal style in their book manuscripts. The University of Chicago Press accepts this practice if an author has consistently employed it. When only place and date are used, a comma (not a colon) follows the place.

3. Charles Akers, *Abigail Adams: An American Woman* (Boston, 1980).
4. Michael David, *Toward Honesty in Public Relations* (Chicago, 1968).

Akers, Charles. *Abigail Adams: An American Woman.* Boston, 1980.
David, Michael. *Toward Honesty in Public Relations.* Chicago, 1968.

15.154 The second alternative, inclusion of date only, is both economical in that it saves space and realistic in that the date is usually the fact of publication most important to the scholar; the publisher of the book cited may be discovered by the interested reader in a library catalog or the current *Books in Print,* available for consultation in most bookstores. The University of Chicago Press will accept this practice in books where it is consistently used and seems appropriate to the subject.

5. Kurt Vonnegut, *Jailbird* (1979).
6. Edmund S. Morgan, *The Birth of the Republic, 1763–89* (1956; 3d ed., 1992).

Vonnegut, Kurt. *Jailbird.* 1979.
Morgan, Edmund S. *The Birth of the Republic, 1763–89.* 1956. 3d ed., 1992.

15.155 For works published in earlier centuries, whose publishers have long since ceased to exist or cannot be determined, either place and date or date alone is entirely acceptable, even when mixed in a list containing modern works accompanied by full facts of publication:

7. William Baldwin, *A Treatise of morall philosophy Contaynynge the sayings of the wyse* (London, 1579).
8. John Bunyan, *A Few Sighs from Hell, or The Groans of a damned Soul* (1658).

Baldwin, William. *A Treatise of morall philosophy Contaynynge the sayings of the wyse.* London, 1579.
Bunyan, John. *A Few Sighs from Hell, or The Groans of a damned Soul.* 1658.

15.156 The inclusion of the publisher's name is, of course, essential in references to quoted material for which permission to reprint has been granted by the publisher as owner of the copyright (see chapter 4).

PLACE

15.157 The name of the city where the publisher's main editorial offices are located is usually sufficient:

New York: Macmillan, 1980.

If the title page of the book cited lists two cities with the publisher's name, the city listed first is the one to use; it is permissible, but not necessary, to use both:

> Chicago: University of Chicago Press, 1991.
> Chicago and London: University of Chicago Press, 1991.

(If "London" does not appear on the title page of the book being cited, it must not be given in the reference.) The University of California Press prefers the use of "Berkeley and Los Angeles" in references to its publications.

15.158 If the place of publication is not widely known, the abbreviation of the state name, region, or country should follow it. Short state names, like Alaska, Iowa, Maine, and Ohio, are given in full (see 14.17).

> Post Mills, Vt.: Chelsea Green, 1992.
> Ottawa, Ill.: Jameson Books, 1991.
> Harmondsworth, England: Penguin Books, 1988.

The distinction between Cambridge, England, and Cambridge, Massachusetts, should be made. In the absence of contrary indications—such as inclusion of the state name or mention of Harvard University or Massachusetts Institute of Technology (MIT)—it will be assumed that the English city is meant. Thus the following are all acceptable:

> Cambridge: Cambridge University Press, 1979.
> Cambridge, 1979.
> Cambridge: Harvard University Press, 1979.
> Cambridge, Mass., 1979.
> Cambridge: MIT Press, 1979.

The English language version of the name of a foreign city, when such a variant occurs, is usually used in the publication facts: Vienna (Wien), Cologne (Köln), Turin (Torino), Rome (Roma), Milan (Milano), Munich (München), Brunswick (Braunschweig), Prague (Praha), The Hague ('s Gravenhage); *but* Frankfurt am Main (*not* Frankfort on the Main).

15.159 When the place of publication is not given on the title page or the copyright page and cannot be determined, *n.p. (no place)* may be substituted for the missing information. Only in the bibliography should *n* be capitalized.

> (n.p.: Evanescent Press, 1840)
> N.p.: Evanescent Press, 1840.

If the place is known but not given, it may be included in brackets:

> ([Wauwatosa, Wis.]: Evanescent Press, 1840)
> [Wauwatosa, Wis.]: Evanescent Press, 1840.

PUBLISHER

15.160 *Single publisher.* The publisher's name may be given either in full, as printed on the title page of the book, or in an acceptable abbreviated form. American publishers' names and the usual abbreviations for them are listed in *Books in Print,* published annually by R. R. Bowker Company, and British publishers' names may be found in *Whitaker's Books in Print,* published annually by J. Whitaker & Sons. An initial *The,* as well as *Inc., Ltd.,* or *S.A.* following the name, is generally omitted, even when the full name is given. The abbreviation *Co.* may also be omitted. The use of either long or short forms of publishers' names must be consistent throughout a bibliography.

15.161 The word *University* in names of university presses may be shortened to *Univ.,* so long as it is done consistently. A place-name that is part of a publisher's name, however, should always be spelled out: Univ. of South Carolina Press. The word *Press* should not be omitted from the name of a university press because the university itself may issue publications independently of its press. Where there is no ambiguity, the word may be omitted; for example, Pergamon as a short form of Pergamon Press.

15.162 Punctuation and spelling of publishers' names should be carefully observed. For example, there is now no comma in Houghton Mifflin Co.; there is a comma in both Little, Brown & Co. and the former Harcourt, Brace & Co., now Harcourt Brace Jovanovich with no comma whatever. There is no capital *M* in the middle of Macmillan; the London firm is Macmillan Publishers Ltd., and the New York firm is Macmillan Publishing Co., Inc.; both are abbreviated "Macmillan."

15.163 Either *and* or & may be used in a publisher's name, regardless of how it is rendered on the title page, provided consistency in the treatment of the conjunction is observed throughout a bibliography:

Harper and Row	*or*	Harper & Row
Duncker und Humblot	*or*	Duncker & Humblot

No part of a foreign publisher's name should be translated, even though the place of publication has been anglicized:

Paris: Presses Universitaires de France, 1982.
Mexico City: Fondo de Cultura Económica, 1981.
Munich: Carl Hanser Verlag, 1980.

If the name of the publisher has changed since the book was published, the name on the title page is the one to use, not the present name; for example, Henry Holt & Co., not Holt, Rinehart & Winston. Such recent additions to title pages as "A Division of —— Corporation" should not be added to the publisher's name in scholarly notes or bibliographies.

15.164 *Publisher not identified.* When the publisher is known but not identified on the title page or copyright page, the name may be added in brackets:

Wauwatosa, Wis.: [Evanescent Press], 1947.

A question mark is added if the identity is uncertain:

> Wauwatosa, Wis.: [Evanescent Press?], 1947.

If the publisher cannot be ascertained, the abbreviation *n.p.* (*no publisher,* in this case) may be used, or the publisher may simply be omitted:

> Cleveland: n.p., 1889.
> Cleveland, 1889.

When neither place nor publisher can be ascertained, a single *n.p.* may serve as notice for both:

> (n.p., 1840)
> N.p., 1840.

15.165 *Copublication and other publishing arrangements.* For copublished books—books published simultaneously by two different publishers, one in the United States, for example, and one in another country—it is permissible, but not necessary, to give both in the facts of publication:

> 9. Marc Bloch, *Feudal Society,* trans. L. A. Manyon (Chicago: University of Chicago Press; London: Routledge & Kegan Paul, 1961).

> Bloch, Marc. *Feudal Society.* Translated by L. A. Manyon. Chicago: University of Chicago Press; London: Routledge & Kegan Paul, 1961.

A bibliography entry or a full note reference in a book published in the United States and addressed principally to American readers should give the American edition of a copublished book, or both—not just the British edition.

15.166 When a book is published under one publisher's name and distributed under another's, use the name on the title page of the book; add the distributor's name only if this information would be useful to the reader:

> 10. James Borcoman, *Eugène Atget, 1857–1927* (Ottawa: National Gallery of Canada, 1984; distributed in U.S. by University of Chicago Press).

> Borcoman, James. *Eugène Atget, 1857–1927.* Ottawa: National Gallery of Canada, 1984; distributed in U.S. by University of Chicago Press.

15.167 When a publishing arrangement specified on the title page suggests something about the background or the nature of the book, it should be included:

> 11. Sophocles, *Oedipus the King,* trans. and adapt. Anthony Burgess, Minnesota Drama Editions, ed. Michael Langham, no. 8 (Minneapolis: University of Minnesota Press in association with Guthrie Theater Company, 1972).

> Sophocles. *Oedipus the King.* Translated and adapted by Anthony Burgess. Minnesota Drama Editions, edited by Michael Langham, no. 8. Minneapolis: University of Minnesota Press in association with Guthrie Theater Company, 1972.

15.168 *Special publications divisions.* Some publishers issue certain categories of books through a special publishing division or under a special imprint. In such instances the imprint may be given after the publisher's name:

> 12. *The Letters and Journals of James Fenimore Cooper,* ed. J. F. Beard, 2 vols. (Cambridge: Harvard University Press, Belknap Press, 1960).

> Cooper, James Fenimore. *The Letters and Journals of James Fenimore Cooper.* Edited by J. F. Beard. 2 vols. Cambridge: Harvard University Press, Belknap Press, 1960.

The same style is used for paperback reprints (see also 15.178–82):

> 13. Jack Fuller, *Convergence* (New York: Doubleday, 1982; Chicago: University of Chicago Press, Phoenix Fiction, 1991).

> Fuller, Jack. *Convergence.* New York: Doubleday, 1982; Chicago: University of Chicago Press, Phoenix Fiction, 1991.

15.169 *Translations.* A citation of an English translation of a work in a foreign language should not include the original edition unless the full citation of the latter is also given:

> 14. Jacques Derrida, *Writing and Difference,* trans. Alan Bass (Chicago: University of Chicago Press, 1978).
> 15. Jacques Derrida, *Writing and Difference,* trans. Alan Bass (Chicago: University of Chicago Press, 1978); originally published as *L'écriture et la différence* (Paris: Editions du Seuil, 1967).

> Derrida, Jacques. *Writing and Difference.* Translated by Alan Bass. Chicago: University of Chicago Press, 1978.

> Derrida, Jacques. *Writing and Difference.* Translated by Alan Bass. Chicago: University of Chicago Press, 1978. Originally published as *L'écriture et la différence* (Paris: Editions du Seuil, 1967).
> *or*
> Derrida, Jacques. *L'écriture et la différence.* Paris: Editions du Seuil, 1967. Translated by Alan Bass under the title *Writing and Difference* (Chicago: University of Chicago Press, 1978).

If the original edition is included in the bibliography entry, the work primarily cited should be given first. The work listed second then becomes an annotation and takes the form used in note citations (see 15.124).

DATE OF PUBLICATION

15.170 *General.* The date of publication of a book means the *year* of publication, not the month or day. Sometimes the date of publication may be found on the title page; more often it appears only on the copyright page. The date of publication is usually identical to the copyright date, but some books carry more than one copyright date. If the work is an edition other than the first, copyright dates of the earlier editions may be carried as well as that of the current edition, especially if some material from the earlier editions has been retained. In such cases the last, or most recent, copyright date usually indicates the publication date. First editions may also carry more than one copyright date, indicating that part of the work was published earlier in another publication (book or periodical). In that case the last date again indicates the publication date of the present book.

15.171 In many modern works, this manual for example, the copyright page carries a publication date as well as a copyright date, which simplifies identification.

15.172 Copyright pages also often list successive *printings* or *impressions,* with the dates of each. These are not new *editions* of the book and therefore should be ignored in determining the date of publication. See figure 1.2, showing a fifth edition published in 1987, a fifth impression of which was issued in 1989. The correct publication date to be used for the fifth edition of this book is 1987.

> 16. Kate L. Turabian, *A Manual for Writers of Term Papers, Theses, and Dissertations,* 5th ed., rev. and exp. Bonnie Birtwistle Honigsblum (Chicago: University of Chicago Press, 1987).

> Turabian, Kate L. *A Manual for Writers of Term Papers, Theses, and Dissertations.* 5th ed. Revised and expanded by Bonnie Birtwistle Honigsblum. Chicago: University of Chicago Press, 1987.

If an edition other than the first is referred to, as in the example above, both the date and number of the edition must be given.

15.173 *Multivolume work published over several years.* A reference to a work of several volumes published in different years should give inclusive dates:

> 17. Paul Tillich, *Systematic Theology,* 3 vols. (Chicago: University of Chicago Press, 1951–63).

> Tillich, Paul. *Systematic Theology.* 3 vols. Chicago: University of Chicago Press, 1951–63.

If the work has not yet been completed, the date of the first volume is followed by an en dash (a hyphen if an en dash is not available):

> 18. Margaret Skelton, *A Critical History of Modern Dance,* 2 vols. to date (Chicago: Terpsichore Press, 1987–).

> Skelton, Margaret. *A Critical History of Modern Dance.* 2 vols. to date. Chicago: Terpsichore Press, 1987–.

15.174 When only one of several volumes is mentioned, only the year of publication of that volume is given:

> 19. Douglas Southall Freeman, *George Washington,* vol. 3, *Planter and Patriot* (New York: Charles Scribner's Sons, 1951).

> Freeman, Douglas Southall. *George Washington.* Vol. 3, *Planter and Patriot.* New York: Charles Scribner's Sons, 1951.

15.175 *Date not indicated.* When there is no ascertainable date of publication in a printed book, *n.d. (no date)* takes the place of the year in the facts of publication. When the date is ascertainable but not printed in the book, it is given in brackets; a question mark is added if the date is uncertain.

> 20. Marjorie S. Phillips, *Book-Trading as a Business* (Excelsior, Minn.: Self-Help Publishing Co., n.d.).
> 21. Sir Oliver Moonbeam, *Memoirs of an Inveterate Procrastinator* (Waiting-upon-Tyme, Wessex: privately printed, [1846]).
> *or*
> . . . privately printed, [1846?]).

> Phillips, Marjorie S. *Book-Trading as a Business.* Excelsior, Minn.: Self-Help Publishing Co., n.d.
> Moonbeam, Sir Oliver. *Memoirs of an Inveterate Procrastinator.* Waiting-upon-Tyme, Wessex: privately printed, [1846].

15.176 *"Forthcoming" or "in press."* When a book is in process of publication, the publication facts should be replaced by either *forthcoming* or, if the book is actually being typeset or printed, *in press.* If the publisher is known, it may be included.

> 22. Melvin Otonski, *The Imagists of Chicago* (forthcoming).
> 23. Viola Mitchell, *The Historian as Prophet* (Chicago: Blackstone Publishers, in press).

> Otonski, Melvin, *The Imagists of Chicago.* Forthcoming.
> Mitchell, Viola. *The Historian as Prophet.* Chicago: Blackstone Publishers, in press.

15.177 A manuscript not yet assured of publication is considered an unpublished work. For the method of citing such work, see 15.270.

REPRINT EDITIONS

15.178 Works that are out of print may be reissued in special reprint editions, either paperback or hardcover. Occasionally works that remain in print as hardcover books are also issued in paperback reprint editions. A reprint edition may be issued by the original publisher or by another publisher who has bought rights from the original publisher or who is reprinting a book no longer protected by copyright. Even if the reprint edition is produced by photo-offset process from the original edition and has the same pagination, it is usual to indicate that the edition referred to is a reprint.

15.179 For reprints of very old books, usually only the year of the original publication is given along with the full publication facts of the reprint. The original publication date precedes the reprint information. In the note, the original date is followed by a semicolon, the word *reprint* or *reprinted,* and a comma. In the bibliography entry, the semicolon is replaced by a period, and *Reprint* or *Reprinted* is capitalized. Since in this case the reprint is the source consulted and the original publication date is included only as an annotation, the bibliography entry is given in regular bibliographic form rather than in the form of a citation in a note (compare 15.124).

> 24. Albert Schweitzer, *J. S. Bach,* trans. Ernest Newman (1911; reprint, New York: Dover Publications, 1966).

> Schweitzer, Albert. *J. S. Bach.* Translated by Ernest Newman. 1911. Reprint, New York: Dover Publications, 1966.

15.180 If the reprint edition contains something new (a foreword, for example) or if it combines two or more volumes in one, that information is added as part of the reprint data, before the name of the city and publisher:

> 25. Robert Small, *An Account of the Astronomical Discoveries of Kepler* (1804; reprint, with a foreword by William D. Stahlman, Madison: University of Wisconsin Press, 1963).
> 26. George Ashdown Audsley, *The Art of Organ Building,* 2 vols. (1905; reprint, 2 vols. in 1, New York: Dover Publications, 1964).

> Small, Robert. *An Account of the Astronomical Discoveries of Kepler.* 1804. Reprint, with a foreword by William D. Stahlman, Madison: University of Wisconsin Press, 1963.
> Audsley, George Ashdown. *The Art of Organ Building.* 2 vols. 1905. Reprint (2 vols. in 1), New York: Dover Publications, 1964.

15.181 In the case of more recently published originals, authors of scholarly works should try to give original publication data as well as reprint data. When the original publication data are included, or the name of a reprint series (Anchor Books, Phoenix Books, Vintage Books) appears in the listing, the word *reprint* may be omitted, although it is sometimes retained for enhanced clarity. Consistency should be observed.

> 27. Neil Harris, *The Artist in American Society: The Formative Years, 1790–1860* (New York: George Braziller, 1966; Chicago: University of Chicago Press, Phoenix Books, 1982).
> 28. Michael David, *Toward Honesty in Public Relations* (Chicago: Candor Publications, 1968; reprint, New York: B. Y. Jove, 1990).

> Harris, Neil. *The Artist in American Society: The Formative Years, 1790–1860.* New York: George Braziller, 1966; Chicago: University of Chicago Press, Phoenix Books, 1982.

> David, Michael. *Toward Honesty in Public Relations*. Chicago: Candor Publications, 1968. Reprint, New York: B. Y. Jove, 1990.

If page references are included, the author should, unless certain that pagination is the same in both editions, identify the edition used:

> 29. Michael David, *Toward Honesty in Public Relations* (Chicago: Candor Publications, 1968; reprint, New York: B. Y. Jove, 1990), 134–56 (page citations are to the reprint edition).

15.182 A paperback edition is not necessarily a reprint edition. Original paperbacks, long published in Europe and other parts of the world, are no longer unusual in the United States. A new impression, or new printing, is also not the same thing as a reprint edition (see 15.172). New impressions are issued by publishers to keep in print books that continue to sell.

NO ASCERTAINABLE PUBLICATION FACTS

15.183 When no publication facts are to be found, the abbreviations *n.p., n.d.* may be used:

> 30. John Burton, *A Deadline to Remember* (n.p., n.d.).
>
> Burton, John. *A Deadline to Remember*. N.p., n.d.

PAGE, VOLUME, PART, AND SIMILAR LOCATING INFORMATION

15.184 The final items to be included in a full citation are page references, volume and part numbers, and similar locating data. The designations *volume, part, number, book, chapter, page(s), note(s), appendix, plate,* and *figure* are lowercased and usually abbreviated as *vol., pt., no., bk., chap., p. (pp.), n. (nn.), app., pl.,* and *fig.,* all in roman type. Plurals for all except *p.* and *n.* are formed by adding *s.* The abbreviation *l. (ll.)* for *line(s)* should be avoided, except in works containing many such references, because the letter *l* on some typewriters is also used for the arabic numeral 1 and may confuse the typesetter (see 15.195). If the abbreviation is used, it is helpful to write "ell" or "el," with a circle around it, above the letter or in the margin, at least the first time it occurs in the typescript. (If the designations are spelled out, the practice should be carried through consistently.)

15.185 *Page numbers.* Page references are more common in note citations than in bibliographies. In the latter, page numbers are listed only when the cited piece is a part of the whole—a chapter or other part of a book, or an article in a journal (for the latter, see 15.213–18). When given, such page references should be inclusive—the first and last pages of the piece.

15.186 The style recommended by the University of Chicago Press for representing inclusive numbers is intended to produce graphic displays that are easy to grasp. In general this style recommends the omission of certain digits that remain the same in beginning and ending numbers whenever this avoids ambiguity and facilitates reading. A detailed explanation of the system may be found at 8.68–73. Examples are offered here:

> 5–17, 32–38, 100–107, 105–9, 132–38, 121–53, 1113–21

If the author has consistently included all digits, however, the editor may not wish to change them.

15.187 Although inclusive pages for chapters or other parts of a book may be provided in a bibliography, it is not necessary to do so, for the part may easily be located through the table of contents. If the author wishes to indicate the extent of the material cited, however, inclusive pages may be helpful. When given, such page references should follow the title of the book and, if applicable, the name of the editor or translator:

> Ogilvy, David. "The Creative Chef." In *The Creative Organization,* edited by Gary A. Steiner, 199–213. Chicago: University of Chicago Press, 1965.

15.188 In notes, page references should be provided whenever specific material is cited. The pages are given after the publication facts, following a comma. Unless ambiguity would result, the abbreviation *p.* or *pp.* may be omitted.

> 1. John Trent, *Education in Colonial America* (Cleveland: Arc Light, 1987), 214, 301–21.

15.189 If an author has consistently used *p.* and *pp.,* however, the editor should not delete them. The University of Chicago Press accepts either practice in a book manuscript, so long as it is followed consistently. When writing for a specific journal, authors should follow the style of the journal in this and other matters.

> 2. John Trent, *Education in Colonial America* (Cleveland: Arc Light, 1987), pp. 214, 301–21.

15.190 References to passages extending over several pages should include the first and last page numbers, following the rules for inclusive numbers mentioned above and described in 8.68–73.

> 3. John Trent, *Education in Colonial America* (Cleveland: Arc Light, 1987), 214, 223–36, 300–307.

15.191 The use of *f. (and the following page)* and *ff. (and the following pages)* after a page number is discouraged, but when they are used, a thin space should separate them from the preceding page number: 22f., 126ff. The term *passim (here and there)* should be used sparingly, and only after inclusive page numbers indicating a reasonable stretch of text or after reference to a whole section such as a chapter or a part. Passim, being a complete word, is not followed by a period unless it falls at the end of a citation. Note also that passim is no longer italicized.

15.192 References to pages numbered in arabic numerals are of course given in arabic numerals; in references to pages numbered with roman numerals, as in the preliminaries of a book, including such pieces as foreword, preface, and acknowledgments, the roman numerals are retained.

> 4. John Trent, introduction to *Education in Colonial America* (Cleveland: Arc Light, 1987), xi–xvi.

15.193 *Signatures without page numbers.* A signature is a group of consecutive pages (usually thirty-two, but sometimes sixty-four, sixteen, eight, etc.) formed by folding a large single sheet of paper bearing printed pages on both sides. The pages are so imposed on the two sides of the sheet that, when the sheet is folded repeatedly, the pages fall into correct sequence. Folded signatures are then trimmed on three sides, gathered into correct order, and bound together to make a book. In some books printed before 1800 these signatures did not carry page numbers; each signature bore a letter, numeral, or other symbol (its "signature") to assist the binder in gathering them in the proper sequence. In citing pages in books of this kind, the signature symbol is given first, then the number of the leaf (or sheet of paper) within the signature (since these are not numbered, they must be counted), and finally, whether the front of the leaf (the recto) or the back (verso) is meant. Thus G6v means the back, or verso, side of the sixth sheet in the signature identified by the letter G.

15.194 *Folios.* In some early books the signatures consisted of folios, that is, one large sheet folded once. Each folio thus has two sheets, or four pages. The sheets are numbered only on the front, or recto, side. The two sides of a numbered sheet must therefore be referred to as either recto (r) or verso (v). The page citation would therefore consist of the sheet number and the letter *r* or *v:* 176r, 231v. The same designations are used for manuscript folios (see 15.282).

15.195 *Lines.* In order to avoid using the somewhat confusing abbreviation *l.* *(ll.)* for *line(s),* the term may be spelled out. If spelled out once, it may not be necessary to do so again if many similar references closely follow one another. In some cases, as in citing passages from Shakespeare's plays, it is understood, for example, that the first number represents the act, the second the scene, and the third set of numbers the lines. Thus, the citation *Love's Labour's Lost* 4.3.354–55 refers to act 4, scene 3, lines 354–55 of the play.

15.196 *Volume and page number.* In a note citation, when a volume number must be given in addition to the page reference, and the volumes of the work were published in different years, the volume number must precede the publication facts, and the page reference is given alone at the end of the citation:

> 5. Edward Banicek, *A History of Indonesia,* vol. 2 (Philadelphia: Ross and Kittredge, 1991), 237–39.

Although it is not necessary, and seldom helpful, to indicate the total number of volumes if only one volume is being cited, the total, if included, should precede the publication facts, and the cited volume number would then precede the page references, from which it would be separated by a colon. If publication of the entire work occurred over several years, the beginning and concluding years are used in the publication facts. The date of the cited volume need not, in that case, be given; but if it is, it may be inserted, in parentheses, between the volume number and the colon:

> 5. Edward Banicek, *A History of Indonesia,* 3 vols. (Philadelphia: Ross and Kittredge, 1988–93), 2:237–39.
> *or*
> 5. Edward Banicek, *A History of Indonesia,* 3 vols. (Philadelphia: Ross and Kittredge, 1988–93), 2 (1991): 237–39.

15.197 If all volumes of a multivolume work were published in the same year, volume and page numbers are given together following the facts of publication. In that case the abbreviation *vol.* is omitted along with *p.* or *pp.* The volume number comes first, then the page reference, and the two are separated by a colon. When publication facts are included, as in the full citation, the volume number should be preceded by a comma.

> 6. Vivian Wurtzberger, *Japan and the Western World* (Baltimore: Roberts, Harvey, and Kyle, 1989), 2:125–32.

Since the bibliography entry would not ordinarily include the page reference, the volume number in that case would resume its usual position following the general title (see 15.138).

15.198 If a volume has its own title and that title is included in the note reference, volume and page number cannot be given together, and the abbreviation *vol.* must be used.

> 7. Deborah Baron, *Advertising in the United States,* vol. 2, *The Twentieth Century* (Cleveland: R. L. Glueck, 1990), 246–301.
> *or*
> 7. Deborah Baron, *The Twentieth Century,* vol. 2 of *Advertising in the United States* (Cleveland: R. L. Glueck, 1990), 246–301.
> *but*
> 7. Deborah Baron, *Advertising in the United States* (Cleveland: R. L. Glueck, 1990), 2:246–301.

15.199 *Notes.* When notes are cited, they are indicated by the abbreviation *n.* or *nn.* The note citation is usually preceded by the number of the page on which the note appears. The note number may also be given, in which case a regular word space is added between the abbreviation and the note number. When the number of the note is not given, the period is omitted from the abbreviation.

> 8. Eleanor Warren and Jane Raudebush, *Women in the World of Broadcast News* (Cleveland: Onaway Press, 1989), 214 n, 221.
> 9. Nathan N. Goodman, *The Strange History of Advocacy Journalism* (Cleveland: Chadbourne Press, 1988), 58 n. 21, 60 nn. 26, 27.

15.200 *Illustrations and tables.* In citing illustrations and tables, the abbreviation *fig.* is used for *figure,* but the terms *map* and *table* are given in full. It is usual, and helpful, to give the page number as well as the illustration or table number. A comma should follow the page number:

> 10. Margaretta M. Lovell, *A Visitable Past: Views of Venice by American Artists, 1860–1915* (Chicago: University of Chicago Press, 1989), 86, fig. 96.

MICROFORM EDITIONS

15.201 Works issued commercially in microfilm, microfiche, or text-fiche (printed text and microfiche illustrations used together) are treated much like books, except that the form of publication is indicated after the facts of publication (if it is not indicated in the name of the publisher) and a sponsoring organization may be listed as well as the publisher. The name of the sponsor is given just before the name of the city and publisher and is separated from these, in a note, by a semicolon; in a bibliography entry, by a period.

> 1. Abraham Tauber, *Spelling Reform in the United States* (Ann Arbor, Mich.: University Microfilms, 1958).
> 2. *The Collected Papers of Charles Willson Peale and His Family,* ed. Lillian B. Miller (National Portrait Gallery, Smithsonian Institution, Washington, D.C.; Millwood, N.Y.: Kraus-Thomson Organization, 1980), microfiche.
> 3. William Voelke, ed., *Masterpieces of Medieval Painting: The Art of Illumination* (Pierpont Morgan Library, New York; Chicago: University of Chicago Press, 1980), text-fiche, p. 56, 4F6–4F10.

In the last note, the page reference is to the printed text (*p.* is used to avoid confusion with fiche numbers); the reference to the microfiche part of this publication gives the fiche number, the letter indicating the *row,* and the *frame* number: 4F6. Even when they are the same, fiche and row are repeated when giving inclusive frame numbers.

15.202 Bibliography entries for the above microform editions would be as follows:

> Tauber, Abraham. *Spelling Reform in the United States.* Ann Arbor, Mich.: University Microfilms, 1958.

Peale, Charles Willson. *The Collected Papers of Charles Willson Peale and His Family*. Edited by Lillian B. Miller. National Portrait Gallery, Smithsonian Institution, Washington, D.C. Millwood, N.Y.: Kraus-Thomson Organization, 1980. Microfiche.

Voelke, William, ed. *Masterpieces of Medieval Painting: The Art of Illumination*. Pierpont Morgan Library, New York. Chicago: University of Chicago Press, 1980. Text-fiche.

15.203 Microform or other photographic processes used only to preserve printed material, such as newspaper files, are usually not mentioned as such in a citation. The source is treated as it would be in its original published version.

PERIODICALS

General Requirements

15.204 Periodicals, that is, publications issued at regular intervals—daily, weekly, monthly, quarterly, and so on—include journals, popular magazines, and newspapers. In general, citations to articles in periodicals include the following information:

> author's name
> title of article
> title of periodical
> issue information (volume, issue number, date)
> page reference

DIFFERENCES BETWEEN NOTE AND BIBLIOGRAPHY ENTRIES

15.205 The differences between note and bibliography entries for periodical citations are similar to those for book citations. In notes, authors' names are given in natural order and the main elements of the citation are separated by commas. In bibliographies, authors' names are inverted, last name first, and main elements are separated by periods, except that the title of the periodical, the issue information, and the page reference (if there is one) are treated as though they were a single element.

NAMES OF AUTHORS AND TITLES OF ARTICLES AND PERIODICALS

15.206 The names of the authors of articles published in periodicals are treated identically to those of the authors of books. The titles of articles are given regular title capitalization and are enclosed in quotation marks, and the titles of the periodicals themselves are capitalized and italicized as are the titles of books.

Journals

15.207 As used here, the term *journal* refers to periodicals that are more or less specialized and that are therefore of less general circulation than the so-called popular magazines. Treatment of some of the elements in journal citations is correspondingly somewhat more specialized.

TITLES OF JOURNALS

15.208 Journal and article titles are usually given in full, although journal titles may be abbreviated, provided the abbreviations are clear to readers and are used consistently, and provided the title consists of more than one word. A useful compendium of abbreviations for journals in many fields is *Periodical Title Abbreviations*, published by Gale Research. Abbreviations of journal titles are most widely used in the various scientific fields, probably because such a large proportion of the research in these fields is published in the form of journal articles, and authors therefore make frequent reference to this literature. Readers in these fields will readily understand the accepted abbreviations. Lists of recommended abbreviations are printed by *Chemical Abstracts* and *Index Medicus*. Titles of foreign and less well known journals are generally best spelled out, and it is never incorrect to spell out all journal titles in a reference list.

15.209 In literature, history, and the arts, abbreviations should be used with caution. With the exception of *PMLA, ELH,* and other abbreviations that are themselves titles of journals, it is usually best to spell out journal names. When abbreviation seems desirable, a list of abbreviations may precede the note section or the bibliography (see figs. 15.1, 15.2). Of limited use as guides to abbreviations are lists published in the annual *MLA International Bibliography* (the average reader without handy access to this list will not recognize these abbreviations) and in the American Historical Association's *Recently Published Articles* (individual words commonly used in titles are abbreviated, not the titles themselves).

ISSUE INFORMATION

15.210 *Volume.* The volume number follows the journal title without intervening punctuation. Arabic numerals are used for volume numbers even when the journal itself uses roman numerals.

> 1. John J. Benjoseph, "On the Anticipation of New Metaphors," *Cuyahoga Review* 24 (1988): 6–10.

> Benjoseph, John J. "On the Anticipation of New Metaphors." *Cuyahoga Review* 24 (1988): 6–10.

15.211 *Issue.* If there is an issue number, it may be included after the volume number, following a comma and introduced by the abbreviation *no.* The issue number may also be enclosed in parentheses, in which case the comma and *no.* are omitted. Whatever choice is made must be followed consistently. Identification of the issue number is required only when each issue is paginated separately—most scholarly journals are paginated consecutively through a volume—but identification is often helpful, particularly in the case of recently published issues not yet bound into volumes.

> 2. Cartright C. Bellworthy, "Reform of Congressional Remuneration," *Political Review* 7, no. 6 (1990): 89, 93–94.
> *or*
> . . . *Political Review* 7 (6): 89, 93–94 (1990).

> Bellworthy, Cartright C. "Reform of Congressional Remuneration." *Political Review* 7, no. 6 (1990): 87–101.

15.212 *Date.* The date, or year, of the issue is given in parentheses following the volume number or, if it is used, the issue number (see also 15.225). If the issue number is given in parentheses, the date follows the page reference, as in the alternative to example note 2 above. The month or season[1] may also be given, if consistency is observed in all citations for the same journal, but in that case the issue number, if there is one, need not be included.

> 3. Manuel Fernandez, "Arbitrating Labor-Management Disputes," *North American Labor Relations* 12, no. 3 (1989): 28–31.
> 4. Jane R. Bush, "Rhetoric and the Instinct for Survival," *Political Perspectives* 29 (March 1990): 45–53.
> 5. Ilya Bodonski, "Caring among the Forgotten," *Journal of Social Activism* 14 (fall 1989): 112–34.

> Fernandez, Manuel. "Arbitrating Labor-Management Disputes." *North American Labor Relations* 12, no. 3 (1989): 14–39.
> Bush, Jane R. "Rhetoric and the Instinct for Survival." *Political Perspectives* 29 (March 1990): 45–53.
> Bodonski, Ilya. "Caring among the Forgotten." *Journal of Social Activism* 14 (fall 1989): 112–34.

PAGE REFERENCE

15.213 Page references ordinarily follow the date. When an issue number enclosed in parentheses appears in the citation, however, the page reference, as illustrated in the alternative to example note 2 above, precedes the date in order to avoid adjoining parenthetical expressions. In note citations, specific pages within the article are usually cited, but occa-

---

1. The thirteenth edition of the *Chicago Manual of Style* showed season names capitalized in journal references. In the present edition, to conform with the usual style for names of seasons (see 7.74), lowercase is recommended.

sionally the reference is to the article as a whole. In the latter case, the first and last pages of the article are given. Such inclusive page numbers are also usually given in the bibliography entry, for they not only help the reader locate the article, but also indicate the article's length. It is also acceptable to omit the page reference in the bibliography entry and, if the reference is to the article as a whole, in the note citation.

15.214 When, as is usual, both volume and page numbers are included in the citation, the page numbers are preceded by a colon, even though issue number and date intervene, and the abbreviations *vol.* and *p.* or *pp.* are omitted. The colon immediately follows the closing parenthesis and is separated from the page reference by a word space (that is, by the space normally left between words): 14 (1969): 339–60.

15.215 When, in references to the article as a whole, inclusive pages are omitted, the abbreviation *vol.* should be used before the volume number to avoid confusion, and a comma then follows the journal title:

> 6. Louise Glueck, "The Quiet Poetic Urgency in Richard Ford's 'Empire,'" *Aeolian Studies,* vol. 1 (summer 1989).

> Glueck, Louise. "The Quiet Poetic Urgency in Richard Ford's 'Empire.'" *Aeolian Studies,* vol. 1 (summer 1989).

15.216 Inclusive page numbers, whether citing the entire article or a section within it, should follow the style outlined in 8.68–69.

TYPICAL JOURNAL CITATION AND ACCEPTABLE VARIATIONS

15.217 The following examples illustrate typical citations for a journal article. Specific page references are given in the note, and inclusive pages in the bibliography entry.

> 7. Noel Robertson, "The Dorian Migration and Corinthian Ritual," *Classical Philology* 75 (1980): 17, 19–20.

> Robertson, Noel. "The Dorian Migration and Corinthian Ritual." *Classical Philology* 75 (1980): 1–22.

In this example no issue number is included, because the journal is paginated consecutively throughout each volume. If desired, however, the issue number may be added. Although unnecessary, the month of issue may also be added; in that case, the issue number would not be required.

15.218 Alternative forms of the issue information in the above example are given below. All are acceptable if followed consistently throughout the work.

> *Classical Philology* 75 (January 1980): 1–22.
> *Classical Philology* 75, no. 1 (1980): 1–22.
> *Classical Philology* 75:1–22 (January 1980).

> *Classical Philology* 75 (1): 1–22 (1980).
> *Classical Philology* 75, 1 (1980): 1–22.

TITLES WITHIN ARTICLE TITLES

15.219 In titles of articles, as in titles of chapters and other short works that are enclosed in quotation marks, titles of other short works are set off with single quotation marks and titles of longer works are italicized:

> 8. Louise Glueck, "The Quiet Poetic Urgency in Richard Ford's 'Empire,'" *Aeolian Studies* 1 (summer 1989): 41, 43.
> 9. Peter Lofton, "Reverberations between Wordplay and Swordplay in *Hamlet*," *Aeolian Studies* 2 (fall 1989): 13–14.

> Glueck, Louise. "The Quiet Poetic Urgency in Richard Ford's 'Empire.'" *Aeolian Studies* 1 (summer 1989): 41–53.
> Lofton, Peter. "Reverberations between Wordplay and Swordplay in *Hamlet*." *Aeolian Studies* 2 (fall 1989): 12–29.

QUOTATIONS WITHIN ARTICLE TITLES

15.220 A quotation within the title of an article is set off with single quotation marks:

> 10. Thomas Gerontion, "Further Reflections of an 'Old Man in a Dry Month,'" *Norton Review* 24 (April 1990): 99.

> Gerontion, Thomas. "Further Reflections of an 'Old Man in a Dry Month.'" *Norton Review* 24 (April 1990): 95–100.

TITLES ENDING WITH QUESTION MARKS OR EXCLAMATION POINTS

15.221 A question mark or exclamation point coming at the end of a title or subtitle of a journal article supersedes the usual punctuation:

> 11. John Tuscarora, "And Still We Ask, 'How Long, Great Spirit, How Long?'" *Pacific Quarterly* 7 (spring 1991): 124, 130.
> 12. Wilma Waznowski, "Help, This Is an Emergency! It May Already Be Too Late," *Journal of Environmental Rescue* 11 (fall 1990): 21–34.

> Tuscarora, John. "And Still We Ask, 'How Long, Great Spirit, How Long?'" *Pacific Quarterly* 7 (spring 1991): 121–32.
> Waznowski, Wilma. "Help, This Is an Emergency! It May Already Be Too Late." *Journal of Environmental Rescue* 11 (fall 1990): 21–34.

ARTICLE PUBLISHED IN INSTALLMENTS

15.222 In citing an article that is published in installments over more than one issue, the number of such installments (parts) is indicated and, in addition to the various page references, changes in volume or issue number or in season or year are also reflected. The following examples provide patterns for such citations:

13. Judith Mills, "Packaging the Client," parts 1 and 2, *Public Relations Review* 14, no. 3 (1990): 97–99, 101; no. 4 (1990): 45–49.

14. Elizabeth Nelson Patrick, "The Black Experience in Southern Nevada," parts 1 and 2, *Nevada Historical Society Quarterly* 22 (summer/fall 1979): 130, 138, 210–13.

15. C. Ross Patch, "The Next to Last Angry Man," parts 1–3, *World's End Review* 8 (1985): 318, 320; 9 (1986): 28, 31, 34, 128–38.

Mills, Judith. "Packaging the Client." Parts 1 and 2. *Public Relations Review* 14, no. 3 (1990): 95–102; no. 4 (1990): 43–52.

Patrick, Elizabeth Nelson. "The Black Experience in Southern Nevada." Parts 1 and 2. *Nevada Historical Society Quarterly* 22 (summer/fall 1979): 128–40, 209–20.

Patch, C. Ross. "The Next to Last Angry Man." Parts 1–3. *World's End Review* 8 (1985): 315–30; 9 (1986): 27–52, 125–42.

ARTICLE APPEARING IN TWO PUBLICATIONS

15.223 When it is desirable to list more than one publication in which an article has appeared, only the publication actually consulted should be given in the note or text. In the bibliography, the publication consulted is listed first, as the main entry, after which the alternative appearance may be cited in the form of an annotation (see 15.124).

16. Richard McKeon, "Dialogue and Controversy in Philosophy," *Philosophy and Phenomenological Research* 17 (1955): 150–56.

McKeon, Richard. "Dialogue and Controversy in Philosophy." *Philosophy and Phenomenological Research* 17 (1955): 143–63. First published in *Entretiens philosophiques d'Athènes* (Athens: Institut International de Philosophie, 1955), 161–78.

PLACE OF PUBLICATION

15.224 Although not ordinarily given, the place of publication should be included for foreign journals of limited circulation and for journals whose titles are the same as or similar to those of other journals published elsewhere.

17. Jack Fishman, "Un grand homme dans son intimité: Churchill," *Historia* (Paris), no. 220 (November 1964): 686–90.

18. Marvin P. Garrett, "Language and Design in *Pippa Passes*," *Victorian Poetry* (West Virginia University) 13, no. 1 (1975): 50–54.

Fishman, Jack. "Un grand homme dans son intimité: Churchill." *Historia* (Paris), no. 220 (November 1964): 684–94.

Garrett, Marvin P. "Language and Design in *Pippa Passes*." *Victorian Poetry* (West Virginia University) 13, no. 1 (1975): 47–60.

NO VOLUME NUMBER

15.225 Some journals are not published as volumes and hence carry only issue numbers. In this case a comma is appropriate after the journal title, and the abbreviation *no.* precedes the issue number to distinguish it from a volume number. If the issues are numbered consecutively from the beginning of publication or from the beginning of a new series, the year, in parentheses, follows the issue number. As in the case of journals published in volumes, a colon precedes the page reference.

> 19. Eva Meyerovich, "The Gnostic Manuscripts of Upper Egypt," *Diogenes,* no. 25 (1959): 91, 95–98.
>
> Meyerovich, Eva. "The Gnostic Manuscripts of Upper Egypt." *Diogenes,* no. 25 (1959): 84–117.

If issues are numbered starting at 1 each year, the year may serve as a volume number. In this case the year follows the title and is not enclosed in parentheses. The issue and page reference then follow the year. As shown below, the year and title are separated by a comma; the year and issue number by a comma and the abbreviation *no.;* and the issue and page reference by a colon.

> 20. Patrick Skelton, "Rehabilitation versus Demolition," *Journal of Urban Renewal,* 1989, no. 3:143, 151.
>
> Skelton, Patrick. "Rehabilitation versus Demolition." *Journal of Urban Renewal,* 1989, no. 3:141–62.

TRANSLATOR

15.226 When a translator is given as well as an author, the citations are as follows:

> 21. Jaqueline Blois, "Bouchard's Empire of Absurdity," trans. W. W. Tissant, *Postmodern Review* 24 (winter 1990): 16–21.
>
> Blois, Jaqueline. "Bouchard's Empire of Absurdity." Translated by W. W. Tissant. *Postmodern Review* 24 (winter 1990): 16–21.

FOREIGN LANGUAGE JOURNALS

15.227 Titles of foreign language articles are capitalized, as are book titles, according to the conventions of their respective languages (see 15.118 and chapter 9). Journal names also follow the foreign language convention, as a rule, but may be capitalized as English titles are (9.4) if an author prefers this system and follows it consistently. Dates and such abbreviations as *no., pt.,* or *ser.* are given in English (but see 15.80).

22. Gérard Bouchard, "Un essai d'anthropologie régionale: L'histoire sociale du Saguenay aux XIXe et XXe siècles," *Annales: Economies, sociétés, civilisations* 34 (January 1979): 118–19.
or
. . . *Annales: Economies, Sociétés, Civilisations* . . .
23. Verdun L. Saulnier, "Dix années d'études sur Rabelais," *Bibliothèque d'humanisme et Renaissance* 11 (1949): 121.
24. Martin Broszat, "'Holocaust' und die Geschichtswissenschaft," *Vierteljahrshefte Zeitgeschichte* 27 (April 1979): 288–90.
25. W. Kern, "Waar verzamelde Pigafetta zijn Maleise woorden?" *Tijdschrift voor Indische taal, land- en volkenkunde* 78 (1938): 272.
26. Marcel Garaud, "Recherches sur les défrichements dans la Gâtine poitevine aux XIe et XIIe siècles." *Bulletin de la Société des antiquaires de l'Ouest,* 4th ser., 9 (1967): 11–27.

Bouchard, Gérard. "Un essai d'anthropologie régionale: L'histoire sociale du Saguenay aux XIXe et XXe siècles." *Annales: Economies, sociétés, civilisations* 34 (January 1979): 106–25.
Saulnier, Verdun L. "Dix années d'études sur Rabelais." *Bibliothèque d'humanisme et Renaissance* 11 (1949): 105–28.
Broszat, Martin. "'Holocaust' und die Geschichtswissenschaft." *Vierteljahrshefte Zeitgeschichte* 27 (April 1979): 285–98.
Kern, W. "Waar verzamelde Pigafetta zijn Maleise woorden?" *Tijdschrift voor Indische taal-, land- en volkenkunde* 78 (1938): 271–73.
Garaud, Marcel. "Recherches sur les défrichements dans la Gâtine poitevine aux XIe et XIIe siècles." *Bulletin de la Société des antiquaires de l'Ouest,* 4th ser., 9 (1967): 11–27.

Note that, as in the Garaud citations above, the first substantive in the title of an organization is capitalized in French.

15.228 If a translation of the article title is offered, it is enclosed in parentheses and given sentence-style capitalization. No quotation marks are used.

27. W. Kern, "Waar verzamelde Pigafetta zijn Maleise woorden?" (Where did Pigafetta collect his Malaysian words?), *Tijdschrift voor Indische taal-, land- en volkenkunde* 78 (1938): 271–73.
28. Gérard Bouchard, "Un essai d'anthropologie régionale: L'histoire sociale du Saguenay aux XIXe et XXe siècles" (A study in regional anthropology: The social history of the Saguenay in the nineteenth and twentieth centuries), *Annales: Economies, sociétés, civilisations* 34 (January 1979): 111–15.

Kern, W. "Waar verzamelde Pigafetta zijn Maleise woorden?" (Where did Pigafetta collect his Malaysian words?) *Tijdschrift voor Indische taal-, land- en volkenkunde* 78 (1938): 271–73.
Bouchard, Gérard. "Un essai d'anthropologie régionale: L'histoire sociale du Saguenay aux XIXe et XXe siècles" (A study in regional anthropology: The social history of the Saguenay in the nineteenth and twentieth centuries). *Annales: Economies, sociétés, civilisations* 34 (January 1979): 106–25.

15.229 If the title of a foreign language article is given only in English translation, the original language must be specified. In this case the translated title is capitalized and enclosed in quotation marks as if it were
the title of an English language article.

> 29. Sunao Hori, "Some Problems regarding Ch'ing Rule over Southern
> Sinkiang" (in Japanese), *Shigaku Zasshi* 88 (March 1979): 1–36.
> 30. M. Kosman, "Evolution of Paganism in the Baltic States" (in Rus-
> sian; English summary), *Voprosy Istorii*, 1979, no. 5:35, 41.

> Hori, Sunao. "Some Problems regarding Ch'ing Rule over Southern Sin-
> kiang" (in Japanese). *Shigaku Zasshi* 88 (March 1979): 1–36.
> Kosman, M. "Evolution of Paganism in the Baltic States" (in Russian; En-
> glish summary). *Voprosy Istorii,* 1979, no. 5:30–44.

NEW SERIES

15.230 As in the case of book series, some journals have attained such longevity that they have begun a new series of volumes or issues. Identification of the series *(n.s., 2d ser., 3d ser., ser. b)* must be made in citations
to these journals. The notation is added between the journal title and
the volume or issue number and is set off by commas:

> 31. "Letters of Jonathan Sewall," *Proceedings of the Massachusetts His-
> torical Society,* 2d ser., 10 (January 1896): 414.
> 32. G. M. Moraes, "St. Francis Xavier, Apostolic Nuncio, 1542–52,"
> *Journal of the Bombay Branch of the Royal Asiatic Society,* n.s., 26 (1950):
> 279–313.
> 33. Jean Filliozat, "Les premières étapes de l'Indianisme," *Bulletin de
> l'Association Guillaume Budé,* 3d ser., no. 3 (1953): 83–96.

> Sewall, Jonathan. "Letters of Jonathan Sewall." *Proceedings of the Mas-
> sachusetts Historical Society,* 2d ser., 10 (January 1896): 411–24.
> Moraes, G. M. "St. Francis Xavier, Apostolic Nuncio, 1542–52." *Journal
> of the Bombay Branch of the Royal Asiatic Society,* n.s., 26 (1950): 279–
> 313.
> Filliozat, Jean. "Les premières étapes de l'Indianisme." *Bulletin de
> l'Association Guillaume Budé,* 3d ser., no. 3 (1953): 83–96.

Popular Magazines

15.231 Popular weekly or monthly magazines are usually (but not always) cited
by date only; page numbers may be omitted, but when they are included
a comma, not a colon, separates them from the date of the issue:

> 1. Scott Spencer, "Childhood's End," *Harper's,* May 1979, 16–19.
> 2. E. W. Caspari and R. E. Marshak, "The Rise and Fall of Lysenko,"
> *Science,* 16 July 1965, 276.
> 3. Robert Karen, "Becoming Attached," *Atlantic,* February 1990,
> 54–55.
> *or*

3. Robert Karen, "Becoming Attached," *Atlantic* 265, no. 2 (February 1990): 54–55.

Spencer, Scott. "Childhood's End." *Harper's,* May 1979, 16–19.
Caspari, E. W., and R. E. Marshak. "The Rise and Fall of Lysenko." *Science,* 16 July 1965, 275–78.
Karen, Robert. "Becoming Attached." *Atlantic,* February 1990, 35–70.
or
Karen, Robert. "Becoming Attached." *Atlantic* 265, no. 2 (1990): 35–70.

15.232   If the article cited begins in the front of the magazine and jumps to the back, inclusive pages are meaningless and should be omitted in the bibliography entry. In the note, however, the specific pages may be cited.

4. Richard Schickel, "Far beyond Reality: The New Technology of Hollywood's Special Effects," *New York Times Magazine,* 18 May 1980, 8, 45.

Schickel, Richard. "Far beyond Reality: The New Technology of Hollywood's Special Effects." *New York Times Magazine,* 18 May 1980.

15.233   Titles of regular departments or features of a magazine are given title capitalization but are not set in italics or enclosed in quotation marks. Usually, no author is given.

5. Currents in the News, *U.S. News and World Report,* 11 February 1980, 5.

In the bibliography such an entry would, like an anonymous book, be alphabetized by its title.

Currents in the News. *U.S. News and World Report,* 11 February 1980, 5.

Newspapers

ELEMENTS OF THE CITATION

15.234   In citations to items in daily newspapers, the day, month (often abbreviated), and year are essential. Because items may be moved or eliminated in various editions, page numbers are usually omitted. For a news item in a large city paper that prints several editions a day, the name of the edition is useful (first edition, city edition, late edition, etc.) because the item might not appear in all editions. (Do not confuse edition with issue, which means any edition published on a specific day. Thus, a newspaper's issue of 22 February 1980 might consist of several editions.) The name of the edition is not included in references to editorials, features, or other material that appears in all editions of the day. If page and column numbers are included, use *p.* and *col.* to avoid ambiguity—for example, p. 3, col. 4. The citation should also include the author's name and the title of the article, if these are given.

1. Editorial, *Philadelphia Inquirer,* 30 July 1990.
2. "Robert Moses, Master Builder, Is Dead at 92," *New York Times,* 30 July 1981, Midwest edition.
3. Albert Finnonian, "The Iron Curtain Rises," *Wilberton (Ohio) Journal,* 7 February 1990, final edition.

15.235 News items from daily papers are rarely listed separately in a bibliography. Rather, the name of the paper and the relevant run of dates may be given either in the general alphabetical list or in a separate section devoted to newspapers.

> *Milwaukee Journal,* 8 February–12 March 1990.

Articles from Sunday supplements or other special sections are treated like listings from popular magazines (see 15.231–33). In a work containing both a bibliography and notes, citations to specific items may be given in the notes or in the text and not listed in the bibliography.

15.236 References to newspapers published in sections—almost all Sunday papers and large daily newspapers such as the *New York Times* and the *Chicago Tribune*—usually include the name, number, or letter of the section.

4. Williams Robbins, "Big Wheels: The Rotary Club at 75," *New York Times,* Sunday, 17 February 1980, sec. 3.
or
4. . . . *New York Times,* 17 February 1980, Business and Finance section.
5. Tyler Marshall, "200th Birthday of Grimms Celebrated," *Los Angeles Times,* 15 March 1985, sec. 1A, p. 3.

15.237 It is often important to identify the edition of the newspaper on a given date, either spelled out (see example note 3 above) or indicated by a letter (often capitalized and in parentheses) following the page number without intervening space.

6. Michael Norman, "The Once-Simple Folk Tale Analyzed by Academe," *New York Times,* 5 March 1984, 15(N).

NAMES OF NEWSPAPERS

15.238 If the city is not part of the name of an American newspaper, it should be added at the beginning of the name and italicized along with the official title.

15.239 If the name of the city is not well known or is the same as that of a well-known city, the name of the state or, in the case of Canada, province should be added in parentheses and italicized:

> *Houlton (Maine) Pioneer Times*
> *Hiawatha (Kans.) Daily World*
> *Wilberton (Ohio) Journal*

Ottawa (Ill.) Times
Saint Paul (Alberta) Journal

15.240 Names of cities not part of the titles of foreign newspapers are added in parentheses after the title and are not italicized:

Times (London)
Le Monde (Paris)

If the city name is part of the title it is italicized:

Frankfurter Zeitung
Manchester Guardian

15.241 For such well-known national papers as the *Christian Science Monitor,* the *Wall Street Journal,* and the *National Observer,* the city of publication is omitted.

15.242 In the titles of English language newspapers, the initial *the* is omitted. In a foreign language title, its equivalent is retained: *Times* (London) and *Le Monde* (Paris).

Reviews in Periodicals

15.243 In citations to reviews in periodicals the elements are given in the following order: the name of the reviewer, if indicated; the title, if any, of the review; the words *review of* followed by the identification of the work reviewed, including, as applicable, the author, composer, director, performer, location, and date; and finally, the listing of the periodical, with relevant information, in which the review appeared. If no author is indicated, the entry begins with the title of the review or, if there is no title, with the words *Review of* plus the identification of the work reviewed. If included in the bibliography, the entry is alphabetized by the first-appearing element.

BOOK REVIEWS

15.244   1. Steven Spitzer, review of *The Limits of Law Enforcement,* by Hans Zeisel, *American Journal of Sociology* 91 (November 1985): 726–29.
      2. David Scott Kastan, review of *Jonson's Gypsies Unmasked: Background and Theme of "The Gypsies Metamorphos'd,"* by Dale B. J. Randall, *Modern Philology* 76 (May 1979): 391–94.
      3. Susan Lardner, "Third Eye Open," review of *The Salt Eaters,* by Toni Cade Bambara, *New Yorker,* 5 May 1980, 169.

Spitzer, Steven. Review of *The Limits of Law Enforcement,* by Hans Zeisel. *American Journal of Sociology* 91 (November 1985): 726–29.
Kastan, David Scott. Review of *Jonson's Gypsies Unmasked: Background and Theme of "The Gypsies Metamorphos'd,"* by Dale B. J. Randall. *Modern Philology* 76 (May 1979): 391–94.

Lardner, Susan. "Third Eye Open." Review of *The Salt Eaters,* by Toni Cade Bambara. *New Yorker,* 5 May 1980, 169.

REVIEWS OF DRAMAS AND TELEVISED PLAYS

15.245   4. Review of *Fool for Love,* by Sam Shepard, as performed by the Circle Repertory Company, New York, *New York Times,* 27 May 1983, 18(N) and C3(L).
5. Review of televised version of *True West,* by Sam Shepard, *New York Times,* 31 January 1984, 22(N).

Review of *Fool for Love,* by Sam Shepard. Circle Repertory Company, New York. *New York Times,* 27 May 1983, 18(N) and C3(L).
Review of *True West,* by Sam Shepard, televised version. *New York Times,* 31 January 1984, 22(N).

MOVIE REVIEWS

15.246   6. Stanley Kauffmann, "Turbulent Lives," review of *A Dry White Season* (MGM movie), *New Republic,* 9 October 1989, 24–25.

Kauffmann, Stanley. "Turbulent Lives." Review of *A Dry White Season* (MGM movie). *New Republic,* 9 October 1989, 24–25.

REVIEWS OF MUSICAL PERFORMANCES

15.247   7. John Rockwell, "Eve Queler Conducts Verdi's *Vespri Siciliani,*" review of concert performance of *I vespri Siciliani,* by Verdi, Carnegie Hall, Opera Orchestra of New York, *New York Times,* Living Arts Section, 18 January 1990, 18(Y).

Rockwell, John. "Eve Queler Conducts Verdi's *Vespri Siciliani.*" Review of concert performance of *I vespri Siciliani,* by Verdi, Carnegie Hall, Opera Orchestra of New York. *New York Times,* Living Arts Section, 18 January 1990, 18(Y).

SUBSEQUENT OR SHORTENED REFERENCES IN NOTES

15.248   After the first, full reference in a note, subsequent references to a source are shortened. A reference may also be shortened even at first appearance when the source is given in full in an alphabetical bibliography.

15.249   There are two acceptable ways to shorten references to books, parts of books, and articles. One method, commonly used in scholarly journals, is to omit the title of the work and give only the last name of the author followed by a comma and the page reference. When more than one work by an author is cited, a short title is also necessary. If two or more authors with the same last name are cited, the first name or initials must also be included. This method works satisfactorily in journal articles because their brevity makes locating first references easier. It is less satisfactory in longer works, however, and is therefore not generally recommended for them.

15.250 The method of shortening references that is preferred for use in book-length works always includes a short title. In other respects it follows the form of the first method. The following paragraphs offer guidelines for shortening citations to books, parts of books, letters in published collections, and articles and other pieces in periodicals. Methods for shortening citations to other specialized sources are more varied and more complicated and will therefore be illustrated in the discussion of each source.

Author's Name

15.251 Only the last name of the author, or of the editor or translator if given first in the full reference, is needed. First names or initials are included only when two or more authors with the same last name have been cited; *ed., trans.,* and *comp.* following a name in the first reference may be omitted from subsequent references. If a work has two or three authors, the last name of each should be given; for more than three authors, give the last name of the first author followed by *et al.* or *and others.*

Short Title

15.252 The short title contains the key word or words from the main title of the work (book, chapter, or article). Abbreviations are not used unless this fact is noted in the first reference (see 15.24, 15.261). The order of the words should not be changed; for example, *Politics in the Twentieth Century* should not be shortened to *Twentieth-Century Politics.* It should, instead, be shortened to *Politics* or to *Twentieth Century.* In general, titles of fewer than five words should not be shortened:

> *Deep South*
> *North of Slavery*
> *Elizabethan and Metaphysical Imagery*

For many titles the omission of the initial *The* or *A* is sufficient:

> *Rise of the West*

Examples of shortened titles:

FULL MAIN TITLE	SHORT TITLE
Health Progress in the United States, 1900–1960	*Health Progress*
The Culture of Ancient Egypt	*Ancient Egypt*
A Compilation of the Messages and Papers of the Presidents, 1789–1897	*Papers of the Presidents*
Kriegstagebuch des Oberkommandos der Wehrmacht, 1940–1945	*Kriegstagebuch*
"A Brief Account of the Reconstruction of Aristotle's *Protrepticus*"	"Aristotle's *Protrepticus*"

In shortening titles in languages other than English, care must be taken not to omit a word that governs the case ending of a word included in the short title.

Use of *Ibid.*, *Idem*, *Op. Cit.*, and *Loc. Cit.*

15.253 *Ibid.* (*ibidem*, "in the same place") refers to a single work cited in the note immediately preceding. It should not be used if more than one work is given in the preceding note. Ibid. takes the place of the author's name, the title of the work, and as much of the succeeding material as is identical. It may therefore be used to repeat the complete preceding citation. The author's name and the title are never used with ibid.

15.254 Ibid. may also be used in place of the name of a journal or book of essays in successive references to the same journal or book of essays within one note.

15.255 *Idem* ("the same," sometimes abbreviated as *id.*) may be used in place of an author's name in successive references within one note to several works by the same person. It is not used for titles, except in legal references. It should not be used in place of ibid. to refer to the complete preceding citation. It should be noted that idem is used much less frequently than it once was and may soon be as outmoded as op. cit. and loc. cit.

15.256 *Op. cit.* (*opere citato*, "in the work cited") and *loc. cit.* (*loco citato*, "in the place cited") have long served as space savers in scholarly notes. Both, used with the author's last name, stand in place of the title of a work cited earlier in the chapter or article. But consider, for example, the frustration of the reader on meeting "Wells, op. cit., p. 10" in note 95 and finding the title of the work by Wells back in note 2 or, in a carelessly edited book, finding *two* works by Wells cited earlier, or none at all. For greater clarity, the University of Chicago Press uses the short-title form described above instead of either op. cit. or loc. cit.

Shortened Book Reference

15.257 In a shortened reference to a book, the shortened book title is given in italics. If the cited book is part of a multivolume work with a single title, the volume number must be added before the page reference. If the individual volumes in a multivolume work have titles of their own, it is sufficient to use a short form of the volume title without the volume number.

> 1. John P. Roche, *The Quest for the Dream: The Development of Civil Rights and Human Relations in Modern America* (New York: Macmillan, 1963), 204–6.
> 2. Broderick Mummerston, *An Introduction to Inca Sports and Rituals,* 2 vols., Ancient American Culture Series (Houston: H. D. Dobbs, 1990), 2:214.
> 3. William Farmwinkle, *Humor of the American Midwest,* vol. 2 of *Survey of American Humor* (Boston: Plenum Press, 1983), 223–24.
> 4. Roche, *Quest for the Dream,* 175.
> 5. Mummerston, *Inca Sports and Rituals,* 1:213–21.
> 6. Ibid., 2:312.
> 7. Ibid., 314.
> 8. Ibid.
> 9. Farmwinkle, *Humor of the American Midwest,* 241.
> 10. Ibid., 243–46.

Chapter or Other Titled Part of a Book

15.258 In a shortened reference to a chapter or other titled part of a book, the short title of the chapter or other part is placed in quotation marks. The title of the book itself is omitted.

> 11. Brendan Phibbs, "Herrlisheim: Diary of a Battle," in *The Other Side of Time: A Combat Surgeon in World War II* (Boston: Little, Brown, 1987), 150–60.
> 12. Ernest Kaiser, "The Literature of Harlem," in *Harlem: A Community in Transition,* ed. J. H. Clarke (New York: Citadel Press, 1964), 218–20.
> 13. Richard Ford, "Sweethearts," in *Rock Springs* (New York: Atlantic Monthly Press, 1987), 55–56.
> 14. Phibbs, "Herrlisheim," 156.
> 15. Ibid., 158.
> 16. Kaiser, "Literature of Harlem," 189.
> 17. Ford, "Sweethearts," 58.

Articles, Reviews, and Other Pieces in Periodicals

15.259 In shortened references to articles, reviews, and other pieces in periodicals, the short title of the piece is enclosed in quotation marks. The title of the periodical and the issue information are not repeated.

> 18. Louise Glueck, "The Quiet Poetic Urgency in Richard Ford's 'Empire,'" *Aeolian Studies* 1 (summer 1989): 44–47.
> 19. J. H. Hexter, "The Loom of Language and the Fabric of Imperatives: The Case of *Il Principe* and *Utopia*," *American Historical Review* 69 (1964): 945–68.
> 20. Glueck, "Ford's 'Empire,'" 45.
> 21. Ibid., 28.
> 22. Hexter, "Loom of Language," 948, 950.
> 23. Spitzer, review of *Limits of Law Enforcement*, 728.
> 24. Review of *Fool for Love*, 18(N).
> 25. Kauffmann, "Turbulent Lives," 25.
> 26. Rockwell, "Eve Queler Conducts."

Letters in Published Collections

15.260 A subsequent reference to a letter or other communication in a published collection lists only the last names (or initials) of the correspondents. If the reference is to another letter in the same collection, however, the full facts covering the letter itself must be given, followed by a shortened citation to the collection.

> 1. Quincemeyer to Lord Wallington Trixton, Salisbury, 6 October 1924, *Selected Letters of Jonathan Quincemeyer, 1908–1933,* ed. Rosemary Winslow (London: Whisper Press, 1953), 211–12.
> 2. EBW to Harold Ross, interoffice memo, 2 May 1946, *Letters of E. B. White,* ed. Dorothy Lobrano Guth (New York: Harper and Row, 1976), 273.
> 3. Ibid.
> 4. Quincemeyer to Trixton, 211.
> 5. Quincemeyer to Fanny Millworthy, Brighton, 26 December 1921, *Letters of Jonathan Quincemeyer,* 119.
> 6. EBW to Ross, 275.

Abbreviations

15.261 If a work is cited frequently throughout a chapter or a book, its title may be abbreviated after its first appearance. The full title should be given the first time it is cited, followed by an indication in parentheses of the abbreviation to be used for it thereafter. An abbreviated title differs from a shortened title in that words may be abbreviated and the order changed.

1. Nathaniel B. Shurtleff, ed., *Records of the Governor and Company of the Massachusetts Bay in New England (1628–86)*, 5 vols. (Boston, 1853–54), 1:126 (hereafter cited as *Mass. Records*).

The parenthetical notation of the abbreviation may be placed directly after the title of the work, but it is easier to find if it comes at the end of the reference. (See also 15.24–25.)

INTERVIEWS AND PERSONAL COMMUNICATIONS

15.262 Interviews and personal communications broadly traverse categories of sources. Some are published in books and periodicals; some appear on radio or television broadcasts; some are preserved on audio or video recording devices, including magnetic tapes, movie film, or disk records; others exist in the form of letters or transcripts; still others only in the notes or memories of those involved. In whatever form such interviews or communications exist, references to them should begin with the name of the person interviewed or the person from whom the communication was received.

Interviews

15.263 Interviews are best cited in text or notes. It is not necessary to include them in a bibliography, but if they are listed, the entries should follow a form similar to that illustrated in the examples that follow.

15.264 After the name of the person interviewed, references to interviews should provide the title of the interview, if there is one; the words *interview by* followed by the interviewer's name (if the author conducted the interview, this should read *interview by the author*); the medium, if any, in which the interview appeared, whether a book, journal, radio or television program, audio or videocassette, or some other form (italicized or in quotation marks as it would be in the first reference to any such medium); identification of the editor, translator, or director, if any; facts of publication, the repository, or such other information as may be required for location of printed and nonprinted sources.

1. Raymond Bellour, "Alternation, Segmentation, Hypnosis: Interview with Raymond Bellour," interview by Janet Bergstrom, *Camera Obscura,* nos. 3/4 (summer 1979): 93.
2. Isaac Bashevis Singer, interview by Harold Flender, in *Writers at Work: The "Paris Review" Interviews,* ed. George Plimpton, 5th ser. (New York: Viking Press, 1981), 85.
3. McGeorge Bundy, interview by Robert MacNeil, *MacNeil/Lehrer News Hour,* Public Broadcasting System, 7 February 1990.

4. Hamid al-Hamad, *Alexandrian Archaeology,* interview by Barker Comstock, videocassette, dir. Nathan Goodhugh, Warberg Films, 1989.

Bellour, Raymond. "Alternation, Segmentation, Hypnosis: Interview with Raymond Bellour." By Janet Bergstrom. *Camera Obscura,* nos. 3/4 (summer 1979): 89–94.

Singer, Isaac Bashevis. Interview by Harold Flender. In *Writers at Work: The "Paris Review" Interviews,* edited by George Plimpton. 5th ser., 81–92. New York: Viking Press, 1981.

Bundy, McGeorge. Interview by Robert MacNeil. *MacNeil/Lehrer News Hour.* Public Broadcasting System, 7 February 1990.

al-Hamad, Hamid. *Alexandrian Archaeology.* Interview by Barker Comstock. Videocassette, directed by Nathan Goodhugh. Warberg Films, 1989.

15.265 References to interviews that have not been published or broadcast should include the name of the interviewee; the name of the interviewer; a description of the type of interview conducted; the place or date of the interview; and, if applicable, the depository of a transcript.

5. Horace Hunt [pseud.], interview by Ronald Schatz, tape recording, 16 May 1976, Pennsylvania Historical and Museum Commission, Harrisburg.

6. Merle A. Roemer, interview by author, tape recording, Millington, Md., 26 July 1973.

7. Tim G. Peterson, interview by author, Long Beach, Calif., 1 August 1989.

Hunt, Horace [pseud.]. Interview by Ronald Schatz. Tape recording, 16 May 1976. Pennsylvania Historical and Museum Commission, Harrisburg.

Roemer, Merle A. Interview by author. Tape recording. Millington, Md., 26 July 1973.

Peterson, Tim G. Interview by author. Long Beach, Calif., 1 August 1989.

15.266 Shortened subsequent note references to interviews may include the last name of the person interviewed plus the word *interview* or, if applicable, the short title of the interview or of the work containing the interview:

11. Bellour, "Interview," 94.
12. Singer, interview, 86.
13. Bundy, interview.
14. al-Hamad, *Alexandrian Archaeology.*
15. Hunt, interview.

Personal Communications

15.267 References to conversations conducted in person or by telephone, or to letters received by the author, may be included in the text or in an informal note:

1. Colonel William Rich informed me by telephone in October 1989 that he was opposed to any . . .
2. When I interviewed her in her home in Oak Park, Ill., on 14 July 1990, Margaret Skelton expressed the opinion that . . .
3. In a letter to the author dated 10 January 1990, Jeanne Cavanagh pointed out . . .

If more suitable, information obtained in such a way might be documented more formally:

4. Colonel William Rich, telephone conversation with author, 12 October 1989.
5. Margaret Skelton, conversation with author, Oak Park, Ill., 14 July 1990.
6. Jeanne Cavanagh, letter to author, 10 January 1990.

15.268 Subsequent note references to personal communications may be shortened as follows:

11. Rich, telephone conversation.
12. Skelton, interview.
13. Cavanagh, letter to author.

15.269 Since personal communications are not usually available to the public, there is little point in listing them in a bibliography. If they are listed, however, personal communications should begin with the name of the letter writer or the person with whom the author has conversed:

Rich, Colonel William. Telephone conversation with author, 12 October 1989.
Skelton, Margaret. Conversation with author, Oak Park, Ill., 14 July 1989.
Cavanagh, Jeanne. Letter to author, 10 January 1990.

UNPUBLISHED MATERIAL

Theses, Dissertations, and Other Unpublished Works

15.270 The title of an unpublished work (manuscript, typescript, machine copy, computer printout) is treated like the title of an article or short work: it is set in roman type, with regular title capitalization (see 15.104), and enclosed in quotation marks. The word *unpublished* is not necessary. Location or sponsoring body or both should appear as well, with a date if possible.

THESES AND DISSERTATIONS

15.271 In a note citation, the identification of thesis or dissertation, the academic institution, and the date are, like publication facts, enclosed in parentheses. In the bibliography, they are not. (Note the capitalization of the abbreviation *Ph.D.*)

1. Andrew J. King, "Law and Land Use in Chicago: A Pre-history of Modern Zoning" (Ph.D. diss., University of Wisconsin, 1976), 32–37, 129.

2. Dorothy Ross, "The Irish-Catholic Immigrant, 1880–1900: A Study in Social Mobility" (master's thesis, Columbia University, n.d.), 142–55.

King, Andrew J. "Law and Land Use in Chicago: A Pre-history of Modern Zoning." Ph.D. diss., University of Wisconsin, 1976.

Ross, Dorothy. "The Irish-Catholic Immigrant, 1880–1900: A Study in Social Mobility." Master's thesis, Columbia University, n.d.

15.272 A dissertation issued on microfilm is treated as a published work (see 15.201–3). If the citation is to an abstract published in *Dissertation Abstracts International,* the form may be as follows:

1. Alice B. Downright, "Narrative Diffusion and the Professional Editor" (Ph.D. diss., University of Chicago, 1992), abstract in *Dissertation Abstracts International* 52 (1993): 3245A.

Downright, Alice B. "Narrative Diffusion and the Professional Editor." Ph.D. diss., University of Chicago, 1992. Abstract in *Dissertation Abstracts International* 52 (1993): 3245A–3246A.

PAPERS READ AT MEETINGS

15.273 In the note, the description of the circumstances for the reading of the paper, including location and date, is enclosed in parentheses. In the bibliography the parentheses are dropped; the description follows a period and ends with a period and begins with a capital letter.

3. Eviatar Zerubavel, "The Benedictine Ethic and the Spirit of Scheduling" (paper presented at the annual meeting of the International Society for the Comparative Study of Civilizations, Milwaukee, Wis., April 1978), 17–19.

Zerubavel, Eviatar. "The Benedictine Ethic and the Spirit of Scheduling." Paper presented at the annual meeting of the International Society for the Comparative Study of Civilizations, Milwaukee, Wis., April 1978.

15.274 Papers printed in published proceedings of meetings are treated like chapters in a book (see 15.120). Working papers may be cited as follows:

12. Nancy Frishberg and Bonnie Gough, "Time on Our Hands," working paper, Salk Institute for Biological Studies, La Jolla, Calif., 1974.

Frishberg, Nancy, and Bonnie Gough. "Time on Our Hands." Working paper, Salk Institute for Biological Studies, La Jolla, Calif., 1974.

UNPUBLISHED DUPLICATED MATERIAL

15.275 The status of duplicated material is somewhat ambiguous. To the extent that it is distributed, even at no cost, it is technically published. To the extent that its distribution is limited, however, it may be said to be unpublished. In any case, in a note citation the location and type of duplication are enclosed in parentheses. In the bibliography they are set off by periods and begin with a capital letter.

> 4. Salvador Florencio de Alarcón, "Compendio de las noticias correspondientes a el real y minas San Francisco de Aziz de Río Chico . . . de 20 de octobre [1777]" (Department of Geography, University of California, Berkeley, photocopy), 19–23.
> 5. United States Educational Foundation for Egypt, "Annual Program Proposal, 1952–53" (U.S. Department of State, Washington, D.C., 1951, mimeographed), 28.

> Alarcón, Salvador Florencio de. "Compendio de las noticias correspondientes a el real y minas San Francisco de Aziz de Río Chico . . . de 20 de octobre [1777]." Department of Geography, University of California, Berkeley. Photocopy.
> United States Educational Foundation for Egypt. "Annual Program Proposal, 1952–53." U.S. Department of State, Washington, D.C., 1951. Mimeographed.

SHORTENED REFERENCES

15.276 Shortened references to theses, dissertations, and other unpublished works are similar to those to articles or chapters in books. The following are shortened references to a few of the full note citations in the paragraphs above:

> 6. King, "Law and Land Use," 82–85.
> 7. Zerubavel, "Benedictine Ethic," 21, 23.
> 8. Alarcón, "Compendio de las noticias," 22.
> 9. Foundation for Egypt, "Annual Program Proposal," 22, 25.

Manuscript Collections

15.277 When citing manuscript materials, a basic difference between documentary notes and bibliography entries should be observed. In the note, the important element is usually the specific item relevant to the discussion, and therefore this is given first, followed by its location. If the specific item is given in the running text, however, the citation in the note may begin with the collection or depository. The element of first importance in the bibliography is usually the collection in which the specific items cited may be found, the author of the items in the collection, or the depository for the collection. Collections, authors, and depositories are therefore entered in alphabetical order. The specific items themselves are not mentioned in the bibliography unless only one item in a collection is cited, in which case the entry may begin with the item.

15.278 The following passage from the *Guide to the National Archives of the United States* is useful in deciding what to include, in both notes and bibliography, when citing manuscript materials:

> The most convenient citation for archives is one similar to that used for personal papers and other historical manuscripts. Full identification of most unpublished material usually requires giving the title and date of the item, series title (if applicable), name of the collection, and the name of the depository. Except for placing the cited item first [in a note], there is no general agreement on the sequence of the remaining elements in the citation. . . . Whatever sequence is adopted, however, should be used consistently throughout the same work. (761)

NOTE CITATIONS

15.279 Note citations of personal letters and diaries, of memoranda and minutes, and of other papers in manuscript form begin with the particular item being discussed in the text. A citation to a letter starts with the names of the letter writer and the recipient, in that order. If the identity of the people is clear from the text, last names only may be used. The names are followed by the place where the letter was written, if known and considered relevant, and by the date of the letter. The word "letter" is unnecessary, but other forms of communication (telegram, memorandum) are specified.

15.280 Numbered letters in printed collections are sometimes referred to by number *(no.)* rather than page. Some manuscript collections have identifying series or file numbers that may be included in the citation, but usually the item and date, with the name of the collection and the depository, are sufficient. A citation to a diary gives the name of the diarist and the date of the entry. A title of a manuscript in a collection is given in quotation marks (e.g., "Canoeing through Northern Minnesota"), but not such descriptive designations as *records* or *report;* when in doubt, omit the quotation marks.

15.281 In titles of manuscript collections the terms *papers* and *manuscripts* are synonymous, and either is acceptable, as is the abbreviation *MSS* when brevity is desirable. Some scholars differentiate between *manuscript* in its original significance of handwritten material *(MS)* and *typescript (TS),* which is produced by typewriter, word processor, or similar machine.

15.282 Older manuscripts are usually numbered by folios *(fol., fols.)*—sheet by sheet—rather than by page (see 15.194). When both sides of a folio have been used, references specify which side, recto (r) or verso (v), thus: fols. 25r–27v. Note that the letters *r* and *v* are set on the line, in roman type, and without periods unless they come at the end of a sentence. Typescripts and modern manuscripts usually carry page numbers, which are of course used in a reference; it is often wise to use *p.*, *pp.* in such references to avoid ambiguity.

15.283 Names of the months in dates may be spelled out, as in the examples below, or abbreviated consistently.

15.284 In a note that includes the first reference to a collection, full identifying information is usually given. This is essential if there is no bibliography. In subsequent note references to items in that collection, the description of the collection may be shortened to a single significant element.

Full first references:

> 1. George Creel to Colonel House, 25 September 1918, Edward M. House Papers, Yale University Library.
> 2. James Oglethorpe to the Trustees, 13 January 1733, Phillipps Collection of Egmont Manuscripts, 14200:13, University of Georgia Library (hereafter cited as Egmont MSS).

Subsequent references:

> 11. House diary, 6, 12 November, 10 December 1918; R. S. Baker to House, 1 November 1919, House Papers.
> 12. House diary, 16 December 1918.
> 13. Thomas Causton to his wife, 12 March 1733, Egmont MSS, 14200:53.

In the full references above, locations of such well-known depositories as university libraries have been omitted, but the locations may be included if the author so desires. Note also that since the item cited in note 12 is from the same manuscript cited first in the preceding note, the name of the collection need not be repeated. Had the item cited not been from the manuscript cited first in the previous note, or if several notes had intervened, it would have been more helpful to repeat the name of the collection:

> 12. R. S. Baker to House, 16 December 1918, House Papers.
> 22. House diary, 16 December 1918, House Papers.

15.285 A shortened reference to a manuscript collection omits the name of the depository unless more than one collection with the same name has been cited; in the latter case, the depository must be given.

> 1. Stevens to Sumner, 26 August 1865, Charles Sumner Papers, Harvard College Library, Cambridge, Mass.
> 2. Minutes of the Committee for Improving the Condition of Free Blacks, Pennsylvania Abolition Society, 1790–1803, Papers of the Pennsylvania Society for the Abolition of Slavery, Historical Society of Pennsylvania, Philadelphia.
> 3. Sterns to Sumner, 28 August 1865, Sumner Papers.
> 4. Minutes, Committee for Improving the Condition of Free Blacks, Papers of the Pennsylvania Society for the Abolition of Slavery.

15.286 The following examples represent full documentary note references to various manuscript items and collections. Subsequent note references would be formed in the manner illustrated above.

> 14. Embree to Swift, 19 March 1929, copy in Dodd Papers, with covering letter, Embree to Dodd of same date, William E. Dodd Papers, Manuscripts Division, Library of Congress.
> 15. Burton to Merriam, telegram, 26 January 1923, Charles E. Merriam Papers, University of Chicago Library.
> 16. Hiram Johnson to John Callan O'Laughlin, 13, 16 July, 28 November 1916, O'Laughlin Papers, Roosevelt Memorial Collection, Harvard College Library.
> 17. Memorandum by Alvin Johnson, 1937, file 36, Horace Kallen Papers, YIVO Institute, New York.
> 18. Minutes of the Committee for Improving the Condition of Free Blacks, Pennsylvania Abolition Society, 1790–1803, Papers of the Pennsylvania Society for the Abolition of Slavery, Historical Society of Pennsylvania, Philadelphia.
> 19. Louis Agassiz, Report to the Committee of Overseers . . . [28 December 1859], Overseers Reports, Professional Series, vol. 2, Harvard University Archives, Cambridge, Mass.
> 20. Undated correspondence between French Strother and Edward Lowry, container 1-G/961 600, Herbert Hoover Presidential Library, West Branch, Iowa.
> 21. Memorandum, "Concerning a Court of Arbitration," n.d., Philander C. Knox Papers, Manuscripts Division, Library of Congress.

(For citations to material in government archives see 15.374–76, 15.402–6.)

15.287 Citation to a microfilm copy in a different library, rather than the original manuscript, may be made as follows:

> 22. John Brownfield to the Trustees, 6 March 1736, John Brownfield's Copy Book, 1735–40, Archives of the Moravian Church, Bethlehem, Pa. (microfilm, University of Georgia Library).

BIBLIOGRAPHY ENTRIES

15.288 The bibliographical sequence most useful for all collections of correspondence and other personal papers named for an individual or group begins with the name of the author of the collected manuscripts or the title of the collection of items being cited and ends with the depository and, where desirable, its location.

> House, Edward M. Papers. Diary and letters. Yale University Library.
> Egmont Manuscripts. Phillipps Collection. University of Georgia Library.
> Butler, Nicholas Murray. Papers. Columbia University Library, New York.
> Women's Organization for National Prohibition Reform. Papers. Alice Belin du Pont files, Pierre S. du Pont Papers. Eleutherian Mills Historical Library, Wilmington, Del.

> Roosevelt, Franklin D. General Political Correspondence, 1921–28. Franklin D. Roosevelt Library, Hyde Park, N.Y.
> O'Laughlin, John Callan. Papers. Roosevelt Memorial Collection. Harvard College Library.
> Pennsylvania Society for the Abolition of Slavery. Papers. Historical Society of Pennsylvania, Philadelphia.
> Harvard University Overseers. Reports. Professional Series, vol. 2. Harvard University Archives, Cambridge, Mass.
> Strother, French, and Edward Lowry. Updated correspondence. Herbert Hoover Presidential Library, West Branch, Iowa.

Thus when a letter, telegram, diary entry, or other specific reference is cited in the text or in a note, the reader will easily locate the collection it came from in the bibliography or reference list.

15.289 A second possible sequence begins with the depository (or its location) and ends with the collection or part of the collection being cited. This sequence is useful when a number of collections from the same depository are cited and it is desirable to list them together in the bibliography reference list.

> Porkola University Library, Nilo Hills, Ohio. Andrew Porkola Papers. Olga Serafina Papers. Letters of Naj Namsorg.

(For additional manuscript referencing see 15.374, 15.402, 15.413.)

15.290 Individual items cited from a collection, such as specific letters or diary entries, are mentioned in the text or in a note. If only one item from a collection has been cited, it may be listed under its own author or title in the bibliography:

> Dinkel, Joseph. Description of Louis Agassiz written at the request of Elizabeth Cary Agassiz. Agassiz Papers. Houghton Library, Harvard University.

Quotation marks may enclose the title of a specific manuscript:

> Purcell, Joseph. "A Map of the Southern Indian District of North America, [ca. 1772]." MS 228, Ayer Collection. Newberry Library, Chicago.

15.291 Titles of collections and descriptive designations such as *diary, correspondence,* or *records* are usually capitalized in a bibliography listing but are not enclosed in quotation marks:

> House, Edward M. Diary. Edward M. House Papers. Yale University Library.

15.292 It is impossible to formulate specific rules applicable to all bibliography listings of manuscript materials because methods of arranging and cataloging differ from one depository to another, and kinds of material differ as well. Librarians and archivists are usually willing and able to explain to an author what is required in citations to the documents in their collections. A publisher's editor may add or delete or rearrange items in listings only with the consent of the author.

SPECIAL TYPES OF REFERENCES

Reference Books

15.293 Well-known reference books are usually not listed in bibliographies. When such reference books are cited in notes, the facts of publication (place of publication, publisher, and date) are usually omitted, but the edition, if not the first, must be specified. References to an encyclopedia, dictionary, or other alphabetically arranged work cite the item (not the volume or page number) preceded by *s.v.* (*sub verbo,* "under the word").

> 1. *Encyclopaedia Britannica,* 11th ed., s.v. "original package."
> 2. *Webster's New International Dictionary,* 3d ed., s.v. "epistrophe."
> 3. *Columbia Encyclopedia,* 4th ed., s.v. "cold war."
> 4. *Dictionary of American Biography,* s.v. "Wadsworth, Jeremiah."

Scriptural References

JUDEO-CHRISTIAN SCRIPTURES

15.294 References to the Judeo-Christian scriptures are usually confined to the text or notes. Note or parenthetical text references to the Bible and Apocrypha should include book, in roman type and abbreviated (see 14.34), chapter, and verse—never a page number. Traditionally, a colon is used between chapter and verse, as in the first three examples, but a period, as in the next two examples, serves equally well and is frequently seen in current works:

> 1. Heb. 13:8, 12.
> 2. 1 Thess. 4:11.
> 3. Ruth 3:1–18.
> 4. Gen. 25.19–37.1.
> 5. 2 Kings 11.12.
> 6. 1 Sam. 10.

The version of the Bible now most frequently referred to in scholarly work is probably the New Revised Standard Version, but other versions are also used, and it is therefore essential to identify which is being cited or quoted. If the work is intended for specialists, the version should be identified by abbreviation; for a broader readership, the version should be spelled out in the first citation and abbreviated thereafter.

7. 2 Kings 11.8 RSV.
8. 1 Cor. 13.1–13 New English Bible.
9. John 3.5–6 NEB.

Abbreviations for the various versions, as well as for the various books, are to be found in 14.34–35.

OTHER SACRED WORKS

15.295 References to the sacred and highly revered works of other religious traditions are treated similarly to those of the Judeo-Christian tradition.

Plays and Poems with Line or Stanza Numbers

15.296 References to plays and poems carrying section and line or stanza numbers need not be listed in a bibliography, and note references to them may omit edition and facts of publication unless these are essential to a discussion of the texts. In the latter case the cited edition may also be listed in the bibliography. (See also 15.311.)

> 1. *The Faerie Queene,* bk. 2, canto 8, st. 14.
> 2. *Hamlet,* Arden edition, ed. Harold Jenkins (London: Methuen, 1982), 1.2.129–32.
> 3. *Hamlet,* 1.5.29–31 (Arden).
> 4. *King Lear,* ed. David Bevington et al. (New York: Bantam Books, 1988), 3.2.49–60.
> *or*
> 4. *King Lear,* Bevington, 5.3.274–79.

> Shakespeare. *Hamlet.* Arden edition. Edited by Harold Jenkins. London: Methuen, 1982.
> ———. *King Lear.* Edited by David Bevington et al. New York: Bantam Books, 1988.

15.297 In works of literary criticism including many such references, the form of citation may be shortened. Note that the comma following the title of the work is omitted:

> 3. *Winter's Tale* 5.1.13–16.
> *or*
> 3. *WT* 5.1.13–16.
> 4. *Faerie Queene* 2.8.14.
> *or*
> 4. *FQ* 2.8.14.

Shortened references with abbreviated titles are best put into the text in parentheses (see 15.24).

Greek and Roman Classical References

15.298   Classical references are ordinarily given in text or notes and are listed in a bibliography only when the reference is to information supplied by a modern editor.

15.299   Abbreviations are used extensively in classical references for the author's name; for the title of the work; for collections of inscriptions, papyri, ostraca, and so on; and for titles of well-known periodicals and reference tools. The most widely accepted standard for abbreviations is the comprehensive list in the front of the *Oxford Classical Dictionary.*

15.300   The numbers identifying the various parts of classical works (e.g., books, sections, lines) remain the same in *all* editions, whether in the original language or in translation. (Exceptions occur in collections of fragments of classical works; see 15.308.) References to these parts therefore should not include page numbers. References to information supplied by a modern editor, however (in an introduction, commentary, note, or appendix), must give page numbers.

15.301   The edition used should be specified the first time it is cited; if several editions of the same source have been cited, the edition must be given in each citation. Credit for a translation should be given in a note accompanying the first use. In a work addressed to classicists, the name of an editor or a translator alone will identify the edition referred to (see example notes 10, 20–22, 32–35 below). In a work addressed to a wider audience, the full title and facts of publication should be given the first time an edition is used, and a full listing may also be included in the bibliography.

15.302   Titles of individual works, collections, and periodicals are italicized, whether given in full or abbreviated form. Titles of unpublished collections are given in roman, without quotation marks. In Latin and transliterated Greek titles, only the first word, proper nouns, and adjectives derived from proper nouns are capitalized.

15.303   In references to individual works there is no punctuation between the author's name and the title of the work or between the title and numerical references to divisions of the work. (In works of a general nature where classical references are mixed with other references, it is quite acceptable to put a comma after the author's name.) The names of these divisions are omitted unless they are needed for clarity. If *ibid.* is used in succeeding references, it is followed by a comma, but the preferred classical form is the abbreviated title.

15.304   Different levels of division of a work (book, section, line, etc.) are separated by periods with no space after the period; commas are used between several references to the same level; the en dash is used between continuing numbers. If explanatory abbreviations are necessary for clarity before the numerical references (bk. 1, sec. 3), commas rather than periods are used to separate the different elements. Arabic numerals are used for all subdivisions of individual works:

1. Homer *Odyssey* 9.266–71.
   or
1. Hom. *Od.* 9.266–71.
2. Plato *Republic* 360E–361B.
3. Lucan *Bellum civile* 3.682
4. Cicero *De officiis* 1.133, 140.
5. Ovid *Amores* 1.7.27.
6. Thucydides *History of the Peloponnesian War* 2.40.2–3.
   or
6. Thucydides 2.40.2–3.
   or
6. Thuc. 2.40.2–3.
7. Pindar *Isthmian Odes* 7.43–45.
   or
7. Pind. *Isthm.* 7.43–45.
8. Aristophanes *Frogs* 1019–30.
9. Sappho *Invocation to Aphrodite*, st. 2, lines 1–6.
10. Solon (Edmonds's numbering) 36.20–27.

15.305 Arabic numerals are now generally used in references to volumes in collections of inscriptions. Periods follow the volume number and the inscription number, and further subdivisions are treated as in other classical references. Although it is not necessary, a comma may follow the title (or the abbreviation of the title) provided the usage is consistent in similar references:

11. *IG* 2^2.3274.
[= *Inscriptiones Graecae,* vol. 2, 2d ed., inscription no. 3274]
12. *IG Rom.* 3.739.9.10, 17.
["IG Rom." = *Inscriptiones Graecae ad res Romanas pertinentes*]
13. *POxy.* 1485.
[= *Oxyrhynchus Papyri,* document no. 1485]

15.306 Some collections are cited only by the name of the editor, in roman.

14. Dessau, 6964.23–29.
["Dessau" = H. Dessau, ed., *Inscriptiones Latinae selectae*]

15.307 Superior figures or letters are used in several ways in classical references. When a superior number is used immediately after the title of a work or the abbreviation of the title, including its final period, but before any other following punctuation, it indicates the number of the edition:

15. Stolz-Schmalz *Lat. Gram.*^{5} (rev. Leumann-Hoffmann; Munich, 1928), 390–91.
16. *Ausgewählte Komödien des T. M. Plautus*^{2}, vol. 2 (1883).

When a superior number or letter is placed after a number referring to a division of a work, it indicates a part, section, column, or other subdivision. An acceptable, and now widely adopted, alternative to using superior letters is to put them on the line, in the text type size. Such letters, when set on the line, may be capital or lowercase according to how they appear in the source being cited. (When in doubt, make them lowercase.)

17. Aristotle *Metaphysics* 3.2.996^{b}5–8.
or better,
17. Aristotle *Metaphysics* 3.2.996b5–8.
18. Aristotle *Nicomachean Ethics* 1177b31.
19. Roscher *Lex.* 2.2223A.15ff.

15.308 Fragments of classical texts (some only recently discovered) are not uniformly numbered. They are published in collections, and the numbering of the fragments is usually unique to a particular edition. It is therefore necessary, in citing fragments, to include the editor's name.

20. Empedocles frag. 115 Diels-Kranz.
21. Anacreon frag. 2.10 Diehl [fragment 2, line 10].
22. Hesiod frag. 239.1 Merkelbach and West.

In subsequent references, the editor's name is usually abbreviated:

32. Anacreon frag. 5.2 D.
33. Hesiod frag. 220 M.-W.

Sometimes a reference includes citations to two or more editions in which the fragments are numbered differently. The additional citations may be given in parentheses following the first, or the citations may be separated by equals signs, with regular word spacing before and after the signs.

34. Solon frag. 4 West (frag. 3 Diehl).
35. Pindar frag. 133 Bergk = 127 Bowra.

Medieval References

15.309 The form for the Greek and Latin classical references may properly be applied to medieval works. It may also be adapted for citations to modern sources occurring in a work where most of the references are classical.

1. Augustine *De civitate Dei* 20.2.
2. Augustine *City of God* (trans. Healy-Tasker) 20.2.
3. *Beowulf* lines 2401–7.
4. *Sir Gawain and the Green Knight* (trans. John Gardner), pt. 2, st. 1, lines 21–24.
5. Abelard *Epistle 17 to Heloïse* (Migne *PL* 180.375c–378a).

English Classics

15.310 The classical reference style may also be adapted for citations to classic English works in which sections (acts, scenes, parts, books, cantos) and lines are numbered. Thus,

> 1. Pope, *Rape of the Lock,* canto 3, lines 28–29.

may be rendered

> 2. Pope *Rape of the Lock* 3.28–29.

15.311 If the work is widely recognized as that of a well-known author, the author's name is frequently omitted. Among such works are the plays of Shakespeare, Jonson, and Marlowe and such well-known long poems as *The Faerie Queene, Paradise Lost,* and *The Ring and the Book.*

> 3. *Twelfth Night* 2.4.1–7.
> *for*
> 3. Shakespeare, *Twelfth Night,* act 2, scene 4, lines 1–7.
> 4. *Paradise Lost* 1.83–86.
> *for*
> 4. Milton, *Paradise Lost,* book 1, lines 83–86.
> 5. "Wife of Bath's Prologue" 105–14.
> *for*
> 5. Chaucer, "Wife of Bath's Prologue," *Canterbury Tales,* fragment 3, lines 105–14.

In citing such classic English works, it is usual to give the edition and facts of publication in the first reference, but these may be omitted in subsequent references. In textual and critical studies of the plays of Shakespeare, it is important to identify the edition used, since variations occur in wording, line numbering, and even scene division. If more than one edition is used in a single study, a short identification of the edition referred to should be included in all citations subsequent to the first, full reference, unless the edition meant is clear from the text.

> 6. *Hamlet,* Arden edition, ed. Harold Jenkins (London: Methuen, 1982), 4.5.17–20.
> 7. *Hamlet,* Arden, 5.2.215–20; Bevington, 5.2.217–22.
> 8. *Othello,* Bevington, 3.3.426–29.

LEGAL REFERENCES

Citations in Predominantly Legal Works

15.312 Citations in predominantly legal works may follow the style set forth in *The University of Chicago Manual of Legal Citation,* edited by the staff of the *University of Chicago Law Review* and by the University of

Chicago Legal Forum and published in 1989. The style presented in
that manual is considerably simpler than the one set forth in *A Uniform
System of Citation,* 15th edition, published by the Harvard Law Review
Association in 1991, although the latter remains an acceptable alterna-
tive. A summary of some of the guidelines presented in the *Chicago
Manual of Legal Citation* follows.

TYPEFACES

15.313 Italic type is used for case names, titles of articles in periodicals and
edited books, titles of books and treatises, uncommon words or phrases
in languages other than English, and words or phrases intended to be
emphasized. (Such well-known legal phrases as *ex parte* and *de facto*
may be set in roman type.) All other material is presented in roman
type.

ABBREVIATIONS

15.314 With a few exceptions, periods may be omitted from abbreviations in
citations. Abbreviations of case names and book or treatise titles retain
periods. No period follows the abbreviation *v* for *versus* in case names,
however, and periods are omitted in acronyms, wherever they are used.

NLRB v Watson Tools, Inc., 399 F2d 543 (2d Cir 1953).

FULL CITATIONS

15.315 As they are in nonlegal works, initial citations to sources are given in
full in legal works. Names of authors or editors are reproduced as they
appear in the source. The names are set in roman type, capitals and
lowercase. When there are either two or three authors (or editors), all
may be listed. When there are more than three, only the first appearing
is listed, followed by *et al* in roman, without a period.

BOOKS

15.316 In citations to books, information is provided in the following arrangement:

author (or editor)/*comma*/volume number (if applicable), title, and subdivision, all without intervening punctuation/and finally, in *parentheses* pub-
lisher/*comma*/edition (if there has been more than one) and year/*period*

Arabic numerals are used for volume numbers. Titles are given in italic
caps and lowercase and may be shortened if excessively long. Subdivisions may be identified with the assistance of such symbols or abbreviations as § (section), ¶ (paragraph), *ch* (chapter), or *n* (note). Page

references are usually not preceded by an abbreviation, but following a designation of a larger subdivision, they may be preceded by the word *at* (see below).

> Patricia Love and Timothy P. Namssorg, 2 *Litigation in Unfriendly Buyouts* § 18.2 at 20 (Castleworth, 1991).
> Caroline D. Allegra et al., *Litigation on Behalf of Political Dissidents* ch 3 at 86 (Cavanagh, 3d ed 1991).
> Nancy Krick, Max Patrick, and Sarah Williamspouse, eds., *Strategies in Plea Bargaining* ch 12 (Castelworth, 1990).

ARTICLES IN PERIODICALS

15.317 The arrangement of elements in citations to articles in periodicals is as follows:

> author/*comma*/article title/*comma*/volume number/title of periodical/opening page number of article/*comma*/cited page number(s)/date in *parentheses/period*

The title of the article is given in italics with headline-style capitalization and may be shortened if very long. The journal title is set headline style in roman. An arabic numeral represents the volume number. The volume number may be omitted, however, if the periodical is commonly identified by date of issue. A generally recognized abbreviation may be used for the journal title.

> Miriam Marlowe, *Judicial Construction of the Constitution*, 14 Porkola U of Law Rev 8, 11–12 (1966).
> Watson McKinley III and T. B. Brust, *Repossession and Its Consequences*, Pacific Coast Monthly 46, 50–51 (Oct 1984).

CASES, OR COURT DECISIONS

15.318 Elements in a citation to a court decision are arranged as follows:

> case name/*comma*/volume of reporter/name of reporter/opening page of decision/*comma*/cited page number(s)/court and date in *parentheses/period*

The case name is given in italic caps and lowercase, with the abbreviation *v.* for *versus*. Arabic numerals are used for the volume number, and the name of the reporter, cited in roman type, is usually abbreviated.

> *Bridges v. California*, 314 US 252 (1941).
> *United States v. Dennis*, 183 F2d 201, 203 (2d Cir 1950).

For state court cases, both the official and the commercial reporters are cited, separated by a comma:

> *Henningsen v. Bloomfield Motors, Inc.*, 32 NJ 358, 161 A2d 69 (1960).

CONSTITUTIONS

15.319 Citations to constitutions, whether state or federal, are given in the following form:

> state or country/the abbreviation *Const* (in roman, without a period)/ *comma*/subdivision(s)/*period*

Article and amendment numbers are given in roman numerals; other subdivision numbers, in arabic.

> US Const, Art I, § 4.
> US Const, Amend XIV, § 2.
> Ariz Const, Art VII, § 5.

ADDITIONAL INFORMATION

15.320 For more extensive consideration of legal citations in legal works, including citations to legislative, executive, and administrative materials and the formation of subsequent shortened references, consult the *Chicago Manual of Legal Citation* or, alternatively, *A Uniform System of Citation*. Either system should be followed consistently throughout a work. Copyeditors should not change the author's style of citation from one method to the other without the author's consent.

Legal Citations in Nonlegal or General Works

15.321 For the recommended style for legal citations in nonlegal or general works see 15.322–411 and, for loose-leaf legal information services, 15.421.

PUBLIC DOCUMENTS

15.322 References to printed public documents, like other references, should include elements needed for location in a library catalog. In general these elements are as follows:

> Country, state, city, county, or other government division issuing the document
> Legislative body, executive department, court, bureau, board, commission, or committee
> Subsidiary divisions, regional offices, and so forth
> Title, if any, of the document or collection
> Individual author (editor, compiler) if given
> Report number or any other identification necessary or useful in finding the specific document
> Publisher, if different from the issuing body

Date
Page, if relevant

15.323 The above elements may not all be essential in note or bibliographic documentation. For example, a work in the field of American history or politics with many references to government publications may omit *U.S.* in its citations, and further abbreviation is often desirable.

15.324 The order in which the elements appear in the citation may differ from work to work, according to preference of authors and relevance to subjects. When a reference is given in a shortened form in a note and in full in the bibliography, it is well to begin both with the same element to avoid confusing the reader.

15.325 Citations to public documents, in other words, may take various forms, from the full formal listing beginning, as does a library catalog card, with the name of the country, state, or other geographical division, to an abbreviated form dictated by the context. Discretion and common sense are useful in deciding in any given case how much information is necessary for the reader to locate the material.

15.326 The number and variety of government publications preclude all-inclusive representation in this manual. The classifications illustrated below are those most commonly encountered in bibliographies and notes.[2] For documents that do not fit these patterns, the author or editor should be able to devise a logical form of citation.

United States

15.327 Publications are issued by both houses of Congress (Senate and House of Representatives) and by the executive departments (State, Justice, Labor, etc.) and agencies (Federal Trade Commission, General Services Administration, etc.). Most government publications are printed and distributed by the Government Printing Office (GPO) in Washington, D.C.; bibliographies, references, and notes may use, consistently, one of the following:

> Washington, D.C.: U.S. Government Printing Office, 1980.
> Washington, D.C.: Government Printing Office, 1980.
> Washington, D.C.: GPO, 1980.
> Washington, D.C., 1980.
> Washington, 1980.

These facts of publication are often omitted when other identifying data are given, such as the data for congressional documents.

---

2. Detailed instructions for citing legislative sources in law publications can be found in *The University of Chicago Manual of Legal Citation* or in *A Uniform System of Citation*.

15.328 In addition to the publications issued by both houses of Congress and by the executive departments and agencies, a large array of technical literature is also listed in the *Monthly Catalog of United States Government Publications,* including government-sponsored research, development, and engineering reports, foreign technical reports, and other analyses prepared by national and local government agencies and their contractors or grantees. Many of these materials are available through such information services as the National Technical Information Service (NTIS) and the Educational Resources Information Center (ERIC). Because of the great proliferation of these materials, citations to them should include dates, serial and print numbers, and other facts of publication, including information-service identifying and accession numbers when these are available.

CONGRESS

15.329 Congressional publications include the journals of both the House of Representatives and the Senate; the *Congressional Record;* committee reports, hearings, and other documents; and bills and statutes.

15.330 Bibliography listings of congressional documents often begin with "U.S. Congress" and include identification of the house ("Senate" or, for the House of Representatives, "House"); the committee and subcommittee, if any; the title of the document; the number of the Congress and session; the date of publication (sometimes omitted when the congressional session is identified); and the number and description of the document (e.g., H. Doc. 487), if available. Because Congress is understood as the comprising body, however, reference to it may be omitted. In that case the listing begins with the identification of the congressional branch: "U.S. Senate" or "U.S. House." As noted above, in contexts where *U.S.* is understood, it too may be omitted.

15.331 Full note references contain similar information but need not begin with the name of the country because this is usually obvious from the text. If the issuing body is also clear from the text, it need not be repeated in the note. When the country and issuing body are not clear from the text, however, the note may need to offer a fuller reference. The note citation may also contain, as its final element, a page reference.

15.332 A Congress ordinarily lasts two years and consists of two one-year sessions. Congress and session must both be identified in a reference:

87th Cong., 2d sess.　　*or*　　87 Cong. 2 sess.

15.333 *Congressional journals.* The journals of the Senate and the House contain motions, actions taken, and roll-call votes and are published at the end of each session. Journal citations in notes and bibliographies take the following forms. Note that *Senate Journal* and *House Journal* are italicized.

> 1. *Senate Journal,* 16th Cong., 1st sess., 7 December 1819, 9–19.

> U.S. Congress. *Senate Journal.* 16th Cong., 1st sess., 7 December 1819.
> *or*
> U.S. *Senate Journal.* 16th Cong., 1st sess., 7 December 1819.

15.334   *Journals of the Continental Congress.* The *Journals of the Continental Congress* were kept from 1774 through late 1788. A complete edition of these journals in thirty-four volumes was published by the Library of Congress from 1904 to 1937. Since volume numbers are included in citations to these journals, the page reference is introduced by a colon. The first full citation for these volumes in a note may be illustrated as follows:

> 2. *Journals of the Continental Congress, 1774–1789,* ed. Worthington C. Ford et al. (Washington, D.C., 1904–37), 15:1341.

In note citations, *Journals of the Continental Congress* is often abbreviated *JCC*.

> 2. *JCC, 1774–1789,* ed. Worthington C. Ford et al. (Washington, D.C., 1904–37), 15:1341.

Subsequent note citations might omit the full publication facts and give only volume, year (of the Congress), and page reference:

> 3. *Journals of the Continental Congress* 25 (1783): 863.
> *or*
> 3. *JCC* 25 (1783): 863.

The bibliography entry would simply list the publication as a whole:

> Continental Congress. *Journals of the Continental Congress, 1774–1789.* Edited by Worthington C. Ford et al. 34 vols. Washington, D.C., 1904–37.

15.335   *Debates.* Since the first session of the Forty-third Congress in 1873, congressional debates have been printed by the government in the *Congressional Record.* Daily issues of the *Record* are bound in paper biweekly and in permanent volumes at the end of each session. A single bound volume of the *Record,* which is regularly divided into parts, therefore covers one complete session (one year) of a Congress. Since material may be added, deleted, or modified when the permanent bound volumes for complete sessions are prepared, the pagination as well as the contents differs from that of both daily and biweekly volumes. Whenever possible, citations should be made to the permanent bound volumes. If it is necessary to cite the daily or biweekly editions, these must be identified.

15.336 In citing a particular volume and part of the *Congressional Record* it is usual to identify the Congress, the session, the year (although this is optional), the volume, and the part. In a note documenting a specific discussion in the text, a page reference, preceded by a colon, should also be included. When both volume and page are cited, the abbreviations *vol.* and *p.* or *pp.* are omitted.

> 4. *Congressional Record,* 71st Cong., 2d sess., 1930, 72, pt. 10:10828–30.

A bibliography entry for the specific volume and part cited would be as follows:

> *Congressional Record.* 71st Cong., 2d sess., 1930. Vol. 72, pt. 10.

The *Congressional Record* may also be cited in the bibliography in full, or with the run of dates consulted:

> *Congressional Record.* Washington, D.C., 1873–.
> *Congressional Record.* 1940–45. Washington, D.C.

15.337 The identity of the speaker and the subject of the speech or remarks included in the *Record*'s account of the debate are usually specified in the discussion in the text. If they are not, it is advisable to identify them in the citation. In that case the citation might be as follows:

> 5. Senate, Senator Kennedy of Massachusetts speaking for the Joint Resolution on Nuclear Weapons Freeze and Reductions to the Committee on Foreign Relations, S.J. Res. 163, 97th Cong., 1st sess., *Congressional Record* (10 March 1982), 128, pt. 3:3832–34.

A subsequent citation of this reference might be shortened as follows:

> 15. Senate, Kennedy, 3833.
> *or if necessary*
> 15. Senate, Kennedy, Nuclear Weapons Freeze, 3833.

15.338 The bibliography entry for this reference would take the following form:

> U.S. Senate. Senator Kennedy of Massachusetts speaking for the Joint Resolution on Nuclear Weapons Freeze and Reductions to the Committee on Foreign Relations. S.J. Res. 163. 97th Cong., 1st sess. *Congressional Record* (10 March 1982), vol. 128, pt. 3.
> *or*
> U.S. Congress. Senate. Senator Kennedy of Massachusetts . . .

15.339 In note citations, *Congressional Record* is often abbreviated *Cong. Rec.*

15.340 Before 1874, congressional debates were privately printed in *Annals of Congress,* covering the years 1789–1824; *Congressional Debates,* covering 1824–37; and *Congressional Globe,* 1833–73. In a bibliography these are usually cited in full; specific page references and date or session numbers are given only in text or notes:

16. *Annals of Congress,* 2d Cong., appendix, 1414–15.
17. *Annals of Congress,* 18th Cong., 1st sess., 358, 361.
18. *Congressional Globe,* 39th Cong., 2d sess., 1867, 39, pt. 9: 9505.

Annals of the Congress of the United States, 1789–1824. 42 vols. Washington, D.C., 1834–56.
Congressional Globe. 46 vols. Washington, D.C., 1834–73.

The bibliography listing for any of these collections of debates may begin with "U.S. Congress" when it is desirable to list them with other congressional publications.

15.341 *Reports and documents.* Reports and documents of the Senate and the House are each numbered serially through one session (one year) or through one Congress (two years). References to these reports and documents, therefore, should include the Congress and session numbers and, if possible, the series number. Since 1817, with the Fifteenth Congress, all these publications have been bound together serially in volumes numbered consecutively and called the serial set. (These volumes are now being issued on microfiche by the Congressional Information Service, which also publishes an index to the contents of the serial set. The microfiche volumes are available at depository libraries. The information is also available through several large computer services.) Citations to these reports and documents are illustrated in the examples following. Note that in the report and document numbers, the abbreviations *Rept., Doc., S.,* and *H.* are used.

19. Senate Committee on Foreign Relations, *The Mutual Security Act of 1956,* 84th Cong., 2d sess., 1956, S. Rept. 2273, 9–10.
20. House, *Report of Activities of the National Advisory Council on International Monetary and Financial Problems to March 31, 1947,* 80th Cong., 1st sess., 1947, H. Doc. 365, 4.
21. *Declarations of a State of War with Japan, Germany, and Italy,* 77th Cong., 1st sess., 1941, S. Doc. 148, serial 10575, 2–5.

U.S. Senate Committee on Foreign Relations. *The Mutual Security Act of 1956.* 84th Cong., 2d sess., 1956. S. Rept. 2273.
U.S. House. *Report of Activities of the National Advisory Council on International Monetary and Financial Problems to March 31, 1947.* 80th Cong., 1st sess., 1947. H. Doc. 365.
or
U.S. Congress. Senate. Committee on Foreign Relations. . . .
U.S. Congress. House. *Report of Activities.* . . .
U.S. Congress, *Declarations of a State of War with Japan, Germany, and Italy.* 77th Cong., 1st sess., 1941. S. Doc. 148. Serial 10575.

15.342 Subsequent note citations to reports and documents issued by the Senate and House of Representatives may be shortened as follows:

22. Senate Committee, *Mutual Security Act,* 9.
23. House, *Report of Activities,* 5.
24. *Declarations of War,* 4.

15.343 *Hearings.* Published hearings offer records of testimony given before congressional committees. Hearings normally have titles, which should be used in the citations. Even if the "author" listed on the publication does not indicate the committee before which the hearings were held, the committee should be named in the citation as the author.

25. House Committee on Banking and Currency, *Bretton Woods Agreements Act: Hearings on H.R. 3314,* 79th Cong., 1st sess., 1945, 12–14.
26. Senate Committee on Foreign Relations, *Famine in Africa: Hearing before the Committee on Foreign Relations,* 99th Cong., 1st sess., 17 January 1985, 53, 57.

U.S. House Committee on Banking and Currency. *Bretton Woods Agreements Act: Hearings on H.R. 3314,* 79th Cong., 1st sess., 1945.
U.S. Senate Committee on Foreign Relations. *Famine in Africa: Hearing before the Committee on Foreign Relations.* 99th Cong., 1st sess., 17 January 1985.
or
U.S. Congress. House. Committee on Banking and Currency. . . .
U.S. Congress. Senate. Committee on Foreign Relations. . . .

15.344 Subsequent note citations to published hearings may be shortened as follows:

27. House Committee, *Bretton Woods Agreements Act,* 13.
28. Senate Committee, *Famine in Africa,* 55.

15.345 *Committee Prints.* Another form of congressional publication is the Committee Print, generally a research report. Committee Prints are usually numbered; if they are, the numbers should be used in the citation; if not, the date will be sufficient for location.

29. House Committee on Interior and Insular Affairs, Subcommittee on Energy and the Environment, *International Proliferation of Nuclear Technology,* report prepared by Warren H. Donnelly and Barbara Rather, 94th Cong., 2d sess., 1976, Committee Print 15, 5–6.
or
29. Congress, House Committee on Interior and Insular Affairs, . . .
or
29. Warren H. Donnelly and Barbara Rather, *International Proliferation of Nuclear Technology,* report prepared for the Subcommittee on Energy and the Environment of the House Committee on Interior and Insular Affairs, 94th Cong., 2d sess., 1976, Committee Print 15, 5–6.
30. House Committee on Foreign Affairs, *Background Material on Mutual Defense and Development Programs: Fiscal Year 1965,* 88th Cong., 2d sess., 1964, Committee Print, 6, 31.

U.S. House Committee on Interior and Insular Affairs. Subcommittee on Energy and the Environment. *International Proliferation of Nuclear*

Technology. Report prepared by Warren H. Donnelly and Barbara
Rather. 94th Cong., 2d sess., 1976. Committee Print 15.
or
U.S. Congress. House. Committee on Interior and Insular Affairs. . . .
or
Donnelly, Warren H., and Barbara Rather. *International Proliferation of
Nuclear Technology.* Report prepared for the Subcommittee on Energy
and the Environment of the House Committee on Interior and Insular
Affairs, 94th Cong., 2d sess., 1976. Committee Print 15.
U.S. House Committee on Foreign Affairs. *Background Material on Mu-
tual Defense and Development Programs: Fiscal Year 1965.* 88th Cong.,
2d sess., 1964. Committee Print.
or
U.S. Congress. House. Committee on Foreign Affairs. . . .

15.346 Subsequent note citations to Committee Prints may be made as follows:

39. House Committee, *Proliferation of Nuclear Technology,* 6.
40. House Committee, *Mutual Defense,* 32.

15.347 *Bills and resolutions.* Congressional bills (proposed laws) and resolutions are published in pamphlet form (slip bills) and are available on
microfiche at many libraries. Bills and resolutions originating in the
House of Representatives are both referred to as House Resolutions
(abbreviated H.R. in citations); those originating in the Senate, Senate
Resolutions (S.R.). Bills and resolutions may be cited to slip bills (as
in the first example below) and, once printed there, to the *Congressional Record.*

15.348 Bills and resolutions are ordinarily cited in the text or notes; they are
sometimes, but not always, listed in the bibliography. The slip bill citation includes the title of the bill, in italics; the congressional session;
and the bill number. The citation to the *Congressional Record,* if available, follows the bill number.

42. *Food Security Act of 1985,* 99th Cong., 1st sess., H.R. 2100.
43. *Food Security Act of 1985,* 99th Cong., 1st sess., H.R. 2100,
Congressional Record, 131, no. 132, daily ed. (8 October 1985): H8461–
66.
or
43. House, *Food Security Act of 1985,* . . .

If it appears in the discussion in the text, the title of the bill or resolution
may be omitted from the note. The note in that event would begin with
the resolution number (H.R. or S.R.):

44. H.R. 2100, 99th Cong., 1st sess., *Congressional Record,* 131, no.
132, daily ed. (8 October 1985): H8461–66.

If the bill or resolution is listed in the bibliography, the citation there
should include the title. The citation may begin with either the originating congressional chamber or the title:

U.S. House. *Food Security Act of 1985*. 99th Cong., 1st sess., H.R. 2100. *Congressional Record*, 131, no. 132, daily ed. (8 October 1985): H8353–H8486.

Food Security Act of 1985. U.S. House. 99th Cong., 1st sess., H.R. 2100. *Congressional Record*, 131, no. 132, daily ed. (8 October 1985): H8353–H8486.

15.349 In shortened citations to congressional bills and resolutions, only the bill title or the bill number need be given:

52. *Food Security Act of 1985*.
or
52. H.R. 2100.

If the citation to the *Congressional Record* is also included in the original reference, as in example note 43 above, a page reference to that publication may simply be added at the end of the shortened reference:

53. *Food Security Act of 1985,* H8463–65.

15.350 *Laws, public acts, and statutes.* Once a bill or resolution has been passed by both houses of Congress and signed by the president, it becomes a law, also referred to as a public law or statute. Statutes are cited in the text or in notes. They may also be cited separately in the bibliography, but often they are not. If a number of laws are referred to in a work, the printed collections in which they appear may be cited as a whole in the bibliography.

15.351 Statutes are first published separately, as slip laws, and then are collected in the bound volumes of the *United States Statutes at Large,* issued annually. Later, the statutes are incorporated into the *United States Code,* which is revised every six years. When cited to slip laws, statutes are referred to as public laws. The citation should include the public law number, the session of the Congress that enacted the law, and the date the law was approved. Inclusion of the title of the law is not necessary, but it may be added, in the note, either after the date or at the opening of the citation. In the bibliography, it may be added either at the beginning or at the end of the entry. In both note and bibliography, the title of the law should be in italics.

54. Public Law 585, 79th Cong., 2d sess. (1 August 1946), 12, 19.
or
54. Public Law 585, 79th Cong., 2d sess. (1 August 1946), *Atomic Energy Act of 1946,* 12, 19.
or
54. *Atomic Energy Act of 1946,* Public Law 585, 79th Cong., 2d sess. (1 August 1946), 12, 19.

U.S. Public Law 585. 79th Cong., 2d sess., 1 August 1946.
or

U.S. Public Law 585. 79th Cong., 2d sess., 1 August 1946. *Atomic Energy Act of 1946.*
or
Atomic Energy Act of 1946. Public Law 585. 79th Cong., 2d sess., 1 August 1946.
or
Public Law 585. . . .

15.352 Shortened citations to public laws may be as follows:

64. Public Law 585, 13–14.
or
64. PL 585, 13–14.
or
64. *Atomic Energy Act of 1946,* 13–14.

15.353 Once the law appears in the *Statutes at Large,* it should be cited to that publication. The citation should include the volume number (without *vol.*), the year in parentheses, and the page reference, preceded by a colon. If desired, the title may be added, as illustrated below.

65. *U.S. Statutes at Large* 60 (1947): 767, 774.
or
65. *Statutes at Large* 60 (1947): 767, 774.
or
65. *Atomic Energy Act of 1946, U.S. Statutes at Large* 60. . . .

U.S. Statutes at Large 60 (1947): 755–75. *Atomic Energy Act of 1946.*
or
Statutes at Large 60 (1947): 755–75.
or
Atomic Energy Act of 1946. U.S. Statutes at Large 60 (1947): 755–75.

15.354 Citations to laws published in the *U.S. Statutes at Large* are sufficiently brief to require no shortening in subsequent references, unless the title of the law has been included, in which case the title itself, with page numbers if applicable, may be used as the shortened reference.

75. *Atomic Energy Act of 1946,* 771–73.

15.355 After the statute has been incorporated into the *U.S. Code,* its citation takes the form illustrated below. Note that the page reference applicable to the *Statutes at Large* has been replaced by a section reference.

76. *Declaratory Judgment Act, U.S. Code,* vol. 28, secs. 2201–2 (1952).

Declaratory Judgment Act. U.S. Code. Vol. 28, secs. 2201–2 (1952).

15.356 Shortened citations to laws appearing in the *U.S. Code* consist of the title of the law and the *Code* section reference:

86. *Declaratory Judgment Act,* secs. 2201–2.

15.357 *Earlier statutes.* The *United States Statutes at Large* began publication in 1874. Before that, laws were published in *Statutes at Large of the United States of America, 1789–1873* (abbreviated *Stats. at Large of USA*), 17 vols. (Washington, D.C., 1850–73). Citations to this collection must include the volume number and the publication date of that volume. Short citations should also include the volume number, but not the publication date. If the title of the law is included in the first citation, that title, itself shortened if too long, may be used for the shortened citation.

15.358 *American State Papers.* Documents printed privately for the early Congresses are collected in the thirty-eight volumes of the *American State Papers* (1789–1838). These papers, comprising both legislative and executive documents, are organized into ten classes—for example, 1. *Foreign Relations;* 3. *Finance;* 8. *Public Lands*—each class having several volumes. In documenting the papers, the class number and class title are both usually given, although the number may be omitted, especially if a volume is cited. When volume and page numbers are cited, as in the examples below, no comma is used between the class title and the volume number. In the note citation, the abbreviation *Am. St. P.* may be used.

> 87. *American State Papers,* 5, *Military Affairs* 2:558.
> *or*
> 87. *American State Papers: Military Affairs* 2:558.

> *American State Papers:* 5, *Military Affairs.* Vol. 2.
> *or*
> *American State Papers: Military Affairs.* Vol. 2.

The entry may also start with the title of the paper cited:

> 88. Mifflin to Washington, 18 July 1791, *Am. St. P.: Misc.* 1:39.

> Mifflin to Washington. 18 July 1791. *American State Papers: Miscellaneous* 1:39–40.
> *or*
> *American State Papers: Miscellaneous.* Vol. 1.

In the bibliography, several classes may be included in a single entry:

> *American State Papers:* 5, *Military Affairs.* 6, *Naval Affairs.*

15.359 Subsequent note citations to *American State Papers* may be shortened by using the abbreviation *Am. St. P.* or, if included in the first reference, the title of the paper.

> 98. Mifflin to Washington, 39.

15.360 *Other collections.* Various other collections of congressional papers exist, but adequate discussion of them would be impractical here. An excellent source covering legislative documents and collections is

Laurence F. Schmeckebier and Roy B. Eastin, *Government Publications and Their Use,* 2d ed. The author or editor may devise references for these additional sources by adapting the general principles presented above. Sufficient information should be given to enable the reader to locate a copy of the document cited.

PRESIDENTIAL DOCUMENTS

15.361 Presidential proclamations, executive orders, and such other documents as addresses, letters, and vetoes are published in *The Weekly Compilation of Presidential Documents.* Presidential proclamations and executive orders are also carried in the *Federal Register,* which is published daily. The issues of the *Federal Register* are available on microfiche.

> 99. President, Proclamation, "Caribbean Basin Economic Recovery Act, Proclamation 5142, Amending Proclamation 5133," *Federal Register* 49, no. 2 (4 January 1984): 341, microfiche.

> President. Proclamation. "Caribbean Basin Economic Recovery Act, Proclamation 5142, Amending Proclamation 5133." *Federal Register* 49, no. 2 (4 January 1984): 341. Microfiche.

15.362 The public papers of the presidents of the United States are collected in two large multivolume works: *Compilation of the Messages and Papers of the Presidents, 1789–1897,* and for subsequent administrations, *Public Papers of the Presidents of the United States.*

> 100. *House Miscellaneous Document no. 210,* 53d Cong., 2d sess., in *Compilation of the Messages and Papers of the Presidents, 1789–1897,* ed. J. D. Richardson (Washington, D.C.: Government Printing Office, 1907), 4:16.
> 101. *Public Papers of the Presidents of the United States: Herbert Hoover, 1929–33,* 4 vols. (Washington, D.C.: GPO, 1974–77).
> 102. Herbert Hoover, *Public Papers of the Presidents of the United States: Herbert Hoover, 1929–33,* vol. 4 (Washington, D.C.: GPO, 1977), 178–83.

> *House Miscellaneous Document no. 210,* 53d Cong., 2d sess. In *Compilation of the Messages and Papers of the Presidents, 1789–1897,* edited by J. D. Richardson. Vol. 4. Washington, D.C.: Government Printing Office, 1907.
> *or*
> *Compilation of the Messages and Papers of the Presidents, 1789–1897.* Edited by J. D. Richardson. Vol. 4. Washington, D.C.: GPO, 1907.
> Hoover, Herbert. *Public Papers of the Presidents of the United States: Herbert Hoover, 1929–33.* 4 vols. Washington, D.C.: GPO, 1974–77.
> Hoover, Herbert. *Public Papers of the Presidents of the United States: Herbert Hoover, 1929–33.* Vol. 4. Washington, D.C.: GPO, 1977.

15.363 Subsequent note citations to presidential documents may be shortened as follows:

109. President, "Caribbean Basin Economic Recovery Act," 341.
110. *House Misc. Doc. no. 210,* 16.
111. Hoover, *Public Papers,* 4:180, 183.

EXECUTIVE DEPARTMENT DOCUMENTS

15.364 *General.* Executive department documents consist of reports, bulletins, circulars, and miscellaneous materials issued by executive departments, bureaus, and agencies. When authors of these publications are identified, they should be included in the citations along with the issuing body. The citation usually begins with the name of the issuing body, but it may also begin with the name of the author. When both personal author and issuing body are included in the bibliography entry, one should be cross-referenced to the other.

113. Treasury Department, Bureau of Prohibition, *Digest of Supreme Court Decisions Interpreting the National Prohibition Act and Willis-Campbell Act* (Washington, D.C.: GPO, 1929), 14–28.
114. President's Commission on Law Enforcement and Administration of Justice, *Task Force Report: Juvenile Delinquency and Youth Crime* (Washington, D.C.: GPO, 1967), 21.
115. Ralph I. Straus, *Expanding Private Investment for Free World Economic Growth,* a special report prepared at the request of the Department of State, April 1959, 12.
116. Department of the Interior, Minerals Management Service, *An Oil-spill Risk Analysis for the Central Gulf (April 1984) and Western Gulf of Mexico (July 1984),* by Robert P. LaBelle, open-file report, U.S. Geological Survey, 83–119 (Denver, 1983), lease offerings microfilm.
117. Department of Labor, Employment Standards Administration, *Resource Book: Training for Federal Employee Compensation Specialists* (Washington, D.C., 1984), 236.

Treasury Department. Bureau of Prohibition. *Digest of Supreme Court Decisions Interpreting the National Prohibition Act and Willis-Campbell Act.* Washington, D.C.: GPO, 1929.
President's Commission on Law Enforcement and Administration of Justice. *Task Force Report: Juvenile Delinquency and Youth Crime.* Washington, D.C.: GPO, 1967.
Straus, Ralph I. *Expanding Private Investment for Free World Economic Growth.* A special report prepared at the request of the Department of State. April 1959.
U.S. Department of State. *See* Straus, Ralph I.
U.S. Department of the Interior. Minerals Management Service. *An Oilspill Risk Analysis for the Central Gulf (April 1984) and Western Gulf of Mexico (July 1984),* by Robert P. LaBelle. Open-file report, U.S. Geological Survey. Denver, 1983. Lease offerings microform.
LaBelle, Robert P. *See* U.S. Department of the Interior.
U.S. Department of Labor. Employment Standards Administration. *Resource Book: Training for Federal Employee Compensation Specialists.* Washington, D.C., 1984.

15.365 *Series numbers.* Many departmental publications are classified in series, and the series number may be a helpful addition to the citation. When the serial number is given, publication facts may be omitted:

> 118. Department of State, *Postwar Policy Preparation, 1939–1945,* General Policy Series, no. 15.

> U.S. Department of State. *Postwar Policy Preparation, 1939–1945.* General Policy Series, no. 15.

15.366 *Census Bureau publications.* Census Bureau publications may be listed under "U.S. Department of Commerce, Bureau of the Census," but this is not necessary. The *National Union Catalog* lists them as below, with a cross-reference under "Department of Commerce."

> 119. Bureau of the Census, *Median Gross Rent by Counties of the United States, 1970,* prepared by the Geography Division in cooperation with the Housing Division, Bureau of the Census (Washington, D.C., 1975).

> U.S. Bureau of the Census. *Median Gross Rent by Counties of the United States, 1970.* Prepared by the Geography Division in cooperation with the Housing Division, Bureau of the Census. Washington, D.C., 1975.

UNITED STATES CONSTITUTION

15.367 The United States Constitution is cited by article or amendment, section, and if relevant, clause. Abbreviations and arabic numerals are used in referring to all parts of the document. Citations to the Constitution are usually given in the text or notes. It is unnecessary to list the Constitution in the bibliography.

> 120. U.S. Constitution, art. 1, sec. 4.
> 121. U.S. Constitution, amend. 14, sec. 2.

PUBLICATIONS BY GOVERNMENT COMMISSIONS

15.368 Bulletins, circulars, reports, and study papers issued by such government commissions as the Federal Communications Commission, Federal Trade Commission, and Securities and Exchange Commission, often classified as House or Senate documents, may be cited as follows:

> 122. Securities and Exchange Commission, *Annual Report of the Securities and Exchange Commission for the Fiscal Year* (Washington, D.C.: GPO, 1983), 42.
> 123. Senate, *Report of the Federal Trade Commission on Utility Corporations,* 70th Cong., 1st sess., 1935, S. Doc. 91, pt. 71A.

> U.S. Securities and Exchange Commission. *Annual Report of the Securities and Exchange Commission for the Fiscal Year.* Washington, D.C.: GPO, 1983.

> U.S. Senate. *Report of the Federal Trade Commission on Utility Corpora-tions.* 70th Cong., 1st sess., 1935. S. Doc. 91.

FEDERAL COURT DECISIONS

15.369 Decisions of the federal courts are cited in text or notes and are rarely listed separately in the bibliography.

15.370 Until 1875, decisions of the United States Supreme Court were com-piled and printed under the names of official court reporters; for ex-ample: William Cranch, *Reports of Cases Argued and Adjudged in the Supreme Court of the United States, 1801–1815,* 9 vols. (Washington, D.C., 1804–17). Since 1875 the decisions have been published offi-cially in the *United States Supreme Court Reports* (abbreviated U.S.), which is the preferred source for citation. They may also be cited to the *Supreme Court Reporter* (Sup. Ct.), or both. The citation should begin with the title of the case in italics, followed by the source, which in-cludes volume, reporter (in roman type), and page reference, in that order; and finally, in the first reference only, the year in parentheses. As illustrated in the following examples, a period is used after the abbre-viation for *versus* in general, nonlegal works. The legal style of omit-ting the period (see 15.318) may also, however, be adopted for general works if followed consistently.

> 124. *Bridges v. California,* 314 U.S. 252 (1941).
> 125. *Associated Press v. United States,* 326 U.S. 1 (1944).
> *or*
> 125. *Associated Press v. United States,* 65 Sup. Ct. 1416 (1944).
> *or*
> 125. *Associated Press v. United States,* 326 U.S. 1; 65 Sup. Ct. 1416 (1944).

15.371 Subsequent citations may be shortened to case titles and page refer-ences if only one reporter is originally cited. If more than one reporter is originally cited, the reporter referred to must be repeated. The year is omitted in subsequent citations.

> 134. *Bridges v. California,* 253.
> 135. *Associated Press v. United States,* 2–3.
> 136. *Associated Press v. United States,* 326 U.S. 3–5.

15.372 Citations of decisions of lower federal courts, such as the Court of Appeals of the Second Circuit (2d Cir.), may be made to the *Federal Reporter* (F.), in which they have their official publication. If a series other than the first is involved, that should be indicated. The court, usually in abbreviated form, and the date are identified in parentheses at the end of the first citation.

> 137. *United States v. Dennis,* 183 F. 2d 201 (2d Cir. 1950).

TREATIES

15.373 Since 1950, treaties have been published in the annual bound volumes of *United States Treaties and Other International Agreements*. The treaties appear in these bound volumes as they were numbered and published in pamphlet form by the Department of State in the series Treaties and Other International Acts (TIAS). Multilateral treaties, those involving more than two countries, appear in the Treaty Series of the United Nations, but usually not until a year or more after their signing. Depending on their nature and date, treaties predating 1950 may be found in one or another of the following: Treaty Series of the League of Nations, Treaty Series and Executive Agreement Series of the Department of State, and *Statutes at Large*. In note and bibliography citations, the titles of treaties are enclosed in quotation marks, as though they were titles of chapters. Subsequent note citations to treaties are shortened in much the same way as are those to articles or chapters in books.

> 138. Department of State, "Nuclear Weapons Test Ban," 5 August 1963, TIAS no. 5433, *United States Treaties and Other International Agreements*, vol. 14, pt. 2.
> 139. "Naval Armament Limitation Treaty," 26 February 1922, *Statutes at Large* (December 1923–March 1925), 43, pt. 2:9–12.
> 140. "Denmark and Italy: Convention concerning Military Service," 15 July 1954, *Treaties and International Agreements Registered or Filed or Reported with the Secretariat of the United Nations* 250, no. 3516 (1956): 45.
> 148. Department of State, "Nuclear Weapons Test Ban."
> 149. "Naval Armament Limitation Treaty," 10–11.
> 150. "Denmark and Italy," 43.

> U.S. Department of State. "Nuclear Weapons Test Ban," 5 August 1963. TIAS no. 5433. *United States Treaties and Other International Agreements*, vol. 14, pt. 2.
> U.S. "Naval Armament Limitation Treaty," 26 February 1922. *Statutes at Large* (December 1923–March 1925), 43, pt. 2.
> United Nations. Treaty Series. "Denmark and Italy: Convention concerning Military Service," 15 July 1954. *Treaties and International Agreements Registered or Filed or Reported with the Secretariat of the United Nations*, 250, no. 3516 (1956).

UNPUBLISHED DOCUMENTS

15.374 Most unpublished documents of the United States government are housed in the National Archives (NA) in Washington, D.C., or in one of its branches. All the materials, including manuscript and typescript records, films, still photographs, and sound recordings, are cited by record group (RG) number. They may be further identified by title and by subsection and file number. Names of specific documents are enclosed in quotation marks. The order of items in note and bibliography citations is not fixed but should be consistent within each work. Either of the following forms may be adopted:

> 151. Senate Committee on the Judiciary, "Lobbying," file 71A-F15, RG 46, National Archives.
> *or*
> 151. National Archives, Files of the Senate Committee on the Judiciary, RG 46, "Lobbying," file 71A-F15.
> 152. National Commission on Law Observance and Enforcement, RG 10, National Archives Branch Depository, Suitland, Md.
> *or*
> 152. National Archives Branch Depository, Suitland, Md., Records of the National Commission on Law Observance and Enforcement, RG 10.

> U.S. Senate Committee on the Judiciary. "Lobbying." File 71A-F15. RG 46. National Archives.
> *or*
> National Archives. Files of the Senate Committee on the Judiciary. RG 46. "Lobbying." File 71A-F15.
> National Commission on Law Observance and Enforcement. RG 10. National Archives Branch Depository, Suitland, Md.
> *or*
> National Archives Branch Depository, Suitland, Md. Records of the National Commission on Law Observance and Enforcement. RG 10.

15.375 Subsequent citations may be shortened as follows:

> 161. Senate Committee, "Lobbying."
> *or*
> 161. National Archives, "Lobbying."
> 162. Law Observance and Enforcement, RG 10.
> *or*
> 162. National Archives Branch, RG 10.

15.376 For a list of the record groups and their numbers see *Guide to the National Archives of the United States.*

STATE AND LOCAL GOVERNMENTS AND COURTS

15.377 *Government documents.* Citations to state and local government documents follow essentially the same form as that used for United States documents. Administrative or legislative reports, gubernatorial or mayoral messages or addresses, and similar documents published in pamphlet form are cited in a style similar to that used for books, except that the publisher is usually omitted.

> 163. California Legislature, Joint Committee on the Twenty-first Century, *Preliminary Report to the Legislature, 1998 Regular Session, on Preparing to Enter the Twenty-first Century* (Sacramento, 1998), 15, 26, 31–34.
> 164. R. Kaufman Wordsmith, governor of Illinois, *Message of Governor*

> *R. Kaufman Wordsmith to the 96th General Assembly, 21 January 2010* (Springfield, 2010), 23, 26.
>   165. Illinois General Assembly, Law Revision Commission, *Report to the 80th General Assembly of the State of Illinois* (Chicago, 1977), 14–18.
>   166. Illinois Institute for Environmental Quality (IIEQ), *Review and Synopsis of Public Participation regarding Sulfur Dioxide and Particulate Emissions,* by Sidney M. Marder, IIEQ Document no. 77/21 (Chicago, 1977).

> California Legislature. Joint Committee on the Twenty-first Century. *Preliminary Report to the Legislature, 1998 Regular Session, on Preparing to Enter the Twenty-first Century.* Sacramento, 1998.
> Wordsmith, R. Kaufman, governor of Illinois. *Message of Governor R. Kaufman Wordsmith to the 96th General Assembly, 21 January 2010.* Springfield, 2010.
> Illinois General Assembly. Law Revision Commission. *Report to the 80th General Assembly of the State of Illinois.* Chicago, 1977.
> Illinois Institute for Environmental Quality (IIEQ). *Review and Synopsis of Public Participation regarding Sulfur Dioxide and Particulate Emissions.* By Sidney M. Marder. IIEQ Document no. 77/21. Chicago, 1977.

15.378 Subsequent citations:

> 173. California, Joint Committee, *Preliminary Report,* 24–28.
> 174. Wordsmith, *Message,* 24.
> 175. Illinois, Law Revision Commission, *Report,* 16.
> 176. IIEQ, *Review and Synopsis.*

15.379 *State laws and municipal ordinances.* Citations to specific state laws or municipal ordinances should be restricted to text or notes. Compilations of state laws (usually referred to as codes) or municipal ordinances may be cited as entities in the bibliography. (In the case of edited or annotated compilations, the editor's or annotator's last name is included with the date in parentheses, but without the separating comma.)

> 178. Ohio General Code (Page 1937), sec. 3566.
> 179. California Civil Code, secs. 29, 34.
> 180. Kentucky *Revised Statutes, Annotated* (Baldwin 1943), sec. 28.

> Kentucky. *Revised Statutes, Annotated* (Baldwin 1943).

15.380 In references to specific laws or ordinances by title, the title is italicized, and the date of the law is added in parentheses after the compilation. Volume and page number or section number then follow in the usual form.

> 181. Ohio, *Judicial Organization Act, Statutes* (1830) 3:1571–78.
> 182. New York, N.Y., *"Good Samaritan" Law, Administrative Code* (1965), sec. 67-3.2.

15.381 Subsequent citations:

> 191. Ohio, *Judicial Organization Act,* 1577.
> 192. New York, *"Good Samaritan" Law.*

15.382 *State constitutions.* References to state constitutions are given in text or notes. The title of the constitution is set in roman type. It is not necessary to list constitutions in the bibliography.

> 193. Arizona Constitution, art. 7, sec. 5.

15.383 Because some states have adopted new constitutions, references to superseded constitutions should include the date, in parentheses. No date is used for current constitutions.

> 194. Illinois Constitution (1848), art. 5, sec. 2.

15.384 *Court decisions.* References to state and local court decisions are made in text or notes only and are cited in a form similar to that used for federal courts (see 15.369–72). Citation to official state reports is preferred. For subsequent citation see 15.371.

> 195. *Williams v. Davis*, 27 Cal. 2d 746 (1946).

United Kingdom

15.385 The British have been keeping records at least since the Norman Conquest of 1066. Among the numerous guides to this vast amount of material for the scholar (and editor) are *Guide to the Contents of the Public Record Office; A Guide to British Government Publications,* by Frank Rodgers; and *The Bibliographic Control of Official Publications,* by John E. Pemberton—all listed in the bibliography of this manual. The following paragraphs attempt only a general description, noting some common abbreviations and some pitfalls to be avoided by copyeditors.

15.386 Like United States government publications, British publications fall into two main categories, parliamentary and nonparliamentary (i.e., departmental). The nonparliamentary publications cover an enormous range of subjects and are usually cited like privately published books and pamphlets: author or issuing body, title (shortened if necessary), series if any, place of publication, publisher, date, and (in notes) page reference.

15.387 Citations to British government documents, as to their counterparts in United States documents, should begin with the name of the authorizing body under which they were issued: Parliament, Public Record Office, Foreign Office, Ministry of Transport, and so on. In bibliography entries, and in notes when it is not clear from the text, the authorizing body should be preceded by "United Kingdom" (U.K.) or "Great Britain" (G.B.). The most recent edition of *Anglo-American Cataloguing Rules* recommends that British government publications be listed under

United Kingdom (U.K.), although Great Britain (G.B.) was widely used until recently and is also acceptable.

15.388 The publisher of most government material in recent years is Her (His) Majesty's Stationery Office (HMSO) in London.

PARLIAMENT

15.389 Parliamentary publications include all materials issued by both houses of Parliament, the House of Commons (H.C.) and the House of Lords (H.L.): journals of both houses (sometimes abbreviated *C.J.* and *L.J.*); votes and proceedings; debates; bills, reports, papers; and statutes.

15.390 *Debates*. Through 1908, House of Lords and House of Commons debates were published together; since 1908 they have been published in separate series:

> *Hansard Parliamentary Debates,* 1st series (1803–20)
> *Hansard Parliamentary Debates,* 2d series (1820–30)
> *Hansard Parliamentary Debates,* 3d series (1830–91)
> *Parliamentary Debates,* 4th series (1892–1908)
> *Parliamentary Debates,* Commons, 5th series (1909–)
> *Parliamentary Debates,* House of Lords, 5th series (1909–)

Although no longer the official name of the parliamentary debates, *Hansard* (sometimes *Hansard's*) is still frequently used in citations to all series of debates. The debates are cited by series and volume number, to which dates may be added; references in notes are to column or page:

> 1. *Hansard Parliamentary Debates,* 3d ser., vol. 249 (1879), cols. 611–27.
> 2. *Parliamentary Debates,* Commons, 5th ser., vol. 26 (1911), cols. 119–26.

> United Kingdom. [*or* U.K.] *Hansard Parliamentary Debates,* 3d ser., vol. 249 (1879).
> ———. *Parliamentary Debates,* Commons, 5th ser., vol. 26 (1911).
>   *or*
> U.K. Parliament. *Debates,* 3d ser., vol. 249 (1879).
> ———. *H.C. Debates,* 5th ser., vol. 26 (1911).

15.391 In notes, the short form below may be used and, if desired, it may be further shortened by omitting the dates.

> 3. *Hansard,* 3d ser., 249 (1879): 613–19.
> 4. *Parl. Deb.,* 4th ser., 13 (1893): 1273.
> 5. *Parl. Deb.,* Lords, 5th ser., 58 (1924): 111–15.
> 6. *Parl. Deb.,* Commons [*or* H.C.], 5th ser., 26 (1911): 225–27.

15.392 The official British style for *Debates* citations in notes is as follows:

> 7. 188 *Parl. Deb.* 4s., cols. 1356–1406.
> 8. 393 *H.C. Deb.* 5s., col. 403.

15.393 Specific items in the *Debates* may be cited as follows:

> 9. Churchill, Speech to the House of Commons, 18 January 1945, *Parliamentary Debates,* Commons, 5th ser., vol. 407 (1944–45), cols. 425–46.
> 19. Churchill, Speech, col. 428.

> Churchill, Winston S. Speech to the House of Commons, 18 January 1945. *Parliamentary Debates,* Commons, 5th ser., vol. 407 (1944–45), cols. 425–46.

15.394 *Parliamentary Papers, Sessional Papers.* The bills, reports, and papers issued separately by Parliament are bound together at the end of each session into volumes referred to as Parliamentary Papers or Sessional Papers. References to items in these volumes include the originating house, the title of the item (in quotation marks), the title and years of the Sessional Papers (in italics), including the divisional title (*Prison Education* in the example below), the date of the item, the volume number, the section or paragraph number, when appropriate, and the page number.

> 20. House of Commons, "Present and Future Role of the Assistant Chief Education Officer," *Sessional Papers, 1982–83, Prison Education,* 25 April 1983, vol. 2, par. 9.14, p. 102.
> 30. Commons, "Present and Future Role," 103.

> United Kingdom. House of Commons. "Present and Future Role of the Assistant Chief Education Officer." *Sessional Papers, 1982–83, Prison Education.* 25 April 1983. Vol. 2.

15.395 Many of the documents in these series are "command papers," so called because they originate outside Parliament and are ostensibly presented to it "by command of Her Majesty." There have been five series of command papers to date:

1833–69	No. 1 to No. 4222
1870–99	C. 1 to C. 9550
1900–1918	Cd. 1 to Cd. 9239
1919–56	Cmd. 1 to Cmd. 9889
1956–	Cmnd. 1–

Note that the form of the abbreviation for "command" indicates the series and so must not be altered by the copyeditor. (Do not add *s* for plural: Cmnd. 3834, 3835.) An individual paper may be a pamphlet or several volumes and may bear a month date or just the year date.

> 31. *The Basle Facility and the Sterling Area,* Cmnd. 3787 (October 1968), 15–16.

> 32. *First Interim Report of the Committee on Currency and Foreign Exchanges after the War,* Cd. 9182 (1918).
> 33. *Report of the Royal Commission on Indian Currency and Finance,* vol. 2, Appendices, Cmd. 2687 (1926).
> 34. Committee on the Working of the Monetary System [Radcliffe Committee], *Principal Memoranda of Evidence,* vol. 1 (London, 1960).
>
> United Kingdom. Parliament. *The Basle Facility and the Sterling Area.* Cmnd. 3787. October 1968.
> United Kingdom. Parliament. *First Interim Report of the Committee on Currency and Foreign Exchanges after the War.* Cd. 9182. 1918.
> United Kingdom. Parliament. *Report of the Royal Commission on Indian Currency and Finance.* Vol. 2, Appendices. Cmd. 2687. 1926.
> United Kingdom. Parliament. Committee on the Working of the Monetary System [Radcliffe Committee]. *Principal Memoranda of Evidence.* Vol. 1. London, 1960.

15.396 Subsequent citations:

> 41. *Basle Facility,* 16.
> 42. *First Interim Report.*
> 43. *Royal Commission.*
> 44. Monetary System, *Principal Memoranda.*

15.397 *Statutes.* More often cited in notes or text than in bibliographies, the Acts of Parliament are identified by title (roman type), date (regnal year through 1962, calendar year after 1962), and chapter (c. or cap.) number (arabic for national, roman for local). Monarchs' names in regnal year citations are abbreviated: Car. (Charles), Edw., Eliz., Geo., Hen., Jac. (James), Phil. & M., Rich., Vict., Will., W. & M. The number of the year precedes the name; the monarch's ordinal, if any, follows it (15 Geo. 6); both are arabic. The ampersand may be used between regnal years and between the names of dual monarchs (1 & 2 W. & M.).

> Act of Settlement, 12 & 13 Will. 3, c. 2.
> Consolidated Fund Act, 1963, c. 1.
> Manchester Corporation Act, 1967, c. xl.

The three chief compilations of statutory material for the United Kingdom are the following:

> *Statutes of the Realm.* Statutes of the period 1235–1948, with the exception of the years 1642–60.
> *Acts and Ordinances of the Interregnum,* ed. C. H. Firth and R. S. Rait, 3 vols. (London, 1911). Includes statutes for the years 1642–60.
> *Public General Acts and Measures,* published annually since 1831 by HMSO.

Examples of note citations to the *Statutes of the Realm,* the most commonly cited compilation, follow. Note that in the second example the calendar date is given in addition to the regnal year.

> 45. King's General Pardon, 1540, *Statutes of the Realm,* 32 Hen. 8, c. 49.
> 46. *Statutes of the Realm,* 31 Vict. c. xiv, 2 April 1868.
> *or*
> 46. *Statutes,* 31 Vict. c. xiv, 2 April 1868.

BRITISH FOREIGN AND STATE PAPERS

15.398 Citations to the *British Foreign and State Papers* include the name of the originating agency, the title of the paper, in quotation marks, and (in the note) the volume number and page reference of the *Papers:*

> 47. Foreign Office, "Austria: Proclamation of the Emperor Annulling the Constitution of 4th March 1849," *British Foreign and State Papers,* 1952–53, 41:1289–99.

> United Kingdom. Foreign Office. "Austria: Proclamation of the Emperor Annulling the Constitution of 4th March 1849." *British Foreign and State Papers,* 1952–53.

REPORTS IN PAMPHLET FORM

15.399 Reports issued in pamphlet form by ministries, commissions, committees, and the like are cited as follows:

> 48. Office of the Minister of Science, Committee on Management and Control of Research, *Report,* 1961, 58.

> United Kingdom. Office of the Minister of Science. Committee on Management and Control of Research. *Report,* 1961.

OTHER PUBLISHED RECORDS

15.400 There are many compilations of British historical records, some of which are transcriptions or calendars of the documents preserved in the Public Record Office. Sample note citations and bibliography entries for a few of these sources are given below. Note that abbreviations for the compilations are used in the note citations.

> 49. *Rot. parl.,* vol. 2 (1341) (n.p., n.d.).
> 50. *Statutes,* ed. A. Luders et al., vol. 7 (London, 1821).
> 51. *Acts,* ed. J. R. Dasent, vol. 17 (London, 1899).

> U.K. *Rotuli parliamentorum . . .* (1278–1504). 6 vols. N.p., n.d.
> U.K. *Statutes of the Realm.* Edited by A. Luders et al. 11 vols. London, 1810–28.
> U.K. *Acts of the Privy Council of England.* Edited by J. R. Dasent. 32 vols. London, 1890–1907.

15.401 Although the early records called *Calendar of . . .* are arranged more or less chronologically, some are of irregular duration. It is therefore essential to give the date of the item. Citations to the calendars begin with "Public Record Office" and include the title of the item, in quotation marks; its date; and the italicized title of the calendar (abbreviated in the note), including the reign and followed by the inclusive dates of the calendar, in roman and parentheses. The item number and page reference may be given in the note citation, following the publication facts.

> 52. Public Record Office, "Queen Mother to Queen," 18 February 1581, *Cal. S.P. For., Reign of Elizabeth [I]* (January 1581–April 1582) (London, 1907), no. 85, 63.

> United Kingdom. Public Record Office. "Queen Mother to Queen," 18 February 1581. *Calendar of State Papers, Foreign Series, of the Reign of Elizabeth [I]* (January 1581–April 1582). London, 1907.

UNPUBLISHED DOCUMENTS

15.402   Unpublished government documents are kept in the Public Record Office (PRO, sometimes RO) in London; in the British Library (BL), before 1973 a part of the British Museum (BM); and in local and private libraries. Documents in the Public Record Office are classified by government departments. References to them usually include the abbreviation of the name of the department or collection, the collection number, the volume number, and in notes, the folio (sometimes called page) number(s). Among classifications frequently cited are Admiralty (Adm.), Chancery (C.), Colonial Office (C.O.), Exchequer (E.), Foreign Office (F.O.), and State Papers (S.P.). These abbreviations often appear without periods, for example, CO, FO, SP.

15.403   Collections in the British Library frequently cited are the Cotton Manuscripts, with subdivisions named after Roman emperors (e.g., Cotton MSS, Caligula [Calig.] D.VII), the Harleian Manuscripts, the Sloane Manuscripts, and the Additional Manuscripts (Addit. or Add.).

15.404   Details of citation vary among documents. The following examples illustrate how some may be cited in notes:

> 53. Clarendon to Lumley, 16 Jan. 1869, PRO, FO Belgium/133, no. 6.
> 54. Hodgson to Halifax, 22 Feb. 1752, PRO, CO 137:48.
> 55. [Henry Elsynge], "The moderne forme of the Parliaments of England," BL, Addit. MSS 26645.
> 56. Minutes of the General Court, 17 Apr. 1733, 3:21, BL, Addit. MSS 25545.
> 57. Letter of a Bristol Man, BL, Addit. MSS 33029:152–55.

15.405   Individual documents are usually cited only in text or notes. More general references to collections from which several items are cited in a work may be listed in the bibliography.

> United Kingdom. Public Record Office. Lisle Papers. S.P.3. 18 vols.
> United Kingdom. Patent Rolls, Philip and Mary. C.66/870. London.

15.406 Abbreviations in the above notes are usually spelled out at first appearance unless a list of abbreviations is included (Public Record Office, Foreign Office, Colonial Office, British Library, Additional Manuscripts). Where there are many references to the same collection, the name of the depository need not be repeated in each note. And in works whose readers will be familiar with the collections cited, the depository need not be named. In the following note citation to a manuscript in the Public Record Office, that depository is omitted because it is assumed to be well known to the reader; the citation includes, however, a reference in parentheses to its place in the printed calendar:

> 58. Patent Rolls, 3 Rich. 2, pt. 1, m. 12d (Calendar of Patent Rolls, 1377–81, 470).

Canada

15.407 References to Canadian government publications in notes need not identify the country unless that is not clear from the context. Entries in the bibliography normally begin with the name of the country, unless the entire work has Canada as its subject.

PARLIAMENT AND EXECUTIVE DEPARTMENTS

15.408 Canadian government documents are issued by both houses of the Canadian Parliament (Senate and House of Commons) and by the various executive departments.

> 1. House of Commons, *Debates,* 2 October 1951, 335–37.
> 2. Senate, Special Committee on the Mass Media, *Report,* 3 vols. (Ottawa, 1970), 2:25.
> 3. House of Commons, Standing Committee on External Affairs, *Minutes of Proceedings and Evidence,* no. 4, 24 April 1956, 8–21.
> 4. "Report of the Royal Commission to Enquire into Railways and Transportation in Canada," *Sessional Papers,* 1917, no. 20g, p. xiii.
> 5. Department of External Affairs, *Statements and Speeches,* 53/30, 11 June 1953, 26–31.

> Canada. House of Commons. *Debates,* 2–6 October 1951.
> Canada. Senate. Special Committee on the Mass Media. *Report.* 3 vols. Ottawa, 1970.
> Canada. House of Commons. Standing Committee on External Affairs. *Minutes of Proceedings and Evidence,* no. 4, 24 April 1956.
> Canada. "Report of the Royal Commission to Enquire into Railways and Transportation in Canada." *Sessional Papers,* 1917, no. 20g.

Canada. Department of External Affairs. *Statements and Speeches,* 53/30, 11 June 1953.

STATUTES

15.409 Statutes are published in the *Statutes of Canada* and are identified by both calendar and regnal year and by chapter *(c.)* number.

> 6. *Statutes of Canada,* 1919, 10 Geo. 5, c. 17.
>
> Canada. *Statutes of Canada.* 1919, 10 Geo. 5, c. 17.

UNPUBLISHED RECORDS

15.410 Unpublished records are housed in the Public Archives of Canada (PAC) and are identified by the name of the record group, the series number, and the volume.

> 7. Public Archives of Canada [*or* PAC], Privy Council Office Records, ser. 1, 1477:147–49.
>
> Canada. Public Archives of Canada. Privy Council Office Records. Ser. 1, vol. 1477.

International Bodies

15.411 Citations to publications and documents of international bodies such as the League of Nations and the United Nations should identify the authorizing body, the topic or title of the paper, and the date. When available, the following information should also be included: the series and publication numbers, the place of publication, and a page reference when applicable. For these documents, it is advisable to retain the roman numerals in the publication numbers. The series abbreviation *L.o.N.P.* is standard for "League of Nations Papers."

> 1. League of Nations, *Position of Women of Russian Origin in the Far East,* ser. L.o.N.P., 1935, IV.3.
> 2. League of Nations, *Monetary and Ecomonic Conference: Draft Annotated Agenda Submitted by the Preparatory Commission of Experts,* II, Economic and Financial, 1933, II.Spec.I.
> 3. League of Nations, *International Currency Experience: Lessons of the Inter-war Period* (Geneva, 1944), II.A.4.
> 4. United Nations [*or* UN], Secretariat, Department of Economic Affairs, *Methods of Financing Economic Development in Underdeveloped Countries,* 1951, II.B.2.
> 5. UN General Assembly, Ninth Session, Official Records, Supplement 19, *Special United Nations Fund for Economic Development: Final Report,* prepared by Raymond Scheyven in pursuance of UN General Assembly Resolution 724B (VIII), A/2728, 1954.

6. UNESCO, *The Development of Higher Education in Africa* (Paris, 1963), 145.

7. General Agreement on Tariffs and Trade (GATT), *Agreement on Implementation of Article VI (Anti-dumping Code)* (Geneva, 1969), 14–21.

League of Nations. *Position of Women of Russian Origin in the Far East.* Ser. L.o.N.P. 1935. IV.3.

League of Nations. *Monetary and Economic Conference: Draft Annotated Agenda Submitted by the Preparatory Commission of Experts.* II. Economic and Financial. 1933. II.Spec.I.

League of Nations. *International Currency Experience: Lessons of the Inter-war Period.* Geneva, 1944. II.A.4.

United Nations [*or* UN]. Secretariat. Department of Economic Affairs. *Methods of Financing Economic Development in Underdeveloped Countries.* 1951. II.B.2.

UN General Assembly. Ninth Session. Official Records, Supplement 19. *Special United Nations Fund for Economic Development: Final Report.* Prepared by Raymond Scheyven in pursuance of UN General Assembly Resolution 724B (VIII), A/2728. 1954.

UNESCO. *The Development of Higher Education in Africa.* Paris, 1963.

General Agreement on Tariffs and Trade (GATT). *Agreement on Implementation of Article VI (Anti-dumping Code).* Geneva, 1969.

MUSICAL SCORES

Published

15.412 Documentary notes and bibliography entries for published musical scores follow rules similar to those for books.

1. Giuseppe Verdi, *Rigoletto: Melodrama in Three Acts by Francesco Maria Piave,* ed. Martin Chusid, *The Works of Giuseppe Verdi,* ser. 1, *Operas* (Chicago and London: University of Chicago Press; Milan: G. Ricordi, 1982).

2. Wolfgang Amadeus Mozart, *Sonatas and Fantasies for the Piano,* prepared from the autographs and earliest printed sources by Nathan Broder, rev. ed. (Bryn Mawr, Pa.: Theodore Presser, 1960).

3. Franz Schubert, "Das Wandern (Wandering)," *Die schöne Müllerin (The Maid of the Mill),* in *First Vocal Album* (for high voice) (New York: G. Schirmer, 1895).

Verdi, Giuseppe. *Rigoletto: Melodrama in three acts by Francesco Maria Piave.* Edited by Martin Chusid. *The Works of Giuseppe Verdi.* Ser. 1, *Operas.* Chicago and London: University of Chicago Press; Milan: G. Ricordi, 1982.

Mozart, Wolfgang Amadeus. *Sonatas and Fantasies for the Piano.* Prepared from the autographs and earliest printed sources by Nathan Broder. Rev. ed. Bryn Mawr, Pa.: Theodore Presser, 1960.

Schubert, Franz. "Das Wandern (Wandering)," *Die schöne Müllerin (The Maid of the Mill).* In *First Vocal Album* (for high voice). New York: G. Schirmer, 1895.

In the Schubert work above, the words and titles of the pieces are printed in both German and English.

Unpublished

15.413 Documentation of unpublished musical scores opens with the name of the composer, then gives the title of the work in quotation marks followed by the identification *score,* the date of composition, and the name of the depository, if any.

> 4. Ralph Shapey, "Partita for Violin and Thirteen Players," score, 1966, Special Collections, Joseph Regenstein Library, University of Chicago.

> Shapey, Ralph. "Partita for Violin and Thirteen Players." Score. 1966. Special Collections, Joseph Regenstein Library. University of Chicago.

NONBOOK MATERIALS

Sound Recordings

15.414 Records, tapes, compact discs, and other forms of recorded sound are generally listed under the name of the composer, writer, or other person(s) responsible for the content. Collections or anonymous works are listed by title. The title of a record or album is italicized. If included, the name of the performer usually follows the title, but in some cases—a comparison of the styles of various performers, for example—the citation may begin with the performer's name. The recording company and the number of the recording are usually sufficient to identify the recording, but when desirable, the date of copyright, the kind of recording (stereo, quadraphonic, four-track cassette), the number of records in the album, and so on may be added.

15.415 If the fact that the recording is a sound recording is not implicit in the designation, that information may be added to the citation by such terms as "sound recording," "compact sound disc," "sound cassette" or "audiocassette," and so on, since discs, cassettes, and tapes may be used to record not only sound but pictures and computer programming, including text to be printed.

15.416 In the following examples, note that the names of such musical forms as the symphony and the mass, usually not italicized, are italicized when part of the title of the recording.

> 1. Dmitri Shostakovich, *Symphony no. 5,* New York Philharmonic, Leonard Bernstein, CBS IM 35854.
> *or*

1. Leonard Bernstein, dir., *Symphony no. 5,* by Dmitri Shostakovich, New York Philharmonic, CBS IM 35854.

2. Johann Sebastian Bach, *The Goldberg Variations,* Glenn Gould, CBS IM 37779.

3. Wolfgang Amadeus Mozart, *Mass in C Minor,* Chorus and Academy of St. Martin-in-the-Fields, Neville Marriner, Philips audiocassette 7300 775.

4. Wolfgang Amadeus Mozart, *Symphony no. 38 in D Major,* Vienna Philharmonic, James Levine, Polydor compact disk 423 086–2.

5. Elliott Carter, "Eight Etudes for Woodwind Quintet," on record 1 of *The Chamber Music Society of Lincoln Center,* Classics Record Library SQM 80–5731.

Shostakovich, Dmitri. *Symphony no. 5.* New York Philharmonic. Leonard Bernstein. CBS IM 35854.

or

Bernstein, Leonard, dir. *Symphony no. 5,* by Dmitri Shostakovich. New York Philharmonic. CBS IM 35854.

Bach, Johann Sebastian. *The Goldberg Variations.* Glenn Gould. CBS IM 37779.

Mozart, Wolfgang Amadeus. *Mass in C Minor.* Chorus and Academy of St. Martin-in-the-Fields. Neville Marriner. Philips audiocassette 7300 775.

Mozart, Wolfgang Amadeus. *Symphony no. 38 in D Major.* Vienna Philharmonic. James Levine. Polydor compact disk 423 086–2.

Carter, Elliott. "Eight Etudes for Woodwind Quintet." On record 1 of *The Chamber Music Society of Lincoln Center.* Classics Record Library SQM 80–5731.

15.417 Recordings of drama, prose or poetry readings, lectures, and the like may be cited as follows:

6. *Genesis of a Novel: A Documentary on the Writing Regimen of Georges Simenon* (Tucson, Ariz.: Motivational Programming Corp., 1969), sound cassette.

7. M. J. E. Senn, *Masters and Pupils,* audiotapes of lectures by Lawrence S. Kubie, Jane Loevinger, and M. J. E. Senn presented at meeting of the Society for Research in Child Development, Philadelphia, March 1973 (Chicago: University of Chicago Press, 1974).

8. Dylan Thomas, *Under Milk Wood,* performed by Dylan Thomas and others, Caedmon TC–2005, audiocassette.

9. Dylan Thomas, *Under Milk Wood,* performed by Dylan Thomas and others, Caedmon CDLS–2005, compact disc.

10. Herman Melville, *Moby Dick,* selected readings, Spoken Arts 850, audiocassette.

11. W. H. Auden, *Poems,* read by author, Spoken Arts 7137, compact disc.

Genesis of a Novel: A Documentary on the Writing Regimen of Georges Simenon. Tucson, Ariz.: Motivational Programming Corp., 1969. Sound cassette.

Senn, M. J. E. *Masters and Pupils.* Audiotapes of lectures by Lawrence S. Kubie, Jane Loevinger, and M. J. E. Senn presented at meeting of the

Society for Research in Child Development, Philadelphia, March 1973. Chicago: University of Chicago Press, 1974.

Thomas, Dylan. *Under Milk Wood.* Performed by Dylan Thomas and others. Caedmon TC–2005. Audiocasette.

Thomas, Dylan. *Under Milk Wood.* Performed by Dylan Thomas and others. Caedmon CDLS–2005. Compact disc.

Melville, Herman. *Moby Dick.* Selected readings. Spoken Arts 850. Audiocassette.

Auden, W. H. *Poems.* Read by author. Spoken Arts 7137. Compact disc.

Written material accompanying the recording may be cited as follows:

12. Archie Green, introduction to brochure notes for Glenn Ohrlin, *The Hell-Bound Train,* University of Illinois Campus Folksong Club CFC 301; reissued as Puritan 5009.

Green, Archie. Introduction to brochure notes for Glenn Ohrlin, *The Hell-Bound Train.* University of Illinois Campus Folksong Club CFC 301. Reissued as Puritan 5009.

Videorecordings

15.418 The many varieties of visual (and audiovisual) materials now available render futile any attempt at universal rule making. The nature of the material, its use to the researcher listing it, and the facts necessary to find (retrieve) it should govern the substance of any note or bibliography citation.

SLIDES AND FILMS

15.419   1. Louis J. Mihalyi, *Landscapes of Zambia, Central Africa* (Santa Barbara, Calif.: Visual Education, 1975), slides.

2. *The Greek and Roman World* (Chicago: Society for Visual Education, 1977), filmstrip.

3. *An Incident in Tiananmen Square,* 16 mm, 25 min., Gate of Heaven Films, San Francisco, 1990.

Mihalyi, Louis J. *Landscapes of Zambia, Central Africa.* Santa Barbara, Calif.: Visual Education, 1975. Slides.

The Greek and Roman World. Chicago: Society for Visual Education, 1977. Filmstrip.

An Incident in Tiananmen Square. 16 mm, 25 min. Gate of Heaven Films, San Francisco, 1990.

VIDEOCASSETTES

15.420   4. *Itzak Perlman: In My Case Music,* prod. and dir. Tony DeNonno, 10 min., DeNonno Pix, 1985, videocassette.

Perlman, Itzak. *Itzak Perlman: In My Case Music.* Produced and directed by Tony DeNonno. 10 min. DeNonno Pix, 1985. Videocassette.

MATERIAL OBTAINED THROUGH LOOSE-LEAF, COMPUTER, OR INFORMATION SERVICES

15.421 Documentation of material obtained through such loose-leaf services as the federal tax services published by Commerce Clearing House (CCH) and Prentice-Hall (P-H) is handled similarly to that obtained from books. For some loose-leaf services, paragraph rather than page numbers are given.

> 1. Commerce Clearing House, *1990 Standard Federal Tax Reports* (Chicago: CCH, 1990), ¶20,050.15.

> Commerce Clearing House. *1990 Standard Federal Tax Reports.* Chicago: Commerce Clearing House, 1990.

15.422 References to material obtained through computer services like Dialog and Orbit and through information services like ERIC (Educational Resources Information Center) and NTIS (National Technical Information Service) are treated like first references to original printed material except that the usual information is followed by the name of the service, the name of the vendor providing the service, and the accession or identifying numbers within the service.

> 2. Susan J. Kupisch, "Stepping In," paper presented as part of the symposium Disrupted and Reorganized Families at the annual meeting of the Southeastern Psychological Association, Atlanta, Ga., 23–26 March 1983, Dialog, ERIC, ED 233276.
> 3. Rosabel Flax et al., *Guidelines for Teaching Mathematics K–12* (Topeka: Kansas State Department of Education, Topeka Division of Education Services, June 1979), 85, Dialog, ERIC, ED 178312.
> 4. D. Beevis, "Ergonomist's Role in the Weapon System Development Process in Canada" (Downsview, Ont.: Defence and Civil Institute of Environmental Medicine, 1983), 8, NTIS, AD-A145 5713/2, microfiche.

> Kupisch, Susan J. "Stepping In." Paper presented as part of the symposium Disrupted and Reorganized Families at the annual meeting of the Southeastern Psychological Association, Atlanta, Ga., 23–26 March 1983. DIALOG, ERIC, ED 233276.
> Flax, Rosabel, et al. *Guidelines for Teaching Mathematics K–12.* Topeka: Kansas State Department of Education, Topeka Division of Education Services, June 1979. 85, DIALOG, ERIC, ED 178312.
> Beevis, D. "Ergonomist's Role in the Weapon System Development Process in Canada." Downsview, Ont.: Defence and Civil Institute of Environmental Medicine, 1983. 8, NTIS, AD-A145 5713/2. Microfiche.

COMPUTER PROGRAMS AND ELECTRONIC DOCUMENTS

Programs, or Software

15.423 References to computer programs, packages, languages, systems, and the like, known collectively as software, should in general include the title, usually spelled out, except for such commonly known programs as FORTRAN, BASIC, or COBOL; such identifying detail as version, level, release number, or date; the short name or acronym, where applicable, along with other information necessary for identification, all in parentheses; and the location and name of the person, company, or organization having the property rights to the software. The author's name may also be mentioned if it is important for identification.

> 1. FORTRAN H-extended Version [*or* Ver.] 2.3, IBM, White Plains, N.Y.
> 2. Houston Automatic Spooling Priority II Ver. 4.0, IBM, White Plains, N.Y.
> 3. International Mathematical Subroutine Library Edition 8 (IMSL 8), International Mathematical Subroutine Library, Inc., Houston, Tex.
> 4. Operating System/Virtual Storage Rel. 1.7 (OS/VS 1.7), IBM, White Plains, N.Y.
> 5. Statistical Package for the Social Sciences Level M Ver. 8 (SPSS Lev. M 8.1), SPSS, Chicago.
> 6. Lotus 1–2–3 Rel. 2, Lotus Development Corporation, Cambridge, Mass.

> FORTRAN H-extended Version [*or* Ver.] 2.3. IBM, White Plains, N.Y.
> Houston Automatic Spooling Priority II Ver. 4.0. IBM, White Plains, N.Y.
> International Mathematical Subroutine Library Edition 8 (IMSL 8). International Mathematical Subroutine Library, Inc., Houston, Tex.
> Operating System/Virtual Storage Rel. 1.7 (OS/VS 1.7). IBM, White Plains, N.Y.
> Statistical Package for the Social Sciences Level M Ver. 8 (SPSS Lev. M 8.1). SPSS, Chicago.
> Lotus 1–2–3 Rel. 2. Lotus Development Corporation, Cambridge, Mass.

Documents

15.424 The proliferation of documents created, stored, and disseminated on computer systems and the burgeoning requirement to cite such documents introduces a need to specify standards for citing such material. The International Standards Organization (ISO) has endeavored to construct, and continues to modify, a uniform system of citing electronic documents. The ISO documentation system, to which the University of Chicago Press subscribes, stresses consistency but allows discretion in the choice of punctuation used to separate elements and in the use of variations in typeface or underscoring to distinguish or highlight certain elements. The ISO recommends that capitalization follow the "accepted practice for the language or script in which the information is given." Although examples are offered below in illustration of the adaptation by the University of Chicago Press of the proposed style, the reader is urged to obtain the latest recommendations of the ISO for a more comprehensive treatment of this exceedingly complex, fluid, and rapidly expanding field of source material.[3]

1. "Acquired Immunodeficiency Syndrome," in MESH vocabulary file [database online] (Bethesda, Md.: National Library of Medicine, 1990 [cited 3 October 1990]), identifier no. D000163 [49 lines].

2. *Belle de jour,* in Magill's Survey of the Cinema [database online] (Pasadena, Calif.: Salem Press, ca. 1989– [cited 1 January 1990]), accession no. 50053, p. 2 of 4; available from DIALOG Information Services, Inc., Palo Alto, Calif.

3. Stephanie R. Peters and Neil C. Silverstein, "Predicting Success in Graduate School," paper presented at the annual meeting of the American Educational Research Association, Seattle, Wash., 21–24 April 1995 [database on-line]; available from DIALOG, ERIC, ED 685923.

4. "Jericho's Walls," in History Log9008 [electronic bulletin board], s.l. 27 August 1990– [cited 15 December 1990]; available from listserv @ FINHUTC.BITNET.

5. Stan Kulikowski, "Readability Formula," in NL-KR (Digest vol. 5, no. 10) [electronic bulletin board] (Rochester, N.Y., 1988 [cited 31 January 1989]); available from nl-kr @ cs.rochester.edu; INTERNET.

"Acquired Immunodeficiency Syndrome." In MESH vocabulary file [database online]. Bethesda, Md.: National Library of Medicine, 1990 [cited 3 October 1990]. Identifier no. D000163. [49 lines.]

Belle de jour. In Magill's Survey of the Cinema [database online]. Pasadena, Calif.: Salem Press, ca. 1989– [cited 1 January 1990]. Accession no. 50053. P. 2 of 4. Available from DIALOG Information Services, Inc., Palo Alto, Calif.

Peters, Stephanie R., and Neil C. Silverstein. "Predicting Success in Graduate School." Paper presented at the annual meeting of the American Educational Research Association, Seattle, Wash., 21–24 April 1995. Database on-line. Available from DIALOG, ERIC, ED 685923.

"Jericho's Walls." In History Log9008 [electronic bulletin board]. S.l. 27 August 1990– [cited 15 December 1990]. Available from listserv @ FINHUTC.BITNET.

---

3. Information on citations to electronic documents may be requested from the ISO at the following address:
ISO TC46/SC 9
Secretariat: Office of Library Standards
National Library of Canada
Ottawa K1A 0N4
Canada

Kulikowski, Stan. "Readability Formula." In NL-KR (Digest vol. 5, no. 10) [electronic bulletin board]. Rochester, N.Y., 1988 [cited 31 January 1989]. Available from nl-kr @ cs.rochester.edu; INTERNET.

CITATIONS TAKEN FROM SECONDARY SOURCES

15.425 References to the work of one author as quoted in that of another must cite both works:

> 1. Louis Zukofsky, "Sincerity and Objectification," *Poetry* 37 (February 1931): 269, quoted in Bonnie Costello, *Marianne Moore: Imaginary Possessions* (Cambridge: Harvard University Press, 1981), 78.

If the purpose of such a reference is to emphasize the secondary author's quoting of the original work, the following style should be used:

> 2. Bonnie Costello, *Marianne Moore: Imaginary Possessions* (Cambridge: Harvard University Press, 1981), 78, quoting Louis Zukofsky, "Sincerity and Objectification," *Poetry* 37 (February 1931): 269.

15.426 In the bibliography entry, the first-mentioned work is cited in the usual style, with the elements separated by periods. If the work is a book, the page reference immediately follows the title, separated from it by a comma. The work mentioned second is treated as a unit, with the elements separated by commas and, in the case of a book, the facts of publication enclosed in parentheses. The name of the author of the second work is presented in normal order.

> Zukofsky, Louis. "Sincerity and Objectification." *Poetry* 37 (February 1931): 269. Quoted in Bonnie Costello, *Marianne Moore: Imaginary Possessions* (Cambridge: Harvard University Press, 1981), 78.
> *or*
> Costello, Bonnie. *Marianne Moore: Imaginary Possessions,* 78. Cambridge: Harvard University Press, 1981. Quoting Louis Zukofsky, "Sincerity and Objectification," *Poetry* 37 (February 1931): 269.

When the quoting work is the primary reference, as in the second example above, page citations should be omitted if there is additional discussion of that work, or if there are citations to other parts of it.

16 Documentation 2
Author-Date Citations and
Reference Lists

INTRODUCTION

16.1   The system of documentation generally most economical in space, in time (for author, editor, and typesetter), and in cost (to publisher and public)—in short, the most practical—is the author-date system. The University of Chicago Press strongly recommends this system of doc-

In the preparation of this chapter, some material has been adapted from *A Manual for Writers of Term Papers, Theses, and Dissertations,* by Kate L. Turabian, revised and expanded for the fifth edition by Bonnie Birtwistle Honigsblum, © 1987 by The University of Chicago.

umentation for all its publications in the natural sciences and most of those in the social sciences. Authors in other fields who are willing to adapt their documentation to this system, and whose documentation is amenable to such adaptation, are encouraged to do so.

16.2   The author-date system of documentation comprises two indispensable parts: the text citation, usually enclosed in parentheses, and the list of sources cited, often called the reference list. Unlike the humanities style of documentation, in which full bibliographic information may be given in both notes and bibliography, the author-date system provides brief identifying information in the text citation and reserves full documentation for the list of references.

Author-Date Text Citations

BASIC FORM

16.3   The basic form of the author-date citation in running text or at the end of a block quotation consists of the author's last, or family, name and the year of publication of the work. In this context, "author" means the name under which the work is alphabetized in the list of references and may thus refer to an editor, compiler, or organization as well as to a single author or to multiple authors. The abbreviations *ed.* and *comp.* are not included in the text reference, but they do appear in the reference list entry. No punctuation is used between the author's name and the date in the text citation. Where the reference list includes two or more works by different authors with the same last name and the same date, it is necessary to include the authors' initials in the text citations.

> (Blinksworth 1987)
> (Collins and Wortmaster 1953)
> (EPA 1986)
> (P. Brown 1991)

16.4   Reference list entries providing complete information for the author-date citations given above might be as follows:

> Blinksworth, Roger. 1987. *Converging on the evanescent.* San Francisco: Threshold Publications.
> Collins, Geoffry, and Matthew Q. Wortmaster, eds. 1953. *The collected works of G. Farthington Pennyloss.* Boston: G. F. Pennyloss.
> Environmental Protection Agency (EPA). 1986. *Toxicology handbook.* Rockville, Md.: Government Institutes.

TWO OR THREE AUTHORS

16.5   For works by two or three authors, all names are included (use *and,* not an ampersand):

(Finburn and Cosby 1990)
(Smith, Wessen, and Gunless 1988)

16.6 In a reference to a work by two family members with the same last name, the name is repeated:

(Weinberg and Weinberg 1980)

The plural of the name may be used in the text when the reference is to the persons rather than the work:

The Weinbergs (1980) maintain that Darrow . . .

MORE THAN THREE AUTHORS

16.7 For more than three authors, use the name of the first author followed by *et al.* or *and others*. Thus, for a work by Zipursky, Hull, White, and Israels:

(Zipursky et al. 1959)

If, as sometimes happens, there is another work *of the same date* that would also abbreviate to "Zipursky et al."—say, a paper by Zipursky, Smith, Jones, and Brown—one must give either the group of names in full or a short title identifying the work cited:

(Zipursky, Smith, Jones, and Brown 1958)
 or
(Zipursky et al., *Brief notes,* 1958)

Another method sometimes used to distinguish such works is to cite the first *two* names followed by et al.:

(Zipursky, Hull, et al. 1958)
(Zipursky, Smith, et al. 1958)

GROUP AS AUTHOR

16.8 When a book or pamphlet bears no author's name on the title page and is published or sponsored by a corporation, government agency, association, or other group, the name of that group may serve as the author in text references and the reference list. Most of these names present no problem and may be used in full:

(International Rice Research Institute 1977)
(Federal Reserve Bank of Boston 1976)

Because of the length or complexity of some group names, text citations to the groups should carry shortened versions. In that case, care must be taken to select a shortened version that agrees with the opening portion of the entry in the reference list. For a discussion of such shortened citations see 16.53–54.

16.9 Government agencies as authors present special and frequent problems in citations because of the length of their names. No body of rules could be drawn up to solve all such problems; citation forms must often be devised ad hoc by author, or editor, using common sense and a regard for the reader's convenience. The same form, once decided upon, must be used for all references to that work throughout a book or article.

PAGE OR OTHER SPECIFIC REFERENCE

16.10 A specific page, section, figure, equation, or other division or element of the cited work follows the date and is preceded by a comma (for treatment of inclusive numbers see 8.68–73). (A colon rather than a comma is sometimes used between date and page number, but the University of Chicago Press prefers the comma, reserving the colon for use in separating volume and page numbers; see 16.12.) Unless confusion would result, the abbreviation for *page* or *pages* is omitted. Abbreviations for other elements or divisions should be included.

> (Blindsworth 1987, 125)
> (Foley 1955, 23, 43, 46–51)
> (Klein 1987, sec. 13.5)
> (Watkins, Brice, and Tissont 1967, fig. 5)
> (Filbert and Arezzo 1975, 146, eq. 24)
> (Foley 1955, app. A)
> (McAndrew 1989, 246 n. 4)

If a reference to a figure, equation, note, or similar item is accompanied by a page reference, the page number is given first.

16.11 When several references to the same page or pages in the same source are made in a single paragraph of text, only one parenthetical author-date citation need be made in that paragraph, at either the first or the last reference. If references to different pages of the same source occur in a single paragraph, the first citation should include author and date, but subsequent citations need include only the page.

VOLUME AND PAGE NUMBER

16.12 When reference to both volume and page number is required, a colon will distinguish between them, and the abbreviations *vol.* and *p.* or *pp.* are omitted:

> (Wazinski 1989, 3:114)

If more than one volume of the author's work is referred to in the same reference, the volumes are separated by commas:

> (García 1987, 2:168, 3:119–23)

16.13 A reference to a volume as a whole, without page number, requires *vol.* for clarity:

> (García 1987, vol. 2)

MULTIPLE REFERENCES

16.14 When two or more references are given together in one parenthetical citation, they are separated by semicolons:

> (Light 1972; Light and Wong 1975; Rooster 1976)
> (Whipsmith 1988, 34; Larisch 1987, 2:150; Ohmstead 1990, 28)

Additional works by the same author are indicated in the citation by date only, the dates being separated by commas. If two or more of the works by a single author or team of authors have the same date of publication, however, additional alphabetical identifiers must be given. (See also 16.27.)

> (García 1941, 1944)
> (Keller 1896a, 1896b, 1907) *or* (Keller 1896a,b, 1907)
> (Knight and Belinski 1987a, 1987b)

When page numbers are given, the references must be separated by semicolons:

> (García 1941, 45–49; 1944, 105)

The order in which multiple references are given is determined by the author who cites them. Editorial rearranging in alphabetical or chronological order without consulting with the author is not recommended.

PLACEMENT OF TEXT CITATIONS

16.15 For ease of reading, an author-date citation in the text should be placed where it will offer the least resistance to the flow of thought. The best location is just before a mark of punctuation:

> Before proceeding with a more detailed discussion of our methods of analysis, we will describe the system of scaling quantitative scores (Guilford 1950).

> What conclusions might they have reached, one wonders, had they been aware of the narrow-aperture principle recently reported (Klein, Cane, and Abbelli 1991)?

If this placement is impractical or confusing, the reference should be inserted at a logical place in the sentence:

> Some investigators (Jones and Carter 1980) have reported findings at variance with the foregoing.

Occasions will arise when all or part of the citation is incorporated in the text. In the example below, the incorporated phrases "in Hudson 1976b" and "in Stockwell, Schachter, and Partee 1973" refer to the works of the authors; the dates as well as the names are part of the incorporation and should not be enclosed in parentheses. "Carter and Jones," however, refers to the authors themselves, and the date of their relevant work is parenthetical. When only the date is parenthetical, it should nevertheless be placed at the grammatically logical position that is closest to the author's name (see also the example in 16.17).

> Jones and Carter (1980) report findings at variance with the foregoing. All I can do is present the daughter-dependency equivalent of the transformational analysis that I advocate in Hudson 1976b. In this paper I argue for an analysis very similar in spirit to the one in Stockwell, Schachter, and Partee 1973, in which the result . . .

AGREEMENT OF CITATION AND REFERENCE

16.16   Care should be taken to ensure that author-date citations in the text agree exactly with corresponding entries in the list of references and that all of the facts are accurate. Accuracy and agreement are the responsibility of the author, but agreement should also be verified by the editor. Discrepancies in the spelling of names or the dates of publication must be rectified before the manuscript is sent to the typesetter. Specific pages included in citations to articles in periodicals or to chapters in edited volumes should be checked to make sure they fall within the span of pages given for the article or chapter in the reference list.

AUTHOR-DATE SYSTEM WITH NOTES

16.17   When explanation or amplification is needed in addition to source documentation, the author may wish to employ footnotes or endnotes as a supplement to author-date documentation. If such substantive notes also contain source citations, the citations should be in the author-date style:

> 1. This notion seems to have something in common with Piaget's concept (1977) of nonbalance and equilibrium in the area of knowledge.

Reference Lists

16.18   To complete the brief form of the text citations that it employs, the author-date system requires a detailed list of sources in which full bibliographic information is given. Such a list of sources may be called Works Cited, Literature Cited, Sources Cited, or simply References. All sources cited in the text must be included in the reference list.

16.19   Reference lists are best placed at the end of the work; in books, just before the index. If there are appendixes or endnotes, these should come before the list of references. Separate lists are sometimes placed at the ends of the chapters to which they apply—in textbooks, for example, and in books whose chapters are contributed by different authors, especially when there are to be chapter offprints.

16.20   The information provided in reference list entries is the same as that provided in bibliographies, and the segments containing that information are, as in bibliography entries, separated by periods. A comparison of the systems was made in 15.69–74, and the reader may wish to review that discussion before proceeding further. A brief summary of the differences between the two systems, however, is provided in the following paragraphs.

DATES: AN ESSENTIAL DIFFERENCE

16.21   The essential difference between reference list and bibliography entries is that in reference lists the year of publication immediately follows the author's name, thus reflecting the content of the text citation and facilitating location of the entry. Other differences in style occur, as outlined below, but they are by no means essential or universally followed.

AUTHORS' NAMES

16.22   In the author-date reference list entry, the author's given name, even if it appears in full on the title page, is sometimes abbreviated; that is, initials are used for first names or for both first and middle names. This distinction is not rigidly followed, however; authors' names may also be given in the form in which they appear on the title page of the work, as they customarily are in bibliographies. Many readers prefer the more helpful practice of providing full given names, and the University of Chicago Press strongly encourages this practice (see also 15.81–82).

TITLES

16.23   Ordinarily titles of books, periodicals, long poems, and so on are italicized, as they are in bibliography style; titles of chapters, articles, short poems, and the like are given in roman type but are *not* enclosed in quotation marks. Titles of periodicals are capitalized in regular title, or headline, style. They are more likely to be abbreviated in reference lists than in bibliographies. All other titles in reference lists are capitalized in the *down,* or sentence, style; that is, only the first word in the title and subtitle and all proper nouns and proper adjectives are capitalized. (See figs. 16.1, 16.2.) This capitalization distinction, however, is not always observed. Titles of works of whatever length are sometimes,

Literature Cited

Alexander, R. D. 1974. The evolution of social behavior. *Ann. Rev. Ecol. Syst.* 5:324–83.

Allen, G. M. 1939. *Bats.* Cambridge: Harvard University Press.

Altmann, J. 1974. Observational study of behavior: Sampling methods. *Behavior* 49:227–65.

Anthony, E. L. P., and T. H. Kunz. 1977. Feeding strategies of the little brown bat, *Myotis lucifugus,* in southern New Hampshire. *Ecology* 58:775–86.

Anthony, E. L. P., M. H. Stack, and T. H. Kunz. 1981. Night roosting and the nocturnal time budget of the little brown bat, *Myotis lucifugus:* Effects of reproductive status, prey density, and environmental conditions. *Oecologia* 51:151–56.

Arata, A. A., and C. Jones. 1967. Homeothermy in *Carollia* (Phyllostomatidae: Chiroptera) and the adaptation of poikilothermy in insectivorous northern bats. *Lozania* 14:1–10.

Arata, A. A., J. B. Vaughn, and M. E. Thomas. 1967. Food habits of certain Colombian bats. *J. Mammal.* 48:653–55.

Armitage, K. B., and D. W. Johns. 1982. Kinship, reproductive strategies, and social dynamics of yellow-bellied marmots. *Behav. Ecol. Sociobiol.* 11:55–63.

Arnold, M. L., R. L. Honeycutt, R. J. Baker, V. M. Sarich, and J. K. Jones, Jr. 1982. Resolving a phylogeny with multiple data sets: A systematic study of phyllostomid bats. *Occas. Pap. Museum, Texas Tech Univ.* 77:1–15.

August, P. V. 1979. Distress calls in *Artibeus jamaicensis:* Ecology and evolutionary implications. In *Vertebrate ecology in the northern Neotropics,* ed. J. F. Eisenberg, 151–59. Washington, D.C.: Smithsonian Institution Press.

————. 1981. Fig consumption and seed dispersal by *Artibeus jamaicensis* in the llanos of Venezuela. *Biotropica (Reprod. Bot. Suppl.)* 13:70–76.

Ayala, S. C., and A. D'Alessandro. 1973. Insect feeding behavior of some Colombian fruit-eating bats. *J. Mammal.* 54:266–67.

Baker, H. G. 1972. Seed weight in relation to environmental conditions in California. *Ecology* 53:997–1010.

Baker, H. G., and I. Baker. 1981. Floral nectar constituents in relation to pollinator type. In *Handbook of experimental pollination biology,* ed. C. E. Jones and R. J. Little, 243–64. New York: Van Nostrand-Reinhold.

Baker, H. G., K. S. Bawa, G. W. Frankie, and P. A. Opler. 1983. Reproductive biology of plants in tropical forests. In *Tropical rain forest ecosystems,* ed. F. G. Golley, 183–215. Amsterdam: Elsevier.

Baker, J. R., and Z. Baker. 1936. The seasons in a tropical rain forest (New Hebrides). 2. Fruit bats (Pteropidae). *J. Linn. Soc. London* 40:123–41.

Fig. 16.1. Opening page of a reference list, here titled "Literature Cited." The list illustrates alphabetical arrangement, location of dates, consistent use of authors' initials, and treatment of various kinds of titles. In this case journal titles are abbreviated.

References

McCourt, Kathleen. 1977. *Working Class Women and Grass-Roots Politics.* Bloomington: Indiana University Press.

Macdonald, Dwight. 1970. "Introduction." Pp. xi–xxiv in *The Tales of Hoffman,* ed. M. Levine, G. McNamee, and D. Greenberg. New York: Bantam Books.

Mailer, Norman. 1968. *Miami and the Siege of Chicago.* New York: World.

Mamet, David. 1984. *Glengarry Glenn Ross.* New York: Grove Press.

Marciniak, Edward. 1981. *Reversing Urban Decline: The Winthrop-Kenmore Corridor in the Edgewater and Uptown Communities of Chicago.* Washington, D.C.: National Center for Urban Ethnic Affairs.

———. 1986. *Reclaiming the Inner City: Chicago's Near North Revitalization Confronts Cabrini-Green.* Washington, D.C.: National Center for Urban Ethnic Affairs.

Marciniak, Edward, and Nancy Jefferson. 1985. "CHA Advisory Committee Appointed by Judge Marvin E. Aspin: Final Report" (December). Chicago. Unpublished.

Mark, Norman. 1979. *Mayors, Madams, and Madmen.* Chicago: Chicago Review Press.

Masotti, Louis, and Samuel Gove, eds. 1982. *After Daley.* Urbana: University of Illinois Press.

Masters, Edgar Lee. 1933. *The Tale of Chicago.* New York: Putnam's.

Mayer, Harold. 1955. *Chicago: City of Decisions.* Chicago: Geographic Society of Chicago.

Mayer, Harold, and Richard C. Wade. 1969. *Chicago: Growth of a Metropolis.* Chicago: University of Chicago Press.

Mayor's Council of Manpower and Economic Advisors. 1977. *Chicago's Economy on the Move.* Chicago: City of Chicago.

Mead, George Herbert. 1934. *The Social Psychology of George Herbert Mead.* Chicago: University of Chicago Press.

Meeker, Arthur. 1949. *Prairie Avenue.* New York: Knopf.

Mencken, H. L. 1917. Untitled article. *Chicago Tribune* (28 October).

Metropolitan Housing and Planning Council. 1982. *Map 2000: Metropolitan Area Plan for the Year 2000.* Chicago: Metropolitan Housing and Planning Council.

Molotch, Harvey. 1976. "The City as a Growth Machine." *American Journal of Sociology* 82 (September): 50–65.

Muller, Chandra. 1983. "Resource Dependency in Community Based Organizations." Master's thesis, Department of Sociology, University of Chicago.

Myerson, Martin, and Edward C. Banfield. 1955. *Politics, Planning and the Public Interest: The Case of Public Housing in Chicago.* Glencoe, Ill.: Free Press.

Neil, Andrew. 1980. "Chicago through British Eyes." *Economist* (Spring). (Republished in the *Chicago Tribune,* 6 April 1980.)

Newman, Oscar. 1973. *Defensible Space: Crime Prevention through Urban Design.* New York: Macmillan.

Nord, David Paul. 1985. "The Public Community: The Urbanization of Journalism in Chicago." *Journal of Urban History* 11 (August): 411–41.

Fig. 16.2. Page from a list of references in the field of sociology, showing authors' names and all titles in the usual humanities style, including full titles for journals. Note, however, that the dates immediately follow the authors' names.

in the author-date system, uniformly capitalized headline style. Whatever style is selected must be followed consistently throughout a work.

16.24   Subtitles of both long and short works are often omitted from reference lists. In one severely concise reference style, used in some scientific journals, not only are journal titles abbreviated, but article titles are omitted altogether. In this style also, italics are dispensed with for book and journal titles. The preference of the University of Chicago Press is to include full given names, full titles, and full publication facts.

VARIATIONS

16.25   So long as a documentary style is clear, effective, and consistently followed, variations and combinations of the basic styles outlined in this manual may be considered acceptable alternatives.

ARRANGEMENT OF ENTRIES

16.26   When the author-date system of documentation is used, the reader is best served by references arranged in a single alphabetical list. There is rarely a need to divide the list into sections; to do so may complicate location. The rules for alphabetizing an index (17.97–131) obtain also in alphabetizing a reference list. Special problems may be resolved by observing the following principles:

> 1. A single-author entry comes before a multiauthor entry beginning with the same name.

> Ramos, Frank P. 1990. Deconstructing the deconstructionists. *Eolian Quarterly* 11 (spring): 41–58.
> Ramos, Frank P., John R. Wizmont, and Clint T. O'Finnery. 1987. *Texts and nontexts.* Philadelphia: Whynot Press.

> 2. All works attributed to one author, editor, translator, or compiler should be listed together in chronological order. The chronological arrangement facilitates location from the author-date citation. (For differentiating among works written, edited, translated, or compiled by the same person or persons see 16.28–29.)

> Alcazar, W. C., ed. 1966. *Microphysiology: New frontiers.* Seattle: Warburton.
> ———. 1967. Dysfunction in pseudopodia. *Bacteriological Quarterly* 17 (winter): 16–21.

16.27   Two or more works by the same author or authors published in the same year are distinguished by roman letters, in alphabetical sequence, following the date without intervening space. The works published in one year are alphabetized by title:

Langston, W., Jr., 1965a. Fossil crocodilians from Colombia and the Cenozoic history of the Crocodilia in South America. *Univ. Calif. Publ. Geol. Sci.* 52:1–157.

————. 1965b. *Oedaleops campi* (Reptilia: Pelycosauria): A new genus and species from the Lower Permian of New Mexico, and the family Eothyrididae. *Bull. Tex. Mem. Mus.* 9:1–47.

THREE-EM DASH FOR REPEATED NAMES

16.28 As in bibliographies (see 15.66–68), the 3-em dash replaces the name of the author, editor, compiler, or translator for successive works attributable to the same person. If another author, editor, compiler, or translator is added, however, the original author's name must be repeated:

Fontanelle, Eric C. 1944. *Preparing for the postwar period.* Columbus, Ohio: W. C. Cartwright and Daughters.

————. 1952. *What really happened when the war ended.* Cleveland: Chagrin Valley Press.

Fontanelle, Eric C., and Valerie Mandible. 1951. Iron despair: Postwar bewilderment. *World Spectator,* 6 April.

Whenever the role of the named person changes (from author to editor or translator, for example), any entries involved are placed after all of the authored works, and whatever new categories are added are arranged in alphabetical sequence—compiled, edited, translated:

Fontanelle, Eric C. 1944. *Preparing for the postwar period.* Columbus, Ohio: W. C. Cartwright and Daughters.

————. 1952. *What really happened when the war ended.* Cleveland: Chagrin Valley Press.

————, comp. 1958. *Prognoses for the Middle East.* Boston: Whipple and Yardley.

————, ed. 1951. *Speculations grand and noble.* Chicago: Tintern Press.

————. 1962. *Mediterranean questions.* Boston: Whipple and Yardley.

16.29 A single 3-em dash may also be used to stand for a group of authors responsible for successive works, provided the authors are given in the same order for each work. The dash may be similarly used for two or more compilers, editors, or translators.

Fredermeyer, Isabelle T., and Terence Maus. 1959. *The Anti-Nazi underground in Berlin.* Lincoln, Neb.: Wattskeld.

————. 1964. Postwar bewilderment and postwar terror. *World Spectator,* 11 November.

————, eds. 1976. *Speculations on the changing nature of the cold war.* Lincoln, Neb.: Wattskeld and Daughter.

————. 1992. *Sequelae to the end of the cold war.* Tulsa: Oklahoma Group.

————, trans. 1989. *Husinga Drinkhaven and the European question.* Seattle: Blinknagen and Klinglemeyer.

Fratanelli, Dominic, Agnes Andersen, and Homer Tristofelli, eds. 1991. *Policies for world order after the cold war.* Atlanta: Myerdahl Press.

Framson, George W.
   1978   The problem of disintegrated confabulations. *Am. J. Soc.* 8:28–37.
   1981   *Fabulous confabulations.* Denver: Press of the Great Divide.
   1989   Calculations modest and spectacular. *Am. J. Soc.* 19:123–31.
———, ed.
   1982   *Casterfield study of microconfabulations.* Boulder, Colo.: Boulderado
        Press.
Furmor, Cedric T., trans.
   1992   *Experimental programs in unburdening.* Atlanta: Willmont and Jorgen-
        son.

Fig. 16.3. Portion of a reference list illustrating form used when many works by single authors or groups of authors are cited. Note the way edited and translated works are handled.

Fratanelli, Dominic, Homer Tristofelli, and Agnes Andersen, eds. 1988. *Hydra-headed threat to world peace.* Atlanta: Myerdahl Press.

16.30   A dash may also be used for institutional or corporate authors, as in a bibliography. The dash stands for as much of the name as is the same:

U.S. Senate. Committee on Foreign Relations. 1919–20. *Investigation of Mexican affairs.* 2 vols. 66th Cong., 2d sess.
———. Committee on Public Lands. 1917. *Leasing of oil lands.* 65th Cong., 1st sess.
———. *Leases upon naval oil reserves.* 1924. 68th Cong., 1st sess.

In the second entry above, the dash stands for "U.S. Senate." In the third it stands for "U.S. Senate. Committee on Public Lands."

16.31   When a reference list has a preponderance of dashes, one might consider the alternative arrangement illustrated in figure 16.3.

BOOKS

Information to Be Included and the Order of Elements

16.32   The list of information to be included in full documentary notes and bibliography entries (15.77) applies also to reference list entries, except that the position of the publication date is changed. In reference lists, the date immediately follows the author's name.

Author

16.33   In reference list entries, authors' names should be given as they appear on the title pages of their books, except that, especially in scientific works, initials often replace first and middle names, even when the full forms appear on the title page. (Note that space is added between initials; see 7.6.) Whether one elects to present all names exactly as they appear on the title page, to use initials for given names, or to use full given names, one should observe consistency as far as possible, unless authors' preferences require variation.

16.34 Degrees and affiliations following names are normally omitted—except *M.D.* for an author of a medical work. If an author's name appears in another entry as a coauthor, editor, compiler, or such, it should appear in consistent form (see also 15.81).

ONE AUTHOR

16.35 In the reference list, where entries are arranged alphabetically by authors' last names, the name is inverted, last name first (see also 15.83):

> Barbour, Ian. 1974. *Myths, models, and paradigms: A comparative study in science and religion.* New York: Harper and Row.
> Woodthrush, Julian R. 1985. *Birdsong and mating behavior.* New Haven, Conn.: George and Lilian Fromson.

TWO AUTHORS

16.36 In the reference list the name of the first author is inverted, that of the second is given in its natural order, and the conjunction is preceded by a comma (see also 15.85):

> Unwin, Liam P., and Joseph Galway. 1984. *Calm in Ireland.* Boston: Stronghope Press.
> Weinberg, Arthur, and Lila Weinberg. 1980. *Clarence Darrow: A sentimental rebel.* New York: Putnam's Sons.

THREE AUTHORS

16.37 See discussion at 15.86.

> Brett, P. D., S. W. Johnson, and C. R. T. Bach. 1989. *Mastering string quartets.* San Francisco: Amati Press.
> *or*
> Brett, P. D.; S. W. Johnson; and C. R. T. Bach. 1989. *Mastering string quartets.* San Francisco: Amati Press.
> Merk, Jane S., Ida J. Fogg, and Charles A. Snowe. 1987. *Astrology for the beginning meteorologist.* Chicago: Darkweather and Clere.

MORE THAN THREE AUTHORS

16.38 When referring to a work by more than three authors, the text citation should give the last name of the first author followed by *et al.* or *and* *others* without intervening punctuation. In the reference list entry, however, it is customary to give all of the authors, in the order in which they appear on the title page.

(Sanders et al. 1989)

Sanders, G. S., T. R. Brice, V. L. deSantis, and C. C. Ryder. 1989. *Prediction and prevention of famine*. Los Angeles: Timothy Peters.

AUTHOR'S NAME IN TITLE

16.39 When an author's name appears in the title of the work cited, such as an autobiography, a collection of letters, or the complete works of that author, both the text citation and the reference list entry should begin with that author's name, even if the title page does not list the author as an author.

(Adams 1918)
(DeLor 1991)

Adams, Henry. 1918. *The education of Henry Adams: An autobiography*. Boston: Houghton Mifflin.
DeLor, Elizabeth. 1991. *The complete poems of Elizabeth DeLor*. Chicago: Seraphim.

ANONYMOUS WORKS

16.40 If the authorship of a work is known but not revealed on the title page, the name is given in brackets:

[Doe, Jane]. 1948. *The burden of anonymity*. Nowhere: Nonesuch Press.

If the identity of the author is merely surmised, a question mark follows the name before the closing bracket:

[Doe, Jane?]. 1948. *The burden of anonymity*. Nowhere: Nonesuch Press.

The text citation in both cases should give the name in brackets. In the latter case a question mark may be included if desired.

([Doe] 1948)   ([Doe?] 1948)

16.41 If the name of the author is unascertainable, the reference entry should begin with the title of the work. The use of *Anonymous* or *Anon.* is to be avoided. The date, in this case, follows the title.

The burden of anonymity. 1948. Nowhere: Nonesuch Press.

In alphabetizing the entry, the initial article is discounted. The article may be transposed to the end of the title, following a comma:

Burden of anonymity, The.

The text reference for such an entry may substitute the title, or a short-ened version of the title, for the author (see 15.252):

> (*Burden of anonymity* 1948)   *or*   (*Burden* 1948)

DESCRIPTIVE PHRASE AS "AUTHOR"

16.42   See discussion at 15.92.

> (Cotton Manufacturer 1869)

> Cotton Manufacturer. 1869. *An inquiry into the causes of the present long-continued depression in the cotton trade, with suggestions for its im-provement.* Bury.
> *or*
> A Cotton Manufacturer. 1869. *An inquiry* . . . [alphabetized under *C*]

PSEUDONYM

16.43   A pseudonym is generally treated in both text citation and reference list as if it were the author's name, unless the sense of the text demands the real name. If known, the real name may follow the pseudonym in brackets in the reference list, but this is not necessary if the pseudonym is well known.

> (Eliot 1977)
> (Le Carré 1982)

> Eliot, George. 1977. *Middlemarch.* Norton Critical Editions. New York: W. W. Norton.
> Le Carré, John [David John Moore Cornwell]. 1982. *The quest for Karla.* New York: Knopf.
> *or*
> Le Carré, John. 1982. *The quest* . . .

16.44   If the author's real name is better known than the pseudonym, the for-mer should be used in both text citation and reference list. The pseu-donym may, but need not, be included in brackets in the reference list.

> (Brontë 1847)

> Brontë, Charlotte [Currer Bell, pseud.]. 1847. *Jane Eyre.* London.
> *or simply*
> Brontë, Charlotte. 1847. *Jane Eyre.* London.

16.45   If the author's real name is not known, the pseudonym may be followed by *pseud.* in brackets in the reference list.

> (Quester 1946)

> Quester, Jack [pseud.]. 1946. *Searching for the real Shakespeare.* London: Grieff Publications.

EDITOR, COMPILER, OR TRANSLATOR

16.46   The name of the editor, compiler, or translator takes the place of the author when no author is listed on the title page. In the reference list, the abbreviation *ed./eds., comp./comps.,* or *trans.* follows the name and is preceded by a comma:

> Wiley, Bell I., ed. 1980. *Slaves no more: Letters from Liberia, 1833–1869.* Lexington: University Press of Kentucky.
> Kamrany, Nake M., and Richard H. Day, eds. 1980. *Economic issues of the eighties.* Baltimore: Johns Hopkins University Press.
> Lenz, Carolyn Ruth Swift, Gayle Greene, and Carol Thomas Neely, eds. 1980. *The woman's part: Feminist criticism of Shakespeare.* Champaign: University of Illinois Press.
> McBurney, William Harlin, comp. 1960. *A check list of English prose fiction, 1700–1739.* Cambridge: Harvard University Press.
> Wang, Jen Yu, and Gerald L. Berger, eds. and comps. 1962. *Bibliography of agricultural meteorology.* Madison: University of Wisconsin Press.
> Williams, Charles, Margaret Skelton, Tim Peterson, Jeanne Cavanagh, and David Michaelson, eds. and trans. 1989. *Letters, stories, and poems from underground suburbia.* Chicago: Namsorg and DeLor.

The abbreviations for editor, compiler, and translator are omitted from the text citations:

> (Wiley 1980)
> (Kamrany and Day 1980)
> (Lenz, Greene, and Neely 1980)
> (McBurney 1960)
> (Wang and Berger 1962)
> (Williams et al. 1989)

EDITOR, COMPILER, OR TRANSLATOR WITH AN AUTHOR

16.47   The edited, compiled, or translated work of an author indicated on the title page is normally listed under that author's name rather than the name of the editor, compiler, or translator. In the reference list the name of the editor, compiler, or translator is part of a new element following the title and a period. The new element is introduced by *Edited by, Compiled by,* or *Translated by.* The abbreviations *Ed., Comp.,* and *Trans.* may also be used, but in this case they stand for *Edited by, Translated by,* and so forth, and therefore the plural abbreviations *Eds.* and *Comps.* should not be used.

> Ariès, Philippe. 1962. *Centuries of childhood: A social history of family life.* Translated by Robert Baldock. New York: Knopf.
> Pound, Ezra. 1953. *Literary essays.* Edited by T. S. Eliot. New York: New Directions.
> Unseld, Siegfried. 1980. *The author and his publisher.* Translated by Hunter Hannum and Hildegarde Hannum. Chicago: Univ. of Chicago Press.

Newton, Isaac. 1976. *The mathematical papers of Isaac Newton.* Ed. D. T. Whiteside and M. A. Hoskins. Vol. 7, *1691–1695.* Cambridge: Cambridge Univ. Press.

Naumov, N. P. 1972. *The ecology of animals.* Translated from the Russian by Frederick K. Plous Jr. and edited by Norman D. Levine. Champaign: Univ. of Illinois Press.

Or, to shorten this last entry:

. . . Trans. F. K. Plous Jr., ed. N. D. Levine. . . .

In text citations for these works, the name of the author is used:

(Ariès 1962)
(Pound 1953)
(Unseld 1980)
(Newton 1976)
(Naumov 1972)

16.48 When matters of editing and compiling are more complicated, they may need to be clarified in the reference list:

Chaucer life-records. 1966. Edited by Martin M. Crow and Clair C. Olson from materials compiled by John M. Manly and Edith Rickert, with the assistance of Lilian J. Redstone and others. London: Oxford University Press.

Note that since these compiled life records cannot be attributed to an author or group of authors, the title is given first in the reference list entry. The title or, if long, a shortened version of it is also used in place of the author in the text citation:

(Chaucer life-records 1966)

16.49 If the editor or translator is more germane to the discussion than is the author, the editor's or translator's name is given first in the reference list and alone in the text citation. Thus, in a work on T. S. Eliot, the citation and reference list entry for the work listed above under its author, Ezra Pound, would be as follows:

(Eliot 1953)

Eliot, T. S., ed. 1953. *Literary essays,* by Ezra Pound. New York: New Directions.

Note that in this case the author's name follows the title in the reference list and is preceded by a comma and the word *by.*

16.50 Amplifications of the editor's or translator's role by such phrases as *Edited and with an Introduction by* or *Translated and with a Foreword by* are usually simplified to *Ed.* or *Edited by, Trans.* or *Translated by.* For example, for a book whose title page reads

The Red Notebook of Charles Darwin
Edited with an Introduction and Notes
by Sandra Herbert

the reference list entry should read as follows:

> Herbert, Sandra, ed. 1980. *The red notebook of Charles Darwin.* Ithaca,
> N.Y.: Cornell University Press.
> *or*
> Darwin, Charles. 1980. *The red notebook of Charles Darwin.* Edited by
> Sandra Herbert. Ithaca, N.Y.: Cornell University Press.

AUTHORS OF FOREWORDS AND INTRODUCTIONS

16.51   Authors of forewords and introductions to works by other authors
should be omitted from reference list entries unless the foreword or
introduction is the item cited. In that case the entry is listed under the
name of the author of the foreword or introduction. The author of the
work itself is given after the title of the work, from which it is separated
by a comma and the word *by:*

> Namsorg, Nodj. 1990. Foreword to *The psychodynamics of chronic stress,*
> by Salvador Mensana. New York: Isadore O'Malley and Son.

The text citation uses the name of the author of the foreword or introduction:

> (Namsorg 1990)

ORGANIZATION, ASSOCIATION, OR CORPORATION AS "AUTHOR"

16.52   If a publication issued by an organization carries no personal author's
name on the title page, the organization should be listed as the author,
even if the name is repeated in the title or series title or as the publisher:

> International Monetary Fund (IMF). 1977. *Surveys of African economies.*
> Vol. 7, *Algeria, Mali, Morocco, and Tunisia.* Washington, D.C.: Inter-
> national Monetary Fund.
> Modern Language Association of America (MLA). 1975. *1973 MLA inter-*
> *national bibliography of books and articles on the modern languages and*
> *literatures.* 3 vols. New York: Modern Language Association of Amer-
> ica.
> International Statistics Institute (ISA). 1964. *Proceedings of the 34th ses-*
> *sion, International Statistics Institute, Ottawa, 1963.* 2 vols. Toronto:
> University of Toronto Press.
> Ohio State University. College of Administrative Science. Center for Hu-
> man Resource Research. 1977. *The national longitudinal surveys hand-*
> *book.* Rev. ed. Columbus.
> Washington University and the Federal Reserve Bank of Saint Louis, Cen-
> ter for the Study of American Business. 1977. *Financing economic*

growth: The problem of capital formation. CSAB Working Paper no. 19. Saint Louis.
or
Center for the Study of American Business (CSAB). Washington University and the Federal Reserve Bank of Saint Louis. 1977. . . .
Hamelin Public Welfare Department. Pest Control Division. Rodent Activities Termination Section (RATS). 1985. *The piper and the rats: A musical experiment.* Report no. 84. Hamelin, Vt.
or
Rodent Activities Termination Section (RATS). Hamelin Public Welfare Department. Pest Control Division. 1985. . . .

16.53   Devising text citations for reference list entries such as the ones above, where the comparative brevity of an author's, translator's, or editor's name is replaced by the longer name of an organization, association, or corporation, presents something of a challenge for the author or editor. For some of these listings acronyms are appropriate, and these have been added in parentheses after the names of the organizations. In other cases, the name of the organization may be shortened. When shortening the name of an organization, choose words as close to the beginning of the name as possible.

16.54   The following text citations are suggested for the examples above:

(IMF 1977)
(MLA 1975)
(ISA 1964)
(Ohio State 1977)   *or*   (Ohio State University 1977)
(Washington University 1977)
(CSAB 1977)
(Hamelin Public Welfare 1985)
(RATS 1985)

In the reference list entries illustrated in 16.52 the acronyms follow the full organizational names. The alternative of placing the acronym before the name is also acceptable:

IMF (International Monetary Fund). 1977. *Surveys* . . .

16.55   Where a reference list includes a number of works published or sponsored by the same organization, some with individual authors and some without, it is helpful to list them all alike, either under the name of the organization or by individual author or title.

Better Books Association. 1988. *The art of bookbinding,* by Clarence Stamp. Centerville, Mass.
———. 1988. *How to prepare a bibliography in seven steps.* Centerville, Mass.
or
How to prepare a bibliography in seven steps. 1988. Centerville, Mass.: Better Books Association.

Stamp, Clarence. 1988. *The art of bookbinding.* Centerville, Mass.: Better Books Association.

Date

16.56   As illustrated in the examples above, the date (year) of publication immediately follows the author's name in both author-date text citations and reference list entries. Other than this difference in location, publication dates for books in reference lists are treated as they are in notes and bibliographies (see discussion at 15.170–77):

> Turabian, Kate L. 1987. *A manual for writers of term papers, theses, and dissertations.* 5th ed. Revised and expanded by Bonnie Birtwistle Honigsblum. Chicago: University of Chicago Press.
> al-Hakim, H. A. 1984–90. *Mammals of the Asian steppes.* 3 vols. Cairo: Ahmad Husayn.
> Cavanagh, Jeanne. 1989–. *Theatrical history of Shakespearean productions.* 2 vols. to date. New York: Hershall Press.
> Rich, William M. 1977. *A history of dentistry in America.* Vol. 1. Cincinnati: Robert Howard Publications.
> Kocinak, John. n.d. *Notes from the field . . .*
> Kahn, Morris. [1924]. *Studies of . . .*
> O'Foalan, Patrick. [1944?]. *Differential diagnosis of . . .*

16.57   For books still in process of publication, *Forthcoming* or *In press* may be used in place of the actual publication date (see 15.176). It is also permissible to use either an announced publication date or *n.d.* in place of the date. While not strictly accurate, n.d. may be more practical than Forthcoming or In press in reference lists and text citations because it fills approximately the same amount of space as a date, and if the actual date becomes available during the proof stage, it may be slipped in without much resetting. If either n.d. or an announced future date is used in this way, either Forthcoming or In press should be added at the end of the reference list entry so that the reader will know the work has not yet been published.

> Sánchez, Miguel. Forthcoming. *Black holes and other unimaginably dense masses.*
> Sánchez, Miguel. 1993. *Black holes and other unimaginably dense masses.* Forthcoming.
> McGinnis, J. P. n.d. *The surprising modernism of "Troilus and Cressida."* In press.

If known, the name of the publisher of the forthcoming book may be included:

> McGinnis, J. P. n.d. *The surprising modernism of "Troilus and Cressida."* Cleveland: Playhouse Press, forthcoming.

16.58   In text citations to the entries illustrated above, dates are treated as follows:

> (Turabian 1987)
> (al-Hakim 1984–90)
> (Cavanagh 1989–)
> (Rich 1977)
> (Kocinak n.d.)
> (Kahn [1924])
> (O'Foalan [1944?])
> (Sánchez forthcoming)
> *or*
> (Sánchez 1993)
> (McGinnis n.d.)

16.59   In the case of reprint editions, the original publication date is usually given in addition to the date of the reprint (see 16.94–95).

Titles

16.60   The various styles in which titles of printed works appear on the title pages of books or the opening pages of chapters or of articles in periodicals may, within limits, be changed to conform to an established style when compiling reference lists. Whereas in humanities-style bibliography entries headline capitalization is used for all titles, sentence capitalization is usually used in the author-date system for all except titles of journals and series (see also 16.23). Sentence-style capitalization, sometimes referred to as *down style,* means that only the first word of the main title, the first word of the subtitle, all proper nouns and proper adjectives, and the personal pronoun *I* are capitalized.

HUMANITIES STYLE

Goodman, Nathan. *The Massacre of Innocents in Timisoara: Unleashing the Romanian Revolution.* 1990.

AUTHOR-DATE STYLE

Goodman, Nathan. 1990. *The massacre of innocents in Timisoara: Unleashing the Romanian revolution.*

16.61   As in the humanities system, titles of books, chapters, and articles may be given in full, including subtitles. In the author-date style, however, the subtitle is often omitted:

Goodman, Nathan. 1990. *The massacre of innocents in Timisoara.*

Needless to say, the choice must be followed consistently. If a subtitle is included, a colon separates it from the main title, and a regular word space follows the colon.

16.62 Titles of chapters, articles, and other short pieces are set in roman type without quotation marks:

> O'Meara, Thérèse. 1988. Irresponsible waste disposal. In *A single inhabitable planet.*

16.63 In all titles, commas are used in the style recommended in this manual (5.57) to separate items in a series.

> Cavanagh, Mark. 1989. *Color, harmony, and rhythm . . .*

16.64 See discussion at 15.110.

> Fistula, C. S. 1966. *Sojourns in the Serengeti, 1950–53.*

16.65 See discussion at 15.111.

> Skelton, Samantha. 1989. *The fate of 1,000 points of light.*
> *or*
> *. . . The fate of one thousand points of light.*
> Hershal, Joseph. 1990. *Medicine in the twelfth century.*

16.66 Titles of both long and short works appearing in an italicized title are usually also given in italics but set off with quotation marks. Titles within titles are capitalized in the same style as are the titles that include them.

> Parker, Joan. 1987. *Rhythm and imagery in "Pied beauty" and other Hopkins exclamations.* Buffalo, N.Y.: Ashtabula Press.
> Plainreader, Jack. 1988. *The month I nodded and plodded through "Finnegans wake."* Stamford, Conn.: John Kocinak.

16.67 Note that some names used to refer to certain works, especially musical works, are not titles in the usual sense (see 7.150) and so are neither quoted nor capitalized (see also 16.201):

> *Another analysis of Mozart's symphony in C major.*
> *but*
> *Another analysis of Mozart's "Jupiter" symphony.*

16.68 If followed consistently, an alternative method of treating titles of long or book-length works within italicized titles may be chosen: they may be set in roman type without quotation marks.

> Arezzo, Anthony. 1978. *The delayed publication of* The origin of species.

16.69 Titles of long works included within roman titles are set in italics:

> Wisma, Gerold. 1987. *Uncle Vanya* in Kansas. In *Traveling with Chekov*. Saint Louis: Thisbe Press.

16.70 Titles of short works within roman titles are set off with quotation marks:

> Masaryk, Eugenia. 1967. From "Winter afternoons" to "Dark mornings." In *A poet's downfall*. Boston: Nadir Publications.

16.71 Names of ships, aircraft, and spacecraft, when included in italicized titles, are also enclosed in quotation marks or, alternatively, set in roman type. Note that the names retain their normal capitalization. Designations of class or make, however, and names of trains and space programs retain their capitalization but are not enclosed in quotation marks or set in roman type. (See also 7.99–100.)

> Finnery, Irmgard, 1989. *What they did with the "Queen Mary."*
> *or*
> . . . *What they did with the* Queen Mary.
>
> Cassowary, Daniel. 1990. *Memories of journeys aboard El Capitán.*

QUOTATIONS WITHIN TITLES

16.72 See discussion at 15.115.

> Gerontion, Thomas. 1972. *Feeling like an "old man in a dry month."* London: Fibber and Fibber.
> Witmore, Fargus. 1976. "But what if she refuses?" he said. In *Tales of the indecisive*. Detroit: Odo Publishers.

TITLES ENDING WITH QUESTION MARKS OR EXCLAMATION POINTS

16.73 See discussion at 15.116.

> Tweeksbury, Irma. 1949. *If only we had known! Confessions of a regretter.* New Orleans: Ash Press.
> Valesquez, Fernando. 1950. *What could we have done?* Toledo, Ohio: I. M. Heartsick.

TITLES IN LANGUAGES OTHER THAN ENGLISH

16.74 See discussion at 15.118.

> Vail, Eugène A. 1841. *De la littérature et des hommes de lettres des Etats-Unis d'Amérique.* Paris.

Cesbron, Henry. 1909. *Histoire critique de l'hystérie*. Paris: Asselin et Houzeau.

Gundert, Wilhelm. 1943. *Japanische Religionsgeschichte: Die Religionen der Japaner und Koreaner in geschichtlichem Abriss dargestellt*. Stuttgart: Gundert Verlag.

Pirumova, N. M. 1977. *Zemskoe liberal'noe dvizhenie: Sotsial'nye korni i evoliutsiia do nachala XX veka* (The zemstvo liberal movement: Its social roots and evolution to the beginning of the twentieth century). Moscow: Izdatel'stvo "Nauka."

Wereszynski, Henryk. 1977. *Koniec sojuszu trzech cesarzy* (The end of the Three Emperors' League; summary in German). Warsaw: PWN.

Pirumova, N. M. 1977. *The zemstvo liberal movement: Its social roots and evolution to the beginning of the twentieth century* (in Russian). Moscow: Izdatel'stvo "Nauka."

Parts of a Book

CHAPTERS OR OTHER TITLED PARTS OF A BOOK

16.75 When a chapter or other titled part of a book is cited, that title is given in roman type, with sentence capitalization, without quotation marks. The title ends with a period and is followed by *In* and the title of the book. If the part is identified by type and number ("Chap. 8 in," "Pt. 1 of"), this information replaces *In* preceding the book title.

> Phibbs, Brendan. 1987. Herrlisheim: Diary of a battle. In *The other side of time: A combat surgeon in World War II*. Boston: Little, Brown.
> McNeill, William H. 1963. The era of Middle Eastern dominance to 500 B.C. Pt. 1 of *The rise of the West*. Chicago: University of Chicago Press.
> Thompson, Virgil. 1971. Cage and the college of noises. Chap. 8 in *American music since 1910*. New York: Holt, Rinehart, and Winston.
> Kaiser, Ernest. 1964. The literature of Harlem. In *Harlem: A community in transition*, edited by J. H. Clarke. New York: Citadel Press.

Text citations to such titled parts may include the page reference, but the part is unnecessary:

> (Phibbs 1987, 117–63)
> (McNeill 1963)
> (Thompson 1971, 231–36)
> (Kaiser 1964, 48, 54)

CHAPTER ORIGINALLY PUBLISHED ELSEWHERE

16.76 See also the discussion at 15.124. The text citation should refer only to the publication listed first.

> (Fromson 1990, 134)

> Fromson, Orlando. 1990. Progressives in the late twentieth century. In *To left and right: Cycles in American politics*, edited by Wilmer F. Turner

(Boston: Lighthouse Press). First published in *North American Political Review* 18 (fall 1988): 627–42.

(Wallowitz 1989, 23–31).

Wallowitz, Kazimir. 1989. The series paintings of Monet. In *Claude Monet and light: New perspectives,* edited by Wallingford Moribundi (Boston: Tetzel and Schumacher). Originally published in Kazimir Wollowitz, *Varieties of impressionism* (Boston: Revere Publications, 1987).

PREFACE, FOREWORD, INTRODUCTION, AND
SIMILAR PARTS OF A BOOK

16.77   See discussion at 15.129–31.

Jacobs, James B. 1989. Introduction to *Drunk driving: An American dilemma*. Chicago: University of Chicago Press.
Zimring, Franklin E. 1989. Foreword to *Drunk driving: An American dilemma,* by James B. Jacobs. Chicago: University of Chicago Press.

LETTERS, MEMORANDA, AND SIMILAR COMMUNICATIONS IN
PUBLISHED COLLECTIONS

16.78   In the author-date system, a letter, memorandum, or similar communication included in a published collection is mentioned in the running text and is then cited to the collection:

In a letter to Charles Milnes Gaskell from London, 30 March 1868, Henry Adams wrote . . . (Adams 1930, 141).

White sent Ross an interoffice memo on 2 May 1946 pointing out that . . . (White 1976, 273).

The commissioners received a letter from the secretary of state dated 27 May 1914 directing them . . . (*Papers relating to foreign relations,* 1928, 509–10).

The collection itself is then listed among the references:

Adams, Henry. 1930. *Letters of Henry Adams, 1858–1891*. Edited by Worthington Chauncey Ford. Boston: Houghton Mifflin.
White, E. B. 1976. *Letters of E. B. White*. Edited by Dorothy Lobrano Guth. New York: Harper and Row.
Papers relating to the foreign relations of the United States, 1914. 1928. Washington, D.C.

Edition

SUBSEQUENT EDITIONS

16.79   When an edition other than the first is cited, the number or description of the edition follows the title in the reference list entry (see also

15.132). If a volume or the total number of volumes is mentioned, this
follows the edition number.

> Smart, Ninian. 1976. *The religious experience of mankind.* 2d ed. New
> York: Scribner's Sons.
> Le Gros Clark, W. E. 1978. *The fossil evidence for human evolution.* 3d
> ed. Edited by B. Campbell. Chicago: University of Chicago Press.
> Weber, M.; H. M. de Burlet; and O. Abel. 1928. *Die Säugetiere.* 2d ed. 2
> vols. Jena: Gustav Fischer.
> Dickens, Charles. 1951. *The life and adventures of Martin Chuzzlewit.*
> New Oxford Illustrated Dickens. London: Oxford University Press.

MODERN EDITIONS OF THE CLASSICS

16.80   When classics are referred to by page number, the edition must be cited
(see also 15.133–34):

> Horace. 1932. *Satires, epistles, and Ars poetica.* Loeb Classical Library.

(Horace 1932, 146)

> Maimonides. 1965. *The code of Maimonides. Book 5: The book of holi-
> ness.* Translated and edited by Louis I. Rabinowitz and Philip Grossman.
> Yale Judaica Series. New Haven: Yale University Press.

(Maimonides 1965, 98)

REPRINT EDITIONS

16.81   See discussion at 15.178–82 and 16.94–95.

Multivolume Works

CITING THE WORK AS A WHOLE

16.82   See discussion at 15.136.

> Wright, Sewall. 1968–78. *Evolution and the genetics of populations.* 4
> vols. Chicago: University of Chicago Press.

CITING A PARTICULAR VOLUME

16.83   See discussion at 15.137–42, 16.12.

> Ncombwai, Numi. 1988. *Epidemiology in Africa.* Vol. 2. New York: Her-
> shall and Son.
> Farmwinkle, William. 1983. *Humor of the American Midwest.* Vol. 2 of
> *Survey of American humor.* Boston: Plenum Press.
> > *or*
> Farmwinkle, William. 1983. *Survey of American humor.* Vol. 2, *Humor of
> the American Midwest.* Boston: Plenum Press.

ONE VOLUME IN TWO OR MORE BOOKS

16.84   See discussion at 15.142.

> Skelton, Margaret. 1988. *A critical history of modern dance.* Vol. 2, bk.
> 1. Chicago: Terpsichore Press.
> Lach, Donald F. 1977. *Asia in the making of Europe.* Vol. 2, *A century of
> wonder.* Bk. 2, *The literary arts.* Chicago: University of Chicago Press.
> *or*
> Lach, Donald F. 1977. *The literary arts.* Bk. 2 of *A century of wonder.*
> Vol. 2 of *Asia in the making of Europe.* Chicago: University of Chicago
> Press.

GENERAL EDITORS AND VOLUME EDITORS OR AUTHORS

16.85   See discussion at 15.143.

> Tancredi, Edmund. 1989. *The letters of Edmund Tancredi.* Edited by Wil-
> liam Tismont. Vol. 2, *The war years,* edited by Arthur Soma. San Fran-
> cisco: Idlewink Press.
> *or*
> Tancredi, Edmund. 1989. *The war years.* Edited by Arthur Soma. Vol. 2
> of *The letters of Edmund Tancredi,* edited by William Tismont. San Fran-
> cisco: Idlewink Press.
>
> Ray, Gordon N., ed. 1959. *An introduction to literature.* Vol. 2, *The nature
> of drama,* by Hubert Hefner. Boston: Houghton Mifflin.
> *or*
> Hefner, Hubert. 1959. *The nature of drama.* Vol. 2 of *An introduction to
> literature,* edited by Gordon N. Ray. Boston: Houghton Mifflin.

Series

16.86   Reference list entries for works in a series include, between the book
title and the place of publication, the title of the series, in roman type
and headline capitalization; series editor, though this is usually omitted;
series number, if other than the first; and volume number and subsidiary
number, if these apply (see also 15.144–46):

> Caldwell, Helen. 1960. *The Brazilian Othello of Machado de Assis: A study
> of "Dom Casmurro."* Perspectives in Criticism, vol. 6. Berkeley and Los
> Angeles: University of California Press.
> Wolf, Theta Holmes. 1938. *The effects of praise and competition on the
> persisting behavior of kindergarten children.* Child Welfare Monograph
> Series, no. 15. Minneapolis: University of Minnesota Press.
> Chapman, Jefferson. 1975. *The Icehouse Bottom Site—40MR23.* Univer-
> sity of Tennessee Department of Anthropology Publication no. 23.
> Knoxville: University of Tennessee Press.
> Hopp, Joachim. 1977. *Untersuchungen zur Geschichte der letzten Attali-
> den.* Vestigia, Beiträge zur alten Geschichte, no. 25. Munich: C. H.
> Back'sche Verlag.

Kendeigh, S. C. 1952. *Parental care and its evolution in birds.* Illinois Biological Monographs, vol. 22, nos. 1–3. Champaign: University of Illinois Press.

Issawi, Charles. 1980. *The economic history of Turkey, 1800–1914.* Publications of the Center for Middle Eastern Studies, ed. Richard L. Chambers, no. 13. Chicago: University of Chicago Press.

Text citations to works that are part of a series give only the author's last name, the year of publication, and, if appropriate, a page reference. The series is not mentioned, nor is the volume or other number within the series. If the work itself consists of more than one volume, however, the volume number must also be included, as in any multivolume work, unless the whole work is being cited (see the following section).

MULTIVOLUME WORK WITHIN A SERIES

16.87   See discussion at 15.147–48.

Mummerston, Broderick. 1990. *An introduction to Inca sports and rituals.* 2 vols. Ancient American Culture Series. Houston: H. D. Dobbs.

Mummerston, Broderick. 1990. *An introduction to Inca sports and rituals.* Vol. 1. Ancient American Culture Series. Houston: H. D. Dobbs.

Wattle, Ralph. 1989. *Economic aspects of professional sports in America.* Vol. 2, *Player salaries and bargaining power.* Trends in American Economy, no. 11. Boston: Flummery Press.

   or

Wattle, Ralph. 1989. *Player salaries and bargaining power.* Vol. 2 of *Economic aspects of professional sports in America.* Trends in American Economy, no. 11. Boston: Flummery Press.

In text references to multivolume works in a series, the volume number is not included unless a particular volume is referred to. If the reference is to a volume as a whole, the abbreviation *vol.* must be used. If the reference is to both volume and page number, a colon separates the two and no abbreviations are necessary.

(Mummerston 1990)
(Mummerston 1990, vol. 1)
(Mummerston 1990, 1:211–21)
(Wattle 1989, 2:31, 56)

SUBSEQUENT SERIES NUMBERING

16.88   See discussion at 15.149.

Boxer, Charles R., ed. 1953. *South China in the sixteenth century.* Hakluyt Society Publications, 2d ser., vol. 106. London.

Palmatary, Helen C. 1950. *The pottery of Marajó Island, Brazil.* Transactions of the American Philosophical Society, n.s., 39, pt. 3. Philadelphia.

16.89   Names of these series are properly part of the publication facts (see 16.90), not series titles reflecting subject categories.

Facts of Publication

16.90   In reference list entries, the element containing the publication facts includes only the place of publication and the name of the publisher, the date of publication having already appeared after the name of the author. The place and publisher are given in that order, separated by a colon, and follow the title and such other descriptive material as the identification of editor, translator, series, or number of volumes, should these apply. The element itself is preceded and terminated by a period.

> Porkola, Olga. 1990. *Contemporary Finnish design and architecture.* Cleveland: Cuyahoga Press.
> Harris, James E., and Edward F. Wente, eds. 1980. *An X-ray atlas of the royal mummies.* Chicago: University of Chicago Press.
> Mellars, Paul, ed. 1979. *The early postglacial settlement of northern Europe: An ecological perspective.* Pittsburgh: University of Pittsburgh Press.
> Schmutki, Itzka. 1991. *Struggles against oppression in Eastern Europe.* 2 vols. Translated by Peter Foldes. Boston: Revere Publications.
> Wolf, Theta Holmes. 1938. *The effects of praise and competition on the persisting behavior of kindergarten children.* Child Welfare Monograph Series, no. 15. Minneapolis: University of Minnesota Press.

16.91   If the city is not widely known, the name of the state, or its abbreviation, should be added, unless the state is part of the publisher's name. If the city is not in the United States and is also not widely known, the country should be identified. (See also the discussion at 15.157–59.)

> Akron, Ohio: T. J. Brice.
> Portland, Oreg.: Pacific Publications.
> Jackson, Miss.: Margolis Press.
> Chapel Hill: University of North Carolina Press.
> Bristol, England: Potiphar Press.
> Pátzuarco, Mexico: Manuel Galdós.
> Helsinki: Laaksonen Press.

Cambridge, England, and Cambridge, Massachusetts, should be distinguished unless the name of the publisher makes it clear (see also 15.157–58):

> Cambridge.
> Cambridge, Mass.
> Cambridge: Cambridge University Press.

Cambridge: Harvard University Press.
Cambridge, Mass.: Wizmer Press.

If the place of publication is not known, this may be indicated by using the abbreviation *N.p. (No place)*. If the place is known but not listed on the title or copyright page, it may be identified in brackets.

N.p.: Evanescent Press.
[London].
[Dallas]: Beckstein Press.

PUBLISHER

16.92   For a full discussion of the style for publishers' names see 15.160–69.

Macmillan.
Harper and Row.
    or
Harper & Row.
Paris: Presses Universitaires de France.
Mexico City: Fondo de Cultura Económica.
Munich: Carl Hanser Verlag.
Chicago: University of Chicago Press; London: Routledge & Kegan Paul.
Cambridge: Harvard University Press, Belknap Press.
Chicago: University of Chicago Press.
    or
Chicago: Univ. of Chicago Press.

ALTERNATIVE FORMS

16.93   See the discussion at 15.152–56.

David, Michael. 1968. *Toward honesty in public relations*. Chicago.
Vonnegut, Kurt. 1979. *Jailbird*.

REPRINT EDITIONS

16.94   In references to reprints of very old books, the original publication date, enclosed in brackets, may precede the reprint date. (See also the discussion at 15.178–82.)

(Schweitzer [1911] 1966, 134–36)

Schweitzer, Albert. [1911] 1966. *J. S. Bach*. Translated by Ernest New-
    man. Reprint, New York: Dover Publications.

(Small [1804] 1963, 111, 213)

Small, Robert. [1804] 1963. *An account of the astronomical discoveries of
    Kepler*. Reprint, with a foreword by William D. Stahlman, Madison:
    University of Wisconsin Press.

In an alternative style, the original publication date may be left out of the text citation and included only in the reference list entry, where it should be placed just before the reprint publication facts and set off by periods rather than brackets:

> (Schweitzer 1966, 134–36)

> Schweitzer, Albert. 1966. *J. S. Bach.* Translated by Ernest Newman. 1911. Reprint, New York: Dover Publications.

16.95   In references to reprints of more recently published originals, it is preferable to give the full original publication facts as well as those of the reprint. In this case, the date of the reprint edition only is given in the text citation:

> (Harris 1982, 211–15)

In the reference list entry, the reprint publication date should follow the author's name; the publication facts of the original edition, including date, in bibliography style, follow the title (and such other descriptive material as is necessary); and finally the city and publisher for the reprint are given. The listing may end with a statement that page references are to the reprint edition.

> Harris, Neil. 1982. *The artist in American society: The formative years, 1790–1860.* New York: George Braziller, 1966. Reprint, Chicago: University of Chicago Press, Phoenix Books (page references are to reprint edition).

> (Flissman 1991, 217)

> Flissman, J. H. 1991. *How the cold war will end.* Translated by William DeLor. New York: Stalwart Press, 1968. Reprint, Los Angeles: Tim P. Johnson.

An alternative way of listing reprints of more recently published originals is to give the publication facts of the reprint first and those of the original edition last. For clarity, the word *Reprint* may follow the reprint date, and in any case the words *Original edition* should precede the original publication facts:

> Harris, Neil. 1982. Reprint. *The artist in American society: The formative years, 1790–1860.* Chicago: University of Chicago Press, Phoenix Books. Original edition, New York: George Braziller, 1966.
> Flissman, J. H. 1991. Reprint. *How the cold war will end.* Translated by William DeLor. Los Angeles: Tim P. Johnson. Original edition, New York: Stalwart Press, 1968.

Microform Editions

16.96   See discussion at 15.201–3.

> (Tauber 1958)
> (Peale 1980)
> (Voelke 1980)

Tauber, Abraham. 1958. *Spelling reform in the United States.* Ann Arbor, Mich.: University Microfilms.

Peale, Charles Willson. 1980. *The collected papers of Charles Willson Peale and his family.* Edited by Lillian B. Miller. National Portrait Gallery, Smithsonian Institution, Washington, D.C.; Millwood, N.Y.: Kraus-Thomson Organization. Microfiche.

Voelke, William, ed. 1980. *Masterpieces of medieval painting: The art of illumination.* Pierpont Morgan Library, New York; Chicago: University of Chicago Press. Text-fiche.

PERIODICALS

General Requirements

16.97   Varieties of periodicals include journals, popular magazines, and newspapers. In the author-date system, text citations to articles in periodicals are identical with those to books: last name of author followed, without punctuation, by the year of publication and finally, after a comma, the page reference. Reference list entries for articles in periodicals contain much the same information as do bibliography entries, but there are differences in order and style. The chief difference is that in reference lists the year of publication immediately follows the author's name.

16.98   In general, the data included in reference list entries for articles in periodicals are as follows:

> author's name
> year
> title of article
> title of periodical
> issue information (volume, issue number, month or season)
> page reference

16.99   The names of the authors of articles in periodicals are inverted in reference lists, as they are in bibliographies, last name first. In reference lists, however, initials often replace all given names. Whether full given names or initials are used, consistency should be observed if possible, but it is also acceptable to mix the two practices in order to accommodate the preferences of the cited authors. Multiple, pseudonymous, and anonymous authorship are treated as in book citations (see 16.36–45).

16.100   Titles of articles are given sentence capitalization and are set in roman type without quotation marks. Subtitles may be omitted, if this is done consistently, and it is also acceptable to omit the whole title, leaving the reader to find the article in the cited volume or issue of the periodical.

16.101   The titles of the periodicals themselves are italicized and given headline, or regular title, capitalization. Periodical titles are sometimes abbreviated, especially in the sciences. For guidelines in the use of abbreviations for periodical titles, see 15.208–9.

16.102 Issue information includes volume and issue number, when applicable, and sometimes the month and day, the month alone, or the season. The year is omitted from the issue information, since it has already appeared after the author's name. Arabic numerals are used for both volume and issue numbers.

Journals

16.103 Journals are specialized periodicals and have more restricted circulation than popular magazines. They are often intended for an academic, or scholarly, audience. It is more important to give volume and issue numbers in citing these publications than in citing magazine articles. Except for the differences outlined above (16.21–25), the guidelines applicable to journal entries in a bibliography generally apply to reference list entries (see 15.207–30). The examples in the paragraphs that follow illustrate the various kinds of journal entries likely to be found in reference lists and the variations in style permissible in such entries.

ARTICLE TITLES AND JOURNAL TITLES

16.104 See discussion at 15.208 and 16.100–101.

> Bennett, John W. 1946. The interpretation of Pueblo culture: A question of values. *Southwestern Journal of Anthropology* 2:361–74.
> *or*
> Bennett, J. W. 1946. The interpretation of Pueblo culture. *Southwestern Journal of Anthropology* 2:361–74.
> *or*
> Bennett, J. W. 1946. *Southwestern Journal of Anthropology* 2:361–74.
> Auerbach, C. 1949. Chemical mutagenesis. *Biol. Rev.* 24:355–91.
> Banks, William. 1958. A secret meeting in Boise. *Midwestern Political Review* 6:26–31.

TITLES WITHIN ARTICLE TITLES

16.105 See discussion at 15.219.

> Lofton, Peter. 1989. Reverberations between wordplay and swordplay in *Hamlet*. *Aeolian Studies* 2:12–29.
> Loomis, C. C., Jr. 1960. Structure and sympathy in Joyce's "The dead." *PMLA* 75:149–51.

QUOTATIONS WITHIN ARTICLE TITLES

16.106 See discussion at 15.220.

> Arbogast, Melvin. 1988. Meeting "a nicens little boy named baby tuckoo": Joyce observed. *Fictive Reviews* 2:23–31.

TITLES ENDING WITH QUESTION MARKS OR
EXCLAMATION POINTS

16.107 See discussion at 15.221.

> Starczak, E. S. 1986. At last! Patience rewarded. *Esoterica* 13:42–49.
> Quimber, Collie. 1977. Did Babbington disclose more than was necessary? *Political Review* 16:71–78.

VOLUME AND ISSUE NUMBERS

16.108 See discussion at 15.210–11.

> Sommerstein, A. R. 1972. On the so-called definite article in English. *Linguistic Inquiry* 3:197–209.
> Meltzer, Françoise. 1979. On Rimbaud's "Voyelles." *Modern Philology,* vol. 76.
> Armstrong, Paul B. 1974. E. M. Forster's *Howards End:* The existential crisis of the liberal imagination. *Mosaic* 8, no. 1:183–99.
> Brain, C. K., and V. Brain. 1977. Microfaunal remains from Mirabib: Some evidence of palaeoecological changes in the Namib. *Madoqua* 10 (4): 285–93.

MONTH OR SEASON

16.109 See discussion at 15.212.

> Orshansky, Mollie. 1965. Counting the poor: Another look at the poverty profile. *Social Security Bulletin* 28 (January): 3–29.
> Martin, Albro. 1979. Uneasy partners: Government-business relations in twentieth-century American history. *Prologue* 11 (summer): 91–105.

ARTICLE PUBLISHED IN INSTALLMENTS

16.110 See discussion at 15.222.

> Rowe, E. G. 1947. The breeding biology of *Aquila verreauxi* Lesson. Parts 1 and 2. *Ibis* 89:387–410, 576–606.
> Mills, Judith. 1990. Packaging the client. Parts 1 and 2. *Public Relations Review* 14, no. 3:95–102; no. 4:43–52.
> Patch, C. Ross. 1985–86. The next to last angry man. Parts 1–3. *World's End Review* 8:315–30; 9:27–52, 125–42.

ARTICLE APPEARING IN TWO PUBLICATIONS

16.111   See discussion at 15.223.

> McKeon, Richard. 1955. Dialogue and controversy in philosophy. *Philosophy and Phenomenological Research* 17:143–63. First published in *Entretiens philosophiques d'Athènes* (Athens: Institut International de Philosophie, 1955), 161–78.

PLACE OF PUBLICATION

16.112   See discussion at 15.224.

> Hughes, A. R., and P. V. Tobias. 1977. A fossil skull probably of the genus *Homo* from Sterkfontein, Transvaal. *Nature* (London) 265:310–12.
> Garrett, Marvin P. 1975. Language and design in *Pippa Passes*. *Victorian Poetry* (West Virginia University) 13, no. 1:47–60.

NO VOLUME NUMBER

16.113   See discussion at 15.225.

> Grabowski, M. M. 1990. After post-modernism. *Journal of the American Aesthetic Association,* no. 3:39–47.

FOREIGN LANGUAGE JOURNALS

16.114   See discussion at 15.227–29. (See also 9.4, including note 1.)

> Bouchard, Gérard. 1979. Un essai d'anthropologie régionale: L'histoire sociale du Saguenay aux XIXe et XXe siècles. *Annales: Economies, sociétés, civilisations* 34 (January): 106–25.
> Saulnier, Verdun L. 1949. Dix années d'études sur Rabelais. *Bibliothèque d'humanisme et Renaissance* 11:105–28.
> Broszat, Martin. 1979. "Holocaust" und die Geschichtswissenschaft. *Vierteljahrshefte Zeitgeschichte* 27 (April): 285–98.
> Kern, W. 1938. Waar verzemelde Pigafetta zijn Maleise woorden? (Where did Pigafetta collect his Malaysian words?) *Tijdschrift voor Indische taal-, land- en volkenkunde* 78:271–73.
> Kosman, M. 1979. Evolution of paganism in the Baltic states (in Russian; English summary). *Voprosy Istorii,* no. 5:30–44.

NEW SERIES

16.115   See discussion at 15.230.

> Barstow, T. S. 1979. Lincoln's literary style. *Plenum,* n.s., 5 (fall): 24–36.
> Morales, Salvador. 1988. A Central American journey. *Hemispheric Policy Review,* 3d ser., 2:62–71.

Popular Magazines

16.116 See discussion covering articles and regular features at 15.231–33.

> Karen, Robert. 1990. Becoming attached. *Atlantic,* February, 35–70.
> Caspari, E. W., and R. E. Marshak. 1965. The rise and fall of Lysenko. *Science,* 16 July, 275–78.
> Currents in the news. 1980. *U.S. News and World Report,* 11 February.

The text citation for the last entry above might be

> (Currents in the news 1980) *or* (Currents 1980)

Newspapers

16.117 In the author-date system, citations to items in daily newspapers are made in running text and are usually not listed individually in the reference list. When introduced in this way, titles are treated as in the humanities style.

> An editorial in the *Philadelphia Inquirer,* 30 July 1990, took the position that . . .
>
> In an article entitled "The Iron Curtain Rises," published in the *Wilberton Journal,* 7 February 1990, Albert Finnonian reported that . . .

16.118 Should the author deem it appropriate to include a newspaper citation in the reference list, an individual entry might be made as follows:

> *Philadelphia Inquirer.* 1990. Editorial, 30 July.
> Finnonian, Albert. 1990. The Iron Curtain rises. *Wilberton Journal,* 7 February, final edition.

(For a discussion of other matters of style in making citations to items in newspapers, see 15.234–42.)

Reviews in Periodicals

16.119 See the general discussion at 15.243.

BOOK REVIEWS

16.120 See discussion at 15.244.

> Spitzer, Steven. 1985. Review of *The limits of law enforcement,* by Hans Zeisel. *American Journal of Sociology* 91 (November): 726–29.
> Lardner, Susan. 1980. Third eye open. Review of *The salt eaters,* by Toni Cade Bambara. *New Yorker,* 5 May, 169.

REVIEWS OF DRAMAS AND TELEVISED PLAYS

16.121   See discussion at 15.245.

> Review of *Fool for love,* by Sam Shepard. 1983. Circle Repertory Company, New York. *New York Times,* 27 May, 18(N), C3(L).
> Review of *True West,* by Sam Shepard. 1984. Televised version. *New York Times,* 31 January, 22(N).

Text citations for the above unsigned reviews might be as follows:

> (Review of *Fool for love* 1983, C3[L])
> (Review of *True West* 1984)

MOVIE REVIEWS

16.122   See discussion at 15.246.

> Kauffmann, Stanley. 1989. Turbulent lives. Review of *A dry white season* (MGM movie). *New Republic,* 9 October, 24–25.

REVIEWS OF MUSICAL PERFORMANCES

16.123   See discussion at 15.247.

> Rockwell, John. 1990. Eve Queler conducts Verdi's *Vespri Siciliani.* Review of concert performance of *I vespri Siciliani,* by Verdi. Carnegie Hall, Opera Orchestra of New York. *New York Times,* Living Arts section, 18 January, 18(Y).

CITATIONS TAKEN FROM SECONDARY SOURCES

16.124   When reference is made to the work of one author as quoted in the work of another author, the reference list entry should include both works. If the discussion emphasizes the original work, that comes first in the entry. If the emphasis is on the use of the original source by the author of the secondary source, the secondary source should be listed first. (See also discussion at 15.425–26.)

> Zukofsky, Louis. 1931. Sincerity and objectification. *Poetry* 37 (February): 269. Quoted in Bonnie Costello, *Marianne Moore: Imaginary possessions* (Cambridge: Harvard University Press, 1981), 78.
> *or*
> Costello, Bonnie. 1981. *Marianne Moore: Imaginary possessions,* 78. Cambridge: Harvard University Press. Quoting Louis Zukofsky, Sincerity and objectification, *Poetry* 37 (February 1931): 269.

16.125   The parenthetical text citation should be to the work mentioned first in the reference list entry; that is, to the work emphasized:

(Zukofsky 1931, 269)
or
(Costello 1981, 78)

INTERVIEWS AND PERSONAL COMMUNICATIONS

16.126 Interviews and personal communications are recorded in a variety of ways (see discussion at 15.262–69). References should begin with the name of the person interviewed or the person from whom the communication was received.

Interviews

16.127 Citations to interviews are best made in running text in the author-date system, but if the author wishes, they may also be listed in the reference list or in an appendix.

PUBLISHED, BROADCAST, OR RECORDED INTERVIEWS

16.128 See discussion at 15.263–64.

> Bellour, Raymond. 1979. Alternation, segmentation, hypnosis: Interview with Raymond Bellour. By Janet Bergstrom. *Camera Obscura,* nos. 3/4 (summer): 89–94.
> Singer, Isaac Bashevis. 1981. Interview by Harold Flender. In *Writers at work: The "Paris Review" interviews,* edited by George Plimpton. 5th ser., 81–92. New York: Viking Press.
> Bundy, McGeorge. 1990. Interview by Robert MacNeil. *MacNeil/Lehrer News Hour.* Public Broadcasting System, 7 February.
> al-Hamad, Hamid. 1989. *Alexandrian archaeology.* Interview by Barker Comstock. Videocassette, directed by Nathan Goodhugh. Warberg Films.

UNPUBLISHED INTERVIEWS

16.129 See discussion at 15.265.

> Hunt, Horace [pseud.]. 1976. Interview by Ronald Schatz. Tape recording, 16 May. Pennsylvania Historical and Museum Commission, Harrisburg.
> Roemer, Merle A. 1973. Interview by author. Tape recording. Millington, Md., 26 July.
> Peterson, Tim G. 1989. Interview by author. Long Beach, Calif., 1 August.

Personal Communications

16.130 Although usually confined, in the author-date system, to references in the text, personal communications may also be included in the reference list (see 15.269). When entered in the reference list, personal communications should begin with the name of the letter writer or the person with whom the author has talked:

> In a telephone conversation with the author on 12 October 1989, Colonel William Rich revealed that . . .

> Rich, Colonel William. 1989. Telephone conversation with the author, 12 October.
> Skelton, Margaret. 1990. Conversation with author. Oak Park, Ill., 14 July.
> Cavanagh, Jeanne. 1990. Letter to author, 10 January.

UNPUBLISHED MATERIAL

Theses, Dissertations, and Other Unpublished Works

16.131 The title of an unpublished paper is treated like the title of an article or other short work. In the reference list, it is set in roman type and given sentence capitalization, but it is not enclosed in quotation marks. (See 16.62.)

THESES AND DISSERTATIONS

16.132   (King 1976, 32–37)
(Ross n.d., 142–55)
(Mann 1968)
(Maguire 1976)

> King, Andrew J. 1976. Law and land use in Chicago: A pre-history of modern zoning. Ph.D. diss., University of Wisconsin.
> Ross, Dorothy. n.d. The Irish-Catholic immigrant, 1880–1900: A study in social mobility. Master's thesis, Columbia University.
> Mann, A. E. 1968. The paleodemography of *Australopithecus*. Ph.D. diss., University of California, Berkeley.
> Maguire, J. 1976. A taxonomic and ecological study of the living and fossil Hystricidae with particular reference to southern Africa. Ph.D. diss., Department of Geology, University of the Witwatersrand, Johannesburg.

If the citation is to an abstract published in *Dissertation Abstracts International,* the form may be as follows:

> (Downright 1993)

> Downright, Alice B. 1993. Narrative diffusion and the professional editor. Ph.D. diss., University of Chicago, 1992. Abstract in *Dissertation Abstracts International* 52:3245A–3246A.

PAPERS READ AT MEETINGS

16.133 See discussion at 15.273. The titles of the meetings (symposia, conferences) are given regular title capitalization.

> (Speth and Davis 1975)
> (Royce 1988)

> Speth, J. D., and D. D. Davis. 1975. Seasonal variability in early hominid predation. Paper presented at symposium, Archeology in Anthropology: Broadening Subject Matter. Seventy-fourth annual meeting of the American Anthropological Association.
> Royce, John C. 1988. Finches of Du Page County. Paper read at 22d Annual Conference on Practical Bird Watching, 24–26 May, at Midland University, Flat Prairie, Illinois.

UNPUBLISHED DUPLICATED MATERIAL

16.134 See discussion at 15.275.

> (U.S. Educational Foundation for Egypt 1951, 28)
> (Downes 1974, 12)
> (Cooke n.d., 4–7)

> United States Educational Foundation for Egypt. 1951. Annual program proposal, 1952–53. U.S. Department of State, Washington, D.C. Mimeographed.
> Downs, W. J. 1974. Systematic grammar and structural sentence relatedness. London School of Economics. Duplicated.
> Cooke, H. B. S. n.d. South African Pleistocene mammals in the University of California Collections. Typescript.

Citations to working papers are as follows:

> (Frishberg and Gough 1974)

> Frishberg, Nancy, and Bonnie Gough. 1974. Time on our hands. Working paper, Salk Institute for Biological Studies, La Jolla, Calif.

Manuscript Collections

16.135 When several manuscripts from a single collection are cited in the author-date system, each manuscript and its author, if known, are regularly identified in the running text, and the collection, if not also given in the text, is identified in a parenthetical reference that is keyed to the reference list. The collections cited in the work, with their locations, or depositories, are then entered in the reference list alphabetically by the name of the collection.

> In a letter to Colonel House dated 25 September 1918 (House Papers), George Creel wrote . . .

> House, Edward M. Papers. Yale University Library.

16.136 No date is given in either the parenthetical reference or the reference list entry, because the collection obviously contains items from various dates. A date is provided only for the particular item in the running text.

> Oglethorpe wrote to the trustees on 13 January 1733 (Egmont Manuscripts) to say . . .

> Egmont Manuscripts. Phillips Collection. University of Georgia Library.

> In a report to the Committee of Overseers, probably written 28 December 1859 (Overseers Reports), Louis Agassiz . . .

> Overseers Reports, Professional Series, vol. 2. Harvard University Archives.

> Alvin Johnson, in a memorandum prepared sometime in 1937 (Kallen Papers, file 36), observed that . . .

> Kallen, Horace. Papers. YIVO Institute, New York.

In the last example, note that a file number is added to the parenthetical reference to assist location.

16.137 If only one manuscript in a collection is cited the manuscript may be entered under its own author or title in the reference list. In this case the date, if given, is included in the text reference:

> There is an interesting description of Agassiz, written at the request of Elizabeth Cary Agassiz (Dinkel n.d.), . . .

> Dinkel, Joseph. n.d. Description of Louis Agassiz. Agassiz Papers. Houghton Library, Harvard University.

> The reply, when it came, was abrupt and unexpectedly discourteous (Hooker 1948).

> Hooker, Rathburn. 1948. Who the devil do you think you are? Memorandum, 17 November. Torrentsworth Papers. Blanchelevre Archives, Blanchelevre, Ariz.

16.138 When several collections contained in one depository are referred to in a work, it may be desirable to include all the collections under the name of the depository and to tailor text references to refer to the depository:

> (Porkola University Library, Porkola Papers)
> (Porkola University Library, Serafina Papers)
> *or*
> Reference is made in a letter from Olga Serafina to Joseph Hershal dated 6 October 1924 (Porkola University Library) . . .

> Porkola University Library, Nilo Hills, Ohio. Andrew Porkola Papers. Olga Serafina Papers. Letters of Naj Namsorg.

(For further discussion of style in documenting manuscript collections see 15.277–92.)

SPECIAL TYPES OF REFERENCES

16.139 In the author-date system, specific citations to material in reference books, scriptures, plays and poems with line or stanza numbers, Greek and Roman classics, medieval works, and English classics are generally made in the text, sometimes in parentheses, following the guidelines set forth in 15.293–311. Such works are generally not included in the reference list.

Reference Books

16.140 See discussion at 15.293.

> In his article on Nebo in the eleventh edition of the *Encyclopaedia Britannica,* Morris Jastrow noted that . . .

Scriptural References

16.141 See discussion at 15.294–95.

> In a letter to the Thessalonians (1 Thess. 4:11), Paul urges the faithful . . .

Plays and Poems

16.142 See discussion at 15.296–97.

> What's past and what's to come is strew'd with husks
> And formless ruin of oblivion.
>
> *(Troilus and Cressida* 4.5.165–66)

> "Ay me, how many perils do enfold / The righteous man," said Spenser
> (*FQ* 1.8.1).

Greek and Roman Classics

16.143 See discussion at 15.298–308.

> Of that battle Thucydides (2.40.2–3) records . . .

> I was astonished to discover in Pindar (frag. 133 Bergk = 127 Bowra) a similar figure of speech.

Medieval References

16.144 See discussion at 15.309.

> That the idea was shared by Augustine is suggested in the *City of God* (trans. Healey-Tasker, 20.2).

English Classics

16.145 See discussion at 15.310–11.

> Massingale's observation may also be applied to a passage in *Paradise Lost* (1.83–86).

16.146 If page citations to particular editions of such works are given, a suitable entry, including publication facts, must be added to the list of references, and a publication date should be included in the text reference. For well-known modern editions of the classics, the name of the edition and the date of the volume are usually sufficient:

> (Horace 1932, 34–41)
> (Dryden 1906)
>
> Horace. 1932. *Satires, epistles, and Ars poetica*. Loeb Classical Library.
> Dryden, John. 1906. *Dramatic essays*. Everyman's Library.

16.147 For less well known editions, editor, place of publication, and publisher should be added:

> (Maimonides 1965)
> (Wharton 1977)
>
> Maimonides. 1965. *The code of Maimonides. Book 5: The book of holiness*. Translated and edited by Louis I. Rabinowitz and Philip Grossman. Yale Judaica Series. New Haven: Yale University Press.
> Wharton, Edith. 1977. *The house of mirth*. Edited by R. W. B. Lewis. Gotham Library. New York: New York University Press.

PUBLIC DOCUMENTS

16.148 For ease of location, the text citation and reference list entry for a public document should begin with the same element. The second element, in the author-date system, should of course be the date. (For a general discussion of the information germane to reference list entries as well as bibliography entries see 15.322–26.)

United States

16.149 For introductory information see 15.327–28.

16.150 *Congressional journals* (see also 15.333). Text citations to the journals of the Senate and the House should include the journal title, in italics, in place of the author; the session year; and the page reference, if applicable:

> (*Senate Journal* 1819, 9–19)
> (*House Journal* 1920, 44–49)

Reference list entries, which must reflect the text citation, should also begin with the journal title, although this may be preceded by "U.S." (or "United States") if the country is not clear from the discussion. In either case, the journal title should be followed by the year of the session covered, the numbers of the Congress and of the session, and the month and day of the entry cited:

> U.S. *Senate Journal*. 1819. 16th Cong., 1st sess., 7 December.
> U.S. *House Journal*. 1820. 16th Cong., 2d sess., 8 April.

It might sometimes be helpful to add cross-references like the following:

> U.S. Congress. *Senate Journal*. See U.S. *Senate Journal*.

16.151 *Journals of the Continental Congress* (see also 15.334). Text citations to the *Journals of the Continental Congress* should include the following information in the order shown: "Continental Congress" as author; meeting year of the Congress (not the year of publication); and the volume and page reference.

> (Continental Congress 1783, 25:863)

The reference list entry should, as would a bibliography entry, list the publication as a whole.

> Continental Congress. 1774–89. *Journals of the Continental Congress, 1774–1789*. Edited by Worthington C. Ford et al. 34 vols. Washington, D.C., 1904–37.

Note that, as in the text reference, the dates following the "author" are the meeting dates, not the publication dates. The latter are given after the place of publication, an exception in the author-date system.

16.152 *Debates* (see also discussion at 15.335–40). In reference lists, the *Congressional Record* may be cited in full (first example below); in part, with the run of dates indicated (second example); or as a specific part of a specific volume (third example):

Congressional Record. 1873–. Washington, D.C.

Congressional Record. 1930–41. Washington, D.C.

Congressional Record. 1930. 71st Cong., 2d sess. Vol. 72, pt. 10.

16.153 Full references or references to a run of dates are useful when the text contains many citations to various volumes or parts of the *Congressional Record*. Such text citations, of course, must provide more specific information: year, volume, part, and pages.

(*Cong. Rec.* 1930, 72, pt. 10:10828–30)

16.154 When few citations to the *Congressional Record* are given in the text, the reference list entries themselves may be more specific, as in the third reference list example above, and the text citations may then be more concise:

(*Cong. Rec.* 1930, 10828–30)

16.155 If the identity of the speaker in a debate is not given in the text, it is usual to do so in the documentation. In this case both the text citation and the reference list entry begin with the name of the speaker:

(Kennedy 1982, 3832–34)

Kennedy, Edward. 1982. Senator Kennedy of Massachusetts speaking for the Joint Resolution on Nuclear Weapons Freeze and Reductions to the Committee on Foreign Relations. S.J. Res. 163. 97th Cong., 1st sess. *Cong. Rec.*, 10 March, vol. 128, pt. 3.

16.156 Text citations to earlier collections of congressional debates may be given as follows (see also 15.340):

(*Annals of Congress* 1791, app., 1414)
(*Annals of Cong.* 1823, 358)
(*Congressional Globe* 1867, 39, pt. 9:9505)

In the reference list, these earlier collections are usually cited in full:

Annals of the Congress of the United States, 1789–1824. 42 vols. Washington, D.C., 1834–56.
Congressional Globe. 1833–73. 46 vols. Washington, D.C., 1834–73.

Note that the session dates follow or, as in the first example, are part of the title; the publication dates, in this case, follow the place of publication.

16.157 *Reports and documents*. See discussion at 15.341.

(House 1947, 4)
(Senate 1956, 9–10)
(Congress 1941, 2–5)

U.S. House. 1947. *Report of activities of the National Advisory Council on International Monetary and Financial Problems to March 31, 1947.* 80th Cong., 1st sess. H. Doc. 365.

U.S. Senate. 1956. Committee on Foreign Relations. *The Mutual Security Act of 1956.* 84th Cong., 2d sess. S. Rept. 2273.

U.S. Congress. 1941. *Declarations of a state of war with Japan, Germany, and Italy.* 77th Cong., 1st sess. S. Doc. 148. Serial 10575.

16.158 *Hearings.* See discussion at 15.343.

(House 1945, 12–14)
(Senate 1985, 53, 57)

U.S. House. 1945. Committee on Banking and Currency. *Bretton Woods Agreements Act: Hearings on H.R. 3314.* 79th Cong., 1st sess.

U.S. Senate. 1985. Committee on Foreign Relations. *Famine in Africa: Hearing before the Committee on Foreign Relations.* 99th Cong., 1st sess. 17 January.

16.159 *Committee Prints.* See discussion at 15.345.

(House 1976, 5–6)
or
(Donnelley and Rather 1976, 5–6)

U.S. House. 1976. Committee on Interior and Insular Affairs. Subcommittee on Energy and the Environment. *International proliferation of nuclear technology.* Report prepared by Warren H. Donnelley and Barbara Rather. 94th Cong., 2d sess. Committee Print 15.

or

Donnelley, Warren H., and Barbara Rather. 1976. *International proliferation of nuclear technology.* Report prepared for the Subcommittee on Energy and the Environment of the House Committee on Interior and Insular Affairs. 94th Cong., 2d sess. Committee Print 15.

or

Donnelley and Rather. 1976. *See* U.S. House. 1976.

16.160 *Bills and resolutions* (see also discussion at 15.347–48). House and Senate bills and resolutions are usually cited in the text by title, including date, or by resolution number; or, if preferred, by both. The title is italicized. Occasionally bills and resolutions are also cited in the reference list. In that case, the text citation is parenthetical and keyed to the reference list entry, or to a cross-reference.

16.161 Bills and resolutions may be cited to slip bills as follows:

(House 1985)
or
(Food Security Act of 1985)

U.S. House. 1985. *Food Security Act of 1985.* 99th Cong., 1st sess., H.R. 2100.
Food Security Act of 1985. See U.S. House. 1985.

16.162 Citation of bills and resolutions to the *Congressional Record* may be made as follows:

> (House 1985, H8463, H8466)
> *or*
> (*Food Security Act of 1985,* H8463, H8466)

>> U.S. House. 1985. *Food Security Act of 1985.* 99th Cong., 1st sess., H.R. 2100. *Congressional Record* 131, no. 132, daily ed. (8 October): H8353–H8486.

16.163 *Laws, public acts, and statutes* (see also discussion at 15.350–55). Slip laws may conveniently be cited in running text, either by public law number or by title. If the text requires it, the citation may be enclosed in parentheses. The date may also be used in the text reference, although it is not necessary, since the public law number or the title will be sufficient to locate the item in the reference list. The reference list entry should of course begin with the same element used in the text reference, or should contain a cross-reference.

>> U.S. Public Law 585. 79th Cong., 2d sess., 1 August 1946. *Atomic Energy Act of 1946.*
>> *or*
>> *Atomic Energy Act of 1946.* U.S. Public Law 585. 79th Cong., 2d sess., 1 August 1946.

16.164 When cited to the *U.S. Statutes at Large,* the text reference should run as follows:

>> (*Statutes at Large* 1947, 767, 774)
>> *or*
>> (*Atomic Energy Act of 1946,* 767, 774)

And the reference list entry:

>> U.S. *Statutes at Large.* 1947. Vol. 60, pp. 755–75. *Atomic Energy Act of 1946.*
>> *or*
>> *Atomic Energy Act of 1946.* U.S. *Statutes at Large* 60:755–75.

Note that if *Statutes at Large* is used as the initial element in the reference list entry, the volume and page references constitute the third element, following the date. Rather than beginning with a numeral, this third element should begin with the abbreviation *Vol.* A comma, rather than a colon, should in that case separate volume and page numbers, and to match the abbreviation for *volume,* the abbreviation for *page(s)* should also be used.

16.165 Once the law has been entered in the *U.S. Code* it may be cited in running text by title. The reference list entry would then begin with the title followed by the date and the *U.S. Code* volume and inclusive section numbers:

> *Declaratory Judgment Act.* 1952. *U.S. Code.* Vol. 28, secs. 2201–2.

16.166 *Earlier statutes* (see also discussion at 15.357). Citations to statutes enacted prior to 1874 may begin by mentioning the title of the statute in running text, followed, in parentheses, by the volume number and page reference of the *Statutes at Large of the United States of America,* abbreviated *Stats. at Large of USA.* The date, in this case, is not necessary. If the statute is not mentioned in the running text, a full parenthetical citation, like the one that follows, may be given:

> (*Stats. at Large of USA* 6:321–23)

The reference list entry might be as follows:

> *Statutes at Large of the United States of America, 1789–1873.* 17 vols. Washington, D.C., 1850–73. Vol. 6, pp. 321–23.

16.167 *American State Papers.* See discussion at 15.358.

> (*Am. St. P.: For. Rel.* 2:115)
> (*Am. St. P.: Mil.* 2:558)
>
> *American State Papers:* 1, *Foreign Relations.* 5, *Military Affairs.*
> *American State Papers: Military Affairs.* Vol. 2.

PRESIDENTIAL DOCUMENTS

16.168 See discussion at 15.361–62. Note that in citations to the House Miscellaneous Documents the document number is sufficient for locating the entry in the reference list and the date is therefore unnecessary.

> (President 1984, 341)
> (*House Misc. Doc. no. 210*)
> (Hoover 1974–77, 4:178–83)
>   *or*
> (Hoover 1977, 178–83)
>
> President. 1984. Proclamation. Caribbean Basin Economic Recovery Act, proclamation 5142, amending proclamation 5133. *Federal Register* 49, no. 2 (4 January): 341. Microfiche.
> *House Miscellaneous Document no. 210.* 53d Cong., 2d sess. In *Compilation of the messages and papers of the presidents, 1789–1897,* edited by J. D. Richardson. Vol. 4. Washington, D.C.: GPO, 1907.
> Hoover, Herbert. 1974–77. *Public papers of the presidents of the United States: Herbert Hoover, 1929–33.* 4 vols. Washington, D.C.: GPO.
>   *or*
> Hoover, Herbert. 1977. *Public papers of the presidents of the United States: Herbert Hoover, 1929–33.* Vol. 4. Washington, D.C.: GPO.

EXECUTIVE DEPARTMENT DOCUMENTS

16.169 See discussion at 15.364. Suggested short text references for the examples presented in 15.364 are offered below:

> (Treasury Department 1929, 14–28)
> (*Task force report* 1967, 21)
> (Straus 1959, 12)
> (LaBelle 1983, 83–119)
> (Department of the Interior 1983, 83–119)
> (Department of Labor 1984, 236)

Reference list entries for the above citations are as follows:

> Treasury Department. Bureau of Prohibition. 1929. *Digest of Supreme Court decisions interpreting the National Prohibition Act and Willis-Campbell Act.* Washington, D.C.: GPO.
>
> *Task force report: Juvenile delinquency and youth crime.* 1967. President's Commission on Law Enforcement and Administration of Justice. Washington, D.C.: GPO.
>
> Straus, Ralph I. 1959. *Expanding private investment for free world economic growth.* A special report prepared at the request of the Department of State. April.
>
> LaBelle, Robert P. 1983. *See* U.S. Department of the Interior. Minerals Management Service. 1983.
>
> U.S. Department of the Interior. Minerals Management Service. 1983. *An oilspill risk analysis for the central Gulf (April 1984) and western Gulf of Mexico (July 1984),* by Robert P. LaBelle. Open-file report, U.S. Geological Survey. Denver. Lease offerings microform.
>
> U.S. Department of Labor. Employment Standards Administration. 1984. *Resource book: Training for federal employee compensation specialists.* Washington, D.C.

16.170 When the publication facts are omitted because such other identifying data as serial numbers are given, the title and issuing body may be mentioned in running text, and the serial number added in the reference list entry:

> Referring to the document *Postwar Policy Preparation, 1939–1945,* issued by the Department of State, the senator hazarded the opinion that . . .
>
> Department of State. *Postwar policy preparation, 1939–1945.* General Policy Series, no. 15.

16.171 Census Bureau publications may be cited as follows:

> (Bureau of the Census 1975)
>
> U.S. Bureau of the Census. 1975. *Median gross rent by counties of the United States, 1970.* Prepared by the Geography Division in cooperation with the Housing Division, Bureau of the Census. Washington, D.C.

UNITED STATES CONSTITUTION

16.172 Citations to the United States Constitution are made in running text, following the guidelines presented in 15.367. The Constitution is not included in the reference list.

PUBLICATIONS BY GOVERNMENT COMMISSIONS

16.173 See discussion at 15.368.

> (Securities and Exchange Commission 1983, 42)
> (Senate 1935, pt. 71A)

> U.S. Securities and Exchange Commission. 1983. *Annual report of the Securities and Exchange Commission for the fiscal year.* Washington, D.C.: GPO.
> U.S. Senate. 1935. *Report of the Federal Trade Commission on utility corporations.* 70th Cong., 1st sess. S. Doc. 91.

FEDERAL COURT DECISIONS

16.174 See also discussion at 15.369–72. Decisions of the federal courts are cited in the text and are rarely listed separately in the reference list. Examples of citations in running text follow:

> In 1941, in *Bridges v. California* (314 U.S. 252), the Court held that . . .
> The United States Court of Appeals, Second Circuit, in *United States v. Katzwallader* (183 F. 2d 210 [1950]), found . . .

TREATIES

16.175 See also discussion at 15.373. Possibilities for treating parenthetical citations and reference list entries for treaties follow. Note that the dates used for locating references are the treaty dates, not the dates of publication or registration.

> (Department of State 1963)
> (Naval Armament Limitation Treaty 1922)
> (United Nations 1954)

> U.S. Department of State. 1963. Nuclear Weapons Test Ban 5. August. TIAS no. 5433. *United States treaties and other international agreements,* vol. 14, pt. 2.
> U.S. Naval Armament Limitation Treaty. 26 February 1922. *Statutes at Large* (December 1923–March 1925), 43, pt. 2.
> United Nations. Treaty Series. 1956. Denmark and Italy: Convention concerning military service. 15 July 1954. *Treaties and international agreements registered or filed or reported with the Secretariat of the United Nations,* 250, no. 3516.

16.176 See also discussion at 15.374. Since dates are frequently unavailable for unpublished documents of the United States government, the parenthetical citation in the text should give the record group (RG) number, following a suitable short version of the author or depository. Suggestions based on the alternative forms presented at 15.374 follow:

> (Senate Committee, RG 46)
> *or*
> (National Archives, RG 46)
>
> (National Commission, RG 10)
> *or*
> (National Archives Branch, RG 10)

Matching reference list entries are as follows:

> U.S. Senate Committee on the Judiciary. RG 46. Lobbying. National Archives. File 71A-F15.
> *or*
> National Archives. RG 46. Files of the Senate Committee on the Judiciary. Lobbying. File 71A-F15.
>
> National Commission on Law Observance and Enforcement. RG 10. National Archives Branch Depository, Suitland, Md.
> *or*
> National Archives Branch Depository, Suitland, Md. RG 10. Records of the National Commission on Law Observance and Enforcement.

STATE AND LOCAL GOVERNMENTS AND COURTS

16.177 *Published reports, messages, and addresses.* See discussion at 15.377.

> (California Legislature 1998, 15, 26, 31–34)
> (Wordsmith 2010, 23, 26)
> (Illinois General Assembly 1977, 14–18)
> (IIEQ 1977)
>
> California Legislature. 1998. Joint Committee on the Twenty-first Century. *Preliminary report to the legislature, 1998, regular session on preparing to enter the twenty-first century.* Sacramento.
> Wordsmith, R. Kaufman. 2010. Governor of Illinois. *Message of Governor R. Kaufman Wordsmith to the 96th General Assembly, 21 January 2010.* Springfield.
> Illinois General Assembly. 1977. Law Revision Commission. *Report to the 80th General Assembly of the State of Illinois.* Chicago.
> Illinois Institute for Environmental Quality (IIEQ). 1977. *Review and synopsis of public participation regarding sulfur dioxide and particulate emissions.* By Sidney M. Marder. IIEQ Document no. 77/21. Chicago.

16.178 *State laws and municipal ordinances* (see also discussion at 15.379–80). In the author-date system, citations to specific state laws or municipal ordinances should be restricted to running text:

> According to section 3566 of the Ohio *General Code* (Page compilation) . . .

Compilations of state laws or municipal ordinances as a whole may be cited in the reference list:

> Kentucky. 1943. *Revised Statutes, Annotated* (Baldwin).

Titles of specific laws or ordinances are italicized:

> The New York *"Good Samaritan" Law* of 1830 . . .

16.179 *State constitutions and court decisions.* Citations to state constitutions and court decisions are made in running text and are not included in the reference list (see also discussion at 15.382–84).

United Kingdom

16.180 For a background discussion of government documents of the United Kingdom, Great Britain, and England see 15.385–88.

PARLIAMENT

16.181 *Debates* (see also discussion at 15.390, 15.393). In parenthetical text references to the various publications containing parliamentary debates, shortened or abbreviated titles are used; the British style of denominating series is used (1s, 2s, 3s), followed but not preceded by a comma; the volume number replaces the date; column numbers follow the volume number, from which they are separated by a colon; the abbreviations *vol.* and *cols.* are omitted.

> (*Hansard* 1s, 32:119)
> (*Hansard* 2s, 112:96–112)
> (*Hansard* 3s, 249:611–27)
> (*Parl. Deb.* 4s, 164:911–31)
> (*Parl. Deb.*, Commons, 5s, 26:119–26)
> (*Parl. Deb.*, Lords, 5s, 58:111–15)

16.182 In the reference list, the entry should begin with "United Kingdom" (U.K.) or "Great Britain" (G.B.); the title of the compilation, which comes next, should be given in full; the abbreviations for the series, volume, and if included, column(s) should be used; the year may be included, in parentheses, immediately following the volume number; the first element ("Great Britain," etc.) is followed by a period, but all other elements are separated by commas:

> United Kingdom. 1879. *Hansard Parliamentary Debates,* 3d ser., vol. 249, cols. 611–27.
> ———. 1911. *Parliamentary Debates,* Commons, 5th ser., vol. 26.

Specific items in the *Debates* may be cited in the more usual author-date style:

(Churchill 1945, 407:425–46)

Churchill, Winston S. 1945. Speech to the House of Commons, 18 January. *Parliamentary Debates,* Commons, 5th ser., vol. 407 (1944–45), cols. 425–46.

16.183 *Parliamentary Papers, Sessional Papers.* See discussion at 15.394–95.

(Commons 1983, 2, par. 9.14:102)

United Kingdom. House of Commons. 1983. Present and future role of the assistant chief education officer. *Sessional Papers, 1982–83, prison education.* 25 April. Vol. 2.

16.184 *Command papers.* See discussion at 15.395.

(Parliament 1968, 15–16)
(Parliament 1918)
(Parliament 1926)
(Parliament 1960)

United Kingdom. Parliament. 1968. *The Basle facility and the Sterling area.* Cmnd. 3787. October.
United Kingdom. Parliament. 1918. *First interim report of the Committee on Currency and Foreign Exchanges after the War.* Cd. 9182.
U.K. Parliament. 1926. *Report of the Royal Commission on Indian Currency and Finance.* Vol. 2, Appendices. Cmd. 2687.
U.K. Parliament. 1960. Committee on the Working of the Monetary System [Radcliffe Committee]. *Principal memoranda of evidence.* Vol. 1. London.

16.185 *Statutes.* Acts of Parliament are best identified in running text. Citations such as "(*Statutes of the Realm,* 32 Hen. 8, c. 49)" may be given in parentheses. (See also discussion at 15.397.)

BRITISH FOREIGN AND STATE PAPERS

16.186 See discussion at 15.398.

(Foreign Office 1952–53, 41:1298–99)

United Kingdom. Foreign Office. 1952–53. Austria: Proclamation of the emperor annulling the constitution of 4th March 1849. *British Foreign and State Papers.*

REPORTS IN PAMPHLET FORM

16.187 See discussion at 15.399.

(Minister of Science 1961, 58)

United Kingdom. Office of the Minister of Science. 1961. Committee on Management and Control of Research. *Report.*

OTHER PUBLISHED RECORDS

16.188 See discussion at 15.400–401.

> (*Rot. parl.* [1278–1504], vol. 2)
> (*Statutes* 1810–28, vol. 7)
> (*Acts* 1890–1970, vol. 17)
> (Public Record Office 1907, nos. 85, 63)
>
> U.K. *Rotuli parliamentorum* . . . (1278–1504). 6 vols. N.p., n.d.
> U.K. *Statutes of the Realm.* 1810–28. Edited by A. Luders et al. 11 vols. London.
> U.K. *Acts of the Privy Council of England.* 1890–1907. Edited by J. R. Dasent. 32 vols. London.
> U.K. Public Record Office. 1907. Queen Mother to Queen, 18 February 1581. *Calendar of State Papers, Foreign Series, of the Reign of Elizabeth [I]* (January 1581–April 1582). London.

UNPUBLISHED DOCUMENTS

16.189 As indicated in the discussion at 15.402–6, citing unpublished government documents of the United Kingdom is a complex and irregular affair. The difficulties are compounded by the requirements of the author-date documentation system, which perhaps render that system less suitable to such documents.

16.190 One solution to the difficulties is to describe the item in running text; list the depository in parentheses, in abbreviated form; and supply the details in the reference list.

> "Clarendon, in a letter to Lumley dated 16 January 1869 (PRO), observed that . . ."
> "Henry Elsynge, the presumed author of 'The moderne forme of the Parliaments of England' (BL n.d.), maintains in that manuscript . . ."
>
> United Kingdom. Public Record Office (PRO). 1869. Foreign Office, Belgium/133, no. 6. Clarendon to Lumley, 16 January.
> United Kingdom. British Library (BL). n.d. [Henry Elsynge]. The moderne forme of the Parliaments of England. Addit. MSS 26645.

16.191 In works citing mainly, or very many, such documents, it may be more suitable to use the humanities style of notes and bibliography entries.

Canada

16.192 See also the discussion at 15.407–10.

PARLIAMENT AND EXECUTIVE DEPARTMENTS

16.193 (Commons 1951, 335–37)
(Senate 1970, 2:25)

(Commons 1956, 8–21)
(*Sessional Papers* 1917, xiii)
(Dept. Ext. Affairs 1953, 26–31)

Canada. House of Commons. 1951. *Debates,* 2–6 October.
Canada. Senate. 1970. Special Committee on the Mass Media. *Report.* 3 vols. Ottawa.
Canada. House of Commons. 1956. Standing Committee on External Affairs. *Minutes of proceedings and evidence,* no. 4, 24 April.
Canada. *Sessional Papers.* 1917. No. 20g. Report of the royal commission to enquire into railways and transportation in Canada.
Canada. Department of External Affairs. 1953. *Statements and speeches,* 53/30, 11 June.

16.194 Note that in the author-date system, for brevity and ease of location, *Sessional Papers* is paired with the date and, in the reference list, precedes the title of the report.

STATUTES

16.195 See discussion at 15.409.

(*Statutes* 1919, 31–34)

Canada. *Statutes of Canada.* 1919. 10 Geo. 5, c. 17.

UNPUBLISHED RECORDS

16.196 Because dates do not appear in references to unpublished records housed in the Public Archives of Canada, a variation from the usual author-date style is necessary in citations to these items. The text reference begins with the archive, usually abbreviated *PAC;* this is followed, without punctuation, by an abbreviation for the name of the record group (*PCOR* for Privy Council Office Records, for example). The citation should then continue with whatever additional information is required to locate the full documentation in the reference list. If items from only one volume are cited, only the page reference need be added. If more than one volume is cited, the volume number should also appear. If more than one series of the record group is involved, the series number must also be added.

(PAC PCOR, 147–49)
(PAC PCOR, 1477:147–49)
(PAC PCOR, ser. 1, 1477:147–49)

16.197 In the reference list entry, the abbreviation of the name of the record group should follow, in parentheses, the full name of the group. Series and volume numbers follow the record group.

Canada. Public Archives of Canada. Privy Council Office Records (PCOR). Ser. 1, vol. 1477.

International Bodies

16.198 See the discussion at 15.411.

> (League of Nations 1935)
> (League of Nations 1933)
> (League of Nations 1944)
> (UN Secretariat 1951)
> (UN General Assembly 1954)
> (UNESCO 1963, 145)
> (GATT 1969, 14–21)

> League of Nations. 1935. *Position of women of Russian origin in the Far East.* Ser. L.o.N.P. IV.3.
> League of Nations. 1933. *Monetary and economic conference: Draft annotated agenda submitted by the Preparatory Commission of Experts.* II. Economic and financial. II.Spec.I.
> League of Nations. 1944. *International currency experience: Lessons of the inter-war period.* Geneva. II.A.4.
> United Nations. Secretariat. Department of Economic Affairs. 1951. *Methods of financing economic development in underdeveloped countries.*
> United Nations. General Assembly. 1954. Ninth Session. Official Records. Supplement 19. *Special United Nations fund for economic development: Final report.* Prepared by Raymond Scheyven in pursuance of UN General Assembly Resolution 724B (VIII), A/2728.
> UNESCO. 1963. *The development of higher education in Africa.* Paris.
> General Agreement on Tariffs and Trade (GATT). 1969. *Agreement on implementation of article VI (Anti-dumping Code).* Geneva.

MUSICAL SCORES

Published

16.199 See discussion at 15.412.

> (Verdi 1982)
> (Mozart 1960)
> (Schubert 1895)

> Verdi, Giuseppe. 1982. *Rigoletto: Melodrama in three acts by Francesco Maria Piave.* Edited by Martin Chusid. *The works of Giuseppe Verdi.* Ser. 1, *Operas.* Chicago: University of Chicago Press; Milan: G. Ricordi.
> Mozart, Wolfgang Amadeus. 1960. *Sonatas and fantasies for the piano.* Prepared from the autographs and earliest printed sources by Nathan Broder. Rev. ed. Bryn Mawr, Pa.: Theodore Presser.
> Schubert, Franz. 1895. Das Wandern (Wandering). *Die schöne Müllerin (The maid of the mill).* In *First vocal album* (for high voice). New York: G. Schirmer.

Unpublished

16.200 See the discussion at 15.413.

> (Shapey 1966)
>
> Shapey, Ralph. 1966. Partita for violin and thirteen players. Score. Special Collections, Joseph Regenstein Library. University of Chicago.

NONBOOK MATERIALS

Sound Recordings

16.201 In the author-date documentation system, sound recordings are mentioned in running text. For musical recordings, the composer, the title of the work, the performers, and the recording company are usually identified. Full documentation may then be given in the reference list, usually under the name of the composer but sometimes under the performer. The title of the recording is italicized. In sentence-style capitalization, letters designating keys are ordinarily capitalized, as exceptions to the rule, but such modifiers as *major, minor, flat, sharp,* and *natural* are not. (See also the discussion at 15.414–17.)

> Shostakovich, Dmitri. *Symphony no. 5.* New York Philharmonic. Leonard Bernstein. CBS IM 35854.
> *or*
> Bernstein, Leonard, dir. *Symphony no. 5,* by Dmitri Shostakovich. New York Philharmonic. CBS IM 35854.
> Bach, Johann Sebastian. *The Goldberg variations.* Glenn Gould. CBS IM 37779.
> *or*
> Gould, Glenn, pianist. *The Goldberg variations,* by Johann Sebastian Bach. CBS IM 37779.
> Mozart, Wolfgang Amadeus. *Mass in C minor.* Chorus and Academy of St. Martin-in-the-Fields. Neville Marriner. Philips audiocassette 7300 775.
> Mozart, Wolfgang Amadeus. *Symphony no. 38 in D major.* Vienna Philharmonic. James Levine. Polydor compact disk 423 086-2.
> Carter, Elliott. Eight etudes for woodwind quintet. On record 1 of *The Chamber Music Society of Lincoln Center.* Classics Record Library SQM 80-5731.

16.202 Recordings of drama, prose or poetry readings, lectures and the like, which often carry the name and location of the publisher and the date of publication or copyright, may be cited as follows in parenthetical text references and reference list:

> (*Genesis of a novel* 1969)
> (Senn 1974)

Genesis of a novel: A documentary on the writing regimen of Georges Simenon. 1969. Tucson, Ariz.: Motivational Programming Corp. Sound cassette.

Senn, M. J. E. 1974. *Masters and pupils.* Audiotapes of lectures by Lawrence S. Kubie, Jane Loevinger, and M. J. E. Senn presented at meeting of the Society for Research in Child Development, Philadelphia, March 1973. Chicago: University of Chicago Press.

If the date is unavailable, the recording is mentioned in the running text, and full documentation, minus the date, is given in the reference list entry:

Thomas, Dylan. *Under Milk Wood.* Performed by Dylan Thomas and others. Caedmon TC-2005. Audiocassette.

Thomas, Dylan. *Under Milk Wood.* Performed by Dylan Thomas and others. Caedmon CDLS-2005. Compact disk.

Melville, Herman. *Moby Dick.* Selected readings. Spoken Arts 850. Audiocassette.

Auden, W. H. *Poems.* Read by author. Spoken Arts 7137. Compact disk.

16.203 Written material accompanying the recording may be listed as follows:

Green, Archie. Introduction to brochure notes for Glenn Ohrlin, *The hellbound train.* University of Illinois Campus Folksong Club CFC 301. Reissued as Puritan 5009.

Videorecordings

16.204 See discussion at 15.418–20.

SLIDES AND FILMS

16.205   (Mihalyi 1975)
        (*Greek and Roman world* 1977)
        (*Incident in Tiananmen Square* 1990)

Mihalyi, Louis J. 1975. *Landscapes of Zambia, central Africa.* Santa Barbara, Calif.: Visual Education. Slides.

The Greek and Roman world. 1977. Chicago: Society for Visual Education. Filmstrip.

An incident in Tiananmen Square. 1990. 16 mm, 25 min. San Francisco: Gate of Heaven Films.

VIDEOCASSETTES

16.206   (*Itzak Perlman* 1985)

Itzak Perlman: In my case music. 1985. Produced and directed by Tony DeNonno. 10 min. DeNonno Pix. Videocassette.

MATERIAL OBTAINED THROUGH LOOSE-LEAF, COMPUTER, OR INFORMATION SERVICES

16.207 For a background discussion see 15.421–22.

(CCH 1990, ¶ 20, 050.15)
(Kupisch 1983)
(Flax et al. 1979)
(Beevis 1983)

Commerce Clearing House (CCH). *1990 standard federal tax reports.* Chicago: Commerce Clearing House.

Kupisch, Susan J. 1983. Stepping in. Paper presented as part of the symposium Disrupted and Reorganized Families at the annual meeting of the Southeastern Psychological Association, Atlanta, Ga., 23–26 March. DIALOG, ERIC, ED 233276.

Flax, Rosabel, et al. 1979. *Guidelines for teaching mathematics K–12.* Topeka: Kansas State Department of Education, Topeka Division of Education Services, June. 85, DIALOG, ERIC, ED 178312.

Beevis, D. 1983. Ergonomist's role in the weapon system development process in Canada. Downsview, Ont.: Defence and Civil Institute of Environmental Medicine. 8, NTIS, AD-A145 5713/2. Microfiche.

In the second reference list entry above, the name of the symposium has been given headline capitalization to set it off from the surrounding text.

COMPUTER PROGRAMS AND ELECTRONIC DOCUMENTS

Programs, or Software

16.208 References to computer software (programs, packages, languages, systems, and the like) are best made in running text. The location and identity of the supplier may be reserved for the full citation in the reference list. The following examples illustrate typical reference list entries for computer software. Because dates are not involved, the entries are identical to those for humanities-style bibliographies (see also the discussion at 15.423).

FORTRAN H-extended Version [*or* Ver.] 2.3. IBM, White Plains, N.Y.
Houston Automatic Spooling Priority II Ver. 4.0. IBM, White Plains, N.Y.
International Mathematical Subroutine Library Edition 8 (IMSL 8). International Mathematical Subroutine Library, Inc., Houston, Tex.
Operating System/Virtual Storage Rel. 1.7 (OS/VS 1.7). IBM, White Plains, N.Y.
Statistical Package for the Social Sciences Level M Ver. 8 (SPSS Lev. M 8.1). SPSS, Chicago.
Lotus 1-2-3 Rel. 2. Lotus Development Corporation, Cambridge, Mass.

Documents

16.209 See discussion at 15.424. Note that the year the document is cited is used in lieu of the date of publication.

("AIDS" 1990, 2)
(*Belle de jour* 1990)
(Moore 1990)
("Jericho's Walls" 1990)
(Kulikowski 1989)

"AIDS." *See* "Acquired Immunodeficiency Syndrome."
"Acquired Immunodeficiency Syndrome." 1990. In MESH vocabulary file [database online]. Bethesda, Md.: National Library of Medicine, 1990 [cited 3 October 1990]. Identifier no. D000163. [49 lines.]
Belle de jour. 1990. In Magill's Survey of the Cinema [database online]. Pasadena, Calif.: Salem Press, ca. 1989– [cited 1 January 1990]. Accession no. 50053. P. 2 of 4. Available from DIALOG Information Services, Inc., Palo Alto, Calif.
Moore, Rich. 1990. "Compaq Computer: COMPAQ Joins the Fortune 500 Faster Than Any Company in History." In Businesswire [database online]. San Francisco: Business Wire, 1986– [updated 9 April 1986; cited 10 March 1990]. Accession no. 000782; NO = BW420. 5 screens. Available from DIALOG Information Services, Inc., Palo Alto, Calif.
"Jericho's Walls." 1990. In History Log9008 [electronic bulletin board]. S.l. 27 August 1990– [cited 15 December 1990]. Available from listserv @ FINHUTC.BITNET.
Kulikowski, Stan. 1989. "Readability Formula." In NL-KR (Digest vol. 5, no. 10) [electronic bulletin board]. Rochester, N.Y., 1988 [cited 31 January 1989]. Available from nl-kr @ cs.rochester.edu; INTERNET.

17 Indexes

INTRODUCTION

17.1 Every serious book of nonfiction should have an index if it is to achieve its maximum usefulness. A good index records every pertinent statement made within the body of the text. The subject matter and purpose of the book determine which statements are pertinent and which peripheral. An index should be considerably more than an expanded, alphabetical table of contents. It should also be something other than a concordance of words and phrases.

DEFINITIONS

Kinds of Indexes

17.2 Because an index should enable a reader to find every pertinent statement made in a book, it usually includes both proper-name and subject entries. Indexed proper names include not only those of persons and other entities discussed in text or notes, but frequently also those of authorities cited (see 17.27). Occasionally, if the material is complex and there is a large cast of characters, two indexes are prepared: one of persons only and the other of subjects and other proper names. This division may be particularly helpful in a large historical work. A still finer division may be useful in a history of literature, art, or music, where the works of the creators may be listed separately. For example, an anthology of poetry in several parts with discursive introductions may require a subject index, an author index, and an index of titles and first lines. For some kinds of scholarly works it is usual to make a separate listing of all authors cited in the text (titled Author Index) as well as a general index (titled Subject Index) of everything else, including names of other persons. Perhaps the rarest is the index of subject matter only, as might be called for in a discourse on philosophy, theology, or mathematics.

The Entry

17.3   The *entry* is the principal subdivision of an index. A simple entry consists of a *heading* and what is technically called a *locator.* The heading identifies the subject of the entry; the locator tells the reader where to find material pertaining to the subject. The locator can be a section number, chapter and paragraph number (as in the index of this volume), or any of several other types of place identification; in most indexes, however, it is a *page number* or sequence of page numbers, and that is what will be referred to in the discussion that follows.

Subentries

17.4   An entry consisting of a heading and a large number of page references is always, in good indexing practice, broken up into *subentries.* These consist of subheadings, each representing some aspect of the main heading, and page numbers. Good subheadings, at once logical and useful to the reader, constitute one of the marks of a superior index.

Headings and Subheadings

17.5   The main heading of an index entry is normally a noun or noun phrase—the name of a person, place, object, abstraction, or such. A sequence of headings in one book on American Indians reads as follows:

tents, skin	Teton Sioux
teosinte	Tewa organization
tepary beans	textiles, cedar-bark
termination	theology, Navaho
Teton Dakota	throwing stick

Each of these headings is a substantive of some sort, and where the keyword—the word a reader is most likely to look under—was not the first word in the phrase, the indexer has inverted the heading. Such inversion is an important consideration in the choice of good headings for an index.

17.6   Obviously, every subheading must bear a logical relation to the heading. Often there is a close grammatical relation as well; that is, it is possible to join heading and subheading in normal order and have the combined phrase make sense grammatically as well as semantically:

> statistical material, 16, 17, 89; marking of, for printer, 176; months in, 65; proofreading, 183; states, territories, and possessions in, 65–66; in tables, 90–91; time of day in, 64; units of measure in, 63

In the foregoing entry, note that the heading and the first subheading unite grammatically to read "marking of statistical material for printer."

17.7   At other times, however, it is more appropriate to use subheadings that are subdivisions or units within a larger category expressed in the principal heading or that have a logical relation to the main heading that does not require grammatical connection as well:

> Native American peoples: Ahualucos, 140–41; Aztecs, 81–84; Chichimecs, 67–68; Huastecs, 154; Mixes, 178; Olmecs, 90–102; Toltecs, 128–36; Zapotecs, 168–72
>
> Loans: collateral, 33–34; default, 38–41; interest rates, 30, 36–37; refinancing, 42, 44; usury, 37

17.8   A *complete entry* consists of the principal heading and page references, all subheadings and page references, and all cross-references.

Page References

17.9   When discussion of a subject continues for more than a page, the sequence of pages is given: 34–36, 192–96, and so on. (University of Chicago Press style for printed indexes calls for en dashes, rather than hyphens, with continued numbers; the number of digits to use is discussed in *f.*, *ff.*, 8.69–70.) Never use the abbreviations *f.*, *ff.*, or *et seq.* in an index: use only the actual sequence of pages. A distinction is sometimes made between continued discussion of a subject (indexed, for example, 34–36) and individual references to the subject on a series of pages (34, 35, 36). If passing references to the subject over a long sequence of pages are actually important enough to index, *passim* may be used (for example, 78–89 passim), but this is a locution seldom used by professional indexers. Passing references are preferably either ignored or gathered under the subheading "mentioned," which is sometimes placed at the end of the whole entry.

Run-in and Indented Typographical Styles

17.10 All indexes are set in what is called *flush-and-hang* style. This means that the first line of an entry is set flush left and the rest of the entry is indented below it. When there are subentries, a choice must be made between *run-in* and *indented* styles. In run-in style the subentries follow one another laterally across the column and are separated by semicolons. Examples of the run-in style may be seen in 17.6 and 17.7. In indented style each subentry begins a new line, indented one em; subentry runovers are indented two ems, and if the main heading runs over, it should also be indented two ems:

> Iraq, the (lower Tigris-Euphrates Valley),
> 48, 125, 138, 245. *See also* Sawad
> under Abbasids, 275, 487
> agricultural investment by Sasanians in,
> 144, 201–3
> Arab conquest of, 301–7

Run-in style takes less space and is widely used in general books, but its use in complicated works whose indexes require great quantities of subentries and, frequently, sub-subentries, should, whenever possible, be avoided in favor of indented style, which is much easier for the eye to follow. Compare, for example, the index samples in 17.15 and the three varieties in 17.143 and 17.145–46. (See also 17.55.)

Cross-References

17.11 Cross-references guide the reader to related information. Properly used, they are extremely helpful adjuncts to an index, but they should never be employed unless they actually lead to *additional* information, not just the same information indexed under other headings. Cross-references are of two general kinds, *see* references and *see also* references.

17.12 *See* references are used in the following situations:

1. When the indexer has chosen one among several keywords or phrases and the reader might look under another:

   Roman Catholic Church. *See*   adolescence. *See* teenagers; youth
   Catholicism

2. When the subject has been treated as a subentry to a principal entry (note that the entry and subentry are separated by either a colon or a comma):

Book of Common Prayer. *See* Church of England: and Book of Common Prayer

Iroquois Indians. *See* Indian tribes, Iroquois

For this type of cross-reference some indexers use the expression *see under,* followed by the principal heading only. The Press does not object to this locution, provided it is clear which subentry the reader is directed to.

3. When an entry has been alphabetized under another letter of the alphabet:

The Hague. *See* Hague, The

van Gogh, Vincent. *See* Gogh, Vincent van

4. When a personal name has been alphabetized under the real surname rather than a pseudonym, name in religion, earlier name, or married name:

Bell, Currer. *See* Brontë, Charlotte

Louis, Father. *See* Merton, Thomas

Lunt, Mrs. Alfred. *See* Fontanne, Lynn

Thibault, Jacques Anatole. *See* France, Anatole

5. When reference is from a popular or shortened form of a term to the "official," scientific, or full form:

Mormon Church. *See* Latter-day Saints, Church of Jesus Christ of

baking soda. *See* sodium bicarbonate

Gray's "Elegy." *See* "Elegy Written in a Country Churchyard" (Gray)

An entry composed merely of a heading and a *see* reference is termed a *blind entry.* The indexer and anyone editing the index must make certain that no blind entry refers to another blind entry.

17.13 *See also* references are used when *additional* information can be found in another entry or subentry. When additional information can be found in more than one other entry, the cross-references follow one another in alphabetical order and are separated by semicolons:

Elizabethan Settlement, 11–15, 17, 43; and Hooker, 13–14. *See also* Catholicism; Church of England; Protestantism

Maya: art of, 236–43; cities of, 178 (*see also* Chichén Itzá; Uxmal); human sacrifice among, 184–87; present-day, 267. *See also* Quiché Maya; Yucatán, Indians of

As with *see* references, when the cross-reference is to a subentry, some indexers use *see also under,* followed by the principal heading. Indexers and editors must make sure that all *see also* references do indeed lead to additional information and that none leads to a blind entry.

17.14 *See also* cross-references pertaining to a whole entry may be placed immediately after the heading or at the end of the entire entry:

LOCATION A

Calumet People (*see also* Lakes People; Prairie People): animal totem, 123, 146; clothing, 126–27; dream dance, 182–86; migration, 112, 136; population, 139; reservations, 137, 139

Calumet People. *See also* Lakes People; Prairie People
animal totem, 123, 146
clothing, 126–27
dream dance, 182–86
migration, 112, 136
population, 139
reservations, 137, 139

LOCATION B

Calumet People: animal totem, 123, 146; clothing, 126–27; dream dance, 182–86; migration, 112, 136; population, 139; reservations, 137, 139. *See also* Lakes People; Prairie People

Calumet People
animal totem, 123, 146
clothing, 126–27
dream dance, 182–86
migration, 112, 136
population, 139
reservations, 137, 139
See also Lakes People; Prairie People

Location A is preferred by many indexers on the ground that it gives the user all the probable headings under which to look for material at the outset. Location B, the older and more traditional way of inserting *see also* references, is preferred by others on the ground that such references usually lead only to peripheral material and should not clutter the opening of the entry. The University of Chicago Press accepts either location, so long as it is consistently used in an index.

17.15 In the style preferred by the University of Chicago Press, when *see* references follow and pertain to a main heading, the word *see* always begins with a capital letter and is preceded by a period (see examples in 17.12). Following and pertaining to a subheading, in either run-in or indented style, the word *see* is lowercased and the reference is enclosed in parentheses. The heading itself is capitalized or lowercased to match the main entry referred to.

government: archives, 38, 44, 103–17; basis of, 19–24; officials, 21, 136–42, 209; programs, 87–92, 210; publications (*see* public documents); responsibilities, 24–32, 157–62

government
archives, 38, 44, 103–17
basis of, 19–24
officials, 21, 136–42, 209
programs, 87–92, 210
publications (*see* public documents)
responsibilities, 24–32, 157–62

17.16 In run-in style, when *see also* references follow a main heading and apply to the entire entry the word *see* is lowercased and the reference is enclosed in parentheses:

> Calumet People (*see also* Lakes People):
> animal totem, 123, 146; clothing, 126–27; etc.

In the indented style, the reference may be similarly enclosed in parentheses, or *see* may begin with a capital letter and follow a period:

> Calumet People (*see also* Lakes
> People)
> animal totem, 123, 146
> clothing, 126–27

> Calumet People. *See also* Lakes
> People
> animal totem, 123, 146
> clothing, 126–27

If such a reference is placed at the end of the entire entry, *see* always begins with a capital letter and the reference is not enclosed in parentheses; in run-in style it is also preceded by a period:

> Calumet People: animal totem, 123, 146;
> clothing, 126–27; . . . reservations,
> 137, 139. *See also* Lakes People

> Calumet People
> animal totem, 123, 146
> clothing, 126–27
> . . . .
> reservations, 137, 139
> *See also* Lakes People

When following and applying to a subentry, however, *see also* references are always enclosed in parentheses and the word *see* lowercased:

> Maya: art of, 236–43; cities of, 178 (*see
> also* Chichén Itzá); human sacrifice
> among, 184–87; etc.

> Maya
> art of, 236–43
> cities of, 178 (*see also* Chichén Itzá)
> human sacrifice among, 184–87

17.17 In cross-references, headings and subheadings should usually be cited in full, with capitalization, inversion, and punctuation exactly as given in the entry referred to. Exceptions are sometimes made, however, for very long headings. A cross-reference to "AAAS (American Association for the Advancement of Science)" could be shortened to "*See* AAAS" without ambiguity. When more than one principal heading is cited, they should be separated by semicolons (17.14); if reference is to a subheading, its principal heading should be given first, followed by a colon or a comma and the subheading (17.12). Multiple cross-references are arranged in alphabetical order (17.13).

17.18   For any kind of cross-reference the words *see* and *see also* are normally set in italic type. If what follows, however, is in italics (a book title, for example), *see* or *see also* may be set in roman to distinguish it from the rest of the cross-reference.

17.19   Both *see* and *see also* references may include generic references, that is, they may refer to a type of heading rather than to specific headings too numerous to list:

> sacred writings. *See under specific titles*
> sacred writings, 125–27, 130. *See also*
> *under specific titles*

Note that such a cross-reference is completely italicized. If the generic reference occurs with other, specific, cross-references, the generic reference comes last (see example in 17.141, under "agriculture").

THE INDEXER

17.20   The ideal indexer sees the book as a whole, both in scope and in arbitrary limits; understands the emphasis of the various parts and their relation to the whole; and, perhaps most important of all, clearly pictures potential readers and anticipates their special needs. An indexer must make certain that every pertinent statement in the book has been indexed in such a way that the reader can easily find the information sought. A good indexer must also have sufficient knowledge of both publishing and typesetting practices to be able to present the data in acceptable editorial and typographic form.

The Author as Indexer

17.21   Clearly, authors know better than anyone else both the scope and the limits of their work and the nature of the audience to whom the work is addressed. It might be supposed, therefore, that authors are their own ideal indexers, and sometimes this is indeed the case. The best scholarly indexes are probably made by authors who have the ability to be objective about their work, who understand what a good index is, and who, having mastered the craft, know how such an index is achieved. But authors are sometimes so subjective about their own work that they are tempted to include in an index even references to milieu-establishing, peripheral statements, and as a result they prepare a concordance rather than an efficient index. Not all authors have mastered the skills or acquired the experience necessary to make a good index.

In such a case, the surest way to attain a suitable index is to enlist the aid of a professional indexer.

The Professional Indexer

17.22 Professional indexers have the advantages of objectivity and experience in many fields of interest and scholarship. The most valued have mastered the craft of indexing, are familiar with the publisher's style and with standard publishing practices, and are accustomed to timely delivery of their product. For the author who cannot prepare an index, or does not wish to, the professional indexer is the logical choice for the task. In much of what follows in this chapter it is assumed, for purposes of fuller explanation, that the author and the indexer are not the same person.

17.23 The indexer should be intelligent, widely read, well acquainted with publishing practices, and capable of working rapidly to meet almost impossible deadlines. Less time is available for the preparation of the index than for almost any other step in the bookmaking process. For obvious reasons, most indexes cannot be completed until page proofs are available. Typesetters are anxious for those few final pages of copy; printers want to get the job on the press; binders are waiting; salesmen are clamoring for finished books—*surely* you can get that index done over the weekend?

17.24 Of course you cannot. No adequate index for a full-length book of any complexity can be—or should be—completed over a weekend, unless the weekend includes several extra days at either end. In addition to requiring intense intellectual concentration, good indexing requires reflection; that is, the indexer should stop frequently, review what has been done, and decide whether both author and reader have been well served by the choices made.

THE MECHANICS OF INDEXING

The Human Factor

17.25 Although we speak of the sequence of tasks we perform when indexing—some of them physical, some mental—as the *mechanics* of the job, the process is far from mechanical in any literal sense. There are, of course, indexes that are mechanically—or better, electronically—produced. One kind of electronic indexing system is referred to as the concordance generator. Such a program provides the computer with a list of words to be excluded—articles, prepositions, and conjunctions, for example—and commands the computer to record every occurrence of every word not excluded. The words are recorded in alphabetical order and, for multiple occurrences, in order of occurrence. The printout is thus indeed a concordance and cannot in any way substitute for a real index prepared with the aid of human intelligence. At present, indexes cannot be electronically made, for the decisions required are of a far higher order than computers are yet capable of.

Computer Assistance

17.26 Although the well-tempered indexer cannot be replaced by a computer, he or she can be assisted by one. The indexer still selects items, headings, and subheadings, and the indexer still keyboards the entries, but the properly programmed computer takes over such operations as alphabetizing the headings, combining like entries, suppressing duplicate headings, checking cross-references, and formatting the entire index. The task of the indexer who uses some such dedicated indexing program as CINDEX or MACREX is made less arduous, less tedious, and less time-consuming. It should be stressed, however, that the indexing functions of present word processing programs do not achieve results that are comparable to those achieved with dedicated indexing software. The sorting routines of word processing programs, for example, are not yet sufficiently sophisticated to conform to either letter-by-letter or word-by-word alphabetization rules. Much of what follows in this chapter applies to indexing done with dedicated computer programs as well as to indexing with the use of pen or pencil and typewriter. When the assistance of the dedicated computer program offers benefit to the indexer, the nature of that assistance will be described.

What Parts of the Book to Index

PRELIMINARY PAGES, TEXT, AND BACK MATTER

17.27 The first decision to be made, what to index (other than the text itself), is relatively straightforward. Much of the preliminary matter—title page, dedication, epigraphs, lists of illustrations and tables, and acknowledgments—should not be indexed. A preface, even a foreword by someone other than the author, may be indexable if it concerns the subject of the book itself and not simply how the book came to be written. A true introduction to the work, which occasionally finds its way into the prelims, is of course fully indexable. Most of the back matter should not be indexed: glossary, bibliography, and so on. Appendixes should be indexed if they contain important material omitted from the main body of the text, but not if they merely reproduce documents (the text of a treaty, for example, or a questionnaire) that are discussed in the text. Authors cited in text or notes are indexed if such practice is customary in the field, since readers may wish to see whether work by important authorities has been taken into account.

NOTES

17.28   Notes, whether at the foot of the page or at the back of the book, may be indexed if they continue or amplify discussion in the text (textual, or reading, notes); those that merely document statements in the text (reference notes) should not ordinarily be indexed. If a note documents an otherwise unattributed statement or idea discussed at some length in the text, however, the cited author may be added to the index (see also 17.27). References to footnotes should normally be by page number and *n* for *note*, alone; for example, 134n (hair space between numeral and *n*, no period after *n*). If there are several notes on a page, the note number may be given (in this instance with a period and a word space following *n*): 134n. 14, 172nn. 17, 19. If there is indexable material in a text passage and in a note that is on the same page but not tied to that passage, separate references may be given: 63, 63n. When notes are printed at the back of the book (endnotes), an index reference is most helpful if it includes the number of the note as well as the page on which it is printed. If the subject discussed in the endnote is not directly identified in the text, citation of the context in which the note reference occurs is nevertheless sometimes helpful. In that case the text page may be added in parentheses following the endnote citation:

> synergy, 224, 238–39, 364n. 12 (193)

If such contextual citations are used, they must be explained in a head-note at the beginning of the index.

AUTHOR-DATE CITATIONS

17.29   Documentation by means of author-date citations (see chapter 16) instead of notes, either in the form "(Madrington 1989)" or "According to Madrington (1989)," is, like documentation in notes, not ordinarily indexed, unless it is customary in the field to do so or there is to be an index of authors or unless the citation documents an otherwise unattributed statement discussed at some length in the text.

TABLES, CHARTS, AND SIMILAR MATERIAL

17.30   Matter in tables, charts, graphs, maps, drawings, photographs, and other illustrative material is occasionally listed in the index when it is of particular importance to the discussion. Index references to illustrations may be of great assistance to the reader who wishes to refer to a reproduction of a painting discussed in an art book. For clarity, references to illustrative material often require inclusion of the illustration or table number:

> 121, 138 fig. 2, 214, 311 table 6

It may sometimes be sufficient, however, to set the page number in italic type when the reference is to an illustration:

> 121, *138*, 214, *311*

In that case it is advisable to add, at the beginning of the index, an explanation of the use of italics.

Workspace and Equipment for Indexing without a Computer

17.31 A word about what an indexer needs in the way of working space and equipment when working without a computer. Abundant desk or table space is essential—the dining-room table is a useful adjunct for indexers who work at home, especially when they come to alphabetizing the index cards, and one cannot have too much desk space for handling proofs.

17.32 Three-by-five-inch index cards are needed, as are alphabetic tab dividers for the cards and a file box to put them in. You will also need a typewriter and standard-size ($8\frac{1}{2} \times 11$ inches), good-quality paper. For a scholarly book of average length and complexity you will need at least a thousand index cards, so don't skimp: they come in packages of a hundred and boxes of a thousand. Preferably, cards for an index should be typed, not handwritten, to obviate later errors arising from misinterpretation of handwritten words or numbers. A special typewriter platen for index cards speeds typing, but is not really necessary, and the long strips of perforated card stock that tear apart into three-by-five cards provide an alternate convenience.

The Process in Brief

17.33 Indexes are usually prepared from page proofs. Much preliminary work may be done with galley proofs, however, if these are to be seen in the manufacturing process. Working on the text and in the margins of the galleys, the indexer can make decisions about headings and subheadings and even start to prepare index cards or, if working with a computer, enter and format the headings and subheadings on disk or tape. Entries cannot be completed, however, until page proofs are available, unless locators are paragraph or section numbers rather than page numbers. Such preliminary work may prove helpful, however, if the schedule is very tight or if the book is of great length and complexity. Except in special circumstances such as these, the more usual course is to await page proofs before beginning work on the index, for there is some duplication of work if the indexer must go back through page proofs to find the locators.

17.34 Occasionally, especially for books with many scattered illustrations and a complex format, dummy pages are prepared by the designer as a guide to the typesetter in page makeup. A dummy consists of cut-up galley or other proofs arranged and pasted, along with copies of the illustrations, into formatted pages. Such a dummy—more usually, a copy of such a dummy—can be used for the preparation of the index before actual pages are available. If any deviations from the dummy prove necessary, however, some adjustments in the index may be required.

17.35 When working without a computer, the indexer prepares index cards from the marked page proofs, one item to a card, and then alphabetizes all of the cards. When all entries and subentries have been amalgamated by combining locators from duplicate cards and suitable cross-references have been made, the cards are edited into final form. Then the entire index is retyped, double spaced, on 8½-by-11-inch paper in a form that can be marked by the editor and set in type for printing. Sometimes, supposedly in the interest of speed, a publisher is willing to accept index copy on cards, but savings are largely illusory: an index costs more to set from cards, and copyediting and proofreading are much slower.

17.36 In computer-assisted indexing, alphabetization is done by the computer, and since the index at any stage may be viewed in alphabetical and formatted order, editing may be performed as the work goes along. Finally, the completed index, double spaced and properly formatted, is printed out by the system's printer. No retyping is necessary.

First Step: Marking the Page Proofs

17.37 The indexing method advocated in this chapter involves doing much of the actual work on the page proofs, before any cards are prepared or computer entries made. This method may not commend itself to professional indexers, since much of the work is done twice, but anyone compiling a full-length index for the first time, whether author or editor, will probably find it more reassuring and less troublesome than other, more sophisticated methods. It also makes changing one's mind and correcting mistakes easier to accomplish.

17.38   Page proofs may be marked up all at once before any cards are prepared or entries keyboarded, or the indexer may prefer to work with one chapter at a time, marking the pages for that chapter, typing the entries, and then moving on to the next chapter. The latter procedure is more agreeable to many people, and as time goes on, the indexer becomes more skilled and self-assured in marking the proofs so that less underlining and fewer marginal notes suffice to dictate what goes into the entry. Marking should not become so skimpy and cryptic, however, that it is impossible to reconstruct from the proofs what is to be indexed and under what headings it should be listed.

17.39   To visualize the method advocated here, suppose you are indexing one of the earlier sections in this book, a discussion in chapter 11 of how to draw up a list of illustrations (see fig. 17.1). You have read through the chapter once and have now gone back to select headings and subheadings for indexing this particular section. You decide that the whole section (11.44–46) will have to be indexed under *List of illustrations, preparing,* so you mark the section head as shown. (In marking the proofs, a colon separates a proposed principal heading from a proposed subheading.) Then you decide that since preparing the list of illustrations is one of the tasks of manuscript editing, this section had better be indexed under *Copyediting* and *Manuscript editor* also, so you add these headings in the top margin, with *list of illustrations* as the subheading proposed for each. Going down the page, you pass over *interstellar particles, Roman architecture,* and *photographs of ancient buildings* without making a mark (though you may be tempted): these are nonindexable examples only. But you decide to include one more subheading under the main heading *List of illustrations;* this is *when to include* (11.44 only). Note that there is no point in making an elaborate breakdown of the main heading, with many specific subheadings, when the subheadings all lead to the same few paragraphs—the reader is already there, so to speak. Continuing down the page, you underline *capitalized* (modifying it to *capitalization*), *sentence style, headline style, plates, figures,* and several other terms as proposed main headings, with *in* (or *for*) *list of illustrations* as subheads. Note how *page numbers* is marked to be inverted (numbers, page) for use as a main heading. It might be argued, of course, that *page numbers* should not be inverted, the assumption being that *page* is the operative word.

17.40   For each heading you choose, you should also supply a *modification,* a word or phrase that narrows the application of the heading. Some of these will become subheadings in the index as finally edited. Some will not. But it is important to have them on hand at later stages in making the index, because if you do not, you may end up with nothing but unmodified headings followed by long strings of page numbers, which make an index all but useless. In computer assisted indexing, the modifications may be retained, altered, or eliminated as the work goes on.

copyediting: list of illustrations

manuscript editor: and list of illustrations

LIST OF ILLUSTRATIONS : *preparing*

11.44 A task that often falls to the manuscript editor (but is more properly done by the author) is preparing the list of illustrations. Not every illustrated book requires such a list. The criterion is, Are the illustrations of interest apart from the text they illustrate? For a scientific monograph on interstellar particles, illustrated largely by graphs, the answer is obviously no. For a book on Roman architecture, illustrated by photographs of ancient buildings, the answer is obviously yes. For some other illustrated books, the answer may not be so easy to give, and the author and editor must decide whether the list of illustrations is worth the space it will take. *: when to include*

Preparing the List

11.45 The list of illustrations follows the table of contents, normally on a new recto page, and is headed simply Illustrations. The titles of the illustrations listed are capitalized in sentence style or headline style in agreement with the style used in the list of tables and so forth. If illustrations are of more than one type, they are listed by category—plates, figures, maps, and so forth—and by number if numbers are used in the text (see 11.28, also fig. 11.4). For figures and maps that print with the text (and hence have folios assigned to them, whether or not the folios are expressed on the page), page numbers are given (*000* or ■■■ in the copy as first prepared). For plates and for maps printed separately, another type of location is given. If plates are to be inserted in groups of four or more pages at one location, each group is listed under the tag *Following page 000* when copy is prepared. If they are to be inserted in the text two pages at a time (each page of plates accordingly lying opposite a text page), the location is given as *facing page 000*. The editor changes the zeros to real numbers once page proofs are out and page numbers are known. *ation : in list of illustrations*

Editing Captions *↗ picture: editing ↗ for list of illustrations*

11.46 It should be remembered that the list of illustrations is a *list*, not a reprinting of the captions and legends. If the captions are short and adequately identify the subjects of the pictures, they may do double duty in the list of illustrations. Long captions, however, should be shortened, and discursive legends should never be used here. *↗ picture: in list of illustrations*

Fig. 17.1. Type proof of three paragraphs from an earlier chapter in this manual, marked for indexing (for explanation of marking see text, 17.39–41)

17.41   If a text discussion extends over more than one page (in this instance, more than one paragraph), as it often does, beginning and ending references have to be given—as with the main entry above. Sometimes you can look ahead and add the closing reference immediately. At other times it is more practical to leave the closing reference open and add the number later.

Second Step: Typing the Entries

17.42   When the preliminary work on the page proofs, whether part or all of them, has been completed, the next step is typing the entries, either on cards or in the digital files of a computer system. The entries typed may essentially confirm the indexing decisions made while marking the proofs, or they may somewhat alter those decisions as the result of further reflection. In any case, entries at this stage should include three elements: a heading, a modification or provisional subheading, and a locator (see 17.3). In the present exercise (see fig. 17.2) the locators are chapter and paragraph numbers rather than the page numbers typical of most indexes.

17.43   After each entry is typed, it should be proofread, either on the card or on the video display terminal, and the content and locator should be checked against the proof. This checking of entries is most conveniently done as you go along, before the examined pages have been returned to their place in the whole body of proof and the cards, if these have been used, have been alphabetized.

17.44   After all the entries have been completed and checked, read quickly through the pages again to see whether anything indexable has been omitted. You may find that unmarked items that seemed peripheral at first now, in the light of themes developed in later chapters, declare themselves significant. It is also possible that entries for important material may inadvertently have been overlooked. Such omission may now be remedied.

Third Step: Alphabetizing the Entries

17.45   Index entries typed on cards may be alphabetized as they accumulate, at the end of each work session, or after all cards have been completed. As the alphabetizing goes on, some preliminary editing may suggest itself, perhaps the addition, deletion, or modification of some subheads or the addition of locators.

17.46   Alphabetization of index entries on cards is usually accomplished in two stages. First, all entries are arranged in alphabetical groups by ini-

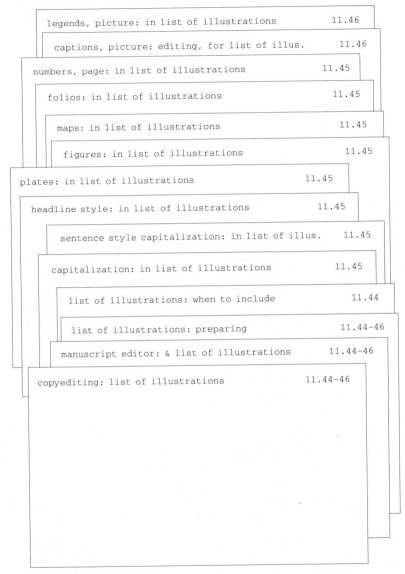

legends, picture: in list of illustrations   11.46

captions, picture: editing, for list of illus.   11.46

numbers, page: in list of illustrations   11.45

folios: in list of illustrations   11.45

maps: in list of illustrations   11.45

figures: in list of illustrations   11.45

plates: in list of illustrations   11.45

headline style: in list of illustrations   11.45

sentence style capitalization: in list of illus.   11.45

capitalization: in list of illustrations   11.45

list of illustrations: when to include   11.44

list of illustrations: preparing   11.44-46

manuscript editor: & list of illustrations   11.44-46

copyediting: list of illustrations   11.44-46

Fig. 17.2. Cards made from the marked proof shown in fig. 17.1. The cards are shown in the order in which they would be filed, and so should be read from the bottom to the top of the illustration.

tial letter. Following this, the entries within each letter group are arranged alphabetically following either the word-by-word or letter-by-letter mode. (For a complete discussion of alphabetizing entries, including the two modes mentioned here, see 17.97–131.)

17.47 When indexing is done with a microcomputer equipped with dedicated indexing software, alphabetization occurs automatically as the entries are keyboarded, and alterations may be performed anywhere in the accumulated index at any time by calling up the desired entries on the video display terminal.

Fourth Step: Editing the Entries

17.48 Whether alphabetization is done mechanically by hand sorting of cards or electronically by computer, the assembled entries must now be edited to a coherent whole comprising clear, concise, and effective parts. Headings must be tailored, subheadings determined, and adequate but not excessive cross-referencing provided, all of which will make the difference between an index that is an efficient, truly complete key to the material within a book and one that is merely a collection of words and page numbers. Some of this editing will already have been performed along the way in computer assisted indexing—perhaps even a bit will have been done while indexing with cards—but much refinement must await the assembled whole. (For a simple example of a sequence of edited cards see fig. 17.3.)

17.49 From the headings and modifications on the cards, or the headings and subheadings stored in the computer, you now have to make final decisions about principal headings and subheadings—main entries and subentries. You now have to make a final choice among synonymous or closely related terms—monarch, king, or ruler; agriculture, farming, or crop raising; clothing, costume, or dress; life, existence, or being—and prepare suitable cross-references to reflect those choices.

17.50 You also have to decide whether certain entities will be treated as main entries or as subentries under a comprehensive principal heading—

Hopi, 00		
Iroquois, 00	*or*	Indian tribes: Hopi, 00; Iroquois,
Kwakiutl, 00		00; Kwakiutl, 00; Mohawk, 00
Mohawk, 00		

painting, 00		
pottery making, 00	*or*	handicrafts: painting, 00; pottery
weaving, 00		making, 00; weaving, 00; wood
wood carving, 00		carving, 00

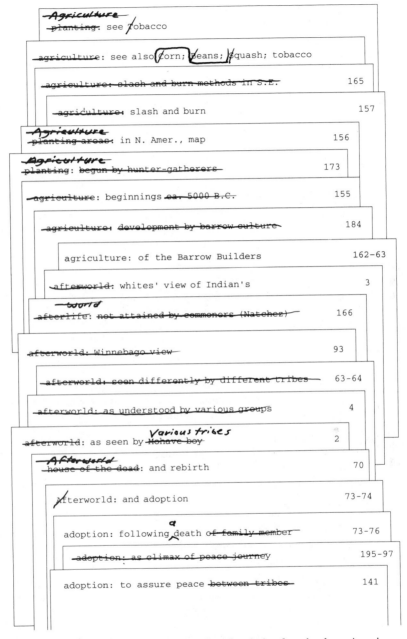

~~Agriculture~~
~~planting:~~ see /Tobacco

~~agriculture:~~ see also |Corn; |Beans; |Squash; tobacco

~~agriculture: slash and burn methods in S.E.~~   165

~~agriculture:~~ slash and burn   157

~~Agriculture~~
~~planting areas:~~ in N. Amer., map   156

~~Agriculture~~
~~planting: begun by hunter-gatherers~~   173

~~agriculture:~~ beginnings ~~ca. 5000 B.C.~~   155

~~agriculture: development by barrow culture~~   184

agriculture: of the Barrow Builders   162–63

~~afterworld:~~ whites' view of Indian's   3

~~world~~
~~afterlife: not attained by commoners (Natchez)~~   166

~~afterworld: Winnebago view~~   93

~~afterworld: seen differently by different tribes~~   63–64

~~afterworld: as understood by various groups~~   4

Various tribes
~~afterworld:~~ as seen by ~~Mohave boy~~   2

~~Afterworld~~
~~house of the dead:~~ and rebirth   70

Afterworld: and adoption   73–74

adoption: following ^a death ~~of family member~~   73–76

~~adoption: as climax of peace journey~~   195–97

adoption: to assure peace ~~between tribes~~   141

Fig. 17.3. Cards for the first three entries of an index for a book on American Indian religion. The completed cards have been alphabetized and edited, ready for typing (the beginning of the file is at the bottom of the illustration). For two typed versions of these entries see figs. 17.4 and 17.5.

again with cross-references if needed in the context. One's main concern here, as everywhere in the preparation of an index, should be to make sure that every pertinent piece of information within the book is recorded, either as principal entry or as subentry, and that the reader will be able to find it without arduous searching.

WHEN TO FURNISH SUBENTRIES

17.51 Main entries unmodified by subentries should not be followed by long rows of page numbers. Such an entry forces the reader to run through many pages before finding the exact information needed. A rule of thumb is to furnish at least one subentry if there are more than five references to any single heading.

17.52 If, for example, the index of a book on medical care included an entry like the one at the left below, it should certainly be broken up into a number of subentries, perhaps as at the right:

hospitals, 17, 22, 23, 24, 25, 28, 29–31, 33, 35, 36, 38, 42, 91–92, 94, 95, 96, 98, 101, 111–14, 197

hospitals: administration of, 22, 96; and demand for patient services, 23, 91–92; efficiency of, 17, 29–31, 33, 111–14; finances of, 28, 33, 36, 38, 42, 95, 112; and length of patient stay, 35, 94, 98, 101, 197; quality control in, 22–25, 31

The original entry would defeat any but the most persistent user, whereas the second, though longer, leads the reader to the information sought with a minimum of leafing through pages.

17.53 Subentries are most effective when they are concise and informative and begin with a keyword or phrase. The rambling and poorly worded subentries in the example at the left below make subject location tiresome. Two methods of improving this example are offered at the right. The first, consisting of fairly inclusive subentries, meets the requirements of economy. The second, appropriate to more generous space allowances, includes sub-subentries. Other solutions, of course, are possible; there is no single and absolutely correct way to construct or improve an index.

house renovation
 balancing heating system, 65
 building permit required, 7
 called "rehabbing," 8
 correcting overloaded electrical circuits, 136
 how wallboard is finished, 140–44

house renovation, 5, 8
 electrical repairs, 129–34, 135, 136
 fireplace, installing, 191–205
 heating system, balancing, 65
 legal requirements, 7, 135, 192
 painting and decorating, 11, 156–58

installing ready-made fireplace, 191–205

painting outside of house adds value, 11

plumbing permit required, 7

removing paint from doors and woodwork, 156–58

repairing dripping faucets, 99–100

replacing clogged water pipes, 125–28

replacing old wiring, 129–34

separate chimney required for fireplace, 192

straightening sagging joists, 40–42

termite damage to sills a problem, 25

three ways to deal with broken plaster, 160–62

violations of electrical code corrected, 135

what is involved in, 5

plaster repair, 160–62

plumbing repairs, 99–100, 125–28

structural problems, 25, 40–42

wallboard, finishing, 140–44,

house renovation, 5, 8

  electrical repairs

    circuit overload, 136

    code violations, 135

    old wiring, 129–34

  heating system

    balancing, 65

    fireplace installation, 191–205

  legal requirements

    electrical code, 135

    permits, 7

    separate chimney for fireplace, 192

  painting and decorating

    painting the exterior, 11

    stripping woodwork, 156–58

  plumbing repairs

    clogged water pipes, 125–28

    dripping faucets, 99–100

  structural problems

    sagging joists, 40–42

    termite damage, 25

  wall and ceiling repairs

    broken plaster, 160–62

    wallboard, finishing, 140–44

ARRANGEMENT OF SUBENTRIES

17.54 Subentries should ordinarily be arranged alphabetically according to the first important word, but a chronological order is also widely used, especially for historical studies and others in which the text itself is structured on a chronological basis. Occasionally, subentries are arranged in mathematical or some other order (see 17.105).

THE PROBLEM OF SUB-SUBENTRIES

17.55 Sub-subentries are best treated in the indented style index, where they and their relation to the subheads can be clearly seen. Unless space must be saved and a substantial saving can indeed be achieved by using the run-in style, all indexes having sub-subentries should be cast in the indented style. True sub-subentries are difficult if not impossible to use in run-in indexes, but if necessary a similar effect can be achieved by repeating an opening word or phrase in a series of subentries or by representing the word or phrase with an em dash:

> Eskimos: language, 18; pottery, 432–37; traditions of, in Alaska, 123; traditions of, in California, 127

> Eskimos: language, 18; pottery, 432–37; traditions of, in Alaska, 123; —, in California, 127

For a more extensive use of the em dash in this way see the example in 17.145.

17.56 Another solution to the problem is illustrated in 17.146, where indented style is used for the subentries and the run-in style for sub-subentries. Following this combined style, for instance, the second method of improving the index example in 17.53 might, instead, begin as follows:

> house renovation, 5, 8
>> electrical repairs: circuit overload, 136; code violations, 135; old wiring, 129–34
>> heating system: balancing, 65; fireplace installation, 191–205
>> legal requirements: electrical code, 135; permits, 7; separate chimney for fireplace, 192

If it looks as though an index is going to require a great many sub-subentries, however, the indexer should check with the manuscript editor before proceeding. The publisher may in that case prefer the more lucid structure of indented style. Almost never should sub-sub-subentries be used.

PUNCTUATION

17.57 The inversion of a phrase used as the heading in a main entry is punctuated with a comma. A comma is also used to separate a heading from a qualifying phrase.

> balance of payments
> *inversion:*
> payments, balance of

> apology, to war victims

If the heading is followed immediately by page references, a comma should appear between the heading and the first numeral and between subsequent numerals:

> payments, balance of, 16, 19

If the heading is followed immediately by run-in subentries, a colon precedes the first subheading:

> payments, balance of: definition of, 16

All subsequent complete subentries are preceded by semicolons:

> payments, balance of: definition of, 16;
> importance of, 19

Discussion of a single point may begin, be interrupted, and then continue on subsequent, widely scattered pages. Such occurrences must be indicated by appropriate punctuation within both main entries and subentries:

> education, higher, 16, 36–38, 64–67,
> 119–20; at Cambridge, 37–38, 119; at
> Harvard, 16, 64–65

Note that there is no punctuation at the end of any complete entry.

17.58 For examples illustrating punctuation in indented-style indexes see 17.10, 17.14–16, 17.143–44.

17.59 For a discussion of punctuation for *see* and *see also* references see 17.12–16.

CROSS-REFERENCING

17.60 Most cross-references are added at this point in the indexing process, after the final form of entries and subentries has been determined and after the principal headings and subheadings have been edited. Cross-references that you inserted while preparing the cards or computer entries should be carefully examined to make certain that they agree with the final form of headings and subheadings. *See* references should be added if for good reason information has been indexed under a heading that would not easily come to a reader's mind. But to add many entries on the pattern of

> psychology, depth. *See* depth psychology

> *or*

> magazines. *See* periodicals

is to be overkind to the reader to the point of cluttering the index with useless headings. You should also consider whether it is not easier to duplicate locators under a second heading than to make a cross-reference to an entry with only two or three locators. That is, not

> youth movements. *See* "jeunesse" organi-
> zations
> "jeunesse" organizations, 45, 67–68

but simply

> youth movements, 45, 67–68
> "jeunesse" organizations, 45, 67–68

17.61 As has already been suggested, all of the editorial functions outlined above may, with the aid of computer software, be performed as the entries are being keyboarded or, with little disruption, at any time after entries have been embedded. Tailoring and arranging headings and subheadings and adding or combining page references can be carried out through comparison with the accumulating index, which is always available for examination and revision. Cross-references and punctuation may also be added or revised as work progresses; indeed, some punctuation—commas before and between page numbers, for example—falls into place programmatically.

Fifth Step: Typing, Proofreading, and the Final Review

17.62 An index prepared on a computer is fully formatted and ready to be printed out. As with all manuscript material, the printout must be double-spaced. An index prepared on cards, however, once editing has been completed and the last cross-reference added, must be typed in final form, double-spaced, on 8½-by-11-inch paper, in one column, with ample margins, so that it can be marked up by the editor and easily followed by the typesetter (see figs. 17.4, 17.5). Principal headings, as well as subheadings, are preferably lowercased unless they are proper nouns or proper adjectives. The alternative style of capitalizing all principal headings is also acceptable. Leave extra space between alphabetic sections (between the *A*s and *B*s, for example). Number all pages, beginning with 1, and write the author's name and the book title on the first page. Add a title (e.g., "Index" or "Author Index") if you know what it is to be.

17.63 When you have finished typing, proofread the typescript against the cards, check the alphabetical order of all entries, and, in general, conduct a final review based on the suggestions listed in 17.134. Computer printouts, of course, cannot be read against cards, since none exist, but the printout itself should be read for obvious errors. The headings and page references should have been carefully checked—perhaps double-checked—as the entries were made, but it is advisable, in this case as in that of a typed index, to make a final review based on 17.134.

17.64 One copy of the final index typed or printed on standard-sized paper should be delivered to the publisher. If the index is recorded on a magnetic disk, the publisher may want a copy of that for typesetting. For

Fig. 17.4. First page of the typed copy for an index in run-in style. Note especially the punctuation of entries. See fig. 17.5 for copy typed in indented style.

```
                              Index


adoption

    to assure peace, 141, 195-97

    following a death, 73-76

afterworld

    and adoption, 73-74

    and rebirth, 70

    as seen by various tribes, 2, 4, 63-64, 93, 166

    whites' view of Indians', 3

agriculture

    of the Barrow Builders, 162-63, 184

    beginnings, 155, 173

    in North America, map, 156

    slash-and-burn, 157, 165

    See also beans; corn; squash; tobacco

alcoholic beverages, 3, 256, 261

    in ceremony, 251

    See also liquor

altar, 40, 146, 210-12, 266

amulets, 12

    See also tokens

angalok, 88

    See also shaman

animals

    attitude toward, 40-45

    and owner, 42-44, 98, 120-21
```

Fig. 17.5. Opening pages of the typed copy for an indented-style index. See also fig. 17.4.

security against loss of the manuscript or disk, and for reference in case of telephone queries from your editor, keep a duplicate manuscript or a backup disk for yourself. As additional resources against queries, hold on to the cards (if these have been made) and the page proofs until you know that the index has been typeset, proofread, and printed. It is likely that you will not have a chance to proofread the index yourself, as this is frequently done in the publishing office to save time, and for the same reason you may not see the final, copyedited form of your index before it appears in the printed book.

Gauging the Length of an Index as You Go

17.65 If you are an inexperienced indexer, you may want some guidance on the approximate size of the index you have undertaken to compile. The most appropriate length for the index will vary according to the complexity of the book: scholarly books generally need longer indexes than popular ones. For a typical scholarly book this might be (in pages) from one-fiftieth to one-twentieth the length of the text, if we assume that the index is set in two-column, run-in style, in a typeface two points smaller than the body type—all usual specifications for such an index. A book of three hundred pages, for example, might need an index of from six to fifteen pages, depending upon how closely written the book is (one printed page of a two-column run-in index generally accommodates about a hundred lines).

17.66 What does this mean in terms of index entries? Again, much depends upon variables such as the typeface chosen for the index and the width of the column in which it is set. But as an extremely rough working figure, the indexer may assume that an average of five references per text page will yield a short index (one-fiftieth the length of the text) whereas fifteen or more references per text page will yield a fairly long index (perhaps one-twentieth the length of the text). As a running check, then, the indexer can count references marked on the pages or typed on the accumulating cards from time to time and from that number estimate the relative size of the finished product.

17.67 The publisher may be able to provide the indexer with a range of pages that is suitable to both subject matter and the number of pages available in the final signature (see 19.66). If enough is known about the typeface, column width, and page length for the index, the publisher may also be able to convert the range of pages into total numbers of index lines and the approximate number of characters that can be accommodated in a line. Such information would be especially helpful to the indexer working with indexing software.

What to Do about Typos You Find

17.68   The indexer must not attempt to edit the book in page proofs; at the same time, obvious typographic or other errors should be corrected on the proofs, and indexing should reflect the corrections. (The page proofs given an indexer are usually not the corrected master set, but an unmarked duplicate set.) Having finished work on the page proofs, the indexer may (sometimes by prearrangement) telephone the manuscript editor with a list of corrections before undertaking later tasks in preparing the index. It is sometimes possible to make corrections even at this late stage in the manufacture of a book if they are important enough. In certain cases it is still possible to make important corrections at the time the editor receives the index, and it is therefore helpful if the indexer encloses a list of errors.

GENERAL PRINCIPLES OF INDEXING

17.69   An index is a working tool for one particular book, and the indexer should hold this fact in mind at all times. By page-proof time, agreement has long since been reached between author and editor concerning style and usage. If British spelling has been used consistently throughout the text, so should it be in the index. Shakspere in the text would call for Shakspere in the index. Hernando Cortez should not be indexed as Cortés, Hernán; Cortes, Hernando; or any other variant. Virgil should not be indexed as Vergil; Sir Walter Raleigh as Ralegh, Sir Walter. Similarly, the spelling of place-names should agree with the text; if the author used the language of origin ('s Gravenhage, Köln), the name should not be changed in the index to the better-known English form (Hague, The; Cologne). Nor should older geographic terms be altered to their present form (Siam, Thailand; Byzantium, Constantinople, Istanbul) unless so used in the text. The use of accents and other diacritical marks should also be observed (Yucatán, Yucatan; Schönberg, Schoenberg). Only in the rare instance in which confusion might arise in the reader's mind should any cross-reference or parenthetical word or phrase be inserted giving "correct" or more widely used forms. In spelling, capitalization, use of italics, and so on, the index should scrupulously reflect the author's usage (but see 17.90).

17.70   Before commencing the actual indexing, an indexer should gain some familiarity with the work as a whole, and the best way to do this is to run quickly through the entire set of page proofs from beginning to end. One need not, cannot, read every word in such a perusal, but one can learn a great deal about the scope of the work, chronological or otherwise, about the author's approach and self-imposed limitations—historical, philosophical, political, clinical, or whatever—and a good deal about the terminology employed. The knowledge thus gained about the work is well worth the time required, in terms of mistakes and false starts avoided.

Choosing Terms for Entries

17.71 In indexing a work indexers should as nearly as possible imagine themselves the eventual readers and try to anticipate needs and expectations. Under what headings will a reader be most likely to look for information? How full should these headings be? Should they be expanded, modified, or broken down? What should be included? What omitted?

17.72 The wording for all entries should be clear, concise, logical, and consistent throughout. Terms should be chosen according to the author's usage as far as possible. If, for example, the author of a philosophical work uses the term *essence* to mean *being, essence* should be in the index, possibly with a cross-reference. If the author uses the terms interchangeably, only one should be chosen for use in the index, and in this instance a cross-reference is imperative:

> essence (being), 97, 109, 119, 246, 359–
> 62, 371–80
> being. *See* essence

Choosing the most useful keywords is important. Sometimes an author's terminology cannot be reduced to a brief heading, and some other term must be substituted. Here it is essential that indexers put themselves in the reader's place and choose words that will most probably come to the user's mind. Common sense is the best guide.

Incidental Items

17.73 Proper names are an important element in most indexes, but there are times when they should be ignored. In a book on the history of the automobile in America, for example, an author might write, "After World War II small sports cars like the British MG, often owned by returning veterans, began to make their appearance in college towns like Northampton, Massachusetts, and Ann Arbor, Michigan." Seeing these two place-names in the paragraph, an indexer might be tempted to underline them and make cards for inclusion in the index. The temptation must be resisted. The identity of the two towns mentioned has nothing to do with the theme of the book, and the names should find no place in the index. The MG sports car, on the other hand, probably should be indexed, given the subject of the work.

17.74 Scene-setting statements employed by the author to establish historical milieu, particularly in opening sequences, should be carefully considered before they are indexed. For example, the first paragraph of John M. Rosenfield's introduction to his *Dynastic Arts of the Kushans* (Berkeley and Los Angeles: University of California Press, 1967) reads: "In the first three centuries of the Christian era, a great inland empire stretched from the Ganges River valley into the oases of Central Asia. This empire was created by a nation of former nomads whose ruling princes gave themselves the dynastic name Kushan. Opulent and powerful men, cast in much the same mold of Iranian princely ideals as Darius the Great, Timur, or Akbar, they governed a land which lay at the junction of three culture spheres—the Indian subcontinent, Iran and the Hellenized Orient, and the steppes of Central Asia." Fine scene setting, impressive cast of characters—but the indexer should pass it by without making a single entry.

Making Choices between Variants

17.75 Despite their importance in an index, or perhaps because of it, names probably cause more trouble for inexperienced indexers than any other aspect of the indexing craft. Particularly troublesome are names that appear within the work in more than one form, or in incomplete form. The paragraphs that follow survey some of the problems that arise frequently and recommend solutions for them.

FAMILIAR FORMS OF PERSONAL NAMES

17.76 Personal names should be indexed as they have become widely and professionally known:

> Lawrence, D. H. [*not* Lawrence, David Herbert]
> Poe, Edgar Allan [*not* Poe, E. A., *or* Poe, Edgar A.]
> Bizet, Georges [*not* Bizet, Alexandre César Léopold]
> Cervantes, Miguel de [*not* Cervantes Saavedra, Miguel de]

(Note, however, that in a biography or critical study of Lawrence, Bizet, or Cervantes, the full name should appear in the index.)

PSEUDONYMS

17.77 Persons who have used pseudonyms professionally should ordinarily be listed under their real names, with suitable cross-references:

> Ouida. *See* Ramée, Marie Louise de la
> Ramée, Marie Louise de la (pseud. Ouida)

Æ. *See* Russell, George William
Russell, George William (pseud. Æ)

There are, however, some exceptions. François-Marie Arouet, for example, is almost always given primary reference under Voltaire; and Samuel Langhorne Clemens is also frequently given primary reference under Mark Twain.

PERSONS WITH THE SAME NAME

17.78 Persons with identical names should be distinguished from one another:

Field, David Dudley (clergyman)	Pitt, William (the elder)
Field, David Dudley (lawyer)	Pitt, William (the younger)

If many persons with the same surname appear in the same book, particularly if they are members of the same immediate family, suitable parenthetical identifications should be furnished in the index. For example, the index to *O'Neill* by Arthur and Barbara Gelb (New York: Harper, 1962) contains the following entries:

O'Neill, Edmund Burke (brother)
O'Neill, Edward (grandfather)
O'Neill, Mrs. Edward (Mary) (grandmother)
O'Neill, Mrs. Eugene (Agnes Boulton O'Neill Kaufman)
O'Neill, Mrs. Eugene (Carlotta Monterey O'Neill)
O'Neill, Mrs. Eugene (Kathleen Jenkins O'Neill Pitt-Smith)
O'Neill, Eugene Gladstone
O'Neill, Eugene, Jr.
O'Neill, Mrs. Eugene, Jr. (Elizabeth Green)
O'Neill, Eugene, III (son of Shane)
O'Neill, James (father)
O'Neill, Mrs. James (mother) (Mary Ellen "Ella" Quinlan)
O'Neill, James, Jr. ("Jamie") (brother)
O'Neill, John (godfather)
O'Neill, Oona (daughter by Agnes) (Mrs. Charles Chaplin)
O'Neill, Shane Rudraighe (son by Agnes)
O'Neill, Mrs. Shane (Catherine Givens)

MARRIED WOMEN'S NAMES

17.79 Many married women are widely known by their birth names and should usually be indexed accordingly. References to married names can, if necessary in the context, be supplied in parentheses or by means of suitable cross-references:

Sutherland, Joan (Mrs. Richard Bonynge)
Bonynge, Mrs. Richard. *See* Sutherland, Joan
Marinoff, Fania (Mrs. Carl Van Vechten)
Van Vechten, Mrs. Carl. *See* Marinoff, Fania

Others, better known by their married names, should be indexed under their married names, with references to their maiden names, husbands' full names, familiar names, and the like supplied within parentheses or by cross-references if needed:

Besant, Annie (née Wood)
Wood, Annie. *See* Besant, Annie
Browning, Elizabeth Barrett

Roosevelt, Eleanor
Truman, Bess (Mrs. Harry S.)

17.80 Occasionally, a woman may play two roles of importance within a single book—as an unmarried person and later as a wife. For example, in a study of the Barrett family, the following index entries might be needed for one person:

Barrett, Elizabeth (later Elizabeth Barrett Browning), 12, 18–36, 79–82. *See also* Browning, Elizabeth Barrett

Browning, Elizabeth Barrett, 128, 143–45, 162–67. *See also* Barrett, Elizabeth

MONARCHS AND POPES

17.81 Monarchs, popes, and others of such rank should be listed according to their "official," not personal, names:

Henry V (king of England)   Gregory VII

If the monarch or pope is referred to in the work by other than the monarchical or papal name (as, for example, both Gregory VII and Hildebrand), a cross-reference from the alternative name should be included. And in a book on English history where only the English Henrys appear, the identifying tag shown in the example may be omitted.

TITLES OF NOBILITY

17.82 Immediate members of royal families, like monarchs, are generally indexed under their given names:

Charles, Prince of Wales   Fabiola, Queen (of Belgium)
Margaret Rose, Princess

Other persons bearing titles of nobility are generally indexed under the title:

Shaftesbury, first earl of   Guise, third duc de
Dunmore, fourth earl of

17.83 Such rules, however, should be tempered by common sense. In a book in which the Villiers family figured prominently, for example, it would be foolish to index the seventeenth-century dukes of Buckingham under Buckingham and other members of the family under Villiers.

17.84   Titles such as Sir, Dame, Lady, or (sometimes) Baron, when used before a name, are usually retained when the name is inverted for indexing (see 17.97):

> Anderson, Dame Judith   Bax, Sir Arnold

CLERICAL TITLES

17.85   Clerical titles like Reverend, Monsignor, Pastor, or (sometimes) Bishop, when used before a name, are usually retained when the name is inverted for indexing, although ignored in alphabetization (see 17.97):

> Jaki, Rev. Stanley S.   Mannierre, Msgr. Charles L.

Anglican and Roman Catholic bishops are generally identified by the titles of their sees or provinces:

> Ussher, James (archbishop of Armagh)
> Lessard, Raymond W. (bishop of Savannah)
> Cranmer, Thomas (archbishop of Canterbury)

ACADEMIC TITLES AND DEGREES

17.86   Academic titles like Professor and Doctor, used before a name, are not retained in indexing, nor are abbreviations of degrees following a name, like Ph.D., M.D., or LL.D.

SR., III, JR.

17.87   A suffix like "Sr." is retained when the name is inverted for indexing but is placed after the given name following a comma:

> Roosevelt, Theodore, Jr.   Moffett, Mrs. James, Sr.
> Stevenson, Adlai E., III

(See also 17.78.)

SAINTS

17.88   Saints are usually indexed under their given, or Christian, names, with identifying tags to differentiate them, when necessary, from others bearing the same names:

> Catherine of Siena, Saint   Thomas Aquinas, Saint
> Thomas, Saint   Becket, Saint Thomas
>   *or*   Borromeo, Saint Charles
> Thomas, Saint (the apostle)   Chrysostom, Saint John

OBSCURE PERSONS

17.89 Persons referred to in the book by surname or given name only should be further identified:

Thaxter (family physician)   John (Smith's shipmate on *Stella*)

FULL FORM OF NAME

17.90 Proper names should be indexed in full, even though the author may use shortened forms in the text:

TEXT	INDEX
the lake	Michigan, Lake
the bay	San Francisco Bay
"Shasta"	Shasta, Mount
"the Village"	Greenwich Village
"Roosevelt," "the president,"	
"TR," *or* "Teddy"	Roosevelt, Theodore
"Wordsworth"	Wordsworth, William

CONFUSING NAMES

17.91 Proper names about which there might be some confusion should be clearly identified within parentheses:

New York (city)   Mississippi (state)
New York (state)   Mississippi (river)

ACRONYMS AND ABBREVIATIONS OF ORGANIZATION NAMES

17.92 Governmental, international, and other organizations that have become widely known under their abbreviated names or acronyms, usually consisting of capital letters, should be indexed according to the abbreviations, particularly if the full names are cumbersome and little known:

| AFL-CIO | OAS | EEC |
| NATO | OPEC | UNICEF |

(For the alphabetization of such abbreviations see 17.101.) Organizations whose abbreviations are not widely known should be listed by their full names. The abbreviation may, if desired, be added in parentheses after the name, especially if the author has used the abbreviation anywhere in the text.

NEWSPAPERS

17.93 Most English-language newspapers should be indexed under the city of publication regardless of how the name appears on the masthead:

Chicago Sun-Times
Cleveland Plain Dealer
Long Beach Press-Telegram
New York Daily News [not *Daily News* or
    Daily News, New York]

There are exceptions. The city of publication should not be included with the title of a newspaper intended for national distribution, and the venue of foreign English-language newspapers, if not part of the title, is added in parentheses after the title:

Christian Science Monitor
Wall Street Journal
Manchester Guardian
Times (London) [in Britain indexed as
    Times, The]

A foreign language newspaper should be alphabetized according to the first word following an article in its title; the place of publication may be included in parentheses:

Aurore, L' (Paris)
Dziennik Zwiazkowy Zgoda (Chicago)
Jewish Daily Forward (Chicago)
Prensa, La (Buenos Aires)

PERIODICALS

17.94 Periodicals are indexed according to the full title, omitting any article that may appear at the beginning:

Nation
Observer
Atlantic

TITLES OF ARTISTIC WORKS

17.95 A reference to a work by an author (or composer or painter) is usually indexed both as a main entry under its title and as a subentry under the main entry for the author. Historical and critical studies often cite the works of many authors, so the author's name should be included, in parentheses, in the main entry for the individual work; if, however, the work is by the principal subject of a biographical or critical study, such identification is not needed:

Look Homeward, Angel (Wolfe), 34–37
Wolfe, Thomas: childhood of, 6–8; early
    literary influences on, 7–10; literary rep-
    utation of, in 1939, 44; *Look Home-
    ward, Angel,* 34–37; and Maxwell Per-
    kins, 30–41

17.96 If there are citations to many works by the same author, the titles of these works as subentries to the main entry for the author can be grouped, for easy reference, at the end of the other subentries:

> Shelley, Percy Bysshe, 167–68, 193–96; and atheism, 195–96; and Blake, 196; and Coleridge, 193–94, 196; and Keats, 194–95; and Platonism, 167, 194–95; and religion, 167. Works: *Adonais,* 194–95, 200; *Defence of Poetry,* 194–96; *Mont Blanc,* 193–94; *Prometheus Unbound,* 196; *Queen Mab,* 193

Works and authors that are discussed in the text should be indexed as shown above; those that are cited in notes only as documentation should not be indexed unless such a practice is customary in the field (see 17.27).

PRINCIPLES OF ALPHABETIZING

The Two Systems

17.97 There are two principal modes of alphabetizing, the *word-by-word* system and the *letter-by-letter* system. All alphabetizing is letter by letter in one sense: in arranging a series of words in alphabetical order, one considers first the initial letter of the word, then the second letter, the third letter, and so on:

> aardvark
> aardwolf
> Aaron
> Ab
> aba
> abaca

The need to choose between the two modes arises when one is alphabetizing not a set of single words but a set of headings, some of which consist of more than one word. In the word-by-word mode, alphabetization is interrupted at the end of the first word. Second and all subsequent words are included only when two or more headings begin with the same word or words. Hyphens, slashes, and apostrophes are treated as continuing the single word (*new-fashioned, new/old,* and *newborn's,* for example, are each considered one word). In the letter-by-letter mode, alphabetization continues across spaces between words and stops at the first comma preceding a modifying element or an inversion. Serial commas, however—that is, commas used to separate items in a series—are ignored. Parentheses enclosing definitions, alternatives, explanations, or cross-references also interrupt letter-by-letter alphabetization. But as in the word-by-word mode, alphabetization continues across hyphens, slashes, apostrophes, and, as already mentioned, serial commas. The columns below illustrate the differences in alphabetical sorting between the two modes. Note, for example, the variations in relative placement of the following pairs: *new-fashioned/New Latin; newlywed/new math; news, lamentable/news conference; newsletter/ news, networks, and the arts; NEWT (Northern Estuary Wind Tunnel)/ New Testament.*

LETTER BY LETTER	WORD BY WORD
New, Arthur	New, Arthur
New, Zoe	New Deal
newborn	new economics
newcomer	New England
New Deal	New Latin
new economics	new math
newel	New Testament
New England	new town
new-fashioned	New World
New Latin	New Year's Day
newlywed	New, Zoe
new math	newborn
new/old continuum	newcomer
news, lamentable	newel
newsboy	new-fashioned
news conference	newlywed
newsletter	new/old continuum
news, networks, and the arts	news conference
newspaper	news, lamentable
newsprint	news, networks, and the arts
news release	news release
newt	newsboy
NEWT (Northern Estuary Wind Tunnel)	newsletter
New Testament	newspaper
Newton, Lady Anne	newsprint
Newton, Isaac	newt
Newton, Rev. Philip T	NEWT (Northern Estuary Wind Tunnel)
Newton, Dame Sylvia	Newton, Lady Anne
new town	Newton, Isaac
New World	Newton, Rev. Philip T.
New Year's Day	Newton, Dame Sylvia

In an alternative version of the letter-by-letter mode, one practiced by some professional indexers, alphabetization continues uninterrupted across commas. In the letter-by-letter example above, for example, *New, Zoe* would come at the very end of the column, far from *New, Arthur.* The University of Chicago Press, however, strongly favors the procedure previously described, in which sorting stops for all commas except serial commas.

17.98   The University of Chicago Press, while preferring the letter-by-letter approach for most books, is willing to accept indexes compiled on the word-by-word principle if that is the preference of the author or the custom of the discipline or the only mode allowed by the computer software.

General Rules

17.99   When a person, a place, and a thing have the same name, they are arranged in normal alphabetical order:

London, England	hoe, garden
London, Jack	Hoe, Robert

17.100   In sorting identical surnames, those with initials in place of given names take precedence over those whose given names, beginning with the same letter, are spelled out:

Oppenheimer, J. Robert
Oppenheimer, James N.
Oppenheimer, K. T.
Oppenheimer, Keven S.

17.101   Acronyms, arbitrary combinations of letters, and most abbreviations, when used as headings, are alphabetized letter by letter. Identification may be added in parentheses:

AARP (American Association of Retired
   Persons)
ACTH (adrenocorticotropic hormone)
ASCAP (American Society of Composers,
   Authors, and Publishers)
EU (European Union)
WFMT (Chicago radio station)
XYZ affair

For some acronyms and abbreviations it may be appropriate to supply a cross-reference from the fully spelled-out name, or to provide an entry consisting of the full name followed by the acronym or abbreviation in parentheses (see also 17.92). When they begin the entry, acronyms and abbreviations are interspersed alphabetically among the other topical entries:

NAACP
nabob
NATO
nebula
Northern Estuary Wind Tunnel (NEWT)
NRA (National Recovery Act)
numerology

17.102 Numerals may be alphabetized as though spelled out, especially when there are few such entries:

> 125th Street (*alphabetized as* one hundred
>   twenty-fifth)
> 10 Downing Street (*alphabetized as* ten)
> 1066 (the year) (*alphabetized as* ten sixty-
>   six)

An alternative system, particularly useful when there are many such entries or when the numbers are complicated, is listing all such entries together in numerical order at the beginning of the index, before the *A*s. When the numerals do not come first in the entry but follow a common element, they should be listed in numerical order.

> section 9
> section 44
> section 77

17.103 Accented vowels and consonants are usually to be alphabetized along with the unaccented letter in a sequence. The Press does not recommend treating *ü, ö, ä,* as *ue, oe, ae,* or *ş* as *sh,* and so on. In an index containing a great many headings beginning with such accented letters it might be best to put them in separate sections following the unaccented letters. But a note at the head of the index should signal that this has been done.

17.104 In alphabetizing subheadings, introductory articles, prepositions, and conjunctions are disregarded (see also 17.131):

> Marinoff, Fania (Mrs. Carl Van Vechten)
>   caricatured by Covarrubias, 128
>   childhood of, in Boston, 45
>   marriage of, 83
>   in *Spring's Awakening,* 133
>   at Stage Door Canteen, 145
>   as Trina in *Life's Whirlpool,* 137

(This Press rule of long standing is based on the assumption that a reader scanning a long list of subheadings is looking for key terms and will find them most readily if they are in alphabetical order. If subheadings are alphabetized according to *and, in, of,* and the like, the reader has to outguess the indexer, since the choice of such introductory words is often arbitrary.)

17.105 Occasionally, subheadings are arranged according to chronological, mathematical, or some other sense, rather than alphabetically (see also 17.54):

> dynasties, Egyptian: First, 10; Second, 12,
>   141; Third, 45; Fourth, 47–49

> Holmes, Oliver Wendell (1841–1935): childhood and youth, 20–26, 40, 125–26; Civil War years, 70–84, 92; at Harvard, 101–7, 246; as writer, lecturer, and barrister, 132–34, 148–56, 160, 170–73; as Massachusetts jurist, 7, 165, 182–93; as U.S. Supreme Court justice, 8–11, 108, 138–40, 196–205
>
> flora, alpine
> at 1,000-meter level, 46, 130–35
> at 1,500-meter level, 146–54
> at 2,000-meter level, 49, 163–74

Personal Names

NAMES WITH PARTICLES

17.106 Family names containing particles often present a perplexing problem to the indexer. Both the spelling and the alphabetizing of these names should follow the personal preference of, or accumulated tradition concerning, the individual, as best exemplified in *Webster's New Biographical Dictionary.* Note the wide variations in the following list of actual names arranged as they should appear in an index:

Ben-Gurion, David	Gogh, Vincent van
Braun, Wernher von	Guardia, Ricardo Adolfo de la
Cervantes, Miguel de	Hindenburg, Paul von
D'Annunzio, Gabriele	Lafontaine, Henri-Marie
de Kruif, Paul	La Fontaine, Jean de
De la Mare, Walter	La Guardia, Fiorello H.
Del La Rey, Jacobus Hercules	Le Maistre, Antoine
Della Robbia, Luca	Medici, Lorenzo de'
De Valera, Eamon	Ramée, Marie Louise de la
Deventer, Jacob Louis van	Thomas à Kempis
De Vere, Aubrey Thomas	Van Devanter, Willis
De Vries, David Pietersen	Van Rensselaer, Stephen
DiMaggio, Joseph	Vries, Hugo Marie de

NAMES WITH *SAINT*

17.107 A family name in the form of a saint's name should be spelled according to the preference of the person bearing the name. Again, if the person is well known, *Webster's New Biographical Dictionary* should help. If spelled with the abbreviation, such names are preferably alphabetized letter-by-letter as they appear, although they may alternatively be sorted as though spelled out. In this regard, they should generally be treated as are personal names beginning with *Mac, Mc,* or *M'* (17.109).

Sorted as They Appear	Sorted as if Spelled Out
Sainte-Beuve, Charles-Augustin	St. Denis, Ruth
Saint-Gaudens, Augustus	Sainte-Beuve, Charles-Augustin
Saint-Saëns, Camille	Saint-Gaudens, Augustus
San Martín, José de	St. Laurent, Louis Stephen
St. Denis, Ruth	Saint-Saëns, Camille
St. Laurent, Louis Stephen	San Martín, José de

In alphabetizing the names of Christian saints, the word Saint never precedes the personal name (see 17.88).

COMPOUND NAMES

17.108 Alphabetize compound surnames, with or without hyphens, according to preferences of individuals or established usage:

Ap Ellis, Augustine	Lloyd George, David
Campbell-Bannerman, Henry	Mendes, Frederic de Sola
Castelnuovo-Tedesco, Mario	Mendès-France, Pierre
Fénelon, François de Salignac de La Mothe-	Merle d'Aubigné, Jean-Henri
	Merry del Val, Rafael
Gatti-Casazza, Giulio	Pinto, Fernão Mendes
Ippolitov-Ivanov, Mikhail	Teilhard de Chardin, Pierre
La Révellière-Lépeaux, Louis-Marie de	Vaughan Williams, Ralph

NAMES WITH *MAC, MC,* AND *M'*

17.109 Personal names beginning with *Mac, Mc,* or *M'* are preferably alphabetized letter-by-letter as they appear. Alternatively, they may be alphabetized as though the full form, *Mac,* were spelled out.

Sorted as They Appear	Sorted as if Spelled Out
Macalister, Donald	McAdoo, William G.
MacArthur, Charles	Macalister, Donald
Macaulay, Rose	McAllister, Alister
Macmillan, Arthur	MacArthur, Charles
MacMillan, Donald B.	Macaulay, Rose
Macmillan, Harold	McAuley, Catherine
McAdoo, William G.	M'Carthy, Justin
McAllister, Alister	Macmillan, Arthur
M'Carthy, Justin	MacMillan, Donald B.
McAuley, Catherine	Macmillan, Harold

SPANISH NAMES

17.110 Almost without exception Spanish names should be alphabetized according to the father's name. The custom in Spain and Latin America is to use a double surname, the first element of which is the father's family name and the second the mother's maiden name (that is, *her* father's family name). A boy named Juan whose father's name is Jorge Sánchez Mendoza and whose mother's maiden name was María Esquivel López is named Juan Sánchez Esquivel. His sister, Juana, is Juana Sánchez Esquivel. In Latin America, a woman often keeps her maiden name after marriage but drops her mother's family name and replaces it with *de* plus her husband's family name. Thus the mother of the two children just mentioned is called María Esquivel de Sánchez. In this example, then, the father, mother, son, and daughter would be indexed, respectively, as

> Sánchez Mendoza, Jorge
> Esquivel de Sánchez, María
> Sánchez Esquivel, Juan
> Sánchez Esquivel, Juana

The two names that form the full surname are sometimes joined by *y* ("and"), but this does not affect use of the first element in alphabetization:

> Ortega y Gasset, José   Leguía y Salcedo, Augusto

17.111 Not all Spanish names precisely fit the pattern described. For example, some persons use only one surname, and two given names are not uncommon. José Murguía and Agustín Pedro Justo are alphabetized (again, by the father's name):

> Murguía, José   Justo, Agustín Pedro

Also, some family names include particles that may make them look like married women's names to the uninitiated: as José María Fernández de Sandoval, for example, or Cristóbal de Torre Redondo, which should be alphabetized as follows:

> Fernández de Sandoval, José María
> Torre Redondo, Cristóbal de

Finally, persons with the conventional compound surname are sometimes known to the world by the mother's name rather than the father's, a well-known example being the poet Federico García Lorca, called Lorca in the English-speaking world. The name, however, is alphabetized

> García Lorca, Federico

and in this instance one would insert a cross-reference under Lorca.

17.112 These are not the only complications presented by Spanish names, and an indexer who is not conversant with Hispanic culture should seek help before trying to index any but the most straightforward examples.

17.113 In Hungarian, personal names appear with the surname first, followed by the given name (Bartók Béla). In English, however, Hungarian names are usually written in English order and reinverted—with the comma—in alphabetizing:

> Bartók, Béla   Molnár, Ferenc

17.114 Most modern Arabic names consist of a given name plus a family name (e.g., Zakir Husain) or a given name plus the given name of the individual's father plus the family name (e.g., Ahmad Hamid Hmisi). Such names are alphabetized under the family name:

> Husain, Zakir   Hmisi, Ahmad Hamid   Mahfouz, Naguib

Family names beginning with *al-* (the equivalent of *the*) are alphabetized under the element following this particle. The particle itself may be placed after the whole inverted name or (the more modern practice) retained before it:

> Hakim, Tawfiq al-   Jamal, Muhammad Hamid al-
> *or*   *or*
> al-Hakim, Tawfiq   al-Jamal, Muhammad Hamid

In either case *al-* is ignored in alphabetizing. Elided forms of the article (*ad-, an-, ar-,* etc.) are treated the same way; the practice of spelling such names in the elided form, however, is discouraged by most Orientalists (see 9.91).

17.115 Arabic names of earlier periods are indexed in the form in which they originally became familiar in the West. In the classical period names consisted of a given name plus one or more other names reflecting place of origin or residence, trade, sect of Islam, and so on. The given name was often followed by a word of relationship such as *ibn, bin,* and so forth ("son of") or *abu* ("father of") and the name of the individual referred to. Such names are alphabetized under the element by which the person is most commonly known, which may be the given name or any of the appended names (consult the catalog of a large reference library in doubtful cases). The familiar Western form of some classical names is often remote from the original: Averroës, for example, actually bore the name Abu al-Walid Muhammad ibn Ahmad ibn Muhammad ibn Rushd, and he is usually listed under the surname Ibn Rushd, *ibn* in that case being capitalized (see 7.12). For later times, too, the principle often holds. The founder of Saudi Arabia, for instance, is indexed under his patronymic, Ibn Saud, capitalized as if it were a surname, but his son and successor is indexed under his given name, Faisal; in both instances these happened to be the forms in which the names first became familiar in Europe and America.

CHINESE NAMES

17.116 In English language texts Chinese names are spelled in Latin characters that suggest the Chinese pronunciation, sometimes according to no particular system, usually according to either the pinyin system (especially since the mid-1970s) or the older Wade-Giles system. The indexer should spell the names as given in the work, making no attempt to regularize them and adding no cross-references unless the author has introduced alternative spellings in the text. Romanized Chinese names often appear in the forms in which they first became familiar to Western readers, so a mixture of systems in the same work is not uncommon.

17.117 Chinese personal names generally consist of three syllables, the one-syllable family name coming first, the two-syllable given name following. In romanized form both names are capitalized; in the Wade-Giles system the given name is hyphenated; in pinyin, closed up (see also 9.95–98):

PINYIN	WADE-GILES
Cheng Shifa	Ch'eng Shih-fa
Li Keran	Li K'o-jan
Zeng Youhe	Tseng Yu-ho
Zhao Wuji	Chao Wu-chi

When alphabetizing Chinese names that are written in traditional form, with family name first, do not invert, and use no commas.

17.118 Some Chinese names, particularly from earlier times, consist of only two syllables. In the romanized forms, there is little consistency about the use of hyphens. These names too should be alphabetized without inversion:

> Lao-tzu
> Li Po
> Sun Fo

Many twentieth-century Chinese with ties to the West have adopted the practice of giving the family name last (Tang Tsou, H. H. Kung, T. V. Soong, etc.). These names should be inverted in alphabetizing:

> Kung, H. H.
> Soong, T. V.
> Tsou, Tang

JAPANESE NAMES

17.119 Japanese names normally consist of two elements, a family name and a given name—in that order. If the name is westernized, as it often is by authors writing in English, the order is reversed. Thus:

JAPANESE ORDER	WESTERN ORDER
Tajima Yumiko	Yumiko Tajima
Yoshida Shigeru	Shigeru Yoshida
Kurosawa Noriaki	Noriaki Kurosawa

In recent years, however, there has been a tendency among authors writing in English on Japanese subjects to use the traditional order for personal names. It is important, therefore, in alphabetizing Japanese names, that the indexer make certain which order the author has used. If a name is in Japanese order, it is left as is, with no inversion and no comma; if in Western order, it is inverted, with a comma, like a Western European name.

VIETNAMESE NAMES

17.120 Like Chinese names, Vietnamese names consist of three elements, the family name being the first (Ngo Dinh Diem, Vo Nguyen Giap). Similarly, the family name is used in alphabetizing, and no inversion is necessary:

> Ngo Dinh Diem
> Vo Nguyen Giap

17.121 Confusion about Vietnamese names arises from the fact that Vietnamese persons are usually referred to—correctly and politely—by the last part of the given name (Premier Diem, General Giap). An exception was Ho Chi Minh, who was originally named Nguyen That Thanh and later took the Chinese name by which he became widely known. He was referred to both in Vietnam and abroad as President (or General) Ho. Although Vietnamese names should always be alphabetized as shown above, a cross-reference from the more familiar part of the name may be inserted for the benefit of readers unfamiliar with the Vietnamese custom.

INDIAN NAMES

17.122 Modern Indian names, of whatever ethnic and linguistic origin, generally appear with the family name last, and this is the name used in indexing. As in other countries, the personal preference of the individual as well as national usage should be observed:

Nehru, Jawaharlal	Narayan, R. K.
Gandhi, Mohandas Karamchand	Bhattacharya, Bhabhani

BURMESE NAMES

17.123 Family names are not used in Burma. The name by which a person is known is a given name, of one or two elements, preceded by a term of respect (*U* is the commonest) or a title, used in alphabetical listing:

Nu, U   Po Lat, U
Thant, U   Than Tun, Dr.

JAVANESE AND OTHER INDONESIAN NAMES

17.124 Indonesians of Javan origin use only a personal name, family names being nonexistent in Java:

Suharto
Sukarno

In other parts of Indonesia family names often exist, although the personal name may still be the one to use in indexing. Also, a person may take an additional name (for Muslims of strong religious bent, often an Arabic name). Indonesians resident in the West may adopt an additional name simply to conform to local custom. Except for Javanese names of the type described above, an indexer should seek expert help in dealing with Indonesian names.

THAI NAMES

17.125 Family names are used in Thailand, but the person is normally known, and addressed, by the personal name. (In Thai order, the personal name precedes the family name.) The personal name is usually used in alphabetizing, but practice varies among students of Thai culture, as shown by the following examples:

Sut Saengwichian   Songsaengchan, Suphat
Damrong Rachanuphap, Prince   Thong-Urai, Prachap

OTHER ASIAN NAMES

17.126 Throughout Asia, many names derive from the European languages and from Arabic, Chinese, and other, less widely known, languages, regardless of the places of birth of the persons bearing the names. In some places, such as the Philippines, names follow a strictly Western order and give precedence to the family name, although the names themselves are derived from local languages and cultures. In many parts of Asia and the Orient, also, names denoting status (such as the Indian castes) and titles often form part of the name as it appears in written work and must be dealt with appropriately. In all these instances an indexer's problems are best solved by querying the author whenever the dependable rules of standard reference works do not answer a specific question.

17.127 When used as names of businesses or other organizations, full personal names are usually not inverted unless the organization is more widely known by the family name only. In cases of doubt, cross-references may be used.

> Benedict Ardmore Recycling Corp.
> *or*
> Ardmore Recycling Corp. *See* Benedict Ardmore Recycling Corp.
>
> Arthur Wistlemacher Co.
> *or*
> Wistlemacher Co., Arthur
>
> Christine D. and Thomas R. Winsome Fund. *See* Winsome Fund
>
> R. K. Bexhalter Co. *See* Bexhalter Co.

Place-Names

17.128 Geographic proper names beginning with *Mount, Lake, Cape, Sea,* and the like that actually refer to mountains, lakes, capes, and seas should be alphabetized according to the part of the name following this element. The name itself is inverted.

> Everest, Mount   Mendocino, Cape
> Japan, Sea of   Geneva, Lake (Switzerland)

Names of cities or towns beginning with these same elements should be alphabetized according to the first element:

> Cape Girardeau, Mo.   Mount Vernon, N.Y.
> Lake Geneva, Wis.   Sea Girt, N.J.

17.129 Place-names beginning with non-English articles, except Arabic *al-* (see 17.114), are usually alphabetized under the article:

> El Dorado   Le Bourget
> El Ferrol   Le Havre
> El Paso   Les Eyzies
> La Coruña   Los Angeles
> La Crosse   Los Michis
> LaPorte   's Gravenhage

17.130 Place-names beginning with the appellation *Saint* or *Sainte* (*St.* or *Ste.*) should be recorded in the index as spelled in the text (Press preference is for the spelled-out form for most such names). The name is preferably alphabetized letter-by-letter as it appears in the text, but it may also be consistently alphabetized as though spelled out. Note that in French place names the saint's name is invariably hyphenated:

> Île Saint-Louis
> rue Saint-Honoré
> Saint-Cloud

Alphabetizing by Computer

17.131 Computer-assisted alphabetizing with dedicated indexing software (see 17.26) can follow either the letter-by-letter system or the word-by-word system. In either system, opening prepositions, articles, and conjunctions can be ignored; and *St.*, *Ste.*, *M'*, and *Mc* can be sorted either as they appear or as though spelled out.

EDITING AN INDEX COMPILED BY SOMEONE ELSE

17.132 Indexes prepared by experienced professionals or by authors who have learned the craft usually require very little editing. Indeed, an inexperienced editor should be wary of tampering with such an index, lest the excellence be marred or the carefully thought-out structure undone. An ill-prepared index, on the other hand, is likely to present serious, if not insurmountable, problems. You cannot, as editor, remake a really bad index yourself. You can often make minor repairs, as noted below, and you can usually impose some typographical and logical consistency, but you cannot turn a basically flawed index into a good one. If an index is so bad that even after improvement it cannot be used, you have two choices: leave it out of the book or have a new one made by a professional indexer—and thereby delay production of the book.

17.133 The following suggestions for editing an index are based on the experience of University of Chicago Press editors, augmented by a checklist that editors at another university press shared with us.

Copyediting Tasks

17.134 Copyediting (apart from markup) should include the following:

> 1. Check the spelling of each heading, consulting the page proofs when necessary.

2. Check punctuation for proper style and mark any end-of-line hyphens that should be set.

3. Look for long strings of unanalyzed locators and break them up, if possible, with subheads (see 17.51–54).

4. Check the reasonableness of page numbers (no "12122" or "193–93"), and make sure that sequences are in ascending order.

5. If some entries seem overanalyzed (many subentries with only one page reference each) try to combine some of the subentries, if that can be managed without the distortion of logic and without sacrificing the usefulness of subheads; do not simply delete subheads and string the page references together in long unanalyzed runs following the main heading. If subheadings are longer and more elaborate than necessary, try to simplify them. (See 17.53.)

6. If "false" sub-subentries appear in a run-in style index, correct them by adding appropriate repeated subheadings or by using em dashes (see 17.55). (For the latter procedure you may have to rekeyboard parts of the copy.)

7. Delete entries that are recognizably trivial, such as references to place-names or personal names used only as examples. (Be careful here. This can be dangerous, and it might involve you in much more work than you bargained for.)

8. Be sure that related information is not scattered through the index without cross-references.

9. Check principal headings for strict alphabetical order. Few indexes are entirely without alphabetization errors, and sorting done by word processors without dedicated indexing software is apt to be marred by numerous misplacements.

10. Check subentries for consistency of order, whether alphabetical, chronological, or other; if extensive reordering is necessary, the desired order may be indicated by means of circled marginal numbers, or the entire entry may be retyped. If "mentioned" or some other such device is used, make sure that the use is consistent.

11. Check cross-references to make sure they go somewhere and that headings are identical. Make sure that they are needed: if only a few page references are involved, add these to the original heading and delete the cross-reference. Also, see that their placement within the entries is consistent.

12. Evaluate the accuracy of page references by a random check of approximately 5 percent of the entries.

Markup

17.135 Marking up an index manuscript for conventional typesetting, or a computer printout accompanied by a disk for electronic processing, should include the following:

1. Identify the job for the typesetter by author and title at the top of the first page—or by whatever device you have been using for earlier parts of the book—and indicate what page the index begins on (if you know).

2. Mark type specifications at the top of the first page of the copy. If setting is to be ragged right, indicate the maximum allowable end-of-line space.

3. Mark en dashes within continued numbers for the first few lines of copy (if that is your style), and write a note to the typesetter asking for this style throughout.

4. Indicate the spacing before and after *n* or *n.* in references to notes.

5. Mark copy for inclusion of blank lines between alphabetic sections of the index (e.g., between the *A*s and the *B*s).

6. Make sure all pages are in order and numbered before sending them off for setting.

TYPOGRAPHICAL CONSIDERATIONS

Type Size and Column Width

17.136 Indexes are usually set in smaller type than the body of a book, often two sizes smaller. That is, if the body copy is set in 10-on-12-point type and the extracts, bibliographies, and appendixes in 9-on-11, the index would probably be set in 8-on-10. Usually, too, indexes are set in two columns; if the type page is 27 picas wide, the index columns are 13 picas wide, with a 1-pica space between. In large-format books, however, the index is often set in three columns or even four.

Justification

17.137 Body copy for most books is set *justified* column; that is, the right side of the column is straight and even, like the left. This effect is achieved by varying the amount of space between words to make all lines the same length. The shorter the lines the more awkward is the justification, resulting all too often in gaping word spaces or excessive hyphenation. Index columns are therefore usually set ragged right, which produces an index that is not only better looking but also easier to set and correct (see 18.27).

Indention

17.138 The distinction between the indented and run-in styles of setting subentries was noted above (17.10). If the indented style is adopted, and if there are sub-subentries (perhaps even sub-sub-subentries), the editor or designer should figure maximum indentions before marking up copy for the typesetter. Subentries might be indented 1 em, sub-subentries 2 ems, sub-sub-subentries 3 ems, and runover lines 4 ems. This may mean, however, that the runover lines are too short for efficient setting and that something else must be done. Indentions could be reduced to 1 en (also called a *nut space*), 1 em, 1½ ems, and 2 ems, or the index set in two columns instead of three, or the sub-sub-subentries run into the sub-subentries, as illustrated in 17.147. It should be kept in mind, however, that sub-sub-subheads should be avoided unless absolutely necessary. Whatever the solution, problems like this should be addressed before any type is set.

Bad Breaks, Remedies, and *Continued* Lines

17.139 What cannot be solved before setting type are the problems connected with page and column breaks. A line consisting of only one or two page numbers should not be left at the top of a column, for example. A single line at the end of an alphabetic section (followed by a blank line) should not head a column, nor should a single line at the beginning of an alphabetic section be allowed to stand at the foot of a column. Blemishes like these (called *bad breaks* by editors and typesetters) are eliminated by transposing lines from one column to another, by adding to the white space between alphabetic sections, and sometimes by lengthening or shortening all columns on facing pages by one line. Another kind of bad break is more easily corrected. In a long index, it often happens that an entry breaks at the foot of the last column on a right-hand page and resumes in the first column on the following, left-hand, page. This is remedied by repeating the main heading, followed by the italicized word *continued* in parentheses, above the carried-over part of the entry:

RUN-IN STYLE	INDENTED STYLE
ingestive behavior (*continued*)	ingestive behavior (*continued*)
network of causes underlying,	network of causes underlying, 68
68; physiology of, 69–70, 86–	physiology of, 69–70, 86–87

87; in rat, 100; in sheep, 22; in	in rat, 100
starfish, 45, 52–62	in sheep, 22
	in starfish, 45, 52–62

If sub-subentries have been used, as in an indented-style index, it may also be necessary to repeat a subheading if the subentry has been broken. The subheading may be repeated at its correct indention, as in the example at the left below, or it may be run in following the repeated main heading, as in the example to the right. In this latter case, care must be taken to begin the new subentry at the correct indention.

house renovation (*continued*)	house renovation, structural prob-
structural problems (*continued*)	lems *(continued)*
termite damage, 25	termite damage, 25

Such continued lines are essential on verso pages, but they are also helpful, and highly recommended, at the head of any column that continues an entry in another column.

Special Typography

17.140 An index to a complicated book can often be simplified if special typography is used to differentiate headings, locators, or both. If, for example, two kinds of personal names need to be distinguished in an index—perhaps authors and literary characters—one or the other might be set in caps and small caps. Page references to illustrations might be in italic and references to the principal treatment of a subject in boldface. Before settling on such a system, however, the author or editor should confer with a representative of the typesetter to make sure the scheme is practicable. One must also remember to provide a key to the significance of the different kinds of type at the head of the index (as in examples 17.142, 17.144, 17.149).

EXAMPLES

A Typical Scholarly Index in Run-in Style

17.141 The following is an excerpt from a typical scholarly index for a long (450-page) study of industrialization in Soviet Russia. Note the alphabetization of the run-in subentries. Note also what are essentially run-in sub-subentries under "annual plans: functioning of." This can occasionally be done without confusion if the sub-subentries are all identical in construction (here, "for such-and-such year") and attach themselves obviously to the preceding subentry. In most circumstances, sub-subentries are possible only in an indented-style index, such as examples 17.143 and 17.144, or by using em dashes, as in example 17.145.

agriculture, 6, 7, 35, 176, 308–58; during *All-out Drive,* 83–85, 96–97, 139; investment in, 84–85, 137, 191, 192, 238, 304; labor in, 310–12, 320, 384–86; during *NEP,* 41–42; during *Post-Stalin,* 329, 432–33; and price system, 287–88, 293; during *Purge Era,* 177, 195–98; during *Stalin Has Everything His Way,* 238, 239, 241–42, 309–10, 343–44; during *Three "Good" Years,* 139–42, 156–58, 176; during *Warming-up,* 55–56. *See also* acreages, sown; animal products; crop production; farm output; farm products; kolkhozy; livestock; peasants; Sovkhozy; *and names of individual commodities*

"all-citizen statistical ration," 282, 384, 410

annual plans: functioning of, 27, 125–26; for 1931, 73, 77–79, 120; for 1932 and 1933, 120–21; for 1935 and 1936, 129–32; for 1937, 184–85; for 1947, 254–56; targets of, 120, 130–32, 183. *See also* control figures

Arden Conference, 178 n

An Index with Boldface and Italic References

17.142 The following is an index in run-in style for a book on animal behavior, showing the use of references in boldface and italic type to distinguish illustrative material. Shown also is one way to locate photographs within inserts. To avoid difficulties in numerical ordering, it is often necessary, as in the example, to list the boldface and italic references at the end of the normal sequence of text references for the entry or subentry.

> *References to drawings are printed in boldface type. Numbers in italics refer to the photographic inserts; the first number is that of the text page preceding the insert, the second that of the page in the insert*

goose: allelomimetic behavior of, **18;** imprinting in, 178, *148–2*

grasshopper population fluctuations, 216

gravity as related to tactile sense, 34

ground squirrel. *See* prairie dog

group formation, 160–61

growth curve, 224–26, **225**

growth of populations, 224–32, *212–2*

guinea pig: female sexual behavior of, 80–81; limited motor capacity of, 32–33; male sexual behavior of, 81–82

gull: nesting territories of, 222; primary stimulus in, 142

gynandromorph, behavior of, 126

habitat selection in deermouse, 243–44, **243**

habit formation, 98; decreases variability, 156; makes behavior consistent, 122; in organization of behavior, 150; versus variability, 108

Habrobracon, behavior of gynandromorphs of, 126

Indented-Style Indexes

17.143 Note the format for subheads and sub-subheads in the indented-style index.

Arcadia, 4
    Early Helladic, 26, 40
    Mycenaean, 269, 306
Argos
    cremation at, 302
    and Danaos of Egypt, 108
    Middle Helladic, 77
    Mycenaean town, 204, 233, 270, 309
    painted tomb at, 205, 299
    shaft graves at, 84
armor and weapons
    attack weapons (general)
        Early Helladic and Cycladic, 33
        Mycenaean, 225, 255, 258–60
        from shaft graves, 89, 98–100
        from tholos tombs, 128, 131, 133
    body armor
        cuirass, 135–36, 147, 152, 244, 258, 260, 311
        greaves, 135, 179, 260
        helmets, 101, 135, 147, 221, 243, 258
    bow and arrow, 14, 99, 101, 166, 276
    daggers, 33, 98, 255, 260
    shields, 98–99, 135, 147, 221, 260
    sling, 14, 101, 260
    spears and javelins, 33, 195, 210, 260
    swords
        in Crete, 147
        cut-and-thrust, 228, 278
        Middle Helladic, 73
        Mycenaean, 175, 255, 260, 279
        from shaft graves, 98
        from tholos tombs, 128, 131, 133, 135
    See also frescoes, battle; metals and metalworking
Arne. *See* Gla
Asine
    Early Helladic, 29, 36
    Middle Helladic, 74
    Mycenaean town and trade, 233, 258, 263
    seals from, 38
    shrine at, 166, 284–88
    tombs at, 300

17.144 Note, in addition to the indented treatment of subentries and sub-subentries, the use of italic type for references to pages on which definitions occur (the index is called "Index to Subjects and Definitions"):

Page numbers for definitions are in italics

brightness temperatures, 388, 582, 589, 602
bright rims, *7*, 16, 27–28. *See also* nebular forms
B stars, *3, 7*, 26–27, 647
bulbs (in nebulae). *See* nebular forms
cameras, electronic, 492, 499
carbon flash, 559
Cassiopeia A (3C461). *See* radio sources; supernovae
catalogs
    of bright nebulae, 74
    of dark nebulae, 74, 120

Lundmark, 121
Lynds, 123
Schoenberg, 123
Herschel's (of nebulae), 119
of planetary nebulae, 484–85, 563
Perek-Kohoutek, 484, 563
Vorontsov-Velyaminov, 484
of reflection nebulae, 74
3C catalog of radio sources, revised, 630
central stars. *See* planetary nebulae
Cerenkov radiation, *668, 709*

chemical composition, 71. *See also* abundances; *and names of individual elements*
of stars and nebulae, 405
Clark effect, *756, 758, 765*
clouds. *See* interstellar clouds
cluster diameters, 170, 218
angular, 184
apparent, 167, 168
cluster distances, 167, 168, 171, 173, 174, 215–16
clusters, 172–73, 181–82
absolute magnitudes, 181

Use of the Dash with Run-in Subentries

17.145 In the following index, dashes are used before what in effect become sub-subentries in the run-in style. The dash stands in for the inclusive element in the subentry, which ends at the comma that introduces the modification serving as the sub-subentry. This treatment of sub-subentries is best restricted to indexes having only a few such entries and to situations dominated by considerations of space and cost (see 17.55–56).

Arcadia, 4; Early Helladic, 26, 40; Mycenaean, 269, 306
Argos: cremation at, 302; and Danaos of Egypt, 108; Middle Helladic, 77; Mycenaean town, 204, 233, 270, 309; painted tomb at, 205, 299; shaft graves at, 84
armor and weapons: attack weapons (general), Early Helladic and Cycladic, 33; —, Mycenaean, 225, 255, 258–60; —, from shaft graves, 89, 98–100; —, from tholos tombs, 128, 131, 133; body armor, cuirass, 135–36, 147, 152, 244, 258, 260, 311; —, greaves, 135, 179, 260; —, helmets, 101, 135, 147, 221, 243, 258; bow and arrow, 14, 99, 101, 166, 276; daggers, 33, 98, 255, 260; shields, 98–99, 135, 147, 221, 260; sling, 14, 101, 260; spears and javelins, 33, 195, 210, 260; swords, in Crete, 147; —, cut-and-thrust, 228, 278; —, Middle Helladic, 73; —, Mycenaean, 175, 255, 260, 279; —, from shaft graves, 98; —, from tholos tombs, 128, 131, 133, 135. *See also* frescoes, battle; metals and metalworking
Arne. *See* Gla
Asine: Early Helladic, 29, 36; Middle Helladic, 74; Mycenaean town and trade, 233, 258, 263; seals from, 38; shrine at, 166, 284–88; tombs at, 300

Combined Indented and Run-in Styles

17.146 The following example represents a compromise between indented and run-in styles. Each subentry under "armor and weapons" starts a new line and is indented. Sub-subentries are run in, runovers being further indented. This style, as well as the style represented in 17.145, is most satisfactory for an index in which a few entries require rather elaborate breakdown, the rest being simple entries (for a similar treatment of sub-sub-subentries see 17.147).

Arcadia, 4; Early Helladic, 26, 40; Mycenaean, 269, 306
Argos: cremation at, 302; and Danaos of Egypt, 108; Middle Helladic, 77; Mycenaean town, 204, 233, 270, 309; painted tomb at, 205, 299; shaft graves at, 84
armor and weapons. *See also* frescoes, battle; metals and metalworking
  attack weapons (general): Early Helladic and Cycladic, 33; Mycenaean, 225, 255, 258–60; from shaft graves, 89, 98–100; from tholos tombs, 128, 131, 133
  body armor: cuirass, 135–36, 147, 152, 244, 258, 260, 311; greaves, 135, 179, 260; helmets, 101, 135, 147, 221, 243, 258

bow and arrow, 14, 99, 101, 166, 276
daggers, 33, 98, 255, 260
shields, 98–99, 135, 147, 221, 260
sling, 14, 101, 260
spears and javelins, 33, 195, 210, 260
swords: in Crete, 147; cut-and-thrust, 228, 278; Middle Helladic, 73; Mycenaean, 175, 255, 260, 279; from shaft graves, 98; from tholos tombs, 128, 131, 133, 135
Arne. *See* Gla
Asine: Early Helladic, 29, 36; Middle Helladic, 74; Mycenaean town and trade, 233, 258, 263; seals from, 38; shrine at, 166, 284–88; tombs at, 300

17.147 If sub-sub-subentries must be used, some space may be saved and appearance improved by running them in following an indented subsubentry:

armor and weapons
  attack weapons (general)
    Early Helladic and Cycladic, 33
    Mycenaean, 225, 255, 258–60
    from shaft graves, 98–100; Bing's excavations, 258; thefts from, 259–60; Tumble's classification of sites, 99; Ungar's theory concerning, 100
    from tholos tombs, 128, 131, 133
  body armor
    cuirass, 135–42
    greaves, 158, 163

Specialized Indexes

17.148 The first example of a specialized index (17.149), from an anthology, *Poetry of the English Renaissance, 1509–1660,* edited by J. William Hebel and Hoyt H. Hudson, combines indexes of authors, titles, and first lines. Such a combination, probably easiest of all on the reader, is less usual for an anthology than are separate indexes—one of authors or of authors and titles, set narrow measure, and another of first lines or titles and first lines, set wide measure, with leaders (see examples in 17.150 and 17.151).

AUTHORS, TITLES, AND FIRST LINES OF POEMS

17.149 The authors' names are set in capitals and small capitals, titles of poems in italics, and first lines of poems in ordinary roman type:

Cermak, it was, who entertained so great astonishment, 819
Certain she was that tigers fathered him, 724
CHESTERVILLE, NORA M., 212
Cinders, Eloise, see them? 112
Come, my way, my truth, my life, 743
Come over the bourn, Bessy, 408
Come, pass about the bowl to me, 872
Come sleep! O sleep, the certain knot of peace, 112
Come, sons of summer, by whose toil, 665
Come, spur away, 693
Come then, and like two doves with silv'ry wings, 647
Come, we shepherds whose blest sight, 768
Come, worthy Greek, Ulysses, come, 280
Come, you whose loves are dead, 394
Coming Homeward Out of Spain, 73
Commemorate me before you leave me, Charlotte, 292
Commendation of Her Beauty, Stature, Behavior, and Wit, 208
Compare me to the child, 73
Comparison of the Sonnet and the Epigram, 521

Complaint of a Lover Rebuked, 29
Complain we may, much is amiss, 47
COMPTON, WILBER C., 96
Confined Love, 463
Confound you, Marilyn, confound you, 469
Conscience, 739
CONSTABLE, HENRY, 229
Content, not Cates, 661
COOPER, ROBERT, 42
Cooper's Hill, 844
CORBET, RICHARD, BISHOP OF OXFORD AND NORWICH, 633
Coridon and Melampus' Song, 386
Corinna's Going a-Maying, 654
CORNISH, WILLIAM, 42
Corpse, clad with carefulness, 80
Corydon, arise my Corydon, 199
Could not once blinding me, cruel, suffice, 766
Country men of England, 426
Courage, my soul! now learn to wield, 859
COWLEY, ABRAHAM, 829
CRAIG, ALEXANDER, 228
CRASHAW, RICHARD, 758, 1025
Crayton, we are not here to further your desires, 774
Crimson radiance overcame him, 61
CRUFFTON, MARTHA, 336
CUPPERBACH, ARTURO, 157

AUTHOR-TITLE INDEX

17.150 Authors' names are in roman type, titles in italic:

Masefield, John, 136
Masked Shrew, The, 105
Master, The, 185
Masters, Edgar Lee, 166
*Mathematics or the Gift of
Tongues,* 72
Melville, Herman, 128
Men Say They Know Many Things,
124
Message from Home, 99
Metropolitan Nightmare, 115
Millay, Edna St. Vincent, 75, 133
Moore, Marianne, 67, 84, 147
Moss, Howard, 181
Motion of the Earth, The, 38
My Father's Watch, 24

Naked World, The, 69
Nash, Ogden, 120

Newton, 158
New York—December, 1931, 149
Nicholson, Norman, 38
Non Amo Te, 119
No Single Thing Abides, 9
Numbers and Faces, 91

Ode to the Hayden Planetarium, 29
Once a Child, 21
*Open Did I First My Heart to Isa-
bel,* 228
Orington, Springfield, 167
Our Little Kinsmen, 107

Physical Geography, 52
Plane Geometry, 87
Pleiades, The, 31
Point, The, 89
Pope, Alexander, 121, 157

INDEX OF FIRST LINES

17.151 This index is set wide measure, with leaders guiding the eye to page
numbers aligned at the right:

God sends his teachers unto every age 388
Good-bye, my Fancy. 474
Good-bye, proud world! I'm going home 309
Gusty and raw was the morning 436

INDEX OF TITLES AND FIRST LINES

17.152 In this index of titles and first lines of poems, the titles are enclosed in
quotation marks. Titles of long poems would be italicized.

Casually, in the midst of fever
"Crumpled Temperaments"
"Deadly Pursuits and Mournful Pleasures"
Dear Lady, I abhor
Did she turn, and will she turn again?

FOR FURTHER REFERENCE

17.153 For an excellent and extensive discussion of indexing and indexes see
Nancy Mulvany, *Indexing Books*.

Part 3

Production and Printing

18 *Design and Typography*

INTRODUCTION

18.1   The purposes of a chapter on design and typography in this manual are two. First, the chapter is intended to give editors some basic facts about bookmaking so they may work more knowledgeably with professional designers, production personnel, and typesetters. Second, it aims to give helpful suggestions to those editors, copywriters, and others who must plan the design and typography of a book, pamphlet, or brochure without the guidance of an expert. It is *not* intended to serve the needs of professional designers, typographers, or production people. For these reasons it deals only with the bare essentials of designing a book.

18.2   The design of a book should complement and enhance the subject of the book. A textbook usually requires a complex design (not to be undertaken by an amateur); scholarly monographs require less complex designs but ones that will accommodate notes, bibliographies, glossaries, and other aspects of scholarly communication.

PRELIMINARY PLANNING

Characteristics of the Manuscript

18.3   At the initial stage of planning a design, the editor who has acquired the book can greatly assist the designer by explaining the nature of the work and the audience for whom it is intended. This editor should also indicate the placement of notes (footnotes or endnotes), the kind and number of illustrations to be included, the number of tables, graphs, or charts, what material is to be in the preliminary pages and what in the back matter, and any other special problems peculiar to the work. Many publishing houses, the University of Chicago Press among them, provide the acquisitions editor with a printed editorial transmittal sheet upon which such information may be included (see fig. 18.1);[1] the sheet goes with a copy of the manuscript to the design and production department. Such fact sheets are often not enough, however, and subse-

---

1. Not to be confused with the production transmittal sheet that later accompanies the edited manuscript to the production department and the typesetter (see fig. 2.3).

Date:

Book Transmittal Acquisitions editor:

Author
Editor/Translator
Full title

General: Author's background and our reasons for publishing book:

Checklist	Herewith	To come	Contract		
	[x]	[date]	Contract no.:	Series:	Series contract no.:
Half title			☐ Book represents all new work by one or more authors under contract to us.		
Series title			☐ Category of book as follows:		
Title page					
Copyright page			**Manuscript Editing**		
Dedication			Manuscript and proof to:		
Epigraph					
Contents			Index to be done by:		
List of illustrations . .					
List of tables			**Rights and Permissions**		☐ Rights specified below
Foreword			☐ We have world rights, all languages, all editions.		☐ Specifics below
Preface			☐ Author(s), editor(s), translator(s) citizens of U.S.		☐ Details below
Acknowledgments .			☐ No permissions needed	☐ Permissions in, free to Press	
Introduction					
Complete text			**Design and Production**		
Notes			☐ Duplicate MS attached	No. words:	If reprint, no. pages:
Appendix(es)			No. line drawings:	No. maps:	No. photos:
Glossary			☐ All straight composition	☐ Special sorts (see below)	No. tables:
Bibliography			☐ Standard trim size OK	☐ Special trim (see below)	☐ Offprints needed
Index			Proposed del. date:	Proposed print run:	Bind (cloth/paper):
All illustrations					
Tables			**Marketing**		
			Publishing season:	Subject:	Cloth:
			Proposed price and discount—	Subject codes:	Paper:

Remarks/Explanations

Fig. 18.1 Transmittal form to be filled in by the acquisitions editor and sent with a copy of the manuscript to the design and production department. A photocopy of the completed form goes to the manuscript editor with the copy to be edited.

quent conferences between designer and acquistions editor or manuscript editor are necessary.

18.4 Before designing a book, the designer must know not only the nature of the subject and the components of the book but also the book's length. The editor's rough estimate of the number of words is usually not enough, nor is the number of manuscript pages. The designer must have an accurate *castoff* (or *character count*), prepared by the production department (in some publishing houses by the editor), giving the number of characters in (*a*) text, (*b*) extracts, (*c*) footnotes or endnotes, (*d*) appendixes, glossary, bibliography, and so on. Physical size as well as the nature of the book will determine the width and length of the type page and the typeface, type size, and leading between lines to be specified.

18.5   The manuscript used by the designer should be *final* (at least so far as the title and the number and nature of the parts are concerned) and *complete* in all essentials. In some publishing houses it is the practice to complete the editing phase of preparation before turning the manuscript over for design. In others (including the University of Chicago Press), to save time, the book is designed from a second copy of the manuscript while the master copy is being edited. If the latter system is used, the editor should quickly inform the designer of any editorial changes affecting the design of the book, such as the addition of a subtitle to the book title or an increase in the number of levels of subheadings, and the editor should point out any special problems the designer might not be aware of.

Castoff

18.6   The most accurate way to estimate the exact length of a printed work from a typewritten manuscript is to count each *character,* meaning each letter, mark of punctuation, and space between words. With heavily edited material this may be the only way. The less time-consuming and more usual way is to count (*a*) the characters in an average line of the manuscript and (*b*) the number of lines, and then to multiply *a* by *b*. If different typewriters have been used in preparing the manuscript—one with elite type, another with pica, for example—the number of characters per line will also be different. A separate estimate should then be made for each type size in the manuscript and the results added together for the total number of characters.

18.7   Estimating the length of a manuscript prepared on a word processor may be simpler. Many word processors use systems able to count and record *(capture)* the characters in a "manuscript," thus providing a quick and accurate estimate of length. Such information should be furnished by the acquisitions editor along with a paper printout *(hard copy)* for the designer's use.

18.8   The designer needs, however, not just a total character count of the work but a count broken down by kinds of material in it. Each kind of material will be set in its own specified type size, in part determined by the amount in a given category. For material such as notes, bibliographies, and glossaries, where each item begins a new line, the number of lines, including runover lines, is often more helpful than a character count. A typical character count might read as follows:

	CHARACTERS	NUMBER OF LINES
Front Matter	5,000	. . .
Text	700,000	. . .
Extracts	50,000	. . .
Appendix	85,000	. . .
Bibliography	. . .	240

The number of tables and illustrations and any peculiarities of size should be included with the character count, although characters in tables and legends need not be counted.

18.9 The designer, with the manuscript and its character count in hand, will decide upon the typeface, the type sizes for each category, and the size of the type page and will thus be able to determine how many characters of each type size will fit on a single printed page. Dividing the figures in the character count by the relevant number of characters per printed page will give a good estimate of the length of the finished book.

PROSE TEXTS

Typeface

18.10 Which typeface and what sizes of type to use for text, notes, and other apparatus in a given book are perhaps a designer's most important decisions. These decisions rest partly on suitability of type to subject and partly on which typesetting process is to be used and the availability of particular typefaces in that process. Among questions to be considered are the following: Is the text peppered with foreign words requiring a variety of diacritical marks? Is it highly technical, containing mathematics or other material requiring symbols? In the field of mathematics, for example, only a few typefaces have all the necessary characters (Times Roman is perhaps the most widely available).

ALPHABETS

18.11 The usual font (all the type characters of one face and size, i.e., a complete *set* of all the characters) contains five alphabets: roman capitals, roman lowercase letters, italic capitals, italic lowercase letters, and small capitals. Some works, however, require seven alphabets, the additions being boldface capital and lowercase letters. For these works a typeface—such as Times Roman or Baskerville—with a related bold-face in the appropriate sizes must be chosen.

18.12 Authors and editors will aid the bookmaking process, both economi-cally and aesthetically, by avoiding wherever possible the use of bold-face or other characters not commonly found in a five-alphabet font. It is not necessary, for example, to introduce boldface numerals in bibli-ographies or reference lists, or in section numbers or subheadings in the text. Where boldface numerals have a real function to perform—as in this manual, where they aid in indexing and cross-referencing—they may well be specified, but only after checking with the typesetter as to the feasibility and cost of adding them to the font.

CHARACTERISTICS

18.13 A previous edition of this manual illustrated various typefaces by show-ing ten specimens, all of them either Linotype or Monotype faces. With the advent of photomechanical and then electronic (CRT) composition, specimen typefaces can no longer serve a similar purpose because no one of them would be universally applicable. For example, this edition of the manual was composed electronically in Times Roman. The same typeface produced by a different typesetting system, though generally similar in appearance, will vary in many minor details.

18.14 Another variation introduced by photomechanical and electronic com-position is that the number of characters per pica in a given typeface and type size is no longer fixed. In film setting, the *set*—how close together the characters appear—can range from moderately loose or *maximum* through standard or *optimum* to very tight or *minimum* (where some letters may actually touch each other).[2] The typesetting operation determining the set is called the *track*—one-track, two-track, three-track:

> Literature is the written expression of those who believe they have something to say that is worth recording and reading by

> Literature is the written expression of those who believe they have something to say that is worth recording and reading by others. It has

> Literature is the written expression of those who believe they have some-thing to say that is worth recording and reading by others. It has occupied an

18.15 Some of the typefaces most commonly available and widely used for bookwork today are Baskerville, Bembo, Garamond, Janson, Palatino,

2. The standard set is the one normally used for castoff and estimate when counting characters per pica.

and Times Roman. The general contours of these faces, and usually the names, are the same as those of their metal counterparts of the previous generation; but because of the many variations in the current versions of these typefaces, the amateur designer should consult the typesetter who is to produce the work before making a final decision on which typeface to use.

Type Page and Trim Size

18.16   The *type page,* also known as the *text page* or the *text area,* includes the area occupied by the running head, the text itself, footnotes (if any), and the page number *(folio).* The dimensions of the type page are measured in picas, one pica equaling approximately one-sixth of an inch. In addition to the width and length of the type page in picas, the number of text lines in a full page and in a chapter-opening page are commonly specified. *Trim size,* measured in inches, refers to the size of the whole page, including all margins.

WIDTH

18.17   As a rule, text matter intended for continuous reading (as opposed to reference material) should be set in lines neither too wide nor too narrow for comfortable reading. Ideally the line should accommodate 65 to 70 characters. Depending upon the size of type chosen, this means a line 22 to 27 picas wide.

18.18   In addition to reference materials, such as dictionaries, various other kinds of books are more economically set in double columns—books of readings, lengthy proceedings, and the like. A double-column format will accommodate considerably more words per page. First, the text page may be wider than is practical for a single column. Second, the shorter reading line in a double-column format permits the use of smaller type and less leading, without impairing readability, than does a typical one-column line. The width of the type page in a double-column format will include the space necessary between the two columns, usually 1 pica. Thus, if the type page is 31 picas wide, each column will be 15 picas wide.

LENGTH

18.19   The length of the type page is determined not so much by readability as by conventional relationships between width and length. Margins set off and enhance the type area in much the same way as does the mount for a drawing or picture. There should, generally speaking, be more margin at the bottom of a page than at the top to avoid the appearance of type falling off the page. The inner margin should be narrower than the outer margin, since a double-page spread is the entity and not two single pages. An old formula for the proportions of the four margins is $1^1/_2$, 2, 3, 4 (inside, head, outside, bottom), but many well-designed books depart widely from this and other formulas.

Spacing

18.20 The following remarks apply to space between words, between letters, and between lines in the text. For vertical spacing with display type see 18.50 and sample layouts.

BETWEEN WORDS

18.21 Spacing between printed words is partly a matter of the mechanics of composition. "Normal" word spacing is about one-third of an em. But when lines of type are justified—each line the same length (see 18.26)—spacing between words will vary slightly from line to line, though all word spacing in a single line should be the same. A line with narrow spacing is called a *close* line, one with wide spacing an *open* line. Excessively wide spacing detracts from readability, is unsightly, and is thus to be avoided. Also, a number of excessively open lines following one another may produce the printing phenomenon called a *river*—wide white spaces meandering vertically down the page and distracting the eye of the reader. Modern composition methods in general, therefore, aim for close word spacing. (For word spacing in unjustified material see 18.27.)

BETWEEN LETTERS

18.22 In display matter (title pages, chapter headings, etc.) and in anything set in full caps or caps and small caps, *letterspacing*—additional space between letters—is often specified by the designer. For subheads in the text the amount of space is likely to be standard, but for large display lines the designer may ask for *optical,* or *visual,* spacing. This means that the typesetter is to insert varying amounts of space between letters, depending upon their form: more, for example, between *N* and *E,* less (or none) between *L* and *A*. Except where so specified, the compositor should avoid letterspacing. All letters within words of a given typeface should be separated from each other by the same amount of space (but see 18.14). Authors and editors should be aware, however, that some combinations of letters, particularly in the italic alphabets, give the illusion of more space between them.[3]

BETWEEN LINES

18.23   The space between lines of type is called *leading,* or *lead,* because in hand or Monotype composition it was originally created by strips of lead inserted between lines of type (see also 2.137–38). To make more space between lines of text is to *lead it,* or to *lead it out.* To *close up* lines—leave less space between them—is to *delete lead.* Leading is measured in *points* (one point equaling one-twelfth of a pica) and is always specified by a designer for each type size used in a book.[4] Where increased leading is necessary—before and after extracts, for example—the number of points is usually also specified. If extra leading is used to mark the divisions between sections, the words *blank line* or *line space* circled in the margin or in the space itself will tell the compositor to insert space equivalent to one full line of type. A space mark *(#)* is usually sufficient to indicate extra space between alphabetic sections in indexes.

18.24   To determine an appropriate amount of leading requires consideration of a number of factors. The first of these, for text matter at any rate, is readability, and this is largely dependent upon the type measurements. The larger the type size, the more leading is required to prevent the eye from being distracted by the lines above and below the one being read. Also, the wider the line of type, the greater the leading needed, because in moving from the end of one line to the beginning of the next the eye takes a long jump, and in closely set material it may easily jump to the wrong line. Another factor to consider is economy. Use of a relatively small type size and reduced leading allows more words per page, making a thinner book and cutting costs of paper, mailing (weight), and so forth, although the cost of composition remains the same. The opposite of this is the desire to make a short work into a longer book. More than the usual number of points between lines will obviously result in fewer lines per page and thus more pages in the book.

18.25   The designer's ultimate concern, in specifying leading as in every other aspect of planning a book, is the nature of the material and the audience for whom it is intended.[5]

3. Garamond offers good examples of this.

4. If 2 points of leading are wanted between lines of a 10-point typeface, the usual designation is *10 on 12,* which in hot-metal composition meant a 10-point letter cast on a 12-point *body.* The same designation is used for modern typesetting methods even though letters consist of film matrices or electronic impulses rather than blocks of metal.

5. For examples of specifications appropriate to various kinds of material see sample layouts at the end of this chapter.

Justification

18.26   A column of type is conventionally rectangular, its left and right edges neatly aligned. To make a line of type, regardless of the words in it, exactly the same length as its fellows is to *justify* the line. This is still common practice in bookmaking. Since words in a language, unlike bricks in a building, are not all the same length, and since a word should not be divided at the end of a line without regard for the rules of word division, the spacing between words in justified lines cannot be exactly the same in each line. The shorter the line, the more acute the problem becomes for the compositor—or for the computer governing hyphenation and justification. In an index, for example, when an entry runs for two or more lines, the runover lines must be indented under the first line, thus making the runover line even shorter. Sometimes there is room for only two medium-sized words on a line. There may be enough space left over to accommodate another, shorter word, but perhaps the next word in the entry is too long to fit on the line and cannot be divided (*through* or *passed,* for example). A large, unsightly space must then be left between the two words to justify the line.

18.27   A solution to this problem, now not only acceptable but often desirable in bookmaking, as in other kinds of printed material, is simply *not* to justify lines of type. The width of the type column is taken as the maximum. The left edge is even—that is, each line begins directly under the line above—but the right edge runs ragged *(ragged right)*. Word spacing is the same in every line, and a line ends with the word falling nearest, but not beyond, the maximum length of the type line. No word except a very long one has to be divided at the end of a line, and thus the reader is not distracted by vertical rows of hyphens. To avoid an excessively ragged look caused by one or more lines set much shorter than the rest, however, it is advisable to specify a *minimum* line length, usually 2 or 3 picas shorter than the maximum; thus for text set to a maximum of 24 picas, a designer might specify 22 picas as the minimum line length.

Subheads

18.28   The typeface and type size used for all subheads (see 1.71–80) are ideally the same as those used for the text. Differentiation of levels is brought about by various combinations of the available five-alphabet font and by placement on the page. For example, A-level subheads might be set in caps and small caps (or in full caps), B-level in small caps, and C-level in italics (lowercase except the first word and proper nouns and adjectives) at the beginning of a paragraph (often called *run-in sideheads*). A- and B-level subheads may be letterspaced 1 to 3 points (see examples in 18.29 and subheads throughout this manual). A-heads might be centered and B-heads flush left, or both might be indented, say, 2 ems (or 2 picas) from the left. Space should be inserted above and below each subhead to set it off from the text.[6] A subhead should never fall at the bottom of a page with fewer than two lines following it on the page. Instead, the page should run short and the subhead should come at the top of the following page. The first line of text following a subhead may begin flush left or be indented by the usual paragraph indention or more.

18.29 The following examples illustrate a common design, described in 18.28, for three levels of subheads.

A-head:

NOMENCLATURE USED IN EASTERN AFRICA

B-head and text following:

BASIC ASSUMPTIONS
The first Pan-African Congress on Prehistory . . .

C-head:

The Kalomo industry. The Kalomo industry, which represents the Iron Age occupation of the Batoka Plateau . . .

Extracts

18.30 Extracts are commonly intended to illustrate points made in the text and are therefore considered part of the text proper.[7] They must, however, not only be identifiable as extracts but also be readable. There are various typographic ways to accomplish both purposes. Whichever method is used, extra space—at least 2 or 3 points—should be inserted both above and below each extract. The amount of space should be specified for the typesetter (see 2.138–40).

REDUCED TYPE

18.31 The traditional method for indicating extracts is to set them in a type size 1 point smaller than that of the text. Leading is also reduced at least 1 point. The extract may then be set to the same measure (width)

---

6. Such spacing should be so specified that the subhead plus the white space above and below it exactly equals a whole number of text lines. If, for example, the text is being set on a 12-point body, a 12-point subhead might be leaded 8 points above and 4 points below. The subhead and its white space thus equal two lines of text.

7. For length and nature of quoted material, here called *extracts,* see chapter 10.

as the text (except a verse extract, which is usually indented or centered), the extra space above and the reduced type serving notice to the reader that this is quoted material. For example, if the text is set 11 on 13, the extracts may be set 10 on 12, or 10 on 11. (Although indention, discussed below, is not necessary when the extract is set in reduced type, it may be employed as an additional means of differentiating the extract.) Modern computer-assisted typesetting methods permit changing type size and leading while setting text, thus avoiding the extra expense of setting different sizes separately as older methods required.

INDENTION

18.32   An alternative way of indicating extracts is to indent them from the left, with either a justified or a ragged right margin, or to indent them from both left and right. Indented extracts may be set in the same type size as the text or in a smaller size; leading in such an extract may also be equal to or less than that in the text.

Notes

18.33   Notes documenting a text are now frequently collected in a section at the back of a book, although footnotes—notes at the bottom of the page—are still a fact of scholarly life. Where notes are to be placed in a given book is usually a decision to be made by the editor, with the author's consent; it is not to be arbitrarily changed by a designer without consultation. (For numbering and placement of endnotes see 1.86.)

TYPE SIZE

18.34   Footnotes are set in type at least two sizes smaller than that of the text, but no smaller than 8-point solid.[8] In most typefaces, 8 on 9 is a good and readable size for footnotes.

18.35   Endnotes at the back of a book or at the end of a chapter are usually set in a type size smaller than that of the text but not as small as that of footnotes. The degree of difference between text and notes is not important here, since the two kinds of printed matter do not appear on the same page.

SPACE

18.36   There must be enough space between the footnotes and the text—at least 4 points—so that they are clearly differentiated. Spacing between

---

8. Notes to tables and the like are often set in 6- or 7-point type.

notes and text is not an entirely rigid matter. In the same book it may of necessity vary, say, between 4 and 6 points to accommodate the exigencies of particular pages in makeup.

HAIRLINE RULES

18.37 In closely set text it is sometimes desirable to insert a 3- or 5-pica hairline rule flush left above the footnotes on each page. This device is optional. When a note must continue on a following page, however, a 3-pica or full-measure hairline rule should always be inserted above the continuation.

CONTINUED NOTES

18.38 When a footnote is continued on a following page, not only should a hairline rule be used above it but the continuation should never begin with a full sentence, because readers may very well think the note has finished on the first page and miss the continuation. This is of course a problem in page makeup and can be checked by the editor or proofreader only in page proofs. The length of the page or the footnote material itself can usually be adjusted easily to avoid such breaks.

NOTE NUMBERS

18.39 Numbers in the text referring to footnotes or endnotes are always superior numerals. Traditionally, the corresponding numbers introducing each footnote or endnote were also superior numerals, a practice still followed by many designers. The University of Chicago Press prefers the more modern and more convenient practice of setting note numbers on the line, in the same type size as that of the notes, and followed by a period. The larger number is easier for the reader to identify. (For unnumbered notes see 15.50–52.)

PARAGRAPHING

18.40 The paragraphing of footnotes or endnotes should be in keeping with the design of the rest of the book. They may be set flush, in regular indented paragraph style, or even sometimes in *flush-and-hang* style.

Indexes

18.41 Indexes are usually set in two or more columns. To determine the width of a column in a two-column index, subtract 1 pica from the width measurement of the type page (to account for the space between the columns) and divide by 2. For example, if the type page is 24 picas wide, the index will be set in columns 11½ picas wide, with a 1-pica space between them.

18.42 Index matter is usually set in 8- or 9-point type, 8 on 9 (1-point leading) being a common specification in most typefaces. Indexes are almost always set ragged right (see 18.27).

18.43 Each main entry begins flush left, and runover lines are indented—flush-and-hang style. The amount of indention for runover lines should be specified. When the index has run-in subentries rather than indented subentries, runover lines are indented 1 em. When subentries are separated from the main entry, they are indented 1 em and all runover lines are indented 2 ems. When sub-subentries are also set on separate lines, they are indented 2 ems and all runover lines are indented 3 ems. (See also 17.10, 17.136–40, and examples in 17.141–52.)

DISPLAY TYPE

18.44 *Display type* means the typefaces used for preliminary pages, or front matter (half title, series title, title page, copyright, dedication, epigraph, etc.), for part and chapter titles, for running heads, and sometimes for subheads. Display type used on the title and half-title pages and for chapter titles need not be the same typeface used for the text but should be compatible with it.

Preliminaries, or Front Matter

18.45 Faced with planning a title page, an untrained person is well advised to keep it simple. Each item should be set on a separate line; all should be centered or all set flush left or flush right: main title, subtitle, author's name, publisher's imprint. The title on the half-title page (p. i) is usually set in the same type style used on the title page.

18.46 Material on the copyright page is set in the same typeface as the text but in a smaller type size—usually 8- or 9-point. The copyright notice may be centered or set flush left. The CIP information (see 1.28–30) should be set substantially as it appears on the library card replica received from the Library of Congress. It may be centered on the page or set flush left to match the placement of the copyright notice, and it is usually set in the same typeface and size as the notice.

18.47 A dedication is normally placed on a recto page by itself (see 1.36–37). It is usually set in the same type size as the text (if only two words, it might be a size larger), either centered or set flush left or right or indented to match other display matter, and placed on the page with the same sinkage (see 18.50) as the first line of text in a chapter.

18.48 An epigraph in the prelims is, like a dedication, usually on a page by itself (see 1.38–39). It may be set in the text type, indented two picas from each side (or flush left or right), and placed on the page with the same sinkage as the chapter text.

18.49 The table of contents (for title see 18.53) is best kept simple: chapter titles flush left, page numbers flush right, all set in text type size. When subheads are given in the contents, they are usually indented one em under the chapter title. Part titles may be set in a larger type size or in the same size but separated from the chapter titles by extra space.

Chapter Openings

18.50 Chapter display type generally is set lower than the top of the type page. The amount of space between it and the top of the page is called *sinkage* or *drop*. The amount of sinkage (in picas) is specified by the designer, and if possible the chapter openings should be checked in page proofs for uniformity in this matter.

18.51 Some books carry only chapter titles, but in most books chapters are also numbered. Any book that contains cross-references in the text to other chapters (as does this manual) must of course have numbered chapters. For some time arabic numerals have been preferred to roman numerals for chapter numbers, but either system is acceptable. Should the number of chapters be very great, however, it might be better to avoid roman numerals, since the less familiar ones may prove uninviting to the modern reader. The word *chapter* is also optional, although in recent years it is more often omitted than not. In most cases the editor is well advised to await the book design before either deleting or adding the word.

18.52 The chapter title should be set in a type size larger than that of the text but not so large as to dwarf the reading matter below it. The designer considers the length of each chapter title in a book before choosing a typeface and type size suitable for chapter titles. If titles require more than one line, as frequently happens, the designer should specify how many characters are allowed in each line and ask the editor to mark the breaks accordingly. But note that titles (and other display type) are never justified even where text lines are so treated, and word breaks should be avoided. When titles are set in full capitals, letterspacing makes them easier to read. In books in which each chapter is by a different author the author's name is included in the display type.

18.53 Titles of parts of the book other than chapters—preface, contents, bibliography, index, and so on—may be set in the same type size as the chapter titles, but they are more often set one or two sizes smaller. In special instances a designer may choose a different type style for them. Sinkage is generally the same as for the chapter openings.

18.54 An epigraph at the head of a chapter may be set in italics in the same size type as the text or in roman a size smaller. It should be set to a shorter measure than the text: when the chapter title is centered, the epigraph may be indented two to three ems from each side; where the chapter title is flush left, the epigraph may be indented (2–4 ems) and set ragged right (18.27). (For examples of epigraphs see 10.33.)

18.55 The beginning of the text in each chapter is also a consideration in designing chapter openings. It is usual, for example, to omit the paragraph indention, setting the first line flush left. (This is often done after subheads also.) When the first line begins flush left, the first letter may be a display initial—either a *stickup initial,* extending above the line it is set on, or a *drop initial,* extending two or more lines below its own line (if it is a three-line drop initial, for example, the second and third lines of text will be set shorter to accommodate it). If a display initial is used, the following word or two—article and noun, single long word, prepositional phrase, or such—may often be set in small capitals.

18.56 In a work with one appendix the word *Appendix* precedes the title (if any) of the appendix, usually on a line by itself and in smaller type than the title. Where there is more than one appendix, each is given a number or a letter (Appendix A, Appendix B, etc.), and the word *Appendix* is generally retained in the display type to avoid confusion with chapters and other parts of the book.

Running Heads

18.57 Running heads must be readable at a glance and distinct from the text.[9] In choosing the type size for running heads, the designer will consider the length of all possible running heads in the particular work, with the understanding that the editor may be able to shorten the overlong ones. If running head and page number are to appear on the same line, sufficient space—at least 2 picas—must be allowed between them.

Folios

18.58 Page numbers (folios) in the text are commonly placed at the top of the page, left on verso pages, right on recto pages. If the typeface provides

9. For selection of material to be used in running heads (normally done by the editor) see 2.159–61.

a choice, old style *(O.S.)* or modern *(lining* or *aligning)* numerals are specified. *Drop folios* (at the foot of the page) are used on the first page of a chapter and other opening pages (appendix, index, etc.) and may be used throughout the book. (Drop folios are common in books without indexes and in reference works, like this manual, that do not use page numbers in their indexes.)

TEXT OTHER THAN PROSE

Verse

18.59 Works such as poems and verse plays differ from prose in that the length of a line is determined by the author, not, as in prose, by the designer. The designer must try to reproduce the author's intention within a stipulated width of the printed page.

18.60 The size of type and the width of the type page should, wherever possible, accommodate the longest line—allow it to be set on one line—so that the shape of the poem on the page helps the reader to understand its rhythmic nature; if more than a few lines must be run over, the shape of the poem may be lost.

18.61 In most books of poetry the individual poems will vary one from another in the length of lines, and, generally speaking, the best way to place them on the page is to center each poem optically within the given measure of the text. Blank verse and poems characterized by a preponderance of long lines are generally not centered but are given a standard indention. No hard-and-fast rules can be laid down here; each book must be considered with its own characteristics in mind.

Plays

CAST OF CHARACTERS

18.62 For the reader's convenience a list of characters (often titled *Dramatis Personae*) is frequently given at the beginning of a play. This list appears between the title and the start of the play itself, either on the same page as the title or on a page by itself following a separate title page. Such a list may be arranged in alphabetical order, in order of appearance, or in order of importance. Any identifying remark about a character, if less than a sentence, follows the name and is separated from it only by a comma (if a sentence or more, it is separated from the name and set as a sentence or several sentences). Both names and remarks are commonly set in the same typeface as the text of the play, in roman or in italics.

ACT AND SCENE NUMBERS

18.63   Act and scene numbers may be designed in the manner described above (18.28) for setting the first two levels of subheads in prose works. A new act does not necessarily begin on a new page, but there should be at least 12 points above and 6 points below the new act number. A new scene should have about 8 points above and 6 points below the scene number. If an act or scene ends so close to the bottom of a page that at least two lines of the following act or scene cannot be accommodated on the page, the bottom of the page should be left blank (short page) and the new division should begin on the following page. Either arabic or roman numerals (in the latter case, capitals for act, lowercase for scene) may be used to designate these divisions.

SPEAKERS' NAMES

18.64   Because the name of each speaker in a play must be easily identifiable and must stand apart from the words to be spoken, names are commonly set in a style different from that of the text—for example, in italics or in caps and small caps or all in small caps—but in the same typeface as the text. They may be placed on a separate line, either centered or flush left, where they are most easily identified. This method, of course, takes more space, and when space is a consideration, especially if speeches are short and change of speaker is frequent, it is better to set the name in the left margin of the text page, followed by a colon or a period (see fig. 15.6 and example in 18.65). Speakers' names may be abbreviated to save space, but abbreviations must be consistent throughout a volume and the speaker easily identifiable by the abbreviation used (an editorial consideration).

STAGE DIRECTIONS

18.65   Like the speakers' names, stage directions must also be differentiated from the text by means of the type. They are usually set in italics and enclosed in brackets (sometimes parentheses). Introductory material setting the scene is also set in italics but not enclosed in parentheses.

Scene iii. *Bohemia. A desert country
near the sea*

Enter Antigonus, *with the* Babe, *and a* Mariner

Ant.   Thou art perfect then, our ship hath touch'd upon
          The deserts of Bohemia?
Mar.   Ay, my lord; and fear
          We have landed in ill time: . . .
Ant.   . . .
          There lie, and there thy character; there these,
          Which may, if Fortune please, both breed thee, pretty,
                              [*Laying down the babe, with a paper and a bundle*]

And still rest thine. . . .
Well may I get aboard! This is the chase;
I am gone for ever.

[*Exit, pursued by a bear*]

LINE NUMBERS

18.66 In verse plays, especially when there are notes or other references to particular lines, it is common practice to provide line numbers for every fifth or tenth line. These numbers are usually set flush right (see fig. 15.6).

LAYOUT, SPECIFICATION SHEET, AND SAMPLE PAGES

Layout

18.67 A *layout* is the designer's blueprint for a book. It shows the exact size of the trimmed page and of the type page and how the display type and text matter will fit within it. Specifications for the typeface and all type sizes and measurements are written by the designer on the layout. Until the advent of the personal computer, desktop publishing programs, and laser printers, a book designer's layouts were rendered by hand. Now that desktop systems are available, many designers are producing layouts on the computer. The days of meticulously hand traced display faces and ruled lines to represent a block of text may soon be gone. Today's layouts look more like sample pages with all typographical elements represented and positioned as they will appear in the typeset pages. Type specifications as well as measurements for drops and spacing are still generally added by hand to the computer-generated layouts.

18.68 A normal layout will include all the preliminary pages where display type is used; a chapter opening; two facing pages showing text, with extracts, subheads, footnotes if any, and running heads and page numbers; back matter, such as a page of an appendix, notes, glossary, bibliography or reference list, and index.

Specification Sheet

18.69 As a supplement to the layout, a comprehensive list of composition and page-makeup specifications should be compiled by the designer. Arranged by categories, such a list, referred to as a *specification sheet* or *spec sheet*, provides detailed information on format, typefaces and type sizes, extracts, tables, notes, subheads, running heads, folios, and so on.

18.70 From the designer's layout and specification sheets, the editor (or a production person) will mark the manuscript for the typesetter (see also 2.135–65). The layout and list of specifications accompany the edited, marked manuscript to the typesetter. Both production department and editor should keep photocopies of the layout in the files.

Sample Pages

18.71 Publishers often ask to see *sample pages* before composition begins. Sample pages, which are prepared by the typesetter following the specifications and layouts prepared by the publisher's designer, show how various typographic elements will look on page proof. The elements to be included are selected by the designer and usually include chapter openings, the various levels of subheads, running heads and folios, prose and poetry extracts, tables, displayed equations, and any other unusual construction found in the book. When sample pages are received, the designer and, usually, the editor will examine them and either approve them or request certain changes. Once the sample pages have been approved, composition proceeds.

Sample Layouts and Marked Manuscript

18.72 Following this chapter are five illustrative pages showing (1) a layout for a chapter opening; (2) a page of manuscript marked by an editor from specifications provided in the layout, and page proof of the typeset material; (3) a layout for a two-page spread of text, with subheads, an extract, footnotes, and running heads; and (4) a layout for a single page containing subheads and a table.

FOR FURTHER REFERENCE

18.73 Nonprofessionals seeking further help in book design and the graphic arts may find it in *Bookmaking,* by Marshall Lee, and in Norman Sanders, *Graphic Designer's Production Handbook.* More detailed guidance may be secured from *Methods of Book Design,* by Hugh Williamson, and *Graphic Arts Manual,* edited by Janet N. Field and others. The last has a good section on book design, including examples from university press books. The CBE Scientific Illustration Committee's *Illustrating Science* covers such topics as camera-ready copy, graphs, maps, computer graphics, and halftone and color printing. All these books are listed in the bibliography.

5

Systems and Sources:
The Mishnah and the Torah
of Moses

Preliminary Observations

Literature is the written expression of those who believe they have something to say that is worth recording and reading by others. It has occupied the mind of men and women to an extent greater than all the other arts summed together. Hence, the importance of the study of all the means, in their several respects and aspects, by which the thought of mankind has been recorded and transmitted. By far the most potent of all these means is the typographic book. The present publication considers the appearance of sheets of vellum (rarely), or paper (usually), impressed from types or letters, mechanically multiplied, composed in a frame, and inked upon a press. The result is a 'print'. This is 'Typography'. If the lines of the types in the frame are so arranged and the corresponding sheet of paper is large enough to be folded, the 'print' falls into 'pages'. When the process is repeated in sequence the result is a series of typographic sheets. When the sheets are gathered together in correct order the intention is fully realised. The result is a 'Book'.

Thus consideration of the 'Typographic Book' excludes single sheets and books printed from engraved plates. The objects under present consideration, therefore, consist of three elementary essentials: paper, type and ink. The binding, so far as this work is concerned, is unimportant since it is an option. A book is a book whether it is bound or not, and the present volume is not concerned with leather-work. For the object to be a 'book' it is only necessary that the sheets should be capable of being bound. When the essential paper, type and ink are skilfully selected and used the result may interest those able to discriminate in terms of quality of production among printed books.

The span of the present set of facsimiles stops short of the latest development in book composition, that is the projection of letters by photographic means. The design and production of a text by photography and its printing, lithographically or otherwise, in a style attractive to discriminating collectors is not an easy task. But it has been achieved. The process, however, is such recent maturity that its date excludes it from the present volume. It is not, however, within the intention

79

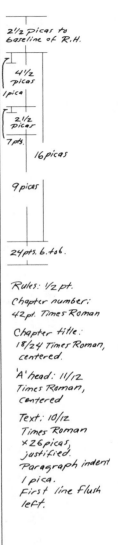

2½ picas to baseline of R.H.

4½ picas
1 pica

2½ picas
7 pts.
16 picas

9 picas

24 pts. b. to b.

Rules: ½ pt.
Chapter number:
42 pt. Times Roman

Chapter title:
18/24 Times Roman,
centered.

'A' head: 11/12
Times Roman,
centered

Text: 10/12
Times Roman
× 26 picas,
justified.
Paragraph indent
1 pica.
First line flush
left.

24 pts. baseline
to baseline.

] 5 [

Chapter V

] SYSTEMS AND SOURCES: [

] The Mishnah and the Torah ⌐ of Moses [

Preliminary Observations. In the long unfolding of diverse versions of
Judaism, one form of Judaism will take up and revise materials of another,
existing one, dropping some available elements, adapting others, as well
as inventing still others. But every sort of Judaism from the beginning
to the present has had to make its peace with the Scriptures universally
received as revealed by God to Moses at Mount Sinai or to the prophets,
or by the "Holy Spirit" to the historians and chroniclers, psalmists
and other writers. Insight into the modes and principles of selection
among all these candidates for authoritative and generative status
will therefore lead us far into the deepest structure and definitive
tension of a given kind of Judaism. From the formation of the Pentateuch
onward, framers of various sorts of Judaism have had to take
measure in particular of the Mosaic revelation and place themselves
in relationship to it. Each version has found it necessary to lay
claim in its own behalf to possess the sole valid interpretation of the
Torah of Moses. All have alleged that they are the necessary and logical
continuation of the revelation of Moses and the prophets. It is not
surprising, therefore, that in behalf of the Mishnah an equivalent claim
was laid down almost from the very moment of the Mishnah's completion
and closure.

The diverse versions of that claim in behalf of the Mishnah indeed

5

Systems and Sources:
The Mishnah and the Torah
of Moses

Preliminary Observations

In the long unfolding of diverse versions of Judaism, one form of Judaism will take up and revise materials of another, existing one, dropping some available elements, adapting others, as well as inventing still others. But every sort of Judaism from the beginning to the present has had to make its peace with the Scriptures universally received as revealed by God to Moses at Mount Sinai or to the prophets, or by the "Holy Spirit" to the historians and chroniclers, psalmists and other writers. Insight into the modes and principles of selection among all these candidates for authoritative and generative status will therefore lead us far into the deepest structure and definitive tension of a given kind of Judaism. From the formation of the Pentateuch onward, framers of various sorts of Judaism have had to take measure in particular of the Mosaic revelation and place themselves in relationship to it. Each version has found it necessary to lay claim in its own behalf to possess the sole valid interpretation of the Torah of Moses. All have alleged that they are the necessary and logical continuation of the revelation of Moses and the prophets. It is not surprising, therefore, that in behalf of the Mishnah an equivalent claim was laid down almost from the very moment of the Mishnah's completion and closure.

The diverse versions of that claim in behalf of the Mishnah indeed constitute one of the complex and interesting problems in the history of Judaism in the Mishnah's version both in the time in which the Mishnah was taking shape and afterward. But the analysis and historical evaluation of those efforts to lay down, in behalf of the Mishnah, a claim of the authority of revelation in the name of Moses and from the mouth of God just now need not detain us (see below, pp. 172–74). The reason is that these theological formations are post facto assertions. They are not data out of the inner history of the formation of the Mishnah itself and the unfolding of its ideas. Later

26 picas

3/4" to
baseline
of running
head

20pts. baseline
to baseline

Verso running
head: 9pt New
Baskerville
C. + S.C.

30pts. baseline
to baseline

18pts. baseline
to baseline

18pts. baseline
to baseline
minimum.
Keep as close
to minimum
as
possible

'A' head: 11/12
New Baskerville
'B' head: 10/12
New Baskerville
italic

21pts. baseline
to baseline

15pts. baseline
to baseline

Extract: 9/11
New Baskerville
indent left
and right
1 pica.

should be rejected as being non-'typographic'. Their exclusion from these pages is no more than a chronological accident. A typographic book is any book in which the letters are multiplied mechanically. When the letters are formed by hand the result is a calligraphic book.

The following facsimiles present, for the pleasure of collectors of typography, and the benefit of practitioners of the art, a selection of books printed since 1450 which have achieved a significant standard of design. Any pleasing attributes these objects may possess arise from the degree of skill with which the letters or types have been designed, engraved, composed, inked and impressed upon the properly prepared vellum or paper. The quality of this achievement is fairly suggested in the accompanying facsimiles.

Repubublican Definitions of Union

It must be admitted that, while a photographic facsimile carefully made (as in the present work), can accurately reproduce the graphic components, that is the type, the decoration and the illustration, it is powerless to indicate the nature of the paper or the degree of skill of the impression. It must be emphasised that the fine paper and skilled presswork are important constituents of the fine typographic book. Hence, no photographic facsimile, however accurate by itself, is a sufficient substitute for the original, unless the paper, too is duplicated, And this is, generally speaking, an impossibility.

> Complete success, moreover, depends in largest measure upon the choice of letter or type. Hence, the selection of examples for reproduction in the following pages has often turned upon the character and quality of letter employed in their composition.

The aim of the present work, therefore, is to inspire readers to make the physical acquaintance of the original editions. Only then will the true quality of the impression be appreciated, as, for instance, a limited number of copies pulled by a skilled printer on a hand-press is work that is markedly distinct from any of the several thousands manufactured on a high-speed rotary press. Similarly, paper has to be seen and touched and judged if the fine book is to be fully appreciated.

An Union of Interests

It has often been pointed out that to collect the productions advertised as éditions de luxe is not equivalent to critical discrimination. The fine book is not identical with 'luxury'. Many of these éditions de luxe normal commercial compositions printed upon unnecessarily thick paper.

Moreover, while a publisher's limitation of his edition to a small number of copies may be relevant to its prospects as an article of trade, it has no connection with its artistic merit, if any.

On the other hand, a commercial book need not be lacking in merit. The anti-industrial convictions of some Victorian printers, combined with the spectacular quality of their productions, has resulted in the paradox that some of the most interesting typography of later generations comes from commercial houses working in the normal course of business. Even so, it must be admitted, the finest quality of book-production is created by the scrupulous use of materials rarely in the stock of a commercial house. Intelligence and skill are always more important to the art of the book than the employment of rare materials or costly processes. The highest standard of the typographic art can be reached only by unusual care. It is vital to bring, in sufficient degree, knowledge and sensitivity to the composition of the page and to its inking and impression upon the chosen material, if full justice is to be done to the letter or type by which the thought of the author, and the comment of the illustrator (if any), are conveyed to the reader.

Complete success, moreover, depends in largest measure upon the choice of letter or type. Hence, the selection of examples for reproduction in the following pages has often turned upon the character and quality of letter employed in their composition.

While, therefore, access to skill and judgement in letter-design are of vital importance to the production of the fine book, no satisfactory, ecumenical, definition of the type best suited to the text in hand is forthcoming. Few printers wish to be limited to one type only. Fewer wish to change the type in every book they print. The creation of a new type is always an arduous and expensive undertaking, but, as the facsimiles prove, the task has been achieved in the past and even recently, in both kinds of letter, that is the old 'gothic' and the modern 'roman', The medieval, heavy, narrow, pointed letter rightly called 'black' is certainly more homogenous as a design and presents itself more majestically on the page than the modern renaissance, light, round, roman letter. Yet the economy, elasticity and versatility of the roman letter makes a general return to 'gothic' impossible. Today only in Germany could a few editions be composed in a form of black-letter. In default of an ecumenical definition of the 'best' type it may be said that a 'good' type is one

23. Hence, the immediate problem before a printer who is ambitious to produce a fine rendering of his text is the choice of the variety of roman type to be used. In the past there was no wide choice. Had Morris found to his hand the number of founts now available, he might have thought twice before cutting the Golden and Troy types. But the conditions be

Handwritten margin notes:

3/4" to baseline of running head

20 pts. baseline to baseline

Recto running head: 9 pt. New Baskerville C. + S.C.

Footnotes: 8/10 New Baskerville × 26 picas justified. Paragraph indent 1 pica use aligning figures.

18 pts. minimum baseline to baseline. Keep as close to minimum as possible.

3/4" to
baseline of
running
head

20pts.
baseline
to baseline

30pts. baseline
to baseline

18pts. baseline
to baseline

21pts. baseline
to baseline

15pts. baseline
to baseline,

18pts. minimum
baseline to
baseline, keep
as close to
minimum
as possible

'A' head:
11/12 Helvetica

'B' head:
10/12 Garamond
book italic

Tables:
8/9 Garamond
Book

234 Strategies of High Uncertainty

books printed since 1450 which have achieved a significant standard of design. Any pleasing attributes these objects may possess arise from the degree of skill with which the letters or types have been designed, engraved, composed, inked and impressed upon the properly prepared vellum or paper. The quality of this achievement is fairly suggested in the accompanying facsimiles

The Problem of Equality and Community

It must be admitted that, while a photographic facsimile carefully made (as in the present work),can accurately reproduce the graphic components, that is the type, the decoration and the illustration, it is powerless to indicate the nature of the paper or the degree of skill of the impression. It must be emphasised that the fine paper and skilled presswork are important constituents of the fine typographic book. Hence, no photographic facsimile, however accurate by itself, is a sufficient substitute for the original, unless the paper, too is duplicated, And this is, generally speaking, an impossibility.

Civil Equality and the Problem of Administration

The aim of the present work, therefore, is to inspire readers to make the physical acquaintance of the original editions. Only then will the true quality of the impression be appreciated, as, for instance, a limitied number of copies pulled by a skilled printer on a hand-press is work that is markedly distinct from any of the several thousands manufactured on a high-speed rotary press. Similarly, paper has to be seen and touched and judged if the fine book is to be fully appreciated.

It has often been pointed out that to collect the productions advertised

Table 4.2 Baccalaureates (Bacs) Granted by Age and Population

Year	General Population (m)	17 yr old Population (m)	Bacs (1000's)	Bacs/1000 (17 yr. olds
1820	30.3	–	3.1	–
1831	32.6	–	3.2	–
1842	34.5	6.1	2.8	5
1854	35.9	6.4	4.3	7
1865	37.9	6.5	5.9	9
1876	36.9	6.4	5.4	8
1887	38.2	6.6	6.6	10
1898	38.7	4.6	7.8	12

Adapted from Ringer, 1979: 316

19 *Composition, Printing, Binding, and Papermaking*

INTRODUCTION

19.1   The processes of composition, printing, and binding, along with the allied arts of papermaking and platemaking, impose limitations on bookmaking that editors ought to be aware of if they are to play their parts well in the publishing enterprise. It is not necessary to understand these processes in all their detail—indeed, advances in the technology occur with such rapidity that any full discussion of them would soon become obsolete—but some knowledge of what happens between the time an edited, marked-up manuscript leaves the editor's hands and a finished book is placed in them is essential.

19.2   This chapter is not intended to serve as a history of printing and its allied arts: much that was of great importance in its time but has now disappeared is totally ignored. Nor is it intended to supply the technical detail and the terminology that a production controller must command to function effectively. It is intended only to supply a reader who knows little or nothing about the technology of bookmaking with enough information to picture what goes on and so avoid the worst mistakes. Those wishing to pursue the history of composition and bookmaking are referred to the sources listed at the end of the chapter.

THE PREPONDERANCE OF OFFSET LITHOGRAPHY

19.3   Earlier methods of composition and printing involved the production of metal type that was then assembled into printing plates, inked, and pressed against paper. This method of printing is generally referred to as letterpress printing. Although such methods remain in occasional use (see 19.56–58, for example), they have been largely replaced in book and journal printing by offset lithography, a process in which printing plates containing no metal type are made photochemically.

19.4   The principle of offset lithography rests on the physical repulsion between water and oil. It is a principle long used by graphic artists to produce multiple copies of an original drawing done on porous stone with a greasy crayon *(tusche)*. The stone bearing the crayon drawing is dampened with water, which clings to the porous open surface of the stone but not to the greasy surface of the image. The lithographer then inks the stone with a greasy ink, which clings to the image but is repelled by the wet surface of the bare stone. Finally, paper is laid on the printing surface, pressure is applied, and the image is transferred from the stone to the paper. In like manner the offset lithographic plate, a thin sheet of grained aluminum bearing a positive, water-repellent image of the text or other matter to be printed, is wetted and inked so that the greasy ink adheres to the dry image and is repelled by the water clinging to the rest of the plate.

Platemaking

19.5   The making of the offset lithographic plate usually begins with the preparation of clean, sharp-imaged page proof by one of a variety of compositional systems. The proof, which in this case is called *reproduction proof* ("repro," for short, or "repro proof"),[1] is photographed, and the resulting negatives or, in some situations, positives[2] are used to transfer the proof images to the grained, photosensitive metal plate that serves as the primary printing surface. Originally reproduction proof was made (or "pulled") from inked metal type, but this process was soon replaced by compositional methods that produce repro without that intermediary. The variety of compositional methods by which repro is now made are discussed below (19.9–24).

19.6   Printing plates bearing two, four, eight, sixteen, thirty-two, or more pages are exposed in either of two ways: stripping or projection. In the *stripping* method, full-sized negatives of all text pages and illustrations are taped down (stripped) over rectangular, page-sized openings in a

---

1. Reproduction proof is also sometimes referred to as *camera-ready copy,* or simply *camera copy.*

2. *Positive,* in this case, refers to a photographic image on film in which the values of light and dark correspond to the original subject. In the ensuing discussion of platemaking, it should be understood that when negatives are referred to, positives may also occasionally be used.

large sheet of somewhat stiff masking paper in such an order (referred to as the *printing layout*) that the printed sheet, when printed on both sides ("backed up") and folded, will constitute a collection, or *signature,* of pages in correct sequence. The assemblage of masked negatives, called a *flat,* is pressed down tightly against the photosensitive plate, and the whole is exposed to light. When the exposed plate is developed, it is ready for printing.

19.7 In the *projection* method of making offset plates, small negatives are made of the page materials in the order and orientation in which the printing images will appear on the plate. These are then projected one by one, at page size, onto the photosensitive plate. The result, when developed, is a plate similar to that obtained by stripping. The projection method, however, cannot be used when the pages contain halftone illustrations.

The Advantage

19.8 The ease with which offset plates can be made and printed accounts for much of the present predominance of offset lithography. The cost of using line illustrations is negligible: once they have been photostated to correct size, they can be photographed along with the text at no extra charge. And good-quality halftones, made with 133- or 150-line screens (see 19.49–50), can print with the text on ordinary book paper. (High-resolution, 300-line halftones do, however, require smoother and denser stock.)

COMPOSITION AND MAKEUP

19.9 Since all that is needed for making a printing plate in offset lithography is an image on paper or film, it really makes no difference how the image gets there, so long as it is sharp and clear. There is no need to set metal type, as was originally done, if an image similar to that of a page of repro proof can be created by other means, and that is what all modern composition systems are designed to do. The simplest mode of composition without metal type—and the first historically to be used— is *strike-on composition.* More complex and sophisticated are the various later methods and systems known collectively as *photocomposition,* or *computer-assisted composition.*

Strike-on Composition

19.10 When typewriter composition first began to be used in commercial printing, it was often referred to as *cold type,* because reproduction copy was produced without the agency of molten type metal. The name has stuck and has even been extended to cover other modern modes of composition. It is more a layman's term, however, than a professional's.

TEXT COMPOSITION

19.11   The simplest form of strike-on composition is that produced by an ordinary office typewriter, and this method is sometimes used by scholarly publishers for special-interest monographs, where the cost of conventional typesetting cannot be justified by the probable sales revenue. The machine commonly used is the IBM Selectric, with its many interchangeable "golf ball" type fonts and carbon ribbon. Such composition lacks proportional spacing (*is* and *ws* occupy the same space) (fig. 19.1) and is usually unjustified, that is, the right margin is irregular *(ragged)* rather than straight (see also 18.26–27).

```
WWWWW  MMMMM  NNNNN  aaaaa  iiiii  lllll  . . . . .
```

WWWWW MMMMM NNNNN aaaaa iiiii lllll .....

Fig. 19.1. Character spacing and typewriter composition. As illustrated by the top line above, the ordinary office typewriter allots the same amount of space to every character—*l, m,* capital letter, lowercase letter, or punctuation mark. Real type, as illustrated by the lower line, produces characters that occupy space according to the width of the character, a capital *M* being three or four times as wide as a lowercase *l,* for example. The spacing of letters in real type is referred to as *proportional spacing.*

19.12   More sophisticated, but now seldom used to produce reproduction copy, owing to the appearance of affordable microcomputer systems, is the MTST (magnetic-tape Selectric typewriter) system, which provides proportional spacing, mixing of fonts, justification, automatic centering of subheads, and some other refinements. MTST does this by storing on magnetic tape the record of up to 4,000 keystrokes, including function commands (such as font changes, line justification, etc.) and using the tape to drive an automatic typewriter. It produces a page or two of typeset matter at a time. Other strike-on systems have similar or greater capabilities.

19.13   The availability of affordable microcomputers has greatly diminished the role of typewriters in strike-on composition. With attached printers and the capability of operating with a wide variety of word-processing software, microcomputers offer such advantages as the proportional spacing of characters, the capacity for justifying margins, and the simplification of the correction process. Corrections that can be confined to one page, even though more than one line is involved, are simply entered in place, and then the entire page is reprinted. Corrections that affect the makeup of more than one page require only that all pages affected (sometimes extending to the end of the chapter or other piece) be reprinted. Another advantage of microcomputer-generated proof is that additional copies can be printed, avoiding the necessity of making photocopies of single printouts from typewriter composition. (For a discussion of microcomputers in desktop publishing see 19.61–63.) While some printers employed by microcomputers operate on the strike-on principle, and thus continue the tradition of strike-on composition, but with greater flexibility and sophistication, others print by means of lenses and laser beams. Such printers, producing copy with greater resolution, cross over into the realm of photocomposition, which will be discussed below (19.19–24).

COMPOSITION FOR DISPLAY

19.14 Since typewriter composition is unsuitable for the production of type large enough for display work, title pages, chapter headings, part titles, and the like cannot be composed by this method. With appropriate software and printer, however, microcomputer composition can produce whatever display is needed. For display work that cannot be done by the compositional system in use, other means must be resorted to. One possibility, seldom used but attractive if there is a calligrapher on the staff, is to have display lines written out by hand. Another is to put them together with the press-on type sold in art-supply stores (Letraset is one example). This type is printed on transparent vinyl backed with adhesive wax and comes in a great variety of faces and sizes. The procedure most commonly resorted to, however, is conventional typesetting.

19.15 If conventional modes of typesetting are resorted to for display work, reproduction proof is produced by means of either metal type or any of the phototypesetting systems capable of display work. In either case the display lines are all prepared at the same time, and the repro is then cut apart and pasted down on the appropriate pages for photographing.

PROOFS AND CORRECTIONS

19.16 With the exception of the microcomputer systems mentioned above (19.13), strike-on composition produces only one copy of the set matter, so conventional proofs are not available. Instead, it is customary to make copies on an office copying machine. Since most typewriter-composed books are typed in page form, the photocopies are the equivalent of page proof. Corrections are marked on these, the typist retypes whatever needs to be corrected, whether words or whole lines, and the retyped copy is pasted over the original. Needless to say, corrections involving transfers of lines from one page to another are discouraged.

19.17 If a book is typed in page form, most of the makeup decisions—avoidance of bad breaks, spacing of subheads, placement of footnotes, and the like (see also 19.40–42)—are made by the typist. If there are to be illustrations, space is left for them. Line work, such as graphs and diagrams, scaled to appropriate size, may be pasted down directly on the typed pages. (Typewriter composition prepared on an office machine is ordinarily reduced 10 to 20 percent when negatives for the printing plates are made; MTST, microcomputer, and other similar composition is usually reproduced same size.) If photographs are to be used for illustrations, the pages are *keylined,* that is, areas are outlined to show the positions and shapes of the illustrations, and the photographs, marked for cropping, are sent to the printer separately.

19.18 When offset negatives of the pages have been made and stripped in position, the printer may make blueprints of the flats if the publisher asks for them and is willing to pay for them (see 3.54, 3.57). Blueprints provide the editor's only chance to check the placement of halftone illustrations and are useful for checking the positioning of typed material on the page and for making sure that everything intended for inclusion in the book is there. Dirt, ink, or a piece of tape on the type area shows up as a blank spot on the blueprint and can be caught and corrected at this time. A scratch shows as a dark line.

Photocomposition

19.19 Because of the high cost of hot-metal composition and the typographic limitations and slowness of strike-on composition, *photocomposition* accounts for most of the book, periodical, and newspaper typesetting done today. In photocomposition, or *phototypesetting,* printing images are produced through the agency of light controlled by digital information stored in a computer.

19.20 All modern phototypesetting systems consist of three basic parts: an *input device* (such as a keyboard), a *computer* (for storage and retrieval of typographic information), and a *typesetter* (which actually creates the type images on the paper or film). Three kinds of phototypesetters are currently in use: the photomechanical typesetter, the CRT system, and the laser imagesetter.

PHOTOMECHANICAL TYPESETTING

19.21 The photomechanical typesetter, the oldest of the three currently employed phototypesetters, forms letters, numbers, and punctuation by passing brilliant flashes of light from a stroboscopic xenon source through a film matrix. The shaped flashes are then projected through a lens system onto the light-sensitive medium. Many changes of point size are made optically, rather than by changing fonts. Some typesetters use several lenses, each for a particular enlargement or reduction of the type image, mounted in a turret that rotates to bring any particular lens into position. Others use a zoom lens (like that of a television camera) for the same purpose.

CRT COMPOSITION

19.22 Phototypesetters of the next generation are entirely electronic. These typesetters use information stored in digital form to generate type images at great speed on the surface of a cathode-ray tube (CRT). The process is analogous to the way a television set uses signals received over the air or from a videotape to generate images on the picture tube.

19.23 Any CRT is in essence an evacuated glass bottle. The screen, at the bottom end, is coated on the inside with phosphors, chemical substances that emit light when bombarded with electrons. A mechanism at the neck end generates and controls a stream of electrons that constantly sweeps the inside of the screen in a pattern of closely spaced lines. If the stream of electrons is continuous, the screen is completely lighted, but if the electrons are emitted in controlled bursts rather than a steady stream, the beam can be made to build up an image on the screen. This is what happens inside a television picture tube and inside the character-generating CRT of an electronic typesetter. The typesetter's "picture" is much finer, and the outside front surface of the CRT is a fiber-optic plate, against which the photosensitive paper or film is held. The image is thus transmitted directly to the paper or film exactly as it is generated, with no magnification or reduction.

LASER IMAGESETTERS

19.24 Still more sophisticated than the CRT system, and now more widely used, is the *laser imagesetter.* In this more recently developed system, information stored in digital form generates type images through the rapid manipulation of a laser beam projected onto photosensitive paper or film as dense configurations of dots. The denser the configuration, the greater the resolution of the character or image. Most imagesetters operate at three levels of resolution—low, medium, and high. Book imagesetting is ordinarily done at medium resolution, which is about 1,270 dots per inch. Imagesetters are also capable of producing line graphics and of integrating these with text.

Integrated Typesetting Systems

19.25   A typesetter is only one part of an integrated system that includes one or more other units that function with the aid of computers. Each typesetter has a small computer built into it that governs its basic internal functioning. Such a machine is far from self-governing, however. In the main it is a "slave," making no decisions on its own but responding to commands from outside. Here "outside" means what industry people refer to as the "front end" of the system—one or more input devices and various computer storage-and-retrieval and processing units.

19.26   Typesetting systems vary greatly in capability and in how their various units integrate with one another. The most sophisticated systems can be programmed to produce completely made-up pages that need no further attention before they are photographed for offset printing. Indeed, some can provide offset negatives of the pages, ready for stripping. Less sophisticated systems produce only the basic typography for a page, which then must be cut up and pasted down on boards, as with strike-on composition.

INPUT DEVICES

19.27   The most usual form of input device in modern integrated typesetting systems is an *input and editing terminal,* also called a *video display terminal,* or *VDT* (fig. 19.2). This consists of (1) a keyboard that includes all the usual typewriter keys plus a number of other keys controlling special functions and (2) a CRT viewing screen on which computer-stored copy can be displayed. As the operator "keyboards" (types) the material to be set, keystrokes are recorded in digital form on magnetic disks and appear as typed copy on the screen above the keyboard. Copy can be edited—additions, corrections, or cancellations made—as it is being recorded, or it can be called up later and edited then.

19.28   Along with the copy itself, the operator inputs other information that will be needed for typesetting. The amount of information needed varies according to the capabilities of the system in use. It always includes *codes* (sequences of letters and numbers) directing a change of typeface, as from roman to italic or from 10-point to 8-point type, or changes of alignment, as at the beginning and end of indented material. It may also include end-of-line hyphenation decisions. The keyboard is then characterized as *counting* and the input is *justified.* Many typesetting systems are capable of making justification decisions on their own, however, and when keyboarding material for such a system, the operator simply types along, without regard to line endings. In that instance a *noncounting* keyboard can be used and the input is *unjustified.* When

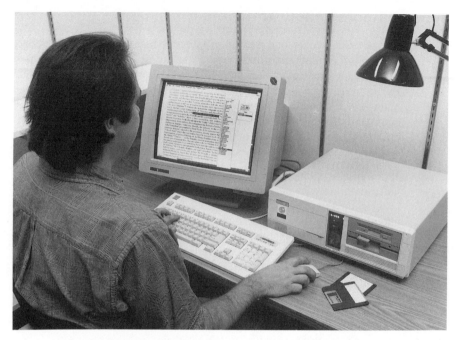

Fig. 19.2. Video display terminal. The operator can check input as it is recorded or call it back for subsequent editing. At the right are two floppy disks.

disks containing unjustified copy, sometimes called *idiot disks,* are run through a typesetter programmed to make justification decisions, the copy produced is justified.

19.29   Systems differ in how they integrate the keyboard. A *direct-input* keyboard or terminal is connected directly to the typesetter. An *off-line* keyboard or terminal is connected to an intermediate storage-and-retrieval unit.

19.30   One of the most ingenious input devices is the OCR (for *optical character recognition*) device. This machine scans the lines of a typewritten manuscript and records the characters in digital form on magnetic tape for use in driving a typesetting system. Appropriate input codes may be included in the original manuscript, or they may be inserted later in the digital input. OCRs are now capable of interpreting digitally a number of different typewriter faces. However ingenious this input device is, one should bear in mind that, even with the cleanest copy, the probability of error is 0.5 percent. That is, in the scanning of two hundred characters, there is likely, on average, to be one that is misread.

19.31   The word processors manufactured by business-machine companies are also capable of producing input for typesetting systems. The computer language they employ, however, is designed primarily for office and scientific use, and it usually has to be "translated" for use as typesetting input.

COMPUTER STORAGE AND PROCESSING UNITS

19.32 Between keyboard and typesetter an integrated typesetting system includes a great deal of computer capacity for the storage and retrieval of information and for manipulating input so as to produce acceptable typeset material. These functions (hyphenation and justification, for example, or basic page makeup) may be performed by individual "stand-alone" units connected electronically, or they may be combined in a *central processing unit* (CPU) that stores all the information and performs all the command functions needed to drive the typesetter.

19.33 Part of the information stored in a central processing unit is in permanent storage (the *master file*) and is seldom, if ever, altered. This information might include the following:

Kerning records (for example, "When *T* is followed by *a, e, o,* or *u,* set the word so the crossbar of *T* overhangs the next letter by so many units")

Logical hyphenation routines—a series of instructions that answers many word-division questions

Exception dictionary—acceptable divisions for many words to which the logical hyphenation routines do not apply

Justification program, for spacing out words to fill the line

Makeup instructions on adjusting spacing, number of lines to the page, and so forth to avoid bad breaks

For driving a digital typesetter, all the characters in all the fonts the machine is capable of setting, in digital form

19.34 Information in temporary storage (the *job file*) would probably include the following:

The text itself in digital form

Specific commands concerning font and point size

Specific makeup instructions—line length, page length, indention of various elements, and so on

CAPABILITIES

19.35 Modern computer-controlled typesetting systems, whether photomechanical or electronic, offer far greater opportunity to control the appearance of the type images in the line than was ever possible with metal. Word spacing ranging from maximum to minimum may be specified for a line or two, a paragraph, or a whole manuscript by giving the simplest of instructions. Space between letters, which formerly could be no closer than the width of the metal type body permitted, can now be made so close that the letterforms are actually tangent, and any letter (not just a few specially designed "kerned" type sorts) may overhang any other when the forms of the letters permit:

Total control is often sought but seldom attained.
Total control is often sought but seldom attained.
Total control is often sought but seldom attained.

Proofs and Corrections

19.36 Because of the completely different way that typeset material is created in a phototypesetting system, the procedures by which the proofs are made and corrections entered are quite unlike those used in hot-metal days, when the set type was placed either in long trays called *galleys* or in shorter trays capable of holding all of the type necessary to produce individual pages. The type in these trays was inked, and either *galley proof* or *page proof* was pulled from it for reading and correction.

PROOFS

19.37 The usual form of proof from a modern system is a photocopy of the typesetter output. This may be the equivalent of a galley proof, showing the typeset material in long columns, or, if the typesetting system is one that produces made-up pages on its own, it may be the equivalent of page proof (see fig. 19.3). In either case it is read by author and editor in the same way as conventional proof from metal type.

19.38 Many integrated systems today include a proofing device, such as the Tegra Proofing System. This system, circumventing the regular typesetter, provides reading proof with simulated typefaces, hyphenation, justification, and other typographic functions. While resembling typesetter output in many ways, such reading proof does not have the same sharpness of character and is not on photographic paper. The advantage of such a proofing system is that it provides reading proof resembling typeset quality without the expense of employing the typesetter.

CORRECTIONS

19.39 The least sophisticated typesetting systems require corrections to be made in the least sophisticated way—by resetting words or lines and pasting these down on the typesetter output, as is done with strike-on

Chapter One

lecting and rearranging pieces of several myths, she had created personal histories that vividly presented her own version of her marriage, the deaths of her children, her husband's infidelities, the arrival of a co-wife, etc. Like entries on a Rosetta stone, Rubak's stories made it possible to lay out with dramatic clarity connections among personal symbols and collective representations, showing how "myth can be regarded as constituting the furthest background of a continuous perspective which ranges from an individual's personal concerns, fears, and sorrows . . . right back into the epoch where a similar fact is imagined to have occurred for the first time" (Malinowski 1954 [1926]:156).

During the next ten years of intermittent fieldwork, *nonekuma* became the key to my understanding of Gimi women's protests—and acquiescence—in the "male ideological hegemony" of Gimi culture. Women may never have had eyes on flutes, or never have done so publicly before the arrival of missionaries, but their myths indicate they have always known the secret. The association of *nonekuma* with women's houses suggests that women may even participate in, or influence, the creation of men's myths—a priority that men's myth seems to recognize in the premise that the first woman invented the flute by herself. Children of both sexes sleep with their mothers, giving males an intimate knowledge of women and women's bedtime stories. But women have no counterpart knowledge of men, as some men point out, because they have no parallel experience in childhood of living for years alone with their fathers: on the contrary, they are traditionally kept apart. *In Oriuma*, or tales of the men's house, may be considered in this light not simply as the male equivalent of *nonekuma* but also as a response or appropriation of the *nene*, incorporating, elaborating, translating into the terms of a male ethic stories men heard in infancy. Whatever the direction—or mutuality—of influence, the tales told "in secret" inside men's and women's separate houses seem to speak to one another across the night.

The Mythic Argument

An interpretation of culture based upon the content of belief is inherently unwieldy. In speaking of two sides of a hidden dispute between the sexes, I have used certain key myths to express the gist of hundreds. To summarize the mythic argument in a preliminary way, I present just two of these key myths, treating them to a kind of diagrammatic reduction in lieu of fuller versions that will appear later on. Aside from deleting narrative complexity, sometimes to the point of parody, such treatment gives the impression that I constructed an argument between the sexes simply by comparing their myths. In fact, I was able to see connections among the myths only through the "detour" of ritual enactment. The myths' relations with each other be-

THE ARGUMENT AMONG MYTHS

came apparent from associations informants made, not among the narratives themselves but between certain mythic events and ritual performances. When I examined the spoken content of a myth, and even accompanying exegeses, in the context of their often multiple ritual correlates, I saw that the myth could hide, distort, or even reverse the meanings it acquired in relation to ritual; and that these hidden meanings were sometimes explicit *premise* of other myths, especially those of the opposite sex. Associations with ritual revealed correspondences among myths and even suggested levels of meaning within a myth. While I follow Lévi-Strauss in "reading a myth as a whole," I do not treat them as a closed system of meaning, as if "myth itself provides its own context" (Lévi-Strauss 1967:311).

My interpretations of myths are tied to the rites of death, birth, marriage, initiation, and sorcery. Like a rite of passage or curing, a Gimi myth always has a central character, one who represents the deceased, newborn, bride, groom, initiate, patient, etc., the one on whose behalf the ritual is performed, though in myth the subject is often "out of sight," behind the scenes, circulating in concealment, as it were, among the objects and episodes of the narrative. In the sense that a myth, like a ritual, always has a hero or heroine, one whose life is at stake or in the process of transformation, it is like a dream or personal narrative: everything in the myth makes—and in that sense depicts—a singular point of view or experience. I present the argument between men's and women's myths in these terms, as if they were concocted by an archetypal boy and girl, or man and woman, and addressed to each other. But the analysis is actually routed through ritual performance: it is ritual that grounds my interpretations of the myths and allows me to speak of a male or female view, of the mutual containment of views, of men's unspoken protest, agreement, or collusion with men, etc.

Let me stress at the outset that the relentless sexuality and violence of most Gimi myths do not translate in any direct or obvious way into behavior. When I propose that complex collaborations among women's and men's fantasies provide the structural basis of kinship and exchange, I do not imply that Gimi are more sexual, incestuous, or death-obsessed in their personal relations than other people. Cunnilingus is alluded to in the flute myth, and in women's myth of the giant penis, although both sexes expressly forbid mouth-to-genital contact. While oral sex is sometimes performed, as far as I know it is hardly the general practice. Symbolic male homosexuality is a more prominent, though covert, theme, in my view, in the myths of both sexes. Indeed, I suggest that symbolic male homosexual incest, an encounter between father and son in the prenatal and primordial past, is the organizing principle of marriage and exchange and a focus of life-crisis rites (see Chaps. 7, 8, and 9). Yet, unlike men in some New Guinea societies (e.g., Williams 1969 [1936]; Kelly 1976; Schieffelin 1976; Herdt 1981), Gimi men do not prac-

Fig. 19.3. Proof from a phototypesetting system. The equivalent of galley proof is shown at top; page proof is shown at bottom. Both kinds are photocopied for proof reading and correcting.

composition. With more sophisticated systems the operator simply calls up on the screen of the video display terminal whatever parts of the text require correction and makes the needed changes directly on the digital magnetic record. If the changes necessitate lengthening or shortening the text, a system with page-makeup capability will then remake pages as necessary, just as a printer would do with metal composition.

Makeup

BAD BREAKS

19.40 Makeup is a highly skilled procedure. If the text is merely divided mechanically into portions of equal length, without regard to where the divisions fall, some of the pages that result are bound to be unacceptable logically or aesthetically: they will incorporate *bad breaks*. Common examples of bad breaks are the following:

A *widow,* that is, a short line—one word or two or three little ones (some say anything less than a full line)—at the top of a page.

A recto page that ends with the first part of a broken word.

A subhead falling at the foot of a page or column. A subhead should be followed by at least two lines of text.

A section break consisting of a blank line (or a type device in an otherwise blank line) falling at the head or foot of a page or column. Such a section break should, if possible, be preceded or followed by at least two lines of text.

An extract beginning on the last line or ending on the first line of a page or column. There should be at least two lines in either place.

A footnote that does not begin on the same page as its reference. At least two lines of the note should fall on the page containing the reference before the note continues onto the next page.

19.41 Bad breaks can often be eliminated without resetting type, by adjusting page lengths. Although a page is intended to have a standard number of lines, the designer usually permits the typesetter to let pages run one line long or one line short, so long as facing pages match. By this means lines can be moved forward or backward to eliminate the bad break.

19.42 An alternative or ancillary method is to lengthen or shorten a paragraph in the vicinity of the bad break. Often a one-word paragraph ending can be pulled up by resetting a line more tightly, or a full line can be reset looser to run it over. ("Save a line" and "Make a line" are the proofreader's directions for these operations.) Sometimes, too, a paragraph can be lengthened or shortened by slight rewording that does not change the meaning. This, of course, requires the cooperation of the author or editor or both, and the device cannot be used with reprinted material. Again, if the subheads are set with a fair amount of white space above and below them, this space can sometimes be reduced or increased to save a line or make a line. This works particularly well when two subheads fall on the same page and the stolen or added space can be split between them. (With computer-controlled typesetting, word spacing for a whole paragraph or page can be easily altered to avoid bad breaks—see 19.35.)

MEASUREMENT

19.43 Type is measured in units that are peculiar to the trade. The size of a typeface is defined in terms of *points,* one point being approximately

¹⁄₇₂ of an inch. The *point size* of a particular face refers to the vertical measurement of the letters—historically, the body on which the characters were set. For most typefaces this is approximately the distance between the tops of the tallest letters—which may be either the capitals or the lowercase letters with ascenders, like *b* and *h*—and the bottoms of the letters with descenders, like *p* and *q* (fig. 19.4). The length of a line of type is measured in *picas,* one pica being equal to twelve points, or about ⅙ of an inch. Space between lines, called *leading* (see 2.137, 18.23), is measured in points.

19.44 The *type page,* or *text page,* of a book is the area that includes the running head at the top and the last line of a full page—or the folio, whichever is lower—at the bottom and extends from the left edge to the right edge of any typeset matter, including folios but not illustrations (which may *bleed* into the margins). The type page is measured in picas. Any internal measurement, such as the drop *(sinkage)* for chapter openings, is based on the limits of the type page. (See fig. 19.5.)

19.45 The *trim size* of a book is the actual size of the page after the sheets have been printed, folded, sewn, and trimmed (fig. 19.5). In the United States and Canada it is measured in inches; in the rest of the world, in millimeters. (Librarians, bibliographers, and those who produce publishers' catalogs often give the approximate size of a book, including its covers, in centimeters, but this is not the actual trim size.)

19.46 The page *margins*—the white space between the type page and the trimmed edges of the page—are specified in either picas or inches. Designers generally give the dimensions of only the back (inside, or gutter) and head margins, because picas, used for the type page, are not exactly compatible with inches, used for the trim size. A manuscript editor ought to possess a *pica rule* (also called *pica stick* and *line gauge*) for checking page and type measurements. A pica rule is always divided along one edge into picas and half-picas (that is, 12- and 6-point divisions) and along one edge into inches. Along other edges (both faces are generally used) may appear scales for other common type sizes, such as 8- and 10-point, and often a scale for agate lines

Fig. 19.4. The point size of type

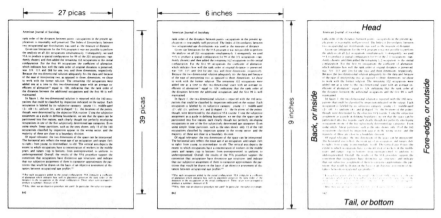

Fig. 19.5. Basic page anatomy. The *type page* (shown at left) is a rectangle, measured in picas, enclosing all the typeset matter on the page. The *trim size* (center) consists of the dimensions of the bound sheets after trimming, measured in inches. The *margins* of a page (right) are the areas of white space surrounding the type page. Clockwise from the top of a right-hand page, they are called the head margin; fore-edge, or outside, margin; tail, or bottom, margin; and back, or inside, margin.

(exactly 14 to the inch), used to measure newspaper advertising space. A reader in possession of such a rule will easily find that the type page of this book measures 27 by about 48 picas and that the trim size is 6 by 9 inches.

PRINTING

The Offset Lithographic Process

19.47   In offset lithographic printing, the pliable lithographic plate, wrapped around and fastened to the plate cylinder (see fig. 19.6), is continuously wetted by the dampening rollers. The water adheres to the background area of the plate but not to the image of the type. The wet cylinder is then inked by inking rollers, and the greasy ink sticks to the dry image of the type but not to the wet background. Continuing to revolve, the plate is pressed against another cylinder bearing a rubber blanket that picks up the ink from the plate and transfers *(offsets)* it to the paper, which is drawn between the blanket cylinder and an impression cylinder that presses the paper against the ink-carrying blanket. (The versatility of the offset method may be noted in the fact that the soft, flexible rubber blanket conforms to the surface it is pressing against, and that it can therefore be used for printing on rough-textured paper or cloth and other materials with relatively uneven surfaces.)

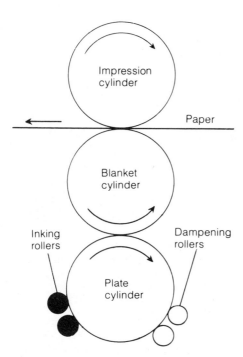

Fig. 19.6. Principle of offset lithography. Five kinds of cylinders and rollers are needed to complete the offset lithographic printing process. Offset presses can be either sheet-fed or web-fed (roll-fed).

Illustrations

LINE ART

19.48   Line art is artwork that consists only of pure blacks and pure whites—pen-and-ink or pencil drawings, bar charts, graphs, prints of engravings or etchings, impressions made from type, and the like. The copy is photographed, transferred to the metal lithographic plate, and printed in the same manner as is the text. For line art that is to be incorporated into the text, measured spaces are left in the text page proofs, the artwork is fixed in the appropriate spaces, and the resulting illustrated pages are photographed for platemaking.

CONTINUOUS-TONE ART: THE HALFTONE PROCESS

19.49   Continuous-tone copy may include pure blacks and pure whites, but it also includes gradations of tone between those extremes, a scale of grays that merges at one end into black and at the other end into white. The most familiar form of black-and-white continuous-tone copy is the photograph. Photosensitive lithographic plates, however, unlike photographic print paper, record only pure black and, by the latter's absence, pure white. No intermediate shades of gray register. The continuous tones of photographic prints must therefore be broken up into tiny black dots whose size depends on the tone of the photographic area being reproduced. If you look at a printed reproduction of a photograph through a magnifying glass, you will see that the black dots in the lightest areas are very small, those in the areas of medium gray are larger, and those in darker areas are so large that they merge, leaving little white dots among them (see fig. 19.7). This is known as a *halftone* reproduction.

19.50   Halftone reproductions are transferred to lithographic plates in the same manner as line art, but the image is first broken up into the requisite halftone dots by photographing the copy through a cross-ruled *screen*. The screen is positioned between the copy and the camera, and the openings between the cross-rules act as little pinhole cameras, bringing the light passing through them to focus on the photographic emulsion as round dots. Halftone screens for the older letterpress work were ruled at from 65 to 150 lines to the inch, the coarser screens being used for newspaper work. For offset lithography, the ruling may run up to 300 lines to the inch.

FOUR-COLOR PROCESS PRINTING

19.51   *Process printing* is a method of printing from three or more halftone plates, each inked with a different color, to obtain a result resembling a

Fig. 19.7. The halftone principle

color photograph or painting. Just as an ordinary halftone gives an illusion of continuous tone in black and white and shades of gray, so process printing gives an illusion of continuous tone in natural colors. If you look at a color illustration in a magazine under a magnifying glass, you will see that the image is composed of tiny dots of pure primary colors, some overlying others but most of them adjacent to one another. The dots of each color vary in size and number across the image, and our unaided eyes, unable to distinguish the individual dots, interpret the patterns they make as natural colors.

19.52   The primary colors used in process printing are not the familiar red, blue, and yellow of a kindergartner's paint box. The yellow is more or less a pure yellow (and so named), but the blue, called *cyan,* is a greenish blue, and the red, called *magenta,* is a purplish red. In color theory, these three hues can be combined in varying proportions to make all the colors of the spectrum, as well as black. But printer's inks are not, and cannot be, perfect theoretical primaries, so a fourth "color," black, is added to the three primaries to help produce the darker shades and the pure black of shadows. Hence "four-color" process printing.

19.53   The halftone plates used in process printing are made from *color-separation negatives,* one for each color plus black. These negatives may be made by shooting the color artwork through filters that blank out all but the one color wanted for that plate or by scanning the artwork on an electronic *color scanner* that separates the colors. As with all halftones, the printing surface is made by shooting through a screen that breaks the image up into dots. For each color, however, the screen is rotated a certain number of degrees so that the resulting dots do not all superimpose on one another or line up in the shimmering, wavy pattern called *moiré (mwa-RAY,* colloquially *maw-RAY).*

19.54   Two ways, among several possibilities, of printing color illustrations are, first, in four passes through a single-color press and, second, in one pass through a four-color press. In the latter, four different color plates are installed serially. In either case, it is simpler and more economical to print the color illustrations in separate signatures, for in that way the entire work need not be run through the expensive color process, and if special coated paper is used for finer reproduction of the color illustrations, that paper need not be used throughout the whole work. Signatures containing only text or text plus black-and-white illustrations can be run through a single-color (black, in this case) press in a single pass. Of the two color processes mentioned, the one requiring a single pass through a four-color press is the more desirable and the more economical, because off-press drying time is required between passes in single-color presses, and the final result is thus delayed.

19.55   In a book containing many color illustrations, it is possible, although more costly, to scatter the illustrations throughout the text. The text, in

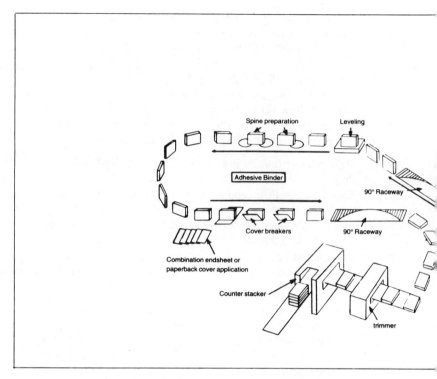

Fig. 19.8. Cameron belt press. This press produces finished paperback books by the letterpress method in relatively short runs at relatively low cost.

that case, is contained on the black plates. Such scattering of color illustrations is more costly because the entire book must be run through the color press.

Giant Modern Presses

THE BELT PRESS

19.56 As the demise of letterpress printing was being confidently predicted, the *belt press* (often called the *Cameron belt press* after one of its manufacturers) made its appearance and changed the outlook for letterpress. The belt press is web-fed (that is, paper is fed to the press from rolls rather than from sheets) and prints from plastic plates carried not on a cylinder but on an endless belt (fig. 19.8). The belt press prints a complete book in one pass and is particularly suitable for paperback books in runs of from 2,000 to 5,000.

19.57 The plastic plates (whose development made possible the belt press) are made from a light-sensitive synthetic material and are acid-etched in

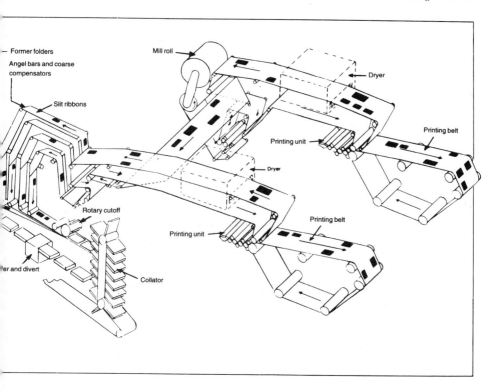

Former folders
Angel bars and coarse compensators
Slit ribbons
Mill roll
Dryer
Printing unit
Printing belt
Dryer
Rotary cutoff
Printing unit
Printing belt
er and divert
Collator

much the same way as metal photoengravings. The plates, which are themselves flexible, are attached to an endless flexible belt that can be lengthened or shortened to suit the job. Usually the plates for several books of ordinary length can be accommodated at the same time. In contrast to conventional letterpress printing, belt-press printing requires very little on-press *makeready,* that is, those frequently difficult adjustments necessary, while the plate is in the press, to ensure that all parts of a plate print evenly. The plastic plates used in belt-press printing are mounted and adjusted before the belt is on the press.

19.58   The belt press has two plate belts, one for each side of the web. As the web of paper goes through the press it is first printed on one side by passing between the rotating plate belt and an impression cylinder, and then the ink impression is dried by heat. Continuing through the press, the other side of the web is printed and dried in the same manner. It is then slit into ribbons of paper two pages wide, and these are folded down the middle and chopped into four-page signatures, which are collated at the delivery end of the press. The signatures of such a book cannot be sewn together for binding; instead, they must be held together with adhesive, as in *perfect binding* (see 19.76). In some installations the collated signatures are fed into an automatic perfect binder (see fig. 19.8), producing finished books, ready for shipping.

WEB OFFSET

19.59 An abundance of the printing for publishers today is done by *web-fed offset lithography,* called *web offset* for short. Web offset presses are in a general way similar to presses used for sheet-fed offset printing but employ only four kinds of cylinders and rollers instead of five and are fed paper in the form of a continuous reel rather than individual sheets (see fig. 19.9). The four kinds of cylinders and rollers are arranged in two similar sets, one for each side of the advancing web. Each set consists of a plate cylinder, dampening rollers, inking rollers, and a blanket cylinder. The web offset press has no impression cylinder, but the two blanket cylinders are tangent to one another, and each acts as the impression cylinder for the other. Both sides of the web are thus printed simultaneously in what is referred to as *blanket-to-blanket* printing. Upon emerging from the printing assembly, the web passes through a gas-fired drying oven, and from there it advances to a folding unit attached to the delivery end of the press. The folder can be adjusted to provide signatures of 8, 16, 24, or 32 pages.

19.60 Web-offset printing is extremely fast and generally uses paper 36–38 inches wide (some presses take webs more than 60 inches wide). As a

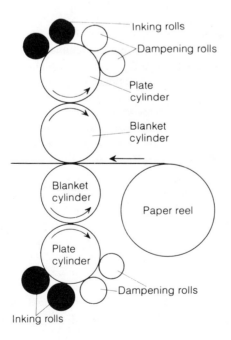

Inking rolls

Dampening rolls

Plate cylinder

Blanket cylinder

Blanket cylinder

Paper reel

Plate cylinder

Dampening rolls

Inking rolls

Fig. 19.9. Web-offset press. The blanket-to-blanket web-offset press dispenses with an impression cylinder, printing both sides of the web at the same time.

consequence, web offset is useful to book publishers chiefly for text-books, dictionaries, encyclopedias, and reference works, where press runs of 15,000 or more are usual. Development of the *miniweb* press, however, with a web less than 30 inches wide, sometimes makes relatively short runs (5,000 or even less) practical.

DESKTOP PUBLISHING

19.61   One of the most important recent developments in low-cost composition and the economical preparation of printed material is the combined operation referred to, somewhat misleadingly, as *desktop publishing.* The term is less than accurate in that not all of the activities associated with publishing are included in such a system. Such operations as acquisitions, binding, and marketing—all very complicated activities— are not part of the process. Moreover, at least at present, large print runs are not possible with such a system. It is important to remain aware of the limited sense in which the term is used in regard to these desktop operations. Another, perhaps less misleading term sometimes used to refer to this combined operation is *electronic imaging.* The integrated system making such combined operations possible consists of a microcomputer, appropriate software, and a compatible printer. At a single work station, a manuscript may be written, revised, edited, designed, composed, and in a limited sense printed. All of this indeed might be performed by a single operator, if that person happens to be skilled in all of the integrated operations.

19.62   Desktop publishing depends first of all on operators proficient in editing, designing, and page makeup as well as in working with computers. It depends next on sophisticated but affordable microcomputers, versatile word-processing software with strong editing features and page-making capabilities, and low-cost printers that provide acceptable-quality printouts. The page-making capabilities enable the operator to design and produce pages with some typographical refinement, including the selection of type style and size, line spacing, line length, and number of lines per page. They also provide automatic kerning, justification, logical hyphenation, and sensible letter and word spacing. A video display terminal presents the text in a form closely resembling the chosen design so that the operator can change word spacing and hyphenation, eliminate bad page or paragraph breaks, and change type font or size before printing out the manuscript. In all these matters, however, the desktop systems cannot yet match the sophistication of expensive typesetting systems, especially in the placement of multiple footnotes and the hyphenation of unusual words.

19.63   Desktop systems are designed to produce attractive documents for office use, for distribution within an organization, and for limited circulation among the public. The printers now available for desktop systems are office printers and are not designed for high-speed printing on large press sheets. The use of desktop systems for book and journal publishing is therefore currently limited to the production of camera-ready copy, either directly by using the system's printer or indirectly by using the electronic file to drive a high-resolution typesetting device.

BINDING

Hard Covers, or Case Binding

19.64 Most trade and scholarly books are bound in hard covers. Such bindings are called *cases,* or *case bindings,* and are usually constructed of laminated cardboard covered with cloth, treated paper, or plastic (see 1.109–10).

19.65 Case binding was the first fully mechanized method to be developed for binding books and is a direct descendant of the highly skilled hand binding prevalent in earlier times and still employed for rare special editions today. Case binding produces machine-bound books that superficially resemble hand-bound books, although the binding differs structurally and is not as strong.

FOLDING AND COLLATING

19.66 Case binding, like all binding methods, begins with the folding of press sheets and the gathering of signatures in order (collating), here done by machine. A *press sheet,* also called a *printed sheet,* bears printed pages on both sides, each side printed from a single plate. The pages are so arranged that when the sheet is folded in half again and again until only one page is showing, all the pages fall into proper sequence (fig. 19.10). Such a folded press sheet is called a *signature.* A signature may comprise 8, 16, 24, or more commonly, 32 pages. Occasionally signatures of 64 pages are printed.

19.67 If separately printed illustrations are to be included in the book, they are added to signatures by *wrapping, inserting,* or *tipping* (see fig. 19.11). In wrapping, one or more folded sheets of illustrations are wrapped around a text signature, and the two groups, or galleries, of illustrations are therefore separated from one another by all of the pages in the signature. Inserted galleries of illustrations are placed either between or within signatures. Tipped-in illustrations are pasted, at their inner edge, to various text pages.

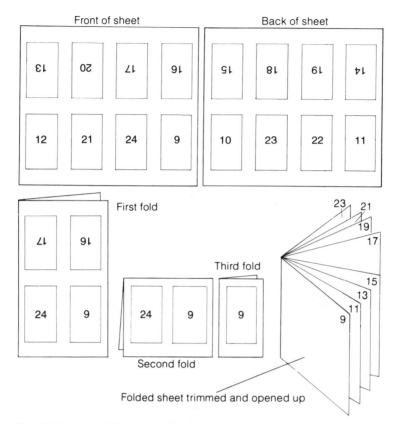

Fig. 19.10. Imposition and the folded sheet. The press sheet schematically illustrated here is printed "eight pages to view," backed up, folded, and trimmed. The imposition, that is, the arrangement of the pages in the form, brings all pages into numerical order after folding. For binding, this folded sheet would probably be slipped inside another 16-page folded sheet (bearing pages 1–8 and 25–32) to make a 32-page signature. The folding sequence (and corresponding imposition) shown here is only one of many variations used in bookmaking.

SEWING THE GATHERED SIGNATURES

19.68   When all of the signatures have been gathered in the proper order, they are referred to as *folded and gathered sheets* (or "f and g's"). The gathered signatures are then sewn together, either by *Smyth* (rhymes with *blithe*) *sewing* or by *side sewing* (fig. 19.12). In Smyth sewing, the signatures are sewn through the folds and to each other. In side sewing, the stiches go through all the signatures at once from the side. Although stronger than those that are Smyth sewn, books that are side sewn will not open flat. By whatever method the signatures are sewn, however,

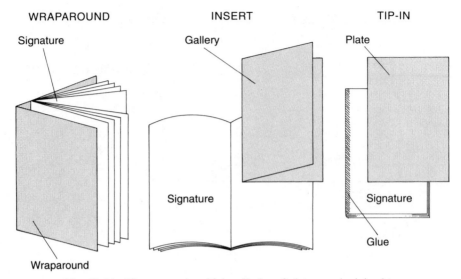

WRAPAROUND   INSERT   TIP-IN

Signature   Gallery   Plate

Signature   Signature

Wraparound   Glue

Fig. 19.11. Three ways in which galleries of plates can be joined to signatures

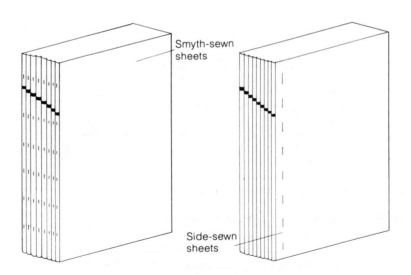

Smyth-sewn sheets

Side-sewn sheets

Fig. 19.12. Two ways of sewing the signatures in machine binding. The black rectangles printed on the signature folds are collating marks. If a signature is missing, duplicated, out of order, or upside down, the error shows up as a variation in the slanted line of marks.

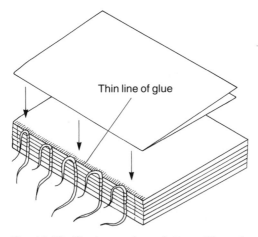

Fig. 19.13. Tipping on the endpapers. The endpapers are tipped, or glued, to the front and back signatures of the sewn book.

the endsheets are then tipped (glued) on (fig. 19.13), the spine is knocked square, and the book is *smashed* (squeezed in a press to remove air).

FORWARDING

19.69 Next comes a sequence of operations known collectively as *forwarding*. These operations include the application of a coating of flexible glue to the spine to help hold everything together. Following this the three remaining sides of the book are *trimmed* to open the folded edges of the signatures. The sewn signatures are then compressed near the spine, which, because of all the sewing, is thicker than the fore edge of the book. The spine is *rounded* to convexity by rollers, the fore edge thus becoming concave, and the book is now of uniform thickness from fore edge to spine (fig. 19.14). The rear folds of the sewn signatures are then *flared* out, creating shoulders against which the front and back covers will come to rest and along which the hinges of the book will be constructed. The construction of the hinges begins with an operation called *lining* (fig. 19.15), in which a piece of stout gauze (the *super*) somewhat wider than the book is thick is glued to the spine with its edges extending outward. A strip of heavy paper the width of the spine is glued down over the super, with the *headbands* tucked between the two layers at the top and bottom. (In hand binding, the headband, a narrow strip of stout cord, vellum, or leather sewn to the top of the spine, was intended to strengthen the spine where it might be strained by a person's finger pulling the book from the shelf. A similar band was often sewn to the bottom of the spine. In the case-bound book,

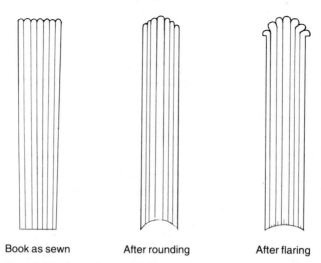

Book as sewn   After rounding   After flaring

Fig. 19.14. Rounding and flaring. After the outer edges of the sewn signatures have been trimmed, compression and rounding compensate for the additional thickness given the spine in sewing. The rear folds are then flared to facilitate hinging and casing in.

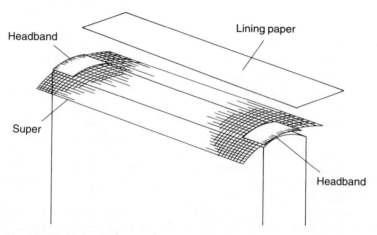

Fig. 19.15. Lining. After the attachment of endpapers, and after trimming, rounding, and flaring, the book is lined as shown here.

headbands are purely decorative and are therefore often left out to save money.)

CASING IN

19.70 The book is now ready to be *cased in,* or enclosed in its cover (fig. 19.16). The case is completely preformed, with boards and paper back-

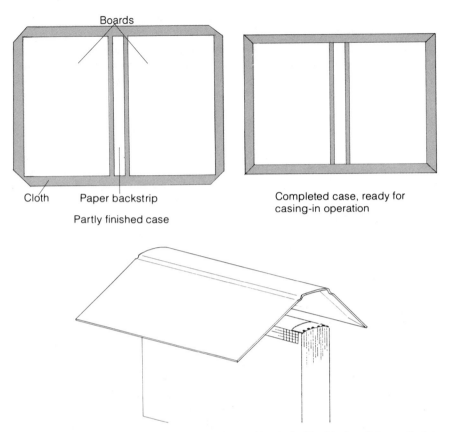

Boards

Cloth   Paper backstrip

Partly finished case

Completed case, ready for
casing-in operation

Fig. 19.16. Casing in. The case is completely finished before it is attached to
the book. The book rides spine side up through the machine; the endsheets are
covered with paste just before the case drops down from above, and the whole
book is squeezed together from the sides.

strip pasted to the printed or stamped cloth. The endpapers are given a
coat of paste just before the case is folded around the book and
squeezed tight. The free edges of the super are thus held between
boards and endpapers, completing the hinging of the book.

BOARDS AND CLOTH

19.71   The materials used in case binding and the ways in which the case is
imprinted and decorated vary widely. The board used for most trade
books, called *pasted board,* is a laminated stock built up of several
thicknesses of cardboard. *Binder's board,* a heavy cellulose-fiber product, is used for fine case bindings, and inexpensive *chipboard* is chiefly
employed when cost is more of a consideration than quality. The cover
material itself may be *binder's cloth,* which comes in a wide range of

qualities, colors, and finishes. Binder's cloth is given body by a *filler,* either the traditional starch or one of the more water-resistant plastic resins. The cover may also be made from one of the various *nonwoven* materials developed as substitutes for cloth. These include extruded synthetics and paper-backed vinyl, as well as paper that has been treated in various ways to increase its durability.

STAMPING AND PRINTING

19.72   The cover is imprinted and decorated by *stamping, printing,* or a combination of the two processes. The dies used for stamping book covers are made of brass or some other hard metal and have a relief surface like that of a woodcut or piece of type. Stamping is indeed identical to letterpress printing except that the pressure is greater, so that the cover is actually indented by the die. Ink may be applied to the die, in which case the cover is *cold-stamped.* Or *leaf* (powdered metal or pigment bonded to plastic film) may be placed between the die and the cover; for this kind of work the die must be heated and the cover *hot-stamped.* *Blind stamping* (no leaf or ink, just the impression of the die) must also be done hot.

19.73   Printed covers, often in more than one color, are usually achieved by offset lithography or by a process called *silk-screen* printing. The latter is a stencil process (something like mimeograph) in which ink is pressed through a sheer fabric on which the nonprinting areas of the design are blocked out. Both processes permit printing on relatively rough surfaces, and silk screen is particularly well adapted to cover printing because of the opacity of the inks.

Alternative Bindings

19.74   A number of different binding techniques have come into prominence in the twentieth century as substitutes for, or supplements to, the traditional case binding. Also a phenomenon of this century is the modern book jacket, a cover for a cover.

SADDLE WIRING AND SIDE WIRING

19.75   Publications like pamphlets and many popular magazines are usually held together by *saddle wiring* (also called *saddle stitching*); that is, they are stapled two or three times from the outside to the inside of the fold. In *side wiring* (or *side stitching*) the staples go through the pages from the side, as in side sewing. Side wiring and saddle wiring permit more than one signature to be held together. The covers of saddle-wired publications are attached with the same staples that hold the pages together. Covers of side-wired publications may be pasted on along the margins of the spine to hide the staples. (See fig. 19.17.) With either type of binding, the pages are trimmed after the wiring operation.

ADHESIVE BINDING

19.76   The method by which most paperback books and city telephone directories are held together is known as *adhesive binding,* of which there are three varieties in use at present: perfect, notch, and burst (fig. 19.18). In perfect binding, the folded and gathered signatures are held tightly and about an eighth of an inch is mechanically roughened off the spine, reducing the book to a series of separate pages. The roughened spine is then coated with a flexible glue, and a paper cover is wrapped around the book. In both notch and burst binding the spine is either scored by a series of notches (notch binding) or perforated (burst binding). The notched and burst spines are then force-fed with glue. Advantages of notch and burst binding over perfect binding are that an eighth of an inch is not lost from the back margin and that signatures remain intact, reducing the risk of pages coming loose. All three types of adhesive binding, however, have become much more dependable in recent years and are widely used both for original trade books (with a hardback case) and for quality magazines that formerly were side-wired.

19.77   Paperback covers are generally printed on flexible stock 8 to 14 *points* (same as *mils,* thousandths of an inch) in thickness, coated on the side that will carry the printing. The surface is usually protected by a transparent coating of some kind—*varnish,* applied with a cylinder printing press; *liquid laminate,* a synthetic resin applied in liquid form; *film*

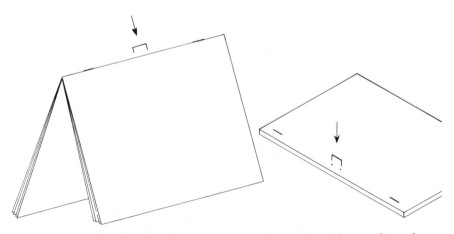

Fig. 19.17. Saddle wiring and side wiring. In saddle wiring, staples go in through the fold; in side wiring they go in from the side.

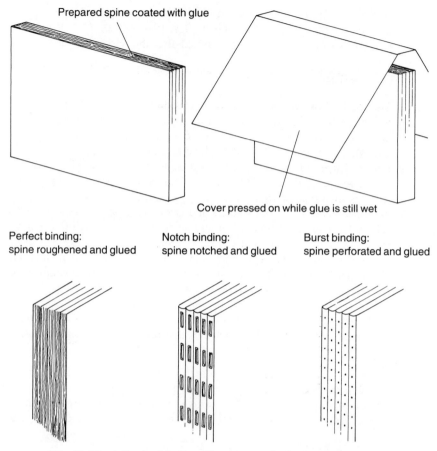

Prepared spine coated with glue

Cover pressed on while glue is still wet

Perfect binding:
spine roughened and glued

Notch binding:
spine notched and glued

Burst binding:
spine perforated and glued

Fig. 19.18. Adhesive binding. Three types of adhesive binding are currently in use. In *perfect binding,* the spine is roughened and glued to receive the paper cover. In *notch binding* the spine is scored by a series of notches, and in *burst binding* it is roughened by perforation. Glue is then forced into the notched or perforated spines.

laminate, a transparent plastic film bonded directly to the printed surface; or any of various other coatings.

MECHANICAL BINDING

19.78   For several types of binding, collectively known as *mechanical binding,* the signatures are trimmed close to the fold (as for perfect binding), and a series of holes is punched through the pages near the back margin. Something is then run through the holes to hold the pages in order. The familiar three-ring notebook and the post binder represent types of mechanical binding, but those commonly used for books (cookbooks, workbooks, and the like) are *spiral* and *comb bindings* (fig. 19.19). Spiral and comb binding are both fully automated processes, but because of the cost of the materials they are considerably more expensive than perfect binding.

BOOK JACKETS

19.79   Originally a simple wrapper provided to keep a cloth binding clean, the book jacket has become in modern times an advertising poster to attract attention to the book in a display and a vehicle for promotional copy intended to help sell the book once it is in a prospective buyer's hands. Even scholarly books are now generally given jackets to attract attention at professional meetings and in college bookstores.

19.80   Jackets are printed in one, two, three, or four colors, generally on a small offset press. Printing is often "two up" or "three up"—meaning that the plate cylinder bears images for two or more copies of the jacket, which then print together on one sheet of paper. The printed jacket may be left as is but is more frequently given a protective coating like those given paperback books.

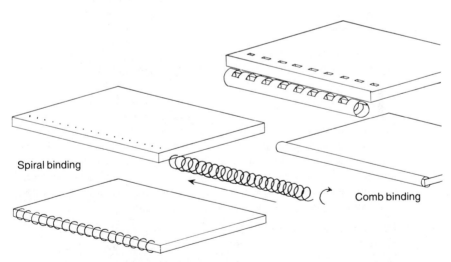

Spiral binding

Comb binding

Fig. 19.19. Mechanical binding. The two types of mechanical binding pictured above involve perforating the back margin of the covers and trimmed sheets with a row of holes. For spiral binding, the holes are small and round, and a spiral of metal or plastic is threaded through them. For comb binding, the holes are rectangular, and teeth or claws of springy plastic penetrate them.

PAPERMAKING

19.81   Paper consists of cellulose fibers felted together into a thin sheet. The source of the fibers nowadays is chiefly wood, but formerly it was rags—originally linen, later cotton—and rags are still used in the manufacture of the very finest papers today. The source materials are reduced to a slurry of fibers floating freely in water, and when the water is removed from a thin layer of this *pulp,* the end product is paper. The machine that forms paper from pulp is called a *fourdrinier* (pronounced *for-drə-near'*), after the English family that financed its development in the early nineteenth century.

Making the Pulp

19.82   Wood is converted into pulp by chemical or mechanical means, or by a combination of both. *Chemical pulp* starts with logs that have been mechanically peeled of their bark and reduced to chips. The chips are boiled in strong caustic solutions that dissolve away those parts of the wood that are not cellulose, such as lignin and resin, and leave the cellulose fibers more or less free. There are two chief varieties of chemical pulp, named after the chemical compounds used in their manufacture. *Sulfate pulp,* also called *kraft,* is made from wood of either deciduous or coniferous trees and produces a very strong paper. Less widely used is *sulfite pulp,* which is made only from coniferous wood and is treated with an acid solution.

19.83   *Mechanical pulp,* or *groundwood,* is made chiefly by stone-grinding peeled logs in a stream of water so that the wood is broken up into fibers. Groundwood contains all the constituents of the original wood, including those considered impurities in chemical pulp. Paper made from groundwood, not very strong to begin with, quickly discolors and becomes brittle. It is used mainly for newsprint. A superior, stronger form of mechanical pulp, called *thermomechanical pulp,* is made from wood chips treated with steam under high pressure. In spite of its impurities and lack of strength, groundwood is often added to the chemical pulps used in making book papers because of its relatively low cost. A paper containing no groundwood is called a *free sheet.*

19.84   Before pulp is ready to be made into paper it is mechanically beaten or refined and, for most purposes, bleached. (Unbleached kraft pulp is used for making grocery bags and heavy wrapping paper.) Other materials are also added to the pulp, depending on the kind of paper to be made. For book papers, fillers such as white clay and titanium oxide may be added to give opacity and extra whiteness, and sizing gives stiffness and smoothness. For tinted papers dyes are also added at this point. The specific combination of pulps and other ingredients used in making a particular kind of paper is called the *furnish* for that paper.

19.85   In the manufacture of most printing and writing papers today, care is taken that the furnish be chemically neutral (registering pH 7 on the acid-base scale). For permanence, paper must be *acid-free,* and any work intended to enjoy a long life should be printed on this type of paper (see 1.35). Librarians and such government agencies as the Library of Congress and the National Endowment for the Humanities have campaigned long and vigorously for the widespread use of acid-free paper in publishing, and advances in manufacturing technology have now placed such paper in a competitive position with regard to the price of acidic paper. Very little acidic paper is in fact produced now, except for such evanescent products as newsprint.

Forming the Pulp into Paper

19.86   At its *wet end* the fourdrinier machine (fig. 19.20) takes pulp that is 99 percent water and, by draining it and subjecting it to suction, pressure, and finally heat, converts it into a continuous web of paper containing only a very small percentage of moisture at the *dry end* of the machine.

19.87   At the wet end the pulp flows continuously onto the surface of a moving endless belt of fine-mesh screening (called the *wire,* though now usually made of nylon). The liquid pulp is prevented from slopping over the sides of the wire by rubber *deckle straps* that move along with it. As the wire moves forward it is shaken from side to side to help the water

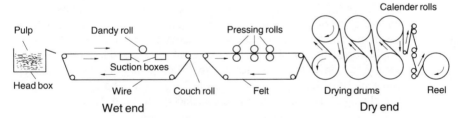

Fig. 19.20. Fourdrinier machine. In reality a complex and enormous (sometimes approaching a city block in length) apparatus, the fourdrinier machine may be represented by the simplified diagram shown here. Wet pulp is continuously poured onto an endless belt supplied with deckle straps to keep the fluid from spilling over. Along this belt, or wire, water is drained and sucked from the pulp, and the drying pulp is pressed by the dandy roll. Another endless belt then carries the drying web through a series of pressing rolls, and delivers it to a series of drying drums that complete the drying process. Finally the web is drawn between a series of calendering rolls and wound onto a reel.

drain through. Toward the end of the wire, suction boxes below the wire pull more water out, and a wire-mesh-covered cylinder (the *dandy roll*) presses on the web of pulp from above. The dandy roll may be covered with plain wire cloth, which imparts a *wove* effect, or with wire in a ladder pattern for the *laid* effect. If there is to be a *watermark,* it is attached to the dandy roll in the form of a wire design.

19.88 As the wire reaches the end of its loop, the web of pulp, now the consistency of very soggy paper, is lifted by the *couch roll* onto an endless belt of wool felt and carried between a series of pressing rollers that squeeze more water from it. It then passes over a series of very large, steam-heated, cast-iron drums that complete the drying process. During drying, the web is held tightly against the hot drums by endless belts of fabric above and below.

Finishing

19.89 After drying, the paper is usually run through a series of highly polished metal rollers *(calender rolls)* that further compact it and smooth the surface. The calender rolls are arranged in pairs, and the rolls of each pair run at somewhat different speeds from each other, thus tending to polish the paper as it passes between them. Depending upon how much if any calendering the paper is subjected to, a variety of finishes can be obtained, ranging from *antique* (the softest and dullest), through *eggshell, vellum,* and *machine finish,* to *english finish* (the hardest and shiniest obtainable without further treatment).

19.90 Further treatment may include *supercalendering, coating,* or *tub* (or *surface*) *sizing.* Supercalendering is a polishing process similar to calendering but done on a separate machine with rollers of different composition. The final finish of coated papers is brushed or rolled on in liquid form; the finish may be matte (as for reproduction typing) or glossy (as on the *enamel* papers for high-quality halftone printing). Most papers include size in the furnish, but for a harder finish additional sizing may be applied to the surface after the paper is made.

Grain and Sidedness

19.91 Machine-made paper has a definite *grain,* tending to fold and tear more easily in one direction than the other, as anyone discovers in trying to tear an article neatly out of a newspaper page. This is because the cellulose fibers tend to align themselves in the direction of travel as the pulp is laid down on the wire—the shaking promotes but does not fully achieve random alignment as it exists in handmade paper. In reeled paper the grain always runs the long way. In sheet paper it may run either the long way or the short way, depending upon how the paper is cut from the reel. For bookwork, sheet paper should be ordered *grain long* or *grain short* so that (depending upon the particular printing and binding machinery) the spine fold will be with the grain and not across it. Books folded cross-grain have an unpleasantly springy feel and tend not to stay closed.

19.92 Like most fabrics, paper has a "right" and a "wrong" side. The bottom of the web—next to the wire at the wet end of the machine (and hence called the *wire side*)—is slightly rougher than the top (or *felt*) side. Consequently, if only one side of the paper is to be used, as is usually true in typing and sometimes in printing, the smoother, felt side is the one commonly chosen. Paper made on a *twin-wire* fourdrinier has either two felt sides or two wire sides, because two webs of pulp are laid down simultaneously and pressed together, same side in, as the paper is dried and finished. (For some purposes the wire side is preferred: though not as smooth as the felt side, it has fewer of the fiber clumps called *fines*, which tend to float to the surface as the paper is formed on the wire.) One-sided paper (paper with two similar sides) is more expensive than ordinary two-sided paper.

Recycled Paper

19.93 Growing concern over the environmental degradation caused by the dumping of wastepaper into landfills has inspired a vigorous recycling movement. The furnish used in producing recycled paper consists of a combination of virgin fiber and preconsumer and postconsumer waste. The proportion of each kind of fiber required to legitimate the label *recycled,* however, is subject to some debate.

Paper Categories

19.94 Paper is made in a bewildering variety of weights, colors, textures, and finishes for a multitude of purposes, including those of the publishing industry. What follows is a brief listing of the chief categories used in bookmaking:

> *Book papers* are intended for book and journal printing and are supplied in either roll or sheet form. Nearly all book papers are now surface-sized for offset lithography (the sizing resists penetration by the water used in offset printing, as well as the *picking* of surface fibers by the tacky offset ink). They are made mainly from sulfate pulp, often with the addition of some groundwood.

Text papers come in many colors and textures, for use in advertising leaflets, endpapers, and the like. They are also sized for offset printing.

Cover papers are heavier papers, made in a wide range of finishes, textures, and colors, for use as covers of pamphlets, journals, and paperback books.

Newsprint is made for printing newspapers, advertising catalogs, inexpensive mass-market paperbacks, and other items that will be read once or twice (if at all) and thrown away. It is made from groundwood pulp, usually with some chemical pulp added for strength.

Bond is made, mainly for office use, in a wide range of qualities, from top-grade papers made from 100 percent rag pulp to low-grade stocks consisting largely of groundwood.

Measurement of Paper

19.95 Paper varies from one kind to another in thickness and in relative weight, and both measurements are used in designating a given paper stock.

19.96 At the mill the thickness of a sheet is known as the *caliper* and is measured in thousandths of an inch *(mils)*. For the purposes of publishers, however, this figure is usually converted into *pages per inch (ppi)*, or *bulk*. Book papers may bulk anywhere from 200 to nearly 1,000 pages to the inch, but the commonly used "50-pound" (see below) machine-finished papers generally bulk in the neighborhood of 500–550 pages per inch. (Remember that each leaf equals two pages.)

19.97 Paper is sold by weight, and different grades of the same type of paper are distinguished by how much some standard quantity of that paper actually weighs. For most of the world the standard quantity is one sheet of paper one square meter in area. In this system the relative weight of the paper (called *grammage*) is given in grams per square meter (g/m^2, or *gsm*), and the same system is used for all categories of paper.

19.98 In the United States, however, an antiquated system of *basis weights*, now abandoned even in England, where it originated, is still used to compare the relative weight of papers. The standard quantity is one ream, or 500 sheets, but the standard sheet size varies from one category of paper to another. For book papers the standard, or *basis*, sheet measures 25 by 38 inches. To describe a paper as "50-pound book paper" means that 500 sheets of that paper, if cut to 25 by 38 inches (never mind the actual size of the paper in hand), would weigh 50 pounds. For cover stocks, on the other hand, the basis size is only 20 by 26 inches, and consequently a single sheet of 50-pound cover paper is nearly twice as heavy as an equal-sized sheet of 50-pound book paper. For bond papers, basis weight is usually referred to as *substance* (note the label on a package of typing paper). The basis size is 17 by 22 inches (which cuts evenly into four standard 8½-by-11-inch sheets), and so a 20-pound bond is approximately equal in weight to a 50-pound book paper. See table 19.1, which compares the common basis weights of the categories of paper described above and gives metric equivalents, and table 19.2, which gives conversion factors for American and metric systems.

Table 19.1 Basis Weights Compared

Book and Text (25 × 38)	Cover (20 × 26)	Newsprint (24 × 36)	Bond (17 × 22)	Grammage (g/m²)
30	16	27	12	44
40	22	36	16	59
45	25	41	18	67
50	27	45	20	74
60	33	55	24	89
70	38	64	28	104
80	44	73	31	118
90	49	82	35	133
100	55	91	39	148
120	66	109	47	178
91	**50**	82	36	135
110	**60**	100	43	163
119	**65**	108	47	176
146	**80**	134	58	216
164	**90**	149	65	243
183	**100**	166	72	271
31	17	**28**	12	46
33	18	**30**	13	49
35	19	**32**	14	52
37	20	**34**	15	55
38	21	**35**	15	57
33	18	30	**13**	49
41	22	37	**16**	61
51	28	46	**20**	75
61	33	56	**24**	90
71	39	64	**28**	105
81	45	74	**32**	120
91	50	83	**36**	135
102	56	93	**40**	151

Source: Table 19.1 is based in large part on a similar table in *Pocket Pal* (New York: International Paper Co., 1979), 158.
Note: Numbers in boldface are the common basis weights in pounds for the various categories of papers. Basis sheet sizes are given in the column headings.

Table 19.2 Conversion Factors, Metric and U.S. Basis Weights

Category and Basis Size	U.S. to Metric	Metric to U.S.
Book and text (25 × 38)	1.480 × lb. = g/m²	0.675 × g/m² = lb.
Cover (20 × 26)	2.704 × lb. = g/m²	0.370 × g/m² = lb.
Newsprint (24 × 36)	1.627 × lb. = g/m²	0.614 × g/m² = lb.
Bond (17 × 22)	3.760 × lb. = g/m²	0.266 × g/m² = lb.

Stock Paper Sizes

19.99 Both in the United States and abroad, paper merchants stock the most popular grades of paper in certain standard sizes, although special sizes may be ordered. Here again, the metric system used in Britain and on the Continent is much simpler than the American system.

19.100 In Europe a series of mutually compatible stock sizes has virtually crowded out the old welter of stock sizes that was formerly offered. The metric *A* series is based on a standard sheet of paper, rectangular in shape (841 mm by 1,189 mm) and one square meter in area. This size is called *A0.* Cutting this sheet in half produces *A1,* and cutting *A1* in half produces *A2,* and so on down to *A6,* which is ¹⁄₆₄ the area of *A0.* (See fig. 19.21 and table 19.3 for the dimensions of the *A* series.) An interesting feature of the series is that all sheets are the same shape; that is, the ratio of short side to long side is identical throughout the series of sizes. There is also a *B* series of sizes that are intermediate between the *A* sizes and two larger sheet sizes that are compatible with *A0.*

19.101 American stock sizes for book paper reflect the sizes of the presses commonly used for bookwork and the most popular trim sizes for books in the United States. See table 19.4 for some of these stock sheet sizes.

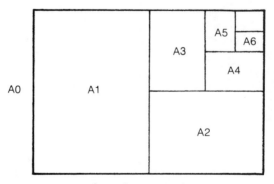

Area=1 square meter

Fig. 19.21. European stock sizes. In the metric *A* series of stock paper sizes, each size is half the area of the next larger, and all are the same shape.

Table 19.3 The *A* Series of Stock Paper Sizes

	Sheet Size	
	Millimeters (approx.)	Inches (approx.)
A0	841 × 1,189	33⅛ × 46¾
A1	594 × 841	23⅜ × 33⅛
A2	420 × 594	16½ × 23⅜
A3	297 × 420	11¾ × 16½
A4	210 × 297	8¼ × 11¾
A5	148 × 210	5⅞ × 8¼
A6	104 × 149	4⅕ × 6

Table 19.4 Some American Stock Sizes for Book Paper (Inches)

Sheet Size	Number of Pages per Sheet	Folds to, before Trimming	Trim Size
Grain short			
35 × 45	64	5⅝ × 8¾	5½ × 8½
38 × 50	64	6¼ × 9½	6⅛ × 9¼
Grain long			
41 × 61	128	5⅛ × 7⅝	5 × 7⅜
44 × 66	128	5½ × 8¼	5⅜ × 8
45 × 68	128	5⅝ × 8½	5½ × 8¼
45 × 69	128	5¾ × 8⅝	5⅝ × 8⅜

Cover papers are generally stocked in smaller sizes, and paper on rolls for web-fed presses comes in various standard widths.

FOR FURTHER REFERENCE

19.102 Readers will find further information about many of the topics discussed in this chapter in *Bookmaking,* by Marshall Lee; *Printing Types,* by Alexander S. Lawson and Dwight Agner; and the *Glossary of Typesetting Terms,* by Richard Angstadt and others.

Glossary of Technical Terms

For unfamiliar terms used in the definitions below, look for entries elsewhere in the glossary, or consult the index for text references. For fuller discussion of computer terms, see computer reference works. (Two computer dictionaries are listed in the bibliography: *Computer Dictionary; Dictionary of Computing*.)

AA, AAs. Abbreviation for *author's alteration(s)*, used in correcting proof. *See* **alteration; author's alteration.**

access. In computer terminology, the ability to reach and make use of electronically stored data. It is often used as a verb, meaning to find and gain access to a particular location in a body of stored data. Data stored on magnetic tape are subject only to sequential access, whereas data stored on disks permit random access.

address. Digitally coded label for a particular location in computer **storage.**

adhesive binding. A binding method employing glue instead of stitching to hold the pages or signatures together. Widely used in paperbound editions. Three types of adhesive binding are currently used: perfect binding, notch binding, and burst binding. *Contrast* **case binding.**

against the grain. Feeding paper to a printing press in a direction across the grain of the paper fibers is said to be feeding *against the grain*. So also is folding paper in that direction for binding. The latter is also called folding, or binding, *cross-grain*.

agate line. A unit of measurement for newspaper advertising space, $^1/_{14}$ of a column inch.

alphabet length. The horizontal measurement, in points, of the lowercase alphabet set in type of a particular face and size.

alphanumeric. Consisting of letters, numbers, and symbols (generally those available on a typewriter)—for example, an *alphanumeric code* for a computer command. *See also* **codes.**

alteration. A change from the manuscript copy introduced in proof, distinguished from a *correction* made to eliminate a printer's error, or typographical error. Alterations are billed as a separate item (in addition to the charge for original composition). Alterations made by the author *(author's alterations, or AAs)*, or some part of them, are customarily charged against royalties.

ampersand. The name for the character &.

arabic numerals. The familiar digits used in arithmetical computation. In many type fonts they are available in two forms: *lining*, or *aligning* (1 2 3 4 5 6 7 8 9 0), invariably used in tabular matter; and *old style*, abbreviated *O.S.* or *OS* (1 2 3 4 5 6 7 8 9 0) and characterized by ascenders and descenders.

artwork. (1) Illustrative material (photographs, drawings, and so forth) intended for reproduction. (2) Additions or corrections made by hand on etch proofs or other reproduction copy.

ascender. The part of a character that extends above the x-height, or top of the letter *x*, as in the letters *d, f, h,* and *k* and the *old-style figures* 6 and 8. *See also* **arabic numerals; descender.**

ASCII. For *American standard code for information interchange*. A computer coding scheme for representing letters, numerals, punctuation marks, and a few nonprintable characters that control tabs, line feeds, carriage returns, and the like. ASCII is used universally in personal computers and workstations.

ASCII file. A text file format that contains only ASCII coded letters, numerals, punctuation marks, spaces, carriage returns, line feeds, tabs, and an end-of-line marker. An ASCII file contains no formatting information encoded through the use of special characters, although it may contain sequences of ASCII characters that can be interpreted as codes controlling formatting. *See also* **SGML.**

A series. Series of stock paper sizes, widely used in Europe, based on a rectangular sheet one square meter in area. Throughout the series stock sizes have the same proportion of short side to long side, namely, one to the square root of two. A supplementary *B series* is cut in sizes between successive *A* sizes.

author's alteration. A change made by the author in proof. *See also* **alteration.**

auxiliary storage. Means for storing data in digital form outside the main computer memory—on magnetic tape, disks, and so forth. *See also* **storage.**

backbone. The spine of a book.

backing. In case binding, applying the backstrip.

back margin. The inner margin of a page; that is, the margin along the binding side of the page. *See also* **gutter.**

backstrip. In case binding, a strip of paper pasted to the back of the sewn sheets after they have been rounded. *See* **rounding.**

back up. To print the back side of a sheet already printed on the front.

bad break. (1) In page makeup, any of various unsightly or misleading arrangements of type occurring at the bottom or top of a page or column, such as a line consisting of only a word or two at the top of a page or column (called a *widow*) or a subheading falling on the last line of a page or column. (2) A word incorrectly hyphenated at the end of a line.

baseline. In type, an imaginary line connecting the bottoms of the capital letters. *See also* **x-height.**

basis weight. The weight in pounds of a ream (500 sheets) of paper cut to a standard size (25 by 38 inches for book papers). Book papers generally range from 40 to 80 pounds. *See also* **grammage.**

belt press. A fast web-fed letterpress machine employing endless belts bearing flexible plastic printing plates instead of plate cylinders. Often called the *Cameron press* after the developer.

Bible paper. Very thin opaque paper often used for Bibles and other books with a great many pages where easy portability is desired. Also called *India paper.*

binary numeration system. A system of numbers in which all values are expressed by various combinations of the two digits 0 and 1. In contrast to the decimal system, which is based on sums of powers of 10, the binary system is based on sums of powers of 2. All modern digital computers employ the binary numeration system.

binder's board. Board made of densely compressed fibers and used in the finest quality book covers. *See also* **boards.**

binder's die. A die made of brass or other hard metal and used in stamping the case of a book. Also known as *stamping die.*

binding. (1) A covering for the pages of a book. (2) The process by which such a covering is attached. Materials include leather, cloth, paper, and plastic. Processes include case binding, adhesive binding, and mechanical binding.

binding cloth. Cloth used in forming the cover of a book. *See also* **cover materials.**

bit. In computer terminology, a *bi*nary digi*t*, the smallest possible unit of information, resulting from a choice between 0 and 1. *See also* **binary numeration system; byte.**

black letter. *See* **text type; type styles.**

blanket. In offset lithography, the resilient rubber covering of the *blanket cylinder,* which receives the ink impression from the plate cylinder and offsets it onto the paper.

bleed. An illustration that runs to the edge of the paper (or "off the page") is said to *bleed.*

blind embossing. Stamping a design in relief without metallic leaf or ink. *See also* **embossing.**

blind folio. A page number (folio) counted but not actually expressed (printed), as on a blank page or a page containing only an illustration.

blind stamping. Imprinting the case of a book with a heated metal die without the use of ink, foil, or other coloring material. *See also* **cold stamping; hot stamping.**

block letter. *See* **type styles,** *gothic.*

block quotation. A quotation set off from the regular text and therefore not enclosed in quotation marks. *Contrast* **run in** (3).

blow up. To enlarge photographically. A photograph, chart, figure, and so forth, subjected to such treatment is termed a *blowup.*

blueprints. One type of photographic proof made from negatives of text or art intended for offset reproduction. Also called *blues. See also* **proof.**

BMI specifications. *See* **NASTA.**

boards. Stiffening material used in bookbinding to form the foundation of the cover. Formerly wood, now generally a paper product such as binder's board (the finest quality), pasted board (often used in case binding), or chipboard (low quality). Redboard is used for flexible bindings. The bare board is sheathed in one of a variety of cover materials. *See also* **cover materials.**

body type. The type used for the text of a work, as distinguished from the **display** type used for chapter openings, subheads, and so forth.

boldface. Type having thick lines and presenting a dark and heavy appearance, like that used for the terms defined in this glossary. *See also* **type styles.**

bond paper. Paper made chiefly for use in offices and as writing paper.

book cloth. Cotton/cloth sized, glazed, or impregnated with synthetic resins, used for book covers and available in a large variety of weights, finishes, colors, and patterns. *See also* **cover materials.**

book paper. Paper made principally for the manufacture of books, pamphlets, and magazines as distinguished from newsprint and from writing and cover stock.

box. A printed rectangle enclosing typeset matter or an illustration. *See also* **slipcase.**

brackets. A device for enclosing material [thus]. In British usage, ( ) are known as brackets, [ ] as *square brackets.*

broadside. A broadside page is one designed to read normally when the book is turned ninety degrees (also called *landscape*). Wide tables and illustrations are often run broadside. In University of Chicago Press practice the *left* side of a broadside table or illustration is at the *bottom* of the page.

brush-coated. Brush-coated paper is coated by being run through a special brushing machine. *See* **coated paper.**

B series. *See* **A series.**

buckram. A heavy book cloth much used for library bindings or for binding large, heavy books.

bulk. The thickness of paper in number of pages per inch; also used loosely to indicate the thickness of a book, excluding the cover. *See also* **caliper.**

bulking dummy. A dummy that resembles the finished book in every respect except that the pages and cover are blank. Such a dummy is occasionally used by the designer as a final check on the appearance and "feel" of the book, as a guide for the size and position of elements on the jacket, and as an indication of the width of the spine (for the stamping).

bullet. *See* **centered dot.**

burst binding. A type of adhesive binding in which the untrimmed spine is perforated, roughened, and force-fed with glue.

byte. A sequence of eight binary digits (bits), typically used in computer work to represent a single character, such as a letter or numeral. *See also* **bit.**

calender. Part of a papermaking machine, consisting of pairs of steel rollers that smooth the dried web of paper before it is reeled up. *Calendering* is the process of running paper through a calender to achieve varying degrees of smoothness. Also called *machine-finishing. See also* **finish.**

caliper. The thickness of a sheet of paper or board, measured in thousandths of an inch (referred to as *mils* in connection with paper and *points* in connection with board). *See* **mil; point.**

camera-ready copy. Artwork, type proofs, typewritten material, and so forth, ready to be photographed for reproduction without further alteration. *See also* **Linotron proof.**

Cameron press. *See* **belt press.**

cancel. A new leaf or signature replacing a defective one or one containing errors; any material substituting for deleted material. To *cancel* is to cut out blank or printed pages.

caps. An abbreviation for *capital letters.*

caps and small caps. Two sizes of capital letters constituting parts of the same **font.**

caret. A sign directing the typesetter where to insert the correction or additional material written immediately above the line (in manuscript) or at the side (on proof).

case. A cover or binding, made by a casemaking machine or by hand and usually printed, stamped, or labeled before it is glued to a book. The process of applying such a ready-made cover is called *casing in. See also* **stamping.**

case binding. The modern, mechanized method of encasing a book in a rigid cover, or *case.* The gathered signatures are Smyth sewn or side sewn together; endpapers are glued to the first and last signatures; a hinge of heavy gauze (the *super*) is glued to the back, or spine, of the sewn signatures; and the case is secured to the book by being glued to the flaps of the super and to both endpapers. *Contrast* **adhesive binding.**

case fraction. Same as *piece fraction. See under* **fraction.**

casing in. The final step in case binding, in which the case is secured to the endpapers of the sewn signatures.

casting off, *or* **casting up.** Estimating the space, or number of pages, that a given manuscript will occupy when typeset. *See also* **copyfitting.**

cathode-ray tube. A vacuum tube with a screen at one end, illuminated by means of an electron beam controlled by magnetic devices at the other end. A television picture tube and the video screen of a personal computer are common examples. Abbreviated *CRT. See also* **CRT composition; video display terminal.**

CD-ROM. For compact disk read-only memory. A high-capacity optical disk on which electronic publications can be mounted. *See also* **epublication.**

centered dot. A heavy dot, •, used as an ornament before a paragraph or an unnumbered item in a vertical list. Familiarly called a *bullet.* A lighter centered dot is used in mathematical composition as a multiplication sign.

central processing unit. A computer, or division of a computer, that performs all the chief functions of the system and generally contains the main data-storage area. Abbreviated *CPU.*

character. A letter, numeral, symbol, or mark of punctuation. In printing type, characters vary in width, as they do on a *variable-spacing* typewriter. On an ordinary typewriter, or on a computer-generated printout, characters are all the same width.

character count. In copyfitting, a character count is made by computing the number of characters and spaces in an average line of the manuscript and multiplying by the number of lines in the manuscript. Many word processors provide character counts for a document when performing such operations as saving the document to a disk. *See also* **casting off.**

character generation. In CRT composition, the formation of type characters on the face of the cathode-ray tube from stored digital information. In photocomposition, the projection of type images from film matrices.

chemical pulp. Pulp for papermaking made from cellulose-containing substances (in the United States, generally wood chips) by chemical means, which remove most impurities. Distinguished from mechanical pulp, or groundwood. *See also* **mechanical pulp; sulfate process; sulfite process.**

chipboard. A low-quality binding material made from wastepaper. *See also* **boards.**

Chromalin. A trade name for a four-color proof made from color separations. Used to check color and register in illustrations or book jackets before printing.

chunk makeup. The making up and proofreading of portions of a page before the whole page is fully made up. *See also* **makeup.**

claw binding. *See* **comb binding.**

clear. In computer technology, to erase stored data and to restore circuits to their beginning state.

clothbound. A book protected by a rigid cover, usually cloth wrapped around boards, is called *clothbound* (sometimes the wrapping is paper of a distinctive pattern). *See also* **paperbound.**

coated paper. Paper to which a surface coating of clay or other opaque material has been applied. Papers may be *coated one side* (*abbr.* C1S) or *coated two sides* (C2S). *Machine-coated* papers are coated with the aid of rollers as the paper comes off the papermaking machine; *brush-coated* papers are run through a special brushing machine. Coated papers range from matte finishes *(dull-coated)* to very shiny *(gloss enamel).*

codes. In computerized typesetting, combinations of letters, numbers, and symbols representing instructions to the computer for formatting output. Codes may also *tag* such logical units of text as paragraphs or subheads. *See also* **SGML.**

cold stamping. Imprinting the case of a book with an inked metal die. *See also* **blind stamping; hot stamping; stamping.**

cold type. A popular term for strike-on, or typewriter, composition and by extension any composition, including photocomposition, not employing hot metal. *Contrast* **hot-metal composition.**

collage. An illustration made by pasting photographs, line copy, type, and so forth in combination.

collate. In bookmaking, to arrange the folded signatures of a book in proper sequence for binding.

collating mark. A short rule is positioned on the press so as to print the collating mark on the outside of the fold of each signature. When the signatures are collated in the proper order, these marks align diagonally. A miss means an omitted signature; two side by side mean a duplication. Instead of a rule, letters, numerals, or a shortened book title may be used. Sometimes a small letter or numeral is printed at the bottom of the first page of each signature (chiefly a British practice).

collotype. A method of printing from a plane surface of hardened gelatin treated so that a greasy ink adheres to the parts of the plate bearing the image and from there is transferred to paper. The process embraces the principle of lithography, the nonprinting areas retaining moisture, which repels ink, leaving the printing areas ink receptive. Collotype, which provides a continuous-tone image, is used principally for the reproduction of pictorial copy.

color printing. *See* **process color printing.**

color separation. Analyzing color copy for reproduction in terms of the three colors (plus black) to be used in printing; separation is achieved by shooting through filters or by electronic scanning. Also, a film negative or positive so produced. *See also* **process color printing.**

column break. *See* **bad break.**

column inch. A unit of measurement for newspaper advertising space, one inch deep and one column wide.

comb binding. A kind of mechanical binding in which the "teeth" of a curled, plastic comb are threaded through rectangular holes punched through the covers and trimmed sheets of a book. Also called *claw binding. See also* **mechanical binding.**

command. *See* **instruction.**

comp. Short for *comprehensive layout,* as for an advertisement or a book jacket. Also for composition, compositor, and in marketing terms, *complimentary copy.*

compose. To set type, whether by hot-metal composition, photocomposition, or typewriter composition.

composition. Typesetting. *See also* **compose; computerized typesetting.**

compositor. One who sets type. In hot-metal composition, a highly skilled person who makes corrections by hand and performs other hand operations, particularly in constructing tables and other technical matter. Also called *operator* and *typesetter.*

computerized typesetting *or* **computer-assisted composition.** Text rendered in digital form is recorded on a magnetic medium (tape or disks) and run through a computer, where line-ending, hyphenation, justification, and other typographic decisions are carried out. The resulting record is used to drive a photomechanical or CRT typesetter. *See also* **CRT composition; photocomposition; photomechanical composition; video display terminal.**

condensed typeface. The characters of a condensed typeface are narrower than normal, permitting more material to be set in a line of the same width.

continuous tone. A continuous-tone image, such as a photograph, has gradations of tone from dark to light, in contrast to an image formed of pure blacks and whites, such as a pen-and-ink drawing or page of type (*see* **line copy**).

copy. Typescript (including computer printouts), original artwork, photographs, and so forth to be used in producing a printed work.

copy block. A number of contiguous lines of type treated as a unit in design or in makeup.

copyfitting. The process of estimating the space required to print a given quantity of copy in a desired type size or of producing a quantity of manuscript which, when printed, will fill a given space. The former process is also called *casting off copy*. The usual method is to estimate the total number of characters in the manuscript (*see* **character count**) and divide (1) by the *number of characters per pica* for the typeface and size to be used (this information appears with the sample in the typesetter's specimen book), (2) then by the *number of picas in a typeset line*, and (3) finally by the *number of lines of type per page*. The first operation forecasts the total number of picas of printed material; the second, the total number of typeset lines this represents; and the third, the *number of printed pages* the manuscript will occupy when set and made up.

corrected proof. Proof upon which corrections or alterations are written and which is then returned to the typesetter for correction. Usually the *master proof* (*see under* **proof**).

cover. The two hinged parts of a book binding, front and back, and the center panel, or spine, that joins them; also the four surfaces making up the covers in this sense, when used to carry printed matter. In a journal or magazine these are often designated *covers 1, 2, 3,* and *4;* cover 1 carries the journal's name and sometimes the contents; covers 2, 3, and 4 may carry information about the journal or advertising.

cover materials. Flexible materials, such as leather, cloth, paper, or plastic, used to form the outer skin of the boards and spine in case binding. In paperbound books, flexible materials that form the cover itself.

cover stock. Paper, generally thicker than book paper, used for the covers of pamphlets, brochures, paperbacks, and so forth.

CPU. Abbreviation for *central processing unit*.

crash. Same as *super*.

crop. To cut down an illustration, such as a photograph, to improve the appearance of the image by removing extraneous areas. Cropping is performed not by physical cutting but by masking, and *crop marks* are placed on the photograph or drawing as a guide to the printer's camera operator.

CRT. Abbreviation for *cathode-ray tube*.

CRT composition. A CRT typesetter, driven by a computer, generates type images on the surface of a cathode-ray tube from digital records of the letterforms and transfers the images to photographic paper or film. *See also* **computerized typesetting**.

cut and paste. The process of cutting up manuscript, proof, illustrative material, and so forth and pasting, taping, or otherwise affixing the cut-up material in a new arrangement on another sheet of paper or proof. *See also* **dummy**.

cut-in head. A heading that cuts across the statistical columns of a table and applies to all tabular matter lying below it.

cyan. A greenish blue, one of the three colors used in process color printing.

dandy roll. Roller covered with metal gauze that presses down on the web of pulp as it moves through a papermaking machine. When a watermark is desired, the dandy roll carries the wire design for that on its surface.

data bank. Information stored in a computer for later retrieval and use.

database. (1) In statistical work, the total number of responses upon which a percentage is based, indicated by *N* or N. (2) A discrete body of structured information in computer storage.

data processing. In computer technology, handling stored information so as to produce some intended result, such as combining keyboarded text copy and makeup instructions with font data to produce a typeset page.

dead copy. Manuscript copy from which type has been set and corrections made on proof.

decision. In computer technology, a choice, or series of choices, between alternatives, made by comparing new data with stored instructions, such as a hyphenation-and-justification program for typesetting.

deckle, or **deckle straps.** In machine papermaking, rubber straps along the edges of the endless belt of fine-mesh screening (called the wire) that prevent the pulp from slopping over the sides.

deckle edge. The untrimmed edge of paper as it comes from the machine, or the rough natural edge of handmade paper. A deckle edge is sometimes artificially produced on machine-made paper to give a handmade effect.

deep-etch plate. In offset lithography, a working plate on which the image is etched very slightly below the nonprinting surface. Deep-etch plates give high-quality reproduction of fine detail and permit very long press runs.

descender. The part of a character that extends below the base line, or bottom of the capital letters, as in the lowercase letters *j, p, q,* and *y* and the *old-style numerals* 3, 4, 5, 7, and 9. *See also* **arabic numerals; ascender.**

dictionary. In computer-assisted typesetting, an exception dictionary.

die. *See* **stamping.**

die cutting. The process of cutting regular or irregular shapes out of paper by the use of specially fashioned steel knives. The result may be a "door," which can be folded back, or a hole in the paper.

digitize. To describe something, such as a letterform or an image, in terms of *binary* digits (*see* **binary numeration system**), so that it can be entered in, and retrieved from, computer storage.

direct-image composition. Any form of typesetting that produces an image directly on paper without the setting of metal type, such as typewriter, filmset, or CRT composition.

disk. In photomechanical typesetting machines, the grid holding the film matrices of the type fonts. In computer technology, a flat storage device for digitally encoded information or instructions. Because disks offer random access to information stored on them, they are widely used in modern composing systems. A number of photomechanical typesetting machines use disks for the film matrices of their type fonts. And in the computer systems used to drive modern typesetters, digitized information for permanent storage is usually carried on rigid magnetic disks, whereas temporarily stored information (such as the text of a book) is generally carried on flexible ("floppy") disks. *See also* **computerized typesetting; photomechanical composition.**

display. To set copy on a line or lines of its own, apart from the regular text, and often in a different type size or style. *See also* **display type.**

display type. Type that is larger than the body type used for setting the text of a printed work. Display faces are used for title pages, chapter openings, subheads, and the like in a book or journal, for headlines in advertising, and so on.

drop folio. A page number, or folio, printed at the foot of the page.

dropout halftone. A halftone in which the highlights have been whitened by the removal of all dots. Also called *highlight halftone.*

dull-coated. Paper coated in a matte finish. *See also* **coated paper.**

dummy. An unprinted or partially printed or sketched sample of a projected book, pamphlet, book cover, or other material to suggest the appearance and size of the completed work. Dummy pages are frequently arrangements of cut-and-pasted galley proofs with representations of illustrations pasted in place. *See also* **bulking dummy.**

duotone. A halftone reproduction consisting of two intensities of the same color, of black and a color, or of black and gray.

dust wrapper. *See* **jacket.**

edition. (1) The original publication of a work and each subsequent reissue in which the work is significantly revised. (2) In another sense, reissues of a work, without significant revision, in paperback, in special format, with new illustrations, or through licensing with another publisher.

eggshell. *See under* **finish.**

ejournal. Short for *electronic journal.* A journal published either exclusively or principally in electronic form. *See also* **epublication.**

elite type. Typewriter type that runs twelve characters to the inch (also called *twelve-pitch*). *Contrast* **pica type.**

em. In typesetting, a unit of linear measurement equal to the point size of the type in question; for example, a 6-point em is 6 points wide. *See also* **measurement; spacing.**

embossing. Forming an image in relief (a raised image), as by stamping. *See also* **blind stamping; stamping.**

en. Half the measure of an *em.*

enamel. *See under* **coated paper.**

endpaper. Folded sheets pasted or, rarely, sewn to the first and last signatures of a book; the free leaves are then pasted to the inside of the front and back covers for the purpose of securing the book within the covers. Also called *endsheet.*

English finish. *See under* **finish.**

epublication. Short for *electronic publication.* A work published either exclusively or principally in electronic form and accessed through a computer. Epublications are mounted on a variety of electronic media ranging from floppy disk to CD-ROM that can be accessed locally with a personal computer or workstation and on workstations and mainframe computers that can be accessed by modem or through a network. Epublications can be multimedia, incorporating text, digitized images, animation, sound tracks, and functioning formulas. They may also use hypertext technology.

etch proof. Final proof for use in photo-offset. Also called *reproduction proof* or *repro. See also* **proof.**

exception dictionary. In computer-assisted typesetting, a list of words acceptably divided, consulted by the computer if the hyphenation routine does not supply the answer to an end-of-line hyphenation problem.

extended typeface. The characters of an extended typeface are wider than normal ("fatter"), so that less material is set in a line of the same measure.

face. *See* **typeface; type styles.**

felt side. The top side of a sheet of paper as it comes from the papermaking machine (the other side is the *wire side*).

figure. (1) An illustration printed with the text (hence also called a *text figure*) in distinction to a plate, which is printed separately. (2) An arabic or roman numeral.

file. In computer terminology any body of related, digitally stored information, as the text of a book.

839

film laminate. A plastic film bonded to a jacket or paperback cover to protect the surface.

filmset. Set by means of a phototypesetter; synonymous with *photoset*.

fines. In paper, blemishes formed of clumps of fibers that remain stuck together through the papermaking process.

finish. The character of the surface of paper, generally achieved by calendering, supercalendering, and sometimes coating. The roughest finish regularly used in bookwork is *antique*. Calendered finishes, in increasing order of smoothness, are *eggshell, vellum,* and *English finish;* generically, calendered papers are called *machine-finished* (abbr. *MF*). Supercalendered papers are smoother and harder. In coated papers, the finish is determined by the material, such as white clay, applied to the surface. *See also* **calender; coated paper; supercalender.**

flaps. *See under* **jacket.**

flat. In offset printing, a large sheet of paper with the negatives or positives taped into position for printing. The offset plate is made from it. *See* **offset lithography.**

flopped. Erroneously inverted, as a photograph, so that a mirror image of the original is produced.

floppy disk. A flexible disk coated with magnetically sensitive material and widely used in computer technology for temporary storage of information.

flush. In typesetting, even margins. Lines set *flush left* are aligned vertically along the left-hand margin; lines set *flush right* are aligned along the right-hand margin. *Contrast* **paragraph; ragged right.**

flush and hang. Copy-setting style in which the first line begins flush left and subsequent, or runover, lines are indented. Also referred to as *hanging indention*.

flyleaf. Any blank leaf at the front or back of a book, except the endpaper pasted to the inside of the cover.

foil. Metallic leaf used in stamping. *See also* **hot stamping; leaf** (2).

folder. A machine that folds printed sheets into signatures for binding, often attached directly to the press at the delivery end.

foldout. An oversize leaf, often a map, an illustration, or a table, folded to fit within the trim size of the book and pasted, or tipped, in. *See also* **tip-in.**

folio. (1) In printing, a page number, often placed at the outside of the running head at the top of the page. If placed at the bottom of the page, the number is a *drop folio*. A folio counted in numbering pages but not printed (as on the title page) is a *blind folio;* any folio printed is an *expressed folio*. (2) In descriptive bibliography, a leaf of a manuscript or early printed book, the two sides being designated *r* (*recto,* or front) and *v* (*verso,* or back). (3) Formerly, a book made from standard-size sheets folded once, each sheet forming two leaves, or four pages.

font. A complete assortment of a given size and style of type, including capitals, small capitals, and lowercase, together with numerals, punctuation marks, ligatures, and the commonly used symbols and accents. The *italic* of a typeface is considered a part of the equipment of a font of type but is often spoken of as a separate font.

fore edge. The trimmed outer edge of the leaves of a book. The outer margin of a page is called the *fore-edge margin*.

form. In most methods of book printing, all the pages that print together on one side of the sheet. (On a belt press forms as such do not exist.) *See also* **imposition; signature; strip.**

format. The shape, size, style, and general appearance of a book as determined by type, margins, and so forth. Formerly, the size and proportions of a book as determined by the number of times the sheets have been folded, as *folio, quarto, octavo,* and so on.

forwarding. In bookbinding, the processes between folding the sheets and casing in, such as rounding and backing, putting on headbands, reinforcing backs, and so forth.

foul proof. Type proof from which corrections have been made and approved by the author or the editor. *See also* **dead copy.**

four-color process. *See* **process color printing.**

fourdrinier. A papermaking machine.

four-up. *See* **two-up.**

fraction. The typesetter will have the commoner fractions (e.g., $\frac{1}{2}$, ½) set on one sort or matrix; these are called *piece fractions,* also *case fractions.* Others may be *built up,* either with full-size lining figures and a solidus (7/8) or with superior and inferior figures, in the latter case called *split fractions.* (^{1}, -, $_2$, $\frac{1}{2}$).

Fraktur type. A type resembling hand lettering. *See also under* **type styles.**

free sheet. Paper free of mechanical pulp.

full measure. The full width of the type page. *See also* **measure.**

function key. On a keyboard, a key that gives an instruction to the machine or computer, as opposed to keys that govern letters, numbers, marks of punctuation, and so forth. On an ordinary typewriter the shift and backspace keys are function keys.

furnish. The specific combination of materials, including the type of pulp, fillers, size, pigments, and so on, that goes into the making of a particular type of paper.

gallery. A group of consecutive pages devoted to illustrative material.

galley proof. Proof before it is made up into pages. *More under* **proof.**

gatefold. A foldout in a book or periodical.

gilding. The application of gold leaf to the edges of book pages for decoration. *See also* **staining.**

glossy. Short for *glossy print,* a photograph with a hard, very shiny finish, preferred for reproduction work.

gothic. A type style without ornamentation. *See also under* **type styles.**

grain. In machine papermaking the fibers tend to align themselves longitudinally with the web as it moves through the machine, thus establishing the *grain* of the paper. For paper supplied in reel form, the grain is always in the direction of the web. Paper supplied in sheets may be cut *grain long* (grain running the long way of the sheet) or *grain short* (grain running the short way).

grammage. In the metric system for specifying the basis weight of paper, the weight in grams of one square meter of the paper, that is, *grams per square meter* (*abbr.* g/m² *or* gsm).

gray goods. Undyed, unfinished book cloth as it comes from the loom (*gray* is a misnomer for *greige*).

grippers. On a printing press, fingers that seize the edge of the paper and pull it through the press. The *gripper edge* of a printed sheet is the edge that goes through first.

groundwood. Same as **mechanical pulp.**

gutter. The two inner margins (back margins) of facing pages of a book.

hair space. A very small space, variously defined as ¼ point, ½ point, or ⅕ of an em, added between characters. Sometimes (incorrectly) called a *thin space* (¼ em).

halftone. A process whereby a continuous-tone image, such as a photograph, is broken up into a pattern of dots of varying size from which a printing plate is made. When printed, the dots of the image, though clearly visible through a magnifying glass, merge to give an illusion of continuous tone to the naked eye. Reproductions of photographs in printed matter, whether letterpress or offset, are called *halftones*. *See also* **halftone screen.**

halftone screen. A grid used in the halftone process to break the image up into dots. The fineness of the screen is denoted in terms of lines per inch, as *a 133-line screen*.

H & J. Abbreviation for *hyphenation and justification* in connection with computer programs for typesetting. *See also* **hyphenation routine; justify.**

hanging indention. A format for a paragraph, or other block of text, in which the first line begins flush left and subsequent lines are uniformly indented. Also referred to as *flush and hang*. *See also* **paragraph.**

hard copy. A printout of text, artwork, or other material that has been stored in digitized form on a magnetic medium, such as tape or disk.

hardware. In computer terminology, machinery, circuitry, and other physical entities, in distinction to *software,* or programming.

headband. Decorative band at the top (and usually also the bottom) of the spine of a book, originally intended to take the strain of a person's finger pulling a book from the shelf.

head margin. Top margin of a page.

hickey. In offset lithography, a blemish in the impression caused by dirt, a blob of ink, and so forth on the plate or blanket.

highlight. The lightest parts in a photograph or halftone reproduction.

highlight halftone. *See* **dropout halftone.**

hinge. In bookbinding, the connection between the covers and the book proper. In hand binding, its strength is due to the tapes or cords to which the signatures are sewn; in case binding, to a strip of gauze (super).

hot-metal composition. Setting cast metal type either by hand or by machine.

hot stamping. Imprinting the case of a book with a heated metal die. Hot stamping may be done with foil or without foil (blind). *See also* **blind stamping; cold stamping; embossing; foil; stamping.**

house style. *See* **style.**

hypermedia. *See* **hypertext.**

hypertext. A computer technique for augmenting the standard linear format of traditional texts by establishing links between related topics. The reader may follow these links in an order that better represents the nonlinear structure of ideas. In addition to text, the hypertext may include images, sounds, animation, and such functioning procedures as equations or formulas. Because the hypertext may incorporate nontextual information, the term *hypermedia* is sometimes used instead.

hyphenation routine. In computerized typesetting, a set of instructions for hyphenating words at the end of a line, usually supplemented by an exception dictionary.

imposition. The process of arranging the made-up pages of a form so that, when the sheets are printed and folded, the pages will be in the proper order. In offset lithography, sometimes called *stripping in.*

impression. The inked image on the paper created during a single cycle of a press; the speed of a sheet-fed printing press is given in terms of *impressions per hour.* Also, in book publishing, a *printing,* that is, all the copies of a book printed at the same time. *Third impression* and *third printing* are synonymous. *Impression* and *edition,* however, are not synonymous.

impression cylinder. In various methods of printing, a cylinder that supports the paper as the impression is made; that is, it presses the paper against the printing surface.

indent. To set a line of type so that it begins or ends inside the normal margin. In *paragraph-style* indention the first line is indented from the left-hand margin and the following lines are set full measure. In *hanging* indention (also referred to as *flush and hang*) the first line is set full measure and the following lines are indented.

inferior figure. *See* **inferior numeral.**

inferior numeral. A small numeral that prints partly below the base line, as in A_2. *See also* **subscript.**

initial. An oversized letter used to begin the first word in a chapter or section. A *two-line* or *three-line* initial cuts down into the text two or three lines; a *stickup* initial aligns at the bottom with the first line of text but extends into the white space above. *Swash* initials, which are available in some typefaces, are a florid version of the standard italic capital letters.

ink-jet printing. In this process the printed image is formed as the paper moves past a row of minute jets that squirt ink in response to electronically controlled signals.

input. To *input* is to enter information, instructions, text, and so forth in a computer system; *input* is the data so entered. *Input devices* include the direct-input keyboard, off-line keyboard, OCR reader, and others.

insert. (1) An extra printed leaf, sometimes folded, sometimes of a paper different from that used for the text, and sometimes a complete signature. Complete signatures are sewn in with the rest of the book; other inserts are usually *tipped* (pasted) in. (2) Additional matter typed on a separate page and attached to the proof, to be set in type and run in.

instruction. A command in digitally coded form to a computer to perform some function in connection with data supplied to the computer. A computer program consists of many such instructions.

interface. The junction between two systems, as between operator and input device, software and computer, computer and printer, and so forth.

italic. Slanted type suggestive of cursive writing. *See also* **oblique; type styles.**

jacket. A protective wrapping, usually paper, for a clothbound book; it carries the *blurb* (promotional copy) on its *flaps,* which fold around the front and back covers. In the rare-book trade it is usually called *dust wrapper (abbr.* d.w.).

justify. To space out lines of type to a specified measure so that both margins are aligned.

kern. In metal type, the part of a letter that extends beyond the edge of the type body and overlaps the adjacent sort, as the *j* in *adjacent* or the *T* in *To. See also* **kerning.**

kerning. In photocomposition, the adjustment of space between characters to avoid excessive separation. *See also* **kern.**

keyboard. To *keyboard* reading matter is to copy it by means of a machine with a keyboard resembling that of a typewriter. The end product may be hard copy, hot-metal type, machine-readable magnetic tape, magnetic disks, or punched paper tape.

keyline. Copy for offset reproduction, with outlines showing the placement of artwork and type, as well as which parts print in which colors. *See also* **mechanical.**

kill. To omit, purposely, text or illustrations in revision of manuscript or printed matter.

kraft. Brown paper, used chiefly for wrapping paper, made from unbleached sulfate pulp (*see* **chemical pulp**).

laid paper. Machine-made laid paper shows a characteristic pattern of widely spaced vertical lines and closely spaced horizontal lines when held up to the light. The laid effect (in imitation of handmade paper) is produced by the dandy roll. *Contrast* **wove paper.**

Latin alphabet. The ancestor of the modern English alphabet, consisting of twenty-one letters (*j, u, w, y,* and *z* lacking). It is the parent of alphabets used in printing western European languages, including the Old English, German *Fraktur,* and Irish forms of letters. *Latin* is also used to distinguish an alphabet like ours from such forms as the Greek, Cyrillic, and Hebrew alphabets.

layout. A designer's conception of how the printed material, including illustrative content, should appear.

leaders. A line of evenly spaced dots designed to carry the reader's eye across the rows of a table, from the chapter title to its page number in a table of contents, and so forth. Seldom used now.

leading. In metal typesetting, space added between lines of type, usually by inserting metal strips called *leads* (pronounced *leds*). By extension, the term is sometimes used to refer to the spacing between lines produced by photocomposition, but a better term in that case is *line spacing.*

leaf. (1) In a bound book, a single sheet of paper comprising two pages, one on each side. (2) Metallic foil or plastic film to which pigment or metallic powder has been bonded, used in stamping book covers (*see* **hot stamping; stamping**).

letterpress printing. Printing from raised surfaces, such as type, photoengravings, and wood or linoleum cuts. The paper is pressed against the inked surface to form an impression.

letterspacing. Adding extra space between letters to improve appearance or ease of reading, as in display lines.

ligature. Certain letters traditionally joined to form a single character, such as *æ, fi, ff,* and so forth. Older, more decorative forms (as *ꜯ*) are known as *quaint characters. See also* **logotype.**

lightface. The ordinary variety, or *weight,* of roman or italic type, in distinction to boldface. *See also* **type styles.**

line copy. Copy for reproduction which contains only solid blacks and whites, such as a type proof or a pen-and-ink drawing.

line negative. A negative made from copy containing only solid blacks and whites. *See* **line copy.**

lineprinter. A machine, driven by a computer, that prints out stored data one line at a time.

line spacing. Spacing between lines of type in photocomposition, measured in points. *See also* **leading** *and, for contrast,* **spacing.**

lining figures. *See under* **arabic numerals.**

Linotron proof. In electronic typesetting, final, or camera-ready, proof.

Linotype. A hot-metal typesetting machine widely used before the predominance of photocomposition but seldom used today. In this process matrices, or molds, of letters and other characters are arranged and spaced out automatically by keyboarding. The line of matrices is then fed with molten metal, and the entire line is cast as one slug, or single metal strip. *See also* **Monotype.**

liquid laminate. A liquid coating for book jackets and paperback covers that when dry gives an effect similar to film laminate.

lithography. (1) Stone lithography, an art medium whereby a number of impressions can be made from an image drawn with a greasy crayon on porous stone, which is then wetted and inked. (2) A generic designation for machine processes similar in principle to stone lithography (*see* **offset lithography**).

location. In computer terminology, the particular place in a storage medium where specific data are to be found, identified by an address.

logotype. Familiarly, "logo"; one or more words, or other combinations of letters or designs, made available as one sort. Often used for company names, trademarks, and the like.

long page. In makeup, a page that runs longer than provided for in the design.

lowercase. The uncapitalized letters of a font (*abbr.* lc). *See also* **uppercase.**

machine-coated. Machine-coated paper is coated with the aid of rollers. *See also* **coated paper; finish.**

machine copy. *See* **photocopy.**

machine-finished. In papermaking, the same as *calendered. See* **calender; finish.**

machine readable. Said of text or of data recorded in digital form with codes appropriate to the particular computer as programmed.

magenta. A bluish red, one of the three colors used in process color printing.

mainframe. In computer terminology, a large central processing unit, as distinct from input and other devices attached to it. The term is commonly reserved for powerful scientific and business-oriented computers.

makeready. In letterpress printing, a series of operations, performed by highly skilled workers, designed to ensure that all parts of a form print evenly. This process requires a varying amount of time, from a comparatively short period for plain type forms to many hours when halftone illustrations are involved. In offset lithography, the analogous operations are simpler and less time consuming.

makeup. The arranging of type lines and illustrations into page form.

margin. The white space surrounding the printed area of a page, including the *back,* or *gutter, margin;* the *head,* or *top, margin;* the *fore-edge,* or *outside, margin;* and the *tail, foot,* or *bottom, margin. See, for contrast,* **type page.**

markup. The process of marking manuscript copy for typesetting with directions for use of type fonts and sizes, spacing, indention, and so forth.

master proof. The set of proof on which all corrections and changes are marked and which is returned to the typesetter for correction.

matrix. Originally, a die or mold for casting type (plural, *matrices*). In phototypesetting, the patterns forming light into printing characters.

matte finish. A dull finish on paper. *See* **coated paper.**

measure. The length of the line (usually in picas) in which type is set. *Full measure* refers to copy set the full width of the type page. *Narrow measure* refers to a block of copy (such as a long quotation) indented from one or both margins to distinguish it from surrounding full-measure copy, or to copy set in short lines for two-column makeup.

measurement. The typesetter's basic unit of measurement is the *point,* approximately $\frac{1}{72}$ of an inch; 12 points equal 1 pica, approximately $\frac{1}{6}$ of an inch. Within a font of type of one size the typesetter commonly measures by *ems*. In 9-point matter, to mark the copy for 1-em paragraph indention means that each paragraph should be indented 9 points (*see* **em**).

mechanical. Board prepared for offset reproduction with all type, artwork, photographs, and so forth statted to size and pasted down. Differs from a keyline in that all camera-ready materials are supplied in place. *See also* **keyline.**

mechanical binding. Category of bindings for books and pamphlets in which the spine fold is trimmed off and the leaves punched to accept some device that holds them together. Spiral, comb, post, and ring bindings are examples.

mechanical pulp. Pulp for papermaking made by grinding debarked logs. Also called *groundwood.* Unlike chemical pulp, from which impurities are removed, mechanical pulp retains all impurities. It is used chiefly for newsprint.

mechanical screen. Thin transparent film printed with white or black dots, placed over artwork to simulate halftone work.

memory. In computer terminology, part of a central processing unit in which digitized information is permanently stored for rapid retrieval. Also, less strictly, any medium for permanent or temporary storage of information.

mil. One-thousandth of an inch; a unit used in the measurement of paper thickness. *See also* **caliper; point** (2).

misprint. *See* **typographical error.**

mnemonic. Mnemonic computer codes are those that are easily memorized, like *TR9* for "9-point Times Roman type."

modem. Short for *modulator/demodulator.* A device that translates the digital signals used by a computer into the analog signals used on a telephone line, and vice versa, for transmission of information from a computer through a telephone system.

modern. The newer of the two basic roman type styles, the older being *old style. See under* **type styles.**

moiré. In color printing, an undesirable wavy pattern caused by poor screen angles. *See* **halftone screen; process color printing.**

molly. Typesetter's term for an *em. See also* **em; nut.**

Monotype. A hot-metal composing machine frequently employed before the predominance of photocomposition but little used today. In this process a roll of paper, perforated by keyboarding, controls a casting machine so that the letters or other characters are cast one at a time and arrayed in lines that are automatically spaced to the proper length. *See also* **Linotype.**

montage. A photograph whose composition is achieved by combining separate or disparate images or designs. Often mistakenly used for *collage.*

multiple input. In computerized typesetting, characterized by permitting several input terminals (such as video display terminals) operating simultaneously to serve the same system. Also called *multiple access* and *multiterminal.*

NASTA. National Association of State Textbook Administrators. *NASTA specifications,* revised periodically, cover manufacturing standards (particularly those pertaining to bindings) required of books intended for sale to schools. Formerly called *BMI* (Book Manufacturers' Institute) *specifications.*

negative. (1) A photographic image in which light values are reversed (i.e., black appears as white); *see also* **positive; right-reading.** (2) Film used in photo-offset.

nonwoven material. Class of synthetic cover materials for bookbinding made by extrusion or felting rather than weaving.

notch binding. A type of adhesive binding in which the untrimmed spine is notched and roughened and force-fed with glue.

numerals. *See* **arabic numerals; roman numerals.**

nut. Printer's term for an *en. See also* **em; molly.**

oblique. Slightly slanted type, more like slanted roman than italic. *See also under* **type styles.**

OCR. For *optical character recognition.* A method of translating typed or printed characters into digital form on a magnetic medium for computer input. The process employs an electronic reader and appropriate software and is used in computerized typesetting.

octavo. An old term for a book made from sheets that have been folded three times, each sheet forming eight leaves or sixteen pages. Sometimes applied to any book measuring about 6 by 9 inches.

offprint. An article, chapter, or other excerpt from a larger work printed from the original type or plates and issued as a separate unit; also called *reprint.*

offset. (1) In printing, the transfer of an inked image to a target surface through an intermediate, or blanket, cylinder. Short for *offset lithography.* (2) The accidental transfer of an impression from a freshly printed sheet to the back of the next sheet; an alternative term is *setoff.*

offset lithography. An adaptation of the principles of stone lithography in which the design or page is photographically reproduced on a thin, flexible metal plate. For photo-offset, a film negative is used. If especially fine quality is wanted, a film positive is used to prepare a deep-etch plate. The metal plate is curved to fit one of the revolving cylinders of the printing press. The design on this plate is transferred to, or *offset* on, the paper by means of a rubber blanket on another cylinder. Other terms for this process are *photo-offset* and *planographic printing.*

Old English. Layman's term for *text* type. *See under* **type styles.**

old style. The older of the two basic roman type styles, the other being *modern. See under* **type styles.**

old-style figures. *See under* **arabic numerals.**

opacity. A property of some papers that minimizes show-through.

opaque. In photocomposition, to paint out on the negative those areas that are not wanted on the plate.

operator. The person who sets copy at the keyboard in any of the various typesetting processes. Often called *compositor* or *typesetter.*

outline halftone. *See* **silhouette halftone.**

output. Whatever comes out of a computer system, or any division of a system, as opposed to input, or what goes in. The output of a keyboard terminal may be digitized information recorded on magnetic tape or disks, and these may become input for a central processing unit or typesetter whose final output is finished typography.

overlay. A hinged flap of paper or transparent plastic covering a piece of artwork. It may be there merely to protect the work, or it may bear type or other artwork intended for reproduction along with what lies underneath. Often used with a mechanical or a keyline.

overrun. More than the quantity ordered, pertaining especially to paper from a mill or presswork from a printer. According to trade custom, usually mentioned in the order, overruns and underruns to a specified maximum are considered acceptable in fulfillment of a contract. The cost of an overrun is added to the customer's bill; the saving on an underrun is subtracted from it.

page. One side of a leaf, or sheet, of paper. *See also* **type page.**

page break. The end of a typeset page. *See also* **bad break.**

page proof. Proof in page form. *See* **proof.**

pagination. In the terminology peculiar to computerized typesetting, page makeup is sometimes referred to as pagination.

paperback. *See* **paperbound.**

paperbound. A publication bound with a paper rather than a cloth-and-board cover. A paperbound book is often called a *paperback. See also* **clothbound.**

paragraph. A *plain* paragraph has the first line indented and the other lines flush. A *hanging* paragraph, or paragraph with *hanging indention,* has the first line set flush and all others indented (*see also* **flush and hang**). A *flush* paragraph has all lines set flush, and extra space is used to separate paragraphs.

pasted board. A binding material made from layers of chipboard pasted together. It is used for the covers of most casebound books. *See also* **boards; case binding.**

pasteup. The assembly of the various elements of type and illustration for photographing in offset printing. *See also* **camera-ready copy; keyline; mechanical.**

PC. *See* **personal computer.**

PE. Abbreviation for *printer's error,* used in correcting proof. *See* **typographical error.**

penalty copy. Copy difficult to compose (heavily corrected, faint, much in a foreign language, and so forth) for which the typesetter charges a certain percentage over the regular rate.

perfect binding. A method of holding together the pages of a book without stitching or sewing. After folding and collating, the backs of the signatures are cut off; the cut edges are then roughened to produce a surface of intermingled fibers to which an adhesive is applied. The books are usually finished with a wraparound paper cover. *See also* **adhesive binding.**

perfector press. A press designed to print both sides of the paper in one pass through the press. Also called *perfecting press.*

personal computer. Frequently referred to as a *PC.* A general-purpose computer designed to be used by one person at a time. Sophisticated personal computers now perform many of the functions involved in computerized typesetting, ranging from keyboarding to page layout, and are capable of driving photocomposition output devices.

pH. Designation, on a scale of 0 to 14, of the acidity or alkalinity of a substance: pH 7 is neutral, lower numbers progressively acidic, and higher numbers progressively alkaline. Paper with a pH value of 7 is desirable for any artwork or printed matter intended to have a long life.

photocomposition. Typesetting performed through the agency of light, as distinguished from hot-metal and typewriter composition. Historically, the term has been used to include both photomechanical composition and CRT composition, but it is now often considered to be synonymous with the former and to exclude the latter. In this manual, however, the term is broadly interpreted to include both methods.

photocopy. A copy of written, printed, illustrative, or similar material made on an office photocopying machine. Often used as proof in direct-image composition.

photomechanical composition. Photocomposition performed by a typesetting machine employing film matrices, as distinct from CRT composition.

photo-offset. An offset printing process in which a negative film print of the copy is used in the photochemical preparation of the metal plate. Photo-offset is known also as *offset lithography, photolithography,* and, loosely, as *planography* and *lithography.*

photoset. Set by photocomposition; synonymous with *filmset.*

photostat. A photographic copy made on a photostat machine; familiarly, *stat.*

phototypesetter. Usually, a typesetting machine that operates by projecting light through film matrices of the type characters upon light-sensitive paper or film. *See also* **photocomposition.**

pica. Twelve points. *See* **point.**

pica em. Twelve-point *em.*

pica type. Typewriter type that runs ten characters to the inch (also called *ten-pitch*). *Contrast* **elite type.**

pick. *Picking* is the pulling loose of paper fibers by heavily inked type; such fibers collectively are called *pick.*

pick up. To reuse previously printed matter as part of a new work. As a direction to the printer or artist, sometimes abbreviated *P.U.* or *PU.*

planographic printing. *See* **offset lithography; photo-offset.**

plastic binding. Type of mechanical binding employing a plastic spiral or comb.

plate. (1) An image-bearing surface that, when inked, will produce one whole page or several pages of printed matter at a time. (2) A printed illustration, usually of high quality and produced on special paper, tipped or bound into a book; when so printed, plates are numbered separately from other illustrations in the book.

plate proof. *See under* **proof.**

point. (1) The typesetter's basic unit of type measurement—0.0138 inch (approximately ½₂ of an inch). (2) One-thousandth of an inch, a unit used in measuring paper products employed in printing and binding. *See also* **caliper; mil.**

positive. A photographic image on paper or film that corresponds to the original subject in values of light and shade.

prepress. In offset lithography, the processes between completion of individual offset negatives of the pages and printing. The processes include stripping (*see* **stripping in**), platemaking (*see* **plate**), and makeready.

preprint. Part of a book printed and distributed before publication for promotional purposes. *See also* **offprint.**

press run. The number of copies printed. Also called *print run.*

presswork. In bookmaking, the actual printing of the book, as distinct from *composition* (*see* **compose**) and makeup, which precede, and binding, which follows. Also called *machining.*

printer's error. *See* **typographical error.**

printout. Output of a lineprinter or other device that produces normal-reading copy from computer-stored data.

print run. Same as *press run.*

process color printing. Halftone reproduction of full-color artwork or photographs through the use of several plates (usually four), each printing a different color. Each plate is made with a halftone screen. *Process colors* are yellow, magenta, cyan, and black. *See also* **halftone screen.**

program. A set of data-processing instructions for a computer. To *program* is to devise and enter such a set of instructions.

progressive proofs. Proofs of process color plates, showing the colors individually and progressively combined, as the plates will print. Colloquially called *progs.*

proof. A print made from plates or negatives for examination and correction before final printing. *Galley proof* is proof of typeset text before it is made up into pages. It is usually in the form of long columns and is used by the proofreader and author for proofreading. It may also be cut into sections for making dummy pages. *Page proof* is proof made from typeset material arranged in regular page format. After corrections have been made, *revised proof* is prepared. Other kinds of proof are as follows: *plate proof* is an impression taken of a completed plate for final checking before printing; *etch proof* (also known as reproduction proof, or repro) is the final proof of a type page or other material for reproduction by photo-offset; *master proof* is the set of galley or page proof carrying all corrections and alterations and destined for return to the compositor for correction; *blueprints, silver prints,* and *vandykes* are photographic prints prepared from negative or positive films of text or art copy that is intended for offset reproduction. *See also* **Chromalin; Linotron proofs; reproduction proof; Tegra proof.**

proofreaders' marks. A system of marking errors on proof evolved over many years and (with minor variations) internationally understood.

proofreading. Reading proof, usually against the manuscript, to check for accuracy of composition. Also called *proofing.*

P.U. *See* **pick up.**

pulp. Material from which paper is made, consisting mainly of cellulose fibers and water, formerly obtained chiefly from rags, now from wood. *See also* **chemical pulp; mechanical pulp; rag paper.**

quad. (1) A large space to be used in setting a line of type; if not otherwise designated, an *em quad,* equal in width to the point size of the type. *En quads* are half that width, and 2- and 3-em quads are also available. (In typesetter's parlance, a *3-to-em space*—that is, one-third of an em—is abbreviated to *3-em space,* and an en quad is called a *nut,* to avoid confusion with *em quad.*) (2) To *quad* is to fill out a line with space, as when a heading has been set flush left, centered, or flush right.

quaint characters. *See under* **ligature.**

quarto. An old term for a book made from sheets which have been folded twice, each sheet forming four leaves or eight pages. Sometimes applied to any book measuring about 9 by 12 inches.

query. On manuscript or proof, a question addressed to the author or editor (*abbr.* qy).

ragged right. Set with the right-hand margin unjustified. *See also* **justify.**

rag paper. High-quality paper made from cotton (formerly linen) rags chopped, boiled, and beaten to pulp.

random access. In computer terminology, the ability to add or retrieve data directly at any desired location, without having to pass through preceding locations. *Contrast* **sequential access.**

range. *Range right* and *range left* are equivalent to *flush right* and *flush left*—chiefly a British usage. *See also* **flush.**

raw data. (1) Statistical results not yet examined to eliminate incomplete, unresponsive, and other flawed data (*see* **database**). (2) Information, usually in digital form, that has not yet been processed by a computer.

ream. The number unit on the basis of which paper is handled—now usually 500 sheets. *See also* **basis weight.**

recto. The front side of a leaf; in a book, a right-hand page. To *start recto* is to begin on a recto page, as a preface or an index normally does. *Contrast* **verso.**

redboard. A thin, pliable material used for flexible bindings. *See also* **boards.**

reel-fed. *See* **web-fed.**

register. To print an impression on a sheet in correct relation to other impressions already printed on the same sheet; for example, to superimpose exactly the various color impressions in process color printing. When such impressions are not exactly aligned, they are said to be *out of register.*

remake. To alter the makeup of a page or series of pages.

repro. Short for *reproduction proof.*

reproduction proof. A fine-quality type proof pulled for use in offset lithography. Now often means final, corrected photocomposed typography (*see* **photocomposition**).

reverse out. When an image of type or of a drawing appears in white surrounded by a solid block of color or black, the copy is said to be *reversed out.* This technique makes possible the use of the white paper as a "color."

revise. A corrected *(revised)* proof.

right-reading. Said of a photographic image in which right-to-left orientation appears as in the original subject; *wrong-reading* is the opposite, that is, a mirror image, and in that case the photograph is said to be *flopped.* The terms are not to be confused with positive and negative, which refer to light values.

river. In composition in which words are widely spaced, an undesirable streak of white space running down through several lines of type, breaking up the even appearance of the page.

roman. The ordinary type style, distinguished from italic. *See also* **type styles.**

roman numerals. Numerals formed from traditional combinations of roman letters, either capitals (I, II, III, IV, and so forth) or lowercase (i, ii, iii, iv, and so forth). *See, for contrast,* **arabic numerals.**

rounding. In bookbinding, imparting a convex curve to the spine.

routine. In computer technology, a set of instructions to be followed in a particular order, such as a hyphenation routine in computerized typesetting.

rule. A printed line.

run. (1) A press run. (2) A quantity of material produced in one continuous operation by a paper or cloth mill. (3) The processing of a given body of data by a computer.

runaround. Type set in short lines to fit around an illustration or a box.

run back. To transfer text from the beginning of one line to the end of the line above it (*abbr.* rb).

run down. To transfer text from the end of one line to the beginning of the next (*abbr.* rd).

run in. (1) To merge a paragraph with the preceding one. (2) To insert new copy (whether an omission by the operator or an author's addition) into the text. (3) To set quoted matter continuously with text rather than setting it off as a block quotation.

run-in sideheads. *See under* **sideheads.**

running feet. *See under* **running heads.**

running heads. Copy set at the tops of printed pages to inform the reader of the location in the work. Such copy is sometimes placed at the bottoms of the pages, in which case it is referred to as *running feet.*

runover. (1) The continuation of a heading, figure legend, or similar copy onto an additional line. (2) In flush-and-hang material, all lines after the first line of a particular item. (3) Text that is longer than intended, running onto another page; or reset material that is longer than the original material it was meant to replace.

saddle wiring. Binding by inserting staples through the folds of gathered sheets, as in pamphlets and magazines. Also called *saddle stitching.*

sans serif. A typeface devoid of serifs. *See* **serif; type styles.**

scale. To *scale* an illustration is to calculate (after cropping) the proportions and finish size of the reproduction, and the amount of reduction needed to achieve this size.

scanner. (1) A device for producing film color separation negatives or positives for process color printing by electronically scanning the copy. (2) Any device that senses alternation in light and dark, such as an OCR input device, or in magnetized and unmagnetized states of a medium, such as various parts of a computer system.

screen. (1) A halftone screen; also the dot pattern in the printed image produced by such a screen. (2) A mechanical screen. (3) The face of a cathode-ray tube.

script. (1) A variety of type imitative of handwriting (*see under* **type styles**). (2) Short for *manuscript* or *typescript*.

self cover. A cover for a pamphlet, offprint, and so forth made of the same paper as the text.

separation negative. A one-color negative or positive achieved in the process of color separation.

sequential access. In computer technology, the ability to add or retrieve data in sequence only; that is, a desired location is attained by passing through all preceding locations, as in data stored on magnetic tape. *Contrast* **random access.**

serif. A short, light line projecting from the top or bottom of a main stroke of a letter; originally, in handwritten letters, a beginning or finishing stroke of the pen. Gothic and sans serif faces lack serifs.

set. The horizontal dimension of type. It is expressed in units on composing machines and is generally spoken of as *condensed* or *extended, thin* or *fat.*

setoff. Intentional or unintentional transfer of wet ink from one sheet of paper to another. Also, an alternative term for *offset.*

sewing. Stitching signatures together as part of the process of *binding.*

SGML. For *standard generalized markup language.* An ISO standard for tagging the structural components of an electronic text. The tagged text is stored as an ASCII text. Tagging conventions for chapters, paragraphs, subheads, and the like are recorded in a *document type definition* (DTD). An SGML editor, or SGML-aware word processor, uses the DTD to verify that the coding is syntactically correct. The SGML-coded text, together with the DTD and a *formatting output specification instance* (FOSI), can be used to drive typesetting equipment and other output devices on a wide variety of computer platforms. Another output specification standard, *documents style semantics and specification language* (DSSSL), is under development.

sheetwise. A method of printing in which a different form is used for each side of the sheet, as distinct from *work-and-turn.*

shingle. In saddle wiring, to vary the placement of the type image slightly from page to page so that, after binding and trimming, the outside margins will be equal in width.

short page. In makeup, a page that runs shorter than provided for in the design.

show-through. An undesirable effect in which printed matter on one side of the sheet shows through the other side.

sideheads. (1) Subheads that are aligned with, or that lie partly outside, the margin of the text and that are set on a line of their own. (2) Subheads that lie wholly outside the text margin. (3) Subheads that begin a paragraph and are continuous with the text. Subheads of the third sort are sometimes called *run-in sideheads.*

side sewing. Sewing books straight through the signatures from the side, close to the spine, before they are bound. Libraries typically rebind books in this manner. A side-sewn book is more durable than a Smyth-sewn book but will not open flat. Also referred to as *Singer sewing. See also* **Smyth sewing.**

side wiring. Binding the signatures of printed matter by stapling them through the side, near the fold, before the cover is glued on.

signature. A sheet of a book as folded ready for sewing. It is often 32 pages but may be only 16, 8, or even 4 pages if the paper stock is very heavy, or 64 pages if the paper is thin enough to permit additional folding. The size of the press also regulates the size of the signature.

silhouette halftone. A halftone in which all or part of the background has been eliminated. Also called *outline halftone*.

silk-screen printing. A stencil process in which ink is forced through the pores of a fabric screen bearing a reverse image of the design to be printed.

silver print. *See under* **proof.**

Singer sewing. *See* **side sewing.**

sinkage. The distance from the top of the type page to the top of the first line of text on a display page such as a chapter opening.

size. Gluelike material added to paper, either in the furnish or on the surface, to make the paper stiffer and more resistant to moisture.

slant. *See* **solidus.**

slash. *See* **solidus.**

slipcase. A protective box in which a book or set of volumes fits. When the books are in the slipcase, their spines are visible.

slip sheet. A sheet of paper placed between printed sheets as they come off the press to prevent setoff from one sheet to another.

slit on press. To cut printed sheets or webs longitudinally before they reach the folder.

small caps. Short for *small capital letters*. Capital letters that are smaller than the regular, or full, capitals of a font (*abbr.* sc). Small caps are usually equal to the x-height of the font.

Smyth sewing. The signatures of a Smyth-sewn book are individually sewn through the fold before being bound. A Smyth-sewn book has the advantage of lying flat when open, unlike a side-sewn or *perfect-bound* book. *See also* **perfect binding; side sewing.**

software. Computer programs. *Contrast* **hardware.**

solid. To set type *solid* is to set it with no additional space (leading) between lines.

solidus. A type sort consisting of a slant line (/), used between the parts of a fraction (5/8), to separate lines of poetry when quoted in run-in fashion, to separate shillings from pence in predecimalized British currency (2/6), and so on. Also called *virgule, shilling mark, slant,* and *slash.*

sort. In hot-metal composition, a body of metal with a character in relief, the printing surface, cast at one end. The nonprinting area of the sort above and below the character is called the *shoulder.* Any part of the character extending beyond the body of the sort is called a *kern.* By extension, whatever produces the image of a particular character, such as a film negative (in phototypesetting) or digital sequence (in computerized setting), can be termed a *sort.*

spacing. Lateral spacing between words, sentences, or columns, and in paragraph indentions. (Vertical spacing between lines is called *line spacing* or *leading.*) Two systems of lateral measurement, based on old methods of hot-metal typesetting, are in common use.

The first system uses the *em quad* (*see* **quad**) as its basic unit, a block of type metal as wide as it is high, varying in dimensions from one type size to another. Thus in 12-point type an em quad (or simply *em,* the word *quad* being understood) is 12 points square, and in 8-point type it is 8 points square. Other spacing is measured in multiples and fractions of the basic em: *2-em, 3-em, 4-em quads,* and so forth; also the *en* (½-em) *quad* and other spaces such as *3-to-em, 4-to-em,* and *5-to-em* (⅓, ¼, and ⅕ of an em, respectively). In this system a *thin space* is usually defined as a *4-to-em space,* and a *hair space* as a *5-to-em space.* Minimum word spacing, depending on the needs of justification, is about that of a thin space.

The second system employs a unit that is ⅟₁₈ of a quad. For most typefaces the quad is an actual em quad, but some faces use a slightly wider quad ("fat" faces) and others a slightly narrower one ("thin" faces). There are always 18 units in a quad, however. Thus for a regular-size face a *9-unit space* is exactly the same as an *en quad,* and *6-unit, 5-unit,* and *4-unit* spaces approximate the *3-to-em, 4-to-em,* and *5-to-em* spaces of the first system.

Two caveats may be in order. (1) Actual shop terminology often differs from that just given. Thus an *em quad* and an *en quad* are usually called a *molly* and a *nut space,* respectively; and *3-to-em, 4-to-em,* and so forth are commonly spoken of as *3-em, 4-em,* and so forth. (2) Also, elements of a third system sometimes appear, with horizontal spacing given in terms of *points,* down to ½ *point* and even ¼ *point,* the latter the thinnest of hair spaces available in any system.

spec. Short for *specification* (plural, *spex* or *specs*).

spine. The "back" of a book, that is, the center panel of the binding, hinged on each side to the two covers, front and back; the part of the binding visible when the book is shelved. Also called the *backbone.*

spiral binding. A kind of mechanical binding in which a metallic or plastic spiral is threaded through holes punched near the back margin of the covers and trimmed sheets. *See also* **mechanical binding.**

split fraction. *See* **fraction.**

spreadsheet program. A computer software program having the capability of distributing information into tabular, or row-and-column, format.

staining. The coloring of the edges of book pages for decorative effect. *See also* **gilding.**

stamping. In case binding, imprinting the spine of the case and sometimes the front cover with hard metal dies. Stamping may be done blind or with foil *(hot stamping)* or with ink. *See also* **binder's die; blind stamping; cold stamping; embossing; foil; hot stamping.**

stat. Short for **photostat.** To *stat up* is to enlarge a piece of copy photographically and to *stat down* is to make it smaller, usually in connection with producing camera-ready copy for offset lithography.

step and repeat. Used to describe a camera or projector that advances one step (frame, page, and so forth) horizontally or vertically for every exposure, according to a preset sequence.

stock. Paper to be used for printing or binding.

storage. To put data in computer *storage* is to record the data in digital form on a magnetic medium, such as tape, disks, or drums, either inside or outside the computer itself.

straight copy. Copy that contains no math, tables, unusual accents, or special display work. *Contrast* **penalty copy.**

strike-on composition. *See* **typewriter composition.**

stripping in. (1) Arranging and securing offset negatives in a *flat* for the purpose of producing the printing plate *(see also* **imposition**). (2) Correcting a negative by cutting out an incorrect line or passage and taping in a corrected one.

style. Rules of uniformity in matters of punctuation, capitalization, word division, spelling, and other details of expression, many of which may vary according to custom. *House style* is the set of rules adopted by a particular publishing or printing house.

subheads. Headings, or titles, for sections within a chapter or article. Subheads are usually set in type differing in some way from the text; for example, in boldface, all capitals, capitals and small capitals, or upper- and lowercase italic. Headings used for subsections are subheads of a lower level and are typographically distinguished accordingly. *See also* **side heads.**

subscript. In mathematics, a small numeral, letter, fraction, or symbol that prints partly below the base line.

substance. Same as *basis weight*. Used usually of bond paper.

sulfate process. A process of papermaking in which wood chips from both deciduous and coniferous trees are cooked in a solution of caustic soda and sodium sulfide to produce the pulp from which the paper is made. Kraft paper is made from unbleached sulfate pulp. *Contrast* **sulfite process.**

sulfite process. A process of papermaking in which wood chips from coniferous trees are cooked in a solution of lime and sulfurous acid to produce the pulp from which the paper is made. Paper made from sulfite pulp generally has fewer impurities and is more permanent than paper from sulfate pulp. *Contrast* **sulfate process.**

super. Heavy gauze used to form the hinge in a casebound book. Also called *crash*. *See* **case binding.**

supercalender. A machine, similar to a calender but separate from the papermaking machine, used to give additional smoothness and hardness to paper.

superior figure. *See* **superior numeral.**

superior numeral. A small numeral that prints partly above the x-height: A^2. *See also* **superscript.**

superscript. In mathematics or tabular material, a small numeral, letter, fraction, or symbol that prints partly above the x-height.

swash letters. *See under* **initial.**

tail margin. Bottom margin of a page.

tearsheet. A page cut or torn from a book or periodical.

Tegra proof. In computerized typesetting, a proof of intermediate quality, not camera-ready, used for proofreading and correction. *Contrast* **Linotron proof.**

T$_E$X. A computer typesetting system originally built to produce high-quality typesetting of mathematical material. It is also frequently used for setting less complicated text, particularly in academic institutions.

text type. (1) A type style resembling the first cast types, which were imitative of hand lettering. Sometimes referred to as *black letter* or *Old English*. *See also under* **type styles.** (2) Also used to refer to any type chosen for the body or main text of a publication.

thin space. In typesetting, a space usually defined as ¼ em ("4-to-em" or "4-em"). *See also* **hair space.**

three-up. *See* **two-up.**

tip-in. A separately printed leaf tipped—that is, pasted—into a book. *Contrast* **wraparound.**

transpose. In proofreading and editing, to switch the positions of two words, sentences, paragraphs, and so forth. Also, simply to move copy from one position to another.

trim marks. Marks sometimes found on repro proof indicating the edges of the trimmed page.

trim size. The dimensions, in inches, of a full page, including the margins.

two-up. In offset lithography, to duplicate the printing image on the plate so that two copies of the piece are printed at the same time. The terms *three-up, four-up,* and so forth are analogous.

typeface. The design or style characteristics of a complete font of type. The various typefaces are designated by name: Baskerville, Caslon, and Times Roman, for example. Typefaces in photocomposition resemble but are often not exactly like their counterparts in hot-metal composition. *See also* **type styles.**

type page. The area of a page occupied by the type image, from the running head to the last line of type on the page or the folio, whichever is lower, and from the inside margin to the outside margin, including any area occupied by side heads. The type page, also called *type area,* is measured in picas.

typescript. A typewritten manuscript. Now also used to refer to a manuscript in the form of a computer printout.

typesetter. A person, firm, or facility that sets type. Also, especially in photocomposition, a typesetting machine.

typesetting. *See* **computerized typesetting; hot-metal composition; photocomposition; typewriter composition.**

type sizes. Before the adoption of the point system, which became general about 1878, type sizes were known by distinguishing names, such as Great Primer for 18-point type. The sizes to which these names referred lacked uniformity among different type founders, particularly in different countries. This confusion led to the immediate popularity of the point system, which originated in France and was then developed in the United States (*see also* **measurement**). In hot-metal composition, the designation of type sizes by points refers to the vertical dimension of the nonprinting surface (*see under* **sort**) of the type body and therefore has no definite reference to the size of the typeface itself. All the different styles of 12-point faces, for instance, are approximately the same size, but there is significant variation. The designation *12-point,* as referring to a particular typeface, means that it is ordinarily cast on a 12-point body and that the actual vertical dimensions of the characters fall within limits that are somewhat less than 12 points, thus providing an irreducible minimum of space between lines of type. The type sizes and minimum interlinear spacing in photocomposition are analogous to those in hot-metal composition. In hot-metal composition the size of the body is often increased to enlarge the space between the lines without having to insert leads for that purpose. Thus a face ordinarily cast on a 10-point body may be cast on a 12-point body to give the appearance of 2-point leading; it is then referred to as "10 on 12." In photocomposition the same effect is achieved by regulating the spacing of the successive lines of optical images, and the same terminology is used.

type styles. Type characteristics on a more general level than those of the various typefaces. The general style of type commonly used in books and all classes of ordinary reading matter is known as *roman.* Although all roman types are essentially the same in form, there are two fairly well defined divisions or styles. The older form is called *old style* and is characterized by strength and boldness of feature, with strokes of comparatively uniform thickness and with an absence of weak horizontal lines. The serifs are rounded, and the contour is clear and legible. Caslon is an example of an old-style face. The other style is called *modern* and is characterized by heavier shading, thinner horizontals, and thin, straight serifs. Bodoni is an example. Although a few typefaces combine certain characteristics of the two styles and are thus called *transitional*, it is usually comparatively easy to classify any particular face as *old style* or *modern*. Aside from *roman*, there are several other general classes, known as *italic, oblique, script, gothic, text, boldface, condensed,* and *extended*.

In *italic* style, all characters are slanted and have a light, flowing appearance, somewhat suggestive of cursive. There is an italic font to match each roman typeface, and a font of roman type for book and magazine work would be considered incomplete without a corresponding font of italic.

In *oblique* style the characters are also slanted, but somewhat stiffly, so that the style is more like roman with a slight slant than italic. Its developers believed that it would be more readable than italic in large quantities.

Script types are formal imitations of handwriting. Their widest use is in the printing of announcements, invitations, and stationery.

Gothic, or *sans serif,* is perfectly plain, with lines of uniform thickness and without serifs. It is sometimes known as *block letter.*

Text is a survival of the first types cast and was originally an imitation of the hand lettering which prevailed before movable types were invented. It is often known as *black letter* or *Old English.* German *Fraktur* resembles it closely.

Boldface characters are thick lined and heavy. All commonly used faces include boldface versions, sometimes in both roman and italic.

Lightface is the ordinary variety, or weight, of roman or italic type, in contrast to *boldface.*

Many typefaces are also available in *condensed* or *extended* versions, that is, the normal characters are made narrower or broader to occupy less or more space.

See also **body type; display type.**

typewriter composition. Text matter produced by typewriter for offset lithography. The typewriter may be a hand-operated office machine or a highly sophisticated proportional-spacing machine with automatic justification, driven by punched-paper or magnetic tape. Good typewriter composition employing "book" typefaces may closely resemble machine work. Also called *strike-on composition.*

typo. *See* **typographical error.**

typographer. A type designer. Also, more loosely, someone who sets type.

typographical error. Colloquially, *typo.* An error made by the compositor; also called *printer's error (PE).* The layman's term is *misprint.* When proof is being corrected, typos (PEs) are strictly distinguished from author's alterations.

underrun. Fewer printed items or less paper than was ordered. *See also* **overrun.**

unjustified. Of lines of type, not justified; that is, with an uneven right-hand margin. Also called *ragged right.*

uppercase. The capital letters of a type font. *Contrast* **lowercase.**

vandyke. *See under* **proof.**

varnish. A shiny protective coating applied to printed matter, such as a paperback cover, to protect it.

VDT. *See* **video display terminal.**

vellum. *See under* **finish.**

verso. The back side of a leaf; in a book, a left-hand page. *Contrast* **recto.**

video display terminal (VDT). In computer technology, an input keyboard with a video screen on which the keyboarded material can be viewed in typed-out form.

virgule. A slant line. *See* **solidus.**

watermark. Design, maker's name, and so forth on paper, produced by thinning the paper slightly with a wire design attached to the dandy roll so that the design shows when the paper is held up to the light. *See* **dandy roll.**

web. On a printing press using paper in reel form, the paper is referred to as the *web.* The same term is also used for paper as it is being made by machine.

web-fed. Applied to printing presses using paper in reel form rather than in sheets. Also called *reel-fed.*

web offset. Short for *web-fed offset lithography. See also* **offset lithography.**

widow. A short paragraph-ending line appearing at the top of a page. It should be avoided when possible by changes in wording or spacing that either remove the line or lengthen it; also, less strictly, a word or part of a word on a line by itself at the end of any paragraph. *See also* **bad break.**

window. A rectangle (of red acetate or black paper or any other material that has a smooth edge when cut and photographs as black) pasted on a repro page in the blank space left for a halftone illustration. When a negative is made of the page, the rectangle becomes a clear opening, or *window,* in the film, into which the halftone negative is stripped, thus combining the type and halftone components on one flat.

wire. A fine-mesh screen in the form of an endless belt that carries pulp through a papermaking machine and which may impart a subtle design to the finished paper. *See also* **deckle; wove paper.**

wire side. The "back side" of a piece of paper, opposite the "top" or *felt side.* It often shows an impression of the wire on which the paper is formed from pulp.

word. In computer terminology, a sequence of binary digits (bits) conveying meaning in combination, often processed as a whole by the computer.

word division. Dividing words at the end of a line. *See also* **exception dictionary; hyphenation routine.**

word processor. A computer program for recording and manipulating text in electronic form. Sophisticated word processors include routines for formatting text for output that allows the user to specify type styles, type sizes, leading, and so forth. Word processors may also include spelling and grammar checking routines, an on-line thesaurus, and tools for aligning mathematical equations.

work-and-turn. To print *work-and-turn,* a form is arranged, or imposed (*see* **imposition**), so that a sheet may be printed on one side, turned right for left, and printed on the other side, to give two copies of the pages when cut in half. In printing *work-and-tumble* the sheet is turned end for end. *Contrast* **sheetwise.**

workstation. In computing, a system comprising input/output devices and computer hardware and designed for use by one person at a time.

wove paper. Machine-made wove paper shows a faintly discernible woven-fabric effect when held up to the light. The effect is produced by the metal screening on the dandy roll as it passes over the wet web of paper during manufacture. *Contrast* **laid paper.**

wraparound. A folded sheet of paper bearing printed illustrations, slipped around the outside of a signature before sewing as a means of adding such illustrations to a book without the necessity of tipping in single leaves. Thus, when a wraparound is placed on a 16-page signature, the two leaves of the wraparound sheet appear 16 pages apart in the finished book. *Contrast* **tip-in.**

wrong font. A type of different size, style, or face from that of the context in which it accidentally appears (*abbr.* wf).

wrong-reading. *See under* **right-reading.**

WYSIWYG. For *What you see is what you get.* Pronounced "wizzywig." Text and graphics shown formatted on a computer screen as they will appear when printed. Also referred to as *previewing a document.*

x-height. In type, a vertical dimension equal to the height of the lowercase letters (such as *x*) without ascenders or descenders. *See also* **base line.**

Bibliography

Abrams, Howard B. *The Law of Copyright*. Looseleaf. New York: Clark Boardman, 1989.

Achtert, Walter S., and Joseph Gibaldi. *The MLA Style Manual*. New York: Modern Language Association, 1985.
  Useful for notes and bibliographies in the humanities style. Many examples.

ALA-LC Romanization Tables: Transliteration Schemes for Non-Roman Scripts. Compiled and edited by Randall K. Barry. Washington, D.C.: Library of Congress, 1991.
  Very comprehensive treatment of transliteration and romanization. Obtainable from the Library of Congress Cataloging Distribution Service.

American Heritage Dictionary. Boston: Houghton Mifflin, latest edition.

American Medical Association Manual of Style. 8th ed. Edited by Cheryl Iverson. Baltimore: Williams and Wilkins, 1989.

American Men and Women of Science: Physical and Biological Sciences. 18th ed. 8 vols. Edited by Jaques Cattell Press. New York: R. R. Bowker, 1992.

American Men and Women of Science: Social and Behavioral Sciences. 13th ed. Edited by Jaques Cattell Press. New York: R. R. Bowker, 1978.

American Psychological Association. See *Publication Manual of the American Psychological Association*.

Anglo-American Cataloguing Rules. 2d ed., 1988 rev. Prepared by the American Library Association, the British Library, the Canadian Committee on Cataloguing, the Library Association, and the Library of Congress. Edited by Michael Gorman and Paul W. Winkler. Chicago: American Library Association; Ottawa: Canadian Library Association, 1988.
  Intended for library catalogers but also useful to editors, especially for the forms and alphabetization of proper names.

Angstadt, Richard, and others. *Glossary of Typesetting Terms*. New York: Association of American University Presses, 1993.

Baron, Dennis. *Grammar and Gender*. New Haven: Yale University Press, 1986.

Bartlett, John. *Familiar Quotations: A Collection of Passages, Phrases, and Proverbs Traced to Their Sources in Ancient and Modern Literature*. Edited by Justin Kaplan. 16th ed., revised and enlarged. Boston: Little, Brown, 1992.

Barzun, Jacques. *On Writing, Editing, and Publishing: Essays Explicative and Hortatory*. Chicago: University of Chicago Press, 1971.
  Cogent essays addressed primarily to writers.

Barzun, Jacques, and Henry F. Graff. *The Modern Researcher*. 4th ed. New York: Harcourt Brace Jovanovich, 1985.
  Although addressed primarily to historians, the practical advice on how to turn research into well-organized, literate exposition goes well beyond the field of history.

Becker, Howard S. *Writing for Social Scientists: How to Start and Finish Your Thesis, Book, or Article*. Chicago: University of Chicago Press, 1986.

Bernstein, Theodore M. *The Careful Writer: A Modern Guide to English Usage*. New York: Atheneum, 1965.
  An alphabetically arranged list of usages, good and bad, with graceful

discussion of why they should be embraced, tolerated, or shunned. A particularly helpful ally of the manuscript editor.

————. *Miss Thistlebottom's Hobgoblins: The Careful Writer's Guide to the Taboos, Bugbears, and Outmoded Rules of English Usage.* New York: Simon and Schuster, 1984.

A wealth of excellent advice for overzealous editors, by a very careful writer with a delightful sense of humor.

Blue Book. See *A Uniform System of Citation.*

Bookman's Glossary. 6th ed. Edited by Jean Peters. New York: R. R. Bowker, 1983.

Covers English language terminology of the book trade and of the graphic arts.

Books in Print: Authors and *Books in Print: Titles.* New York: R. R. Bowker. Published annually.

The standard annual listing of books published by American publishers. Publishers' addresses, telephone numbers, and other data are listed in a separate volume. An editorial office should have the current edition plus at least a selection of earlier volumes for reference. Published from a computerized database and not to be used as final authority for spelling or dates.

British Books in Print. Title changed in 1988. See *Whitaker's Books in Print.*

Butcher, Judith. *Copy-Editing: The Cambridge Handbook for Authors, Editors, and Publishers.* 3d ed. Cambridge: Cambridge University Press, 1992.

The new edition is an extensive revision of the highly regarded second edition. Like the earlier edition, this is a well-organized, lucid account by the former head of the copyediting department at Cambridge University Press of what a copyeditor does in Great Britain, plus excellent advice for authors and indexers. Highly recommended for American copyeditors, authors, and indexers as well.

Cambridge World Gazetteer: A Geographical Dictionary. Edited by David Munro. New York: Cambridge University Press, 1990.

An excellent source and supplement to *Webster's New Geographical Dictionary.*

CBE Scientific Illustration Committee. *Illustrating Science: Standards for Publication.* Bethesda, Md.: Council of Biology Editors, 1988.

A beautifully illustrated and excellent guide for publishing illustrative material, covering such topics as camera-ready copy, graphs, maps, computer graphics, halftone printing, color illustrations, and legal and ethical considerations. Also includes glossary and annotated bibliography.

CBE Style Manual Committee. *Scientific Style and Format: The CBE Manual for Authors, Editors, and Publishers.* 6th ed. New York: Cambridge University Press, 1994.

The standards of the *CBE Manual* are followed by a great many journals and are acceptable to most publishers of scientific books. This edition extends the manual's coverage from the biological and medical sciences to chemistry, earth sciences, mathematics, physical sciences, and social sciences. Except in a few details its recommendations follow those of *The Chicago Manual of Style.*

Chicago Guide to Preparing Electronic Manuscripts. Chicago: University of Chicago Press, 1987.

Computer Dictionary. Redmond, Wash.: Microsoft Press, 1991.

An excellent dictionary to use by itself or in tandem with *Dictionary of Computing.*

Concise Dictionary of American History. New York: Macmillan, 1983.
  A convenient desk book for editors of historical works.
Concise Dictionary of National Biography. 3 vols. London and New York: Oxford University Press, 1992.
  These three volumes contain shortened versions of all the entries in the complete *Dictionary of National Biography* and all of its supplements.
Council of Biology Editors. *See* CBE.
Day, Robert A. *How to Write and Publish a Scientific Paper.* 4th ed. Phoenix, Ariz.: Oryx Press, 1994.
Dictionary of American Biography. 17 vols. and 8 supplements to 1988. New York: Macmillan.
  A standard reference work (does not list living persons).
Dictionary of Canadian Biography. 12 vols. Toronto: University of Toronto Press, 1966–88.
Dictionary of Computing. 3d ed. New York: Oxford University Press, 1990.
  An excellent and comprehensive dictionary/encyclopedia of computer terms.
Dictionary of National Biography. Edited by Leslie Stephen and Sidney Lee. 22 vols. with 11 supplements to date, prepared under various editors. London and New York: Oxford University Press, 1885–1993.
  A standard sourcebook for British biography from the first century A.D. to 1985. Includes emigrants from and immigrants to the British Empire or Commonwealth. Covers only the deceased. See also *Concise Dictionary of National Biography.*
Directory of American Scholars. 8th ed. 4 vols. Edited by Jaques Cattell Press Staff, Tempe, Ariz. New York: R. R. Bowker, 1982.
  Biographies of scholars in history, English, languages and linguistics, philosophy, religion, and law.
Ebbitt, Wilma R., and David R. Ebbitt. *Index to English.* 8th ed. New York: Oxford University Press, 1990.
  A widely used college textbook on expository writing, including entries on sentence and paragraph construction, spelling, punctuation, and various types of papers. Revision of the original by Porter G. Perrin.
Field, Janet N., and others, eds. *Graphic Arts Manual.* Salem, N.H.: Ayer, 1980.
Follett, Wilson. *Modern American Usage: A Guide.* Edited and completed by Jacques Barzun and others. New York: Hill and Wang, 1966.
  An excellent dictionary of usage, with illuminating essays on a number of questions of concern to authors and editors.
Fowler, H. W. *A Dictionary of Modern English Usage.* 2d ed. Revised by Ernest Gowers. Oxford: Clarendon Press, 1987.
  The classic work on English usage for discriminating writers. A necessity in any university press editorial office.
Goldstein, Paul. *Copyright: Principles, Laws, and Practice.* Boston: Little, Brown, 1989.
Gould, S. H. *A Manual for Translators of Mathematical Russian.* Rev. ed. Edited by R. P. Boas. Providence, R.I.: American Mathematical Society, 1991.
Gowers, Ernest. *The Complete Plain Words.* Edited by Sidney Greenbaum and Janet Whitcut. Boston: Godine, 1990.
  An elegant and witty guide to precise writing by the eminent reviser of Fowler's *Modern English Usage.*

Guide to Reference Books. 10th ed. Compiled by Eugene P. Sheehy. Chicago: American Library Association, 1986.

Standard guide on how to look things up.

Guide to the National Archives of the United States. Washington, D.C.: National Archives and Records Service, General Services Administration, 1987.

An indispensable tool for anyone working with archival materials in United States history. Includes a numerical list of the record groups by which materials are classified in the National Archives. Quarterly supplements are issued in *National Archives Accessions.*

Harman, Eleanor, and Ian Montagnes, eds. *The Thesis and the Book.* Toronto: University of Toronto Press, 1976.

This series of articles, which appeared originally in *Scholarly Publishing,* offers much useful advice to those who aspire to turn Ph.D. dissertations into publishable books.

Hart, Horace, ed. *Hart's Rules for Compositors and Readers at the University Press, Oxford.* 39th ed. New York: Oxford University Press, 1983.

Harvard Guide to American History. Rev. ed. Edited by Frank Freidel, with the assistance of Richard K. Showman. 2 vols. Cambridge: Harvard University Press, Belknap Press, 1974.

Authoritative lists of titles in American political, social, constitutional, and economic history; especially useful for government publications.

Hopkins, Jeanne. *Glossary of Astronomy and Astrophysics.* 2d ed. Chicago: University of Chicago Press, 1980.

Compilation of scientific terms used in the *Astrophysical Journal.*

ILMP (International Literary Market Place). New York: R. R. Bowker. Published annually.

International paperback directory of current publishing personnel and services in 160 countries, including book publishers, book clubs, literary prizes, and trade events of the year.

International Who's Who. London: Europa Publications. Published annually.

Biographical information on currently eminent persons throughout the world.

ISO (International Standards Organization). *General Principles concerning Quantities, Units, and Symbols.* ISO 31-0:1981. Geneva: International Standards Organization, 1981.

Comprehesive treatment of international standards for the typographical representation of mathematical and physical quantities; for example, scalars, vectors, and tensors.

Katz, Michael J. *Elements of the Scientific Paper: A Step-by-Step Guide for Students and Professionals.* New Haven: Yale University Press, 1986.

Kenkyusha's New English-Japanese Dictionary. 5th ed. Tokyo: Kenkyusha, 1980.

Lamon, William E. *The Metric System of Measurement: A Handbook for Teachers.* Edited by Garry Kargel. Portland, Oreg.: Continuing Education Press, 1981.

Latman, Alan, and others. *Copyright for the Nineties.* 3d ed. Charlottesville, Va.: Michie, 1989.

Lawson, Alexander S., and Dwight Agner. *Printing Types: An Introduction.* Rev. ed. Boston: Beacon Press, 1974.

Lee, Marshall. *Bookmaking: The Illustrated Guide to Design, Production, Editing.* 2d ed., rev. and enlarged. New York: R. R. Bowker, 1979.

A well-written, clearly illustrated, and easily understood book on the mechanics of bookmaking (composition, engraving, platemaking, printing, etc.) for authors, editors, designers, and production people.

Li, Xia, and Nancy B. Crane. *Electronic Styles: A Handbook for Citing Electronic Information.* 2d ed. Medford, N.J.: Information Today, 1996.

LMP (Literary Market Place). New York: R. R. Bowker. Published annually.

A comprehensive directory of current publishing personnel and services, including lists of book publishers, book clubs, literary awards, reviewers, translators, and trade events of the year. See also *ILMP.*

Luey, Beth. *Handbook for Academic Authors.* Rev. ed. Cambridge: Cambridge University Press, 1990.

Maggio, Rosalie. *The Dictionary of Bias-Free Usage: A Guide to Nondiscriminatory Language.* Phoenix, Ariz.: Oryx Press, 1991.

———. *The Nonsexist Word Finder: A Dictionary of Gender-Free Usage.* Boston: Beacon Press, 1989.

Manual for Authors of Mathematical Papers. 8th ed. Providence, R.I.: American Mathematical Society, 1990.

Manual for Translators of Mathematical Russian. See under Gould, S. H.

Manual of Foreign Languages, for the Use of Librarians, Bibliographers, Research Workers, Editors, Translators, and Printers. 4th ed. Edited by Georg F. von Ostermann. New York: Central Book Co., 1952.

Somewhat outdated but still useful for spelling, capitalization, diacritics, and basic grammatical forms of the major languages of the world. No longer in print, but may be available in some libraries.

Maroon Book. See University of Chicago Manual of Legal Citation.

Miller, Casey, and Kate Swift. *The Handbook of Nonsexist Writing: For Writers, Editors, and Speakers.* 2d ed. New York: Harper and Row, 1988.

A guide to what constitutes sexism in language and sensible advice on how to avoid it.

Modern Language Association. *The MLA Style Manual. See under* Achtert, Walter S., and Joseph Gibaldi.

Monmonier, Mark. *Mapping It Out: Expository Cartography for the Humanities and Social Sciences.* Chicago: University of Chicago Press, 1993.

Monthly Catalog of United States Government Publications. Washington, D.C.: Government Printing Office.

Mulvany, Nancy. *Indexing Books.* Chicago: University of Chicago Press, 1993.

New York Times Manual of Style and Usage. Edited by Lewis Jordan. New York: Random House/New York Times Book Co., 1982.

A dictionary of names and terms primarily for newspaper writers. Useful for spelling and capitalization.

Nimmer, Melville. *Cases and Materials on Copyright and Other Aspects of Entertainment Litigation Illustrated, Including Unfair Competition, Defamation, Privacy.* 3d ed. American Casebook Series. Saint Paul, Minn.: West, 1985.

———. *Nimmer on Copyright.* 4 vols. New York: Matthew Bender, 1978. Looseleaf updates.

Indispensable for keeping up with the latest developments in copyright.

Oxford Classical Dictionary. 2d ed. Edited by N. G. L. Hammond and H. H. Scullard. Oxford, New York, Toronto: Oxford University Press, 1970.

Patry, William F. *The Fair Use Privilege in Copyright Law.* Washington, D.C.: BNA Books, 1985.

Pemberton, John E., ed. *The Bibliographic Control of Official Publications.* Elmsford, N.Y.: Pergamon, 1982.

Periodical Title Abbreviations. 7th ed. Vol. 1, *By Abbreviation.* Vol. 2, *By Title.* Detroit: Gale Research, 1989.

Covers periodicals and selected monographs in art, business, education, engineering, the humanities, law, library science, medicine, religion, science, the social sciences, and many other fields.

Perle, E. Gabriel, and John Taylor Williams. *Publishing Law Handbook.* 2d ed. Englewood Cliffs, N.J.: Prentice-Hall Law and Business, 1992.

Perrin, Porter G. *Reference Handbook of Grammar and Usage.* New York: William Morrow, 1972.

Perrin's new handbook is derived from his earlier *Writer's Guide and Index to English.* The latter has been recast into an eighth edition by Wilma and David Ebbitt. *See under* Ebbitt, Wilma R., and David R. Ebbitt. *Index to English.*

Pipics, Zoltán, ed. *The Librarian's Practical Dictionary in Twenty-two Languages.* New York: State Mutual Book and Periodical Service, 1980.

List of English language bibliographic terms translated into the major foreign languages, with an index in each language.

Publication Manual of the American Psychological Association. 4th ed. Washington: American Psychological Association, 1994.

Random House Dictionary of the English Language. 2d ed. New York: Random House, 1987.

Rodgers, Frank. *A Guide to British Government Publications.* Bronx, N.Y.: H. W. Wilson, 1980.

Very thorough, well-organized account of a complex subject.

Sanders, Norman. *Graphic Designer's Production Handbook.* Illustrated by William Bevington. New York: Hastings House, 1982.

Schmeckebier, Laurence F., and Roy B. Eastin. *Government Publications and Their Use.* 2d ed. Washington, D.C.: Brookings Institution, 1969.

Helpful in citing U.S. government publications. Now out of print but available from Books on Demand, University Microfilms International, Ann Arbor, Mich.

Scholarly Publishing. Journal published quarterly by the University of Toronto Press.

Full of valuable information for editors and authors of university press books.

Smith, Datus C., Jr. *A Guide to Book Publishing.* Rev. ed. Seattle: University of Washington Press, 1989.

A well-regarded, clear presentation of the general principles of publishing.

Stainton, Elsie Myers. *The Fine Art of Copyediting.* New York: Columbia University Press, 1991.

A concise, helpful guide to copyediting.

Statesman's Year-Book: Statistical and Historical Annual of the States of the World. Edited by John Paxton. New York: St. Martin's Press. Published annually.

Particularly valuable to the editor for its up-to-date information on Commonwealth countries and international organizations, including the United Nations.

Stedman's Medical Dictionary. 25th ed. New York: Macmillan, 1990. Illustrated 25th ed. Baltimore: Williams and Wilkins, 1990.

Steenrod, N. E., and others. *How to Write Mathematics*. Providence, R.I.: American Mathematical Society, 1983.

Strong, William S. *The Copyright Book: A Practical Guide*. 3d ed. Cambridge: MIT Press, 1990.

A succinct and well-written analysis of the law and a practical guide to its application.

Strunk, William, Jr., and E. B. White. *The Elements of Style*. 3d ed. New York: Macmillan, 1979.

A short classic that offers excellent practical advice on achieving a clear and graceful expository style; should be required reading for all authors and editors.

Swanson, Ellen. *Mathematics into Type: Copyediting and Proofreading of Mathematics for Editorial Assistants and Authors*. Rev. ed. Providence, R.I.: American Mathematical Society, 1986.

Includes instructions on all phases of producing a book or an article in the field of mathematics: preparation and submission of manuscript, editing and marking, design and typesetting, proofreading and page makeup, and more.

Tufte, Edward R. *Envisioning Information*. Cheshire, Conn.: Graphics Press, 1990.

An excellent and extensively illustrated guide to the presentation of information in graphic form.

———. *The Visual Display of Quantitative Information*. Cheshire, Conn.: Graphics Press, 1983.

A classic presentation of the theory and practice of graphic representation of quantitative data. Copiously illustrated.

Turabian, Kate L. *A Manual for Writers of Term Papers, Theses, and Dissertations*. 5th ed. Edited by Bonnie Birtwistle Honigsblum. Chicago: University of Chicago Press, 1987.

Intended for students and other writers of papers not written for publication. Useful material on notes and bibliographies.

Ulrich's International Periodicals Directory. New York: R. R. Bowker, 1979–90. Updated annually. Supplemented by *Ulrich's Quarterly*.

A listing by subject of serials published throughout the world. Indexed.

A Uniform System of Citation. 15th ed. Cambridge: Harvard Law Review Association, 1991.

Also known as *The Blue Book*. Citation forms and abbreviations used by many law reviews.

United States Government Printing Office. *Style Manual*. Rev. ed. Washington, D.C., 1984.

The University of Chicago Manual of Legal Citation. Edited by the staff of the *University of Chicago Law Review* and the University of Chicago Legal Forum. Rochester, N.Y.: Lawyers Co-operative Publishing Co., 1989.

Also known as *The Maroon Book*. A concise set of guidelines for a simplified system of legal citation, stressing clear presentation of the central elements of any citation.

Webster's Dictionary of English Usage. Springfield, Mass.: Merriam-Webster, 1989.

Webster's Guide to Abbreviations. Springfield, Mass.: Merriam-Webster, 1985.

Webster's New Biographical Dictionary. Springfield, Mass.: Merriam-Webster, 1983.

Indispensable for checking spelling and alphabetization of personal names.

Webster's (now *Merriam-Webster's*) *Collegiate Dictionary.* Springfield, Mass.: Merriam-Webster, latest edition.

Based on *Webster's Third New International Dictionary,* the *Collegiate* is the best desk dictionary for author or editor to have at elbow. The *Collegiate* rather than the big dictionary should be followed for word division whenever possible: prepared after the parent work, it represents the later thinking of the editors on the principles of word division and frequently departs from the divisions given in the unabridged dictionary.

Webster's New Geographical Dictionary. Springfield, Mass.: Merriam-Webster, 1984.

The first source to consult in checking the spelling or alphabetization of place names.

Webster's Standard American Style Manual. Springfield, Mass.: Merriam-Webster, 1985.

Webster's Third New International Dictionary of the English Language, Unabridged. Springfield, Mass.: G. & C. Merriam, 1964.

The standard for spelling of English words and a basic reference work for any editorial library. "Webster 3" has been criticized for abandoning the attempt to define the "standing" of English words (bookish, colloquial, substandard, etc.) or to suggest that usages are "good" or "bad." Whether it is the province of a dictionary to do so is a separate question, but the 1935 *Second International* did and is still useful for those purposes.

Whitaker's Books in Print: The Reference Catalogue of Current Literature. London: J. Whitaker & Sons. Prior to 1988 titled *British Books in Print.* Published annually.

Serves the same purpose for British books as *Books in Print* (which see) does for American books. Supplemented by *The Bookseller,* a weekly periodical published in the United Kingdom by J. Whitaker & Sons.

Who's Who: An Annual Biographical Dictionary. New York: St. Martin's Press.

A useful listing of living notable persons, mainly British. See also *International Who's Who.*

Who's Who in America. Chicago: A. N. Marquis. Published biennially.

A useful listing of living Americans.

Williams, Joseph M. *Style: Toward Clarity and Grace.* Chicago: University of Chicago Press, 1990.

A precise, lucid, and practical guide to achieving coherence, concision, clarity, and elegance in writing.

Williamson, Hugh. *Methods of Book Design.* 3d ed. New Haven, Conn.: Yale University Press, 1983.

Words into Type. Based on studies by Marjorie E. Skillin, Robert M. Gay, and other authorities. 4th ed. Englewood Cliffs, N.J.: Prentice-Hall, 1992.

An excellent manual of printing practice for authors and editors. The sections on grammar and use of words are particularly helpful.

World Almanac and Book of Facts. Edited by Mark S. Hoffman. New York: Pharos Books. Published annually.

An enormous compilation of names and facts about the world—government agencies, population figures, laws, events, etc.—with a comprehensive general index.

Zinsser, William. *On Writing Well: An Informal Guide to Writing Nonfiction.* 4th ed. New York: Harper and Row, 1990.

Useful pointers on style, usage, and organization for the professional writer.

Zweifel, Frances W. *A Handbook of Biological Illustration*. 2d ed. Chicago: University of Chicago Press, 1988.

A highly useful guide for authors, editors, and artists on preparation of various kinds of illustrative materials for scientific publication.

Index

References are to paragraph numbers except where specified otherwise (i.e., table and figure numbers). Running heads in the text include paragraph numbers. Definitions of technical terms are found in the glossary (pp. 831–59), which is not indexed here.

indexing
  computer assisted, 17.25–26, 17.36, 17.40,
    17.42–43, 17.47–48, 17.61–62, 17.64,
    17.67, 17.98
  equipment for, 17.31–32
  general principles of, 17.69–96
  manual, 17.31–33, 17.35, 17.42–43, 17.45–
    46, 17.48–49, 17.62, 17.66
  marking page proofs for, 17.33, 17.37–41,
    17.64, 17.68, fig. 17.1
  marking up for typesetter, 2.118, 2.147–48,
    17.135
  mechanics of, 17.25–68
  See also indexer; indexes
Indian names, 17.122
indirect
  discourse, 5.78, 10.38, 10.42
  questions, 5.18, 5.27, 10.35, 10.38
Indonesian names, 17.124
inferior characters. *See* subscripts
infinitives
  capitalization of, 7.127, 15.104
  split, 2.98n
information services, 15.328, 15.421–22,
  16.207
ing, word division and, 6.52
initials
  alphabetizing, 17.100–102
  with author's name, 1.13
  in citations, 15.73, 15.82, 15.260
  display, 2.136, 10.33, 18.55
  period with, 14.4
  with personal names, 1.13, 6.53, 7.6, 7.9,
    14.4, 17.100
  spacing of, 7.6, 14.2, 15.82
  used alone, 6.89, 7.6, 14.4
  and word division, 6.53
  See also acronyms; letters (of alphabet)
in press, 15.176, 16.57
insertions, 2.36, 2.67, 2.71–74. *See also* corrections; cutting and pasting
inserts, foldout, 12.55
institutions. *See* organizations
integrated typesetting systems, 19.20–35. *See
  also* photocomposition
interior speech, 5.76, 10.43–47
interjections, punctuation with, 5.45–56
international bodies, citation of, 15.41, 16.198
International Standard Book Number (ISBN),
  1.3, 1.30–32, 1.115
International Standard Serial Number (ISSN),
  1.32
International Standards Organization (ISO),
  1.31
  date and, 8.46, 8.50
  electronic document citations and, 15.424
  mathematical copy and, 13.31

International System of Units (SI), 7.124,
  14.41–49
interpolations, in quoted material, 2.102,
  5.128, 10.21, 10.64–68
interrogation point. *See* question mark
interviews, citation of, 15.262–66, 16.126–29
introduction
  citation of, 15.101, 15.129–31, 15.300,
    16.51, 16.77
  content of, 1.51
  indexing of, 17.27
  location of, 1.3
  in new editions, 1.21
  page numbering of, 1.52
  to parts, 1.67
introductory phrases, with quotations, 10.17–19
introductory remarks, punctuation with, 5.102
inversion
  in alphabetizing, 17.97
  of authors' names, 15.70, 15.76, 15.83–86,
    15.88, 15.205, 16.99
  of Chinese names, 7.13, 17.117–18
  of Hungarian names, 7.15, 15.84, 17.113
  in index headings, 17.5, 17.17, 17.39,
    17.57, 17.84–85, 17.87
  of names for indexing, 17.20, 17.106,
    17.113–14, 17.117–18, 17.127
  of Spanish punctuation marks, 9.73
irony, quotation marks for, 6.63, 6.78
ISBN (International Standard Book Number),
  1.3, 1.30–32, 1.115
ISSN (International Standard Serial Number),
  1.32
issue, in journal citations, 15.211–13, 15.217–
  18, 15.222, 15.225, 16.102–3, 16.108
Italian, 9.46–55
  apostrophe in, 9.48, 9.54
  capitalization in, 9.46
  names in, 7.8, 7.10, 7.48
  punctuation in, 9.47–49
  special characters in, 9.55
  word division in, 9.50–54
italics
  added to quotations, 10.67–68
  for bill or law, 7.70, 15.351
  in Chinese, 9.100–101
  for court cases, 7.72, 15.318
  in cross-references, 17.18–19
  deletion of, 2.83
  embellishment of, 13.13
  for emphasis, 6.63–64, 10.67–68
  with enumerations, 8.75
  for epigraphs, 18.54
  for foreign words, 6.15, 6.65, 6.67–70,
    9.100–101
  for genus and species, 7.102–4
  in Hebrew, 9.108

1

NDX

negatives
for color separation, 19.53
in integrated phototypesetting systems, 19.26
for mathematical copy, 13.7
in offset lithography, 3.54, 3.57, 19.5–7, 19.18
typographical errors on, 3.55
newspaper features, titles of, 7.139
newspapers
citation of, 15.203–4, 15.234–42, 16.117–18
city name with, 15.238–42, 17.93
foreign, 15.240, 15.242
indexing of, 17.93
names of, 6.14, 7.133, 7.135–36, 15.238, 15.242
number style in, 8.3n
the with names of, 7.135–36, 15.242, 17.93–94
nicknames, 7.29, 7.153
nobility, 7.12, 7.16, 7.23–24, 7.27, 17.82–84. *See also* monarchs; titles of persons
nonbook material, citation of, 15.414–20, 16.201–6
Norwegian, 9.63–64
notation, mathematical. *See* mathematical copy
note references, 15.3, 15.6–14, 15.52
checking of, 2.44–45, 2.107
clarity of, 15.23, 15.33
with display type, 1.62, 1.78, 15.11
for illustrations, 15.14
letters or symbols for, 2.26, 12.49–52, 15.14, 15.46, 15.48
location of, 1.78, 2.145, 12.73, 15.8–14, 18.39
manuscript typing and, 2.22
marking of, 2.72, 2.145
with quotations, 10.7, 15.10, 15.18
renumbering of, 2.107, 15.7
repeated, 15.13
and running heads, 15.37–38
and subheads, 1.78, 15.11
for tables, 2.26, 12.51–52, 12.73, 15.14
typography for, 12.51–52, 12.73, 15.3, 15.8, 18.39
See also notes, unnumbered
notes
with author-date citations, 15.3, 15.46, 16.17
and bibliographies, 2.45, 2.109
checking of, 2.44–46
citation of, 15.199
content of, 15.27–34, 15.45, 15.75–76, 15.77, 15.98–99, 15.43, 15.146–48
copyediting of, 2.95, 2.103–10, 2.167, 18.33
cross-references to, 2.44, 15.13, 15.29
discursive material in, 2.106, 15.44, 15.53

dual system of, 15.46–49
editor's, 15.47–48
to entire chapter, 1.62, 15.50–52
full citations in, 15.27–28, 15.75–203, 15.315, 15.322–26, 15.330–31
illustrations and tables cited in, 15.200
indexing of, 17.27–28, 17.96, 17.135
keyed to line or page, 15.52, figs. 15.5–7
legal (*see* legal citations)
location of, 1.3, 1.86, 15.35, 15.52, 18.33
marking of, 2.145
in new editions, 1.21
numbering of, 2.22, 2.26, 2.44, 2.107, 2.174, 12.49–52, 12.73, 15.6–14 (*see also* note references)
page references in, 15.44, 15.184–200
in previously published material, 2.166, 2.174
punctuation in, 15.32, 15.83–86, 15.97–99, 15.106–10, 15.112–17, 15.143, 15.149, 15.162, 15.175, 15.201, 15.205, 15.210, 15.214, 15.219, 15.221, 15.225, 15.231, 15.275, 15.297, 15.303, 15.314–15, 15.318–19
and quotations, 10.7, 10.67, 15.18–19, 15.32–33
reduction of, 15.15–26
running heads and, 1.86, 1.97, 15.37–40, figs. 15.3–4, fig. 15–9
shortened citations in, 2.103, 15.22, 15.26–27, 15.53, 15.57, 15.75, 15.117, 15.248–62, 15.266, 15.268, 15.276, 15.284–85, 15.297, 15.342, 15.344, 15.346, 15.349, 15.352, 15.354, 15.356–57, 15.363, 15.375, 15.378–81, 15.391, 15.396
source (*see* source notes)
substantive, 2.106, 15.46, 15.53
to tables, 2.26, 2.112, 4.68, 12.46–52, 12.60, 12.72–73, 15.14
tables in, 2.106, 15.20
translator's, 15.47–48
typesetting of, 15.41–43
type specifications for, 2.145, 15.42–43, 18.33–40
typing of, 2.21–22
unnumbered, 1.57, 1.62–63, 2.145, 15.11, 15.50–52
See also author-date citations; documentary-note style; endnotes; footnotes; note references; source citations
notes (musical), 6.84–87, 7.128, 7.150
notices, 7.155
not only . . . but also, 5.55
nouns
attributive, 6.23
coined, 6.16
compound, 6.8–9, 6.22
foreign, 6.66

900

The Chicago Manual of Style

Designed by Dennis Anderson, revised from an original design
by Cameron Poulter
Diagrams by R. Williams and Dennis Anderson
Photographs by Ted Lacey
Composed at Graphic Composition, Inc.
in Linotron Times Roman and Baskerville by the PENTA system
Printed by the Maple Press Company
on 50# Glatfelter Offset
Bound by the Maple Press Company
in Holliston Roxite Linen